Irwin Allen's *Lost in Space*
The Authorized Biography of a Classic Sci-Fi Series

ALSO BY MARC CUSHMAN

I SPY: A History and Episode Guide of the Groundbreaking Television Series

These Are the Voyages – Star Trek, TOS: Season One

These Are the Voyages – Star Trek, TOS: Season Two

These Are the Voyages – Star Trek, TOS: Season Three

Irwin Allen's Lost in Space: The Authorized Biography of a Classic Sci-Fi Series, Volume Two

Irwin Allen's *Lost in Space*
The Authorized Biography of a Classic Sci-Fi Series
Volume One

Marc Cushman

Foreword by Bill Mumy

Edited by Mark Alfred

Jacobs Brown Press
San Diego, California

LIBRARY OF CONGRESS CATALOGING-IN-PUBLICATION DATA
Cushman, Marc
Irwin Allen's *Lost in Space: The Authorized Biography of a Classic Sci-Fi Series, Volume One*
Marc Cushman, with a foreword by Bill Mumy;
Edited by Mark Alfred,
with Thomas C. Tucker and Sondra Johnson
Publisher: Matthew Williams Brown

Includes bibliographical reference

ISBN 978 0 692 75018 6
First edition soft cover, August 1, 2016

Library of Congress Control Number: 2016946778

Cover Design: Zack Korn
Interior Design: Andrew Johnson
Back photo of author: Mike Hayward Photography

Soft cover edition manufactured in the United States of America

Jacobs Brown Press
An imprint of Jacobs Brown Media Group, LLC
San Diego, Los Angeles, and Frazier Park, California
www.JacobsBrownMediaGroup.com

To Irwin Allen, for offering us an escape.

To Kevin Burns, for his contributions of material and contacts, making much of what follows possible.

Acknowledgments

Beyond Kevin Burns, my appreciation to those who gave further encouragement, guidance and support:

To the staff at the UCLA Special Collections Library, for their safeguarding and providing access to the *Lost in Space* and *Voyage to the Bottom of the Sea* show files.

To Ron Hamill for joining me in digging through the Irwin Allen Papers Collection, archived by Legend Pictures. And Dereck Thielges in Legend Pictures / Synthesis Entertainment office.

A special thank you to those who kindly granted interviews over the course of many years: Michael Allen, Kevin Burns, Roger C. Carmel, Mike Clark, Paul Comi, Joe D'Agosta, Barbara Eden, Harlan Ellison, Lew Hunter, Bryna Kranzler, Marta Kristen, Barbara "BarBara" Luna, Steve Marlo, Vincent McEveety, Lee Meriwether, Bill Mumy, Herman Rush, Malachi Throne, Guy Williams, Jr., and Francine York.

Sadly, many of those who helped to make *Lost in Space* are no longer with us. In an effort to include their voices in this documentation I relied on hundreds of period newspaper and magazine articles, as well as dozens of books. A full list of these sources can be found in the bibliography, but I wish to give special mention here to the following books and their authors: *Hitchcock's Partner in Suspense: The Life of Screenwriter Charles Bennett*, by Charles Bennett; *Irwin Allen Scrapbook, Volume One* and *Two*, Edited by William E. Anchors, Jr.; *Irwin Allen Television Productions, 1964-1970*, by Jon Abbott; *LISFAN* fanzines, edited by Flint Mitchell; *Lost in Space Design: "No Place to Hide,"* by Robert Rowe; *The Lost in Space Encyclopedia II*, edited by Flint Mitchell and William E. Anchors. Jr.; *Lost in Space Forever*, by Joel Eisner and Barry Magen; *Lost in Space: The True Story*, by Ed Shifres; *Lost in Space 25th Anniversary Tribute Book*, by James Van Hise; *Seaview: A 50th Anniversary Tribute to Voyage to the Bottom of the Sea,* by William E. Anchors, Jr. and Frederick Barr, with Lynne Holland; *Seaview: The Making of Voyage to the Bottom of the Sea,* by Tim Colliver; *Science Fiction Television Series*, Volumes 1 and 2, by Mark Phillips and Frank Garcia; and *Special Effects: Wire, Tape and Rubber Band Style*, by L.B. Abbott.

For those who have either shared in the past year of work or have given their support and encouragement in other meaningful ways: Jim Alexander, Mark Alfred, Mike Clark, Doug Diamond, David Jennings, Andrew and Sondra Johnson, Steven Kates, Mike Makkreel, Susan Osborn, Chris Pappas, Mark Phillips, and Thomas C. Tucker.

Author's Dedication

To those who still feel a childlike "sense of wonder" – as did Irwin Allen – as do I – this book is for you.
— *Marc Cushman*

Editor's Dedications

For Mary Lou the reader, and for Joyce the ever-patient.

Dedicated to Charlie, who showed what was right; and his grandchildren, who are making him proud.

In honor of English teachers everywhere, specifically Ruth White and Della Craighead.
— *Mark Alfred*

TABLE OF CONTENTS

Foreword

"Danger, Will Robinson!"

I thought I knew pretty much everything about *Lost in Space* having worked on the series most everyday of its production. But Marc Cushman's massive thousand page book [in two volumes] has proved me wrong. Turns out, I knew very little.

He has dug deep and discovered blueprints and budgets from various technical departments. His sleuthing has unearthed shooting schedules and the Nielson ratings for every single episode that aired back in the halcyon days of the mid-nineteen sixties – a time when there were only three major networks; no cable channels; no DVRs or internet to stream shows on; and no Blu-rays or DVDs to purchase and watch anytime you wanted; a time when an average of forty million people watched a handful of network broadcast television shows collectively every night and then they talked about the episodes they'd absorbed the next day at school or work. Mister Cushman has provided fifty-year-old fan letters as well as conducting at length interviews with everyone from cast members (like myself) to former network people. "Never fear, Cushman's here!" This guy has seriously walked the walk and now he's talking the talk.

I was only ten years old when I was cast by Irwin Allen to co-star in his groundbreaking, extremely expensive, bold science fiction adventure television pilot. But I had already been working prolifically as an actor alongside legendary performers, directors and producers for half of my short life. My acting career was in high gear by nineteen sixty-five, and I'd had the rare opportunity to play almost every type of character you can imagine in almost every type of genre. Being locked into the same character for five years on a series was something my parents and agents had frowned on, until *Lost in Space* came along.

I jumped at the opportunity to join the project and portray "Will Robinson." The character was literally everything I'd ever wanted to play. As a four-year-old with a broken leg, I sat in a wheelchair in my Beverlywood living room and watched Guy Williams as "Zorro" and George Reeves as "Superman" on our black-and-white made-in-America television set. Seeing those dynamic actors as caped adventurer "super heroes" motivated me at that young impressionable age to "get inside the TV" and be like them. I truly hounded my parents to make it happen. And, you can't escape your destiny. It was meant to be.

I loved every day working on *Lost in Space*. I loved it as from an actor's perspective and I loved it from a kid's perspective and I bonded with the cast and crew so deeply that I am still extremely close with them to this day, more than half a century later.

Imagine having been inspired to become an actor by Guy Williams, and then find yourself working opposite him as he played your father for three years. It was great. *He* was great. He never disappointed me. He was generous and playful and strong and tall and handsome and funny. He taught me how to fence. Yep, I learned the basics of swordplay from Zorro in a spacesuit.

June Lockhart was and is one of the brightest and boldest humans I've ever had the pleasure to know. She constantly kept my fertile young mind fed by playing word games with me.

Mark Goddard is and has been as long as I've known him, a big little kid. We really had a lot of fun together and we really did get into some trouble. We pulled some pranks that, when I think back on them now, were kind of crazy.

Marta Kristen is one of the sweetest and gentlest souls I've ever known and she turned me on to a lot of great music during our years on the series.

But it was Angela Cartwright who stole my heart and became my obsession and my partner in crime during the show. Words can't begin to describe how close we were and have continued to be as our lives have progressed. Very few people can truly understand or relate to the unique experience of being child stars, and Ange and I went through that together and we bonded from day one.

The six of us filmed the ambitious pilot together and we became like a real family. Irwin Allen's initial vision for *Lost in Space* was full of danger, magnificent props and special effects, great makeup, impressive sets and bizarre alien creatures. His manner as the creator, executive producer and director was old school and impressive. Irwin was part Barnum & Bailey and part Cecil B. DeMille. He shouted through a bullhorn and banged on a metal pail to direct us as we lurched from side to side amidst sparks, flames, smoke, torrential flooding and falling rocks. I wish Irwin had chosen to direct more than just the pilot. He did a sensational job.

Irwin's best work was his ability to find and assemble the right people. The right cast, the right cinematographers, crew, designers and certainly composers. *Lost in Space*'s themes by John Williams, billed as "Johnny Williams," more than stands the test of time; they remain some of the very best musical cues ever composed for television in my opinion.

And then along came a robot and a character the audience grew to love to hate; Jonathan Harris was added to our cast after the pilot to join the series as a foil, a constant nemesis to threaten the stability of the family… "Doctor Zachary Smith." "Indeed!" Within a handful of episodes, Jonathan changed the tone of the series and became the breakout star of the show.

CBS mandated that because the show aired during the "family hour," it must be tamed so as not to scare children. With that order standing, the character of Smith shifted from a nefarious saboteur into a sniveling, selfish, lazy, over the top comedian. And along with the Robot, brilliantly brought to life physically by Bob May and vocally by Dick Tufeld, a trio emerged as the focal point of the series … Dr. Smith, the Robot and Will Robinson.

It's almost like there were two completely different series called "Lost in Space". The black-and-white show, an ensemble adventure series pitting a family against the unknown alien environment on a strange planet they were marooned on, and the campy, super colorful, over the top, pop art fantasy series that revolved around the bumbling antics of the always self-serving Smith, the naïve but brilliant young Will Robinson who consistently got Smith and the rest of the group out of trouble, and the Robot who played the straight man and absorbed the brunt of outrageous alliterative insults hurled at him multiple times per episode by Smith. (ALL written personally by Jonathan Harris!) Needless to say, I loved Jonathan dearly and I miss him every day.

Marc Cushman's book will reveal some rancor and unhappiness from cast members regarding the shift in direction the series took. Some felt this way, but I am here to assure you that while on the set, the cast of *Lost in Space*, every single one of us, got along fine. Always. It was a very professional and pleasant environment and there were no temper tantrums thrown on our soundstages. Communications and negotiations between agents and business affairs are one thing, but on our sets, when we were filming the show, there was always a nice vibe.

I look back on those years with nothing but affection.

Lost in Space was a groundbreaking television series. There was absolutely nothing like it on the air before it debuted on CBS, at seven thirty p.m., Wednesday, September 15, 1965. It paved the way for a plethora of further ensemble science fiction shows set in the future. It created a template that survives to this day.

I am proud and grateful to have been a part of it.

And thanks to Marc Cushman's tenacity and literary skill, you can now discover more than you ever could before about *Lost in Space*.

Oh, the pain!

Bill Mumy
Laurel Canyon, Los Angeles, California
January 19th, 2016

Preface

On September 15, 1965, I was a typical American 10-year-old boy. At least, a typical 10-year old country boy. I was raised on a dairy farm outside of Hebo, Oregon, which, in turn, was outside of Tillamook, where all the farmers in the region took their milk to market. Like many baby boomers, after I'd done my chores and my homework, I watched TV. Television was a window to the rest of the world – especially on that dairy farm that seemed to me to be a million miles from anywhere.

I remember the wholesome family shows like *Lassie*, *Father Knows Best* and *Leave It to Beaver*; the westerns like *Wagon Train*, *Gunsmoke* and *The Rifleman*; the shows parents left kids alone to watch between 7:30 and 8 p.m. like *Gilligan's Island*, *The Munsters*, *The Addams Family*, and *My Favorite Martian*; and the fantastic shows that parents would rather kids not watch, but we somehow did anyway, such as *The Twilight Zone*, *The Outer Limits* and *Voyage to the Bottom of the Sea*. I watched my dad relive World War II once a week on *Combat!* And I remember the variety shows, where the world of parents and their kids would collide every week – where Broadway show tunes shared a stage with teen idols, jugglers and animal acts – and that included watching The Beatles on *The Ed Sullivan Show*, who were either a rock band or an animal act, depending on whether you asked the kids … or their parents.

It was a great time to be young in America.

The year that surpassed all the years that had come before in our brief lives was 1965. The songs on the radio kept getting better, the movies at the local theater were more colorful, and it was the year that television came alive with series that were both imaginative and distinctive. New on the tube in '65: *I Spy; Green Acres; Get Smart; Hogan's Heroes; The Wild, Wild West; The Avengers; Secret Agent; I Dream of Jeannie;* and *Lost in Space*. In the afternoons, after school, there were *Where the Action Is* and *Dark Shadows*. All of this and more on only three channels – your local affiliates for ABC, CBS and NBC. These three channels were often two channels too many when we had no means of recording the shows we missed, and there were so many worth watching. You had but one chance – unless you lucked out and caught that particular episode during summer reruns.

My chance – the show I would pick if allowed to watch only one – aired every Wednesday night from 7:30 to 8:30 p.m. on CBS. I would sit spellbound in front of the family's TV set for an hour watching images and ideas unlike anything I had experienced before. Granted, at the ripe old age of ten, I hadn't seen a great deal. But nothing wowed me like *Lost in Space* – a family launched into space; a robot programmed to destroy; a saboteur trapped onboard a spaceship he had rigged for destruction; freezing tubes; meteor storms, a gigantic derelict space ship populated by strange "bubble creatures"; a flying saucer spaceship crash landing; a giant Cyclops hurtling boulders; a chimpanzee with an enlarged cranium, and all of that was in only the first four episodes! The sights and sounds were dazzling; the action unrelenting. When the picture froze at the end of each episode and we were told to wait an entire week to find out what would happen next, that week seemed to take *forever*.

One year later, when NBC launched *Star Trek*, the adventures on *Lost in Space* seemed to pale in comparison. They were also getting sillier by that point, detracting from the reality that perhaps only a 10-year-old could buy into. But millions of us still watched. As Mark Goddard would say, "*Lost in Space* was a show from the heart. *Star Trek* was a show from the head. It didn't matter that we weren't logical." (MG-TVG97)

Although *Star Trek* had plenty of heart, too, *Lost in Space* had it beat in this one crucial area, at least with us pre-teens – this was a show about a family. It involved kids – Will and Penny, and the biggest and naughtiest kid of them all, Dr. Smith. It had a robot. The guy who played Zorro was the dad. Timmy's mother from *Lassie* was the mom. That cool young good-looking guy from *Johnny Ringo* and *The Detectives* was the pilot of the spaceship. The little boy who sent people he didn't like into the cornfield on *The Twilight Zone* was the son. The big-brown-eyed girl from *The Danny Thomas Show* and *The Sound of Music* was the younger daughter. And, for those boys in the audience who were entering into their teens, there was that super hot blonde, Marta Kristen. I appreciated her, too, although I wasn't quite sure why at the time. Well, maybe I had a hunch.

As 1965 turned into 1966, I was disappointed to see the show shift from what I believed to be serious science fiction (even if the adults were laughing) to silly comedy and outlandish fantasy. I still marveled over the imaginativeness of the stories, and, come the fall of 1966, the startling color that radiated from every new episode. Even *Walt Disney's Wonderful World of Color* had nothing over *Lost in Space* when it came to color.

I'm 60 now. But I wouldn't trade places with anyone younger than myself. I grew up with the best music, the best TV, and, in the movie houses, Sean Connery as 007 and Steve McQueen trying to jump a barbed wire fence on a stolen Nazi motorcycle. If I could live as a child again, in any time or place, I would wish to do it the same as I had before, in America, in the 1960s. And, on Wednesday nights from 7:30 to 8:30, you know where I'd be.

Marc Cushman
West Hills, California
September, 2015.

Author's Note

There were many in the 1950s and '60s. On occasion, *Variety* conducted its own ratings survey, but more often was content to report the audience numbers arrived at by Arbitron, A.C. Nielsen Media Research, and TvQ. Nielsen was certainly the industry leader by the time *Lost in Space* was airing, and remains so to this day. But no single Nielsen ratings report was definitive. You see, Nielsen conducted two, three, sometimes four different surveys for each and every week. There was the overnight report (also called Trendix), which would depend on telephone surveys in a handful of major U.S. cities. Then there was the 12-City report, which came a few days later. Its audience numbers would certainly differ from the overnight report. Then, days after that, the 30-City report was issued to the networks and other paying customers. Sometimes they were even printed in the trades or, even more rarely, in newspapers. But Nielsen wasn't done. A week later, it would issue the National report, which, in addition to counting noses in cities, would also factor in rural communities. Most of the information in the later came from "Nielsen families," who kept viewing logs and mailed them to Nielsen once a week. Bottom line, the audience numbers found in any one of these survey reports would invariably differ from the other reports, if only marginally.

The ratings information presented in this book came from a variety of sources, including *Variety*, *Daily Variety*, *Broadcasting*, and other trade magazines, but mostly from Arbitron and Nielsen themselves, in the reports kept in the Irwin Allen Private Papers Collection in Los Angeles, California. We endeavor in this book to identify each report – as Trendix, or 12-City survey, or 30-City survey, or National report.

1

The Way It Was ... 1965

In their respective series *The Twilight Zone* and *Star Trek*, producers Rod Serling and Gene Roddenberry balanced story twists with allegory, character with social relevance. On any given week viewers were likely as not to find, along with adventure, a commentary on the world or the human condition. The producers of *The Outer Limits*, Joseph Stefano and Leslie Stevens, were less concerned with telling stories that related to social issues of the day. Nonetheless, they were dealing on a weekly basis with the human condition in non-political arenas. *The Outer Limits* was not only monster-driven, but immensely character-driven. Each episode provided a striking emotional character arc, with a generous helping of inner conflict, played out against a ticking clock.

Irwin Allen, on the other hand, offered sheer escapism through spectacle.

The social turbulence of the 1960s left many of us seeking temporary escapism. Even grade-schoolers were aware of the world's unrest.

The realities of the world were all around us – in the morning newspapers, on nightly news, in weekly doses on the covers of *Life*, *Look*, *Time*, and *Newsweek*, and hour by hour on the radio. It was unrelenting. A few years after we had experienced the anguish of President Kennedy's murder, 1968 brought the assassinations of civil rights leader Martin Luther King and Senator Robert Kennedy in the space of just a couple of months. The horrors were being played out right in front of us: with the escalating Cold War, including the Cuban Missile Crisis and the nuclear arms race; the Vietnam War; the "Pueblo Incident" with North Korea; with race riots and anti-war protests ripping America down the middle; and more tears in the fabric of a nation with the constant clash between the Hawks and the Doves; the widening Generation Gap; the Battle of the Sexes; and books such as *The Population Bomb*, warning of overpopulation and global annihilation. The grim revelations were bombarding us from every direction. Even the songs on the radio were becoming more political, and pessimistic, with titles such as "Eve of Destruction," "Paint It Black," "Revolution" and Country Joe & the Fish's "I-Feel-Like-I'm-Fixin'-to-Die Rag."

There was little refuge ... except into the surreal world of America's 1960s entertainment TV. Shows like *The Munsters*, *The Addams Family*, *Bewitched*, *I Dream of Jeannie* and *Gilligan's Island* provided comfort food for the mind ... and the soul. And the slice of apple pie that came with the meal was the three ring circus of Irwin Allen's initial foray into television – *Voyage to the Bottom of the Sea*, *Lost in Space* and *The Time Tunnel*. While some say that Allen liked his *Time Tunnel* best, that third-ring of his TV circus was the least successful, lasting only one season, from 1966 to '67. The big impact was two-fold: *Voyage*, which launched in the fall of 1964 and had a healthy four-season run, amassing more than 100 episodes; and *Lost in Space*, blasting off in the fall of '65 and staying in the cosmos for three seasons.

From time to time Allen's series included stories with political angles or even a degree of gloom.

Voyage had a handful of episodes which dealt with impending nuclear war and the possible end of mankind. *Lost in Space* began with an Earth of 1997, overpopulated to the point that the scientific community and the U.S. government could come up with no other solution but to send families into outer space. Also in *Lost in Space* was the enemy agent named Colonel Zachary Smith, who intended to sabotage the mission and destroy the Jupiter 2, including the entire family on board.

Allen's series often started on a dark note, but soon settled in to stories about heroism, patriotism, family, and good triumphing over evil. More often than not, the adversary was a monstrous being who bore little resemblance to the evildoers and foreboding news that appeared on our doorstep every morning with the newspaper. There was certainly a hunger for such escapist fare as featured in comic books, movies, and TV shows like *Voyage to the Bottom of the Sea* and *Lost in Space* in the 1960s.

Both *Voyage* and *Space* ceased production at the same time, in the spring of 1968, leaving their respective networks and moving into syndication in the early fall. Allen would replace them with *Land of the Giants* and extend his reign in TV another two years. But his heyday on the small screen had already passed. Baby boomers, and the rest of popular taste, had moved on.

Yet the reruns remained, for which we should be grateful. *Star Trek*'s Mr. Spock once stated that the more complex the mind, the greater the necessity of simple play. As we grew up into the complexities of adulthood, we could always find a welcome time-out: a voyage to the bottom of the sea; or become lost in space; or take a trip through a tunnel in time, thanks to the brilliance and wonderfully irrelevant worlds of Irwin Allen.

2

Irwin Allen

Irwin Allen, circa mid-1970s.

Don Richardson, director of more *Lost in Space* episodes than anyone else (twenty-six, to be exact), said, "At about the end of the second year, Irwin called me into his office and said that he was going to fire Jonathan Harris. I looked at him in amazement, as I considered him a very bright guy, very inventive guy, and I couldn't understand how he could be so stupid as to not realize that if he fired Dr. Smith, he had no show. Now, you could not say this to him.... [And] he had a guy named Professor La Tourette, who was a professor at UCLA in the theater department, who was his flunky. La Tourette used to stand behind Irwin when he talked and Irwin would always turn to him and say, 'What did he say, La Tourette?' And La Tourette would repeat.... So, I said, 'Irwin, don't you realize you are P.T. Barnum?' He replied, 'What did he say, La Tourette?' La Tourette replied, 'He said you're P.T. Barnum.' Then Irwin said, 'That's right, I am. I *am* P.T. Barnum.' I said, 'P.T. Barnum never fought with his lions. You hire the lions and they do their job, and you crack the whip. You're P.T. Barnum.' He said, 'That's right, I am P.T. Barnum; I shouldn't fight with my lions. Let them kill each other.' And that's how Jonathan stayed another year." (DR-LISF)

With *Star Trek*, Gene Roddenberry often wanted to be a modern-day Jonathan Swift, using faraway times and places to comment on present society. In contrast, Allen was content to play the role of a modern-day circus ringmaster.

Entertainment legend Phineas Taylor Barnum was an American showman who made a name for himself by promoting celebrated hoaxes and human curiosities through his P.T. Barnum's Grand Traveling Museum, Menagerie, Caravan & Hippodrome. Some thought it an interesting showcase and strange mix of ragged and exotic oddities. Others considered it a crude parade of freaks and monsters. Either way, it was a hit.

Barnum was also a journalist, author, editor and publisher. For his autobiography, he wrote: "I am a showman by profession ... and all the gilding shall make nothing else of me."

In 1919, after Barnum's death, his enterprise joined with James Anthony Bailey's Cooper and Bailey's Circus to become "The Greatest Show on Earth," The Ringling Brothers Barnum & Bailey's Circus.

A quarter-century after Barnum's passing, Irwin Allen arrived, destined to embody a similar flamboyant showmanship in the mass media arena of film and television.

Born in New York City on June 12, 1916, Irwin Allen's name then, and for the first twenty-two years of his life, was Irwin Grinovit. He was the youngest of four brothers – along with Rubin, George, and Fred – born to a Russian Jewish immigrant who worked as a tailor. Allen's cousin, Al Gail, told interviewer Kevin Burns, "The era was, unfortunately, depression days – '30s and '40s – [but] we both grew up in what you would call normal middle-class families. Not poor – we always had something to eat. Not wealthy, of course, especially during the depression years. [There] was a lot of struggle – his father and my father – but, as kids, you didn't realize that times were tough. Everyone was in the same predicament." (AG-KB95)

The times were more difficult for the Grinovit family than cousin Al realized. Al Gail lived on Coney Island; Irwin Grinovit and his family lived in the Bronx.

Nephew Michael Allen disclosed, "They were typical of people who lived on the Lower East Side of New York at that time. His father was a relatively recent immigrant. English was clearly a second language. They had limited means. They lived in one of those tenement flats, and they took in boarders. My father [Rubin] eventually went to work as a window decorator. My uncle Fred was a piano cleaner. George was a superintendent – a janitor. They were all working men, not of means." (MA0AI15)

Irwin Grinovit was determined to become a man of means. And, once he found that means, he never spoke of his earlier hardship or the worries and insecurities he may have harbored. That time and place were merely something from which to escape.

Even Sheila Matthews Allen, Irwin Allen's longtime companion, who later became his wife of seventeen years, admitted, "Irwin was a very private man, and I don't really know that much about his childhood. I think you learned more by talking to his cousin [Al Gail] than I ever knew.... But I know they weren't a well-to-do family. If anything, he had to think at an early age about what he was going to do, and he did. He followed his dream." (SM-KB95)

Michael Allen was not surprised to hear this. He observed, "Irwin was extremely conscious of not doing anything that he would have to hide. That mattered to him a lot, perhaps more than you might think. But this was part of the way he was brought up. My father [Irwin's brother Rubin] was much the same way. I would think my uncles George and Fred were probably the same way, as well. Irwin was private... so taking someone into his life didn't constitute an opening of conversations that would be uncomfortable. Quite the contrary, Irwin was very conscious of *not* doing anything ever that he would be uncomfortable about afterwards." (MA-AI15)

That included discussions of his poor background. Michael Allen said, "Irwin used to say he didn't care as much about weeds as he did about flowers. That was his way of avoiding the issue. He really had no interest and didn't talk about his early childhood or his early adulthood; of his various family relationships, whether they were good, bad or indifferent, male or female. And the same with business associates. Those people he did business with – and raising money was a big part of that – were all very private, and he didn't transcend those rules. That was a conscious effort on his part. I can say my father was exactly the same way, and I can presume that my grandfather and grandmother

[Irwin's parents] were. Assuredly that can be traced back to them being Russian/Jewish immigrants. Those were difficult times." (MA-AI15)

Al Gail said, "As the youngest of four boys, he pretty much had to make his own way, in which he did. You know the phrase of 'pulling yourself up by your own bootstraps' – that was Irwin. Because he never had any help, from the very beginning to his eventual success. He did it all on his own." (AG-KB95)

Like P.T. Barnum, Allen studied journalism. Al Gail had a sense early on about his cousin's inclinations: "Something literary, because in his high school days he wrote a column for the high school newspaper, [and] he did some freelance work on local newspapers. He was always interested in writing, advertising, publicity." (AG-KB95)

Allen escaped the Great Depression through his keen interest in books. Gail disclosed, "He was an avid reader. He read all the ones we all read in those days – Frank Merriwell, Nick Carter, Horatio Alger, Tom Swift – and we were both, of course, enamored by Richard Halliburton, the travel writer.... I think most of the reading in those days, when we weren't studying or going to school, or playing football or stoop ball, or roller-skating or bicycling, was adventure books, science books, science fiction – Jules Verne. I guess it was the excitement, the adventure, the creativity of the writers. And we always sought to emulate them if possible. We all wanted to be writers in those days, and many of us *became* writers." (AG-KB95)

Gail said of his cousin, "He'd come down on weekends, because he lived in the Bronx and I was on Coney Island. And we'd sit on the beach and we'd look at some of these tremendous ocean liners coming from Europe, coming into New York Harbor, and we'd say, 'Someday!,' because then it was just a wild dream. Who could afford that kind of a luxury of traveling on the ocean steamer? But he said, 'Someday we'll make it, and we'll do all those things. You'll see.'" (AG-KB95)

Gail was older, and his first step in that dream of "someday" came sooner for him. He said, "I went to University of Alabama. Irwin wanted to go there, too, and I was hoping he'd be able to. But, unfortunately, as I say, with depression times, his family just couldn't afford it. So he went to night school. He went to Columbia." (AG-KB95)

Allen's nighttime study at Columbia University included courses in advertising and journalism. He also took free community college classes at City College of New York. During the day, and between classes, he earned money by writing publicity material for nightclubs in Greenwich Village and on 52nd Street. When Gail returned after four years of college, Allen was working in a low-level position for an advertising agency.

Gail stressed, "Somehow, it seemed to be a dead end. There was really nothing happening. We had a cousin in Los Angeles, and one day we're sitting around and [Irwin] said, 'What the hell, let's go to California and see what's doing.' Within a week or so, we were on our way. We were hopeful to land something either in the movie industry or advertising, or one of the allied arts, and make our own way. We really had no specific target – just to get a job; start working and see where it goes from there." (AG-KB95)

Sheila Matthews Allen said, "He always wanted to be associated with the circus in some way. So, I guess when he came out here, he was running away to *join* the circus." (SMA-KB95)

According to Al Gail, it was on the trip to California that Irwin Grinovit decided to change his name. Gail said, “Grinovit was an old family name, and it was a difficult name. It was a harsh name, and people had trouble remembering it. So, when we came out here, we decided to change it to something that’s more easily spoken and remembered, and we came up with ‘Allen.’ A schoolmate of mine in Alabama had changed his name to Allen, and I said, ‘Well, it’s a good name, and easy to say, and easy to remember.’ So, he liked it. He decided on *Irwin Allen*.” (AG-KB95)

Nephew Michael Allen remembered the deciding moment differently, saying, “He probably changed his name around 1936 or ’37. He came to Boston to visit my father, and we lived on Allen Street in the West End of Boston. And he thought he would change his name to help him in his profession and liked the sound of Allen.” (MA-AI15)

In time, other family members would adopt the new surname, as well.

Allen’s father died shortly after his ambitious son left for Los Angeles. Michael Allen said, “My grandmother did not live very much longer, either. She passed away probably in the early 1940s.” (MA-AI15)

It was actually earlier, in 1938, when Irwin Allen was twenty-two.

The jobs Allen and his cousin Al found were with a magazine called *Key*, which served as an entertainment directory and nightclub guide. Gail said of Allen, “He had a very agile mind. And he was a great salesman. So we came out and we started to work for a local entertainment magazine. We were always a team. He did what he did best and I did what I did best. I was basically a writer. He was a presenter, a talker, a salesman, and very creative on his own. He was also a writer. I wrote a column, and he sold advertising in the magazine, and did very well.” (AG-KB95)

Irwin Allen’s radio career began in Los Angeles as an all-night disc jockey and announcer for KMTR, circa 1939.

Driven to succeed, Allen ventured into other areas of media, first as an all-night disc jockey at local radio station KMTR, followed by a gig as the station’s announcer. Then, with uncanny speed, he had his own radio program. It was called *Hollywood Merry-Go-Round*, heard on Los Angeles’ KLAC for 15 minutes each week. Cousin Al served as producer.

Shortly after starting *Hollywood Merry-Go-Round*, Allen also became a newspaper columnist for Hollywood Features Syndicates. With his “On the Set” column in the early 1940s, he mixed curious tidbits and humor, segueing into showbiz gossip and news.

Allen worked tirelessly. He rose before the sun and toiled after it had set. And, like the sun, he never took a day off. It was a work ethic which would bring success, but also bred harsh critics within Allen’s own inner circle. Famed screenwriter Charles

Bennett, who co-wrote many movies with the brash producer-director, would lie in wait until Allen's death before venomously claiming that his former employer was not a writer at all, and, more so, did *not* write. Bennett said Allen only took credit. Yet Allen's "On the Set" column would indicate otherwise.

One example of Allen's prose, from his syndicated column, circa 1943:

> According to the best available records, murder is the least profitable of all indoor sports. It's also unpatriotic. It's also old fashioned. Just in case that agile mind of yours has recently been running along the lines of "doing away" with your married mate for the sake of the insurance money, forget the mayhem and go to a movie instead. If nothing else, the seat at the local Bijou is less hot than the one at the Big House. Whatever you do, don't underestimate those insurance guys. They've caught more money-mad-murderers than most of the cops in the country. And since you've publicly admitted to being something less than an Einstein, don't bank on being the guy who pulls the "perfect job." No one ever does!
>
> A pet stunt of all insurance killers is to take out a "Double Indemnity" policy on their loved ones. To definitely prove how fascinating and how stupid the whole thing is, Paramount is now turning out a thriller with that very title. Barbara Stanwyck, Fred MacMurray and Edward G. Robinson are cast in a switcheroo of character. Stanwyck and MacMurray are seen as killers while Robinson plays the role of the cop.

Allen soon traded up from Hollywood Features Syndicates' "On the Set" to a daily column for the Atlas Features Syndicate, entitled "Hollywood Merry-Go-Round," named after his radio program, and appearing in seventy-three newspapers around the world.

By 1945, in addition to *Hollywood Merry-Go-Round*, Allen had a second radio series – a weekly program entitled *Story of a Star*. Each episode featured the biography of a well-known entertainment personality.

In the fall of that year, Allen's weekly *Hollywood Merry-Go-Round* radio program began broadcasting to a national audience. The September 13, 1948 issue of *Daily Variety* reported:

> After nine years on local indie KLAC, Irwin Allen has conceived a new gimmick that sends his *Hollywood Merry-Go-Round* airer coast-to-coast. Allen has been running sound tracks from various films on his program, a gimmick occupying about four minutes of air time. Listeners are invited to identify the picture from which the scenes come. Completely new idea brought an instantaneous station response after the initial airing and, as a result, Allen branched out last night to KYA, Frisco, with 14 other outlets around the country set to pick up the program by Oct. 1.

Irwin Allen's *Hollywood Merry-Go-Round*, TV's first known panel show (KLAC-TV, circa late 1948).

KLAC radio was so impressed that they launched a video version of the program four days later on their sister station, KLAC-TV (Channel 13). As with the radio show, Allen's cousin Al performed producer's duties. However, there was never any question that Irwin Allen was in charge.

From November of 1948, Allen told columnist Albert H. Grogan, "When you're as close to radio as I've been for the past ten years, it's not too hard to become a bit suspicious of a brand-new medium. I'm not saying now that radio will be a half-forgotten era five years hence, but after studying television today, I had to admit that it's here and here to stay." (IA-TV48)

Reviewing Allen's new television program on September 24th, *Daily Variety* said:

> Allen corralled Hugh Herbert, Ellen Drew, George Tobias and Irving Cummings, Jr., for the initialer. An excellent opportunity for light banter and humor was missed by adhering too closely to a somber "guessing game" script. Quartet were asked to identify stills, soundtracks from recent pictures, a mystery guest, and a personality by tracking him or her down through 20 questions. Allen raced through the telecast too rapidly, killing what interest could have been provoked.

Allen (center) with panel guests for one of his *Hollywood Merry-Go-Round* broadcasts (KLAC-TV, circa late 1940s).

Allen defended his grab bag of gimmicks and rapid-fire approach, saying at the time, "It's not so easy to switch a radio show to television as it may appear. Listening is one thing, but watching me sit at a mike reading Hollywood news items doesn't add up to a good show.... Just because there's a picture star with me, it doesn't necessarily follow that people at home are going to glue their eyes to the receiver watching the star do *nothing*!" (IA-TV48)

Even though the results were mixed, Allen was justifiably proud. He later boasted, "I invented the panel show *and* the mystery guest!" (IA-DV64)

In 1949, Allen traded his television program *Hollywood Merry-Go-Round*, which had been losing popularity, for a new incarnation, called *Irwin Allen's Hollywood Party*. It was a different title, but was a show that contained pretty much the same parlor tricks. *The Billboard* trade paper reviewed the new series on December 10, 1949, saying:

> A few years ago *Hollywood Party* might have been a novel idea; today it's another tired charade show which suffers by comparison. Irwin Allen's stanza has been a feature of KLAC-TV since the station's inception, the latest offering having undergone surgery to make it more palatable. The chief objection is that the show goes nowhere, lacking both cohesive continuity or good production.

Radio and television were becoming more discerning. The critics were more scrutinizing and were tired of Allen's stilted format. With his thinly-disguised Bronx accent, and his tendency for scripted banter over natural conversation, Allen was suddenly out of favor. To him, this fall from critical acceptance probably didn't matter. What he really wanted was to produce films.

Double Dynamite (1951)

Irwin Allen hadn't confined his efforts to writing newspaper columns and being the producer/host of radio and television programs. In 1947, while still appearing regularly on radio and TV, the ambitious workaholic branched out even further by becoming a Hollywood agent. The first step was taking on a position as head of the Radio Department at the Orsatti Agency. A short while later, Allen began wearing a second hat at the talent agency – as a story editor. This position was what Allen was really after. As a story editor, his job entailed finding writers and, in particular, specific stories – books and scripts worthy of representation by the agency. For such an avid reader, this position was a natural for Allen. By May 1948, he resigned from the Orsatti Agency to open an office under his own name.

Allen wanted to produce films. To his way of thinking, the best way to accomplish this would be to find a hot property, option it, and go in search of a studio or other financial backers. After years of being a Hollywood columnist, and a radio and TV personality, there were few people in Tinseltown who would not take a phone call from Irwin Allen.

Al Gail said, "One day he had a script that he liked, and he decided to see if he could package it – that is, get a director, a star, and backing from one of the studios." (AG-KB95)

Sinatra, Russell and Marx in Irwin Allen's first co-production, the suggestively titled *Double Dynamite* (RKO, 1951).

The working title of the script was "It's Only Money," by Leo Rosten, a humorist in the areas of journalism, story writing, and, more recently, screenwriting. Allen was struck by the title – a phrase he would jokingly use throughout his career as he planned multi-million-dollar disaster films. He also liked this quirky tale of a bank employee who bets on the horse races to earn the money needed to marry his sweetheart, only to be suspected of embezzling when he starts showering his fiancée with presents purchased with his race-track winnings.

Allen had become friendly with Irving Cummings, Jr., who was a screenwriter in his own right, and, more importantly for Allen's needs, the son of Irving Cummings, Sr., who had directed many of child star Shirley Temple's movies. Cummings, Jr. liked Leo Rosten's story and agreed to partner with Allen in attempting to get it produced.

The first step for Allen and Cummings, Jr. was to create a buzz concerning the project around Hollywood. Allen booked Cummings, Jr. for the premiere broadcast of his KLAC-TV *Hollywood Merry-Go-Round* television program to "talk shop," which would conveniently include mentioning "It's Only Money."

The start of a lifelong friendship – between Irwin Allen and Groucho Marx. Pictured: Sinatra and Marx (RKO, 1951).

Irving Cummings, Sr. was watching the program that night, and it didn't take long for him to reach out to his son and offer to direct the project. Financing and studio distribution were quickly arranged.

Irwin Allen already had "first money" investors lined up, and a studio in mind for matching first dollar with second, as well as the distribution of their film.

Al Gail said, "That was in the era of [studio mogul] Howard Hughes. And Irwin liked Howard; Howard liked Irwin. They knew each other. And, he would occasionally see Howard at odd times and at strange places." (AG-KB95)

At one of these "odd times and strange places," Hughes agreed to distribute the movie through his RKO Studios. As a boost for the film, he handed over his biggest studio asset – contract actress Jane Russell – for the lead female role. Along with Cummings, Sr. to direct, RKO to distribute, and Russell as female lead, the package soon included Frank Sinatra and Groucho Marx, both with openings in their schedules, should Allen and Cummings start production between Thanksgiving and New Year's when activity at the studios was at a low. The deal was announced in the Hollywood trade papers on October 15th, with the stars already inked.

Groucho Marx with Miss "Double Dynamite," Jane Russell (RKO, 1951).

Melville Shavelson, a future Oscar winner and a writer known for speedy screenwriting turnarounds, was snatched up after completing the screenplay for the upcoming Bob Hope comedy, *Sorrowful Jones*, and put to work rewriting the script for "It's Only Money," tailoring it to the talents of Sinatra, Marx and Russell. Meanwhile, songwriters Jule Styne and Sammy Cahn were commissioned to pen a comical title tune for Sinatra and Marx to sing.

Irwin Allen's first big star cast: Russell, Sinatra and Marx (RKO, 1951).

Hollywood worked faster in those days, but both Cummings, Jr. and Sr. had never witnessed the type of drive displayed by Allen, the former Bronx salesman who was eager to plow into the picture business.

On November 22, 1948, principal photography began for "It's Only Money." With Allen in the front office, the film's production raced at the same clip with which it had sailed during its pre-production phase. The film finished three days ahead of schedule, on December 18th, and for $100,000 below its projected cost of $1 million.

"It's Only Money" was kept on the shelf for more than a year as Howard Hughes waited for what he felt would be just the right moment, and just the right title. The one he eventually picked was *Double Dynamite*, named after Jane Russell's obvious feminine assets. The film bearing that title and those assets was finally let loose in late 1951.

On November 17, 1951, a film critic for *Variety* opined:

> This is a lightweight hodgepodge with comedic intention that will have to depend on what business can be scared up by the names of its costars, Jane Russell, Groucho Marx and Frank Sinatra. It is formula comedy with a slapdash air that doesn't build sufficiently on the laugh line to carry it through to more than just moderate success.

Variety's sister trade paper, *Daily Variety*, printed its assessment the same day, saying:

> Unfoldment is pretty static, lacking imagination as well as zip.... Miss Russell, per usual, looks okay and part is no strain on her acting ability.... Marx is the picture's standout, dishing out his familiar line of patter for number of laughs.

TIME magazine gave its verdict on November 26, saying:

> *Double Dynamite*, originally called "It's Only Money," got its new title as a leering tribute to the extraordinary physical endowments of actress Jane Russell. The movie, however, cheats on RKO's full-bosomed advertising. Actress Russell is cast as a demure bank clerk named Mibs Gooding [sic], who aspires to nothing more glamorous than marriage with Frank Sinatra, the bank teller in the next cage.

With the heavy ad campaign of $85,000 (which equates to nearly $800,000 in 2015), and all the hype about the lead actress's double dose of TNT, the movie was the sixth top moneymaker over the Christmas and New Year's holidays. For the month of January, 1952, and, as *Variety* commented, "confounding the [critics] who did not expect it to fare so well," *Double Dynamite* inched up to the Number 5 box office slot.

By this time, Allen's second film project was filmed and released – a production which seemed more suitable for a man who would later specialize in nail-biting suspense, or at least relentless action and adventure.

Where Danger Lives (1950)

Even though *Double Dynamite* was still more than a year away from release, Howard Hughes was impressed by the ability of Cummings and Irwin Allen to shave

10% off both the budget and the production schedule. Allen had found another story he wanted to package – again written by Leo Rosten – with a working title of "A White Rose for Julie." This was an atypical tale from Rosten the humorist. "Rose" was a romantic crime drama about a young doctor who falls hard for a mysterious "dame," then learns that she has a husband, leading to a fight, a death, and a run for the border. A different type of screenwriter would be needed for this project, and producer Irving Cummings, Jr. had someone in mind.

Faith Domergue and Robert Mitchum in film noir *Where Danger Lives*, Allen's second as co-producer, and first to be released (RKO, 1950).

Charles Bennett was best known as the primary writer on seven popular films by Alfred Hitchcock (written *with* the two Hitchcocks – Alfred and his wife Alma). These cinematic landmarks included England's first talkie, *Blackmail*, and both versions of *The Man Who Knew Too Much* (1934 and 1956), as well as *The 39 Steps* and *Foreign Correspondent*, the latter of which brought Bennett an Academy Award nomination. He also wrote the popular films *Reap the Wild Wind*, starring John Wayne and Ray Milland, as well as *Black Magic*, starring Orson Welles. Bennett's future would involve scripting numerous movies for Irwin Allen, including *The Lost World* and the big-screen version of *Voyage to the Bottom of the Sea*. However, at this time – the early 1950s – Bennett could not even imagine the relationship going that far.

Bennett's chance encounter with Allen was innocuous enough. He said, "I had been directing a lot of television for Hollywood in England. When I came back, Irving Cummings was going to produce a picture called *Where Danger Lives* with Robert Mitchum and Claude Rains, and I was asked to write it." (CB-SL93)

Mitchum, Rains, Domergue – top-star, top-notch launch for Irwin Allen as co-producer (RKO, 1950).

Bennett was also asked to appear on *The Irwin Allen Show*, as it was now called. On the same program was Vincent Price, with whom Allen would soon work in motion pictures, and Allen's film-making partner, Irving Cummings, Jr. While appearing

Faith Domergue and Robert Mitchum – film noir screen chemistry (RKO, 1950).

on the program, Bennett was surprised to learn that the TV host would also be helping out with the production of the film. He said, dismissingly, "Irwin Allen knew somebody who worked for Howard Hughes, and Hughes owned RKO, so it was somehow finagled into him being associate producer." (CB-SL93)

Bennett completed his screenplay "A White Rose for Julie" (later to be called *Where Danger Lives*) in early September, 1949, freeing Cummings, Jr. and Allen to seek out the film's director and stars. The man they eventually chose to direct was 45-year-old John Farrow, husband of actress Maureen O'Sullivan. Farrow had won the 1942 New York Film Critics Circle Award for the Brian Donlevy-William Bendix starrer, *Wake Island.*

This time out, in order to find stars to the liking of Howard Hughes, the development period was longer. While "It's Only Money"/*Double Dynamite* raced through the process in a matter of two months, "A White Rose for Julie" took six months in order to allow Hughes' newest contract girl, Faith Domergue, to finish another film project – *Vendetta*. Hughes had been personally overseeing the making of *Vendetta*, the production of which slowed to a crawl as the studio boss fussed over every detail for both the film and his latest femme discovery. Domergue was 25. She reached her greatest success after leaving RKO, as leading lady in B-westerns for Universal opposite the likes of Audie Murphy and Jeff Chandler, and receiving first or second billing in the monster mashes *It Came From Beneath the Sea*, *This Island Earth* and *The Atomic Man.*

Star-struck Irwin Allen with Claude Rains and Robert Mitchum during filming of *Where Danger Lives*.

Production on "A White Rose for Julie" finally began on January 9, 1950. Robert Mitchum was cast in the lead as Dr. Jeff Cameron. He was 34, and had received an Oscar nomination for his supporting role in 1945's *The Story of G.I. Joe.*

Domergue and Mitchum, in *Where Danger Lives* (RKO, 1950).

Claude Rains was 52 when cast as Mr. Lannington. He had already received four Best Supporting Actor Oscar nominations – for 1939's *Mr. Smith Goes to Washington*, 1942's *Casablanca*, 1944's *Mr. Skeffington* and 1946's *Notorious*.

Maureen O'Sullivan was 39, and cast to play Nurse Julie Dawn. Besides being married to the film's director, O'Sullivan was best known for playing Jane opposite Johnny Weissmuller's Tarzan, between 1932 and 1942.

On the January 26, 1950 episode of KLAC-TV's *Irwin Allen's House Party*, the host devoted his show to the production crew unit from "A White Rose for Julie," allowing the public to see them talk about the movie and their craft. The artists and technicians who explained their work to the TV audience were Irving Cummings, Jr., assistant director Sam Ruman, makeup artist Layne Britton, costumer Virginia Tutwiler, prop man George McGonigle, and director John Farrow.

Workaholic Allen still kept his other day job, as host of TV's *Hollywood Merry-Go-Round*, now called *The Irwin Allen Show* (KLAC-TV, 1950).

As had happened with Allen's first movie, his second one also underwent a title change, this time to *Where Danger Lives*.

In May, Allen resumed production of his TV talk show, awaiting the release of *Where Danger Lives* and the critical and box office verdicts that would tell him if he had a future as a movie producer.

On June 16, 1950, after a tradeshow screening, the film critic for *Daily Variety* reported:

> As a vehicle to introduce Faith Domergue, *Where Danger Lives* is by no means sock [short for socko]. It is a rambling, confused feature that will lean heavily on the draw value of Robert Mitchum.... Both John Farrow's direction and the script by Charles Bennett shroud the melodrama with too much confusion and the pacing is uneven.... Production by Irving Cummings, Jr. and Irwin Allen emphasizes [melodrama] factors in the story,

> mounting it physically in keeping but falling short on realizing the best from the Leo Rosten original.

Sister trade *Variety* chimed in on June 21st, calling the film "just a fair mystery melodrama."

Time magazine, from December 18, 1950, said:

> *Where Danger Lives* gives movie audiences, at long last, a chance to see highly publicized Faith Domergue, latest graduate of the Howard Hughes straining-bodice school of dramatic art. Hughes discovered Faith in 1941, put her in a strenuous training program for stardom. Like Jane Russell, another Hughes discovery whom she somehow resembles, Faith bloomed unseen except in leg and torso art poses.... Actress Domergue smolders and storms like an overheated Theda Bara, gets some ludicrous lines to read (and gives them the delivery they warrant), builds up fast to an overpowering impression that she has done her best work in publicity stills.

On January 6, 1951, Jesse Zunser, of *Cue* magazine, wrote:

> There is no excuse for a picture as bad as this one. In all departments – writing, direction, performance – it just doesn't rate.

It wasn't the big hit Hughes, Cummings or Allen were hoping for, failing to make the Top 10 box office lists for November and December, then trailing into 1951 with additional releases in less vital markets. But *Variety* ranked it as doing "pleasing" box office in San Francisco, "nice" in Boston, "rugged" (which meant good) in Omaha, "favorable" in Cincinnati, "good" in Providence, and "fancy" in Los Angeles (following a premiere week there where it was rated as "solid"). Thus, Irwin Allen survived his first two motion pictures.

For his third shot at being a big-time big-screen producer, Allen turned back to comedy ... and Groucho Marx.

A Girl in Every Port (1952)

Hitting movie screens one month after *Double Dynamite*, Film Number Three would represent the third and final pairing of Irwin Allen and Irving Cummings, Jr. as co-producers, hitting the movie screens one month after *Double Dynamite*. This time Allen, clearly moving up and taking charge, took first

William Bendix, Marie Wilson and Groucho Marx (RKO, 1952).

chair as producer, leaving Cummings with a lesser role.

In October 1950, Allen, who had become friendly with Groucho Marx, began selling him on the property he was trying to package as his next film, and his first as top producer, which would be based on the humorous short story, "They Sell Sailors Elephants," by Frederick Hazlitt Brennan. Feeling it would make a good vehicle for his new friend, Allen optioned the story.

Thirty days later, *Daily Variety* reported Marx was locked in while Allen and Cummings, Jr. were "avidly awaiting Howard Hughes' okay" to announce Marie Wilson as the leading lady, William Bendix as co-star, and Chester Erskine as director.

Marie Wilson and uncredited actress as car-hop girls (RKO, 1952).

Marie Wilson was 33 and had been starring in her own TV series, as title character Irma Peterson in *My Friend Irma*, and then brought to the big screen as a pair of movies which also starred Wilson (1949's *My Friend Irma* and 1950's *My Friend Irma Goes West*).

Bendix was 44, and had been nominated for an Oscar as Best Supporting Actor for 1942's *Wake Island*. He was a star at the time, having had the title role for 1948's *The Babe Ruth Story*, as well as playing blue-collar factory worker Chester A. Riley in 1949's *The Life of Riley*, later developed into a TV series, also starring Bendix.

Writer/director Chester Erskine was 46, and had adapted the short story into a screenplay. He was from the stage, but had recently made the transition to film, writing, directing and producing the 1947 hit *The Egg and I*, starring Claudette Colbert and Fred MacMurray.

The holdup was Marie Wilson. Hughes wasn't going to green-light a film that didn't prominently exploit one of his well-endowed studio contract starlets, or, in

Bendix, Wilson and Marx (RKO, 1952).

Wilson's case, a well-endowed actress he was contemplating putting under contract. It would take until June 1951 before Wilson was available, and film could start running through the camera.

Unfortunately for Allen, he was cutting his teeth as a producer in a studio that had become an industry joke. RKO had been a great studio in its glory days, decades previously. Now, under millionaire Hughes, its reputation had become tarnished. Hughes liked to "discover" buxom starlets and place them under contract. Some he would rush onto the screen, such as Faith Domergue. Other actresses were featured in films that sometimes sat on the shelf for years until Hughes felt that the time was right. One such example of the latter is Jane Russell's *Double Dynamite*. Or he might pick movie titles that were exploitative, having nothing to do with the story, only the measurements of the leading lady.

Allen in conversation with Marie Wilson, while Marx and Bendix sit in background.

This time Howard Hughes did not hold up the show (although he did change the title), and *A Girl in Every Port* was in movie houses in time for the Christmas box office boom.

On December 20, 1951, *Daily Variety* said:

> Basic yarn is a fragile framework on which to project the merry adventures of two gobs, Marx and Bendix, who become owners of a racehorse. Although lacking in explosive laughs, pic maintains a fairly steady humorous pace, mainly generated by Groucho's quick-triggered cracks and double-takes.

On the same day, the *Hollywood Reporter* echoed:

Although *A Girl in Every Port* fails to generate the hysteria expected of a comedy in which Groucho Marx is the headliner, the Irwin Allen-Irving Cummings, Jr. production shapes up as average laugh fare, able to fill the bill in secondary and family situations.

KLAC's *The Irwin Allen Show*, circa 1952. Allen is second from right. Among guests: Vincent Price (fourth from left) and, to Price's right, Don DeFore, who appeared in *A Girl in Every Port*.

Taking the counterpoint, on February 16th, *Cue* magazine said:

> A very funny story – "They Sell Elephants to Sailors" – has been movie-murdered by a dull script and duller directions – for both of which [Director] Chester Erskine must be held responsible.

On February 25th, *TIME* said:

> *A Girl in Every Port* (RKO) has Groucho Marx, but not much else, in its favor.

Despite reviews that leaned from mixed to negative, business at the box office was surprisingly good.

A Girl in Every Port took its time moving across the nation, playing the neighborhood movie houses. On the national scene, it never made the Top 10, having to settle for the fifteenth place, but earned back its costs a few times over.

The Sea Around Us (1953)

Irwin Allen had risked much in turning his focus away from the comfort zone of radio and TV to become a movie producer. Perhaps his instincts, along with increasingly harsh reviews and diminishing ratings, convinced him that his days of *Hollywood Merry-Go-Round* and its successor, *Hollywood Party*, were numbered. Perhaps they had merely been stepping stones toward what he really wanted to do – direct, produce, and create.

But the types of movies Allen had been making were not going to take him where he wanted to go – the top of the showbiz heap. So, after apprenticing under Irving Cummings, Jr., and with three films on his resume, Allen went solo.

Of his cousin's determination to succeed, Al Gail said, "We all had interest in films, obviously, where you'd go to the Saturday afternoon serials, and all the movies in the local houses. So he recognized the opportunity, and he had the ability. And he learned how to become a director, producer and a writer for films – *specialized writing* – all on his own, with no help from anyone above him. No nepotism involved anyplace." (AG-KB95)

National Book Award presentation, Hotel Commodore, New York City, 1952. Left to right: recipients Marianne Moore, James Jones, and Rachel Carson, with toastmaster James Mason Brown (Photo from the Associated Press).

Allen had been interested in science and oceanography from an early age. When he read *The Sea Around Us*, a seemingly impossible project to adapt from book to screen, he became determined, even obsessed, to see it realized. And then Allen, the salesman who rarely took "no" for an answer, began pursuing the author of the book.

The Sea Around Us was marine biologist Rachel Carson's second published book (and the second of her "Sea Trilogy"). It was considered by many as "poetic," and in its day described as "revealing the science and the poetry of the sea while ranging from its primeval beginnings to the latest scientific probing." It remained on *The New York Times* Best Seller List for an impressive eighty-six weeks, and won both the 1952 National Book Award for Nonfiction, and a Burroughs Medal in nature writing.

Al Gail said of Allen's fascination regarding *The Sea Around Us*, "It was the project that somehow appealed to him, and he had a lot of trouble getting an okay from Rachel Carson, the writer. She didn't want to do anything in Hollywood with it. But he flew to New York, saw her in New York, with her agent and attorneys, and talked her into it, telling her pretty much what he had in mind. And she was satisfied he wouldn't desecrate it." (AG-KB95)

Allen's idea was to break the immense story down into vignettes, combining new footage with that already filmed by various scientific researchers. At the time of the film's release, he told United Press: "I wrote to 2,341 institutions of oceanography, and told them what we had in mind. I kept four secretaries busy for fourteen months with 6,000 pieces of correspondence."

Allen posing with assistant, reviewing film footage for *The Sea Around Us* (RKO, 1953).

Allen said he wound up with 1,622,363 feet of film (the equivalent to 350 miles) – an amount of film that would take twelve 24-hour days to show. From this, he edited a one-hour-and-two-minute movie. He said, "About 75 percent of the movie was shot just for us, and the rest was scientific film these institutions had in their vaults. Some was 16mm film that had to be enlarged [to 35mm]. The film was shot in every color process known, and some we hadn't heard of, so our laboratory had to fix it so the colors in the different sections matched." (IA-UP53)

The January 14, 1953 review in *Daily Variety* reported:

> Footage used is from actual scientific expeditions and filmed marine studies, all edited to take up most of the categories covered in the book and arranged so as to hold the attention throughout. Subjects range from microscopic life, invisible to the naked eye, to the huge whale, largest of all mammals.... For thrills, picture shows a fight between an octopus and a shark; for chuckles there are clips of the eye-brow raising professions of shark-walking and crab-herding.... Film's ending sounds an ominous note, observing that if all the ice and snow of the world's glacier areas should melt, the present level of the oceans would be raised 100 feet, covering most of the Earth.

A two-page ad in the January 19, 1953 issue of *Daily Variety*, paid for by Allen, trumpeted the good notices:

The *Hollywood Reporter* called *The Sea Around Us*: "Thrilling... amazing spectacle... unforgettable theatrical experience..."

Showman's Trade Review said: "Producer Irwin Allen... has achieved a near-miracle..."

The Film Daily said: "Gripping... definite Academy Award contender..."

Motion Picture Daily said: "May well be best documentary ever produced..."

Edwin Schallert of the *Los Angeles Times* said: "Bound to make audiences starry-eyed..."

The Los Angeles Independent said: "Undersea masterpiece... strong Academy contender..."

Joe Hyams of *The Los Angeles Citizen-News* said: "Must-seeing for everyone in the family..."

Boxoffice magazine said: "Engrossing... Impressive... Exciting..."

The Los Angeles Exhibitor said: "Superb entertainment… Most important contribution… New prestige for motion pictures…"

Dick Williams of the *Los Angeles Mirror* said: "One of the unusual film features of the year… will snag Academy Award nomination…"

One review Allen did not choose to cite was from *TIME*. The magazine's film critic said:

> *The Sea Around Us* is an attempt to do in pictures what Rachel Carson did with words in her bestseller about the eternal mother of the world, the sea. Picture for picture the feature-length film is quite as good as the book is word for word…. And yet, taken as a whole, the film is inferior to the book. For while author Carson saw the sea as a poet might, with the inward eye, director Irwin Allen sees it mostly through a very expensive anastigmatic lens. Though the movie is all about water, it strangely does not flow. The camera concentrates on episode after episode, like an observer stepping from tank to tank in an aquarium, not like a diver roaming through the stopless ocean.

The harshest critic was Rachel Carson herself. According to author Linda Lear in *Rachel Carson: Witness for Nature*, Allen sent Carson the film script, which included the bridging narration which would link all the vignettes together, offer commentary, and even serve as comedy relief in many instances. Carson's response was not favorable.

In a letter to Shirley Collier, her film agent in Hollywood, Carson wrote:

> Frankly, I could not believe my first reading, and had to put it away and then sneak back to it the next day to see if it could possibly be as bad as I thought. But every reading sends my blood pressure higher.

Jeff Stafford, in an article for the internet site Movie Morlocks in 2011, wrote:

> Carson was shocked that instead of sticking to the atmosphere and basic concepts of her book and presenting the authoritative scientific knowledge of the ocean as she had, Allen's script was full of outmoded, unscientific concepts, presented in a distressingly, amateurish manner. She particularly objected to the anthropomorphism of the language Allen used to describe ocean creatures and their relationships with each other.

Allen had also scripted many of the narrative passages in an attempt to inject playful humor, even giving human voice to some of the animals on display.

Illustrating Carson's dissatisfaction, her letter to Shirley Collier continued:

> [T]he practice of attributing human vices and virtues to the lower animals went out of fashion many years ago. It persists only at the level of certain Sunday Supplements.

While Carson's reservations were understandable, she missed an important point. Her book had been addressed primarily to the educated. Conversely, Allen's intent was to convey this message to a much larger audience, by means of a sensational presentation. The humanistic dialogue, and Allen's arranging events into narrative vignettes, were necessary to engage a mass movie-going audience. As any successful preacher knows, you have to get the audience into their seats before they will listen.

Beginning in late January, Allen embarked on tour of fifteen key cities throughout the United States to promote *The Sea Around Us*. Hitting the road to plug a new movie was a task studios usually assigned to the film's stars, not its director. But this film had no stars. Therefore, Irwin Allen himself would become the name above the title. With this movie, Allen began a routine of meeting and schmoozing the major motion picture exhibitors, smooth-talking them into booking his product, and even outlining ways they could better attract a mass audience to their theaters with his films. Allen showed himself to be a master of the promotional gimmick, with ideas often outside-of-the-box for the typical motion picture Public Relations man.

For one newspaper interview, Allen said, "I made [*The Sea Around Us*] against everybody's advice, but it emerged as entertaining and palatable. I'd had some previous success, so the powers said, 'If he's nutty enough to want to do this thing, let him go ahead.'" (IA-IAPC62)

Belying his reputation as a man with no sense of humor, Allen told another interviewer, "This is the first time a textbook was made into a movie. I've got a hot script working on an algebra book, too." (IA-UP53)

The 25th Academy Awards ceremony was held on March 13, 1953, at the RKO Pantages Theatre in Hollywood, California. Irwin Allen was in attendance, dressed to the nines. He was hopeful, yet understandably nervous. His first film as a solo producer, as well as writer and director, had been nominated for Best Documentary of 1952. The nomination had brought Allen his first taste of artistic respect from the Hollywood community. This maker of lowbrow comedies and disposable melodramas, for a once prestigious studio that had become less favored in the industry's eyes, was suddenly receiving public praise from the show business elite.

The Sea Around Us had been the favorite of many film critics, yet its victory was far from assured. The film was competing against Dore Schary's *The Hoaxters*, a red-scare look at communism in the United States. It had been a hit with the public, and the conservative crowd was certainly pulling for the MGM production which had been narrated by an impressive stable of celebrities, including Howard Keel, George Murphy, Walter Pidgeon, Barry Sullivan, Robert Taylor, and James Whitmore. Also vying for the prestigious award was Hall Bartlett's *Navajo*, the story of a Native American boy faced with cultural conflict when he rejects "the white man's school." Many among the Hollywood liberal crowd favored this one.

In spite of any politics at play, Irwin Allen went home that night a triumphant bearer of an Oscar. The little man from a humble beginning, who had come to Hollywood with no connections and hardly any prospects, and affected a Bostonian accent in place of one from the Bronx to suggest an upbringing in Massachusetts, had climbed a great distance as a result of his own tenacity and drive.

Nephew Michael Allen said, "Irwin understood the importance of that moment. That award changed the nature of his career dramatically." (MA-AI15)

After harvesting the 1953 Academy Award for Best Documentary, *The Sea Around Us* found an even wider reception. Interviewed by United Press immediately following his Oscar win, a joyful Irwin Allen said, "Everyone said I was crazy when I announced that I was going to make a picture from Rachel Carson's best seller. But that book topped the best seller list for seventy weeks! How could I lose? I figured if people were that interested in fish and other marine life, they'd sure as shootin' want to see it on the screen." (IA-UP53-2)

Jean Hersholt presents Irwin Allen with his Oscar at the 25th Academy Awards ceremony held on March 19, 1953, at the RKO Pantages Theatre in Hollywood, California.

This success inspired Allen's eagerness to use stock footage, which he would utilize in many of his movies and TV series to come. He said, "If we had shot this film from scratch, it would have cost us four-and-a-half-million dollars. This way, we brought it in for a little over $200,000." (IA-UP52-2)

Striking five hundred prints, RKO gave *The Sea Around Us* a deliberately slow release schedule for the duration of 1953. In Los Angeles, where *Variety* said it was "displaying surprising strength," *Sea* was rated as "socko" and settled in for a long eight-week stay at the Fine Arts Theater. Most movies played one to two weeks in movie houses in this day. A two-month run was a rare occurrence, even for a small house such as the Fine Arts, which seated only 631 people. The story was the same elsewhere. On Broadway, *The Sea Around Us* stayed at New York's 458-seat Trans-Lux at 60th Street for eight weeks. In Philadelphia (where it also was ranked "socko"), it held on for six weeks in a single theater. It rated "big" during its premiere engagement in San Francisco, but this was only big because it was in the small 370-seat Stage Door. In Chicago, at the Surf Theatre, with its 685 seats, *Sea* rated "nice," and stayed for six weeks. In Portland, at the 400-seat Gould, it was classified as "very good."

Irwin Allen had gambled more than a year of his life in the making of a documentary, and that gamble paid off with him being handed Hollywood's most prestigious award for his efforts. Allen's career would eventually become a roller coaster ride of risk-taking. On this occasion, he rolled the dice and won.

Dangerous Mission (1954)

Within a couple of months of winning his Oscar, Irwin Allen had already set up his next film with RKO. The prestige he'd gained allowed him to survive a massive shakeup at the studio during the end of 1952 and the start of 1953. Only five producers were able to maintain their contracts – Edmund Grainger (best known for *Sands of Iwo Jima*), Harriet Parsons (*I Remember Mama*), Sam Wiesenthal (*Cry Danger*), Robert Sparks (the *Blondie* film series), and Allen.

By July 1953, Allen had begun his next picture, with a working title of "The Glacier Story," filmed in Technicolor for an early 1954 release. The story came from author James Edmiston (who wrote the book *Home Again*, about the treatment of Japanese Americans during World War II), with a script by Horace McCoy (who had written 1942's *Gentleman Jim*), and a rewrite by W.R. Burnett (who had received an Academy Award nomination for 1942's *Wake Island)*. Louis King, who helmed of the popular *Bulldog Drummond* film series, was tapped to direct.

***Dangerous Mission* for William Bendix, Piper Laurie, Victor Mature, and Vincent Price (RKO, 1954).**

By the time Burnett's rewrite of McCoy's rewrite of James Edmiston's story went before the camera, "The Glacier Story" was renamed "Rangers of the North." And then, with another rewrite by yet another writer, "Rangers of the North" became *Dangerous Mission*.

Charles Bennett, who had written the screenplay for *Where Danger Lives*, was the last to touch the script, and again found himself in the company of Irwin Allen. He said, "My second involvement with Irwin was on *Dangerous Mission*, which W.R. Burnett helped write before I came to it, and which was a complete mess. It

Piper Laurie and Victor Mature share a *Dangerous Mission* (RKO, 1954).

was already in production when the director Louis King implored me to straighten it out." (CB-HPIS14)

Robert Mitchum was originally envisioned for the film's lead. When a scheduling conflict arose, the starring role of the ex-marine Matt Hallett went to forty-year-old Victor Mature.

Mature had been a silver screen leading man since the end of World War II, with a standout role in John Ford's 1946 film *My Darling Clementine*, the leads in 1947's *Kiss of Death* and Cecil B. DeMille's 1949 epic *Samson & Delilah*, as well as other high profile appearances, such as 1953's *The Robe*.

Piper Laurie was cast as Louise Graham, the damsel in distress. She was twenty-one, and had already played opposite leading men such as Donald O'Connor, Tony Curtis and Rock Hudson.

William Bendix had worked for Allen in *A Girl in Every Port*. He was one year shy of making the move to TV for the first of 217 episodes of *The Life of Riley*.

Forty-one year-old Vincent Price was just finding his niche playing sinister characters, as he had in 1946's *Dragonwyck* and 1953's *House of Wax*.

The story for *Dangerous Mission* was perhaps best described in a dismissive tone by a *Boxoffice* magazine critic, who, in the February 27, 1954 issue, summed up the plot concisely:

> Piper Laurie, the only witness to a brutal gangland killing in New York, flees to Glacier National Park, where she gets a job in a hotel. The mobsters dispatch Vincent Price, a gunman, to the park to rub out Piper so she cannot be subpoenaed as a witness in the New York murder. Also sent to the area is Victor Mature, of the Manhattan police, whose job it is to bring Piper back east unharmed. Mature and Piper become romantically inclined, she not suspecting the nature of his mission.... Into its comparatively brief footage is packed, in king-size quantities, a diversity of story ingredients – mobsters on the lam, outdoor action, forest fires, avalanches, romance and what else would you like?

With that as its blueprint, the film was shot in 3-D. This cumbersome process was the movie industry's latest attempt to woo audiences away from their television sets and back into vacant theater seats. However, by the time *Dangerous Mission* had a trade show screening and was scheduled for general release, the timing was no longer good for cashing in on the 3-D craze that had begun only a couple of years earlier.

The problem was not so much a loss of interest among the public, but that exhibitors were balking at being double-billed for the movies they booked (two separate films and two projectors were required to screen a single 3-D title). Theater owners were coming to the conclusion that they could reap more profit by exhibiting a 3-D movie with standard projection equipment, which completely eliminated the 3-D effect. In fact, Allen's movie would have far more play dates in 2-D than 3-D.

Vincent Price in the first of four roles for Irwin Allen (RKO, 1954).

With *Dangerous Mission* having to stand on its own merits, and not on the added gimmick of 3-D, the critics sharpened their pencils.

For its February 24, 1954 issue, the critic for the *Hollywood Reporter* said:

> With the bulk of the film taking place in Montana's Glacier National Park, *Dangerous Mission* has plenty of impressive scenery to offer, beautifully photographed in Technicolor and 3-D by William Snyder. It also has a story that strains credulity… among [the writers] they have worked out a string of episodic adventures that carry little conviction but do successfully utilize the beauties of the locale.

Filmindia, from May 1954, said:

> *Dangerous Mission* is another ill-tasting concoction served in a Technicolored goblet. Portrayed against some interesting natural scenery, the picture is filled with disgusting contents and deals with crooks and criminals, their criminal, violent activities, and their victims. The theme, of course, is murder. Beginning with one murder, the rest of the picture is devoted to showing a long, sinister, planned attempt by a criminal to commit another murder…. What a useful, instructive and educative story!

With these reviews, and a generic-sounding title, Allen's first attempt as a commercial producer of action films tanked. *Variety* and its sister trade paper, *Daily Variety*, tracked the film's performance at the box office. It started on a good note on March 8th (albeit, not a great one), ranked as "fairish" at the 950-seater Holiday Theater in New York (one of the smaller premiere houses on Broadway), then up to "fine" the following week, and then "good" for its third. Elsewhere, it was rated merely as "average" in Providence; "okay" in Cincinnati; "fair" in Chicago; "slow" in Los Angeles; "mild" in Minneapolis; "poor" in both Montreal and Cleveland; "dull" in Seattle; "light" in Toronto; "thin" in San Francisco; and "limp" in St. Louis. These weren't the adjectives that Allen and RKO wanted to hear in connection with *Dangerous*. In its best week during a three-month first-run tour, it ranked at Number 20 on the national box-office register.

Fortunately for Irwin Allen, by the time *Dangerous Mission* was faltering in the movie houses, he had his next project in development ... at a different studio.

The Animal World (1956)

Daily Variety reported on January 13, 1954:

> Two producers abruptly resigned from RKO yesterday as the studio appeared to be entering another full-scale economy drive.... Exiting producers are Irwin Allen and Sam Wiesenthal. Both make their resignations effective within the next few weeks to give themselves time to clean up their desks. Allen reported immediately that he would enter independent production... Allen, who wrote and produced the Academy Award-winning feature length documentary, *The Sea Around Us*, is finishing up *The Dangerous Mission*, his final assignment after five and one-half years as a writer-producer. He owns three properties which he intends to produce independently.

Allen wasn't waiting for the reviews for *Dangerous Mission* to hit before setting up his next picture deal. In early March 1954, he formed his own company – Windsor Productions – and hired former Cinerama treasurer Ernest Scanlon to arrange financing out of New York for a movie that his investors were banking might bring about a second Academy Award acknowledgment. *The Animal World* was pitched to them as a sequel to *The Sea Around Us*, following the evolution of life from the ocean to the land.

Interviewed by United Press for an April 1955 wire-service article, Allen said of *The Sea Around Us*, "It was the biggest financial success RKO had – twice as big as Jane Russell – and *it* won an Oscar! So I decided to make another picture without actors – a documentary on animals.... I love to make pictures without actors. No temperament and they're always on time in the morning because they're the only actors you can lock away at night." (IA-UP55)

Irwin Allen, planning a production (above) and with Oscar-winning animator Willis O'Brian (below) (Warner Bros., 1956).

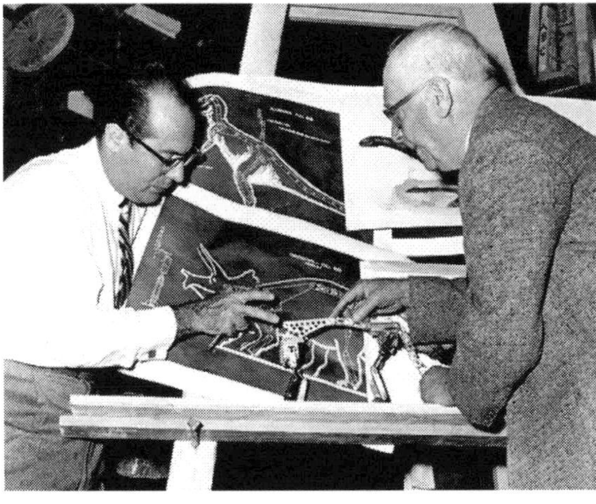

On September 2, 1955, the trades announced that Allen had closed a deal, allowing Warner Brothers to distribute *The Animal World.* He would have to vacate his free RKO digs immediately, but that was fine with Allen. His Windsor Productions moved in to their new complimentary offices at Warner Brothers the next day.

Allen obsessed over this new project, taking two years from inception to distribution. Eighteen months alone were spent in active production. For a workaholic like Irwin Allen, this was an inordinately long period of time to make and arrange for the release of a single picture. He explained, "We had to secure film from sources all over the world. A total of more than 3,000,000 feet was exposed in order to obtain the material that we wanted from many different points of origin.... It required all of two and a half years to bring *The Animal World* to fulfillment. About a year and a half was needed for camera work, preceded by a year of research. However, that is comparatively little to spend on a film which attempts to cover some two and a half billion years in its story – that is, if we assume there have been living things on this Earth for that long." (IA-LAT56)

Ray Harryhausen (Warner Bros., 1956).

As part of that production, seventy-three days alone were needed to create the sequences involving dinosaurs. Using stop-motion animation, Ray Harryhausen, working from designs by Willis O'Brien, carefully and painstakingly moved their models a fraction of an inch for each exposed frame of film, producing the illusion of movement when the footage was projected at normal

Allen playing with his latest toys, with assistance from model and film technicians (above and below: Warner Bros., 1956).

speed. Those seventy-three days created only twelve minutes of the finished film. In comparison, Harryhausen's shooting time was nearly double the typical forty days of principal photography for an ordinary live-action film of the same period.

More delays resulted when Allen and the studio agreed a two-hour running time was perhaps thirty minutes too much. Months passed as the film was edited down to a manageable length – eighty-one minutes. This meant a previously proposed Christmas 1955 release was delayed until early summer 1956.

For a March 16, 1956 *Variety* article, writer Fred Hift said:

> Has Hollywood run out of variations on the seven basic plots? Indie Irwin Allen, who releases through Warner Bros., thinks maybe the time is at hand, and he knows just what to do about it. He started solving the problem with *The Sea Around Us* and he's now following up with the as yet unreleased *The Animal World*, which traces animal history and the animal world's relationship to man. In Gotham last week, Allen said it was his aim to entertain and educate.

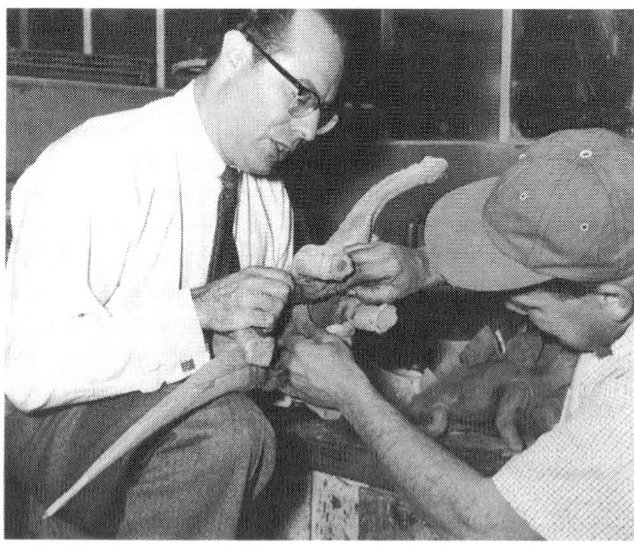

Allen told Hift, "If we can sugarcoat a piece of information, and get them to like it, we've accomplished something." (IA-V56)

Interviewed by Oscar Godbout of *The New York Times* while filming scenes at the Museum of Natural History, Allen bucked at Godbout's description of the film as a documentary on the "evolution of animal life." He said, "We don't use the word 'evolution.' We hope to walk a very thin line. On one hand we want the scientists to say this film is right and accurate, and yet we don't want to have the church picketing the film. However, I think we're safe, since both science and the Bible agree on the fundamental point: life began in the sea." (IA-NYT56)

Allen added, "The first two-thirds of the film will be a panoramic survey of the generation and growth of life. The latter third will show man's relationship to animals through the ages. Man's pretty recent, you know, and the animals get so little credit. Think about Paul Revere. Has anybody ever given any credit to his horse? Where would he have been without the horse? They don't even know the horse's name. See what I mean?" (IA-NYT56)

On June 2, 1956, Jesse Zunser, of *Cue* magazine, said:

> Writer-producer Irwin Allen has set himself the enormous task of trying to picture in 82 minutes the development of animal life on Earth (exclusive of man) from almost the beginning of time. Considering the difficulties, he's done a fairly creditable job – although to many this film may seem more like a grab-bag of odds and ends of briefly interesting film clips, then a cohesive zoological record.

Less impressed, for its June 1956 issue, *Films in Review* said:

> Irwin Allen, who put together *The Sea Around Us*, has put quite a bit of hodge and podge together in *The Animal World* – footage left over from *The Sea Around Us*, other nature footage acquired from various sources, and special effects involving dinosaurs made specially for this film.... Some of his box office ruses are naïve, and a few are vulgar. The narration is anthropomorphic gush, and is spoken by a variety of voices. The placation of Bible fundamentalists is ludicrous, and the truckling to those who fear the kiddies will click to the truth that "nature is raw in tooth and claw" while seeing this film, is venal drool (about a once-upon-a-time land where animals are friends because "no one ever told them they are enemies"). However, Allen is not the fatuous fast-buck chaser such intellectual immorality suggests. Much of his animal footage is objectively interesting, provided you put your fingers in your ears to exclude the irrelevancies, exaggerations and lies which spout without let-up from the sound track.

Warner Brothers launched *The Animal World* wide. It went into hundreds of theaters across North America simultaneously, as the "A" feature in a double bill. Warners ran a newspaper ad campaign touting the film as being "Two Billion Years in the Making." And, unlike *The Sea Around Us*, which was booked into smaller movie houses, *The Animal World* went into medium-size theaters of that day, ranging from 1,000 to 3,000 seats.

On May 30th, Allen flew to New Orleans on the first leg of a 28-day cross-country tour promoting his new film. The last documentary he made had won critical praise and an Oscar. This one needed to win something more tangible – money. As it transpired, *The Animal World* brought home the bacon for Warners and Allen.

The June 27th issue of *Variety* tallied the box office take: Business was "hefty" in Cincinnati; "fine" in Buffalo; "good" in Cleveland; and also doing good business in Providence, Washington D.C. and St. Louis. The film did well enough across the nation to claim the No. 2 slot in the *Variety*'s National Box Office Survey for the week ending June 26th.

Allen had conquered the animal world and was now ready to have another shot at the biped kingdom.

The Story of Mankind (1957)

For his next film, Irwin Allen mixed science fiction and fantasy with pseudo-history, co-writing *The Story of Mankind* for Warner Brothers with Charles Bennett.

Bennett grumbled, "Irwin Allen was the living end! After *Danger*, I wrote his every picture until *The Poseidon Adventure* [1972]. I was his favorite writer, but I couldn't *stand* him – an impossible man with the most horrible swollen head." (CB-HPIS14)

Yet Bennett was always happy to accept work from Allen, who appreciated and felt friendly toward the writer. Sadly, the feeling was hardly returned.

After Allen's death, Bennett scoffed, "*Nobody* could ever be a personal friend of his. But he had tremendous respect for me, and he never dared cross me in any way.... He would come to my house for drinks occasionally, yes, but then, so did many people." (CB-SL93)

Irwin Allen and art department assistant pose for studio publicity photo during pre-production for *The Story of Mankind* (Warner Bros., 1957).

In truth, Allen had many close friends, including Groucho Marx, Red Buttons, Ernest Borgnine, Henry Fonda, Steve Allen, Robert Wagner, Roddy McDowell, Fred Astaire, and Walter Pidgeon. And Allen believed that Bennett was a friend, or at least a friendly and appreciative collaborator. As with many of his long-term employees, Allen was loyal to Bennett, hiring him to co-write many feature films and, later, episodes of TV's *Voyage to the Bottom of the Sea*. Sadly, Bennett's very words betray his own unsavory nature – a man who showed different faces to different people. He was quick to take his employer's money, but was also inclined to attack their characters, question their talents, and demean their works – after the target of his vitriol had died and couldn't answer. The bitter writer saw

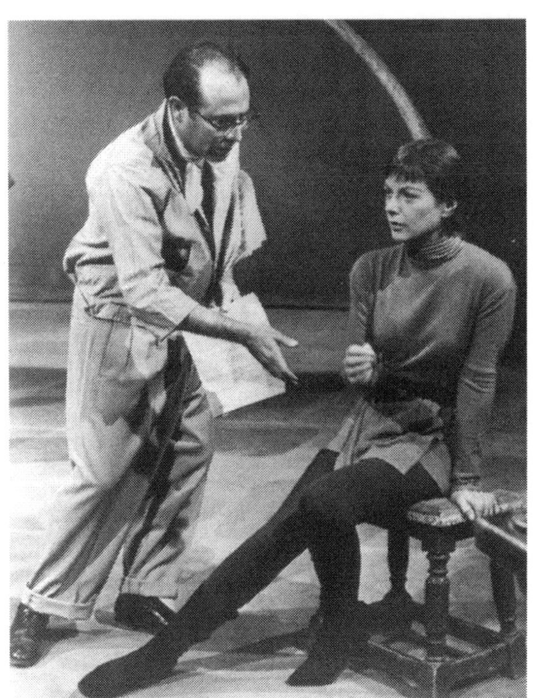

Allen giving direction to Hedy Lamarr for *The Story of Mankind* (Warner Bros. 1957).

himself as above those he worked for, and while many may agree with his assessment of *The Story of Mankind*, it nonetheless said more about the speaker than the filmmaker when Bennett fumed, "That dreadful picture! I came back from England, and Irwin Allen implored me to work on that thing. I didn't realize quite how dreadful it was going to be, or when I was starting off that it was really going to be just a collection of snippets from old pictures and things like that. I *hated* the picture. But I'm a writer; I wrote it; I was being paid quite handsomely, so that was that." (CB-SL93)

Allen had also paid the estate of Hendrik Willem van Loon handsomely for the rights to the title and book to serve as the basis for the film. However, the film had little or nothing to do with the book besides its title.

When asked by interviewer Tom Weaver if the script followed the book, Bennett snapped back with a laugh, "Certainly not! In fact, I never read the book – and I don't think Allen did, either!" (CB-SL93)

A syndicated Associated Press article carried in Michigan's *Kalamazoo Gazette* on December 9, 1956, caught the real Irwin Allen at work (or play, depending on one's perspective), saying:

> Nothing seems to faze the films these days. Now they're attempting to tell the entire story of man. The man behind this ambitious project is Irwin Allen, an energetic young radiocaster turned film producer. He is directing *The Story of Mankind* for Warner Brothers. As a film-maker, Allen is strictly out of the TV dramas about Hollywood. He dashes from a countryside set of a pirate ship followed by a crew of technicians. He climbs to high points for inspiring camera angles. He alternately yells at his underlings and pats them on the cheek fondly. As he leaves the stage, he spies an elaborate window grill in a pile of props. "I like that," he exclaims. "Find me a scene I can shoot through it." Then he rumbles off in his high-priced car to his office. He shouts orders to more underlings and gazes at the gallery of his historical figures on his office wall. "All of them will be portrayed in the picture," he explains. "By the time we finish, we expect to have a bigger cast than Mike Todd had in *Around the World*."

Explaining his approach in telling the story of mankind, Allen told the AP correspondent, "We start with the Hendrik van Loon book. Van Loon had a rare ability to put history into popular terms, to make it understandable to children. But with all due respect to van Loon, history is still something like hearing a joke for the second time. The punch is gone out of it. So, we have added a gimmick. We start out with two stars in the sky. They pulsate as they talk to each other and tell how the people on Earth have developed the gamma bomb, which with one blow could destroy the world. Should it be exploded? Now, we go to someplace in outer space. It's not heaven, because we wouldn't want to offend any religious groups. Here, a trial is held to determine whether Earth should be destroyed. Many of the heroes and the villains of history appear to testify, and we flash back to see their deeds." (IA-AP56)

A trial in the cosmos, with legal rivals and moral opposites played by Vincent Price and Ronald Colman (above and below: Warner Bros., 1957).

The "gimmick" could have been used in any episode of Allen's *Lost in Space*. In fact, it was, in a 1966 episode entitled "Prisoners of Space." A similar cosmic trial of humankind provided the plot for the 1986 pilot episode of *Star Trek: The Next Generation.*

The Story of Mankind was the first of Allen's big, all-star vehicles. The cast included Ronald Colman, Hedy Lamarr, Vincent Price, Peter Lorre and John Carradine (whom Allen would later cast in an episode of *Lost in Space*), among other celebrities. The film was also notable for being the last in which Groucho, Chico, and Harpo Marx appeared together … albeit in separate scenes.

Bennett said, "I don't know that [Vincent Price] enjoyed playing the Devil in *The Story of Mankind*; I don't think anybody enjoyed any part of it. I know Ronald Colman

Groucho Marx, Eden Hartford and Abraham Sofaer in scene from *The Story of Mankind* (Warner Bros., 1957).

hated it, and I don't think Vincent Price liked it either. Nobody liked it. It was just a revolting picture, and it should never have been made." (CB-SL93)

But Irwin Allen liked it and labored over it endlessly. Al Gail said, "I'll quote Groucho Marx. One day, Little Irwin was very upset about something that had gone wrong, or doing something with the picture, and Groucho said, 'Why are you getting excited? It's only a movie!' In other words, 'That's not real life. There's no tragedy here. It's a movie. Have perspective.' And I guess perspective was what Irwin didn't have." (AG-KB95)

On May 6, 1957, *Newsweek* said:

> If there is anything to the Hollywood theory that one way to get people into the theaters is to stun them with sheer size, the beaches this August are going to be deserted. For last week, Irwin Allen, producer and director of Warner Brothers' *The Story of Mankind*, had finished shooting on the most pretentious-sounding movie in recent history. He figures to have the whole thing wrapped up and ready for the public in time for the summer slump. The grandiose movie is based on historian Hendrik Willem Van Loon's best seller, which producer Allen has, of course, consulted ("I enjoyed the whole million years in history," he says. "Each one became a challenge.")

Allen, quoted further in the *Newsweek* piece, remarked, "I said to our research department, 'Find me the giants of history – those people who affected mankind more than anyone else. We found four hundred so-called giants. Obviously, if we were to devote only a minute to each of these giants it would be impossible to tell the story. We boiled it down to fifty-eight people." (IA-NW57)

On October 8, 1957, *Daily Variety* ran the headline, "WB *Story* Winds A-Bomb Pix Race, Declares Allen." Allen told the trade that *The Story of Mankind* was coming at "psychologically the right time" with all the worry in America about a nuclear war with Russia. He was also proud to divulge that his new movie was made with 100% Warner Brothers financing. And yet, he was earmarked for 25% of the profits.

One day later, in sister trade *Variety*, Allen was talking again, projecting that *The Animal World* should clear between $500,000 and $1,000,000 in profits worldwide. He was feeling confident *The Story of Mankind* would do even better, with its sixty-two speaking parts, and many of those assigned to Hollywood stars. "A star," said Allen, "is a name personality whose name is quickly recognized by the public. In recent years, the term ‘star’ also has come to mean someone who can ‘sell’ a picture. It’s almost like a brand name.” (IA-DV57)

Daily Variety gave exhibitors and Hollywood insiders their first peek at *The Story of Mankind* with a review from October 23, 1957. The critic wrote:

Helmut Dantine and Virginia Mayo (Warner Bros., 1957).

> For more than a generation, Hendrik Willem Van Loon’s monumental *Story of Mankind* has been second only to the Bible as a non-fiction best-seller. Now, it has been brought to the screen in a name-dropping production that provides a kaleidoscope of history from the Pleistocene man to early Plutonium man. In the process, however, producer-director Irwin Allen seemed unable to decide whether to do a faithful history of man’s development into a thinking being, a debate on whether man’s good outweighs his evil, or a compilation of historical sagas with some humor dragged in for relief.

On the same day, James Powers, writing for *The Hollywood Reporter*, said:

> It is difficult to tell sometimes if Allen is playing it straight or tongue-in-cheek, and the dialogue does not always help.... The most serious criticism of *Story of Mankind* is that it does not live up to its title. How could it be a presentation of mankind, which means the human race, and omit Christ, Mohammed, Buddha, Plato, Galileo, Luther, Marx and Lenin? This *Story of Mankind* is a Sunday supplement of a story in which the characters have been chosen for their superficial glamour rather than any other value.

Charles Bennett said, “[I]t was way too long. I remember the sneak preview at a theater in the Valley, and the wretched Jack Warner – who owned Warner Bros. – was there. At the end, we all went and talked about it around a table in a pub, and I said, ‘It has to be cut. This is no good in its present form.’ Jack Warner said, ‘Oh, let’s just put it out.’ And all his yes-men said, ‘Yes, Jack’s right, let’s put it out.’ So, they did.” (CB-SL93)

Al Gail said of his cousin Irwin: “He liked it. We felt, naturally, that some of the reviews were unfair. But the film did fairly well. No blockbuster, but, for the type of thing it was, it did fairly well.” (AG-KB95)

Not really. The movie to beat in November was *Around the World in Eighty Days*, Mike Todd’s adventure epic with David Niven at the head of an all-star cast. Irwin Allen’s “all-star epic” wouldn’t even make the national Top Ten list. The adjectives describing its performance in various big-house theaters across the country were: "poor" and "a new low" in Philadelphia; "drab" in Boston; "mild" in Chicago and San Francisco; merely "okay" in Washington D.C.; "terrible" in Seattle; "so-so" in Buffalo; "sad" in Denver; and "wobbly" in Los Angeles.

Allen could not accept that he had made a bad film. Trying to explain the failure, he told a newspaper reporter, "I think the title scared the customers away." (IA-IAPC62)

Allen's nephew, Michael, said, "It was a lousy movie. It bothered Irwin a lot because he wasn't used to losing. He was a winner in a whole lot of different ways. And he was a competitor. And when you lose due to your own failings, it is no fun at all." (MA-AI15)

Unknown studio executive with Irwin Allen (Allied Artists, 1959).

The Big Circus (1959)

Irwin Allen's next film seemed to be the one that he ran off to Hollywood to make. Nephew Michael Allen said, "Irwin had a love and a passion for the circus, because it was great show business. And he loved show business. He understood the nature of the circus, and entertainment, in general." (MA-AI15)

For its day, *The Big Circus* featured an impressive cast.

Victor Mature, who had starred in Allen's *Dangerous Mission*, was given the lead.

Red Buttons was 40, and had been a star on Broadway, as well as having his own TV series, 1952's *The Red Buttons Show*. Now he was a hot item in the movies. For his role in the 1957 Marlon Brando film *Sayonara*, Buttons won an Oscar as Best Supporting Actor. Several months later, he went to work for Irwin Allen.

Rhonda Fleming was 35. She had starred in many popular films, such as 1949's *A Connecticut Yankee in King Authur's Court*, opposite Bing Crosby; 1957's *Gunfight at the O.K. Corral*, co-starring with Burt Lancaster and Kirk Douglas; and 1953's *Pony Express*, opposite Charlton Heston.

Paul Zastupnevich, Irwin Allen's personal assistant and wardrobe designer for three decades, said of his boss, "At one time he was a disc jockey. He had a program from the old Hawaiian Theatre in Hollywood, on the boulevard there. It was at that time that he met Marilyn Lewis, who was Rhonda Fleming. While he was doing his program with her, he said, 'One of these days I'm going to put you in a picture.' And that's how Rhonda agreed to be in *The Big Circus*." (PZ-KB95)

The Big Circus **was Irwin Allen's first movie spectacle and all-star cast. From left to right: Vincent Price, Gilbert Roland, Rhonda Fleming, Victor Mature, Red Buttons, Kathryn Grant, David Nelson, and Peter Lorre (Allied Artists, 1959).**

Kathryn Grant – Mrs. Bing Crosby – was 26. She was top-billed in the 1957 sci-fi film *The Night the World Exploded*, then starred opposite Jack Lemmon that same year in *Operation Mad Ball*. She had the female lead in 1958's *The* 7th *Voyage of Sinbad.*

Irwin Allen said, "Bing actually acted as Kathy's agent for this part. He read the script and told her, 'Take it. It will make you a star." (IA-RMN59)

Gilbert Roland and Kathryn Grant, doing many of their own stunts (Allied Artists, 1959).

Vincent Price was 48, and had worked for Irwin Allen before, in *Dangerous Mission*, and then played the Devil in *The Story of Mankind*.

Gilbert Roland, cast as flying trapeze performer Zach Colino, was 54, and had been a leading man in Hollywood since the late 1930s. His most famous screen character was arguably the Cisco Kid, which Roland played in six films, beginning with 1946's *The Gay Cavalier*.

Peter Lorre gained fame in

Irwin Allen recalled Peter Lorre approaching him in a barber shop and saying, "Why not make *me* the clown?" (Allied Artists, 1959)

1931 with the lead in the German-produced thriller, *M*. Alfred Hitchcock cast him in his first English-speaking part – another good villainous role – for 1934's *The Man Who Knew Too Much*. That standout performance brought Hollywood calling. Lorre was soon starring in his own film series, as the crime-solving Mr. Moto, beginning with 1937's *Think Fast, Mr. Moto*. Irwin Allen was impressed with Lorre's turn in the 1954 sci-fi film *20,000 Leagues Under the Sea*, and cast him for a cameo in *The Story of Mankind*.

Regarding the role for *The Big Circus*, Allen said, "Peter Lorre plays a clown – and a wonderful one. But I never would have thought of casting him in the part. It happens that Lorre and I have our barber appointments in the same shop at the same time, in adjoining chairs. One day we were talking about the picture, and he jokingly said, 'Why not make *me* the clown?' I thought it was a great idea." (IA-RMN59)

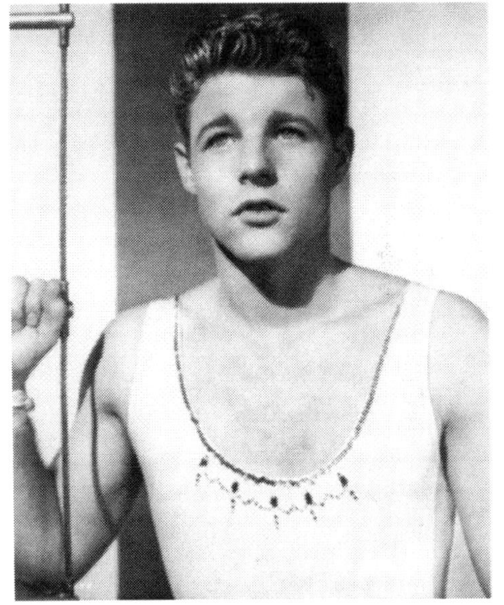

David Nelson found his second calling – trapeze flying – while filming *The Big Circus* (Allied Artists, 1959)

Also in the cast was David Nelson, son of Ozzie and Harriet Nelson. David had been overshadowed on *Adventures of Ozzie and Harriet* by his younger brother Ricky, who was an immensely successful pop singer, second in popularity and chart success only to Elvis Presley. Before the movie's release, Irwin Allen said, "Maybe David can't sing, but he has a million dollar personality. When I signed him, his father asked me for 50 percent of the billing [in respect to the size of Nelson's name compared to the film's lead actors]. We said we would have to wait until he made the picture. Now that the picture is finished, he gets 100 percent and is billed equally with Vic Mature, Red Buttons and the other top stars." (IA-ADB59)

As a result of making *The Big Circus*, David Nelson became an active aerialist. From the June 1960 issue of *TV Month*:

> Total sales of Rick Nelson records by now have exceeded 13 million. The records have showered a rain of gold on the young boy to the tune of 1,000 dollars a week in salary from the record company, Imperial Records, plus the usual royalties. In addition,

> Rick became a "hot" concert artist, wanted for personal appearances all over the country at fees of additional thousands of dollars a week. To Dad Ozzie, who has managed and masterminded the four Nelsons since the radio service started, Rick's special career has become an important sideline, even more lucrative than the popular TV series itself. Brother Dave? Somehow, the older Nelson boy was lost in the shuffle. Dave couldn't sing. Nor did he possess a magnetic personality like Rick. He was good at acting, but he didn't register as especially outstanding. "It wasn't fair," says Ozzie Nelson, "but these are the ways of fame." It hurt dad and mum to see Dave pushed into the background, but it hurt Rick even more. Then, last year while working for Allied Artists, *The Big Circus*, Dave discovered his calling.
>
> Cast as a "catcher" in an aerialist act, he found that he could do what was required of a "catcher" without resorting to tricks or help from a stuntman. The aerialists in the picture were Del and Babs Graham, stars of "The Flying Viennas" trapeze troupe that appeared with the Ringling Circus for three years.
>
> The Grahams had been hired to "double" for the stars, including Dave Nelson, and to serve as technical advisers on the picture. "Dave showed so much natural ability as an aerialist," Del Graham recalls, "that when the film was finished we offered to stick around." Dave became a Graham protégé. He practiced with them every weekend and occasionally during the week when he had no TV scenes to film. "His progress was amazing," Graham says. "It was so unusual that one day I told him that if he'd ever want to join my troupe as a 'catcher,' the job was his. So he said, 'What's wrong with right now?'"

David talked his brother Ricky into training with him, then appearing together in the fall of 1959 before an audience at the Great Western Livestock Show in Los Angeles. The flying trapeze act was sprung as a surprise on the thousands who had settled around the arena to watch a circus in action.

"It was Dave's idea," Rick told *TV Month*. "I simply went along."

Ozzie Nelson then featured his sons repeating their flying trapeze act in a celebrated episode of *The Adventures of Ozzie and Harriet*, aired in January 1960. One of the biggest pop stars in America, second only to Elvis Presley at the time, performed again without a stunt double. And all because of Irwin Allen's *The Big Circus*.

Allen said he would offer the film to Warner Brothers for distribution. But this was before the release of *The Story of Mankind*. With that disaster, Warners took a pass on *The Big Circus*, and Allen went distributor shopping.

Harry Cohn and his Columbia Pictures stepped up to the plate next, but they quickly dropped out as the budget for the film approached $2,000,000.

Director Joseph M. Newman, Victor Mature, Irwin Allen, Rhonda Fleming, and Peter Lorre (above) and Fleming (below), doing many of her own stunts (Allied Artists, 1959).

On December 10, 1958, it was announced in the trades that Allen had secured a deal with Allied Artists to distribute his new big-event film. At this point, the movie had surpassed the $2,000,000 mark, and was not yet complete.

Al Gail said the only other director doing Irwin Allen-type movies during this period was Cecil B. DeMille. Or, more correctly, Allen was doing Cecil B. DeMille-type movies. Gail said of Allen, "DeMille and he were also, in a sense, compared to Samuel Goldwyn, because Goldwyn, as you know, took great pride in his sets and his costumes, and everything [to do with] the look. And so did Irwin. And we were always under a lot of pressure, because we always ran over budget, because he wanted it to look right. Sure, you could save money by cutting this and cutting that, or taking 20 people out of a crowd scene, but that was not his way. He said, 'If you're going to do it, you do it right.' And that led to front office problems." (AG-KB95)

For a January 11, 1959 *New York Times* article, writer Thomas M. Pryor wrote:

> … Irwin Allen promises [*The Big Circus*] will be a "colorful, big, blary, noisy show – the biggest circus ever seen anywhere." … The producer, who also wrote the screenplay with Charles Bennett, was not the least inclined to backtrack when reminded that Cecil B. DeMille didn't spare the tanbark in filming *The Greatest Show on Earth.* Mr. Allen just smiled and pointed to a slogan nearby that proclaimed "The *Biggest* Show on Earth."

For a syndicated newspaper article, Allen stressed, "The DeMille movie, remember, was made before VistaVision and CinemaScope. [My] picture was filmed in the biggest tent in the world – 400 feet long, and specially constructed on MGM's biggest sound stage. In it we have tried to recreate the circus as it is seen through the eyes of a child – one of the most beautiful things in the world, seen in a kind of fantasy-scope." (IA-RMN59)

Interviewed by the *Denver Post* by Larry Tajiri for a July 1, 1959 article, Allen boasted, "I believe we have the biggest, most colorful circus film ever made. Ours is no ordinary three-ring tent show. It is the circus of our childhood dreams, when everything was greater and grander than they could be in real life. This is the most commercial film I have ever produced, but one which I believe has elements which will appeal to every age group." (IA-DP59)

Beginning with *The Big Circus*, Irwin Allen would never again make a movie or television program without his right-hand man at his side – personal assistant, artist, wardrobe designer, and occasional actor, Paul Zastupnevich.

This was the movie for which Paul Zastupnevich joined Irwin Allen's team as a wardrobe designer. He was a native of Pittsburgh, Pennsylvania, and was active in local theater and opera, designing costumes and acting in supporting roles for the Civic Opera. After helping to produce musical comedies that entertained World War II troops stationed at Ft. Benning, Georgia, Zastupnevich borrowed from the G.I. Bill program in order to further his studies at the Pasadena Playhouse in California. For five years he worked on 75 productions, creating costumes, but he also acted, under the name of Paul Kremin. Being cast in the role of an Amish man for one production resulted in his growing his mustache and goatee, which he would keep throughout his career. And, with a last name that was a challenge for most people to remember and pronounce, he also became known as "Paul Z." During this time, as a wardrobe designer, Zastupnevich learned to create costuming out of makeshift materials, ideal training for television.

Performing and designing costumes for the theater was creatively satisfying work, but was hardly paying his way. For this reason Zastupnevich was close to giving up on a career in show business. And that's when Irwin Allen entered his life.

Zastupnevich admitted, "I had been in Los Angeles just over nine years at the time, and had given myself until Christmas. If I didn't make it, I was going home to Pittsburgh. I had a boutique in Beverly Hills, doing gowns and dresses for actresses, and was introduced to Rhonda Fleming, who needed a gown for a TV awards ceremony within four days! I created a gown with a special feature that showed off her legs when she walked, and it was a hit. Rhonda then told me that she and the costume designer on her new picture, *The Big Circus*, weren't getting along. She suggested that I give it a try and said she would get me in to see the producer, Irwin Allen." (PZ-SL93)

Zastupnevich created a "presentation" folder with watercolor illustrations of his designs, including drawings of Fleming in several different outfits. Each drawing had the actress' name, the name of the character, and the presentation had a hand-lettered *Big Circus* title on its cover. Zastupnevich declared, "Irwin loved it! He looked at me and said I had 'showmanship.' I was on cloud nine, because it was unheard of at the time for an unknown to walk in and get a picture." (PZ-SL93)

Ringmaster Vincent Price (Allied Artists, 1959).

Zastupnevich said of Allen, "My first dealing with him was through my agent, who at that time was Harry Bernsen. And Harry said to me, 'Whatever *he* says, he's right, and he's never wrong. Don't ever argue; just agree with him.' So I got to the point where I learned all of his little idiosyncrasies. I knew his color preferences; I knew what kind of shirts he liked to wear; I went shopping with him at times. That was a very funny thing about him – every time he went away on a trip, he never took a laundered shirt; he had to have brand new shirts. We would go to Carol's and Monty Factor's and get him a half a dozen shirts to pack in the suitcases. Everything had to be brand new – new shirts, new socks, new everything. I don't know what that was all about. I think that harks back to the days when he was a little boy and didn't have much. He came up the hard way." (PZ-KB95)

Zastupnevich added, "The job was supposed to be for only three weeks. I ended up staying approximately thirty-two years. I'm like the proverbial man who came to dinner – I never left. A lot of people say to me, 'Why did you put up with him? Why did you stay if you were so unhappy at times?' And I said, 'Well, you know, after all, I had been in Hollywood for nine years knocking on the doors; I'd been at the Pasadena Playhouse doing things; I'd been an actor and whatnot, and this was the first time that I got a chance to do a picture. He gave me a three million dollar picture! I hadn't done any movie work up till this time. But, on the basis of that presentation of mine, he gave me the chance." (PZ-KB95)

Allen and Price on set of *The Big Circus*, their third of four projects together (Allied Artists, 1959)

The Big Circus was Allen's first time working with Winton Hoch, who had won three Academy Awards as Best Cinematographer – for 1948's *Joan of Arc*, 1949's *She Wore a Yellow Ribbon* and 1952's *The Quiet Man*. He had also been the director of photography on other classics, such as 1955's *Mister Roberts*, 1956's *The Searchers* and 1959's *Darby O'Gill and the Little People*. Allen was so impressed with Hoch's work that he arranged his production schedule to be sure the talented D.P. could shoot the rest of his 1960s films – *The Lost World*, *Voyage to the Bottom of the Sea* and *Five Weeks in a Balloon*. He would also convince Hoch to make the move to television, as cinematographer for fifty-one episodes of the television version of *Voyage*, as well as several episodes of *Lost in Space* and all the episodes of *The Time Tunnel*.

The Big Circus was released in early July, 1959. On July 8th, the film critic for *Variety* said:

> Irwin Allen's *The Big Circus* is a rousingly lavish film, stocked with tinted elephants, snarling lions and three rings of handsome production. While at times it looks too much like Hollywood's view of the big top, rather than reality, it is shrewdly calculated to satisfy the peanut-and-sawdust yen of the millions to whom circus-going is a less frequently available diversion than in past generations.

Bosley Crowther, writing for *The New York Times*, laid out his verdict on July 18th, and sniffed:

> There is nothing very subtle about a circus. If you will keep this fact in mind – and also the fact that the world's record in spectacular circus films is held by a most unsubtle champion, the *Greatest Show on Earth*, of the late Cecil B. DeMille – then you can better be prepared for the beating you are going to have to endure when you take the kids to see Irwin Allen's *The Big Circus*, which opened at the Roxy yesterday. One hour and forty-nine minutes of riotous clichés – that's what you're in for, ladies and gentlemen and children of all ages, as they say, with the tiresome assurance of old showmen who persist in thinking you can't insult the intelligence of a kid. One hour and forty-nine minutes of acts, among which, we must say, the [animal] ones are a little more convincing than the ones performed by the human beings!

On August 3rd, *TIME* said:

> *The Big Circus* often looks like a gaudily colored CinemaScope production of *The Ed Sullivan Show*.

Philip K. Scheuer, writing for the *Los Angeles Times* on August 6th, said:

> Allen's whole picture is on the same level of elementary thinking. It's hokum, but DeMille's *Greatest Show on Earth* was hokum, too. The difference was that DeMille had a showman's instincts. Nor has Allen the cinematic gift of a Carol Reed, whose *Trapeze* camera floated through the air with the greatest of ease.... There is

> nothing exceptional about *The Big Circus* – except, maybe, its use of the word "big." A greater artist [Charlie Chaplin] was once content to call his concept simply *The Circus*.

Although the reviews were mixed, and sometimes savage, *The Big Circus* gave Allen the box-office hit he'd been striving for. It was "wow" at Denver's 2,043-seat Orpheum; "excellent" in Washington, D.C., at the Uptown, with 1,100 seats; "loud" in Baltimore at the 2,300-seat Hippodrome; "swell" in Detroit, at the Palms theatre, with 2,296 seats; "fine" in Portland, at the Orpheum, with its 1,600 seats; "big" in Indianapolis, at the Circle, with 2,800 seats, "fancy" in Buffalo, at the Lafayette, with 3,000 seats; "socko" in Omaha, at the Omaha Theater and its 2,066 seats; "great" in Kansas City, at the Uptown, with 2,093 seats; and, on Broadway, rocking the Roxy, with the theater's biggest first day, biggest second day, biggest third day, and biggest fourth day. For its July 22, 1959 issue, *Variety* ranked *The Big Circus* as the seventh highest-grossing movie in America. One week later, it was the fourth. A week after that, down to fifth place.

Irwin Allen could now reach for a bigger brass ring – a production deal with one of Hollywood's true "majors."

The Lost World (1960)

For Allen's next film, the 20th Century-Fox press release from August 1960 promised:

> Stranger then the wildest science fiction dreams is the land of the "lost world" where Jurassic monsters from 150,000,000 B.C. roam at will, where dinosaurs rule the land and man-eating plants reach out at every bend in the trail.
>
> This is the untamed and untouched place that zoology professor Challenger (Claude Rains) takes his unforgettable expedition to. Accompanying him on this journey into the past are Lord Roxton (Michael Rennie), a playboy and big game hunter; Jennifer Holmes (Jill St. John), daughter of an executive who finances the venture; David Holmes (Ray Stricklyn), Jennifer's brother; Ed Malone (David Hedison), American newsman, and Professor Summerlee (Richard Haydn), a scientist. Joining the expedition at a remote trading post on the Amazon are Gomez (Fernando Lamas), who pilots the helicopter to the plateau of *The Lost World*, and Costa (Jay Novello), a jungle agent and guide.

> Unknown animals menace the party at every turn. A large animal blocks their path upon arrival and knocks the helicopter over a cliff. It is identified by Prof. Challenger as a brontosaurus, but still the party plunges deeper into the unknown....
>
> *The Lost World*, Irwin Allen's remarkable production of Sir Arthur Conan Doyle's gripping story of a trip to a prehistoric land, filmed in CinemaScope and DeLuxe Color...

Screenwriter Charles Bennett said, "It was as simple as the fact that somebody suggested to Irwin that he should make *The Lost World*. He liked the idea of prehistoric monsters and things like that, so he asked me to write the script.... I knew the novel by heart; I know *all* Conan Doyle's stuff by heart. I loved him." (CB-SL93)

Io November 6, 1959, in *Daily Variety*, staffer Ron Silverman wrote:

> The price of thrills has gone up, according to producer-director Irwin Allen, who yesterday termed his forthcoming *The Lost World* the most expensive "exploitation" picture ever made. He said the 20th-Fox release will cost a minimum of $2,000,000. The film will abound in prehistoric monsters, Allen pointed out, and kids want to be fooled by them, but he explains it takes more to fool them these days. "The special effects, the story and the entire production must be done with such expertness that audiences accept them even though they know it couldn't happen." That, opined Allen, can't be done satisfactorily on a small budget. The filmmaker admitted a $100,000 exploitation pic can get back its cost by appealing to only a small segment of the motion picture public. "But to return a significant profit, the film must appeal to the entire family," he added. "We start off by saying, 'I want to get the kids into the theaters,' and we know that every third kid is going to bring an adult. By giving adults something that will entertain them, we'll get other adults."

This time out, Allen would be allowed to direct, as well as produce and co-write the screenplay. For a July 6, 1960 *Variety* article, the trade said:

> Whenever possible, a producer should serve as his own director. "It's part of the modern way of filmmaking," according to producer Irwin Allen who directed his current 20th-Fox release, *The Lost World,* as well as his 1957 production, *The Story of Mankind*, released by Warners. By functioning in this dual capacity, a producer simplifies the chain of command, Allen said in New York last week, "eliminating all those little frictions which are bound to arrive in the course of a production between a producer and a director." There should always be great harmony between a producer and a director and "what better way to achieve this than by having the harmony in one beast?"... As to the future of theatrical films, he is optimistic. The population is exploding all

over the place, and more customers are being born than are being lost through death or other unnatural causes.

David Hedison, Michael Rennie and Claude Rains (above) and Hedison (below) (20th Century-Fox, 1960).

Allen hired Michael Rennie to play the playboy game hunter who had an ulterior motive for going on the adventure. Rennie was fifty, and had starred as Klaatu in the 1951 sci-fi classic, *The Day the Earth Stood Still.* Immediately following *The Lost World*, he would have his own television series, *The Third Man*, which co-starred Jonathan Harris (later to play Dr. Smith in *Lost in Space*). Later, Allen would hire Rennie for *Lost in Space*'s only two-part episode, "The Keeper."

Jill St. John was 28 when cast as the girl along for the ride. She had made her big screen debut in 1958's *Summer Love*. She moved up from fourth billing to third, and then second, with her next few films.

David Hedison met Irwin Allen with this acting job, playing the newspaperman assigned to accompany the adventurers. He was thirty-one, and, as Al Hedison, had already been featured prominently in the 1957 hit *The Enemy Below*, and given the lead in the 1958 sci-fi classic, *The Fly*. Immediately following *The Lost World*, he would star in his own hour-long TV series, *Five Fingers*, as a U.S. Intelligence agent working in Europe.

Fernando Lamas played the helicopter pilot, who, like others in the movie, had ulterior reasons for joining the expedition. He was forty-three, and had been a film star in his home country of Argentina before being brought to America with an MGM contract. The studio featured him as a romantic lead in 1952's *The Merry Widow*, opposite Lana Turner, 1953's *The Girl Who Had Everything*, opposite Elizabeth Taylor, and during the same year, *Dangerous When Wet*, opposite Esther Williams.

Popular character actor Richard Haydn was added for comedy relief. He was fifty-four, and known for playing pompous types. He is perhaps best remembered as the freeloading theatrical agent Uncle Max, from 1965's *The Sound of Music*.

The beautiful native girl was played by twenty-two-year-old Vitina Marcus, who would become close to Irwin Allen and work often in his productions. She said, "I was a dancer, and I'd studied with Lee Strasberg, learning Method Acting for four years. I had one small part [on stage], and then starred in a live television show in New York." (VM-AI15)

Allen's second film spectacle with an all-star cast. Left to right: Fernando Lamas, Jay Novello, Michael Rennie, Richard Haydn, Claude Rains, Jill St. John, David Hedison, Ray Stricklyn, and Vitina Marcus (20th Century-Fox, 1960).

She was Dolores Vitina then, appearing on Christmas night, 1957, in the *Kraft Theatre* presentation of "The Other Wise Man." She followed that with an episode of *Schlitz Playhouse*, then played John Drew Barrymore's sister in the 1958 Barrymore/ Steve McQueen starrer, *Never Love a Stranger*. A handful of TV westerns followed, including *Have Gun – Will Travel*, *Death Valley Days* and *Wagon Train*, in which she was usually cast as an American Indian. In 1960, Dolores Vitina became Vitina Marcus.

Marcus recalled, "After that, Jackie Gleason's manager signed me up. He wanted to put me under contract with one of the studios, even though I never wanted that. But he sent me to Hollywood and my agent there took me to 20th Century-Fox for an audition. A short while later he took me back, this time to meet Irwin Allen. Irwin asked me if I knew why I was there. I said, 'No,' just that my agent brought me. He had me sit down in his office and he told me this little story about how he had seen me at 20th once before, but only from the back when I stepped into an elevator." (VM-AI15)

After getting that glimpse of Marcus, Allen learned her name from a security guard. Then he contacted her agent. Marcus said, "He wanted me to test for *The Lost World*. That was fine with me, until I saw the costume he wanted me to wear! I had actually just had a baby six months prior to that. Fortunately, I had been able to get my figure back. As it turned out, Irwin used that costume I wore in *The Lost World* in three different shows. The first three times I worked for him, I wore the same outfit!" (VM-AI15)

The next two turns in the skimpy outfit were for episodes of *Voyage to the Bottom of the Sea*. After that, Allen would have Marcus painted green and costumed in glistening tights for a pair of *Lost in Space* episodes. He would also cast her in two episodes of *The Time Tunnel*.

For the top-billed role in the movie, Charles Bennett recommended his friend Claude Rains. Rains was 59, and had already been nominated four times for an Oscar: as Best Supporting Actor, with 1940's *Mr. Smith Goes to Washington*, 1944's *Casablanca*, 1945's *Mr. Skeffington*, and 1947's *Notorious*. He was also the first to play *The Invisible Man* (in 1933).

Pre-production artwork (above) and lizard shot from low camera angle (below) to realize the artist's rendition (20th Century Fox, 1960).

Regarding Rains, Paul Zastupnevich groaned, "[Irwin Allen] chastised me once for calling Claude Rains 'Claude,' and proverbially bawled me out. Claude overheard and said '<u>I</u> made the request. I want Paul to call me Claude. I don't want to be called Mr. Rains, it makes me feel like an old man, and I want to feel young.'" (PZ-KB95)

Allen didn't think it was respectful for underlings to address stars of movies, or for that matter, celebrity producers, by their first names. Rains may have been fine with it, but Allen was not. However, in Hollywood of this era, it was acceptable, and even traditional, to address major film producers and studio moguls by their initials. Zastupnevich revealed, "So, I never called him 'Irwin.' I never referred to him as 'Mr. Allen.' I always used his initials whenever I had any dealing with him. I always called him 'I.A.' He just didn't want to be on a personal relationship with you." (PZ-KB95)

Someone else who went by their initials was L.B. Abbott, 20th Century-Fox's special effects/photographic effects wizard. His friends called him "Bud," but Allen did not. This was L.B.'s first dealing with I.A.

Abbott was 50, and worked exclusively for Fox at this time. He would soon receive an Academy Award for his effects in the studio's 1960 feature film, *Journey to the Center of the Earth*. Before retiring, he would win the award on three more occasions, including Allen's 1972 film, *The Poseidon Adventure*. He would also win three Emmys, all as a result of his involvement with Allen. Two were for the TV version of *Voyage to*

Jim Donaldson handling two of the lizards used during filming (above) and composite shot combining footage of David Hedison with a lizard (20th Century Fox, 1960).

the Bottom of the Sea, and the third was for *The Time Tunnel* series. Abbott also worked on *Lost in Space*.

Abbott later said, "I personally feel that a great many of us in the industry owe Mr. Allen a sincere 'thank you' for all the employment his tireless organizational efforts provided for us." (LBA-SE84)

For his book, *Special Effects: Wire, Tape and Rubber Band Style*, Abbott wrote of his first encounter with Allen, saying, "One evening at about six in the late summer of 1959, my boss, Sid Rogell, called and asked me to come posthaste to the production meeting room. When I entered the room, I was confronted by ten strangers. Everyone, including Sid, nodded, and I sat down. After some thirty minutes of listening, I realized that the leader of the group was a gentleman named Irwin Allen. He held an option on a property called *The Lost World*, based on the novel by Sir Arthur Conan Doyle. The issue was that the option would expire in New York about two-and-a-half hours hence. The studio's involvement, as I recall, meant an immediate investment of $10,000. Mr. Rogell turned to me and asked, 'Bill, can we make this picture?' I said, 'Yes.' That ended my dialogue and I was excused…. Little did I imagine that my one word commitment was the start of the Irwin Allen syndrome for me." (LBA-SE84)

Now that he had the job, Abbott had to find a way to realize the commitment that he had made. He revealed, "Having experienced problems with the rhinoceros iguanas in *Journey to the Center of the Earth*, I had a talk with Jim Donaldson, an animal man in the industry who is well-versed in the reptile field. Inasmuch as we needed a variety of

monsters, I concurred with his suggestion and we used monitor lizards from the Singapore area for the large dinosaurs. They are six to seven feet long and weigh 70 to 150 pounds. Unlike the iguanas, they are voracious flesh eaters descended from the ancient line of varanian reptiles which, in prehistoric times, attained gigantic size. They naturally move the way monsters should." (LBA-SE84)

Irwin Allen (far left) holding court with cast and crew on the set (20th Century Fox, 1960).

For scenes featuring the lizards moving through the tropical terrain and joining in combat, a large miniature tabletop jungle set was built, twenty feet deep and forty feet wide. It was raised three feet above the stage floor, with a sloping "apron" in the front. The raised set helped to contain the lizards, but also gave the camera operator a better chance to follow the subjects.

Abbott admitted, "On the second day of shooting, I stupidly put myself in a precarious position. I was standing close to a camera that was set up near the foreground apron. The lizard was being very cooperative as it trudged left to right through the jungle, knocking down the upside-down grape vines. When it got directly in front of the camera it stopped to look either at the camera or me. It apparently decided that one or the other should be destroyed, and suddenly it charged us. As it lunged down the slope of the apron, I impulsively grabbed the lizard by the scruff of the neck. Luckily, my grasp was close enough to the back of the monitor's head that he couldn't turn and get his teeth into my arm. The monitor's teeth are formidable, being sharp both at the front and back, like those of a shark. I'm certain that I would have lost the struggle but for the increased flow of adrenaline. As it was, before the lizard could have its way with me, my friend Jim grabbed its tail and jerked it back into the set. Believe me, I was very grateful." (LBA-SE84)

As graphic as the lizard fights were, Abbott recalled that none of the animals featured in the movie were injured.

The Lost World was released during the summer of 1960. On July 6th, *Variety* said:

> Watching *The Lost World* is tantamount to taking a trip through a Coney Island fun house. Like the latter, the Irwin Allen production should appeal primarily to teenagers which, what with the World War II and post-war birth rate, is a good group to be appealing to these days, from a fiscal standpoint. Although basically as plodding and cumbersome as its dinosaurs, the 20th-Fox release contains enough exploitable spectacle and innocent fun to generate a respectable box office return.

For its July 9th issue, *The Motion Picture Herald* said:

> While the picture is a bit slow in getting started – it's about one-third of its running time before the adventurers meet their first dinosaur – it more than makes up for this in the closing reels. The prehistoric animals are presented with fierce realism and should draw gasps from all audiences.

On July 18th, the film critic for *TIME* quipped:

> *The Lost World* exhibits Claude Rains in a red fright-wig, and Jill St. John in – just barely – a pair of pink slacks. These wonders notwithstanding, the most intriguing performers, as is only proper in a Good-Lord-Professor-Can-It-Be? film, are several dinosaurs. Their eyes blaze, their mattress-sized tongues flick menacingly, and their lank green hides glisten in squamous grandeur. They thrash about like lovers in a French art film, roar like convention orators and, when they are hungry, give new depth and meaning to scenery chewing. When two of them duel, Fairbanks-fashion, on the edge of a cliff, they very nearly succeed in bringing to life this tired old Sir Arthur Conan Doyle story of scary Jurassic doings way off in the Amazon rain forest. The human supporting cast, which includes Michael Rennie and Fernando Lamas, adds very little. But then, the reptiles get all the good lines.

David Hedison himself was one of the film's harshest critics. He said, "It was terrible. The alligators with horns and the rhinoceros iguanas were the stars of that picture. Irwin totally wasted the top-notch cast: Michael Rennie, Claude Rains, Fernando Lamas, Jill St. John. We spent the whole film running around from one contrived disaster to another. None of the relationships were thought out or even that conflicted." (DH-DM13)

Regardless, the movie-going public ate it up.

The Lost World opened in New York on Broadway and was proclaimed as a "smash" by *Variety*. A week later, in Washington D.C., in two key movie houses, *Variety* called the picture "socko." In Detroit, at the immense 5,000-seat Fox, business was "swell." In Buffalo, the take was ranked as "great." In Los Angeles, business was "sharp." When the film was held past its original engagement on Broadway, its reception was called "bang up." At the Denver theatre, the take was "lofty" (a good thing in *Variety*-speak); a "smash" in Philadelphia; "fast" in Portland; and "good" in Boston. In other cities, and always booked into large theaters, *Variety* deemed *The Lost World* to be "big," "fat," "bright," "loud," "happy," "socko," "boffo," and "solid." During the film's peak week, *Variety*'s National Boxoffice Survey ranked it as the fifth biggest in the nation.

This was certainly Irwin Allen's greatest triumph to date, solidifying his deal with new partner 20th Century-Fox. Allen would have no resistance from the studio when he announced plans to direct his next feature.

Voyage to the Bottom of the Sea (1961)

On November 1, 1960, and carried by the *Lubbock Avalanche-Journal*, among other newspapers, Louella O. Parsons wrote:

> Any movie these days that earns $10,000,000 profit for a company, as *Lost World* has for 20th Century-Fox, deserves a repeat call on the services of its producer – in this case, Irwin Allen. [Fox executive] Bob Goldstein, who is closing so many deals he's a one man boom in himself, has signed Allen to produce and direct *Voyage to the Bottom of the Sea*, which Allen also co-authored with Charles Bennett.

As with Allen's other projects, this one began as a simple high-concept topic. Screenwriter Bennett claimed, "Irwin's girlfriend had said, 'Why not a movie about a big submarine?' and he told me that this was a good idea for a movie." (CB-SL93)

Charles Bennett, again happy to take Allen's money, continued to pay him little respect. Al Gail was a different story. He said of Irwin Allen and *Voyage to the Bottom of the Sea*, "It was an original idea. It was probably an off-shoot of Jules Verne, but it was an original idea of *his*, and we just developed it as you would normally develop a script." (AG-KB95)

Quoted by Kevin Kelly in *The Boston Globe* on June 14, 1961, Allen said that the concept for his new movie began with a dream. "I had a nightmare," he told Kelly, "Not last night; several months ago. I got up, wrote it down, and turned it into the story that's the basis of the film. You see, there are two belts of radiation surrounding the Earth which were discovered by a scientist named Dr. Van Allen, and I dreamed that one of the belts caught fire. I got to thinking what would happen to a space ship trapped in the blaze at the 300-mile level. I wrote the story and set it in 1967, and if you want to know the solution, you'll have to see the film." (IA-BG61)

Allen had read the reviews of *The Lost World*, which criticized the movie for being sluggish in its first third. Now, he was rewriting the script for Voyage and deleting sections of dialogue that he felt might delay the audience in seeing the spectacular effects awaiting them.

Robert Sterling, Walter Pidgeon, Joan Fontaine, Howard McNear, and John Litel (20th Century-Fox, 1961).

Al Gail said, "He liked excitement. He liked explosions. He liked train wrecks. He liked things that would give you a jolt if you were a moviegoer. And he didn't have too much patience for 'talk scenes,' so our scripts were never overloaded with conversation. He was primarily an action producer, and our audience *wanted* action. And we gave 'em action." (AG-KB95)

Allen avoided the "talk" and then mixed four of his favorite things: sci-fi spectacle, underwater photography, special effects, and an all-star cast. He co-wrote with Bennett, and then, as producer, hired himself to direct.

The cast assembled by producer/director Allen was impressive.

Walter Pidgeon, hired to play Admiral Harriman Nelson, was 53, and had been a star since 1941 when, after nearly 20 years of working his way up on stage and in films, he had the lead in the popular and critically-acclaimed film *How Green Was My Valley*. The following year, he was nominated for an Academy Award as Best Actor in a Leading role for *Mrs. Miniver*. He received a second nomination as Best Actor for 1943's *Madam Curie*. Allen fancied casting Pidgeon because of the actor's lead role in the 1956 sci-fi classic, *Forbidden Planet*.

Peter Lorre was 56 when Allen tapped him to play Lucius Emery. The two had worked together for 1957's *The Story of Mankind* and 1959's *The Big Circus*.

Charles Bennett said, "[W]hen an actor was as good as Lorre, you would naturally employ him whenever you possibly could! It was as simple as that. But, Irwin couldn't always get the actors he wanted. For example... we

Left to right: Director Allen, cinematographer Winton Hoch, Joan Fontaine, Robert Sterling, Barbara Eden, and Frankie Avalon (20th Century-Fox, 1961).

had wonderful actors in [*Voyage*], but none of 'em played again for Irwin Allen, except Lorre, because they didn't like Irwin. Joan Fontaine was in it, and she couldn't stand him!" (CB-SL93)

Again, as with many remarks made by Charles Bennett, this was untrue. Barbara Eden returned to work for Allen again in his next movie, *Five Weeks in a Balloon*; she spoke highly of the producer/director when interviewed for this book. Vincent Price often worked for Allen, and returned in the later 1960s to guest star in an episode of *Voyage to the Bottom of the Sea*. Many other stars became "repeaters" for Irwin Allen projects: Victor Mature, in two films; Groucho Marx; Paul Newman; William Holden, Richard Chamberlain; Robert Wagner; and many others. Ernest Borgnine and Red Buttons worked for Irwin Allen often, as did countless others who were among those in Allen's acting stable. It's too bad that no writer has seen fit to rebut Bennett's slanderous statements … until now.

Joan Fontaine, however, who only worked for Allen once, was cast here as Dr. Susan Hiller. Fontaine had been catapulted to stardom thanks to her role in Alfred Hitchcock's 1940 horror/romance epic, *Rebecca*. It was the first of three Academy Award nominations as Best Actress in a Leading role. The second, for Hitchcock's 1941 suspense thriller, *Suspicion*, brought her the Oscar. Fontaine's third Academy Award nomination was for her lead performance in 1943's *The Constant Nymph*. By 1960, when *Voyage* began production, Fontaine was 43.

Barbara Eden and Robert Sterling (20th Century-Fox, 1961).

Barbara Eden was 30 when cast as Lt. Cathy Connors. She had second billing (under Merry Anders) in the 1957-1959 sitcom *How to Marry a Millionaire*. She also had second billing and played opposite Elvis Presley in the 1960 film, *Flaming Star*. Her most famous role was four years away when she'd begin a five-year run with *I Dream of Jeannie*.

Eden said, "That was my first movie with Allen, and it was a good experience. The only thing I was a little bit uncomfortable with was the camera zooming in on my bottom. I thought, 'Why are we doing this?' I was under contract to Fox, so I didn't say 'yea or nay' about anything. But I think that was something the audience liked. And the reviews said the best part of the film was Joan Fontaine and myself in high heels on this submarine! They just zeroed in on our legs. And so Irwin was going to show those legs, and those high heels." (BE-AI15)

Allen wanted David Hedison to play Captain Crane. Hedison admitted, "[1960] was the most depressing time of my life. I was very low; went home every night depressed, because I was working with Irwin Allen in a film called *The Lost World.* It was one of those pictures that the studio wanted me to do and I felt I had to do, [because] I didn't want to go on suspension…

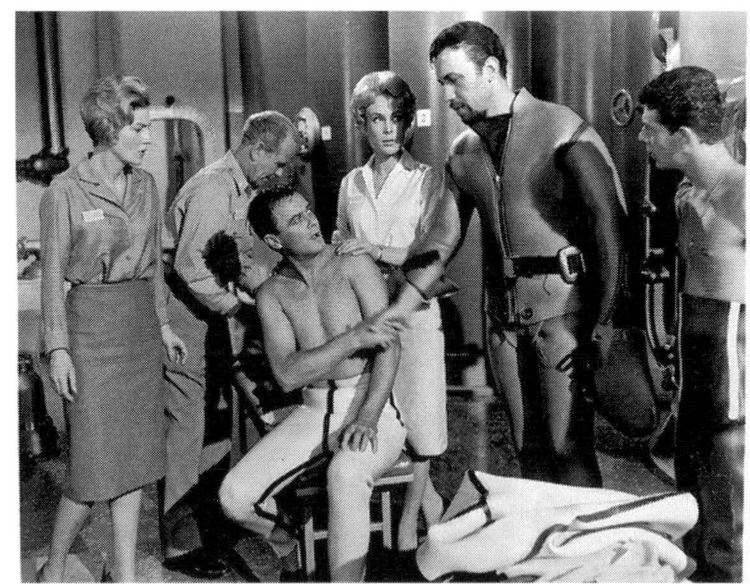

Joan Fontaine, Regis Toomey, Robert Sterling, Barbara Eden, Michael Ansara, and Frankie Avalon (20th Century-Fox, 1961).

I didn't believe in the script. I'd get on the set and I'd see Jill St. John in pink tights, holding a poodle, and [she] was supposed to go on this expedition, you know, and the dinosaurs. I was on that film for about eight weeks or so, and I was truly, really, really depressed. So, about a year later, I wasn't depressed anymore, but Irwin called, and he wanted me to do a film called *Voyage to the Bottom of the Sea.* And, after my experience on the *Lost World*, I just couldn't face it, because it was basically the same thing." (DH-TCF07)

Allen had no problem finding someone else.

Robert Sterling was 43 when cast as Captain Lee Crane. In the 1940s, Sterling had been married to Ann Southern, with whom he co-starred in 1941's *Ringside Maisie.* After divorcing Southern in 1949, Sterling married actress Ann Jeffreys and the two were cast to star as mischievous ghosts in the TV series *Topper* (1953-1955), where they tormented Leo G. Carroll.

Michael Ansara was 38 when cast to play Miguel Alvarez. He had starred in his own television series, as noble Indian Chief Cochise in the 1956-58 western *Broken Arrow.* He had the lead in a second series, the half-hour western *Law of the Plainsman*, for the 1959-60 TV season. He was married to Barbara Eden during the time that *Voyage* was made.

Frankie Avalon had just turned 21 when he played Lt. Danny Romano, and sang the title song. He'd begun acting the year before, with fourth

Irwin Allen and Frankie Avalon (20th Century-Fox, 1961).

Regis Toomey, Paul Zastupnevich, and Robert Sterling (20th Century-Fox, 1961).

billing in *Guns of the Timberland*, under Alan Ladd, Jeanne Crain and Gilbert Roland, and also fourth billed in *The Alamo*, under John Wayne, Richard Widmark and Laurence Harvey. Avalon's entrée into acting came via his popularity as a pop singer. He scored Top 10 hits in 1958 with "DeDe Dinah" and "Ginger Bread." In 1959, "Venus" hit No 1 in the pop charts, followed by a second No. 1 hit, "Why," and three more Top 10 entries: "Bobby Sox to Stockings," "A Boy Without a Girl" and "Just Ask Your Heart."

Also in the cast:

Howard McNear, playing Congressman Parker, was seen often in television and films, and is best known as Floyd the barber on *The Andy Griffith Show*.

Del Monroe played Seaman Kowski (as the name was spelled in the film). He was 24 here, and would be brought back, as Kowalski, for the TV version, appearing in 98 episodes.

Mark Slade played Seaman Jimmy "Red" Smith. He was 21 at this time, and would return for the TV version of *Voyage*, appearing in five episodes. Slade is best remembered for playing Billy Blue Cannon in the 1960s western *The High Chaparral*.

Slade remembered watching Allen direct. He told interviewer Mark Phillips, "Irwin's focus was on the spectacle, not the performances. He was a no-nonsense director and expected actors to be prepared. He and his technicians took months to prepare every detail. He became quite volatile if things didn't go his way. He was also a problem-solver. When Frankie Avalon had trouble with a very technical speech, Irwin shouted for cue cards to be made up. They were rushed in and Frankie did the scene perfectly." (MS-TVC99)

Barbara Eden said of Allen, "He had a lot of energy; he *loved* what he was doing; and got a hundred percent enjoyment out of it. I didn't really know him socially. It was all about work. They were long days; even for *that* time they were long. But I think the thing that stands out in my memory the most is that Irwin didn't say 'Action,' he shot his pistol. And hopefully they were blanks. He'd come on to the set with the boots, and the ballooned pants that directors used to wear, and his pistol, and then 'Boom!' Peter Lorre would jump ten feet and curse, 'What's the matter with that man?! Can't he just say Action?!'" (BE-AI15)

Voyage was breaking records long before its release. On April 10, 1961, *Daily Variety* reported:

> Producer-director Irwin Allen and special effects man L.B. Abbott wound up the longest and most expensive special effects shooting schedule in 20th-Fox history Friday. In winding Allen's *Voyage to the Bottom of the Sea*, 20th had spent $860,000 and 36 days recording undersea and outer space sequences.

L.B. Abbott said, "*Voyage to the Bottom of the Sea* provided a challenge somewhat greater than that of *The Lost World*.... The story required a submarine presumably 350 feet long, utterly unique in design and visually exciting. It also had to be theoretically feasible. The onus for the design fell on Jack Martin Smith and Herman Blumenthal, the art directors." (LBA-SE84)

Smith and Blumenthal built three models of the submarine, dubbed the Seaview – one was seventeen feet, two inches long, and used for surface shots (although some press releases from Fox listed the large model as nineteen feet in length); another was eight feet long and used for underwater shots; and a third, measuring four feet, was used during the battle with a giant octopus.

The miniature work on the *Voyage* feature (as opposed to the TV series) was filmed on "Lake Serson," named after the studio's prior special effects head, Fred Serson. Disney also used this location for *20,000 Leagues Under the Sea*. Lake Serson was not an actual lake – it was a small body of water on the Fox backlot, with a large sky backdrop and an area for pumps to create waves.

Abbott said, "The scene near the opening [of the movie] when the submarine thunders to the surface at a 30 degree up angle, rising half its length out of the water like a jumping swordfish before the bow crashes back into the sea, is very exciting. We had miniature icebergs in the old tank and a blazing red backing. We had dug a pit in the tank floor some years before in order to sink the Titanic in the picture of that name. The Seaview was sunk in the pit, riding on rails that came to within three feet of the surface. These rails gave it the 30 degree up angle. Attached to the sub's stern were two steel cables that ran underwater over pulleys to the rim of the tank where they were fastened to a truck. On cue, the truck would make a fast start, run the proper distance, and make a quick stop. This made it possible to make the sub leap to the surface. Added to this for effect there were several high pressure fire hoses placed in the hull and directed at the ports of the ballast tanks. These made it appear that the tanks were blown as the ship came out of the sea. The concept of the shot was Irwin Allen's, stemming from his having viewed some U.S. Navy film on Polaris submarines in which a Polaris did a maneuver similar to the Seaview's action." (LBA-SE84)

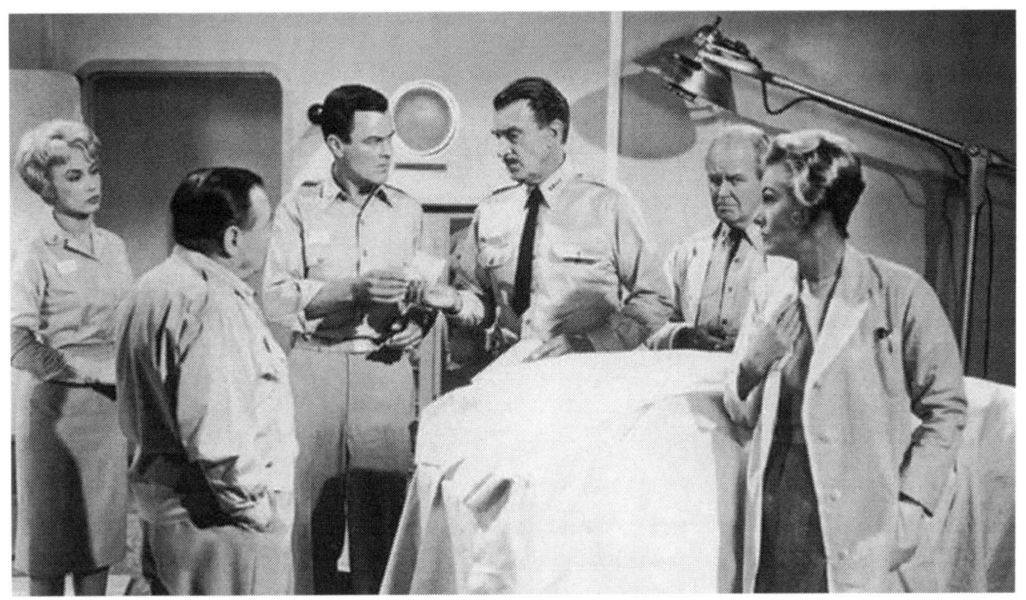

Another Irwin Allen all-star cast. Left to right: Barbara Eden, Peter Lorre, Robert Sterling, Walter Pidgeon, Regis Toomey, and Joan Fontaine (20th Century-Fox, 1961).

Another memorable effects shot involved a giant octopus attacking the Seaview. Abbott said, "The reason for using a four foot model of the Seaview for shooting the octopus attack was that the only octopus available at the time were just slightly larger than one's hand, and the four foot model made the octopus appear huge. We shot the sequence in a tank eight feet by four feet by four feet on a stage. This amount of water was easily filtered and also easily cooled and salinated to make the octopus feel at home. Before each take, the handler would place the octopus we were going to use in a large tub and tease it until it expended its supply of ink. The handler would then, very slowly and carefully, place the octopus on the nose of the sub, which was being held by its tail by an effects man standing in the tank just off screen. Obviously, the octopus would not get on the submarine's nose of its own volition. When it seemed attached to the sub, the handler would make an exit very slowly, and the effects man would carefully position the sub for the camera. Often the octopus would fall off the sub before we had any usable footage and the handler would retrieve it in a net and the procedure would be repeated." (LBA-SE84)

This continued for an entire day. For the scene of the octopus attacking the sub, a fall-off shot in reverse was used.

While he was out promoting his new film, Allen told theater exhibitors and the members of the press, "The filmmakers never had so great an opportunity to profit from television's shortcomings as they do today. The reason is that TV can't produce anything better than stuff for mass communications and it frankly isn't good. What's more, it isn't likely to get better." (IA-EB61)

At least, not until Irwin Allen returned to TV.

Interviewed by Brooks Yarborough for North Carolina's *Charlotte News*, Allen talked about his all-star casting technique, saying, "The pressure is on in Hollywood. When we put two million dollars into a movie as we did in this one, we've got to make over four million to even break even. We do everything possible to ensure that four million, too. That's why, perhaps, the unknown might not get as good a chance as someone even a little known. We've got to do everything we can to sell a picture. It's a product. We're businessmen, first of all."

Allen admitted to loving the pressure of the entertainment business, saying, "I'd probably fall apart without it. I really don't know what I'd do if I *weren't* under pressure."

Allen's respect for his peers came across when he told Yarborough, "They're a group of good, hard-working people out there. They have to be. It's a terrifically competitive business. I'll say this: Most of the actors and actresses who're working are talented people or they couldn't keep on working. And they're earnest people. You know, I don't know how a lot of the crazy ideas about Hollywood get started. For example, I don't think any publicity is good publicity. In fact, believe it or not, we're a real publicity-shy bunch. And I don't think any more marriages fail in Hollywood than in any other town. You just hear about them. A lot of people don't even know Mr. and Mrs. John Jones who got a divorce. But let Gregory Peck get a divorce and it's splashed in headlines everywhere, and three or four times."

As to why he had never been married, Allen rationalized, "Haven't had time to get married. When you're shooting, I may leave home at 4:30 a.m. and get back at 11 p.m. Now, how could I expect a wife to keep a light burning in the window all that time? A wife doesn't have to get jealous of another woman, you know. It can be a career." (IA-CN61)

As for the title, *Voyage to the Bottom of the Sea*, Allen said, "You read the title and you immediately know what the film is about. My business is to entertain and that's just what I try to do. I have no deep message for the public. I promise them no psychological probe, no social study. Just fun." (IA-AJC61)

Talking to Nora E. Taylor, of *The Christian Science Monitor*, Allen said, "Messages are for Western Union. Films are to make money." (IA-CSM61)

Allen was borrowing. The origin of this saying has been attributed to both Samuel Goldwyn and Moss Hart.

Asked by interviewer Mike Clark as to what kind of movies he personally liked, Allen coyly responded, "I like successful pictures." (MC-AI15)

Early indications were that he was about to have another one.

Philip K. Scheuer of the *Los Angeles Times* caught the trade show preview, and wrote for his newspaper's June 18, 1961's edition:

> *Voyage to the Bottom of the Sea* – for such, indeed, it is – seems to me very probably the most effective big-scale science-fiction film since *Journey to the Center of the Earth* and *The Time Machine*…. For *Voyage* is crammed with climax after climax; the initial rain of ice rocks in the Arctic; encounters with not one but two octopuses; the second wider across than the sub itself; the slow-speed penetration of a floating mine field, and the destruction of the Seaview's mini-sub itself when it collides with one such mine; and even an attack by another sub which pursues a zig-zagging, fleeing Seaview with irrevocable orders from the United Nations to shoot (torpedoes) to kill. More, Adm. [Walter] Pidgeon is harassed not only by a saboteur or saboteurs on board but also by a growingly rebellious crew who finally persuade even the handsome young

> captain (Robert Sterling) that the admiral ought to be relieved of his command, and by a religious fanatic of a passenger (Michael Ansara) who keeps shouting that "what will be, will be" and that Pidgeon is flouting the will of God by his high-handed actions.... [O]f all the artists assisting Mr. Allen the loudest salute should probably go to Jack Martin Smith and Herman A. Blumenthal, who have designed such a practical, workable sub that even *we* get a pretty good inkling as to what those knobs and levers and flashing dials are all about.

Jack Muffitt, writing for *Motion Picture Limelight* on June 29th, raved:

> This fine adventure story, which 20th is releasing for saturation booking, is so good that it may reasonably be expected to do *20 Thousand Leagues* business. Produced, directed and written by Irwin Allen (who adapted it in collaboration with Charles Bennett), it is a new, convincing type of science-fiction, in which blobs, monsters and ladies who turn into crocodiles are fortunately absent. Laid in the near future, it deals with conditions whose possibilities already are causing many people a shivery concern – the predicted melting of the Polar ice caps and the ignition of the recently discovered Van Allen radiation belt which, 3000 miles out in space, encircles our Earth.

Jonah M. Ruddy, writing in *The Hollywood Diary* on July 1st, declared:

> Irwin Allen will probably be acclaimed as this generation's Jules Verne of the Mighty Screen. Highly imaginative, marvelously composed with all the magic of special effects and miniatures, his *Voyage to the Bottom of the Sea* is universal entertainment. It's a blend of the sublime and the ridiculous.... In brief, [the film] is swell, submarine science-fiction and by far the most fascinating nuclear-powered submarine – since the Polaris – that we have seen on the wide, wide screen.

Voyage kicked off to good box office. Given the ballyhoo of its promotional campaign, how could it fail to "open big"?

In Washington D.C., at the massive 3,420-seat Capitol, *Variety* rated the movie as "tall." In Toronto, at the 3,348-seat Imperial, and in Detroit, at the huge 5,041-seat Fox, it was "good." In Denver, at the Centre with its 1,270-seats, *Voyage* was "big." And the film was playing in New York City on Broadway, at the 3,665-seat Paramount, where it was rated as "nice." Irwin Allen's movie was the eleventh biggest in the nation.

The following week, it moved up to the seventh spot in the box office derby. The new city to get *Voyage* was St. Louis, where the colossus Fox Theater, with 5,000 hungry seats, reported business was "fine."

In *Voyage*'s fourth week of release, *Variety* ranked it as the seventh top-grossing movie in the nation. In Chicago and Los Angeles the film was "boffo." In Portland, it was "fast."

On August 11th, *Variety* reported that Fox said the movie had made in excess of $1,000,000 in its first four weeks of release. That left $3,000,000 additional revenue to hit "break-even" (between film costs, advertising costs, and exhibitor shares). Then, once there was a profit to post, Fox would have to split that down the middle with Irwin Allen.

In week five, *Voyage* slipped down to tenth place on the national scene. It was new in Kansas City, at the 2,043-seat Uptown and the 1,217 seat Granada, where the word was "fancy." In St. Louis, at the big 5,000-seat Fox, business remained "fast." In Chicago, patronage was "solid."

Allen displays Boxoffice magazine's Blue Ribbon award, presented to *Voyage to the Bottom of the Sea.*

Boxoffice magazine presented Irwin Allen with its Blue Ribbon awards, acknowledging that the magazine's editors and critics felt *Voyage to the Bottom of the Sea* had the most potential of both creating family entertainment and, at the same time, earning exhibitors money.

Nephew Michael Allen remembered, "Irwin was very pleased with *Voyage to the Bottom of the Sea*. It was the first of his disaster style movies, with an all-star cast. He felt very strongly about that – that it was the closest to the course his future was going to take." (MA-AI15)

Five Weeks in a Balloon (1962)

After completing *Voyage to the Bottom of the Sea*, the second of back-to-back "one-off" picture deals with 20th Century-Fox, Allen began negotiations with legendary producer Joseph Levine, founder and head of Embassy Pictures. The buzz around Hollywood indicated a deal was close at hand. On June 7, 1961, *Variety* reported:

> Whether producer-director Irwin Allen will accept what he terms to be a "fabulous" offer from Joe Levine to join Embassy Pictures, or will continue on with 20th-Fox, will be decided within the next week or so, Allen said in New York Monday.... Allen said he expected his agent to meet on the

> coast [Los Angeles] either yesterday (Tues.) or today (Wed.) with 20th-Fox prexy Spyros P. Skouras to receive 20th's counteroffer for his future services.... A new deal, he said, would certainly be a multiple pic arrangement. No matter with whom he signs, Allen intends next to make Jules Verne's *Five Weeks in a Balloon.*

The real intent behind the talks with Embassy was to get a better deal out of Fox. On June 27th, *Variety* reported:

> Turning down Joe Levine and two others, producer-director-writer Irwin Allen wrapped up new five-pix deal at 20th-Fox. Returning yesterday from cross country tour before exhib groups plugging *Voyage to the Bottom of the Sea,* Allen said [Fox] prexy Spyros P. Skouras' offer was best of all; too good to be ignored. Two pix are set under new pact, each to cost $2,000,000: *Five Weeks in a Balloon* and "Passage to the End of Space." Allen will direct and do screenplay with Charles Bennett, who has done eight others with him.

At this time, the studio was thrilled with *Voyage to the Bottom of the Sea* and expected it to be the hit of the summer season. Allen, always a shrewd negotiator, inked the deal while expectations were high and before the excitement of *Voyage*'s opening had faded. *Voyage*, despite doing respectable business, never rose higher than No. 7 in the *Variety*'s National Box Office Survey, and failed to earn enough to post a profit in 1961.

The mood at the studio began to shift against Allen. About the same time, Allen's mood began to shift, as well. Always a strong believer in research surveys, his own polls told him that the problem was the science fiction genre itself. After the incursion of cheap sci-fi B-films throughout the 1950s, an oversaturated public was leaning toward other genres.

Interviewed for a newspaper article at this time, Allen said, "My back goes up when I'm identified with science fiction. I'm a commercial movie-maker, and I enjoy making money at my job. I enjoyed making *Voyage to the Bottom of the Sea*; but something happened that I don't want ever to happen again – mature women and teen-aged girls stayed away in droves. They stay away from all science fiction films. So, remember, *Voyage* was my one venture into that field." (IA-IAPC62)

Allen didn't consider *The Lost World* science fiction, or, for that matter, *The Story of Mankind*, with its tribunal taking place in "The Great Court of Outer Space." Allen maintained that these films were fantasies.

This point was driven home in a studio press release from August 1962. It said:

> *Five Weeks in a Balloon* is straightforward adventure-comedy, without the science fiction elements that so preoccupied Verne later in his career. It details the hilarious adventures of seven would-be explorers (five men, two women) who stage a madcap, 4,000-mile balloon race across Africa. Suspense is built and maintained as the adventurers progress from Zanzibar to Timbuktu in an effort to reach the Gold Coast and plant the British flag before the whole region falls into the hands of slave traders.

Meanwhile, the executives at 20th Century-Fox were looking in the other direction. Paul Zastupnevich said, "They didn't pay that much attention to Irwin. They were too wrapped up in *Cleopatra* and the problems that they were having. I always felt they tolerated him, because his product did make some money for them and it was keeping them afloat. And it gave a semblance of activity at the studio." (PZ-KB15)

Five Weeks in a Balloon was the last film Charles Bennett would co-write with Irwin Allen, although Bennett would return to contribute scripts to the TV incarnation of *Voyage to the Bottom of the Sea*. The writer said, "Eventually, I became irritated at continually seeing Irwin's name co-credited with mine, and I finally rebelled after I wrote my final film for him – *Five Weeks in a Balloon*. I insisted that my name only be mentioned as screenwriter, but he *still* placed his name after mine as screenwriter.... You can hire someone to write something, but that doesn't give you the right to say that *you* wrote it. No, hiring a writer does not give the producer or anyone hiring the writer to a credit as screenwriter. But Irwin did it." (CB-LISTTS96)

The latest all-star cast: Fabian, BarBara Luna, Richard Haydn, Sir Cedric Hardwicke, Peter Lorre, Barbara Eden, and Red Buttons (above), and Eden and Buttons (below) (20th Century-Fox, 1962).

Of course, Bennett was happy to take several script assignments on the TV version of *Voyage to the Bottom of the Seas*. By 1966, Allen appeared to be the only producer in Hollywood still willing to give work to the embittered writer. And Allen would be the last – assigning Bennett a script job in 1968 on *Land of the Giants*.

Next, Allen set about finding his players.

Red Buttons was given the lead. He had previously appeared in Allen's 1959 film, *The Big Circus*. Now he had the lead as Donald O'Shay.

Fabian was only nineteen when hired to play Jacques. He had started his film career as the lead of 1959's *Hound-Dog Man*, then received second billing under Bing Crosby in the 1960 musical comedy *High Time*, and in that same year was cast in the John Wayne comedy/western *North to Alaska.* For 1961, he shared top billing with another teen idol, Tommy Sands, in the musical comedy *Love in a Goldfish Bowl*. Fabian was also a pop star, with three Top Ten singles in 1959: "Turn Me Loose," "Tiger" and "Hound Dog Man."

Interviewed at the time of filming, Irwin Allen said, "This kid wants to be an actor, and he's a *good* actor. We even had to persuade him to sing the title song." (IA-IAPC62)

Barbara Eden had appeared in Allen's previous movie, *Voyage to the Bottom of the Sea*. Here, she was cast as Susan Gale.

Sir Cedric Hardwicke was sixty-nine when hired to play Fergusson. He was a successful character actor who had third billing in classics such as 1935's *Les Misérables*, 1939's *Stanley and Livingston*, and 1941's *Suspicion*. He also played the High Judge in Allen's *The Story of Mankind*.

Peter Lorre was now fifty-eight, and had appeared in *The Story of Mankind* and *Voyage to the Bottom of the Sea*. He was given the role of Ahmed.

Peter Lorre's third time with Irwin Allen (above), with first timers Barbara Luna and Fabian (below) (20th Century-Fox, 1962).

Richard Haydn was fifty-seven, and had worked for Allen in *The Lost World*. For this new film, he played Sir Henry Vining.

BarBara Luna (billed as Barbara] was only twenty-two when cast to play Makia. She had already made a couple of dozen appearances on TV, including four episodes of Guy William's series *Zorro*.

Luna joked, "My audition was really tough. 'Irwin Allen wants to meet you.' 'Okay.' So I go to the office and he says to me, 'Say Me Makia.' So I said, 'Me Makia.' He said, 'Okay, I want you to do my film.' He liked my look. But I had to do something that to this day, if I ever see *Five Weeks in a Balloon* on the TV, I shudder, because he had a thing about hair. He didn't want hair flying all over the place, because we were going to be outside. In fact, I think we were outside *all the time*. And up in the balloon *all the time*. And he didn't want hair blowing in my face. So he made me wear an invisible hair net. You know, like those things that waitresses had to wear back at that time. So, if you look at my hair, you'll see that it never moves, because it was plastered down with this horrible net. And that was a deal breaker. 'Either you wear the hair net or you're not in the movie.' That was his attitude. Actually, come to think of it, that was his attitude about everything." (BL-AI15)

Also featured in the cast, but uncredited, as one of the harem girls, was Sheila Mathews. She would later date Irwin Allen and, in the mid-1970s, become his wife. She was 33 in 1962.

Paul Zastupnevich said, "That was the first thing that Sheila did. Irwin met her and became enamored of her, and, at that time, Sheila was slim enough that I was able to put her in a costume that had been made for Susan Hayward, and re-adapted it for her. So, she was very trim in those days and quite beautiful. She has a gorgeous singing voice, which later was utilized in *Lost in Space*." (PZ-KB95)

Billy Gilbert and Peter Lorre (20th Century-Fox, 1962).

Mathews recalled, "We were introduced at a restaurant by a mutual friend, and he [Allen] invited me out to the studio. He was shooting *Lost World* at the time. So, he sat me in his director's chair, and let me watch the shooting. After about an hour, he said, 'You can leave your picture and resume with my secretary.' So I did. About a year later, I was out there being interviewed for something, and I was looking for the office I was to go to, and I was standing downstairs in what later became the Irwin Allen building. I was reading the board, and three or four men walked in and Irwin said, 'Can I help you?' I turned around and I said, 'Yes, I'm looking for so-and-so's office.' And he said, 'Oh, that's upstairs and down the hall.' As he turned to go up those stairs, he looked familiar, and I said, "Pardon me, but aren't you Irwin Allen?' He said, 'Yes. Have we met?' I told him we'd met a year ago, and he said, 'Well, when you're finished with your interview, why don't you stop up and see me. I'm right upstairs, and let me know how you've been doing.' So, I actually did; I stopped in and we had a chat, and two weeks later he invited me out to dinner, and my dinner date was at Groucho Marx's house, which was quite interesting, to say the least. So then we started dating." (SM-KB95)

Nephew Michael Allen explained, "Groucho reminded Irwin a lot of my father [Irwin's brother Rubin]. They looked a lot alike, and had the same kind of attitudes. And Irwin and my father liked one another. Groucho liked that Irwin was young, brash, bright, and heading for success. And I also think he was always respectful of Groucho." (MA-AI15)

Mathews said, "I feel Groucho was almost like a second father to Irwin. And they had a really good time together. Groucho was, of course, quite funny. And Irwin had his moments, too. But they really enjoyed each other for many, many years. I guess we had dinner at Groucho's about three times a week. Evidently Groucho figured I was okay, because I don't think we would have been seeing each other if it hadn't worked out [on that first dinner with Groucho]." (SM-KB95)

That first date with Allen, and a nod from fatherly Groucho Marx, led to Mathews being cast in *Five Weeks in a Balloon*.

As for working with Allen, BarBara Luna said, "Thankfully, everything I did was okay – it was not problematic. I don't remember him ever yelling at anybody, other than he just yelled, in general, before a take. He would just scream. And this was a comedy, or, at least, it was supposed to be a comedy. I don't know if it ended up being funny. But he was definitely a screamer. If I remember, he was a Gemini. Not that I have anything against Geminis, because I have great fun with all of my Gemini friends, but they are especially hyper. And, he was from New York. He knew exactly what he wanted and it was his way or the highway." (BL-AI15)

Barbara Eden concurred, saying, "He was always high energy, so you didn't know if he was nervous or if he was happy. But he got everything done. And he was never mean spirited. Never. But it is also a matter of how flexible you can be. The older actors, like Peter Lorre, even though he worked with Irwin a lot, were just aghast over his style. The gun that he would fire instead of calling 'Action' was one reason. I don't remember him using the gun in the scenes with the lion, but, otherwise, that gun was always on set. And Peter would jump every time and curse and mumble about it. Irwin also had one of those things you'd talk through – a megaphone. But he was enjoying every minute of it. I've never seen anyone enjoy their job so much. And he got it done." (BE-AI15)

BarBara Luna said of Allen, "I don't ever remember getting direction. I'd already done a fair amount of TV, not that you get a lot of direction in TV, but I don't remember Irwin ever really directing me, other than technical. And it was a very technical film, obviously. He was about, 'Let's just blow up everything!' But who's really going to direct Peter Lorre or Cedric Hardwicke? It was such an interesting cast. So I think that Irwin Allen maybe, *maybe* might have been at his very best behavior because of the actors in that."

Luna added, "Despite Irwin's craziness, it was fun, because the people were so much fun. I think once you get that massive dose of Irwin Allen, you just kind of know what you're in for. But it is tough being a director. In a sense, the director is in *every* shot. But, yes, he would fire a gun instead of saying 'Action!' My gosh, what a character." (BL-AI15)

Five Weeks in a Balloon was released in early August 1962.

Margaret Harford, writing for the May 24, 1962 issue of the *Los Angeles Times*, yarned:

> Although *Five Weeks in a Balloon* seems more like five years (to adults), it isn't because producer Irwin Allen hasn't loaded this color aerial fantasy with a full gondola of Hollywood actors (Fabian, Red Buttons, Herbert Marshall, etc.) and enough African wildlife footage to stock three or four "Tarzan" pictures.... *Five Weeks in a Balloon*, now at local theaters and drive-ins, is mostly hot air, an adventure film inflated from an early Jules Verne novel and sent aloft as a summertime family film. It fills that bill nicely. Children will enjoy it, but adults may find the whimsy heavy and repetitious before the balloon bursts.

On August 15th, *Variety* said:

> Allen has taken a conventional balloon-adventure and dealt with it tongue-in-cheek style – in effect approaching Verne in a kind of

> wild "Road" picture vein. Goal of the kidding approach seems to be to make it more palatable for adults.... At any rate, *Five Weeks in a Balloon* has been designed with a something-for-everybody, "whole family" commercial concept: spoofery for the adults, romance and high adventure for the older youngsters, African wildlife and aerial fantasy for the tykes. There is, however, an inherent danger in the film that aims, a bit too ambitiously, to span and please all age groups. Each separate facet tends to subtract from the impact of the others.

On August 18th, the movie critic for *Cue* magazine groaned:

> Jules Verne's science fiction fantasies have for 60 years provided drama and amusement for movie audiences. However, there is nothing in the Verne public domain to suggest that his work need be brought down to kindergarten level; and that is what, with no apologies, producer Irwin Allen has done here.

In early October, *Boxoffice* magazine singled out *Five Weeks in a Balloon* as a movie the editors and critics felt had the most potential of both creating family entertainment and, at the same time, earning exhibitors money. It was awarded the magazine's Blue Ribbon Award for September.

Five Weeks in a Balloon peaked in the *Variety* National Box Office Survey in seventh position.

During its fourth week of release, *Five Weeks* slipped down to the ninth spot in *Variety*'s National Box Office Survey. One week later, it was missing from most first-run downtown theaters. The neighborhood houses would get it next, and business in those venues was spotty. When all was said and done, it would take overseas sales and, later, television, to turn this one into a moneymaker.

With the marginal returns of *Five Weeks in a Balloon*, Allen's next two feature film projects at Fox – the sci-fi "Passage to the End of Space" and the costume adventure "The Big Pirate" – appeared to be stalled.

It seemed the time was ripe for the former radio host, TV host, newspaper writer, literary agent, movie producer, and documentary maker to reinvent himself once again, this time for a return to the small screen.

3

A Plunge into TV: *Voyage to the Bottom of the Sea*

Irwin Allen had been mired at 20th Century-Fox for some time trying to get his next movie made. *Voyage to the Bottom of the Sea* and *Two Weeks in a Balloon* had both made money, but considering the costs of production, and the further costs of promoting and distributing the movies, the profit margin was not as high as a studio with the *Cleopatra*-blues needed.

Irwin Allen, the real commander of the Seaview (1963).

Cleopatra – the Elizabeth Taylor-Richard Burton epic movie – had become a runaway train, and a runaway drain of resources. Its production spanned 1961 and '62, with massive cost overruns and production troubles, including changes in directors, cinematographers, actors, and locales. Health problems with Taylor delayed the production more than once. Sets were built, discarded, and then built anew. *Cleopatra* is believed to be the most expensive movie ever made up to that time, and it nearly bankrupted the studio. Even though a hit when released in 1963, it couldn't possibly return its combined production and marketing cost of $44,000,000. In 2015, this cost equates to over $348 million.

Richard Burton and Elizabeth Taylor nearly destroy a studio with *Cleopatra* (20th Century-Fox, 1963).

At the same time, another Fox production hemorrhaging money was *Something's Gotta Give*, which paired Marylyn Monroe and Dean Martin. Again, the problem seemed to be the health of the female star – both physically and mentally.

Monroe caused delays on a daily basis, and the production descended into a costly debacle. After weeks of script rewrites on the Monroe picture, and very little progress, Monroe was fired, then rehired and promised a hefty bonus upon the completion of filming. She would never finish the movie, found dead on August 5, 1962. Doris Day replaced Monroe, prompting the exit of Martin. The film was finally completed the following year and released as *Move Over, Darling,* starring Day and James Garner.

In the meantime, Fox sold its back lot (now the site of Century City) to Alcoa in an effort to raise cash needed to complete both films. Despite this, in 1962, the studio released nearly all of its contract stars, including Jayne Mansfield.

The situation at 20th Century-Fox was bleak. Al Gail said, "Up front, the executives kept turning over. You never knew when you came back into work the next day who was running the studio. They were in bad shape. *Cleopatra* almost knocked them out completely. It was strange but, when we'd go out to lunch, we'd never go out the front gate; we'd always go out the back. We didn't want to remind them [that we were still on the lot], because they had no money.... We'd all climb into [Irwin's] Rolls Royce, and we'd sneak out the back gate and hope none of the executives saw us." (AG-KB95)

The studio would soon have a lifeline thrown its way from television. This was ironic, since throughout the early and even mid-1950s the major studios had been snubbing the bastard child of motion pictures. Most TV was produced by production companies established solely for that purpose – ZIV (*Highway Patrol*, *The Cisco Kid*, *Sea Hunt*), Desilu (*I Love Lucy*, *The Andy Griffith Show*, *The Dick Van Dyke Show*, *The Untouchables*), Mark VII (*Dragnet*, *The D.A.'s Man*), Filmways (*The Bob Cummings Show*, *The Beverly Hillbillies*, *Petticoat Junction*) Revue (*Wagon Train*, *Leave It to Beaver*, *Alfred Hitchcock Presents*) and Four Star (*The Rifleman*, *Wanted: Dead or Alive*, *Richard Diamond - Private Detective*). These companies would lease studio or stage space from the majors. However, until the last half of the 1950s, that was as close as Paramount, Warner Brothers, Universal, MGM, United Artists, RKO, Columbia and 20th Century-Fox consented to come. Television remained the motion picture industry's lower-class relation.

But television was hungry for product, and the major studios were hurting for revenue.

The door to producing for television opened a crack when the studios began selling off their older movie libraries to TV distributors. Columbia was the first to take a bold step toward making TV in the mid-1950s, but did so by setting up a new studio – Screen Gems. They made *Father Knows Best*, *The Adventures of Rin Tin Tin*, *Jungle Jim*, *Dennis the Menace*, *The Donna Reed Show* and *Naked City*, among others – all hits in their day, and destined for long lives in syndicated repeats.

Twentieth Century-Fox tested the television waters in the fall of 1955 with *My Friend Flicka*, which spent one year on CBS and one on NBC, and *The 20th Century-Fox Hour*, which had a two-year run on CBS. Neither hit big, but *Flicka* would stick around on Saturday mornings for a few years entertaining the kids in syndication. In 1957, the studio sold the half-hour western *Broken Arrow* to ABC, where it stayed for two years. The kids loved it, so much so that even after suspending production, the series stayed around for another two years on the network in the early evening as repeats, earning Fox an extra return on its investment.

In the fall of 1959, Fox undertook a major push to break through into TV. It had *Five Fingers* on NBC, starring David Hedison, but only for a half season. Also starting, and doing better, were *The Many Loves of Dobie Gillis* for CBS, and *Adventures in Paradise* on ABC. The latter starred Gardner McKay as the captain of a freelance schooner, traveling the South Seas in search of passengers, cargo and adventure.

William Self, circa 1964 (20th Century-Fox promotional photo).

The Many Loves of Dobie Gillis, starring Dwayne Hickman and Bob Denver was the studio's only hit series (20th Century-Fox promotional photos, 1960).

Bob Chandler, for his *Daily Variety* "Sound and Pictures" column on June 26, 1959, said:

> 20th's TV activities have been somewhat shaky since the start, when the company first went into production with *Twentieth Century Fox Hour* and *My Friend Flicka*, neither of which were exemplary examples of television production.

As for *Paradise*, the critic for sister trade *Variety* called it an "elementary hour which took off … like a lead balloon."

But then Fox stole the head of development from CBS – William Edwin Self.

Bill Self started as an actor. During an eight-year period, he appeared in many movies, including *Red River*, *The Thing (from Another World)* and *Adam's Rib*. But Self remained a background player, never a lead. He said, "I worked enough to support my family, but at length I realized what I'm sure many others had grasped much sooner – that I was never going to be a star. It was Spencer Tracy, a close friend for many years, who gave me the clincher. 'Bill,' he said, 'acting is great if you're a star, but if you aren't it's no good.'" (WS-B64)

Rhodes Reason and Marilyn Maxwell of Fox's *Bus Stop* TV series, failed to click, as did *Hong Kong*, with Rod Taylor and Lloyd Bochner (20th Century–Fox, 1961).

Self used his showbiz contacts to get a job on the 1952 TV series *China Smith* as assistant to the producer. Later that year, he became associate producer on the *Schlitz Playhouse*. By 1954, he had advanced on *Playhouse* to the producer's chair and stayed until 1956. During 1957 and '58, Self was producer on *The Frank Sinatra Show*. CBS hired him after that, as a production executive to oversee the making of *The Twilight Zone* pilot. He had been there less than a year when a better offer came his way.

At the end of 1959, Self made the move to 20th Century-Fox, as "executive producer" for all its current series except *Dobie Gillis*. His first task was to revamp *Adventures in Paradise* and try to improve its audience numbers. At the same time, he oversaw the start of a new series, *Hong Kong*, also for ABC. It starred Rod Taylor as an American journalist living in the Far East. The supporting cast included Lloyd Bochner (later to guest star on *Voyage to the Bottom of the Sea*) and Jack Kruschen. They made the cover of *TV Guide*, and the series scored positive reviews, but missed in the Nielsens and closed after one season. *Adventures in Paradise,* less liked, would drift along into a third season on ABC.

In 1961, two more series were launched, with Self also serving as executive producer. *Bus Stop* was set at a diner in Sunrise, Colorado. The series mostly told individual tales involving people whose travels by bus included a brief stop at the diner. That bus, and the series, left the ABC schedule after one season. The second series for the fall of 1961, also on ABC, was *Follow the Sun*, about two handsome young magazine writers who worked the news beat in Hawaii for the *Honolulu Sun*. The stories were not interesting enough and the series folded after only one year, leaving only *Dobie Gillis* in production.

At this point, Roy Huggins, who was head of the TV division, stepped down to concentrate on making pilots, and Bill Self stepped up into the top spot. Now it was his job to make the studio a contender in the TV arena.

Several pilots were made – "The Commuters," about those making the daily Connecticut-to-Manhattan trek; "Misty," a half-hour comedy based on the 20th-Fox film from the previous year; "Three Coins in the Fountain," also based on a library title; "Deadline: San Francisco," a newspaper series; and "The Great American Family," a comedy. "Halls of Montezuma," also based on a 20th-Fox film, likewise failed to find a sponsor.

Come November 1963, the studio was growing desperate. William Self put three more pilots into production. This time out, all would make it to series. One starred Anthony Franciosa – a comedy called *Valentine's Day*. Executive producer Quinn Martin had a green light to make *12 O'Clock High*, starring Robert Lansing. And a certain studio feature film producer who hadn't gotten a project off the ground in more than a year was going to make the move to television, writing, directing and producing a pilot that would take us to the bottom of the sea.

Al Gail said, "[Bill Self] appreciated us. But the front office had so many problems they never knew how safe their job was, so they never had time to think about television. They were trying to avoid the process servers. So we just kept out of their way until the storm blew over and, fortunately, it did." (AG-KB95)

Irwin Allen had been considering television as far back as 1960, prior to Hurricane *Cleopatra*. It was part of the new and improved deal he had obtained from the studio after his flirtation with Embassy Films. *Variety* had the scoop on October 12, 1960, reporting:

> Producer-director Irwin Allen has completed initial plans on a $9,000,000 motion picture and television production slate to encompass the next two years. First project will be [the feature film] *Voyage to the Bottom of the Sea.* Following *Voyage* and being launched almost back-to-back will be Jules Verne's *Five Weeks in a Balloon* and "The Big Pirate." No distribution deal has been set for either film, though it's likely the pair will be released via deals with 20th. On Allen's TV slate are "Safari," an African adventure series, and "The House of Ghosts," a spook [show]. Allen has held talks with 20th Century-Fox Television head Pete Levathes regarding the two projects.... "Pirate" [written by Carey Wilber] is another Allen original and will be filmed next fall at Jamaica Cove, home base of most of history's more notorious pirates.

The studio could not find interest at the networks for Allen's "Safari" or "The House of Ghosts." "The Big Pirate," as a film project, was left adrift, as well. The same fate came to his expensive sci-fi property – "Passage to the End of Space."

Finally, in late summer 1963, Allen had a green light for one of his projects, which would begin his voyage into television science fiction adventure.

Irwin Allen's television agent, Herman Rush, began representing him in 1962. He pointed out, "Irwin was a workaholic. He liked to work. In the picture business, you make one picture, and you work very hard during that production period, but there's always a hiatus between one picture and another. In television, you do an hour series, you work seven days a week, as he did, and you work every week for as long as that series stays on the air. So the accelerated pace of television appealed to him. In addition, he saw the value and the importance of television as a medium, and felt it could be as lucrative as

A new look for Allen as he reinvents himself again, with a move back to television.

motion pictures. Another reason he chose to go into television, I think, is that I and others who represented him had the opinion that he *should*, and that he could be a pioneer; he could be an initiator; and he could use his motion picture expertise in this new medium of television. And I think the combination of those reasons is what got him to do it." (HR-AI15)

Al Gail said of Allen, "He was always fond of television, and he had been comfortable in television [with *Hollywood Merry-Go-Round* and *Irwin Allen's Hollywood Party*]. We had a television background. He was happy being in action – that was the important thing. So, when the opportunity came, he took it. He got the idea for *Voyage to the Bottom of the Sea* and 20th Century-Fox thought it was a good idea and said develop it." (AG-KB95)

Herman Rush elaborated, "In the case of *Voyage to the Bottom of the Sea*, and only in the case of Irwin Allen, he had saved in storage all of the sets from the motion picture. That was a big plus in getting a network interested in the property, because the cost factor would not be as high as if you had to create and build all those particular sets." (HR-AI15)

Paul Zastupnevich commented, "I think he realized that television was the up and coming thing and that films were not going to be that predominant, right at that particular moment. And where the buck was, that's where he went. I think he was approached by his agent, that this would be a good time to go into a TV series. And they had felt that *Voyage to the Bottom of the Sea* would make a proper jump off. They had all the component parts from the main picture. They would be able to do a TV series for peanuts, supposedly – and we did. You know, it's surprising, if you look at *Voyage to the Bottom of the Sea* and you check the budget out, compared to *Star Trek* and other things that came later, you'll find that it was done on a shoestring. And, because he had all those pieces around, and the various component parts – wardrobe, whatnot – he was able to utilize everything, and cut [costs]. He proved that he could do a series for a low figure, and Fox went for it." (PZ-KB95)

In August, the Hollywood trades announced that Allen would write, produce and direct a pilot film based on his movie version of *Voyage to the Bottom of the Sea* for 20th Century-Fox TV, and that ABC-TV had "already manifested interest in the project."

Allen worked on his teleplay throughout August, and continued to tinker with it as late as November 1963. He also played around with alternative titles for the series in order to differentiate it somewhat from the movie, but also to open up the series concept to allow for stories away from the submarine. The ones he considered were "Voyage to the Unknown," "Voyage to Danger," "Dangerous Voyage" and, simply, "Voyage."

In September, *Daily Variety* reported that Walter Pidgeon would be repeating his role as Admiral Nelson from the feature film. Irwin Allen seemed to want it that way at first. It seemed Pidgeon did too. But the announcement which had leaked from Allen's office was premature. The problem was not entirely over money. Pidgeon's asking price to do a TV series was $5,000 per week (with a raise each season that could get him as high as $7,000). This was at the extreme high end of what was considered normal at the time. In the end, it was more a consideration of age and stamina – selecting an actor who could survive the long days spread over several months a year that television production demanded.

Al Gail said of Pidgeon, "He couldn't do it. He wasn't ready to do television. It was too tough for him in those days." (AG-KB95)

Another tool for Allen in making the decision was research, as exemplified in audience surveys. He wanted to know who the average television viewer most wanted to see in the role.

Come October, even without a star signed – or, at least, a human star, since the true "lead" in the series would be the submarine -- it was announced that the pilot film, to be written, directed and produced by Allen, would begin filming on November 18th. The October 15th press release read:

> Shooting starts Monday, November 18 on the season's biggest and most expensive pilot for the new adventure series "VOYAGE" which Irwin Allen will direct and produce in partnership with 20th Century-Fox for airing over the ABC Network.
>
> The announcement was made by William Self, 20th Century-Fox Television production chief, and Richard Zanuck, Vice President in Charge of the Studio. Self reported that the hour-length shows will be filmed in color at both the main studio and a half-dozen local locations. The big-budget project is scheduled for televising during the 1964-65 season. Allen, who had produced and directed a long list of exploitation-adventure feature motion pictures, will serve as producer of the series, as well as write and direct every fourth segment.
>
> The Academy-Award winning producer-director-writer said "VOYAGE" would be "an explosive combination of science-fiction and action-adventure, with generous sprinklings of the Ian Fleming school of romantic espionage." …
>
> An all-star cast will be announced within a week.

Allen and Fox were not exaggerating the cost of the pilot. The projected budget, from October 25, 1963, was $284,772. It was only this low because the main sets – those of the Seaview – were already built. Additionally, to keep costs down, Allen planned to extract several effects shots from the film for use in the series. These sequences included the Seaview in action; a giant squid attack; and crumbling ice falling onto the ship.

By November 4th, the budget had climbed to $339,545, despite the producer taking a pay cut to $7,669, from $10,750.

Also by the start of November, Allen and 20th Century-Fox had set their sights on Richard Basehart for the role of Admiral Nelson. Both Allen and William Self were scheduled to take Basehart and wife to dinner at Dominick's restaurant in West Hollywood, a favorite hangout of Frank Sinatra and his Rat Pack, followed by an 8:30 p.m. screening of the *Voyage* movie at Fox.

After years of jumping from one movie project to another, and often from one country to another as he did them, as well as traveling with touring stage productions, Basehart felt he was ready to commit to a series. He told syndicated entertainment columnist Harvey Pack, "I can still remember the time when I liked living in hotel rooms. But I'm cured. Actors are always knocking the old days when they were under contract to major studios and had to make a certain amount of pictures every year. Now that I look back on my contract days, it really wasn't so bad. At least you went home every night."

On the other hand, in the same interview he added, "I just can't see myself playing the same part every week in just another series. Of course, there have been offers, but nothing exciting." (RB-HT60)

There lay the key – it would have to be something other than "just another series," and a format, or genre, which would allow the actor to play variations on his character. Perhaps sci-fi would prove to be the answer.

The dinner meeting between Richard Basehart, Irwin Allen and William Self went well, as did the screening of the *Voyage* movie later that night on the Fox lot.

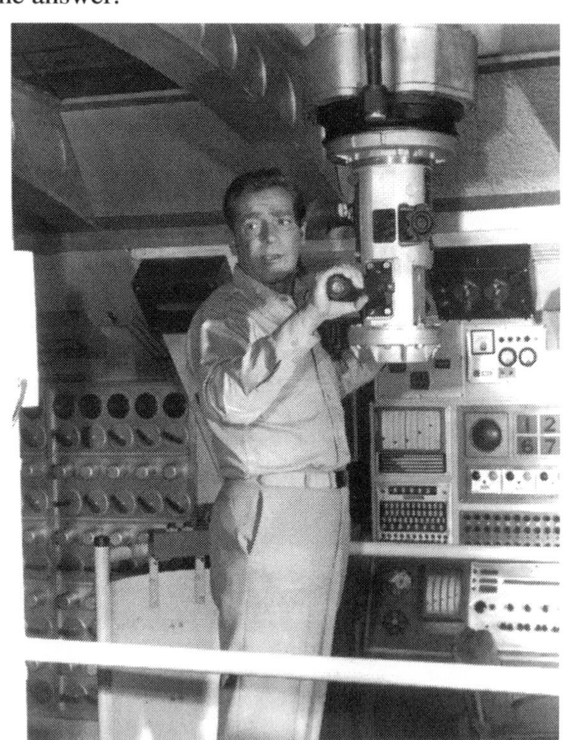

Allen chooses acclaimed stage and screen actor Richard Basehart to be his first TV star (1964).

Paul Zastupnevich said, "The reason he went for Richard Basehart is that, at that time, before Sheila, he was dating a gal by the name of Jodi Desmond. Now, Jodi came from Italy and she knew Basehart, and she mentioned to Irwin, 'Why don't you get Richard Basehart?,' because she was friendly with Basehart and his former wife, Valentina Cortese." (PZ-KB95)

A deal was soon struck. And it was a good deal for Basehart – $7,000 per episode – top dollar for 1964. Two years later, William Shatner would be making $5,000 per episode of *Star Trek*, a sum more in line with industry standards at the time. Then again, Shatner was given a small piece of the action – a five percent ownership in the series. For cash-poor Desilu Studios, it was the only way to bring in a medium-sized fish like Shatner. Irwin Allen and 20th Century-Fox weren't interested in sharing ownership. Herman Rush said, "I am not familiar with anything that we did with Irwin where a star had a cut; a participation. To give out a partial ownership was absolutely an unusual arrangement back then." (HR-AI15)

A bigger paycheck was offered instead. And it was one of the biggest for its time. Basehart, at age 49, was being treated like the movie star that he was.

Assistant casting director Larry Stewart said, "Richard got himself screwed up with the amount of money he had to pay for his divorce. *Voyage* was a way to make money." (LS-SFTS2)

A short while later, while interviewed for a *Los Angeles Times* article and asked why he agreed to do a series, the Shakespearean actor said, "I was surprised myself – still am – but the deal offered was too good to resist. It came at a time when the last half dozen pictures I made weren't satisfying experiences; so I'd done a few guest shots, enough to convince me the medium now had possibilities." (RB-LAT66)

The next big question was, who would play Captain Crane?

On Friday, November 1, as dinner and a movie were still being arranged with Richard Basehart and wife, Allen wrote to William Self:

> Dear Bill: The moratorium "not to panic" over the casting of Captain Crane for the pilot of "VOYAGE" expires at 6 PM tonight. To avoid such panic I am reviewing herewith the situation so that we might mutually move forward to a quick decision.
>
> Together with [studio casting director] Cliff Gould and additionally on my own, I have interviewed, seen on film or still pictures, virtually all the young leading men in town who would be available, believable and within the budget. While there are still three or four pieces of film I hope to see with Cliff before the day is over, I do not have much hope of filling the bill by the deadline hour. You are even more aware than I am that every such young actor is being sought by every television operation in town.
>
> All of the above brings us to the David Hedison situation.
>
> 1) Hedison has been approved by ABC which simply means that we can move forward immediately with a deal without showing them film on any new player and going through all the requirements of the presentation problem.
> 2) Hedison has turned down our first offer (which was $3,500 for the pilot and $1,500 per segment).
> 3) I propose that we make a new offer to Hedison as follows:
>   a) $3,500 for the pilot. (We will also pledge to use our good offices to secure two or three guest appearances on other Fox TV shows over the course of the next year to make up the additional monies he wanted guaranteed from the pilot.)
>   b) $2,500 per episode.
>
> I have reason to believe that Hedison may very well accept this offer over the weekend which would wrap up our casting problem and leave us free to move forward on the thousands of other details that need our attention.
>
> Please advise. Regards, Irwin.

Come Monday, Allen was again writing to William Self:

David Hedison is in London and is supposed to let the producers of "ESPIONAGE" know whether or not he will do a guest spot for them. His doing this show would eliminate him from doing "VOYAGE." He has promised not to give them a commitment until he hears from us by cable tomorrow. May we meet and discuss this sometime today?

David Hedison and Luciana Paluzzi in *Five Fingers* (above, 20th Century-Fox, 1960), and Hedison (below) in his second series – *Voyage to the Bottom of the Sea* (1964).

Herman Rush said, "I think his biggest supporter was Bill Self. I think they understood each other. They weren't friends, but they worked together very closely, and Irwin always accepted whatever was being advised by the studio. He debated it, he argued it; he talked about it; but he never got pissed off and said, 'I'm going to pay no attention to it.' It was a very good relationship." (HR-AI15)

Allen had always wanted David Hedison for Captain Crane. He'd first caught glimpse of Hedison as Lt. Ware, the Executive Officer of the U.S. Navy Destroyer commanded by Robert Mitchum in the 1957 classic *The Enemy Below*. He was Al Hedison back then (his real name), and had third billing. Hedison looked good in the Navy Officer uniform, and Allen was sure he was the right man to serve as the Captain of the Seaview.

In 1958, Hedison was named "Most Promising Newcomer" for his role in an off-Broadway play, *A Month in the Country*. That acknowledgement got him the lead in the film *The Fly*. This led to a contract with 20th Century-Fox.

The studio continued to develop Hedison. A short while later he was starring in his own TV series for NBC, as an American counterspy in Europe with the code name "Five Fingers." The hour-long series was also called *Five Fingers*, and co-starred Paul Burke as Fingers' American contact. For this TV assignment, per the network, Al became David.

Hedison recalled, "They said they wanted me, with the stipulation that Fox change my name. They hated Al. They said, 'We can't make him a star with the name of Al. It was absolutely ridiculous. So they said, 'How about John Hedison?' I said, 'If we are going to change it, use my middle name, which is David.' So I became David Hedison." (DH-LAT11)

Five Fingers premiered opposite the top-rated CBS line-up of half-hour westerns *Have Gun – Will Travel* and *Gunsmoke*, and, on ABC, the popular *Lawrence Welk Show*. It was formidable competition with *Gunsmoke* and *Have Gun* having ranked No. 1 and No. 3, respectively, in the previous year's Nielsens (as they would in both this and the following year-end tallies). Production stopped after sixteen episodes and *Five Fingers* left the network in January.

Shortly after getting his pink slip, Hedison went to work for Irwin Allen in *The Lost World*. Then, in 1961, during the casting period for the big-screen *Voyage to the Bottom of the Sea*, Allen sent a copy of the script to Hedison. However, the actor felt the part of Crane was "a one-dimensional bore," so he passed and took second billing in a war movie for 1961 called *Marines, Let's Go*.

Irwin Allen made his submarine movie without Hedison, but had been disappointed in his second choice (Robert Sterling), and was determined to get the right Crane aboard the Seaview for the TV incarnation.

Hedison said, "He called me for *Voyage to the Bottom of the Sea* – the series. I turned that down. I said, 'Irwin, I'm grateful that you think of me for this part, but I really feel I'm not right for it and I'm looking for something else – something a little different; something with a little more dimension for an actor.' And the guy wouldn't let go. I went to New York; he called me in New York. I went to London and I did a show with Roger Moore – *The Saint*; I was guesting on that – and Irwin called me in the middle of the night and, you know, pursued it. For some reason he wanted me. I don't know why, because God knows there were terrific actors in Hollywood at that time. But he had made up his mind that he wanted me to play the part." (DH-TCF07)

Harry Harris, who would soon start directing for Irwin Allen on all his 1960s TV series, said, "When he wanted you, if he wanted you for something, and you said, 'No, I can't,' it drove him crazy. He had to have you! If he wanted somebody, he stuck in there until he got you. I don't care whether it was an actor or director, whoever, he would never take no, till the very last. I mean, he'd hang in there." (HH-KB95)

Hedison wanted to be a serious actor, and now had a chance to do a play. He struggled with his decision, then went to Roger Moore for advice. Moore was the star of *The Saint* and, according to Hedison, "Roger thought I was crazy. 'The play will last two weeks,' he said. 'Irwin is television; the series would not only pay good money, but could run for several years. What choice is there?' What really clinched it was that Richard Basehart would be playing Nelson. I figured that if Basehart, who I admired for a long time, could play the Admiral, I could play the Captain. I called Irwin and confirmed the deal." (DH-SL86)

On November 10th, William Self announced he had signed Basehart for the role of Admiral Nelson, and Hedison as the Captain of the Seaview. It was a last-minute arrangement, with the pilot set to begin filming in eight days.

While Allen wore three hats as writer, director and producer, he wasn't in the trenches by himself.

Costume designer Paul Zastupnevich was also the production illustrator, and worked as Irwin Allen's assistant in nearly all ways. Allen depended on "Paul Z." for much. The two had worked together since *The Big Circus*.

Al Gail would serve as assistant to the producer, shouldering a vast variety of duties. In time, he would also be elevated to a writing post, as assistant story editor, and then occasional script writer.

Gaston Glass would serve as production manager. He was a Fox man, having performed this duty for some of the studio's other series: *Hong Kong*, *Adventures in Paradise*, *Bus Stop* and *Follow the Sun*.

Winton C. Hoch was the director of photography. He had worked for Allen as cinematographer on *The Big Circus*, *The Lost World*, *Five Weeks in a Balloon* and the big-screen *Voyage to the Bottom of the Sea*.

Jack Martin Smith, one of two art directors responsible for the Seaview, inside and out, had worked for 20th Century-Fox for decades, and was among a team of set designers who shared an Oscar for their work on the studio's 1963 *Cleopatra*. He would also work on the studio's sci-fi epic *Fantastic Voyage*, a few years later.

William J. Creber worked with Smith, and was more directly answerable to Irwin Allen, staying with *Voyage* for thirty-seven episodes, and was instrumental in establishing the look of the series. Creber was a chip off the old block – his father, Louis H. Creber, had been an art director at Fox for the last few decades. Allen would also use William Creber to help launch *Lost in Space* and *The Time Tunnel*. Before this, Creber had served as art director on *Rio Conchos* and *The Greatest Story Ever Told*.

Walter M. Scott decorated the sets. He was a 20th Century-Fox man, having worked on many of the studio's films and all of its TV series.

L.B. Abbott provided the photographic effects, including the work done with the various Seaview models (mostly lifted from the movie). He had also served Allen well, for *The Lost World*, the big-screen *Voyage* and *Five Weeks in a Balloon*. And, being a Fox man, he had also worked on *Cleopatra*. He had already won an Oscar for his work in *Journey to the Center of the Earth*, and there were more to come.

Lionel Newman would supervise the music for the series. As vice president in charge of music for Fox, he selected composers and at times conducted. He had composed title themes, including those for *The Many Loves of Dobie Gillis* and *Daniel Boone*.

Paul Sawtell was Irwin Allen's choice as staff composer. He provided the score, including the memorable theme and title music. He had been composing movie soundtracks since the late 1930s and had worked on several of Irwin Allen's films – *The Sea Around Us*, *The Story of Mankind*, *The Big Circus*, *Five Weeks in a Balloon* and the big-screen version of *Voyage*. He also scored David Hedison's sci-fi hit, *The Fly*. Another sci-fi cult classic featuring Sawtell's music was 1958's *It! The Terror from Beyond Space*. On TV, he wrote the theme song for Michael Ansara's series, *Broken Arrow*. He would work for Allen again on *The Time Tunnel* and *Land of the Giants*.

In putting together his story and pilot film, Allen harvested a great deal of footage from the 1961 feature film version of *Voyage*, including the depth charges, along with many resulting shots of the crew inside of the ship being rocked and falling (such as scenes in the kitchen and corridors). Then, during the scenes involving the reattachment of the sonar antenna, Allen planned to include film sequences showing shark and squid attacks. Finally, he would use footage revealing the large chunks of ice raining down in front of the observation windows. This thrifty practice seemed a perfect way to add big-picture production values to the TV footage. As time progressed, Allen's necessary thriftiness in reusing or recycling costumes, sets, and even storylines from previous works became either a blessing or a curse, depending on your opinion of the resulting hybrid.

***

Production began on Monday, November 18th on 20th Century-Fox Stage 5.

Of his first day on the Seaview, David Hedison said, "They were great sets. Very well done. I wasn't in awe, but I could appreciate the hard work that went into them." (DH-CB12)

On the fourth day of filming, Hedison experienced his first round of the Seaview lurching from side to side. He later said, "There was a guy on set with a metal pail and a hammer. When he hit the pail the first time we all lurched to the right. On the second hit we'd fall to the left as the camera tilted to the right. A hammer and an old tin pail. Can you imagine!" (DH-CB12)

Irwin Allen directing pilot for *Voyage to the Bottom of the Sea*, November 1963.

On the fifth day of the production, work was interrupted by breaking news out of Dallas Texas. At 10:40 a.m. (Pacific Time), Walter Cronkite interrupted the broadcast of *As the World Turns* on CBS-TV to announce, "Here is a bulletin from CBS News. In Dallas, Texas, three shots were fired at President Kennedy's motorcade in downtown Dallas. The first reports say that President Kennedy has been seriously wounded by this shooting.... More details just arrived. These details about the same as previous: President Kennedy shot today just as his motorcade left downtown Dallas. Mrs. Kennedy jumped up and grabbed Mr. Kennedy, she called 'Oh, no!' The motorcade sped on. United Press says that the wounds for President Kennedy perhaps could be fatal. Repeating, a bulletin from CBS News, President Kennedy has been shot by a would-be assassin in Dallas, Texas."

Actor Mark Slade said, "I was walking outside the soundstage. Someone said President Kennedy had been assassinated. I ran back to the stage and told an older crew member. He got angry and said, 'That's not funny!' A few minutes later, everyone knew it was true. The reaction on the set of the Seaview was the same as it was around the country." (MS-SFTS2)

As word spread through the company, work slowed, then stopped, as radios and TV sets were switched on.

Walter Cronkite was the first to break the news to a national television audience, saying, "We just have a report from our correspondent Dan Rather in Dallas that he has confirmed that President Kennedy is dead. There is still no official confirmation of this.... The two priests who were with Kennedy say that he is dead of his bullet wounds. That seems to be about as close to official as we can get at this time."

Above, from left to right: David Hedison, Henry Kulky, Irwin Allen, Richard Basehart, and Christopher Connelly; Below: Basehart, Robert Dowell and Hedison.

Production on *Voyage* was cancelled for the rest of the day. Cast and crew were released to go home.

Numb production personnel and performers returned to 20th Century-Fox on November 25 to pick up where they had left off on the previous Friday. The final shots for the pilot were taken on Friday, December 6.

Regarding taking direction from Irwin Allen, David Hedison said, "He was wonderful to his 'stars.' You know, 'Where are my starrrrs?' All of that stuff. He was terribly generous. But he couldn't direct actors. He loved photo effects; he loved all that kind of thing, but he didn't know what to say to an actor. But he was wonderful; he was great to me; I liked him. But we were always arguing. I'd say, 'Irwin, what a great idea it would be if we tried it this way.' He thought I was mad. I think Irwin was a great salesman; a great producer, but not a director." (DH-TCF07)

In post production, Allen brought in Dick Tufeld to provide the narration for the opening of the first episode. Tufeld would also serve as the narrator (and the voice of the Robot) on *Lost in Space*.

According to *Variety* (September 1, 1965 issue), the pilot film for *Voyage to the Bottom of the Sea* was the most expensive filmed so far, costing $550,000. It was shot in color, though aired in black and white.

***

Irwin Allen (second from right) and Winton Hoch (far right) film a pilot as America mourns the loss of a President (November 1963).

It was an easy sell to ABC. Network executive Lew Hunter said, "The presentation was made on film. Afterwards, I complimented Bill Self on selling the show. I asked him, 'Was that particularly hard?' He said, 'No, I have the tendency to show the pilot to the suits,' whom I was one, 'and then stand up and ask if there are any questions.' And I said, 'Yes, but you didn't go on about the show.' He said, 'One: I thought the show spoke for itself. And, two: I have seen a lot of people talk themselves out of a sale. And I was not going to do that.' That's the kind of man he was. And Irwin would sit there with a smile on his face, wearing those coke-bottle glasses. And he'd say, 'Wasn't it great?!' And then someone would usher him out of there." (LH-AI15)

The first order of business was to hire a rewrite man or two for the series. And before they would be rewriting scripts, they would be working with Allen writing the series bible, also known as the Writer's Guide.

William Welch was a meat-and-potatoes writer, and had cut his teeth on TV series which attempted to spook the viewer, such as *Lights Out* (from 1950 and '51), and those that appealed to youth, such as *Sky King* (in 1957 and '58). He wrote the screenplay for a 1963 low-budget and somewhat trashy Jayne Mansfield movie called *Promises, Promises*. He also tried his hand at being a playwright, with the 1960 way-off Broadway sci-fi *How to Make a Man*, starring Peter Marshall (later of *Hollywood Squares* fame) as a robot. On December 30, 1960, *Daily Variety* said:

> *How to Make a Man*, a new comedy by William Welch which premed tonight at the Cass Theatre [Detroit], provides an ironic lesson in how not to make a play. In attempting to show the difference between man and robots, the comedy carries with it all the faults of man which tend to make him robot-like. Thus, it is obvious that most of the creative effort went into material things – ingenious moving stages, a wondrous home electronic console with a widescreen rear projection color TV set that was an important part of the action, stunning, futuristic sets and gorgeous costumes. Unfortunately, very little substance was given to the words and actions of the human actors.

It could have been, and certainly sounded like, a typical review for a comparable Irwin Allen production. Welch sighed, "Through a combination of incredible circumstances which merit a book of their own, the venture was a cataclysmic bomb which all but destroyed anyone who had anything to do with it. As the author, I was the particular target of vengeance." (WW-TWTD75)

And that meant Welch needed a job.

By virtue of his varied writing background, Welch was a perfect fit for the Allen TV production company, and was signed up to serve as script editor.

Al Gail had been working closely with his cousin Irwin since the two had moved to Los Angeles in the late 1930s. Without credit, he worked with Allen on his various movies, and now he would again be at Allen's side with this new venture, as Welch's assistant.

Welch and Gail worked with Allen, fleshing out the series and committing ideas to paper to serve as a road map for the freelance writers who would be given script assignments.

Allen, ever the showman, was making a big show of trying to intrigue and educate the writers he would use for the series. Every TV series has a series bible, but, with Allen's first series, it was more of an entertainment package. The work of Allen, Welch and Gail grabbed the prospective writers with the bold title, "NOW THAT YOU'VE SEEN THE PILOT…" The first page was THEME. Perhaps a better heading, considering what was to follow, would have been LACK OF THEME. It said:

> *Voyage to the Bottom of the Sea* is an exercise in action-adventure. It has dash … verve … an honest, high-hearted approach to exciting entertainment. In spirit, each episode contains the rapidly sputtering fuse, the breathless, desperate race against the clock, the gripping suspense of overwhelming danger.
>
> Obviously, then, this is not a show of social crusades, satirical comments or probing searches into the human psyche. Such themes, fascinating and worthy as they may be, are outside the province of a series dedicated to the heady business of high adventure.
>
> But the very fact that the themes required are straightforward and fundamental means that great skill is called for in their development. Motivations must be clear. Events must proceed logically. Plausibility is a key note.
>
> In a practical sense, themes may be divided into three broad areas: struggle against the forces of nature; struggle against the enemies of mankind; any combination of the two. Such themes lead naturally to stories of pure adventure, stories of mystery-adventure and stories with overtones of science fiction-adventure.

Sheila Mathews Allen said of her long-time companion, and husband of seventeen years, "He loved to put people in jeopardy, and have them rise to the occasion and succeed…. He was a very moral, ethical man, and he was making pictures in the days that he did, when it was a little different than it is today. We didn't have to deal with as much, you know, sex. Can we say that? And that would not have been his cup of tea, really. So he was a very moral movie-maker. I don't think you can find anything in anything he ever did that was not acceptable to all, the whole range of audience." (SMA-KB95)

The next subject in the series bible was "Style." Allen and his helpers wrote:

> The style of writing desired for the series is deceptively simple. Its main ingredients are action, pace, economy and tense excitement. Talk for talk's sake – even talk for the development of depth of character – [is] considered expendable.... The language used must have the ring of authenticity and dialogue exchanges will be used in all cases to advance the story, heighten the tension, increase the excitement, grip the audience. Taut drama is the prevailing mood. When there is romance, it must impel, not hinder, the relentless progress of the story. Humor is welcome but it must proceed from the action and be part of the headlong dash that carries the viewer from the intriguing teaser to the crashing climax of each show.

Another page in the bible had the heading of "Characters." The first name in the character list was *Seaview*.

Allen wrote:

> Although, strictly speaking, not a character, Seaview is definitely a strong motivating force in the series. It is a huge, radically designed nuclear submarine which carries a complement of twelve officers and one hundred twenty-five men. Its most distinctive feature is a fantastic glass nose which makes the forward lounge an ideal place from which to view the awesome wonders of the undersea world. It is the great glass nose which gives the ship its distinctive look of a "Submarine of Tomorrow." But even more important, although less immediately apparent, are its other features ... its missile room with its arsenal of nuclear warhead rockets ... its mini-sub which permits two men scouting trips below the operating range of the deepest diver ... its escape hatch which permits individual frogmen to explore ocean bottoms ... its rows of efficient computers which can perform all the magic of the new machine brains ... and its amazing ability to dive deeper and move faster than any ship ever designed. These are a few of the features making Seaview the world's most efficient device for scientific research, exploring and defense.

On a separate page, in a box devoted to "Taboos," Allen told his future writers:

> The taboos are few but implacable.
>
> A. All the ordinary taboos set up in the interest of taste and morality;
> B. No spy stories in which the adversary is a representative of any recognizable governments, even by implication (Gamma

is the adversary we use in stories with an international spy flavor);

C. No supernatural stories;

D. No story in which the element of romance, psychological study or personal drama are permitted to bring the action to a halt.

In his summary, the key points Allen highlighted were:

- "The action takes place a few years in the future, giving wide latitude in technical matters";
- "There is a James Bondian flavor to the series, which, of course, means that seductive attractive women often play a part and may involve Crane, Nelson, Chip Morton or – in fact – any one of the twelve officers and 125 crewmen of the sub";
- "The teaser of each episode is vitally important. It must shock the audience – grip them – literally force them to watch the show";
- "And the keynote is … ACTION!"

The struggle at this point was to make sure "Voyage" (or, as it was now being again called *Voyage to the Bottom of the Sea*) could be produced on a TV budget, and delivered on a weekly basis to the network without danger of missing air dates. It would be the same battle for *Lost in Space* one year later, and *Star Trek* a year after that. Television had never produced a one-hour dramatic science fiction series with recurring cast members and regular sets, on a weekly basis. Certainly anthology series had been attempted in this genre before, with shows such as *The Twilight Zone* and *The Outer Limits*. If either of those series fell behind, they could shoot different episodes simultaneously, since the same sets and cast members would not be needed in each. But in many ways Allen was attempting to conquer uncharted lands in television production. Each *Voyage* episode would be the equivalent of half a science-fiction movie. These requirements for futuristic sets, costumes and props, as well as not to mention special effects, loomed as nigh-impossible tasks. Allen would be the pioneer in this new territory of television production, and it is fair to say that without *Voyage to the Bottom of the Sea*, there likely would not have been a *Lost in Space* or a *Star Trek* for many years to come.

Allen's agent, Herman Rush, was involved in much of the wrangling with the network and studio in setting a budget for the series – the magic number that was just high enough, but that wouldn't waste a single thin dime. He said, "The budgets were different for different shows, depending on the time period they would be put into. ABC needed programming for, in those days, 7:30 time periods, where they were getting a young audience. But they had limited budgets. I think ABC had lower budgets than CBS and NBC would have had. But one of Irwin's great assets was the ability to make things on a budget that other producers had difficulty with. Irwin had a system; he had a way of addressing these things. Whatever the budgets were, he would meet them. Those budgets were a little higher than the licensing fee that the network was paying, with 20th Century-Fox doing a little deficit financing, recouping that loss in the foreign sales which took place with this kind of content. What helped him with those small budgets was 20th

Century-Fox had the back lot (which is now Century City) and that included the water area [known as 'The Moat'] where he had filmed portions of the movie version of *Voyage to the Bottom of the Sea* [sic]. So he was able to use that same setting to do the television series, saving money and thereby making it a feasible venture to the thinking of the studio and network executives." (HR-AI15)

Once the potential series had been structured to appear feasible as a TV production, and with the network already impressed with the pilot film, a deal was struck between Irwin Allen Productions, 20th Century-Fox Studios and the ABC television network to partner up on the making of a series, with a commitment for sixteen one-hour episodes, and options in place for ABC to extend that order to twenty-six or more for the first season. Thomas Moore, former president of ABC, said, "Allen was one of the most creative people in the science fiction arena. He grasped the Jules Verne material with an immediate recognition as to its convertibility to television. He surrounded himself with talented young writers, directors and special effects people." (TM-SFTS2)

Allen had one more thing going for him – he was remarkably impassioned.

Dave Kaufman of *Daily Variety* was struck by Allen's enthusiasm. Interviewed for Kaufman's May 5, 1964 column, Allen said, "Like every motion picture producer, you're dying to bring to TV a motion picture technique. They say you don't have the time or money in TV. I think it can be done. In my movies, I've always had about 2,000 sketches made on each project – sketches of all the action in pictures. This is literally cutting a picture before it goes on stage. This way, every department – wardrobe, special effects and so on – knows exactly what I need, and they know long in advance of production. It keeps hysteria to a minimum. I am doing the same thing on the series." (IA-DV64)

Regarding the scope of his first television project as compared to his 1950s panel show, Allen told Kaufman, "I have 21 permanent sets. We will have a second unit on location all over the world. We plan extensive use of miniatures. Our 102-foot submarine will go into the block-long moat -- now occupied by Tiki, the *Adventures in Paradise* ship, which will be removed. We have seven smaller subs, in different sizes for proportionate shooting. We can run them by remote radio. They are the most expensive toys ever made. We will reproduce the sub in sections for indoor shots. We even have a Polaris missile room in the sub; largest in the world. In the pilot, we had an advanced seismograph, which foretold earthquakes. Since we made it, the government has revealed they are just a step away from such an instrument." (IA-DV64)

Allen's excitement for this new project was contagious. Hedison said, "Irwin had fantastic enthusiasm for his projects and got you excited, too. He took you into his office and showed you his sketches, models and costume designs. You got caught up, and it was just fantastic." (DH-SL86)

Allen was having a ball with his expensive toys. However, to his disappointment, it was dictated that the show, including his much-hyped sets and props, would be filmed in shades of gray.

In April, 1964, *Variety* reported "No Tint for 20th's *Bottom of the Sea*." It had been calculated that color processing would have added another $20,000 cost per segment, amounting to about $600,000 over the season. The conclusion, from the studio and network, was that there simply were not enough color sets in America to warrant this added expense.

Black and white could, if nothing else, give *Voyage to the Bottom of the Sea* a *film noir* look. And with the theme Allen had in mind, this might not be an entirely bad thing. Allen told *Daily Variety* that his *Voyage* would be "a damp cloak-and-dagger series, centered about the glass-nosed sub."

Divers prepare one of the Seaview miniatures for underwater filming in the Fox Green Tank. Irwin Allen was disappointed that ABC decided not to pay the extra money needed to film First Season sequences such as these in color (1964).

He added, "In the series, the sub is owned and operated by a Santa Barbara institute as an oceanography lab, but actually that's the cover for 'the top CIA of that day.'"

The sub would be manned by "the super-commandos of the world, the most brilliant scientist-soldiers ever created."

Allen was planning on writing and directing three episodes out of every thirteen, and believed he was making a series that would appeal to adults as much as children. He told *Daily Variety*, "While we hope we will have the teenage kids, we are also reaching for an adult audience. Youngsters alone can't support a show." (IA-DV64)

For the Fall from Fox: Robert Lansing in *12 O'Clock High*.

***

Twentieth Century-Fox was suddenly back in the TV game, with four series scheduled for 1964-65. NBC was taking the one-hour *Daniel Boone* from Fox. And ABC had ordered three hours per week from the studio: *Peyton Place* (one hour broken into two segments), *12 O'Clock High* and *Voyage to the Bottom of the Sea*.

For a June 28, 1964 *Los Angeles Times* article, Cecil Smith wrote:

> The biggest resurgence of television production in Hollywood is at 20th Century-Fox, the studio that went suddenly from nowhere to be the second largest producer of programs on the networks next season. Though still far behind the production of the Universal-Revue colossus, which will supply 8 ½ hours

Along with *12 O'Clock High* and *Voyage to the Bottom of the Sea*, the fall of 1964 saw two more new series from Fox: Fess Parker, Patricia Blair and Darby Hinton in *Daniel Boone* (above), and (below) Mia Farrow in *Peyton Place* (20th Century Fox Television, 1964).

weekly to the networks, the 4 hours from Fox is a major coup. It's also very gratifying to young [studio head] Richard Zanuck, who says, flatly, no major film studio today can survive without a strong television arm, and to William Self, who guides its TV fortunes.

Jack Hellman interviewed Irwin Allen and then filed a report for his July 9, 1964 *Daily Variety* "Light and Airy" column. Irwin told him that with TV's *Voyage to the Bottom of the Sea*, his goal was "every week, *Perils of Pauline*!" Hellman reported:

No show next season can boast such far-flung production as *Bottom*. Four units will be at work on every segment and seven cameras will be used ("more than in feature pictures"). One unit will work in the Bahamas, where the water is crystal clear, and another around Catalina. Says Allen, "If this sounds like a kid show, well and good, but once the elders take a look they'll be confirmed repeaters. Similar pictures of mine have always drawn a family trade and the nights were just as strong as the Saturday matinees. It's targeted, however, for adults and our 11 sponsors are confident they'll be selling their wares in the right places."

Bob Suhosky, TV Publicity Director for 20th Century-Fox Television, got busy next, telling the TV press corps:

No producer in history ever approached a television series with more knowledge of his subject and the materials for making the subject into an exciting series than has Academy Award winner Irwin Allen, producer, director and writer for his 20th Century-Fox Television series, *Voyage to the Bottom of the Sea*, for ABC-TV. *Voyage* has been a preoccupation with Allen for five years, from the time he first began researching an original story about a submarine of the future ("Let's say the late 1960s or early 1970s," said Allen) and this grew to the fantastically successful motion picture, *Voyage to the Bottom of the Sea*, which was a blockbuster for 20th Century-Fox. It is important to the series that *Voyage* initially was a motion picture, for Allen will be the first to admit

> that it would be impossible to obtain the production values for the TV series had it not been for the motion picture version absorbing the initial costs of sets, props, costumes and underwater film to say nothing of such intangibles as research, drawings, conception and a myriad of etcs. "For example," Allen pointed out, "the three main underwater sections of our Seaview submarine cost more than $400,000 to build – more than most television pilot films in their entirety. Yet when we were ready to make the television pilot we had at our disposal, and in perfect working shape, the intact sections of the control room, the viewing room (the only submarine with a glass nose) and the missile and torpedo rooms fully equipped with more than two dozen of the latest atomic warhead-carrying missiles."

For the pilot film, "Eleven Days to Zero," Allen had 1,100 sketches prepared to guide the production. He was approaching the making of a TV series with the kind of strategic planning only seen in motion pictures – until now.

It also had the expensive miniatures made for the motion picture version, as well as sets, uniforms, and stock footage.

Irwin Allen said, "Call us lucky. No other series has ever been handed a million dollars' worth of sets and props to work with right from the start." (IA-TR64)

Richard Basehart told interviewer Erskine Johnson, "Fighting the submarine – that's the challenge to all the actors in this show. With all those lights and dials the submarine is bigger acting competition than a child or a dog.... With our crazy glass-nosed sub, no one will notice the actors in the first show. After that, my only problem will be to make the character believable. SOMETHING has to be believable in this show." (RB-ARN64)

Over the next couple of years, things would only get more challenging.

***

When *Voyage to the Bottom of the Sea* premiered on the ABC Television Network on Monday, September 14, 1964, with "Eleven Days to Zero," it received mixed reviews.

On September 15th, Cynthia Lowry reviewed the premiere episode for the *Warren Times Mirror*, in Warren, Pennsylvania, saying:

> This 60-minute drama was so full of various elements on so many fronts it was pretty hard to follow the plot, if any. There was a super-powerful nuclear submarine and its brave crew on a secret mission to the Arctic to balance with atomic explosions a couple of earthquakes that were going to destroy the Western world. There was also the evil "powerful worldwide force" that wanted the disasters to occur, represented by shadowy bald-headed men with Oriental features. The hostile force -- unidentified -- kept bombing the submarine and shaking up the crew but didn't seem to hurt things much. There was also an undersea battle between

> divers and the biggest, phoniest octopus ever seen on the small screen. Small boys of all ages may find it fun.

Los Angeles Times critic Don Page was the most vicious, with the headline in the newspaper's September 15th edition: "ABC Sinks to New Depths with *Voyage to the Bottom of the Sea*." He wrote:

> *Voyage* was released Monday night as part of the network's Wide World of Entertainment (slogan for ABC's new season). Well, stop the world, we want to get off. Richard Basehart, an outstanding actor, and David Hedison are co-stars of this disaster and must be secretly cringing at every cliché in the script.

If the pilot didn't make David Hedison cringe, the L.A. Times review certainly did. His reaction: "What can I say? I thought that was obviously the end of the series." (DH-DM13)

Terry Vernon, with his "Tele-Vues" column in the September 21st edition of the California-based *Long Beach Press-Telegram*, said:

> [T]he series has going for it good acting, photography and action. However, the storyline in the opener attempted to encompass too much. As a result, the continuity was ragged. The whole thing just didn't hang together – or maybe it did hang itself. My final impression is that the series should succeed. If it ever finds that missing continuity, it has one big factor to its advantage – it offers lots of action and adventure in a relatively adventureless season.

The reviewer for *TIME* magazine was onboard, saying:

> For one hour, on land and at sea, machine guns chattered, torpedoes schlurped through the deep, and missiles sang in the air. *Voyage* is all it tries to be: fast-moving calisthenics for young eyeballs.

TV syndicated columnist Bob Foster called *Voyage* "a better than average adventure series." For his review, printed in the September 15th edition of the *San Mateo Times*, he added:

> It isn't exactly a science-fiction story in the true sense, but it has a bit of the future in it. In fact, what we saw was supposed to have happened about 10 years hence. *Voyage to the Bottom of the Sea* will have its followers, and plenty, too. This is a natural for the older teenagers and the younger "elder citizens" as well, as all those who so enjoyed *Outer Limits* which formally occupied the time slot.

The critic known as "Pit," writing for the trade magazine *Variety*, in its September 16th edition, said:

> No question but that triple-credit [writer, director, producer] Irwin Allen has the credentials for all that sci-fi jazz herein abundantly displayed. Expectedly from this cinema craftsman of the Jules Verne genre, all the imposing folderol was in place and slickly mounted – but then virtually squandered by a script that was Saturday serial stuff. For all that, *Voyage* stands a Nielsen chance precisely because of its obvious play-to-the-kids strategy as ABC's Monday night tee-upper. Yet even the kids might get wise to the conning in double-time, and if that happens, the super A-sub Seaview of this 20th-Fox bromide goes down for keeps. The Allen formula calls for paper-mache characterizations, blinking gizmo lights, a sinister unspecified "enemy power" (who's either back-to-camera or faceless in the shadowy light), and frequent cuts of the sub nosing down to ocean bottom.

On the same day, "Daku," writing for sister trade *Daily Variety*, said of *Voyage*:

> Richard Basehart plays the Admiral with restraint and skill, and is given a good assist by his co-star, David Hedison, as Captain of the sub.... Technical credits, particularly the camera work and special effects, are top-drawer. There is an exciting fight wherein a helicopter attacks a car; an enemy drone plane attacks the sub; there is an underwater fight with an octopus; and, finally, a walloping finale at the North Pole, where the mission is carried out successfully. With its combined elements of futuristic inventiveness, science, intrigue, suspense, *Sea* is off to an excellent start.

ABC's premiere of *Voyage to the Bottom of the Sea* was pitted against the CBS one-two punch of *To Tell the Truth* from 7:30 to 8 p.m., followed by *I've Got a Secret*, from 8 to 8:30. This was the fifth year for *To Tell the Truth* in the lead-off Monday evening position and it had always been a winner for the network.

Ironically, on NBC this night, for one of the last of its Monday Night at the Movies, was, of all things, a repeat showing of Irwin Allen's *The Lost World*, co-starring David Hedison.

Voyage won hands down with a 39.6% audience share, compared to 23.4% for the movie. As for the competition on CBS, the panel shows did not fare well. The previous season, *To Tell the Truth* finished No. 24 out of more than eighty prime time series. *I've Got a Secret* had placed at No 12. Now, with *Voyage* as their opposition, neither show would make it into the Top 30.

The question the network and many in the cast were asking: Would the audience return for a second voyage after experiencing Irwin's Allen's approach to presenting sci-fi action-adventure on television?

For "The City Beneath the Sea," the second episode to air, the numbers from A.C. Nielsen were even better, with *Voyage* winning its time slot with a 42% audience share, compared to the 24.1% that tuned in *I've Got a Secret* on CBS and the 21.9% that watched the NBC Monday Night at the Movies presentation of *The Wings of Eagles*, starring John Wayne.

"The Fear-Makers," the third broadcast episode, again put ABC into top position, with a peak audience of 36.4% as opposed to the 26.9% watching the panel show on CBS and the 25.7% turning the dial to the romantic comedy *Ask Any Girl*, starring David Niven and Shirley MacLaine, on the NBC Monday Night at the Movies.

As October turned into November, and then December, *Voyage* continued to dominate its time slot. On its worst night (October 12th), it was still in first place, with a 29.2% audience share. On its best (November 2nd), it soared to 42.7%.

The Nielsen Top 20 report for the week covering September 28 through October 4, 1964, as printed in the October 12 issue of *Broadcasting* magazine, ranked the most popular of nearly ninety prime time series this way:

1. *Bewitched* (ABC)
2. *The Fugitive* (ABC)
3. *The Addams Family* (ABC)
4. *My Three Sons* (ABC)
5. *Peyton Place II* (ABC)
6. *Valentine's Day* (ABC)
7. *The Patty Duke Show* (ABC)
8. *The Bing Crosby Show* (ABC)
9. *Ben Casey* (ABC)
10. *McHale's Navy* (ABC)
11. *Bonanza* (NBC)
12. *No Times for Sergeants* (ABC)
13. *The Munsters* (CBS)
14. *Wendy and Me* (ABC)
15. *Peyton Place I* (ABC)
16. ***Voyage to the Bottom of the Sea* (ABC)**
17. *Combat!* (ABC)
18. *The Beverly Hillbillies* (CBS)
19. *The Dick Van Dyke Show* (CBS)
20. *The Saturday Night at the Movies* (NBC)

Voyage was an unmitigated hit.

***

While *Voyage to the Bottom of the Sea* was depicted as taking place ten years in the future, it didn't start out as full-fledged sci-fi. Many of the first season episodes, and even a sprinkling of shows in the later seasons, were devoted to Man Against Man/espionage themes, as well as Man Against Nature. But, as the series progressed, Allen snuck in more sci-fi.

With its October 12, 1964 episode, "The Price of Doom," *Voyage* presented its first all-out sci-fi/horror tale with a story by noted science fiction author and screenwriter Harlan Ellison. The plot featured a mysterious batch of plankton which invaded the Seaview and grew to enormous size, infesting the ship and swallowing terror-stricken men and women in its path. For this first foray into fantasy, an espionage subplot was thrown in along with the growing plankton in hopes of holding the attention of the adults watching along with their kids.

The nod toward 1950s monster movies like *The Blob* did not chase away the audience. On this night, as the featured monster swelled, so did the viewership, rising from a 29.2 share in the first half-hour to a 31.7 in the second, again winning the hour for ABC.

On October 19, 1964, *Voyage* presented its first episode in which the crew of the Seaview encountered beings from another planet. On October 18, the day before "The Sky Is Falling" first aired, entertainment columnist Bill Sheriton, in the *Cullman Times*, serving Cullman, Alabama, said:

> Did you ever think about the scientific phenomena involved with *Voyage to the Bottom of the Sea*? Well, in Monday night's episode at 6:30 over Ch. 6, you will see what happens when the Seaview uses its atomic power to destroy an enemy spaceship that sank to the bottom of the ocean. Regulars Richard Basehart and David Hedison also portray spacemen in this story!

The syndicated column "TV Key Previews," carried on October 19 in the *Tucson Daily Citizen*, among other newspapers, said:

> Pretty exciting science fiction hokum. A disabled spaceship falls into the sea and our first thought is that it's an invading enemy. When contact is established and help solicited, a trigger-happy admiral (Charles McGraw) wants to proceed with the attack anyway. Richard Basehart and David Hedison are at their noble best and the show benefits tremendously from some well executed special effects.

Many of those watching television between 7:30 and 8:30 pm approved of the further shift toward more fantastic stories. A.C. Nielsen estimated the audience numbers this way:

Nielsen ratings report from Oct. 19, 1964:	Rating:	Share:
7:30 – 8 p.m.:		
ABC: *Voyage to the Bottom of the Sea*	**25.8**	**38.1%**
CBS: *To Tell the Truth*	16.4	24.2%
NBC: *90 Bristol Court: Karen*	15.0	22.1%
8 – 8:30 p.m.		
ABC: *Voyage to the Bottom of the Sea*	**28.0**	**40.3%**
CBS: *I've Got a Secret*	17.7	25.5%
NBC: *90 Bristol Court: Harris Against the World*	13.1	18.8%

The following week, Irwin Allen presented an episode which harvested scenes of dinosaurs fighting from his *The Lost World* movie, incorporated in another all-out sci-fi entry, called "Turn Back the Clock."

Syndicated "TV Previews," carried by *The Daily Reporter*, from Dover, Ohio, on October 26, 1964, said:

> This could make a good science fiction "B" picture. Somewhere in the bowels of the Antarctic, the Seaview, in its search for the missing members of a scientific expedition, comes across a prehistoric world, complete with savages, monsters and active volcanoes. The cast effectively goes through the motions of pretending to believe all of this and if parts of the show look familiar, they should. They've been used in earlier films. Credit goes more to the editing than to the special effects.

A.C. Nielsen ratings service again declared *Voyage* the winner in its ratings survey report from October 26th, with the sci-fi series peaking with a 39.2% audience share, tromping CBS, which only managed a 22.5% share for its panel shows, and NBC which had pulled in 23.5% for its new *90 Bristol Court* series.

With each new extraterrestrial or monster story, both Allen and ABC saw the ratings spike.

Lew Hunter said, "We went along with the change to 'monster of the week.' We didn't discourage it. I guess I must have been pretty much involved and encouraging the monster of the week, and the toys that went crazy on the submarine, and the things invading the submarine. I think Irwin was going to do it anyway, but I was saying, 'Go, go, go! Keep it going. That's wonderful.' We weren't doing quality television. That was something we all kind of hung our heads a little bit about. But we were serving popcorn. And Irwin would be the first person to tell you, 'I'm serving popcorn; you can get the caviar from Gene Roddenberry.'" (LW-AI15)

Happy to have a hit series, ABC seemed eager to please Allen even more than he wanted to please the network. For the 1965-66 television season, besides bringing *Voyage* back for a sophomore year, the network was hoping to add a second hour-long sci-fi series created and produced by Allen to its schedule. Allen had an idea for a new one, which would switch the focus from inner space to outer space. But he, along with agent Herman Rush and 20th Century-Fox, had set their sights on a bigger fish – the top broadcaster in the United States, respectfully called, "The Tiffany Network."

4

Countdown to Creation

Irwin Allen had been thinking about *Lost in Space*, or an early forerunner to it, as early as 1962. While preparing *Five Weeks in a Balloon* for release during that year, he announced that his next feature film, planned for 1963, would be "Passage to the End of Space." At first he conceived it as *Voyage to the Bottom of the Sea* meets *Five Weeks in a Balloon* ... transferred to a space environment. He described it as "eleven incompatible persons accidentally fired into the wild blue in the first space transport." (IA-IAPC62)

In May 1964, even before *Voyage to the Bottom of the Sea* had had its network premiere, Allen told *Daily Variety*'s Dave Kaufman, "I'm hooked on TV. I'm already flirting with seven new projects." (IA-DV64)

Despite this announcement, and for the same newspaper article, he said, "I enjoyed making *Voyage to the Bottom of the Sea*, but something happened that I don't want ever to happen again – mature women and teen-aged girls stayed away in droves. They stay away from all science fiction films. So, remember, *Voyage* was my only venture into that field."

Allen considered *Five Weeks in a Balloon* to be "a period-piece comedy" with action and adventure. *The Story of Mankind* and *The Lost World*, he said, were fantasies. He was planning "Passage to the End of Space" to be a combination of action adventure, comedy, and fantasy. Regarding the various elements, he remarked, "They are unrelated to one another, or oddly related."

His philosophy: "Make the movie as a total escape, purely for entertainment, in a form that can be duplicated by no other medium. If enlightenment and uplift come into the picture, they must do so secondarily." (IA-IAPC62)

By 1964, the television version of *Voyage to the Bottom of the Sea* was well underway. Allen, per the wishes of 20th Century-Fox, was looking for a TV property he could place with CBS. The studio had done a great deal of business with ABC, and some with NBC, but had never placed product with "The Tiffany Network." And CBS was top dog in television.

It was felt the best way to establish an association with CBS was to partner up with a producer who already had a solid relationship with the network. The one who was the most responsive to a potential collaboration with Allen was Guy della-Cioppa, who was in partnership with Red Skelton, one of CBS' top stars. This in effect made Skelton Allen's associate in the venture as well.

Allen said, "Red Skelton was my partner at the time. He was as silent as you could be. He was almost a silent movie." (IA-MC95)

CBS prided itself in being the "family network" – offering shows that the entire family could watch together, such as Red Skelton's show, *Lassie*, *The Andy Griffith Show*, *The Lucy Show*, *The Beverly Hillbillies*, *The Dick Van Dyke Show*, and *The Ed Sullivan Show*, to name a few. Many of these depicted families, even if they were oddball ones, such as *The Munsters*, or thrown-together families, such as the castaways on *Gilligan's Island*. Irwin Allen had a property in mind which featured a family, which would have instant viewer recognition, as well as offering the possibility of action/adventure excitement. Even more attractive to Allen, he believed the property was in the Public Domain. He said, "*Swiss Family Robinson* had been on my mind for a long time." (IA-MC95)

Guy della-Cioppa, ever the careful and efficient business man with a strong legal background, looked into the possibilities. He engaged a Washington, D.C. law office specializing in copyright law.

On June 24, 1964, attorney Fulton Brylawski wrote to della-Cioppa's attorney, Edward Blad, of Pacht, Ross, Warne, Bernhard & Sears:

Promotional poster for Disney's 1960 film version of *Swiss Family Robinson*. Allen's idea to transplant the father, mother, three children, and pets from the Pacific to outer space was a brilliant, simple concept (Walt Disney Productions, 1960).

> Replying to your letter of June 22, I find that the title SWISS FAMILY ROBINSON has been used for the following:
>
> Fictional classic, written by Johann David Wyss, who died in 1836. A great many editions of this work have been published in the past hundred and fifty years.

Unpublished and unproduced play by Ethelrada Lewis, copyrighted by the author, March 10, 1934.

Play by J. Ralph Corbett, produced on the *Junior Radio Playhouse* program, January 4, 1938.

Photoplay in ten reels [approximately 100 minutes], based on the novel by Johann David Wyss, copyrighted by RKO Radio Pictures, Inc., February 16, 1940. This picture was widely shown on TV in 1955 and 1956.

Story published anonymously in *Boys Life* magazine, April, 1957.

Television series, scripts written by Harold J. Smith and Edgar G. Ulmer, for Trans-World Artists, based on the book by Johann D. Wyss. Two of these scripts were copyrighted by Trans-World Artists – LOST IN THE JUNGLE, January 3, 1958 and SHIPWRECKED AND ALONE, Jan. 3, 1958 [but unaired].

The Hollywood Reporter of March 10, 1960 announced that Filmaster had acquired the pilot film of SWISS FAMILY ROBINSON from Trans-World Artists and would commence production of the TV series. Reference to announced production of the series were carried in the trade journals in 1961 but so far these have not materialized.

Feature photoplay (126 min.) copyrighted by Walt Disney Productions November 8, 1960. This was distributed by Buena Vista Distributing Company, the releasing company for Disney films.

Allen's television agent, Herman Rush, said, "There was an interesting history behind *Lost in Space*. It started out to be the *Swiss Family Robinson*. He was developing *Swiss Family Robinson* for television, but it did not have monsters, *per se*, and it did not have tremendous disasters. It was much more along the lines of a 'classic story.' The network resisted that, and somebody said – and I can't tell you who that somebody was – 'Let's take *Swiss Family Robinson* and put it up into space.' And that was the background. Now, as soon as that happened, then you have the potential for special effects, and then you have tremendous disasters, and then you have monsters, and then those elements became much more important in that story telling. And Irwin recognized that was what was needed for the audience out there." (HR-AI15)

Allen merely said, "*Lost in Space* was a combination of things that were happening in the early 1960s." He was referring to "the space race" between the U.S. and the Soviet Union, and Cold War espionage between the two super powers, as well as the concerns about overpopulation, the sudden interest in cryogenics and the immense success of Disney's movie version of *Swiss Family Robinson*, among many other things. He added, "And, of course, I have been a science-fiction fan all my life, and space was – and still is – the last frontier."

Allen added, "In 1964, America had become very space-minded, and CBS was interested in a family show, so we took the space and family ideas and combined them. That and a conglomeration of other things defined what we were going to do with *Lost in Space*." (IA-SW85)

Attorney Brylawski's notes concerning previous media use of the Swiss Family Robinson concept seemed to give the go-ahead for Allen to utilize it too.

Next, Allen set about putting his ideas to paper. At some point over the weeks to come, he wrote a seven-page treatment (undated). The title for the proposed series: "Space Family Robinson." The first story was "The Shipwreck." Allen wrote:

> The scene: A space port someplace in the United States. Television cameras are trained on a gleaming silver spaceship poised on a launching pad.
>
> A T.V. commentator is speaking. As he reveals the following background exposition, the T.V. screen shows the interior of the spaceship – the people – and the preparations being made for the take-off.
>
> The commentator reveals ----
>
> --- that the space ship had been under construction for two years – ever since space station D.O.Z. had made contact with an alien intelligence on Orion.
>
> --- that Orion is incapable of space flight, but would warmly welcome visitors from Earth.
>
> --- that a special Presidential fact-finding committee had been set up years ago to plan the most minute details of the projected trip. The committee was involved not only in scientific planning but also responsible for sifting through the mass of volunteers and making specific suggestions for final Presidential approval.
>
> --- that in the present year of 1984, space travel is not uncommon. Pioneer colonies already exist on the Moon and on Venus. Mars has been temporarily shelved as a colony site until further environmental studies can be made. Major emphasis has been placed on Venus and Moon projects. However, this trip to Orion has gripped the imagination of the world as it will be the first trip out of the solar system to meet face to face with aliens.
>
> --- that the President of the U.S. chose the Robinson family because of the unique qualities of Dr. Robinson. He is in perfect health. He is a pioneer in space travel, a gifted inventor who helped develop the interstellar drive so that such a trip is possible, an amazingly well-rounded scientist whose specific degrees range from anthropology to zoology AND he has four remarkable children ages six to nineteen (two girls, two boys) and a scientifically oriented wife who are willing and anxious to brave

dangers of the unknown and leave the Earth, possibly forever, to visit an alien world.

(NOTE: While the commentator speaks of the family, the children, etc., the camera will be following each on his appointed task inside the capsule as his or her brief background is revealed.)

--- that the space ship is stocked with every item, both scientifically and otherwise, that astute and imaginative planning can conceive of.

--- that the only passenger not a member of the family is a young twenty-four-year-old scientist who has been Dr. Robinson's assistant for the past three years.

The gleaming silver space ship is poised on the launching pad. Inside the seven passengers settle themselves into their contour chairs, strap themselves in, and tensely listen to the count-down over the p.a. system.

… three – two – one – Blast Off!

The mighty space ship quivers like a thoroughbred greyhound at the starting gate, then lifts off the pad and hurtles through the Earth's atmosphere and into space.

The space travelers unbuckle their straps and quickly leap to their appointed tasks. All are busy … Father, Mother, two girls, eighteen and twelve years of age; a boy of sixteen and a boy of about six. Assisting Father at the instruments is a young scientist of twenty-four. Two dogs and a parrot make up the rest of the space ship's complement.

The Father now announces everything is in readiness for the next big step. The automatic pilot is hooked into the electronic brain. Mother hands out dimethyl sulfoxide pills as the young scientist explains to the kids that it will slow down the chemical and biological processes of the body to an almost undetectable rate … and also protect them from the effects of the "deep freeze." The deep freeze will bring their body temperature down to about 270 degrees Centergrade [sic] … which reduces the rate of metabolic activity to a trillion times slower than normal.

The purpose of the "deep freeze" is now revealed. Inasmuch as the interstellar voyage to Orion will take an estimated 50 years to complete, the space travelers will make the trip in suspended animation.

As a result of the drugs and the freezing, they will eventually waken in pretty much the same condition as when they went into suspended animation. Biologically, they will age only slightly during the fifty years.

All now take their places in special glass-like containers. Father sets the timer for 60 seconds. As the last second ticks off, a cloud of milky gas envelopes all the bodies and in an instant, they are all frozen solid as a block of ice.

Under the control of the magnetic brain and the automatic pilot, the Space Ship speeds toward its eventual destination of Orion.

Suddenly, the ship is caught up in a tremendous solar storm. Meteorites smash into the hull, bouncing the vehicle mercilessly. Finally, the electronic brain pulls the ship out of the vortex, feeds emergency information to the automatic pilot which heads the ship for the nearest land mass containing atmosphere and other conditions suitable for the support of human life.

The ship hits the atmosphere like a flaming star – drops down – skips across a vast sea and crashes against a rocky shore.

The instruments take over feeding antidotes to the passengers.

Passengers revive. They are shocked by the sight of smashed instruments – general chaos. Partial readings on instruments indicate that they are far off their mark – but just where they landed is a complete mystery. How long have they been in suspended animation? A week…? A year…? Ten years…? No one can answer that question until they determine where in space they are.

First order of the day is attempt to repair as many instruments as possible. The radio is a pile of junk so any attempt to contact the Earth is impossible.

Visual observations through the portholes are hardly encouraging. All they can see is a bleak, forbidding landscape. No vegetation, no trees, the ground swept by bitter winds is an eerie yellow-orange color. Sand sweeping by has reddish tint indicating it's heavily oxidized.

With some instruments repaired, vital information is fed into the computer such as: temperature at sunset is zero, midnight it is 90 degrees below zero F, at noon it runs between 50 and 70 degrees F.

Father dons space suit. The atmosphere is thin – but breathable without oxygen mask. Taking a short leap, he soars through the air. Estimation is that the surface gravity is about one third of Earth's gravity … or, in another way, 100 pounds on Earth would weigh thirty-eight pounds here.

> Observation indicates two moons revolving. One, the inner, takes seven hours to revolve; the other, the outer, takes thirty hours to revolve.
>
> As the mass of data is fed into the machine, Father has a pretty good idea of where they landed. However, despite the barrage of questions, he refuses to answer until the computer analyzes the facts and figures.
>
> Finally, the big moment arrives. The computer spews the answer.
>
> They have landed on ... Mars ... just weeks – not years – after leaving Earth.

Before Allen could show his treatment to Guy della-Cioppa, he received a letter from his partner, dated July 28, 1964. Della-Cioppa wrote:

> Dear Irwin: Here I am rushing off some notes to you on our space adventure, a few hours prior to takeoff for Europe. I had hoped for a detailed discussion, but know you will understand.
>
> A bit ago I sent along a letter from the Washington people, outlining the copyright history of *Swiss Family*. While the original property appears to be in public domain, I hope you will agree there need be no clearing away of legal approvals in building your new approach to a Swiss family. I don't think we need *Swiss Family* as a foundation, in view of our last meeting on hillside Allen [Allen's Bel Air home in Los Angeles].
>
> <u>CONCEPT</u>: Pioneer family headed by famed scientist has been seeking a new world, and as the first family in space crash land on Mars. Aboard is Dr. _____, the father image of our series (45); his wife (40); daughter of 18; son of 14; daughter aged 12; and infant son. Two dogs, male and female. And one non-family member of the party, young scientist assistant of 24.
>
> Our father-scientist had been convinced that life abounds in the Universe beyond our solar system. And that man has long been scientifically ready to launch exploration and settlement. The take-off from Earth was widely heralded, and aboard the space-craft were scientific gear – gifts of Earthmen in all forms – books, paintings, seeds, medical instruments – you name it. Even a helicopter. But alas, on landing far short of the Constellation Orion where modern man knew life existed, the space-craft wreck destroyed much of the cargo. Worst of all, all radios are gone beyond repair.
>
> On Mars, the air is thin and water scarce. Slowly a stockade is built, the seeds from Earth are planted, a new life begun. And strange creatures begin to appear. Hope of contact back home is

> constant, but none can be made. And romance begins to bud between daughter and assistant. I can only briefly touch the imagination here, as modern scientific minds cope with a weird new environment; the scope of your imagination is boundless.
>
> FIRST SCRIPT: Should not be the first story – the one you would first broadcast. But rather Episode 7 or 18. A dramatically exciting first episode should be relatively easy to prepare, but leaves the critical comment "where do you go from here." Rather, should our pilot script have a brief prologue of the crash and the family emerging alive, gathered on the edge of the wilderness, in anticipation. Main title and dissolve to any episode.
>
> Irwin, I know these are the most sketchy of hurried thoughts, hardly contributing at this point. But perhaps helpful in your early planning. As the General said, "I shall return" ... in about two weeks. Ready to wade in as you may desire. Meanwhile – Warmest good wishes, Guy della-Cioppa.

What della-Cioppa was asking for was a pilot film that would be typical of an average episode. As he stated, it would open with a recap of the backstory. A brief montage would depict the situation on Earth; the reason for the expedition; the take-off; the problem that would shorten the journey and force the spaceship to have a hard landing on Mars; and the family coming out of the ship to behold their new world. After this, and for the remainder of the hour (or minimum of 50 minutes), a story would follow that could be, as della-Cioppa said, Episode 7 of the series, or Episode 18, or "any episode."

Allen went back to work, writing a new treatment for what he imagined could be Episode 7. He followed della-Cioppa's request and presented what could be an average episode, with the title "No Place to Hide." For its Teaser, after briefly establishing the backstory, Allen wrote:

> The group is almost ready to leave on their next Great Adventure into the unknown – a long, arduous move to the warmer climate of the equator.
>
> The approaching winter in the Northern Hemisphere would be too severe ... generally 150 degrees below Zero F. It is doubtful that they could survive the six months to spring.
>
> Their amphibious vehicle and trailer is being loaded with items necessary for life at the Equator. The space ship – damaged beyond repair – will remain where it is. When necessary they can return to it to replenish supplies, instruments, etc.
>
> Snowflakes are beginning to drift down, heralding an approaching winter storm.

> The youngest Robinson – six-year old Bobby – wanders idly off. The first warning of impending disaster comes when the two dogs, barking frantically, dash toward the youngster. All are horrified to see a grotesque Martian flying beast, slowly descending in ever-shortening circles above the head of the unsuspecting youngster … its claws extended to rip and tear flesh to bits.

The character Bobby would later become Will. The springboard of the family having to move south to avoid the cold was used in the pilot and also used in the fourth broadcast episode. Allen continued, with Act I of the story:

> As the flying monster dives at the boy, it's knocked head-over-heels by one of the dogs. The other dog pounces on the beast that is screaming in rage over the loss of its prey. A talon inflicts a cruel gash along the dog's back. The sigh of blood drives the beast berserk … and it attacks the wounded animal.
>
> The other dog now enters the fray – and is knocked groggy by the swipe from the gigantic wing. The beast now grasps the bleeding dog in one huge claw … rises off the ground and swoops for the youngster standing nearby – frozen in terror.
>
> By this time, Father John Robinson is running toward them, carrying a powerful rifle. As the beast dives toward the boy, John shoots. It's a perfect shot! The beast hits the ground, flutters spasmodically, then lies motionless.
>
> The youngster is quickly comforted in his mother's arms. The dog suffered only a superficial wound and is quickly up and about, tail-wagging in delight over the affectionate pats and caresses from all. There is little doubt that the youngster would have been severely injured, if not killed, had it not been for the alertness and courage of the two dogs.
>
> Packing is now complete … and the vehicle, pulling a trailer full of supplies, starts off into the gathering snow storm.
>
> The fury of the storm mounts frighteningly. Within the vehicle, the radiant heating system fights a desperate battle against the encroaching cold. All have their electrically heated jump-suits turned to "emergency high", but still they shiver and shake as the biting cold sweeps into the very marrow of their bones.
>
> The vehicle tops a ridge … then starts down. Slipping and sliding, it picks up momentum. The brakes are frozen solid … and all can do little more than hold their breath and pray as their vehicle hurtles downhill.
>
> Peering ahead, Father realizes they're sliding down a huge bank toward a river. As they reach the bottom of the snow chute, Father

> switches the amphibious vehicle off "land" to "water" … and it smoothly makes the transition.
>
> Now … they're moving down the river. All congratulate each other on their narrow escape. But they're far from safe … as in the distance an ominous sound can be heard, the sound of seething rapids.
>
> Again, their speed picks up and they're hurtling toward the rapids at breath-taking pace.

The action Allen described could not have been filmed on a TV budget … or, perhaps, even a feature film budget from this era. But a scaled-down version of the Chariot crossing an inland sea and encountering a whirlpool was filmed for the pilot and included in the fifth broadcast episode. Act II of Allen's treatment began:

> Father has the wheel – and it is only his amazing skill that keeps them from destruction and a watery grave. Somehow … they ride out the rapids. Bruised and battered … black and blue from the buffeting … the travelers drift gently downstream.
>
> They are cheered by the sight of the snow clearing up … starting to turn to rain. But again they face a new threat as the rain turns to hail and pieces of ice the size of boulders strike the vehicle like bullets.
>
> Reeling under the terrible pounding from the gigantic ice cubes, Father attempts to leave the river and head for some shelter. He knows the vehicle will not long withstand the brutal punishment pelting down from the Martian skies.
>
> Finally making the shore, he switches off "water" to "land", and drives up the bank. As they top the rise, all are awestruck to see – in the near distance – an amazing "castle-like" structure. Shifting into top speed, they make a dash for the protection of the "castle".
>
> Inside the structure, they are amazed to find evidence that intelligent creatures lived on Mars at some time in the past. Artifacts that took great skill and imagination in both conception and execution are strewn about. Interior storehouses containing seeds – well preserved – of flowers, fruits and vegetables.
>
> They discover what was apparently a frozen food locker deep in the earth containing vegetables which – upon thawing – are found to be delicious.
>
> All around are the remnants of some intelligent lost civilization – but there is no hint to the "why or wherefore" of the mysterious disappearance.

> For several days, the weary travelers rest and recuperate … and try to decide whether to push on toward the equator or spend the winter in this ancient castle.
>
> Although the women – tired from their arduous experiences – vote to remain, the two men are uneasy. Don especially is disturbed by the slant of the cracks in the castle and the direction in which the rows of vegetation is growing outside. He draws Father's attention to it, explaining that his knowledge of geology indicates this is a volatile earthquake area. John is concerned, inclined to agree despite the protestations of the women who do not want to move on.
>
> The young scientist is on the receiving end of some cold treatment from the ladies, especially from the eighteen-year-old who questions Don's knowledge and courage.
>
> That night … the ground trembles … and heaves and tosses the stone columns around like pebbles. Earthquake!

Some elements of the story were used in the episode "There Were Giants in the Earth." Don, as described in Allen's early take on the series, was a scientist, not a pilot. Beyond that, the characters were undefined, even nameless … other than Don, Father John, and little Bobby.

With Act III, Allen wrote:

> They're all lucky to escape with their lives. They manage to get out and to the safety of their vehicle just as the castle collapses. The earth splits … and the remains of the ancient civilization disappears into the gaping fault.
>
> The vehicle gets away just in time … with all hands effusively apologizing to the young scientist for doubting him.
>
> The vehicle and the weary travelers finally arrive at the Equator. The weather is a comfortable 80 degrees F. They drive slowly along a sandy sea court … to where a bubbling spring flows through an area of tropical trees and rich, verdant growth.
>
> At this inviting oasis they decide to set up their summer home. They start to unload the trailer when screams of terror are heard from the girls who had gone into the glade to seek a home site. The two men grab their rifles, start forward when the frightened girls come running out. Lumbering after them is a gigantic, crab-like creature about the size of a medium tank. Everyone hides in the vehicle as the monster approaches. It snakes out a claw, cuts through the wheel on the trailer with the ease of a power saw.

> As it moves toward the vehicle, the men fire. The bullets bounce off the creature's hard shell like peas off a tin roof. If it ever gets its claw into the vehicle, they're all dead.

These crab monsters alone would have blown an entire episode budget. Allen was indulging his imagination with little regard for a means to realizing his colorful ideas.

From Act IV:

> Father rips open a box of super-powerful grenades that were to be used for construction, to blast out home sites in rock. One … two … then three grenades explode under/over the giant crustacean. When the sand and dust settles … the monster lies dead.
>
> The destruction of the monster, however, doesn't solve the problem. Their Garden of Eden is infested with monster sand crawling beasts.
>
> During the next few days, they keep a sharp watch on the habits of the gigantic crabs. They enter the sea in the morning, later they return to deposit their huge eggs, then sleep at night amid the cool comfort of the floating trees.
>
> It is decided that if the pattern can be broken and the creatures scared off, they will go elsewhere to lay their eggs.
>
> A trench is dug between the sea and the trees – then filled with gasoline taken from their precious supplies. All now align themselves behind the trees with hand grenades except the two men who go down near the water's edge with flame throwers. As the creatures crawl ashore, they hit them with blasts of searing flame. In a few minutes, the sea is a hissing turmoil as the monsters lash around in their death throes. Some of the creatures now get ashore – threaten to cut off the two men – who start to retreat. As they turn to run, Don falls. Before a creature can snap him up, John blasts the giant crab with flame.
>
> Now, they cross the trench and watch closely as the creatures form a line and move purposefully forward. As they crawl through the trench, a grenade is tossed into the gasoline and the creatures become a flaming pyre. As others try to crawl through, they are rocked with a fusillade of exploding grenades. That turns the tide and the remaining monsters turn and high-tail it back to the safety of the sea.
>
> The threat from the giant crabs has been met and satisfactorily contained. Now, the family can relax … and start to build their new home on Mars.

Not even Producer Irwin Allen could find a way to film what Writer Irwin Allen had imagined as the seventh episode of "Space Family Robinson." Nor would the TV censors allow the horror of watching numerous giant crab creatures burned to a crisp in a gasoline filled trench. But Allen's treatment was both imaginative and effective enough to convince Guy della-Cioppa that he and his producing partner had the makings of a historic and potentially successful series for CBS.

On August 3, 1964, the attorney for Van Bernard Productions, Inc, drew up a one-page "deal memo" to link his client and Irwin Allen for a series unlike anything ever attempted before on television – a special effects-driven one-hour action-adventure science-fiction with continuing characters for the primetime family hour – the one that would go into space. It was well beyond the 1950s cheap kiddie fare like *Tom Corbett, Space Cadet*; *Captain Video*; *Rocky Jones, Space Ranger* and *Space Patrol*, or primetime anthology series such as *The Twilight Zone* and *The Outer Limits*. It was akin only to Allen's *Voyage to the Bottom of the Sea*, which was still a month away from its television premiere, and would be an Earthbound series. The deal memo forming the alliance between Van Bernard Productions (the business partnership between Red Skelton and Guy della-Cioppa, with ties to CBS) and Jodi Productions (a DBA for Irwin Allen, with ties to 20th Century-Fox), began:

> Gentlemen: Concurrently herewith you and we are entering into an agreement (herein called "the Joint Venture Agreement") for the formation of a joint venture under the fictitious firm name of "Space Productions," for the development, production and exploitation of a television pilot program and series tentatively entitled "Space Family" or "Lost in Space."

This was the first mention of "Lost in Space" as a possible title. However, months later, when presented to CBS, the preferred title had reverted back to "Space Family Robinson " In time, this had to be changed (as covered in Chapter 5).

On September 3, and after discussions with CBS, Guy della-Cioppa and TV agent Herman Rush drafted a letter to Allen, identified as "Notes for Discussion 'Space Family Robinson.'" They said:

> Standard Prologue should be planned for each episode, illuminating the background for the viewer. How the family reached Mars. In essence, an extract from a projected first show for broadcast – of approximately one minute, 30 seconds.
>
> Pilot Script should be a typical episode about 10 shows into the series, rather than the first story to be broadcast.
>
> Mars as our planet offers more advantages than disadvantages. Accepted fact about Mars should be distorted (air too thin, no water, gravity variation, etc.). Our family should not wear helmets and space suits, or special weighted boots. The creatures we meet, the unusual flora and fauna, [and] the terrain will be sufficient to create the reality of a new world. Against these we should play our

people as real as possible, for viewer ease of identification and personal involvement.

Pilot Story should contain:

Clear character delineation so we may meet and like all family members and the young scientist.

Glowing belief in the family resources to survive – courage, determination, pioneer spirit.

Orientation of wrecked space ship and stockade, the permanent home – food and water supplies and sources, power supply, etc.

Examples of gifted human ingenuity, i.e., food devised from natural sources, a mock-up electric plant, water reservoir, gasoline refining from raw oil drip, etc.

Reference leading to suspense potential that beings of human capability may be present on Mars.

Reference to hope of rescue and discussion or remote possibility. No means of communicating.

No horror creatures or fearful weird beings, in direct conflict.

Friendly or benign animals – perhaps to be domesticated for food, clothing, transport.

Constant suspense of the unknown, thru nature's forces, or distant contact with fearful weird subject matter: An ever present feeling the group stands against the mysterious unknown.

Brief moments of reflection exposition; Father concerned for family, mother courageous but for the moment of despair, children full of spirit, Don's excitement scientifically, etc., knowledge that human life exists on Orion with other pioneer families to follow – if no rescue, what will happen to the children on Mars.

In October, Irwin Allen, accompanied by Guy della-Cioppa and Herman Rush, made a presentation to CBS, armed with concept sketches. *Voyage to the Bottom of the Sea* had been airing on ABC for a few weeks now and was winning its time slot in the ratings, destroying the competition on NBC and badly bruising the CBS' early Monday-evening panel shows *To Tell the Truth* and *I've Got a Secret*. The network already enjoyed a successful relationship with Red Skelton and Guy della-Cioppa. They hoped to establish something similar with Irwin Allen.

It has long been believed that Producer Gene Roddenberry, while shopping his proposal for *Star Trek*, met with CBS after Irwin Allen had sold *Lost in Space*. Roddenberry often told the story of his pitch meeting at CBS. He claimed that the execs pumped him for information about how to make a successful space series, and then dismissed him with the claim that they already had okayed a space show – *Lost in Space*. Roddenberry felt that the CBS suits had asked for his ideas solely to use them for Allen's show, and felt like saying: "You S.O.B.s, if you wanted technical advice and help, hire me and pay me for it!"

He complained, "It's like calling a doctor and having him analyze you for two hours and then telling him, 'Thank you very much for pinpointing what's wrong, I've decided to go to another doctor for treatment.'" (GR-MOST68)

As the years passed, even former Desilu executive Oscar Katz began to believe Roddenberry's rewrite of the historical events, and said, "We were in a dining room with six or seven executives, one of whom questioned us rather closely about what we were going to do with the show. We answered his questions and it turned out that his interest was due to the fact that they developed a science fiction show of their own." (OK-STC94)

While it is true that the two men did pitch *Star Trek* to CBS, their meeting took place in May of 1964, more than a month before Irwin Allen even started talking to Guy della-Cioppa about developing a TV version of *Swiss Family Robinson*, and nearly two months before he and della-Cioppa decided to retool the classic adventure into science fiction as "Space Family Robinson." Allen and della-Cioppa's first meeting with the network didn't take place until October.

The reality behind Roddenberry's and Katz's tale is perhaps simpler. They didn't like rejection. Roddenberry's pride was better served by his tale of brain-picking and subterfuge by evil network sneaks.

After failing to interest CBS in *Star Trek*, Roddenberry, now teamed with Desilu executive Herb Solow, chose not to go to ABC because the "alphabet network" already had *The Outer Limits* about to go into its second and final season, and *Voyage to the Bottom of the Sea*, due to premiere in the fall. Surely two hour-long science fiction series were enough for any one network in 1964. The next stop, then, would be NBC, in June, and even that occurred four months *before* CBS would first hear about "Space Family Robinson."

NBC would go with *Star Trek*, but not because they wanted to have further dealings with Gene Roddenberry. They had butted heads with him before while he was producing *The Lieutenant*. However, the network *was* interested in establishing a business relationship with Lucille Ball, president of Desilu and the Golden Girl of CBS.

Meanwhile, over at CBS, the same thinking was in place – lure away the competition's biggest stars. And Irwin Allen was considered a star - a "star producer." Having a hit show on ABC made him all the more attractive to CBS. Beyond this, with *Voyage to the Bottom of the Sea*, Allen was proving himself capable of producing a science fiction series, perhaps the most difficult of all genres for television. At this time, he was delivering episodes on time and on budget. Unlike Roddenberry, who seemed in constant rebellion against his network host, Allen seemed content to work "within the system." He was giving ABC what they wanted, with few complaints, no major battles, and very little hesitation. Lastly, he was showing himself to be wise by partnering up with a production executive whom the network already respected and had good rapport with – Guy della-Cioppa.

Immediately following the meeting with CBS, with the network agreeing to pay for the writing of a *Lost in Space* pilot script, Allen engaged the services of Shimon Wincelberg to co-write the pilot episode with him.

On October 30, 1964, Guy della-Cioppa wrote to Allen:

> First of all, congratulations for the splendid success of "Voyage," for your superb part in the presentation [of "Lost in Space"] before the CBS "assembly" and for our coming order on "Space".
>
> I did not want to bother you further in the midst of your very busy days on a purely technical matter – that of filing a draft concept of your "Lost in Space" project with the Writers Guild. [But,] under the Guild provisions it is necessary to first file the concept before following up with the Writers Employment Agreement and other documentation they require in order to avoid "Separation of Rights" on the part of the author who co-scripted the pilot with you. In simple terms, the Guild requires a presentation to include format, theme or themes and basic characters and we have put together the simple attached presentation, based on notes of yours. In this manner the basic property is protected for you and thereby for us for such rights we may have acquired by our arrangement with you. A copy of the brief presentation is attached.
>
> Also attached is a copy of an acknowledgment note from Wincelberg stating he has read the presentation and that the presentation included the required Guild concept areas to protect Separation of Rights.
>
> I am also enclosing our check to Jodi Productions to cover the services of the other author of the pilot script, that distinguished gentleman with whom we are proud to be associated, Mr. Irwin Allen.
>
> With warm good wishes. Cordially, Guy della-Cioppa.

Della-Cioppa was reminding Allen that his concept must be registered with the Writers Guild before any other writers' names were officially attached to the project. Otherwise, that writer might be entitled to a co-creator credit (and residuals) for the entire show.

Allen quickly responded by phone. Documentation shows he took this warning seriously. Della-Cioppa's October 30 letter had come as a revelation to him. Allen had written the pilot script for *Voyage to the Bottom of the Sea* on his own in 1963. But now, while deep in production with that series, he couldn't free up the time needed to write the script for *Lost in Space* by himself. He needed Wincelberg, and it had not occurred to him that, by involving a collaborator who would be doing the lion's share of the writing, he could jeopardize his claim to the sole creator of the series. He was already allied to Guy della-Cioppa, Red Skelton, and Van Bernard Productions. He wanted employees, not more partners.

Days later, on November 2, Cioppa again wrote to Allen, with cc to Herman Rush, saying:

> Following up our talk I am attaching the pertinent excerpts from Article I of the WGA TV Basic Film Agreement, governing the employment of writers on film for an episodic series such as LOST IN SPACE. Unless these provisions are followed, your co-author of the pilot script would have had continuing rights in any further exploitation of the basic property LOST IN SPACE, i.e. theatrical, in pictures, publications, etc. Hence it was necessary to file the basic concept with the Guild.
>
> In simple summary: Jodi Productions is under contract to Van Bernard insofar as the pilot script is concerned to supply the services of Irwin Allen as co-author of that pilot script. Shimon Wincelberg is under contract to Van Bernard to write as co-author of that pilot script. Since Jodi also controls the basic property and since you in effect are Jodi, there would have been no question of protecting your rights as creator and author. But since Wincelberg is under contract to Van Bernard as co-author, it was necessary to file the concept for this episodic series in order to protect Jodi and hence Van Bernard from any claim for further separation of rights.
>
> Such claim would not have been entered by Wincelberg but rather by the Guild in his behalf since an author cannot give away those potential rights if he has in any way participated in the creation of the series; the only way to provide that the Guild cannot make such a claim is to file the concept as provided under the Guild Agreement.
>
> Hope this clarifies the picture for you. Warm good wishes. Cordially, Guy della-Cioppa.

Allen took the necessary steps to protect himself. Once satisfied that he would have the sole “created by” credit, he let Wincelberg do most of the writing … with plenty of feedback from Allen, of course.

5

The Other "Space Families Robinson"

Gold Key *Space Family Robinson*, issue No. 1, December 1962, as reissued by Dark Horse comics.

Just as space fever seemed to have commandeered the research labs of the U.S and U.S.S.R., it also consumed the popular consciousness. And just as Philip Wylie's and Edwin Balmer's 1933 science fiction novel *When Worlds Collide* was filmed for Paramount in 1951, it seemed that the idea of a family catapulted into new worlds was destined to arise from Johann David Wyss's 1812 novel *Swiss Family Robinson*. As many as four different groups of writers were working to market the concept of a family adrift in outer space, whether for print, film, or television.

Space Family Robinson Comic Books

The first futuristic, outer-space themed version of the "Swiss Family Robinson" to make it to market was the Gold Key comic book series, created by Del Connell, with the first issue hitting newsstands in December 1962.

In the comic books, the Robinson clan was led by scientist father Craig Robinson, scientist mother June, son Tim and daughter Tam (both in their early teens), and pets Clancy (a dog) and Yakker (a parrot). Their home in space was called "Space Station One," a spacious moving craft with hydroponic gardens, an observatory, and two small shuttle craft, called "spacemobiles." The family was selected by computer as the most mentally and physically qualified to man the space station. They left Earth in the year 2001. In the second issue, dated March 1963, a cosmic storm hurled the Robinsons far from Earth where they became … "lost in space." In fact, "Lost in Space" was the name of that second story, under the heading of the series title, *Space Family Robinson.*

Interviewed for this book, film and television producer Kevin Burns, who, along with his friend and business partner Jon Jashni, now shepherds the creative fate of the Irwin Allen intellectual properties through their company, Synthesis Entertainment, set the record straight: "A lot of people have said Gold Key's *Space Family Robinson* was owned by Disney. It was not. A lot of people have said Disney commissioned it. They didn't. But Western Publishing of Racine, Wisconsin – Gold Key comics, Dell comics, Whitman books – had licensed properties [such as *Zorro*, with Guy Williams on the covers; *Lassie*, with June Lockhart on many covers; *Johnny Ringo* and *The Detectives*, with Mark Goddard on various covers; and *Make Room for Daddy*, with Angela Cartwright on many covers] and they also had original things like *Turok: Son of*

Stone. Well, the movie *Swiss Family Robinson* had come out, based on a public domain source, and it had been a big children's hit. So, it didn't take a giant leap to transpose *Swiss Family Robinson* to *Space Family Robinson*, and say, 'What a cool concept for the space age; a family in space.' A great idea; brilliant concept; and I totally credit the people at Western Publishing with that." (KB-AI16)

Issue No. 3 was published in June 1963, with issue No. 4 following in September, and issue No. 5 in December. From that point on, for more than a decade, Western Publications put out a new issue on an average of three times a year. In 1966, due to the popularity of the TV series, Gold Key changed the title for all future comics to *Lost in Space: Space Family Robinson*, even though there was no apparent tie in to the television show.

"Swiss Family 3000," the Motion Picture Treatment

In 1996, Del Connell told author Ed Shifres, "After a few issues of *Space Family Robinson* were out on the stands, our Beverly Hills office was informed by the legal staff in Racine, Wisconsin, that a woman had made an agreement to make *Space Family Robinson* into a TV show, and Western Publishing was to receive a percentage of the profits. I don't recall the woman's name, nor do I know if she was acting on her own or if she was an agent for someone else." (DC-LISTTS96)

The woman was Hilda Bohem. Her husband, Endre Bohem, was one of the producers on the CBS western series *Rawhide*, as well as a writer for movies and TV. Hilda was a story analyst who had also sold a couple of scripts to television (for series such as *The Adventures of Jim Bowie* and *The Cisco Kid*). Under the name of Jan Winters, she had also written several scripts for *Rawhide*. Using a pseudonym was important so not to have it appear that Hilda's husband was showing favoritism in giving her script assignments. As for whether or not she was "acting on her own" or "if she was an agent acting for someone else," the latter seems to have been the case.

Hilda, and likely her husband as well, were friendly with an East Coast office business affairs executive at CBS – Bud Groskopf. According to author Ed Shifres, who interviewed Groskopf, the CBS man wanted to get into producing and came upon the idea of doing a science fiction version of a public domain property – *Swiss Family Robinson*. Groskopf commissioned Hilda to write a screen treatment based on the basic concept. She called it "Swiss Family 3000." Groskopf then took it to his friend Steve Broidy, who was president of Allied Artists Motion Pictures. Broidy expressed interest and put Groskopf in touch with Earl St. John, chairman of J. Arthur Rank Motion Picture Company in England, in hopes of getting co-financing for the project. St. John was interested, and a co-production deal between Allied Artists and Rank was arranged.

The May 28, 1964 issue of *The Hollywood Reporter* ran a small blurb announcing:

> Allied Artists has purchased "Swiss Family 3000," original science-fiction by Hilda Bohem, wife of TV producer Endre Bohem. Negotiations are under way with Annette Funicello to star in the post-dated adaption of *Swiss Family Robinson*.

As it turned out, "Swiss Family 3000" never made it before the cameras. Earl St. John retired, and all of his pending deals were cancelled by Rank. The summer of '65 found Annette Funicello in a "beach party" movie instead – *How to Stuff a Wild Bikini.*

By this time, Groskopf had been transferred by CBS to Los Angeles, where he circulated Hilda Bohem's screen treatment to several agents and discovered that the *Space Family Robinson* comic book series had beaten him to market by a year and a half. Groskopf then contacted Western Publishing and took an option on the live-action screen rights for the series. In all likelihood, CBS was not aware of the efforts of one of its business affairs employees to develop a big-screen version of "Swiss Family 3000."

Kevin Burns said, "In those days, the fact that a modestly successful television writer was developing a creative property with a business affairs executive at CBS wasn't going to impress anyone – not on the motion picture or network television side of things, anyway. Besides, at that time, comic books were considered the lowest form of art. The concept of sending the Swiss Family Robinson into space may have been ingenious – but without someone to properly execute it, it would have meant virtually nothing to a major network." (KB-AI16)

"Space Family Robinson" TV Property

What *would* have meant something to CBS was that Irwin Allen was doing something that had previously been believed impossible – producing a one-hour science fiction series with a recurring cast, and futuristic sets, props, and costumes. The fact that he was managing to do so on a restricted TV budget and schedule – for a rival network – made him all the more newsworthy to CBS. In television, the other man's grass is always greener, and networks love to lure away their competitor's hottest stars and producers. To this end, CBS wanted Irwin Allen.

Kevin Burns said, "This was not Irwin going to CBS; this was CBS going to Irwin." (KB-AI16)

As addressed in the previous chapter, in June 1964, CBS was already in conversations with Guy della-Cioppa, Red Skelton's business manager, to develop a new version of *Swiss Family Robinson* for television, with Irwin Allen producing.

Burns said, "I think CBS was trying to talk Red into staying on the network. They probably thought they would later gift the property to Red in order to keep him on board. This would be the same type deal that had Bing Crosby owning *Hogan's Heroes.* Or Phil Silvers owning *Gilligan's Island*, which a lot of people don't know – Gladysya Productions was Silvers' company. Danny Thomas was still doing *The Dick Van Dyke Show*, with Sheldon Leonard, and they also had *Gomer Pyle*. These were all CBS shows. Another thing most people don't know is that Lucille Ball owned *Star Trek*!" (KB-AI16)

In fact, the primary reason NBC was interested in *Star Trek* was the Lucy connection. She was CBS's Golden Girl and NBC wanted a relationship, just as CBS now wanted a relationship with Irwin Allen and 20th Century-Fox.

Burns said, "I believe what happened was, CBS developed it as 'Space Family Robinson.' They didn't have to make a deal with Western Publishing because it was based on an underlying property, which is why Guy della-Cioppa was researching the copyright of *Swiss Family Robinson*, and found that it's all public domain. So, it's based on a P.D. property, they are not going to use Tim and Tam [from Gold Key's *Space Family Robinson*]; they're not going to use Space Station One; they were just taking the original source premise of a P.D. property and making it a space show. And Irwin takes it from there." (KB-AI16)

Allen had been thinking along the lines of a space age version of *Swiss Family Robinson* for more than a year already. Point of fact, Allen registered the title "Lost in Space" with the Association of Motion Picture and Television Producers, Inc. on July 17, 1963.

"Space Family Robinson," the Film Treatment

Meanwhile, writer and director Ib Melchior, who, among other credits, wrote the screenplay for 1964's *Robinson Crusoe on Mars*, wanted to follow that success with his own version of *Swiss Family Robinson* in space. He registered his treatment with the Writers Guild of America on February 28, 1964. Then, from May to July of that year. Melchior negotiated with Jim Allen Trudeau Associates (known as JATA Productions, Inc.) to develop his story as a possible motion picture property.

In Melchior's treatment, the story took place in the year 1997. The spaceship was called the Alpha. On board: 15-year-old Jimmy Robinson, his 19-year-old brother, Mark, and their 16-year-old brother Frank. Their parents were David and Elizabeth Robinson. And they had a dog named Scout. Also on board was Crewman Tate. When the Alpha was damaged by an explosion, the family, as well as Tate, fled in an escape craft. They managed to land on Titan, one of Saturn's moons, where they would remain, shipwrecked. Once there, they found a girl (Jane Winfield), who said she was a passenger on the Alpha. Only she and her brother Edward had survived the crash.

The areas of similarity between Melchior's screen treatment and the Irwin Allen/Shimon Wincelberg screenplay called "Space Family Robinson" (Shooting Final, dated November 11, 1964) were numerous, but, considering both were a futuristic take on *Swiss Family Robinson*, it should only be expected.

Interviewed by Scott Halper in 1996 for a public access TV show, Melchior said, "I did make a comparison between the original 'Space Family Robinson' script of mine, and the submitted 'Space Family Robinson' script which was created by Irwin Allen."

Among the similarities:

- The title "Space Family Robinson," with the family naturally named Robinson;
- The family consisting of a father, mother, and three teenage children;
- The family is accompanied by one non-family crew member;
- The story takes place in 1997;
- Their objective: colonization of outer space;
- The spaceship is hit by a meteor, then sent hurtling into outer space at great speed, leading to a crash landing on planet which has adequate oxygen and near normal gravity;

- Outdoor shooting was suggested for selected nearby locations, including Trona, California, therefore the planet is barren, desolate, and has strange rock formations;
- The mother manages to plant and cultivate a vegetable garden;
- The castaways find signs of menacing alien life.

It would be hard to imagine the development of a "Swiss Family Robinson" in space concept without such similarities. Of course it would be called "Space Family Robinson," since it was patterned after *Swiss Family Robinson*. Of course there would be a mother and father with teenage children, as there were in *Swiss Family Robinson*. Of course they would be pioneering colonists. Of course they would suffer a shipwreck (and, in outer space, a meteor strike seemed the easy solution for sending a spacecraft hurtling toward a planet). For budget reasons, the family would of course need to be planet-bound, and this planet would need to have Earth-like oxygen and gravity. Of course there would be alien creatures, taking the place of the pirates in the original public domain property. And, to survive on this alien world, of course the castaways would have to be able to plant a garden and harvest food ... and find water... and domesticate animals ... just as the castaways in *Swiss Family Robinson* did.

As for the location of Trona, California, and, as documented in the previous chapter, it was art director Bill Creber who brought that natural yet very alien-looking setting to Irwin Allen's attention during preproduction planning. Allen flew out by helicopter to inspect the area personally, and then congratulated Creber for his find.

The only really suspicious similarity between the proposed properties was their common liftoff date, 1997. On the other hand, who would "borrow" another's idea without changing such a basic attribute?

When merging a classic work of literature with a different genre – as Melchior did when he turned *Robinson Crusoe* into *Robinson Crusoe on Mars*, or Disney did two years later when they turned *Robinson Crusoe* into the Dick Van Dyke vehicle *Lt. Robin Crusoe, U.S.N.*, it is easy to grasp how numerous writers, unbeknownst to one another, could be – and often are – working on similar projects simultaneously

Kevin Burns said, "Too often writers think, 'I have a great idea for a TV series!' and they come in with one line. And they think that's the show. Or several lines, and they think *that's* the show. It ain't. It takes execution, execution, execution, not just concept. Concepts are not copyrightable; concepts are not trademarkable; concepts are not protectable. Period. Never were, still aren't. Titles are trademarkable, but not copyrightable." (KB-AI16)

The fact is, Irwin Allen was not alone in developing the concept and script for the *Lost in Space* pilot. As documented in the previous chapter, he was addressing feedback from Guy della-Cioppa, as well as collaborating on the screenplay with respected playwright Shimon Wincelberg. CBS was also giving plenty of notes as to how they wanted to see the property developed. Was this a conspiracy against Ib Melchior? Likely not.

Regardless, Hollywood's space race was in full flight.

On July 30, 1964, *Daily Variety* reported that Melchior's "Space Family Robinson" was in preparation. *The Hollywood Reporter* made the same announcement for its July 31, 1964 issue.

As discussed in Chapter 4, the Irwin Allen/Guy della-Cioppa version of "Space Family Robinson" was in development at the same time. Predating the trade announcement concerning Melchior's project was Allen's registration of the "Lost in Space" title in July, 1963; then a letter dated June 22, 1964 from Guy della-Cioppa to attorney Fulton Brylawski requested information concerning the public domain status of *Swiss Family Robinson*. Brylawski's reply, from June 24, tracing all known screen treatments based on the work or using the title, whether completed and exhibited or not, made no mention of Ib Melchior, since his project was still more than a month away from being announced in the Hollywood trades.

Next, Allen wrote his treatment for "Space Family Robinson" (undated, but clearly pre-dating July 28, 1964, when della-Cioppa sent notes to Allen based on that screen treatment, two days *before* Melchior's "Space Family Robinson" was first announced in a Hollywood trade magazine). Further, in his letter, della-Cioppa referenced previous meetings at Allen's Bel Air home in Los Angeles where the two had been actively discussing the concept.

Additional communications concerning the property, between della-Cioppa and the attorney for Van Bernard Productions, and then between della-Cioppa and Herman Rush, were dated August 3, 1964 and September 3, 1964, respectively. Two months later, Ib Melchior learned of Irwin Allen's space age version of *Swiss Family Robinson*.

On November 30, 1964, attorney Don Leon wrote to Hunt Stromberg, Jr., at CBS, with cc to Irwin Allen, saying:

> This office represents Mr. Ib J. Melchior, who is the owner of a format and story treatment entitled 'Space Family Robinson' and who is presently in the process of preparing a feature-length theatrical motion picture based on his property. He has informed this office that his property has been registered for many years and was previously submitted to various producers as the basis of a television series, which submissions included submission to CBS.
>
> It has come to his attention that you are contemplating the preparation of a television series entitled 'Space Family Robinson.' While it is assumed that you are not using any of his material, I wish to take this opportunity to alert you to the above facts and to go on record as informing you that any use of his material without his express written permission would cause him extensive damage, for which he would seek legal redress.

Ib Melchior said during a TV interview in the mid 1990s, "At that time I still did not know how extraordinarily close Mr. Allen's script was to mine. But since the name of his project was the same as mine, and even though you cannot protect a name, it occurred to me that there was a possibility that the concept and execution of that concept could be similar, and I wanted Mr. Allen to be aware of the fact that I already had a registered project with that same premise." (IMJ-LIS-TRS96)

Registration with the Writers Guild of America merely assigns a recorded date to a property, but does not determine whether other similar properties are in development elsewhere. Similarly, Allen's registering of the title "Lost in Space" seven months previously, with the Association of Motion Picture and Television Producers, didn't cause any warning flags to arise.

On November 30, 1964, the same day that Leon wrote his letter to Hunt Stromberg, Jr, with cc to Allen, *Boxoffice* magazine reported:

> "Space Family Robinson" will be a $250,000 production of Al Williams of WMA Productions. Carthay Center stages will be used. Ib Melchior's script provided the story. Dave Hewet [sic] is doing the special effects.

Kevin Burns said, "I think that prompted the title change in December for the pilot from 'Space Family Robinson' to 'Lost in Space.' With the announcement in the trades that Melchior was going to use 'Space Family Robinson' as the title to a movie – and we found that announcement from *Variety* in Irwin's files, *circled* – I think they said, 'Id Melchior is coming up with the same idea.' Well, it didn't take a genius, since there was a comic book which anybody could get! I'm sure Irwin had gone through the comic books and probably said, 'There's nothing here.' And so I think they said, 'We'd better change the title; let's call it *Lost in Space*.' I don't think anybody at CBS knew there was a sub-heading to one of the *Space Family Robinson* comic books that said 'Lost in Space.' And that's not protectable, that the words 'Lost in Space' appear as an episodic title in one of the comics. Who protects episodic titles to comic books? Irwin just fell in love with 'Lost in Space.' He wasn't sitting there thinking, 'I'm going to steal it from Western Publishing.' He probably never even knew that it existed as a story title on one of those comics. By the way, *I never knew that it existed*! And also, Irwin Allen, who I knew to be more than a little paranoid, wasn't going to risk his reputation, or that of CBS, or that of Red Skelton, or that of Guy della-Cioppa, or that of 20th Century-Fox, on a purloined property. He didn't need to.

"I think what happened is that he developed it, utilizing the notes from Guy and CBS, then he further developed it with Shimon, then they find out about an Ib Melchoir project – 'Holy shit, we've got to change the title!' – and they do a hasty title change. But Irwin was highly competitive. What he probably also said was, 'Let's make sure we get there first.' That's what happened with *Towering Inferno*." (KB-AI16)

It is well known Hollywood lore how in 1973 Allen and 20th Century-Fox had taken an option on a book entitled *The Glass Inferno*, while Warner Brothers purchased an option on another book, *The Tower*. The stories of the two books were very much alike. To Allen's credit, it was his idea that Fox and Warners combine forces and make an epic movie – *The Towering Inferno* – rather than compete against one another for box office revenue.

The announcement regarding the change in the title for the CBS-TV version from "Space Family Robinson" to *Lost in Space* first appeared in the Hollywood trades on December, 3, 1964. It was also announced that June Lockhart had been cast.

On December 4, after failing to get a reply from CBS, Don Leon tried again, this time writing to Guy della-Cioppa of Van Bernard Productions. He told della-Cioppa:

> Having read the article in today's *Daily Variety* concerning your association with Irwin Allen and Hunt Stromberg, Jr., in connection with a new series called 'Lost in Space,' I want to alert you to the rights of my client, Mr. Ib J. Melchior, and for this purpose I am enclosing a copy of a letter I have sent recently to CBS-TV, Messrs. Stromberg and Allen.

More announcements in the Hollywood trades:

On December 8, in *Daily Variety*, and December 9, in weekly *Variety*, the new Irwin Allen series was again referred to as *Lost in Space*. But on December 11, *Daily Variety*, referred to it as "Space Family Crusoe." Then, on December 29, the same trade was back to calling it "Space Family Robinson." On December 30, *Daily Variety* switched back to *Lost in Space*.

As had happened when Guy della-Cioppa researched the usage of *Swiss Family Robinson* as a screen property, and its standing as a public domain property, great diligence was taken to clear the title "Lost in Space."

On March 4, 1965, John D. Garr of 20th Century-Fox wrote to William Self:

> We have received a title report from New York regarding our intention to use the title "LOST IN SPACE" for a television series.
>
> Fred Gebhardt's Four Crown Productions announced that they would film a motion picture "LOST IN SPACE" on June 15, 1961, although we have no indication that this film was ever completed.
>
> Windsor Productions (controlled by Mr. Irwin Allen) has had the title on registration at the Association of Motion Picture and Television Producers, Inc. since July 17, 1963.
>
> It would appear that the title is available for our use.

A little more than three months after that, on June 15, 1965, a final decision was finally made. Robert L. Brenner, an attorney for the firm of Pacht, Ross, Warne, Bernhard & Sears, representing Van Bernard Productions, wrote a file copy letter, with cc to Irwin Allen and Guy della-Cioppa, saying:

> About two weeks ago Jack Purcell of CBS Legal Department took the position that the title "Lost in Space" should be dropped as the series title, since one of the comic books in which Hilda Bohem is claiming ownership, bears the same title. CBS Program Department went along with Purcell's decision, and Purcell informed Irwin Allen that this decision had been made. (Herman Rush later told me about it several days later.)

> I called Purcell to ask him about this, and he advised me that "Lost in Space" was used as the title of one of the comic books in the regular "Space Family Robinson" series of comic books. In view of this coincidence, he felt this would be a substantial determinant in the mind of a jury, that Mrs. Bohem's property had been infringed.
>
> We then spoke with Irwin Allen about this, and he told us that he wanted to continue using the title "Lost in Space" and wanted us to do everything possible to enable him to do so.
>
> A meeting was held on Friday, June 11, to attempt to resolve this issue. It was attended by Purcell, John Garr of Fox, Bud Roethke and Tony Liebig, representing CBS' insurance underwriters, and myself. After discussion of Irwin Allen's prior registration of the "Lost in Space" title and other merits of the issue, Purcell retreated from his position. It is now agreed that the series will be titled "Lost in Space," and CBS will be indemnified if this title violates anyone's rights, except to the extent (if any) that any infringement is the result of a submission by or through a CBS employee. John Garr has advised me that Fox's insurance carrier is in accord, and will insure with respect to such an indemnity to CBS. John has also confirmed that, in view of a $2,500 deductible provision in the insurance policy, Fox will pay the deductible amount, which will then be changed as a production cost of the series.
>
> I have also confirmed this with Bill Whitsett of CBS Legal Department, who is also in accord.

***

Two more months passed.

In a letter dated August 10, 1965, and sent to Ib Melchior, American International head Samuel Z. Arkoff wrote:

> As you know, we have been very much interested in considering your SPACE FAMILY ROBINSON project. However, I have recently heard disquieting rumors that a certain television project called LOST IN SPACE, which is apparently scheduled to be telecast this fall, is very similar to your project. If this is true and perhaps you can acquaint me further, this would seem to destroy the possibility of our proceeding with your project.

Arkoff was not insinuating misconduct on anyone's part. He was an old Hollywood pro and knew how fluid ideas were, especially when based on previous works such as *Swiss Family Robinson*. He was merely stating the obvious – it appeared the race had been run and Melchior came in second.

Ib Melchior later said, "I was fairly new in Hollywood, just establishing my career here – still had to make a name for myself. I contacted a few lawyers who specialized in motion picture matters, and who advised me that one does not take on the big boys without suffering the consequences. I had no choice but to believe them – right or wrong. I might, of course, have gone ahead anyway, but I was told that a case like that could be in the courts for a decade and cost a considerable amount of money, which at that time I did not have, and with no guarantee of eventual collection on a possible judgment for another decade. The legal picture painted for me was bleak indeed." (IMJ-LIS-TRS96)

Kevin Burns said, "I have great respect for Ib Melchior and was a big fan of his work, but I honestly don't think there is a 'smoking gun' here. After Irwin passed away in 1991, Mr. Melchior came forward with his assertion that Irwin stole his treatment, etc. When asked why he never pursued his case while Irwin was alive to defend himself, Melchior claimed that Irwin was too powerful at the time. But that is simply not true. Ib Melchior was every bit as successful and credible a film producer as Irwin was at that time – much more so than Hilda Bohem, in any case. Had he made a stink – and had there been credence to his claim – he would have likely received a settlement of some kind. The fact is, 'The Space Family Robinson' of Ib Melchior's screen treatment and *Lost in Space* as seen on CBS bear virtually no similarity – outside of the general premise, of course." (KB-AI16)

***

As for Bud Groskopf and Hilda Bohem, and as attorney Robert L. Brenner's June 15, 1965 letter indicated, they hadn't dropped out of the picture. Even though CBS had announced the title change from "Space Family Robinson" to *Lost in Space* in early December, Hilda nonetheless lawyered up. However, because he worked for CBS, Bud Groskopf decided that Hilda would have to file a lawsuit on her own. On December 9, 1964, the law office of Prinzmetal and Maizlish agreed to represent her.

In any race – into space or onto a TV or movie screen – some will tell you, "If you can't beat them, sue them." Or, at least, threaten to sue and then be happy to receive a settlement.

When discussing the matter with writer Ed Shifres in the mid-1990s, Bud Groskopf recalled that the amount paid by CBS and Irwin Allen (and very likely 20th Century-Fox) was in the neighborhood of $20,000. A "gag order" prevented Hilda Bohem from talking about the settlement.

Although a gag order did prevent Bohem from talking about the settlement at the time, the fact is she received $7,500 for her efforts (the equivalent of about $55,000 today). Western Publishing also was given permission to change the name of their Gold Key comic book to *Lost in Space: Space Family Robison* (which they eventually did) and include the characters from the Irwin Allen television series (which they did not).

"This explains why," according to Burns, "there was no official, *Lost in Space* comic book made at the time. There were no Whitman coloring books or paper dolls. The whole affair must have made everyone a bit bitter and legally paranoid." (KB-AI16)

***

When watching *Lost in Space*, we see little that resembles Gold Key's *Space Family Robinson*. And, considering the tone of *Robinson Crusoe on Mars*, it is unlikely the *Lost in Space* we know would have much in common with Ib Melchior's version of *Swiss Family Robinson* in space, if it had ever been made. Nor would there have been any consequential resemblance to a movie called "Space Family 3000" starring Annette Funicello, provided it was ever made. What we do see is *Swiss Family Robinson* as interpreted in that unique and surreal place that could only be The Fantasy Worlds of Irwin Allen.

6

An All-Star Cast

On December 8, 1964, Hunt Stromberg, West Coast Program Vice President, CBS, announced that the network had ordered a pilot for *Lost in Space*. It would be a joint project between Irwin Allen's Jodi Productions, Red Skelton's Van Bernard Productions, and 20th Century-Fox Television, in association with CBS-TV. The pilot was scheduled to begin filming in two weeks, even though only one of the roles had been cast. The following day, *Variety* reported:

Series deals with exploits of a Swiss Family Robinson… and June Lockhart has been signed as one of the femme leads. She will play the biochemist wife of the pilot of the spacecraft. Their three children, ages 18, 12 and 8, and another scientist, round out the [recurring] roles, now being cast. Allen will produce the pilot. He collaborated with Shimon Wincelberg on the script. Guy della-Cioppa will rep VB Productions as production exec, and 20th productions chief Bill Self will rep that studio.

Of course, ABC was not happy that Allen was casting his net into another sea.

Herman Rush said, "There was a major battle with ABC when *Lost in Space* went to CBS. Now, that was a *big* battle. It had high points and low points. ABC wanted to have an exclusive on Irwin Allen. Irwin had all his other shows on ABC in the 1960s, and yet something called *Lost in Space* ended up on CBS. ABC wasn't happy about that." (HR-AI15)

ABC executive Lew Hunter said, "I remember very clearly that we were pissing and moaning about, 'How can he sell this show to CBS when we have the relationship with him and Fox?' I don't think he even gave us a chance to buy it, which was probably a smart move on his part. But we were upset, no questions about that. Irwin had a relationship with Mike Dan over at CBS. Of course, Irwin had a relationship with everybody that he wanted a relationship with. It wasn't what ABC wanted, but we didn't allow it to cause a strain between us; we just shrugged our shoulders and went on trying to win whatever battles we could in persuading Irwin on what he was doing." (LH-AI15)

In the final days of 1964, the casting process began. Casting Director Joe D'Agosta recalled, "When Irwin sold *Lost in Space*, he summoned me to his office, and he had all these drawings of all these monsters. It was all these poster-sized paintings all around his office, on chairs, on tables, on his desk, and he says, 'I want to introduce you to my new cast.' And he meant the monsters. He was like a kid in that way." (JDA-AI15)

With the planned production dates looming before them, there wasn't much time to assemble the remainder of the cast. But Irwin Allen wanted *Lost in Space* to be an all-star vehicle. This put added strain on D'Agosta.

D'Agosta said of Allen, "He worked me from 7 in the morning till 11:30 at night. I didn't mind. I loved my work. I was the same as Irwin in that regard. I loved Monday mornings and hated Friday afternoons. I didn't like *not* going to the studio. And I understood that about Irwin. That's what I respected. The fact that he was a little rigid, I didn't care about. And I didn't care that he was a bit of an emperor, for lack of a better term, with his Napoleonic way. I didn't mind that. I like tough guys. You know what you're dealing with. It's the nice guys that criticize you behind your back that you have to worry about. So I always liked working with him."

Even though D'Agosta respected Allen, and enjoyed working long days with him, there was a stumbling block that soon arose. He recalled, "One thing Irwin wanted from his employees, other than that they agree with him, was absolute exclusive loyalty. When I went to Fox, my deal was that I would cast features as well as television. So, I was assigned *Stagecoach* by my boss, Cliff Gould, the head of casting. And Irwin saw me on the grounds of Fox with the script. He said, 'What's that?' I said, 'I'm casting a movie; it's a remake of the John Wayne movie.' I was very proud when I said it. But he walked away off that comment, and the next thing I get is a call from my boss. I was asked into his office, and he said, 'Irwin wants to meet with us.'"

The junior casting director was about to see how the emperor tested his subjects. D'Agosta recalled, "We went into this meeting, and there was this long table – probably 10 to 15 feet long – and on one end sat Irwin, and on the other end sat my boss. And on one side of the length of the long table sat Frank La Tourette, an associate producer who I always had casting sessions with, and Harry Harris, a director who worked on many of the episodes. I sat on the other long side. Irwin proceeded to talk about how he wasn't getting enough of my time, and then turned to the associate producer and said, 'You tell Cliff Gould what it is like to work with Joe.' And this guy went on with a bunch of complaints about my unavailability; how it took me a little longer to get the interviews set up. I don't remember the arguments, but he had a whole list of things that he was programmed to complain about. Then Irwin turned to director Harry Harris and said, 'Tell Cliff about how it is to work with Joe,' and a similar list was presented. I was a young man at the time, around 26. I sat there and I just started shaking, and my lip was tightening, and my anger was building. And Irwin just sat there, very superior like. Finally, I got up and I stared out the window. I tried to hold my temper, but, when Irwin started to speak again, I verbally attacked him. I put my finger right up to his nose, and said, 'Let me tell you something, you! I come here; I work with you till 11:30 at night. I've got a family at home, but I'm *here* at 7 o'clock in the morning, pulling your casting together.' He just sat there; he froze, and he wouldn't meet my stare. He knew that I was ready to explode. I was scary. I scared *myself*. And it was all because I was hurt. I was *hurt* that I'd been set-up – with that table and the way he placed us and then presided over that kangaroo court. I just attacked him, verbally, then I walked right out the door. As I passed Cliff, I said, 'I'm sorry, Cliff, I couldn't keep it in,' because Cliff was a gentlemen; a truly nice guy, and I felt bad for whatever trouble this would create for him."

Anyone who knew Joe D'Agosta, and this author has met many, consistently describe him as friendly and even tempered. But Irwin Allen had pushed the young casting director's buttons and evoked a response that even surprised D'Agosta. He said, "I went back to my office, and I was shaking. I thought, 'That's it; I'm done here,' because Irwin Allen had more shows on the air than any company in town. I was doing three shows with him [*Voyage*, *Space* and the pilot for *The Time Tunnel*]. So, the phone rings, and Cliff says, 'Can you come in to my office?' I went into his office and said, 'Just fire me. Don't worry about it, Cliff. I'm sorry; I just couldn't hold it in.' He said, 'Boy, you sure can get mad.' I told him, 'Cliff, I worked my ass off for that guy, blah, blah, blah, blah.'"

After apologizing to Gould for losing his temper, D'Agosta prepared himself to an abrupt end of his once-promising career. To his surprise, Gould said, "Well, can you work with him again? … He wants nobody but you."

D'Agosta asked Gould about the casting assignment for *Stagecoach*. Would he be allowed to keep that if he returned to work for Allen? The answer was "yes." Allen had conceded on all points without any prompting from Gould or anyone else.

D'Agosta said, "Now, if Irwin was the emperor I thought he was, he could have had my head chopped off. I would have been finished in the business, not just at Fox. So, I went back to Irwin and, from that point on, he never made a casting decision based on the director's or the associate producer's opinions, but only on my opinion. He'd say, 'What do you think, Joe?' And we had this father/son relationship that was just amazing. It always remained a professional relationship; we didn't hang out; it was within the walls of the office, but when I say father/son, I'm saying he treated me kindly, with respect, and he wouldn't make a move in casting without getting my approval." (JDA-AI15)

The first cast member signed to *Lost in Space* was the easiest for CBS to say "yes" to – she was already held in high esteem at the network.

In Search of Maureen Robinson

Named after the month of her arrival, June Lockhart was born into entertainment on June 25, 1925. Her father was Gene Lockhart, a veteran vaudeville performer, as well as stage and film actor, who had been nominated for an Academy Award in 1938 as Best Actor in a Supporting role for 1938's *Algiers*. He was also a writer, having penned numerous plays and popular songs.

"[Performing] was how my father made his living," June Lockhart told *Starlog* writer Tom Weaver in 1994. "He was awfully good at it and he really loved it – but when he came home, he was concerned with his writing and his correspondences and what happened in the house, and he was *always* outwardly motivated towards people and causes." (JL-SL94)

Besides having a show business dad, June Lockhart's mother Kathleen was an actress. Her grandfather on her father's side, John Coates Lockhart, was a concert singer. Entertainment was both in her blood and her home.

Lockhart said, "And the people my parents entertained were journalists, physicians, publishers, singers, composers, columnists – they were there every Sunday, playing badminton! Growing up in this sophisticated atmosphere was really an extraordinary thing to be able to do. And the laughter in the house; all the time, *such laughter*!" (JL-SL94)

When June Lockhart was eight, she was singled out from her dancing class to play Mimsey in the Metropolitan Opera's production of *Peter Ibbetson*. She made her screen debut at 13, in MGM's 1938 version of Charles Dickens's *A Christmas Carol*, appearing with her parents. She said, "It was lovely to be working with my mother and father, and it just seemed quite a natural thing to do because all my life we had always celebrated Christmas with a reading of *Christmas Carol*, done concert style. My father

June Lockhart (left) in her first screen role, *A Christmas Carol* (above), with parents Gene and Kathleen Lockhart. Also pictured: Terry Kilburn (MGM, 1938). For her second screen appearance (below; standing), she worked with Bette Davis in *All This, and Heaven Too* (Warner Bros., 1940).

wrote the script and the dinner guests would take parts, and we would play it. I played Tiny Tim until I got old enough to be one of the sisters. My mother and father were Mr. and Mrs. Cratchit, and Leo G. Carroll would play Scrooge, because he was always a dinner guest. We had done this all my life and it was lovely, and then there we were doing it at MGM!" (JL-SL94)

Two years later, Lockhart was offered a second screen role for *All This, and Heaven Too*, starring Bette Davis and Charles Boyer. She said, "I was at Marlborough School, which was one of the two top schools at the time in Los Angeles. Daddy went to Miss Blake [the principal] and said, 'June would like to do this part for the experience, regardless of whether she becomes an actress when she grows up. This is a really lovely opportunity for her, and a first-class production.' Miss Blake listened to all this. He went on, 'What I would like, please, is if you would arrange so that June can keep up with her class by doing the class work on the set with the tutor.' At that point, Miss Blake said, 'Well, Mr. Lockhart, I personally would have no objection to June doing the film, but I really don't think the parents of the other girls should want *their* children going to school with anybody in the *movies*.' There was a pause, and then my father turned to me and said, 'June, go to your locker and get your books.' By the time I got back, I was no longer a Marlborough student."

Lockhart explained, "Daddy was an educated man; he was an author and a composer, and just the most marvelous gentle man. And the insult that she had slapped him with was really, really awful. As we drove home after that, he said, 'Well, June, today you experienced the disregard with which the acting profession is held in some circles.' Marlborough School was 'old Los Angeles money,' which meant probably 70 years – old oil money. So, I went to an interim school, Immaculate Heart, which I had

Above: June Lockhart with Peter Lawford in *Son of Lassie* (MGM, 1945). Below: as the title character in *She-Wolf of London* (Universal Pictures, 1946).

been at before – and loathed! – and then I went finally to Westlake, the other top school, which I adored; it was wonderful." (JL-SL94)

By the time Lockhart graduated high school, she was being offered film roles before she had even made a conscious decision to become an actress. She said, "My opportunities came along so easily that there was never any sweating and striving and anxiety over it all." (JL-SL94)

Among those opportunities, in 1941, was *Adam Had Four Sons*, starring Ingrid Bergman, and the 10-time Academy Award nominated *Sergeant York*, for which Lockhart was cast as Gary Cooper's sister, Rosie York. The following year, she appeared in *Miss Annie Rooney,* starring Shirley Temple. The parts were all minor, but led to a contract with MGM in 1943, where Lockhart was cast in a supporting role in 1944's four-time Oscar nominee *Meet Me in St. Louis*. In 1945, MGM cast Lockhart in *Keep Your Powder Dry*, starring Lana Turner and Laraine Day, about life in the Women's Army Corps. Also in 1945, Lockhart and Peter Lawford were upstaged by a collie in *Son of Lassie*. The following year, on loan to Universal, she had her first lead role, in 1946's *She-Wolf of London.*

Daily Variety said:

> *She-Wolf of London* stacks up favorably with horror bills, carrying a plot which builds suspense as a girl is made to believe she is an insane murderess.... Miss Lockhart does excellently with somewhat thankless role...

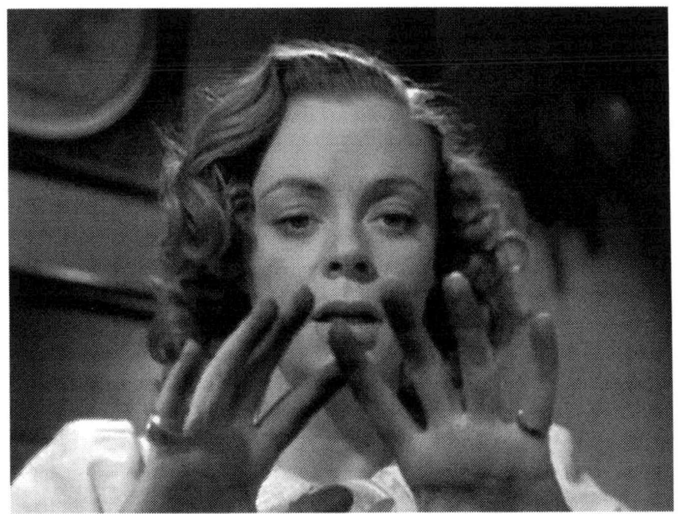

"Oh, *She-Wolf* was fun to do," Lockhart said. "I did it, and was not very good in it. But, the following year, I was the hot ingénue on Broadway in a wonderful comedy, so I guess all I needed [in *She-Wolf*] was good direction." (JL-SL94)

During this time, while "still learning the technique of film acting," Lockhart was being guided by her father. She later said, "We would go to see a play, then afterwards I'd find little notes about the work of people in the cast pinned up in a closet or tucked away in a drawer. Something like, 'A sustained performance because she looked like she was thinking when she wasn't talking.' Things like that." (JL-BDE47)

Released from her contract with MGM, Lockhart signed a seven-year pact with Eagle-Lion. The new film company cast her in its first production, with third billing in *It's a Joke, Son.* The film starred Kenny Delmar as Senator Beauregard Claghorn, a role he created on radio's *The Fred Allen Show*. By now you have probably deduced that this character was the inspiration for the Warner Bros. cartoon character Foghorn Leghorn.

June Lockhart, Eagle-Lion Pictures contract player, circa late 1940s.

Two more Eagle-Lion films followed – 1947's *T-Men*, and a B-film, *Bury Me Dead*, both featuring Lockhart in secondary roles.

Lockhart's big break came in late 1947 when offered the lead role in a new Broadway stage production, *For Love or Money*. Interviewed at the time by E.J. Strong for the *Los Angeles Times*, she gave credit to F. Hugh Herbert, author of the play: "Mr. Herbert's two daughters, Diana and Pamela, were students at Westlake School for Girls, which I attended. He wrote a little theater skit for the school in which I took part. He liked my work in it and asked me to read the first act of a play he was writing." (JL-LAT47)

F. Hugh Herbert said, "When I saw June act, I felt instinctively that I had found an actress who would get attention on Broadway, and I wrote the rest of the play around and for her." (FHH-LAT47)

Lockhart said, "I read the part and Mr. Herbert played all the other parts, and he liked me in it. Then he asked me if I'd like to play it. Bryan Foy, the executive producer at Eagle-Lion, is from an old theater family. He knew what it meant to me and arranged a leave of absence." (JL-SHJ47)

The play's director, Harry Ellerbe, said, "June has a great natural talent and an intense love for her work. We were sitting with other members of the cast after the New Haven opening and June exclaimed, 'Just think, tomorrow we can do the show again!'" (HE-LAT47)

The play was a hit in New Haven, and then moved to Broadway. Lockhart's leave of absence from Eagle-Lion lasted a full year.

The critics raved. According to an Associated Press article, carried in the November 23, 1947 edition of the *Syracuse Herald-Journal*, the accolades included: "June Lockhart is the brightest American ingénue since Margaret Sullivan"; "Miss Lockhart's debut is as exciting as Helen Hays' was in *Dear Brutus* and Ruth Chatterton's in *The Rainbow*"; and "She even dominates the proceedings when she is an innocent and mute bystander."

Aware of all the positive reviews from her fellow critics, writer Jean Meegan, for the *Syracuse Herald-Journal* article, wrote:

> The notices June Lockhart received were not just enthusiastic commendations and applause. They were love letters. All of us told her rapturously that she was not only a delightful young actress giving a most attractive performance, but the most wonderful girl in the world, and that we are crazy about her.

The best accolade came from Gene Lockhart: "Before, Gene and Kathleen Lockhart had a daughter. Now we're the parents of June Lockhart." (GL-SHJ47)

Interviewed in November 1947, Lockhart said, "I never, never thought it would be like this. Chemically I'm not put together for anything like this. I'm not sexy. I honestly thought if I did steady, sensible work, that maybe when I was 30 or 35 I would get approval as a good actress."

Always crediting her parents, Lockhart added, "When I go up there, all the gentle hints I got from mommy and daddy came back to me. They taught me to gesture and walk and sit smoothly; to listen and think what the other actors are saying; to hold the picture until the thought is conveyed." (JL-SHJ47)

Louella O. Parsons wrote for her syndicated column, carried in the January 4, 1948 edition of the *Charleston Gazette*:

> Even if that exciting young charm doesn't come off the same way in the movies, she will never have to worry if she never makes another picture, because the line has formed to the right with producers who have Broadway plays that are just right for June. Not since the advent of Helen Hayes has any girl had such unanimous acclaim, nor been so publicized. June, herself, can hardly believe it. She's been photographed and interviewed, and New York has taken her right to its heart as its own, ignoring the fact that, after all, she's a Hollywood product.

Lockhart told Parsons, "Isn't it wonderful? I sat up all night the first night to read the reviews, and Mommy and Daddy, who came for my opening, were so surprised and as excited as I was over what the drama critics wrote. I never dreamed they would say such things about me. I got Daddy out of bed to go to Times Square and pick up the morning newspapers. I even telephoned one of the newspapers and asked them to read me the review in advance." (JL-LP48)

Gene Lockhart told Parsons, "Kathleen and I so wanted her to have good notices, but we never hoped for such extravagant praise. If they were indifferent, as critics can be, we hoped she wouldn't take it too much to heart, because she's a wonderful youngster. But when they all used such superlative adjectives as 'captivating' and 'appealing' – I guess I did more of a dance of joy than the child." (GL-LP48)

Finding they suddenly had a star in their next film release, which had been completed before Lockhart left for Broadway, Eagle-Lion began using Lockhart's name to promote the pictures. George Phair, writing for July 24, 1947 issue of *Daily Variety*, commented:

> Supersonic speed is here, but it is still a long way from Broadway, where June Lockhart is starring on the stage, to Hollywood, where she plays secondary role in a "B" picture, quaintly titled *Bury Me Dead.*

Jimmie Fidler, for his syndicated Hollywood column, carried in the November 19, 1947 edition of Missouri's *Joplin Globe*, wrote:

> I'm puzzled – just as I've often been puzzled before now – by the case of June Lockhart, who's being acclaimed by Broadway critics as one of the finest young actresses in the history of the New York stage. Why did she have to go to New York in order to have her ability recognized; why didn't movie studio bosses, who have known her since she was a toddler, see her potential?

June Lockhart, circa early 1950s.

Lockhart was only 22.

In May, it was announced that Lockhart was being recalled by Eagle-Lion. She had been ordered to leave the stage production of *For Love or Money* to return to Hollywood on June 1 for a starring role in a movie with the working title of "The World of Little Willie," billed as "a provocative modern story of a beautiful young school ma'am, a precocious pupil and a crusading young newspaperman."

Once back in Hollywood, Lockhart remained on the sidelines, idle. Eagle-Lion failed to come up with the bank loans needed to make the movie. The studio looked into loaning Lockhart out, but, despite her Broadway success, the offers were not forthcoming – at least not fast enough, and not in the price range that Eagle-Lion wanted.

On May 20, 1949, the *Denton Record-Chronicle*, in Denton, Texas, carried a United Press story, saying:

> June Lockhart is the unhappiest girl in town. She still hasn't worked in a picture after being called back from her Broadway sensation over a year ago. She is still under contract to Eagle-Lion, which has been embroiled in financial troubles.

Three months later, while waiting for her contractual problems with the studio to be resolved, Lockhart took to the stage for a Los Angeles production of *John Loves Mary*. Edwin Schallert, for an August 9, 1949 *Los Angeles Times* review, said it had "all the ingredients to yield one of the best entertainments recently offered," and that Lockhart "has unusual charm and freshness in her portrayal."

In October, Eagle-Lion dropped its option on Lockhart, allowing her to become a free agent.

In January 1950, Lockhart was on the stage again, this time in Wilmington, Delaware, but with seventh billing in *The Paragon*. Weeks later, she married for the first time, to Dr. John Francis Maloney, a New York physician.

In May 1951, Lockhart took part in a TV event, a reunion between her and her father, for "House of Seven Gables," aired as part of *Robert Montgomery Presents*. *Variety* said:

> With Gene Lockhart and his daughter, June, teaming for the first time in a video show to top the cast, Montgomery and his production crew made the Hawthorne story as suspenseful and eerie as any of the modern whodunits and supernatural programs on TV. Fact that they retained much of the original Hawthorne dialog gave the show considerably more flavor and literate atmosphere. Lockhart [senior] registered with an exceptionally strong performance as the greedy Col. Jaffrey Pyncheon, last of the ill-fated families to fall under the ancient curse. But it was his daughter who carried most of the show, turning in a top job as the young Phoebe whose faith finally broke the spell.

Gene Lockhart with wife Kathleen and daughter June, circa 1953.

June Lockhart would appear with her father on a second *Robert Montgomery Presents*, in 1952, called "The Biarritz Scandal," and a third, in 1953, called "The Burtons," in which she shared the screen with both her father and mother.

Over the next several years, spanning the early and mid 1950s, Lockhart made the rounds to all the major anthology series beamed live out of New York, including six more appearances on *Robert Montgomery Presents* and five on *Studio One*. This was the Golden Age of television anthology shows, and Lockhart was in big demand. She had the lead in the TV movie *Mistress of the White House* as Dolly Madison, and starred with Eddie Albert and Jack Klugman on *The Philco-Goodyear Television Playhouse*. She also appeared with Carl Betz and Henry Jones (later a guest star on *Lost in Space*) on *Appointment with Adventure*. She was paired with Jason Roberts on *Star Tonight*; with Agnes Moorehead on *Studio 57*; and played the sister of real-life sisters (and silent movie stars) Lillian and

Dorothy Gish, on *The Alcoa Hour*. She played opposite Charlton Heston three times: on *Schlitz Playhouse*, then *Shirley Temple's Storybook* for a production of "Beauty and the Beast," as well as on one of her *Robert Montgomery Presents* appearances. She worked with Henry Jones again, and Ward Bond, on a second *Schlitz Playhouse*, and with Richard Carlson and Whit Bissell (later of *The Time Tunnel*) on a third. She starred with James Whitmore on *The Ford Television Theatre*, and with Richard Kiley on *Kaiser Aluminum Hour*, then with Robert Preston on *Lux Video Theatre*. Her acting partners were Gig Young and Eva Gabor on *Climax!* Among her many unusual roles, Lockhart played a mute spinster who becomes a Mail Order Bride in an episode of the *U.S. Steel Hour*.

Lockhart also worked on filmed series originating from Hollywood, including playing Dr. Phyllis Thackeray, the love interest of series star Richard Boone, in two episodes of *Have Gun – Will Travel*. She was the title character in "The Sarah Drummond Story," on *Wagon Train*, and a mentally disturbed nymphomaniac in "Dirt," a startling and dark episode of *Gunsmoke*.

During all of this, Lockhart also kept busy on the stage. She starred opposite John Dall for a production of *Dear Ruth*, played the title role in *Claudia*, and then starred with her father in a production of *Our Town*.

In 1955, Lockhart returned to Broadway, opposite John Newland, for the lead in *The Grand Prize*. Critic Mark Barron, writing for the January 27, 1955 edition of *The Corpus Christi Caller-Times*, said:

> In the principal role of Lucille Cotton, a role which demands beauty and humor, June Lockhart has both to offer – and does. She is a stunning blonde and has a suave sense of comedy reminiscent of Gertrude Lawrence.

In addition, Lockhart became a regular panelist on the *Who Said That* quiz show, beginning in 1955 and remaining for three years. During the same period, she also frequently sat on the panel for a second New York City based quizzer – *Down You Go*.

On August 15, 1956, Hollywood syndicated columnist Gene Handsaker led his column with the title, "June Lockhart Shows Hollywood She Is 'The Type.'" Handsaker wrote:

> What does a beautiful and young actress do when Hollywood tells her she's "not the type"? June Lockhart went to New York and became a star in top television dramas and a panelist on the quiz shows *Down You Go* and *Who Said That?* Now she's back on the sound stages doing a film which, though it's for TV, could mean a rebirth of her Hollywood career. She's co-starring with Dennis O'Keefe in one of CBS' *Playhouse 90* hour-and-a-half plays starting on the air in October.

On March 3, 1957, Hedda Hopper wrote in the *Los Angeles Times*:

> Richard Widmark caught a TV performance by June Lockhart and was so impressed he gave her a top role in his first independent

> production, *Time Limit.* June plays the part of Dick Basehart's wife – he's accused of collaborating with the enemy during the Korean War.

Dick Basehart was the same Richard Basehart who would go on to star in Irwin Allen's *Voyage to the Bottom of the Sea* TV series.

Weeks later, on March 31, 1957, Gene Lockhart died from a heart attack at age 65. Daughter June told columnist Hal Boyle, "Father was a very versatile, talented and kind man. He was a doer and a giver, and he gave more of that thing that is most precious to all of us – time.... He was a very dedicated man – dedicated to his fellow human beings. He used to spend hours every day helping people with their problems. He had tremendous drive and a great capacity for work. After a long day at the studio, he would write most of the night on plays, sketches, songs, letters to people in trouble. He never sloughed off a job, no matter how small.... We had a very full relationship as father and daughter, and nothing that should be done was left undone, and therefore I did not grieve too much when he died. We had done so much together. We were very close." (JL-MET59)

Come May, June was yearning to do something different. Charles Mercer, in a syndicated newspaper story carried in the May 20 edition of the Bridgewater, New Jersey *Courier News*, wrote:

> June Lockhart has an interesting idea. "Why," she asks, "shouldn't there be a regular woman news commentator on television? A woman with a feeling and respect for news could give it a presentation that would interest everyone."
>
> The next question, obviously, is why shouldn't June Lockhart try it? She's willing – eager, in fact, to try it. An accomplished actress in the theater, movies and television, she confesses that for years a part of her heart has belonged to journalism. For three years she was a panelist on the NBC-TV news quiz show, *Who Said That?* She has written and worked for the publication *Guideposts.* Last year she traveled with both presidential candidates as what she calls "a journalistic buff." She can list numerous other qualifications. So why not give Miss Lockhart a try as a TV commentator?

Lockhart told Edwin Schallert of the *Los Angeles Times*, "I have often thought I would like to undertake a news program. I believe that a woman with a feeling and respect for news could give it an interesting presentation on TV." (JL-LAT57)

Many sources say that the "interesting presentation" on television began two years later when Wanda Ramey might have been the first TV news co-anchor, for the *Noon Show* on KPIX, Channel 5, in San Francisco. Lisa Howard was given her own show, *Lisa Howard and the News with a Woman's Touch* on ABC in 1963. Barbara Walters began sharing the news desk on the *Today Show* in 1964. By the late 1960s, women were familiar figures behind a news desk. But June Lockhart hosting the news in 1957 was a radical concept.

Lassie, June Lockhart and Jon Provost (CBS-TV, 1958)

Lockhart said, "I read newspapers all the time, and I really am a political journalism buff, and I love it… [but] at the time I had the opportunity to pursue television journalism, I was already supporting two children and, economically, it is not as remunerative as acting." (JL-LISF3)

On April 1, 1958, Lockhart was in the news for a personal matter. The *Los Angeles Times* said:

> St. Patrick's Day was a solemn occasion for Actress June Kathleen Lockhart Maloney in Santa Monica Superior Court yesterday. She divorced Dr. John Francis Maloney, 45, a New York physician. Wearing a black dress, trimmed with a white fur collar – and no traditional green – Miss Lockhart said her husband drank to excess and stayed away from home several nights a week. The couple separated June 6, 1956, when Miss Lockhart moved to California with her two children, Anne Kathleen, 4, and June Elizabeth, 2, after a marriage of five years.

Lockhart was now 32.

By June 1958 she was free of this marriage-gone-bad. Not wanting to shuffle her daughters cross-country while she took various roles, Lockhart signed for her first continuing dramatic TV role. She told Dave Kaufman of *Daily Variety* that she had actually been offered the role of the mom on *Lassie* two years earlier.

This story of a boy and his dog had begun as a series on CBS in September 1954, with Tommy Rettig as young Jeff Miller, Jan Clayton as his widowed mother Ellen, and George Cleveland, as "Gramps," who shared his farm with them. Rettig was growing up fast, so in the spring of 1957 a runaway orphan named Timmy (played by Jon Provost) joined the family. That fall, actor George Cleveland passed away, and the series likewise announced that the character Gramps had died suddenly. Ellen Miller found that she and Jeff could not work the farm alone, so she sold the property to new characters Ruth and Paul Martin, and moved with her son to the city. Lassie and her new master Timmy remained behind in the care of the Martins.

Lockhart was the producer's first choice to play Ruth Martin, but she had turned the role down. Cloris Leachman was then hired to play Ruth, and Jon Shepodd was cast as her husband, Paul. By the end of one season with the series, Leachman wanted out, citing the increasing emphasis on the dog/boy relationship as reason. Producer Jack Wrather again approached Lockhart, who later told Dave Kaufman, "This time when they offered me the role, I accepted eagerly. It's a good series. It has dignity. It has a big company for a sponsor [Campbell's Soup] and it means financial security for me and my baby. What could be nicer? I have been doing eight to ten live shows a year, and about the same number of TV films. I will be better off in the series and it's nice to know I won't be unemployed at the end of a show." (JL-DV58)

"Chan," writing for the September 9, 1958 issue of *Daily Variety*, reviewed the fifth season premiere (Lockhart's first episode), saying:

> *Lassie*, it seems, is indestructible as a television property. Although the show's moppet lead has changed once, his parents twice, the supporting farmhand once and the production auspices once, the sponsorship has remained the same through four years and into a fifth. In these days of fickle sponsors and fickler audiences, that's an enviable standing. The latest cast changes don't appear to have made a difference, either to credibility or continuity. June Lockhart and Hugh Reilly, as young Jon Provost's new folks, are distantly warm and reassuring enough to let the focus remain on the boy and the dog.

The ratings were good, with *Lassie* easily out pulling its competition on ABC (the audience participation show *You Asked for It*) and NBC (the detective series *Mark Saber*). *Lassie* often made Arbitron's Top 10 viewer survey lists, such as in Birmingham, Alabama. According to the May 6, 1959 issue of *Daily Variety*, *Lassie* scored 41.2% of the viewing audience. In Miami, Florida, it drew 36.3%. In Tampa, Florida, *Lassie* held 34%.

Concerning her new assignment, Lockhart told Associated Press columnist Charles Mercer, "I'm not worried about becoming typed, because I've already done such a variety of roles. I've played just about everything in the theater, movies and television. I've been an ingénue, a mother, an old maid, a prostitute, a nymphomaniac. If I'm ever desperate, I'm pretty sure I can get another prostitute's role on a western." (JL-CDS58)

At the end of her first year on *Lassie*, Lockhart was nominated for an Emmy for Best Actress in a Leading Role in a Dramatic Series. Some may have thought Lassie had the Lead Actress role in the series ... but Lassie was played by a male dog. Competing for the trophy was Phyllis Kirk of *The Thin Man*, Jane Wyman for *Jane Wyman Presents the Fireside Theatre*, and Loretta Young for *The Loretta Young Show*. The Emmy went to Young.

Between seasons, Lockhart married for the second time. Her new husband was LA architect John Lindsay.

For the 1959-60 TV season, Lockhart's second year, *Lassie* again won its time slot. The competition was now the westerns *Riverboat* on NBC and *Colt .45* on ABC. Arbitron gave *Lassie* a 20.0 ratings, to *Riverboat*'s 13.8 and *Colt .45*'s 12.4.

For the 1960-61 season, the competition again changed, with ABC countering against *Lassie* with *Walt Disney Presents*, and NBC with *Shirley Temple's Storybook*. It was a perilous fight, but *Lassie* was declared the champ, and the only of the three series to hold in the Sunday night time slot for the coming season. *Disney* would jump networks (from ABC to NBC) and start half an hour later to avoid direct competition. *Shirley Temple* was cancelled.

Interviewed at this time by Vernon Scott for a United Press International syndicated story, Lockhart said, "The *Lassie* series provides plenty of opportunity for drama and creativity. The show is the first security I've had in more than 10 years in show business. And that's what almost everybody wants – a steady job. I can't understand why performers in a series suddenly complain about the long hours or being stuck in a single role. It's part of being grown-up to know when you're well off." (JL-SND60)

For the 1961-62 TV season kickoff, *Daily Variety*'s September 12 review said:

> Nothing is more fool-proof for the junior lookers than a boy and his dog. No such thematic teleplay, however, has enjoyed the success of *Lassie*, starting its eighth year for Campbell Soups. From the looks of Sunday's season opener, dog heaven is a long way off for the trained pooch. For the kids who control the set at 7 p.m. it's a gasser and worth an adult look, too.
>
> The trio that keeps the show a Sunday evening must in most families is as earthy and next-doorish as you'll find in a week of dialing. Jon Provost, an adventurous moppet, with the acting skill of a grownup, invariably gets trapped so that Lassie can lead his rescuers. June Lockhart, gentle and motherish, and, occasionally, Hugh Reilly, the doting pater [father], keep the family circle warm with togetherness, the kind you'd like to have in your block.

According to A.C. Nielsen, *Lassie* finished out the season at No. 15. Its competition, *Maverick* on ABC and *The Bullwinkle Show* on NBC, didn't make it into the Top 25.

Lockhart gave an interview for a UPI syndicated newspaper story at this time, saying, "There's only one Lassie, contrary to some fabrications. But technicalities arise. For instance, on long shots, we have another dog named Duke, who's a good runner. He doubles. It would be pretty grinding on poor Lassie if he had to run hard for a long distance, then go through a sensitive closeup. Then we have Laddie, Jr., who's a good fighter and is kind of a stuntman. And there's a collie that stands in for Lassie during the normal setting up of shots, and so forth." (JL-TR61)

In another interview from this period, Lockhart said, "I'm one of the few people in the business who is happy in a series, and I revel in it. It fills all my needs. I have a good deal of freedom and no responsibilities because I'm neither the owner nor the star of the show. It gives me plenty of spare time to be with John and the kids, and I can do lots of reading, my bookkeeping and Scrabble playing. And at the same time, I can help my family have the luxuries we all enjoy." (JL-SGM61)

Lassie and Lockhart, promoting National Dog Week, September 22-28, 1963.

Lockhart talked to Hedda Hopper for the latter's syndicated column, in March 1962. She said, "Kids of all ages can look at [*Lassie*] and grownups do because the kids do. I think is has the aura of a fairy tale. It's everybody's image of what it must be like to be raised on a farm where life is simple and you heard 'Greensleeves' music playing." (JL-LAT62)

Lockhart often referred to the title music from *Lassie* as being "Greensleeves," the traditional Irish folk song. It wasn't, although the *Lassie* theme is reminiscent of "Greensleeves." For the six-year period that she was on the show, the opening and closing title music was an original melody written by Les Baxter, and copyrighted as "Lassie's Main & End Title." The whistling was performed by Muzzy Marcellino, nicknamed "The Whistler," who would also whistle the 1968 movie theme and pop hit, "The Good, the Bad and the Ugly."

Regarding her fourth season with the show, Lockhart joked, "I was the ingénue in the second *Lassie* film at Metro in 1941. Now I'm playing the mother and, if the series goes on long enough, may eventually play the grandmother."

When asked why she was willing to stay on with a series for more than a few years, Lockhart said, "This past year we hit our highest rating of any time since it went on the air. I believe if you stay with a series until it's dropped you can go and do other things. But there's a bad taste left in people's mouths when someone quits." (JL-LAT62)

Lockhart would bring this same work ethic to her next series, *Lost in Space*.

Lassie again won its time slot for the 1962-63 season, ranking No. 19 out of all primetime series for the entire season. Its competition, *Father Knows Best* on ABC and *Ensign O'Toole* on NBC, failed to make the A.C. Nielsen year-end Top 25 list.

Lockhart began her sixth season with *Lassie* in 1963. In the fall, for its October 1st issue, *Daily Variety* again assessed the series, and again gave it a thumbs up. Trade critic "Helm" wrote:

> What makes the stories so palatable to all ages is that the simplification provides as much impact as the more involved [dramas on other series]. As with most westerns, it can be enjoyed in relaxed comfort. For the parents it serves a dual purpose; that of entertaining the tykes and teaching them good manners with a sense of charity for the less fortunate.

For this TV season, ABC gave up the fight and didn't bother to program anything opposite *Lassie*, letting the local affiliates come up with their own alternate programming. NBC programmed *The Bill Dana Show*, co-starring Jonathan Harris (soon to become famous as Dr. Zachary Smith in *Lost in Space*). *Lassie* won, jumping up to No. 12 when all the primetime series were ranked by A.C. Nielsen. *The Bill Dana Show* failed to make the Top 25.

Despite the excellent ratings, the producers of *Lassie* had more than enough episodes in the vault (close to 240) featuring Jon Provost and June Lockhart to make an excellent syndication package. They also feared they had played out the potential storylines for a dog and her family on the farm. On May 24, 1964, for her *Los Angeles Times* column, Aleene MacMinn wrote:

> Don't expect to find June Lockhart on the *Lassie* series next fall. She won't be there. Neither will Jon Provost, or any part of the present format. *Lassie* is being revised and will return for her 11th year with a new master and a new look.

Lockhart told MacMinn, "It was a good six years, probably the happiest six years I've ever had professionally. But, at the same time, there is a sense of release. I can do and say things now that I wasn't permitted to – by contract – while I was on the series."

During the entire run, she had only one complaint: "Driving that pick-up truck. It has no second gear and I never did find reverse. Then the steering wheel went out and I couldn't find the road!" (JL-LAT64)

In the show's restructuring for the 1964-65 season, the Martins moved to Australia. They were not allowed to bring Lassie, so she was left in the care of an elderly couple who had been neighbors. Soon after, the older man became injured and turned Lassie over to a U.S. Forest Ranger.

Interviewed by Charles Witbeck for a syndicated story, Lockhart talked of the future, saying, "I want to play *chic*, sophisticated ladies. And I would like word to get around that I do have a sense of humor."

When asked if she thought the new format for *Lassie* would be successful, Lockhart answered, "Frankly, no. I don't think Lassie can save a U.S. Forest Ranger from fires all the time. It's just incredible." (JL-SGM64)

Lockhart underestimated the TV audience's love for a dog. The series persevered, ranked by Nielsen at No. 17 for the 1964-65 TV season. While the ratings slowly dropped over the next decade, *Lassie* remained in production through 1974.

It didn't take long for Lockhart to find more work. On August 23, 1964, Hal Humphrey wrote for the *Los Angeles Times*:

> During the past 24 weeks, June Lockhart has sat on 37 panel game shows. At an average of $500 per show, June is sitting pretty and says she loves every minute of it.... With all the panel-sitting, June has learned a number of tricks, which is one reason she is in demand by the producers of these shows.

Lockhart told Humphrey, "For a woman, the important thing is how she looks from the waist up, or, really, just from the bosom up. I like a gown with a ruffle in the back of the neckline and cut low in front. It must be attractive to every male viewer and not offensive to the female viewers. Earrings are very important. They should be long ones, and dramatic, but not distracting. If they catch the light and reflect it, that's not good."

She explained the best way to handle sharing the panel with another woman, such as Zsa Zsa Gabor: "One doesn't get coy with Zsa Zsa. I simply call her up and ask, 'Darling, what are you going to wear tonight?' And she tells me."

Lockhart was enjoying the change, and added, "It was the first time I've had my mink out since becoming Lassie's momma, and it felt good. I've decided I'll be the fur-bearing animal from now on." (JL-LAT64a)

Lockhart did not confine her work activities to panel shows. She dropped by for a *Perry Mason*, then for a *Bewitched*, a *Man from U.N.C.L.E.*, and an *Alfred Hitchcock Hour*, as well as a handful of other popular series, including one produced by Irwin Allen. She said, "I did my last episode of *Lassie* in February 1964. Then, I went back to episodic television, doing about one guest shot a month. In September, I did an episode, 'The Ghost of Moby Dick,' of Irwin Allen's *Voyage to the Bottom of the Sea*. After seeing the first day's rushes, he came on the set and said, 'I'm doing a new series called 'Space Family Robinson,' and I would like you to read the pilot script. If you like it, I want you to do it.' I read it, said 'yes,' and became the first one cast. I continued doing guest actor shots until we made the pilot in December, and then, we went right into production." (JL-ST83)

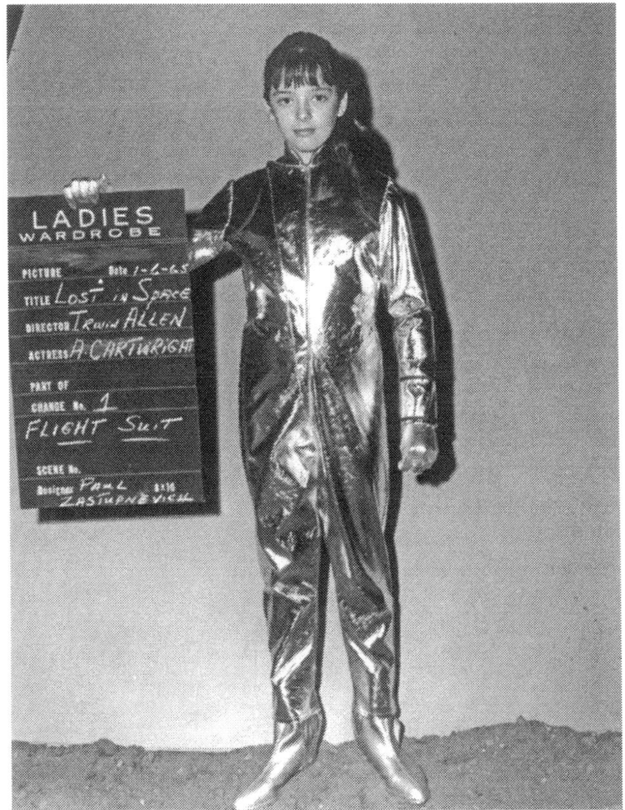

In a different interview, Lockhart observed, "I think at that point, anything that involved space was interesting, and the woman was very much a leader of the family in the initial concept. She was a biophysicist who was doing medical tests, and things like that." (JL-LISF3)

In Search of Penny Robinson

On December 30, 1964, it was reported in the Hollywood trades that Angela Cartwright was the second cast member to be signed for *Lost in Space*. Also, that Sobey Martin, not Allen, would direct the pilot. The plan was to have Allen direct the action sequences, with Martin co-directing, without credit, the dialogue scenes. This would later change, with Allen handling all directorial chores.

Angela Cartwright was born September 9, 1953, and began appearing in front of the camera almost at the same time as she had learned to walk. She said, "Totally by accident, I was sent on an interview for a Sparkletts Water bottle label. I got the job. It was my first modeling job, at the age of three." (AC-WS15)

Also in 1956, Cartwright appeared in her first film. She said, "Robert Wise had cast me in *Somebody Up There Likes Me* when I was three. I played Paul Newsman's daughter. [Wise] had given me a toy stuffed mouse when I finished the shoot. On *The Sound of Music* [in 1964], I just asked him one day if he would sign it for me. He didn't remember I was the three-year-old he had cast." (AG-AF15)

Among the modeling assignments in the late 1950s, Cartwright posed for the cover of the April 1957 issue of *McCall's* magazine.

Angela Cartwright, Danny Thomas and Rusty Hamer for the fourth season of *The Danny Thomas Show* (CBS-TV, 1959).

That same year, Cartwright's older sister Veronica began acting. And little Angela joined the cast of the popular *The Danny Thomas Show*.

Thomas, a real-life travelling nightclub entertainer, played Danny Williams, who was also a piano playing singer and comedian who toured. The series, as originally presented on ABC with the title *Make Room for Daddy*, was a mirror image of Thomas' own life, picking up when he would return home from touring to his wife and two precocious children – Rusty and Terry (played by Rusty Hamer and Sherry Jackson). The king of the castle was actually the stranger in the home. In real life, Thomas' wife would tell his children to "make room for daddy," hence the title.

After the first two seasons on ABC, Jean Hagen, who played Thomas' wife, left the series. For the third season, the title was changed to *The Danny Thomas Show*. The new format depicted Danny Williams as a widower whose well-meaning children tried to dictate his love life, in hopes of finding the right stepmother. The winner was Kathy (played by Marjorie Lord), who had a young daughter of her own – Linda (played by Cartwright). With the new additions to the cast in place, the series moved to CBS.

On October 9, 1957, the television critic for *Daily Variety* wrote:

> Danny Thomas, who moved from ABC to CBS to take over the niche held for so long by *I Love Lucy*, proves on the basis of his opening show a most logical successor to the high-rated *Lucy*. It's certainly too early to predict how high Thomas will climb in the new spot on a new network, but the qualitative funfest he teed off with would seem to assure what may be the best season for his series, particularly in light of CBS' wider coverage [with more affiliated stations than ABC]. In a season when the trend is [shifting toward westerns] and situation comedies are no longer fashionable, Thomas conclusively socks over a rollicking half-hour of heart and humor.... Miss Lord doesn't have too much to do in the opening show, but handles her role well and should make an ideal "wife" for Thomas in this series. Sherry Jackson and Rusty Hamer, Thomas' "kids," are very good, and so is the newest adjunct to the family, moppet Angela Cartwright.

As for "how high Thomas will climb," his retooled series topped the A.C. Nielsen Trendex survey beginning in November 1957 as the most watched program on Monday nights. When the year-end tally was assessed by Nielsen, *The Danny Thomas Show* was the second most popular series on TV, bested only by *Gunsmoke*. It would remain a Top Ten contender for the remainder of its seven-season run on CBS.

Cartwright said, "I thought Danny was hilarious and he was always cracking me up. He was loud and gregarious, nothing like my real Dad, who is far more reserved than that. So, it was fun to be able to make smart remarks and get away with it. I would never have talked to my real parents that way, but in the make-believe world of the Williams family I got away with that."

Being in a hit TV series brought many perks. Her TV wardrobe was featured in a children's clothing line, and a doll based on her character was marketed. She said, "I was pretty young to remember my exact reaction, but what little girl wouldn't want a doll made in her likeness? I never thought the 'Linda doll' looked an awful lot like me, though, but it was cool that the Linda doll came in three different sizes. One was even big enough that she walked with you." (AC-CAFE13)

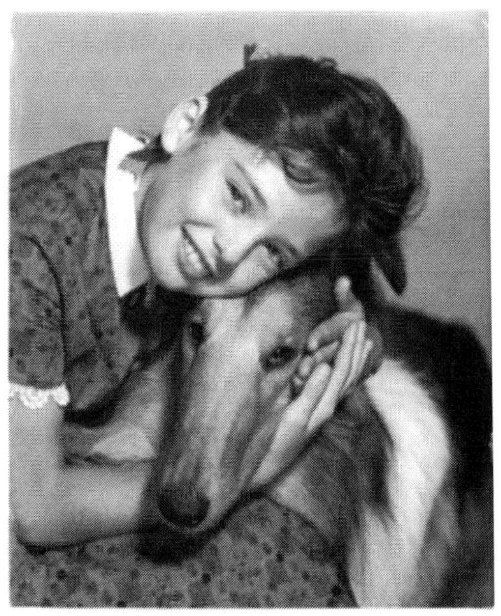

Angela Cartwright with her own Lassie – a boy this time, for *Lad: A Dog* (Warner Bros., 1962).

During breaks in filming, Cartwright had guest appearances in numerous series, including *The Lucy-Desi Comedy Hour* (as her Linda Williams character, in an episode called "Lucy Makes Room for Danny"), and another Desilu series, *Whirlybirds*, as well as *Shirley Temple's Storybook*, *The Red Skelton Hour*, and *Alfred Hitchcock Presents*.

In 1961, during the summer hiatus from *The Danny Thomas Show*, Cartwright played the daughter of Carroll O'Connor in the film *Lad: A Dog*. She said, "[It was] a story of a collie named Lad, who saves me from a rattlesnake, gets me out of my wheelchair and able to walk again, and heroically saves the day during a fire.... I love animals and working with Lad and the puppies was a dream come true for this nine-year-old. I fell in love with this breed of dog and own a Sheltie Collie today." (AC-WS15)

Reviewing the film on May 2, 1962, the critic for *Daily Variety* wrote:

> [The story] describes, with unabashed sentiment and a good degree of conversational redundancy, how Lad manages remarkably to help restore, through affection and a keen, alert sniffer, the functions of a little girl's legs.... Little Angela Cartwright, as the youngster who regains her ability to walk, is accomplished at expressing emotion.

By 1964, after a total of 11 seasons (between the ABC and CBS), Danny Thomas decided it was time to bring his series to a close. During her seven years, Cartwright had appeared in 222 episodes. Her next job was in the biggest movie of 1965 – *The Sound of Music.*

Cartwright said, "[When] I went on an interview for the part of Brigitta, I was still filming *The Danny Thomas Show*, but I knew the series was coming to an end. After several auditions, I was the first von Trapp cast. I asked Danny Thomas if he would let me out of my contract so I could be in the movie and he was very gracious to let me out of the last show of the season. He didn't have to do that and I am very grateful he did.... I was thrilled to get the part of Brigitta and I totally enjoyed making *The Sound of Music*. Singing and dancing and playing with other kids while running around Salzburg, Austria, with Julie Andrews was a fantastic experience. How could you not enjoy that?" (AC-CAFE13)

Prior to leaving for Austria, the cast had much to do in Hollywood. Cartwright said, "I think we were in rehearsal for about six months. We rehearsed the dance numbers over and over and went in the recording studio to do the songs. It's different though to rehearse on an empty set and then put life into it in the Alps."

The company spent three months on location in Austria. Cartwright said, "Robert [Wise] had the patience of a saint, and was always up and loving to us kids. We did many scenes over and over and he always gave us the energy to give it our all."

Of the film's star, Cartwright said, "We really loved Julie.... She was funny and sang with us... and we all looked at her as our friend.... She would joke around with us and make us laugh. It shows in the movie how much we liked her.... Julie taught us how to sing 'Supercalafragilististicexpialidoucious' backwards... and I still remember how to say it to this day. She won the Academy Award for *Mary Poppins* when we were shooting the boat scene." (AC-AF15)

Cartwright added, "Being turned over in the boat was certainly a memorable experience... I can just remember wanting to get out of the water as soon as I could because there were leeches on the bottom of the pond." (AC-CAFE13)

Despite the excellent Rogers and Hammerstein songs in the movie, the young cast members spent more time singing songs of a different type and era. Cartwright said,

"We were Beatle fanatics. We used to drive everybody crazy on the set with our Beatle-isms." (AC-EPT13)

When released in March 1965, *The Sound of Music* quickly became the box office champ, and retained that crown throughout the remainder of 1965, finishing as the top-grossing film of the year. It won five Academy Awards, including Best Picture and Best Director.

Cartwright said, "*The Sound of Music* was just such an honor to be in, because it was a movie that appeals to so many people, and they just loved it so much. And they still love it to this day. And I know that for generations to come, people will still love it. People all over the world have seen that movie, and it really strikes a chord in them. They love the music, they love Julie, they love the kids, and so it's great to be a part of something like that." (AC-SFO14)

Cartwright was about to be part of something else that would be loved for decades to come.

Sheila Matthews Allen, Irwin Allen's girlfriend, and future wife, said, "With Angela… [Irwin] had seen her in *The Danny Thomas Show*, growing up as a little girl, and he was quite taken with her. He thought she was darling." (SMA-KB95)

Cartwright said, "I was 13 by the time I finished *The Sound of Music*, and Irwin called me in to talk about the new show he was doing. I hadn't had any experience with science fiction before that, but the original pilot script was so good that I wanted to go ahead and do it. He said, 'I'd like you for the part,' so that was that." (AC-SL79)

Left to right: Nicholas Hammond, Kym Karath, Angela Cartwright, Julie Andrews, Christopher Plummer, Charmian Carr, Heather Menzies, Duane Chase, and Debbie Turner, in *The Sound of Music* (20th Century-Fox, 1965).

Searching for Major Don West

On January 4, 1965, it was announced in the Hollywood trades that Mark Goddard and Marta Kristen had also been signed to join Lockhart and Cartwright. Billy Mumy was added to the cast at this time, as well.

Mark Goddard was born in Lowell, Massachusetts, and then raised in a "great little town" called Scituate. His father owned a five-and-ten-cent store. Goddard told syndicated entertainment writer Alice Pardoe West (for a January 23, 1966 article in the *Ogden Standard-Examiner*) that he had no intention of ever going into show business … until he failed to make the varsity basketball team at Holy Cross College. West wrote:

> He was so shattered with the disappointment of it, that he lost all interest in college. Then one evening he happened to wander into the campus auditorium during a rehearsal of a student Shakespearean production and ended up with a non-speaking part in it. Just carrying his spear across the stage convinced him that the theater was what he wanted.

Goddard told *Starlog* writer Tom Weaver that he had studied acting at Holy Cross for three years when the head of the dramatic society "took notice of my acting and said, 'Hey, you've got something special. It seems to come across the footlights.' Those were his exact words. And that was all the encouragement I needed – I was off to New York! That was 1958. James Dean died when, '55? And that was still a big influence. When I was doing dramatics in college, I felt like, 'Jeez, I'm gonna be the next Jimmy Dean.' And when I went to New York, there were about 500 Jimmy Deans runnin' around. We all had our red jackets and our little motorcycles. I lived at the Iroquois Hotel where Dean had lived and got my hair cut by his barber. It was like everybody was trying to be Jimmy Dean!" (MG-SL93)

At this point, Goddard was attending the American Academy of Dramatic Arts by day and working at night as a floorwalker at Woolworth's at 45th and Broadway. He said, "At Woolworth's, I had to wear a suit. I had *one suit* – an old, funny-lookin' suit and tie. I remember taking my jacket off to help move some cartons, and somebody stole my jacket! So, I was the floorwalker and I didn't catch anyone stealing, but I lost my jacket."

As for his New York stage training, Goddard related, "Basically, what I was doing was running the lights and painting the scenery – I didn't get to do much acting.

That was my apprenticeship. I have a firm belief that you have to serve before you can *be* served; that you have to put that time in." (MG-SL93)

Goddard moved to Hollywood in 1959, which, by then, was the capitol of television and film production, having stolen the thunder away from New York City, which dominated the early and mid 1950s live TV period.

Goddard recounted to writer Micheline Keating, "The first thing I did here was write a letter to Joseph Anthony, who was directing a motion picture at Paramount. No one had told me that movie people get dozens of such letters every day and mostly ignore them. So I didn't know anything unusual was happening to me when Anthony asked me to come over to the studio for a chat." (MG-TDC61)

Anthony was impressed enough by Goddard's intelligence, looks and spunk to make a phone call on the wannabe actor's behalf to the top talent agency in town.

Goddard said, "I was with William Morris, which also represented Dick Powell at Four Star Television, and, while I was a client of theirs, they had *The Rifleman* with Chuck Connors. That was the first show I did – just a small part. I may have had one line. I was part of a posse and I got shot. I had to get on a horse for the first time and ride, and I didn't know how to do that, and the horse ran away with me! But, like I say, you learn as you go!" (MG-SL93)

Mark Goddard, Karen Sharpe, and Don Durant as *Johnny Ringo* (Four Star Productions for CBS-TV, 1959).

For the following season, Four Star had another half-hour western on TV, this time for CBS. *Johnny Ringo* starred Don Durant as an ex-gunfighter turned town sheriff. In the pilot episode, called "The Loner," aired in March 1959 as an episode of *Zane Grey Theater*, Durant was introduced as the famed gunfighter, who in turn was based on a real famed gunfighter who tried to go straight in the old west. It was a fittingly mediocre kickoff for Aaron Spelling in the producer's chair (his first series, after working as an actor and then writing episodes of *Wagon Train* and *Zane Grey Theater*). *Daily Variety* said:

> So there's this fast draw, a killer but a clean-cut, decent young guy. It's not his fault, but

everybody keeps finding him and challenging him to the draw. He's tired of running and hiding and he wishes they'd let him alone. His name is Johnny Ringo. Sound familiar? And that, plus the attempt to characterize one of the west's worst outlaws as a decent chap are what makes this Aaron Spelling script nondescript.

Goddard was nowhere in sight at this point, nor was he in the first episode when "The Loner" launched as *Johnny Ringo*, and Ringo became a town Marshall with a drunkard as a deputy.

By the second week, Goddard made his entrance, as Ringo's newly-hired young deputy, Cully. Director Joe Anthony had made the introduction to Aaron Spelling and Spelling agreed that Goddard was just what his "formula sagebrush" (as *Variety* called it) needed to liven things up.

For his syndicated entertainment columnist, Hollywood correspondent Erskine Johnson said:

> Fans of Ed Byrnes can start blowing their jets. The new TV season has brought another young Kookie-type character (steady now, because you may not dig this), in Aaron Spelling's 1850-period western. The Sunset Strip can take it, but can the West? Well, anyway, this Kookie-type character has a jar full of jive talk like "Who's been spreading sawdust?"; "Where is the tally?" (girl); "Who is the door-knob?" (boy); and "I've been stacking the word packets" (books). Spelling claims it is 1850 carnival lingo, and that he has the research books to prove it. I suspect he's fudging it a little, but who is going to argue about which "Kookie" was cut from where – unless lawyers are still haggling over the question of priority? "It's Ringo lingo," Spelling grinned.
>
> The lad who spouts it as Ringo's deputy on the show is a handsome, black-haired New Englander named Mark Goddard. Mark never saw the West until he drove to California six months ago from his home in Scituate, Mass., but you should hear and see him now. He's flipping jive words like pancakes and, with a plot that says he is a former carnival trick shot, he's twirling a pair of 45s so fast they look like pinwheels. Six weeks of lessons went into that. Mark is also TV's "Mr. Luck" this year.

Johnny Ringo was given the Thursday 8:30 to 9 p.m. slot on CBS, up against ABC's *The Real McCoys*, a carry-over hit from the year before, starring Walter Brennan and Richard Crenna, and, on NBC, *Johnny Staccato*, starring John Cassavetes as a jazz pianist who moonlights as a private eye.

For its opening week, *Ringo* came in third in the Nielsens, with a 13.9 rating, to *McCoys*' 21.5 and *Staccato*'s 16.2. One week later, *McCoys* pulled further ahead, with a 24.5, but the two Johnnys had switched places, with *Staccato* dropping to third place, with an 11.9, and *Ringo* up to second spot, with a 15.9. A month after that, *McCoys* boasted a 20.6 Nielsen rating, while *Ringo* managed a 16.8 and *Staccato* trailed with a 13.9.

In January, *Johnny Ringo* received a consolation prize: *Fast Draw* magazine proclaimed it as the "Best New Half-Hour Western Series" (for the 1959-60 TV season).

However, with marginal ratings, both Johnnys (*Staccato* and *Ringo*) were axed.

"I did a pretty good job on that," Goddard said. "It only lasted one season, but in those days we used to shoot 39 episodes a year. You would be on the air for 39 weeks, and then in the summertime just 13 weeks of reruns.... [W]hen it went off the air, Dick Powell, who had been like a father-figure, called me into his office. He was a wonderful man and he had a generous heart, and his office door was always open. Actors, craft service people, grips, anybody that worked in his company could go into his office anytime they wanted and talk to him. He told me, 'Mark, *Johnny Ringo* is going off the air, but I have a new show coming on called *Michael Shayne* with Richard Denning, and there's also a part opening up on *The Detectives*, starring Robert Taylor. Which one would you like to do?' I chose *The Detectives*, because I really wanted to work with Robert Taylor, whom I admired very much. I knew that he was the ultimate professional and that I would learn a lot from him. I was very happy and very fortunate to work with him for three years." (MG-SL93)

The series was now called *Robert Taylor's The Detectives*, and ABC slotted it from 10 to 10:30 Friday nights opposite *The Twilight Zone* on CBS and the first half-hour of *Michael Shayne* (the series Goddard had turned down) on NBC. Goddard was cast as Sgt. Chris Ballard.

Robert Taylor takes on a new man for *The Detectives* (NBC, 1960).

Goddard said, "When I went into that show, it was like I was the star and Robert Taylor was the sidekick as far as the publicity was concerned. They threw a lot toward me during that first year. They wanted another 'Kookie' Byrnes [the popular young co-star of *77 Sunset Strip*]; they wanted that 'look.' It wouldn't work today, but in those days, it did." (MG-SL93)

The critic who used the moniker "Helm," writing for the September 19, 1960 issue of *Daily Variety*, said:

> Taylor and his producers have given the show a new look, not content to stagnate the old formula. Mark Goddard and Ursula Thiess (Mrs. Taylor) are added starters to provide both youth and glamour to the police beat. Goddard, a fav with the younger element, becomes a new man on the force, and Miss Thiess a police reporter. Both came off well and suited to their roles. It takes some of the load off Taylor and gives him a romantic interest ... [and he] let his two new aides carry much of the story.

Two days later, "Art," writing for sister trade weekly *Variety*, said:

> Having learned to their own satisfaction that motion picture stars – even stars of Robert Taylor's fame – are not necessarily TV box office, the veteran producers of *The Detectives* have introduced to the team of Taylor's detectives an addition who might appeal to teenagers and who looks quite young enough to be a teenager himself, only he's a policeman instead. Producers Jules Levy, Arthur Gardner and Arnold Laven have also introduced sex more liberally than last season. The new man, who, naturally, is handsome, is Mark Goddard, who was featured last season in Four Star's *Johnny Ringo*. His role in the first program of the new season on Friday (16), didn't call for much. Ursula Thiess, as the sex element... served best as a demonstration of offbeat casting.... Maybe when the two new characters are established, the program will improve again. Meantime, it's a case of lowering standards to raise the audience.

Mark Goddard, Robert Taylor and Ursula Thiess in *The Detectives* (NBC, 1960).

In October, *The Detectives* pulled in a 19.0 rating, compared to the 16.7 for *The Twilight Zone*, and 13.0 for *Michael Shayne*. In November, which was typical of the season, *The Detectives* again won its time slot with a 19.6 rating, to 15.1 for *The Twilight Zone* and 14.3 for *Michael Shayne*. Goddard had chosen well – *The Detectives* received an order for a third season, moving to NBC and expanded to an hour-long format.

Goddard was now a TV star. For an article called "He Came and Conquered," *Tucson Daily Citizen* Entertainment Editor Micheline Keating wrote:

> Hard luck stories come a dime a dozen in Hollywood. That's what makes Mark Goddard so

> refreshing. He's had nothing but good luck in the two years since he arrived in the cinema city – uninvited, unknown and unknowing.

Goddard told Keating, "I did everything you're supposed to *not* do. Only I didn't know I was going about it in the wrong way. So here I am with a steady job in a role that is a good challenge for me and working with actors of experience. Some of their know-how must be brushing off on me. I'm very lucky to be in this particular series. Naturally, I'm overshadowed by Robert Taylor and I like it that way. He is so good, you can't beat him. And that is good for me. The important thing now is for me to have training. And that's what I'm getting, working with people in this show every day. TV is a great training ground for the young actor.... I think *The Detectives* is the best-written show in its category. And I like doing it better than westerns. I have no regrets about anything. I think if it had been meant for me to be a lawyer, I would have continued at Holy Cross. I'm sure acting is what is right for me." (MG-TDC61)

Mark Goddard in *The Detectives* (NBC, 1961).

Goddard was content with his co-starring status, alongside Tige Andrews, Russell Thorson and Adam West, the other young detectives serving under Robert Taylor. Interviewed by Terry Vernon for a 1961 newspaper article, Goddard said he was happy to have time to "learn my craft better and advance more slowly." He added, "Too many guys out here have come too far too fast. They're picked out of a gas station and overnight they get star billing. They're nothing but puppets with someone else pulling the strings. You know the type – they come out here from nowhere; all of a sudden they're stars and, just as suddenly, when the series folds, they're forgotten. I aim to be around for a while. If my acting career should fizzle, I'll become a drama teacher. I mean to stay with it in one capacity or another." (MG-PT61)

Goddard's good fortune seemed to even extend to his personal life. Recently married, he related, "I met Marcia when she interviewed me for a TV magazine. We started dating. Now we're married." (MG-TDC61)

And Marcia was expecting. A daughter was on the way.

Of *Robert Taylor's The Detectives* (as it was called in its third year), "Art," reviewing the series for the October 4, 1961 issue of *Variety*, said:

> Against the established action-adventure plays of *Route 66* on CBS-TV and the change of pace *The Flintstones* on ABC-TV, the new 60 minute version of *Robert Taylor's Detectives* is going to have rough going. First episode of the NBC-TV stanza, seen at 8:30 Friday (29) was utterly typical of the standard detective fare on video nowadays, but if this particular batch of detectives even

> remotely resembled the genuine article then the city they inhabit would be in desperate danger of annihilation by the criminal element. Led by an unduly patient and stony faced captain of detectives (Robert Taylor) is a crew of the youngest police sergeants and police lieutenants on record anywhere, and, furthermore, they are as emotional as they are immature, flaring up frequently at the straw men and false melodramatic situations that were set in their path the first night of the new series.

"Art" was right. *The Flintstones* was the surprise Friday night hit of the season, with 38% audience share in the October sweeps, to *Route 66*'s 33.4%. *Robert Taylor's Detectives* trailed in third spot, with 29% of the viewing audience – excellent numbers by anyone's standards, except those of NBC. The series was cancelled at the end of its third year.

Now without a steady role, Goddard had no trouble finding guest spots. Aaron Spelling brought him out for a *Zane Grey Theater*, a highly promotable episode called "The Mormons," pairing his young discovery opposite Tuesday Weld. Weld played a Mormon girl being persecuted by a wealthy and powerful rancher, whose son, played by Goddard, comes into dispute with his father.

Goddard also appeared in an episode of *Burke's Law*, and Four Star hired him for a second turn on *The Rifleman*. Desilu cast him in a TV pilot called "Maggie Brown." It was supposed to be a vehicle for Ethel Merman, presenting her as a lovable proprietress of a South Seas bistro. From the September 25, 1963 issue of *Daily Variety*, critic "Tube" called the pilot "about as corny, cliché and unimaginative a setup as could possibly have been conceived." He added:

> Unlike Molly [Brown], "Maggie Brown" was sinkable. Unsold as a pilot, she sank officially Monday night as the last of the *Vacation Playhouse* installments in full view of everyone tuned to CBS at 8:30.... Others involved in the pilot were Susan Watson as the teenage daughter whom Merman seeks to shelter from the 1,500 Navy men stationed on "Lobster Island," [and] Mark Goddard as the most eligible seaman in view...

Goddard also turned up on *The Rebel*, *The Virginian* and a pair of *Perry Mason* episodes. He was top guest star in an episode of *The Beverly Hillbillies*, as well as one for *The Fugitive*. For an episode of *Gunsmoke* (under the direction of *Lost in Space*'s Harry Harris), Goddard acted with Michael J. Pollard (who would guest on *Space*) and series co-star Burt Reynolds.

The guest spots continued to come his way, and Goddard was in an episode of the drama *Channing*, opposite fellow guest star Joey Heatherton, and then appeared in a pair of episodes of *The Bill Dana Show*, which co-starred Jonathan Harris.

Goddard was cast in a third series – the sitcom *Many Happy Returns* for the 1964-65 TV season. John McGover starred as manager of a returns and complaints counter in a department store. He shared a home with his daughter (Elinor Donahue), her husband (Goddard) and the couple's small daughter.

Mark Goddard and Elinor Donahue in *Many Happy Returns* (CBS-TV, 1964).

The series appeared to be a success. It won its time slot against *The Bing Crosby Show* (on ABC) and *The Andy Williams Show* (on NBC), coming in at No. 28 in the October Nielsen sweeps. This was good. But not according to CBS, when its lead-in programs on the network were *The Andy Griffith Show* (No. 12) and *The Lucy Show* (No. 16). Renewal was "iffy."

Goddard didn't care. He wanted out. In mid-October, he told *Daily Variety* columnist Army Archerd that he wasn't being given enough to do. By mid-November, Archerd reported that Goddard had been given his release and that he immediately tested for the "young pediatrician lead" in a pilot called "Baby Makes Three."

By this time, *Many Happy Returns* had filmed 26 episodes. That was all there would be. Goddard had managed to quit right before being laid off. He was now looking for his next TV series.

Goddard said, "I was with the General Artists Corporation agency and they represented Irwin Allen, whom I didn't know at the time. My agent, David Gerber, came to me and said, 'How would you like to do a pilot? A space pilot?' I said, 'I'm not really into space too much.' David said, 'Well, you've been everything else – you've been a detective, a cowboy, you've done comedy. This is about a family going into space, and there are gonna be adventures; earthquakes…' I said, 'Gee, I don't know. I'm not sure, because of the subject matter.' And David said, 'Well, listen, you just do it and don't worry about it. Take the money. Because nobody's gonna see it and it'll never sell.'" (MG-SL93)

Goddard had his wife Marcia and their two-year old daughter Melissa to think of. He said "yes" but hoped this was one pilot that would never fly.

Searching for Judy Robinson

Marta Kristen was born Birgit Annalisa Rusanen, in Norway, during the final year of World War II. Her mother was Finnish; her father a German pilot.

Kristen said, "My mother had travelled when she was pregnant with me, and had already had a child by the same birth father, and had to leave her behind. She went to Norway, hid her pregnancy, and birthed me in her room. Then she took me to the hospital, and immediately put me in an underground orphanage [in Oslo, Norway], because they were afraid that I'd be taken by the Germans. They were taking all the blonde, blue-eyed children, and putting them in homes in Germany. It was at the very end of the war, so it must have been a hell hole of a place to be in Norway. They were murdering right and left. It was a scorch and burn situation. So the news got out that I was half German. They were trying to hide that in the orphanage, but you know how children are. I have memories of being called 'the German child' while there.

"I couldn't be adopted within the country because of my German heritage. That's when I became, I think, an actress, because I just performed. I'd say, 'Oh, listen to this,' and I'd sing and dance, because that would lessen the hatred that was being heaved toward me. It was an escape; a catharsis." (MK-AI15)

In 1949, a social worker named Marta Bentzen sent a picture of the pretty blonde haired war orphan to a Detroit couple – Professor and Mrs. Harold Soderquist. Professor Soderquist taught philosophy at Wayne State University. At 53, he was classified as being too old to adopt a child from an American orphanage and had therefore been corresponding with agencies in Europe. It took a year of cutting through red tape to get the four-year-old Birgit brought to America.

Kristen said, "I had to fly by myself from Norway to New York. In fact, I have a photo of me being held by the stewardess in front of a Scandinavian airline. And I was in the newspaper and everything. I didn't know what was happening. You know, as a child, you just think this is an adventure. I was told I was going to get parents. And when my mother first saw me, she said I walked toward her like Charlie Chaplin. We obviously had seen some Charlie Chaplin movies in the orphanage, and I probably did it to endear them to me, just to offset the other stuff that was going on. Then, I started to cry, and my mother didn't know what to do, so she got out her lipstick and her nail polish. So, those were my first two American words – I said, 'lip'a'stick' and 'nail'a'polish.'"

Her new father spoke Swedish, and was able to teach Kristen to speak English. She recalled, "I told him, 'Don't speak Norwegian to me; just English,' because I wanted to fit in. So I picked it up fast, and with no accent. I didn't want to be different from everyone else. My mother was a fourth grade teacher, and a business woman. And I immediately went to school – to kindergarten. The woman who sent me here, I called her Tanta Marta. So I took her name." (MK-AI15)

During Kristen's early years in Michigan, the name Marta was spelled "Martha" to sound more American – Martha Soderquist.

Of her new home, Kristen said, "We had five acres in Michigan. And we had an old farm house. It was a wonderful place to grow up; it was idyllic. I played softball; I was outside climbing trees; and my father built us a slide between two elm trees. We had an apple orchard and we played hide and seek. I was always outside."

To get along with the other children in her new home town, Kristen used the technique that had worked well for her while in Norway. She said, "I started entertaining friends and family, just as I had in the orphanage. And my parents immediately got me involved in theater, and dance, and singing and piano. I told them that's what I wanted.

The first thing I did in first grade, or even kindergarten, was *Romeo and Juliet.* I remember being on a balcony. I don't know how I knew *Romeo and Juliet*, but I did. So, I was leaning over the balcony and saying, 'Romeo, Romeo,' at the age of six."

For a girl who had spent the first five years of her life in an orphanage, Kristen was now in paradise. But every garden had a serpent. She said, "I was sexually abused by somebody who was close. My parents didn't know. I kept it to myself for years and years. So, in a way, it's interesting, because I always sort of split myself in two. Not that I'm schizophrenic, and I know it may sound crazy, but I do split myself in two. And I would have tantrums once in a while. My parents couldn't understand why."

A second upset came when Kristen learned the full story of her past. She said, "To tell you the truth, I never knew very much about myself until I was 12. I knew I had been adopted, but I always thought I was Norwegian by birth. Then one evening I began to rummage around in the desk drawers, and I found a letter which the social worker from the orphanage had written to my foster parents. It explained that my real father was a German soldier, one of those who had occupied Norway during the war, and that my mother was a Finish lady who had now gone back to Sweden. I cried and cried, then I ran up to the bedroom where my parents were and I shouted, 'Thanks a lot for telling me about myself!' My father took me in his arms and said, consolingly, 'We were going to tell you as much as we knew, but gradually, and at what we considered the proper time.'" (MK-CRG62)

Kristen continued to throw herself into acting. By 14, she was playing in *Taming of the Shew* and *Little Women* at the Will-O-Way Theatre in Birmingham, Michigan.

One year later, Kristen experienced another big change in her life. She said, "I was only with my parents in Michigan for ten years, because my father took a sabbatical and we came to California. I was only 15. And I started working as an actress, because James Harris, the producer of *Lolita*, discovered me at a restaurant in Santa Monica. I think when you've been sexually abused that there is something sexual about you – perhaps an awareness, so when he was watching me, I became what I felt he wanted to see. And he wanted me for *Lolita*. But my parents didn't think that was the right role for me."

Even after turning down the part, Harris played a key role in bringing about the next chapter in Kristen's life. She said, "Without any strings, he started me working. He got me with the best agency in town. First it was Lillian Small, but then it was Elizabeth Taylor's agent."

First order of business was a name change. Martha Soderquist became Marta Kristen. With a new agent and a new name, the work soon came her way. Kristen said, "I did all the television shows. I was the 'go to' person for anything young. I did print ads and a great layout with Fabien." (MS-MI15)

At 15, Kristen appeared in an episode of *The Loretta Young Show*. At 16, she was seen in on *Leave It to Beaver*, *The Dick Powell Theatre* and two episodes of *Alfred Hitchcock Presents*, including "Bang! You're Dead," which was directed by Hitchcock himself and featured Billy Mumy as a make-believe young cowboy, who happens to have a real gun in his holster.

Kristen said of Hitchcock, "All I did was sit in the corner and stare at him. I was terrified and in awe of him, although I see the show now and none of that came through. I was amazed to see how natural I am. Hitchcock never said anything more to me than 'action' and 'cut.' I wasn't looking for anything more than that, so it never bothered me."

Regarding her future *Lost in Space* co-star, she said, "Billy was so cute then. He must have been about eight, but he was *really* good." (MK-SL88)

In her first two years in Los Angeles, Kristen achieved enough success to make staying a viable option. She said, "My parents knew what I wanted; I really wanted to stay here; I didn't want to go back to Michigan, which felt like a closed box for me. I felt that if I went back there, I'd never be able to express who I was. And the abuse situation back there, which, again, my parents knew nothing about, was something I didn't want to return to. So my parents stayed for a year, and then my mother stayed on and off with me for a year. After that, I stayed with a girlfriend named Nikki whose mother was a terrible alcoholic. My parents didn't know. I didn't know until I started living with them. She would hide bottles under all the cushions. Nikki and I would come home from school and we'd go find the bottles while her mother was working, and pour everything out in the sink. Her mother would come home and she'd scream and she'd yell, and then go out and buy more booze. It was quite horrible in some ways, but you just sort of survive." (MK-AI15)

A big stepping stone for Kristen came when she was hired by Walt Disney Productions. A widely circulated press release written by Lloyd Shearer, and which was picked up as a filler article by dozens of newspapers across America, including the September 23, 1962 edition of the *Cedar Rapids Gazette*, touted Kristen as "Disney's newest discovery." Shearer wrote:

> Walt believes in Rebecca of Sunnybrook Farm, Robinson Crusoe, Mark Twain, dogs, children, apple pie, American history, and family entertainment. No such brooding stars as Marlon Brando, Frank Sinatra, Warren Beatty and Elizabeth Taylor for him. Walt goes for the healthy, wholesome, corn-fed youngsters like Hayley Mills, Tommy Kirk and Kevin Corcoran. Take his latest "discovery," for example, Marta Kristen. Marta is a 17-year-old blue-eyed blonde with a cute nose-tilt, an outgoing personality, a trim little figure, 5 feet 4, 107 pounds and still growing – and an almost perennial smile. Disney is starring her in *Savage Sam*, a sequel to *Old Yeller*. It's the story of a dog, a boy and a girl taken captive by the Apaches in Southwest Texas in the 1870s. Marta's the only female in the film, for which she is earning $450 a week, a combination of money and opportunity which is transforming her into a contemporary Cinderella.

Kristen told Shearer, "A few weeks ago, my agent took me out to Disney's – I just idolize Walt Disney – and they signed me for the role in *Savage Sam*. It's my first motion picture job, and I don't want to gush but I'm so excited I can hardly stand it. I know I can act and all I want is to be a really good actress. I shouldn't say, 'All I want.' I also want to get a college degree. My father's taught philosophy for the past 37 years and when a girl's had that sort of educational environment, a lot of it wears off."

Photos (above and below): Marta Kristen in *Savage Sam* (Walt Disney Productions/Buena Vista Distributing Company, 1963).

Kristen admitted that she also wanted to get married … "but not just yet." She had a boyfriend named Richard Thornton, and said, "We've talked it all out, and he's willing to wait seven or eight years for me. When I'm 25, that's when I'll be ready to settle down. But right now I'm flying. I'm way up on Cloud Nine." (MK-CRG62)

Kristen later recalled, "It wasn't a great movie, but I just loved being outside, riding the horses, and I loved the wranglers. Oh my God, every Monday morning I'd go on set and there would be some guy – one of the cowboy wranglers, with a broken arm and scratches. It was because they would go to the bars and get into horrible fights. That's just what they did. But they taught me things. This one wrangler would ride the horse and pick me up and throw me behind him on the horse. It was fun; I enjoyed it so much. There was one time when the guy who was playing the Indian was leading me, and he dropped the reins, and something spooked the horse and that horse took off with me, and with the reins hanging down in front. And I thought for sure that horse was going to step on the reins and trip and I'd be flying. I had no saddle; I just had the stirrups that were hidden under the blanket. That was it! But I had spent years around horses, so I just grabbed the reins, and then I started hysterically laughing. I could not stop laughing because I saw this tree that he was heading towards at the top of this hill, and I thought, 'This is it!' I just kept thinking, 'This is crazy.' And they're all behind me, shouting, 'Slow down! Slow down!' And the wranglers and everybody else are running up the hill, and I'm just laughing like crazy. And just as the horse got to the tree, he stopped. They all came running up, and they

said, 'Are you all right?' I just sort of rolled over off the horse, and I continued hysterically laughing. I think they thought, 'She's lost it.' But they were so relieved." (MK-AI15)

On May 22, 1963, the critic known as "Tube," of *Daily Variety*, said of *Savage Sam*:

> It will take all the intrinsic drawing power of the Walt Disney banner to counteract the inadequacies of this undernourished western and bail it out at the box office. *Savage Sam* is one of the least satisfying items to emerge from the Buena Vista hopper in years.... [T]he film is a depiction of the efforts of half-a-dozen Texans led by a hound named "Savage Sam" to catch up with a band of Apaches who have taken prisoner a couple of children. At the root of the picture's problem is the incongruous air of levity with which the scenarists and director Norman Tokar have approached in what is obviously a dead serious situation. This clash confuses the audience throughout and makes it impossible to take the story seriously. As a result, there is never any genuine concern for the characters, nor is there ever any doubt as to the outcome.

"Tube" felt Brian Keith underplayed his role as the posse leader, but that Tommy Kirk (a Disney favorite) was "appealing," and "pretty Marta Kristen, the only female in the film, is satisfactory."

Kristen's publicist tried for damage control, with a filler piece in the July 4, 1963 edition of the *Los Angeles Times*, using the title, "Newcomer Sacrifices for Her Art." We were told:

> Pretty Marta Kristen, screen newcomer, sacrifices her appearance for her art in Walt Disney's Technicolor production, *Savage Sam* ... The blonde Norwegian beauty spends most of the time in the picture clad in a drab, shapeless pioneer dress with her face streaked with dirt. Actually, Marta is a true peaches and cream girl with plenty of glamour and fresh personality to go with it.

The tease worked in getting Kristen various newspaper interviews and feature articles, including one that came in the July 13 edition of the *Los Angeles Times*. Art Seidenbaum used the title, "Marta Kristen's Life Like a Movie."

Kristen told Seidenbaum that she would be a part time actress, and a part-time student, attending Santa Monica City College. She said, "I like ideas too well. Actors always revert to themselves – 'How do I look today? Do you like my new teeth? My new nose?' – and I wind up uncomfortable or bored." (MK-LAT65)

Shortly after the release of *Savage Sam*, Kristen played an unwed pregnant teenager in a two-part episode which bridged two different series. She said, "Jack Smight directed it – a wonderful director. It was really an award-winning quality show. And the first two-parter on television, starting on *Dr. Kildare* and then ending on *The Eleventh Hour*, which was a show about emotional and psychological problems. It really touched the sense of loneliness and loss that I could connect to from my earlier life. There was one scene where I'm alone in the room, and I've tried to abort the child, and failed, and I wake up in the hospital. That's when Dr. Kildare talks to me. You couldn't say 'pregnant' on television. I was 'expecting.' And this show is about teenage pregnancy, and abortion, and the right to a woman's body, and all of those different issues that were being presented in this one two-parter. It was so daring. For me, with my biological mother who had given me up for adaption, I was connecting with all those emotions." (MK-AI15)

Cecil Smith, writing for the November 23, 1963 edition of the *Los Angeles Times*, said:

> One of the most interesting two-parters of the season begins tonight on *Dr. Kildare* and winds up next Wednesday on *The Eleventh Hour*.... The theme is somber – pregnancy in a teenage girl, the emotional crises of the boy involved and the two families. But Jerry de Bono's script is anything but somber – it bristles with the sort of urgent, throbbing vitality that he alone seems to be able to get into TV writing. Its dialogue is full of stings and whips.

Days later, in the November 26 issue of *Daily Variety*, "Tube" said:

> Much has been made of the plight of the unwed mother in theatrical and TV film dramas of recent years, but the tendency has been to dismiss that other guy hovering around in the shadows – the unwed father. "Four Feet in the Morning" rectified the situation, and did so in a highly dramatic fashion certain to please those viewers addicted enough to primetime set-watching to be in front of their magic boxes Thursday of one week and Wednesday (upcoming) of the next. If nothing else, this unusual presentation deserves an Emmy for "best single dramatic show presented in two parts on two series in two weeks with two sets of stars in continuing roles appearing on both programs." Surely there is such an Emmy?... *The Kildare* half is concerned primarily with the girl's recovery after attempting an early self-abortion, and the *Eleventh Hour* half principally with the emotional repercussions on the boy of his impending fatherhood and his involvement in the bickering between his own parents and their relationship with the girl's parents....
>
> The [regular] stars of the two series (Richard Chamberlain, Raymond Massey, Ralph Bellamy and Jack Ging) play essentially secondary roles on this two-ply exercise. The focal character of the youthful father provides Tony Dow – the older brother on the erstwhile *Leave it to Beaver* series – with what must be his most important and challenging role to date, and he plays it with sensitivity and conviction. A promising young actor, his popularity with teenage femmes is apt to zoom after this assignment.

Also in the cast, as the parents, Ruth Roman and Andrew Duggan. "Tube" said "Marta Kristen is fragile, feminine and sympathetic as the unwed mother."

Marta Kristin's new, very-non Disney image (above and below), for *Beach Blanket Bingo* (MGM, 1965).

Soon after this role, Kristen decided not to put off marriage after all. She wed Terrance Treadwell, a grad student who was eight years her senior. Kristen later said, "I guess he was some sort of father figure, and I made him the *only* person in my life. That was a big mistake." (MK-SL88)

In 1964, Kristen gained attention for a highly-promoted episode of *Mr. Novak*, a series starring James Franciscus as a high school English teacher. Kristen played a "scatter-brained girl who matures into an adult" for the episode "The Senior Prom."

Also in '64, Kristen returned for a third *My Three Sons*, and an episode of *The Man from U.N.C.L.E.*

Filmed in 1964, but not aired until early 1965, was "The Wanda Snow Story," on *Wagon Train*. Kristen played the title character, a clairvoyant whom some on the travelers thought was a witch.

In 1965's *Beach Blanket Bingo*, Kristen played a mermaid that rescued a handsome boy – who promptly fell in love with her. She said, "In that story, I would get legs every night at midnight, and I remember shooting day-for-night in Paradise Cove in November, having to be out in the freezing surf to make my entrance. I'm trying to look pleasant and pop up out of the water, while trying also to keep from being dashed against some nearby rocks. But I'm the only one who didn't get sick during the shoot – something about that cold water, I guess!" (MK-SL88)

For its April 4, 1965 issue, *Variety* said:

> It is incredible how much director William Asher and his cowriter Leo Townsend have been able to fit into the newest bundle of beach tomfoolery. Every notion that might appeal to what the box office has indicated is the current teenage taste is there. Not all of it is well done, polished, credible or even desirable in the normal sense of film development and construction. If tunes with a beat, sloppy storylines with action and sentimental young romance and a bevy of half clad boys and girls with delicious looks are the points that satisfy, [the producers] will probably be again counting on a

picture that strictly caters to the inanities of youth.

Margaret Harford, writing for the April 9th edition of the *Los Angeles Times*, was kinder, but said basically the same thing – that writer and director "crammed everything that could conceivably interest the kids into this one," and "some of it is pretty silly, but there are a lot of attractive bikini beauties to look at while trying to sort out the plots and subplots."

The stars were Annette Funicello, Frankie Avalon and Linda Evans, with comedy provided by Paul Lynde and Don Rickles. Marta Kristen wore the fish tail.

Another acting job from this time was in the circus series *The Greatest Show on Earth*. Being a fan of the circus, Irwin Allen was watching. Kristen said, "I had done *The Greatest Show on Earth*, which was fun, because it was a comedy and I played a girl who was great on the high wire, but once she got on the ground she was constantly falling and tripping and dropping things. Irwin had seen that. He said, 'I want that girl!' And Irwin always got what he wanted.

"I was with General Artists Corporation at the time, which is now CAA, and they were packaging *Lost in Space*. I was doing all the shows on television at that time, and, of course, I did a lot of theater, and I was thinking that I would go to New York and do some serious work. But I went to meet him, and I was wearing these big dangling earrings, and I wore a bright pink suit, and he just loved me. But I said, 'I read the script and I'm just going to be put in the background. What are you going to do with my character?' He said, 'Marta, I have it all set up, and your character wanted to go on stage.' I thought, 'Well, that's good,' because I loved quoting Shakespeare, and I thought I could bring that into Judy's character. But I went home and thought about it and I said, 'No, I can't do this. I've just started and I can't get pigeonholed into this one part.' All my instincts said 'Don't do it.'

"So, Irwin called me every day for two weeks. He would say, 'Marta, have you made up your mind yet?' I'd say, 'Irwin, I'm not going to do it.' And he'd say, 'Are you sure?' I said, 'Irwin, I really don't know.' But I finally said, 'Okay, Irwin, I'll do it. And it turned out that it's such a wonderful thing that happened to me." (MK-AI15)

In Search of Will Robinson

Charles William Mumy, Jr. had been on television since the age of four. His father, Charles Mumy, owned a cattle ranch at Bishop, California. His mother, the former Muriel Gould, had worked as a secretary at 20th

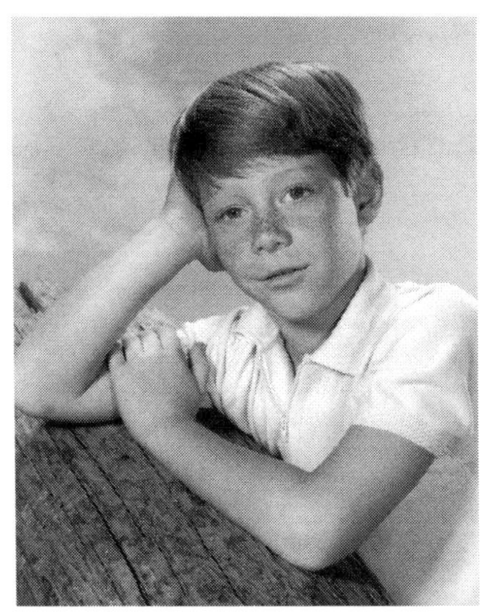

Century-Fox for 11 years prior to marrying, but said she had never planned on being a movie mother. In 1964, Billy Mumy told entertainment columnist Hedda Hopper, "I was hurt in a fall and had to stay in bed for a while, and used to watch a TV show with nothing but kids. I wanted to be in it, and they said if I did everything the doctor told me to do, I could. But I couldn't get into the show then because all the players had to be over four. I went back right after my fourth birthday and got a job." (BM-HH64)

The fall that put Mumy in bed happened as a result of him playing superhero. The show he eventually landed on was *Romper Room.*

Mumy said, "Well, the very, very, very first [prime time] show I ever did was an episode of a television series called *Riverboat*, and that was in 1959. I was five… and then the next year, 1960, I started doing a bunch of the featured roles – starring roles – things like *Loretta Young* and *The Twilight Zone*, and *Alfred Hitchcock*." (BM-LISW)

Mumy was six when he appeared in his first TV-Land classic: "Long Distance Call" on *The Twilight Zone*, in which a toy telephone became a link between a small boy and his dead grandmother.

In an October 1961 episode of *Alfred Hitchcock Presents*, Mumy was the star of a tale with a possibly tragic ending. "Bang! You're Dead!" featured the seven-year-old as a make-believe cowboy who suits up for play and heads outside. The audience knows what little Jackie does not: It's a real gun loaded with live bullets.

Of Alfred Hitchcock, Mumy said, "I hated him. He scared me to death. I never ever, ever, ever wanted to look at him again after that. Until he died, every time I was at Universal, I would go the long way around several soundstages to bypass his office."

Billy Mumy in "Bang! You're Dead!" episode of *Alfred Hitchcock Presents* (NBC-TV, 1961).

Most adults who took direction from Hitchcock found him amusing. Not Mumy. He said, "Whether or not he had an acerbic sense of humor, it definitely wasn't shared well with me when I was seven years old. He told me he was going to take a nail and nail my feet to the floor, and blood would come pouring out like milk. And he said it in a whispery tone in my ear – it wasn't like he was kidding around. I remember telling my mother what he said, and she said, 'Oh, honey, it was late, they were going to lose you in a few minutes and he had to get the shot – that's just his sense of humor.' Well, I didn't think it was funny." (BM-SL91)

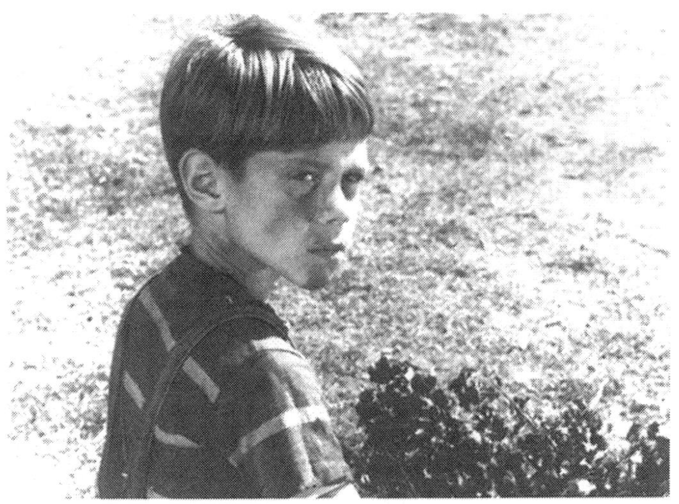

Above: Billy Mumy with a look that could send you into the cornfield, in "It's a Good Life" episode of *The Twilight Zone* (CBS-TV, 1961). Below: With Lucille Ball in "Lady in Limbo" episode of *The Greatest Show on Earth* (ABC-TV, 1963).

Weeks later, Mumy appeared for the second time in *The Twilight Zone* – one of the most famous and chilling episodes. "It's a Good Life" was about a small boy who, when angered, could send people into "the corn field" where they would never be heard from again.

In 1962, Mumy was the subject of "The Boy Who Wasn't Wanted," appearing with Dana Andrews for an episode of the anthology series, *Alcoa Premiere*. Later in '62, he played the son of Robert Culp and Patricia Barry for "Sammy the Way-Out Seal," a two-parter on *Walt Disney's Wonderful World of Color*. He also appeared on *Dr. Kildare*, *Have Gun – Will Travel*, *The Jack Benny Program*, *Wagon Train* and *The Alfred Hitchcock Hour*, although, to his relief, this segment was not directed by Hitchcock.

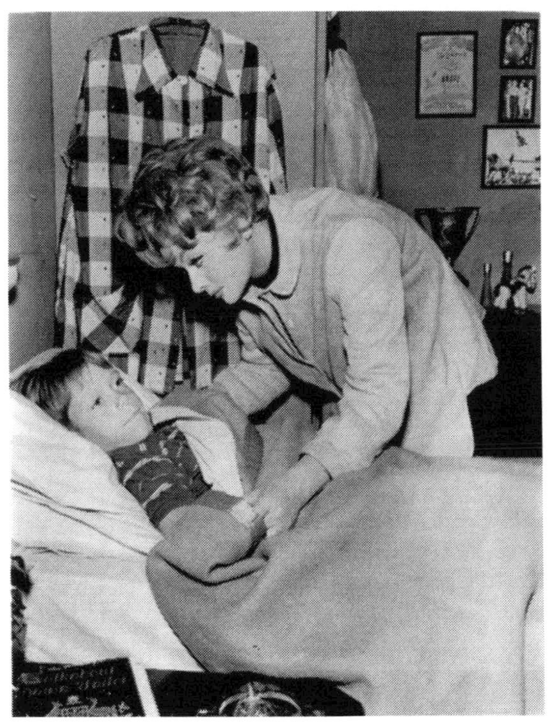

In 1963, Mumy played the son of Lucille Ball in one of her few dramatic turns, for a startling episode of *The Greatest Show on Earth*. Next, he played Jack Klugman's son in a third episode of *The Twilight Zone*: "In Praise of Pip."

Mumy said, "I loved *The Twilight Zone*. This sounds a little silly, but I think they're my favorite pieces of child acting that I did, in a sense. I mean, I can't compare what I was doing at six to what I would do at 25; it's just a different category. But I really like *The Twilight Zone*, and I feel proud of those things." (BM-LISW)

Mumy also appeared in *Perry Mason* during 1963. And, on the big screen, in *Palm Springs Weekend*, with Troy Donahue, Connie Stevens, Ty Hardin, Stefanie Powers, Robert Conrad and Jerry Van Dyke. In *A Ticklish Affair*, he played the son of Shirley Jones, who was investigated by the Navy after one of her boys accidentally sent an SOS signal using a set of window blinds.

In 1964, Mumy worked with one of Irwin Allen's good friends, Red Buttons, for an episode of *The Eleventh Hour*, for a serious treatment dealing with the effects of divorce on small children in a family. He played Dr. Richard Kimble's young nephew in an episode of *The Fugitive*. As an orphan boy who doesn't believe in Santa Claus, Mumy visited the Darrin Stephens family for Christmas, in *Bewitched*. He also appeared in three episodes of *The Adventures of Ozzie & Harriet*. In a second two-part Disney program, called "A Taste of Melon," Mumy played one of two country boys relocated to a larger town where they are drawn into a "battle of pranks" with the local boys.

Mumy said, "Working for the Disney studio was always a pleasure…. When Walt was alive and I was working out [of] the theater, he called me into his office a couple of times just to see if I was having fun, and to tell me that the stuff we were doing was going well. He told me to call him 'Uncle Walt.'" (BM-LISW)

In 1965, Mumy was the title character in "Come Back, Little Googie," in *The Munsters*, as a bratty friend of Eddie Munster who has a surprising visit to the strange family's home. He had actually been offered the role of Eddie Munster one year earlier, but, going by the advice of his parents, turned it down because of the makeup that would become a daily ritual for him.

Billy Mumy with James Stewart in *Dear Brigitte* (20th Century-Fox, 1965).

Next, Mumy returned to *Bewitched* to play a younger version of Dick York when a spell turned Darrin into a boy. And, in *I Dream of Jeannie*, he was a neighborhood boy who witnessed Jeannie doing her magic. He also appeared in *Ben Casey* and *The Virginian*. His greatest exposure that year came from *Dear Brigitte*, for the big screen, as the math prodigy son of Jimmy Stewart who had a crush on French film star Brigitte Bardot, and began corresponding with her to surprising results.

In a United Press syndicated newspaper article, carried by the *New Castle News* on July 22, 1965, Vernon Scott wrote:

> It was Brigitte Bardot's first love scene with an America actor, and she was making the most of it. With an ardent gleam in her sensuous Gallic eyes, she caressed the back of his neck and kissed him squarely on the face. Did our American boy return the passion? He did not. He murmured, "Golly, gee." He blushed and giggled. He looked around self consciously and fled at the first opportunity. This tower of jelly was Billy Mumy and his excuse for such bizarre behavior is that he is only ten years old and inclined to giggle when any girl kisses him.

When asked what he thought of Bardot, Mumy told Scott, "Take a guess." After munching on his cheese sandwich, he added, "She's really neat. She not only kissed me for the cameras, she kissed me a couple of times for nothing."

Brigitte Bardot with Mumy in *Dear Brigitte* (1965, 20th Century-Fox).

When asked what his American girlfriend thought of him traipsing around with the likes of Bardot, Mumy answered uneasily, "I don't discuss those things." He then added, "Miss Bardot is too old for me anyhow. She's 30 and has a kid three years old. She also has a penthouse and a country home. If she was 20 years younger, though. I might have a chance."

Mumy's father chimed in, "Billy falls for all the stars he works with. It was the same with Shirley Jones and Loretta Young."

Scott wrote that Mumy "shot his father a resentful glance and changed the subject." (BM-UPI64)

Regarding Bardot, Mumy told entertainment columnist Hedda Hopper, "She's real nice; real neat, but Shirley Jones is still my favorite." (BM-HH64)

Decades later, Mumy told Mike Hall of *The Indianapolis Star*: "One week I'd be the evil mutant on *Twilight Zone*, the next I'd be running off to France to play Jimmy Stewart's son and kiss Brigitte Bardot in *Dear Brigitte*. You can't turn on '60s TV without seeing Ron Howard or I as the kid.

"When you go from project to project like that, you get a different mindset than if you're young and land on a TV series where you come in, grab cookies and milk and say a line of two for three or four years. You think of yourself as an actor, not a star." (BM-IS96)

By December 1964, Mumy had been contacted about the *Lost in Space* pilot. Mumy recalled, "My agent at the time, Howard Rubin, called and asked me if I would like to do a series. Up until then, [I'd] been so busy and versatile in the shows that I was doing, we'd always felt that locking me into a series would be a mistake. However, when I heard it was a science fiction show, I really got excited. I've been an avid comic book collector and reader since 1960. Anyway, I met with Irwin Allen and that was that." (BM-LISW)

For a boy who collected comic books and loved science fiction, Mumy was about to take the ride of a lifetime.

In Search of John Robinson

The last of the cast members for the pilot to be approved by CBS was Guy Williams. Irwin Allen knew he wanted Williams almost from the start of the casting process, but the network would need convincing. This might seem surprising, since, even more than June Lockhart, Williams carried true star status. CBS didn't question that. Nor was the network concerned about his reputation as an actor – regarding both his talent and professional conduct. The network just wasn't sure if Williams had "the right look."

Born Armando Joseph Catalano in New York on January 14, 1924, Guy Williams' parents were Italian-Americans, having come from Sicily. They nicknamed him "Armand." At the time *Lost in Space* was being made, a friend of Williams, writer Berne Giler, told a *TV Guide* writer that the man who played Zorro, and Sindbad, and Professor Robinson, was "a real Sicilian." Giler said, "He has all the polish and temperament of a true Sicilian and the tremendous pride and ego to go with it." (BG-TVG66)

With his looks and physique, and six-foot, three-inch height, Williams was an imposing presence.

Armand Catalano wanted to act, but he needed an actor's name to match his agenda.

Son Steven Catalano (aka Guy Williams, Jr.) and daughter Toni Catalano, told how the name Guy Williams came to be. Steven said, "When he first started in the business… his agent wanted to send him to New York to an interview, and they said, 'Well, no, no, don't bother sending Armando Catalano; too ethnic.' So they changed the name to Guy Williams there." (GWJ-LISBR15)

Terri interjected, "I think it was in the same phone conversation. [His agent] said, 'Oh, okay, well I have Guy Williams here.' She saw the name in a paper somewhere. And they said, 'Okay, let's see him.'" (TC-LISBR15)

Armando Catalano was sent to New York as Guy Williams, and got the job.

Williams later said, "Guy Williams was about as non-specific as I could imagine!" (GW-SL87)

The newly christened Guy Williams began studying at the famed Neighborhood Playhouse in New York City. To pay the bills, he took jobs as a male model, later saying, "I'd work only a few hours a week. It was kind of like loafing pays." (GW-TVG1)

The modeling work brought dividends – Williams met his wife Janice while loafing. She was a Powers model.

Williams did a little theater, and live television which was beamed out of New York, such as a 1951 episode of *Studio One*. He later said, "I guess you could say I got into acting through modeling. But, actually, I got into acting by a process of elimination. I backed into it by backing away from other things." (GW-LAT58)

Guy Williams, actor/model, circa early 1950s.

Williams ended up backing up all the way across America, stopping in Hollywood in 1952 where he was signed to Universal Pictures and put into the studio's apprenticeship program. His first role was in the B-film *Bonzo Goes to College*, starring Maureen O'Sullivan and a chimpanzee. It also featured Gene Lockhart, the dad of his future space wife, June.

This was not a happy period for Williams. Universal wasted him in minor roles in lesser films, such as *The Mississippi Gambler* and *The Man from the Alamo*, both released in 1953 and quickly forgotten. He said, "They put you under contract on a yearly basis, and used you in little filler spots… walk-throughs and such. If the part was of any consequence, they would usually pick someone from outside to play it." (GW-SL87)

Once his "walk-through" contract was fulfilled, Williams walked out. He did slightly better as a free agent, taking minor guest roles on lightweight TV fare such as *The Lone Ranger*, *The Mickey Rooney Show* and *Highway Patrol*. And he still made a quick dollar or two in movies. He later said, "I used to do window-trimming parts, like being Lori Nelson's brother in *Sincerely Yours* at Warners." (GW-DV58)

It was a movie that had to be seen to be believed. Liberace played a popular pianist who, on the eve of a career-high concert at Carnegie Hall, is stricken deaf.

In 1957, Williams had a small role as a cop in *I Was a Teenage Werewolf*, which starred Michael Landon in the title role. At that time, Williams saw an announcement in the Hollywood trades saying that Walt Disney Productions would be filming a half-hour adventure series for ABC-TV based on *The Mark of Zorro*. The part of Zorro had yet to be cast and the studio was looking for an unknown.

Williams had a leg up – besides his good looks and powerful build, he said, "My father learned fencing as a young man in Europe and he began giving me lessons when I was a boy." (GW-LAT59)

Father knew best, and Williams won the role that had been played in the 1920s silent film by Douglas Fairbanks, Sr., and, more recently by Tyrone Power in 1940. Williams approached the part differently than Power had, saying, "Power played Don Diego as a sissy, a real gay caballero. It was okay for him to do that once in a movie, but I knew that wouldn't work every week on TV. It would get tiresome, not to mention this was the '50s and a show with an audience including kids. So I had to play Don Diego

***Zorro* was an instant hit when it premiered October 10, 1957. Below: Walt Disney conferring with Guy Williams on the set of *Zorro* (Walt Disney Productions, 1957).**

'neutral,' which is difficult because it means *nothing*. How do I make 'nothing' interesting?" (GW-SL87)

Williams came up with his own take on Don Diego, the son of a wealthy Mexican rancher in early 1800s California. Though a bit of a dandy, this quick-witted caballero moonlighted as a caped crusader fighting the tyranny of local authorities. With the black hat, mask, cape, and horse, the one thing that would always shine through was Williams' pearly white smile. Even so, it took some trial and error to find the character. Williams said, "I had auditioned with a heavy Spanish accent, knowing I could drop it instead of starting out light and adding on. For the first couple of weeks, somebody would be tapping me on the shoulder as I'm walking around the set, and it would be Walt. He would say, 'Can you bring it down a little, Guy.' He didn't know what he wanted, so I kept 'bringing it down.' One day, I finished the show and Walt didn't tap me on the shoulder. And that was the accent I kept." (GW-SL87)

Disney spared little expense to make *Zorro* a hit. *El Pueblo de Nuestra Senora la Reina de los Angeles*, a sleepy Spanish village (and forerunner of modern L.A.) on the Disney backlot, was recreated at a cost of $100,000. This equates to approximately $850,000 in 2015 currency. Each episode (39 per season) was budgeted at $50,000. As low as this sounds today (equating to about $425,000 in 2015), the budget was actually on the high side for a 30-minute western in 1957 … especially when on the network that was low man on the totem pole – ABC.

Disney spent more money throwing a party for the press prior to the series premiere. The entertainment correspondents were led into the pueblo courtyard set to meet the cast. Walter Ames, writing for the *Los Angeles Times* on October 10, 1957, said:

Suddenly the huge gates of the make-believe pueblo were

> pushed open. In rushed the village commandant, Monastario, and his sword-wielding bodyguards. They pushed the crowd back. From a two-story window balcony emerged our hero, Zorro, played by Guy Williams. The guardsmen rushed him. One was pushed off the balcony, landing on his back in a pit. Some women in the crowd screamed; it was that real. Suddenly Zorro and Monastario were locked in a fierce fencing duel. It lasted several minutes. Then Zorro stepped back and said, 'Let's have a beer.' The crowd relaxed and applauded. It was one of the outstanding events of a party-filled premiere season and only Disney had the foresight to actually stage a scene from his series.

Zorro was also going to test a formula never tried on primetime television before – one that would later be resurrected for *Lost in Space*: the cliffhanger.

On February 16, 1957, *The Billboard* magazine reported:

> The first cliffhanger produced for TV will be testing an ABC-TV proposition that adventure serials can build larger permanent audiences than current episodic shows, when the [network] unveils *Zorro* next fall. The Disney-produced series, based on *The Mark of Zorro*, will have a running plot and continuing characters, with a tense climax each week designed to carry over home TV viewers with maximum suspense to the next week's episode. It is Walt Disney and ABC's belief that the result will be a smaller percentage of transient audience and a much bigger percentage of permanent viewers, as was true in the heyday of movie theater serials. "It hasn't been done in TV, except for soap operas, plus a few low-budget kid movies transplanted in the early days of television," says a Disney spokesman. "But we are convinced this can revolutionize the pattern and formats of mystery, adventure, dramatic and Western series, and even situation comedies."

Williams seemed born to play the role of *Zorro* (ABC-TV, 1957).

Disney was attempting to give Zorro a fighting chance. ABC appeared to be doing the opposite.

Every year since its founding, ABC had finished dead last in the ratings. For the TV season now coming to an end, ABC only had two series in the Nielsen Top 25 – *Disneyland*, which was about to get a name change to *Walt Disney Presents*, peaking at No. 13, and *The Life and Legend of Wyatt Earp*, at No. 18. Not seeming to give *Zorro* a fair chance in the ratings sweepstakes, ABC scheduled it to go head-to-head against one of NBC's top series – Groucho Marx's *You Bet Your Life*, still running strong after seven previous seasons. Four seasons earlier, it placed at No. 3, bested only by *I Love Lucy* and *Dragnet*. One year later, it sat at No. 4, allowing only *The Jackie Gleason Show* to stand with Lucy Ricardo and Sgt. Joe Friday ahead of it in the TV ratings line.

Zorro's competition on CBS was *Harbormaster*, a crime thriller starring Barry Sullivan.

Of the premiere episode, trade magazine *Broadcasting*, for its December 16, 1957 issue, wrote:

> Unadulterated adventure with all the daring that could be mustered was the formula Johnston McCulley used three decades ago in presenting Zorro through the pages of the old dime Argosy magazine and later in the movie series starring the late Douglas Fairbanks, Sr. In bringing the series to TV, Walt Disney has lost none of that touch. Zorro remains the masked rider of early California days who fights tyranny, for the most part perpetrated by the local Mexican army authorities. He camouflages his activities by assuming the role of a lackadaisical son of a well-to-do Mexican ranch owner. The secret passageway from ranch to stable where his horse and disguise are hidden, and other such gimmicks, may seem on the implausible side to today's more sophisticated audience, but the fast pace of the scripting tends to whisk the viewer past such questions.

On October 14, the critic called "Daku," for *Daily Variety*, reported:

> Walt Disney's new series *Zorro*, based on the character created by Jonathan McCulley, is a well-produced, actionful entry which should capture a combined adult/juve following. Series intros a newcomer, Guy Williams, as the masked hero; he's [a] handsome, competent actor seemingly glove-fit for the role.... Williams is excellent in the dual role of Diego and Zorro; he displays a flair for the flamboyance called for in this 19th century version of Robin Hood.

On the same day, *The Billboard* opined:

> If suddenly it should happen that [a] "Z" epidemic breaks out among the kids, don't be alarmed: It's not the effect of Zputnik, the Russian moon. It's just Zorro, who's arrived. Zorro is the hero of the new Walt Disney series, which zips along with zest and zing. There's hardly a moment to catch one's breath in the action-packed adventure. It's a great show for kids, and should even hold the adults, as long as they're not given time to think; Disney sees that they're not.... Slotted opposite Groucho Marx, much of the success of the program may depend on whether the kids can control the dial that late [8-8:30 p.m.].

As it turned out, the kids did control the dial. *Zorro* was a success in the ratings from the outset. During the season's first "Sweeps Week" rating survey (October 4-10, 1957), *Zorro* was the third most popular of the new series, under *The Restless Gun*, a western starring John Payne, and *Alcoa Theatre*, an anthology which rotated five big screen stars each week: David Niven, Robert Ryan, Jane Powell, Jack Lemmon and Charles Boyer. So popular was *Zorro* that it was out-pulling other new series destined for long network runs, such as *Perry Mason*, *The Price Is Right*, *Wagon Train*, *Have Gun – Will Travel* and *Maverick*. And the numbers continued to climb with each new week.

On October 14, *Daily Variety* reported:

> Groucho Marx, who has had things pretty much his own way for most of his TV years, had a scare thrown into him by ABC-TV's *Zorro* Thursday night, when the swashbuckler checked in with 19.4, a mere three points off the comedy quizzer. *Harbormaster* was fogged in at 8.6.

Using Nielsen's numbers, *Broadcasting* magazine painted a fuller picture: *You Bet Your Life* had attacked 44.1% of the people watching television during that time period. *Zorro* grabbed 36%. *Harbormaster* settled for 15.9%.

The climb continued. On October 21, *Daily Variety* said:

> If the lads at ABC, from [President] Leonard Goldenson down to the mail boy, have that contented look, it was put there by the ratings. For instance, last Thursday night the Trendex checkers had their shows in the thick of it. *Zorro* keeps crowding Groucho Marx, 21.4 to 25.6.

On October 28, *Daily Variety* reported:

> Walt Disney's *Zorro* continues to nip at the heels of Groucho Marx in the overnight Trendex [ratings report]. Last Thursday's markers read like this: Groucho 24.7; *Zorro* 22.5; *Harbormaster* 9.9.

By early November, when CBS and NBC preempted their early Thursday night shows to carry an address by President Dwight D. Eisenhower concerning the missiles crisis between the U.S. and Russia, ABC dared to delay the President's message until a later hour, and continued to cater to the kids instead. On November 11, *Daily Variety* reported:

> Even with all the publicity and interest in missiles, Ike's TV talk last Thursday was out-rated by *Zorro*.... Pulling 19.2 on CBS and 16.1 on NBC, the margin, however slight, went to *Zorro* at 19.3.

In a ratings survey published in *Variety* on March 3, 1958, the Top 10 shows stacked up this way:

1.	*The Perry Como Show*	38.3
2.	*Gunsmoke*	35.7
3.	*Maverick*	32.8
4.	*Tales of Wells Fargo*	32.5
5.	*Sugarfoot*	32.3
6.	*The Restless Gun*	31.2
7.	***Zorro***	**30.0**
8.	*G.E. Theatre*	28.0
9.	*Chevy Show*	27.7
10.	*The Real McCoys* / *Wagon Train* (tie)	27.7

On May 18, 1958, Williams was featured in a *Los Angeles Times* article with the title, "WHHHTT, WHHHTT, WHHHTT!: Williams Making Mark (Z) as Zorro." Boots LeBaron wrote:

> Actor Guy Williams, who plays the swashbuckling masked swordsman Zorro on KABC (7), Thursday nights at 8, is Walt Disney's television answer to Douglas Fairbanks, Sr. Fairbanks, of course, was the most famous actor-stuntman of his era. He was the first motion picture Zorro. And, in a way, this handsome young actor, Guy Williams, is following in his footsteps, via television. There isn't an actor on the video screens today who takes on as many hazardous jobs as Guy. He does all his own fencing and fights and usually does his own riding.

Williams told LeBaron, "Any fight is simple after you conquer the art of fencing. Fencing makes the biggest demand on your coordination."

Those demands were even greater when acting for the small screen. Williams said, "You can't compare television with movies. TV is a rush business. Tyrone Power had a marvelous sword fight scene in his

Zorro movie. It took five weeks of practice. In five weeks we produce five shows! We only have a few hours to practice our fights." (GW-LAT58)

Zorro filmed Monday through Friday with each episode shot in four days. Williams said, "Friday was 'fight day,' so we would do all the stuff you could get injured in. If you banged your head or hurt your arm, you had until Monday to recuperate. All of our visitors would come on Friday to watch the fighting." (GW-SL87)

In early 1958, Williams told the *Los Angeles Times* that the show received more than 1,200 fan letters each week, and it had approximately 20 million people tuning in. By this time, they had finished 39 episodes for Season One, and were about to begin a second batch of 39 half-hours for the second year.

Williams was suddenly a TV star, and a top draw at rodeos. His publicity appearances as Grand Marshal at several parades netted him an average of $2,500 each.

From the June 8, 1959 issue of *The Billboard*:

> The Arkansas-Oklahoma Rodeo, aided by television's Zorro as the featured name, racked up a new all-time record during its six-day run ending Saturday (30). The turnout, according to Bill Harder, president of the sponsoring Chamber of commerce, was close to 60,000, a new high for the 26-year-old event.... Harder said Zorro was instrumental in pulling thousands of youngsters to the event.

Williams was even given a 2.5% royalty on the merchandising rights associated with *Zorro*. He said, "It would have been more, but [Disney] was determined to make sure that I never would receive what Fess Parker got in Davy Crockett merchandising revenues. " (GW-SL87)

Attendance at Disneyland surged whenever an appearance of Guy Williams as Zorro was announced.

Walt Disney and his brother Roy were renowned for being unfairly tight-fisted when it came to salaries or profit participation deals. And they were masters when it came to making money for themselves. The Disneys explored and exploited every possible area of merchandising, from lunch pails to Whitman coloring books, Dell comic books (eleven featuring Guy Williams on the cover), storybook records, and Zorro costumes and toys. In *Zorro*'s first season alone, it has been estimated that the merchandising brought in over $11 million.

By its second season, in October 1958, *Zorro* was often beating the old champ, Groucho Marx. In a ratings report published in the October 13 issue of *Daily Variety*, *Zorro* posted a 19.2 rating, topping both *December Bride* on CBS, which had 14.6, and *You Bet Your Life* on NBC, which settled for a 17.7.

Two days later, sister trade weekly *Variety* reviewed the second season kickoff, saying:

> Seven-Up and AC Spark Plugs are riding a swashbuckling winner into its second year, and there's good reason to suppose, with the way *Zorro* caught on last year, that the mask-and-cape heroics will grow on the fancy of the juve trade now that the series is established. The Spanish western hasn't a single feature that is really unique, but it's so well done that it is standout among the garden variety costume actioners. To coin a phrase, if it's Disney it's got to be good.... Guy Williams, in the title role, has the same dashing good looks and derring-do he had last year...

In November, another ratings report was released to the trades. *Zorro* had new competition on NBC. Groucho had been pushed to a later time slot on the Thursday night schedule and old-time comedian Ed Wynn was given a show, and a showdown, with the masked crusader. *Zorro* again led its time period, with a 19.5 rating. *December Bride*, on CBS, was second, with 16.9. *The Ed Wynn Show* lagged behind with a 9.4.

A week later, a *Variety* ratings survey conducted in Cleveland, Ohio, ranked the prime time Top 10 shows as follows:

1.	*Gunsmoke*	33.2
2.	*Maverick*	31.8
3.	*The Perry Como Show*	30.3
4.	*The Real McCoys*	29.3
5.	*The Lawrence Welk Show*	29.2
6.	***Zorro***	**26.9**
7.	*Leave it to Beaver*	26.5
8.	*The Danny Thomas Show*	26.2
9.	*Wagon Train*	25.8
10.	*The Adventures of Ozzie and Harriet*	25.5

Another survey conducted by *Variety* in December, this time in Wichita, Kansas, again ranked *Zorro* at No. 6. Out of 114 primetime series, it trailed behind only *Gunsmoke*, *The Life and Legend of Wyatt Earp*, *Maverick*, *The Real McCoys*, *The Rifleman* and *Sugarfoot*.

On December 1, *Daily Variety* reported:

> The personal appearance of Zorro (Guy Williams) and his air waves troupe brought out record-busting crowds to Disneyland over the weekend. Included in the mob Sunday was Williams' own six-year-old son, Steve (the Williams also have a six-month-old dotter [sic]). His p.a. [public appearance] at the park also included a battle atop Frontierland roofs, and on the top deck of the Mark Twain – battles which top anything seen on the filmed Disney show!

According to the trade, Williams was now receiving 2,000 fan letters a month, "with quite a few including proposals from teenagers."

NBC pulled *The Ed Wynn Show* from the schedule, cancelled after only three months, and tried an adventure show based on a cartoon strip: *Steve Canyon*. The change didn't help the network which, a year-and-a-half earlier, owned the time period. A Nielsen ratings survey covering the first week of the new year reported that *Steve Canyon* came in third, with a 15.2 rating, below that of CBS's *December Bride*, with a 19.3. *Zorro* again reigned, this time with a 22.1 rating.

Variety, in its ratings survey from late January, listed *Zorro* as No. 9 of all primetime series. A pair of *Variety* regional reports from February ranked it as No 6 in Cincinnati, Ohio, and No 8 in Milwaukee, Wisconsin. NBC cried uncle. *Steve Canyon* was moved to a different time slot in March.

Guy Williams in saber duel with young visitor at Disneyland.

In the meantime, for the *Zorro* crew, the grind continued. Williams said, "We called the actors 'stuntmen' because the scripts were being changed at the last minute, and to learn new dialogue and film it immediately was the real stunt. The work on *Zorro* was interesting. Nobody was doing any better fencing than we were, and working with the production people was fun. I could have kept doing it on and on." (GW-SL87)

In mid-February, it was announced in the Hollywood trades that *Zorro* had finished filming its second season, and that prior to resuming production in July for a third year, Disney would star Williams in a theatrical film called *Gold*. Neither the film nor a third season of half-hour *Zorro* episodes would come to be.

On April 24, 1959, *Daily Variety* ran the headline, "Sponsors Balk Over *Zorro*'s Price Hike." Disney now wanted $50,000 from each of *Zorro*'s sponsors – Seven-Up and the AC Spark Plug Company; an amount they each refused as too high. The two advertisers opted to go with *The Donna Reed Show* instead, which would be given *Zorro*'s time slot. ABC talked of moving *Zorro* to Sunday nights, as a lead-in for *Maverick*. It would have made an unbeatable line-up … except for one hurdle. ABC's intended spot for Zorro was owned by Best Foods, who wanted to stick with its current series, *You Asked for It*.

With no other time slots available, ABC announced it would air *Zorro*'s third season half an hour earlier on Sundays – in a pre-primetime slot from 6:30 to 7 p.m.

On May 20, *Daily Variety* broke the bad news for *Zorro* fans and Guy Williams with the headline: "ABC Says Tag Too High, So Disney Kills *Zorro*." The trade reported:

> Walt Disney will discontinue production of his *Zorro* series, following inability of the studio and ABC-TV to get together on a price for the show. Disney had submitted a final price of $49,500 per episode on the series. ABC felt the tag too high, arguing that [the planned early Sunday night time period] is essentially a fringe time property, with audience potential not large enough to justify the costs.

In a similar dispute, production had ceased on Disney's *Mickey Mouse Club* for ABC's weekday afternoon schedule.

Walt Disney wasn't worried. He was certain he could make a quick deal to place *Zorro* on NBC, which had expressed interest in that series as well as hoping to inherit *Walt Disney Presents* in two years when the current ABC contract for that series ran out. And, unlike ABC, which was an all-black-&-white broadcaster, NBC was talking about presenting Disney's product in color. ABC cried foul and promptly threw a monkey wrench into Disney's plans.

On July 2, 1959, with the fall TV season still three months in the distance (starting in October back then), the top headline on the front page of *Daily Variety* proclaimed, "Disney Antitrust Suit Vs. ABC." The trade reported:

> Walt Disney Productions today filed an antitrust action against ABC-TV, charging it with restraint of trade and seeking to invalidate contracts with the network covering *Zorro* and *Mickey Mouse Club* shows. Suit is believed the first of its kind – a producer charging a network with antitrust violations. Disney charges that ABC has attempted illegally to prevent it from offering the two programs to other networks in the wake of ABC's refusal to carry the shows next season. Complaint alleges belief that the network has contacted other networks and stations warning them against accepting the programs. Although it's been generally known that ABC-TV and Disney have been having disagreements over pricing of programs, the lawsuit came as a surprise in light of the close relationship between two companies.

It was a close relationship that would soon end. Roy Disney said, "Although we do not dispute ABC's right to discontinue these or any other programs on their own network, we will certainly fight ABC's maneuvers to suppress these programs from public exhibition over other television stations." (RD-DV59)

On July 7, *Broadcasting* magazine revealed ABC's side of the dispute. The trade reported:

> ABC countered by charging in its statement that Walt Disney Productions "has been making concerted efforts over the past six months to change the conditions of the [ABC-Disney] agreement and modify the exclusivity provisions" and "now seeks to avoid its obligations." … As explained by ABC, the network and Walt Disney Productions entered [into] an agreement in 1954 stipulating that for seven years Disney had granted an exclusive on his TV programs to ABC. This was "in exchange" for ABC's financing of Disneyland Park (in California) and "agreeing to buy *Disneyland* TV program (now called *Walt Disney Presents*) for seven years with very substantial minimum guarantees." The network said it had "lived up to its agreement in all respects" and that under the agreement Disney has "certain financial obligations to ABC."

During August of 1959, even after the reported cancellation, another *Variety* ratings survey, this time conducted in Honolulu, Hawaii, placed *Zorro* in the Top 10 of all primetime programs, sitting at No. 7.

Days later, the Hollywood trades announced that 20th Century-Fox wanted to buy Guy Williams' contract from Disney and star him in a film based on the 1958 book *The King Must Die*. Williams would play the lead as Theseus, a hero from Greek mythology.

But this too was not to be. Disney, convinced of a victory in court and the right to continue *Zorro* on NBC, refused to release Williams. The movie was never made and Williams would sit home, on full salary, watching a hot acting career quickly turning cold.

Zorro left the ABC network a short time later, and would not be seen on television again until 1965 when it was finally placed into syndicated reruns.

Blocked from making more half-hour *Zorro* episodes, it was announced in October 1959 that Disney would string together multiple segments into a feature film for big-screen release in 1960. *Zorro* was the perfect series to work with in such an experiment, since its episodes often ended with cliffhangers and had story arcs which spanned numerous programs. Recycling the series in this way would help keep *Zorro* a viable property.

On February 3, 1960, Larry Tubelle, reporting for *Daily Variety*, wrote:

> THE WORST FORM OF PAYOLA: That's roughly the way Guy Williams sums up his current relationship with Walt Disney Studios. With four years to go on his exclusive seven-year contract with Disney, Williams has been warming the bench for the past year or so, and is anxious to get back in the starting lineup. In fact, television's inactive Zorro threatens to "resign the business" altogether if the option for his services for another year is picked up (in May) with nothing in view in the way of work. "I wouldn't want to attempt to survive another year like this," Williams avers. The actor, who starred for two seasons as Disney's Zorro on ABC-TV, prior to the year of layoff-with-payoff he's currently observing, sees his predicament as a new and devastating kind of a problem for actors – where, for reasons that have nothing to do with their acting abilities, their careers are short-circuited. There is talk of Zorro returning to a network niche this fall, but as of now the series is off the air altogether – is neither a first-run nor re-run attraction – with the result that Williams is in temporary professional limbo.... As Williams says, "The fact that I could now be doing a series at much more than I'm getting doesn't bother me as much as the fact that I'm not working. My biggest concern is getting back to work."

Within months, Williams would be put back to work. First up, filming a handful of short scenes to help tie together the storylines being worked into a pair of feature films from half-hour *Zorro* episodes. One film, released abroad, was given the title *Zorro the Avenger*. A second, *The Sign of Zorro*, had a running time of 90 minutes. In addition, scripts were also being prepared for four to six new one-hour episodes of *Zorro* to be aired on *Walt Disney Presents*.

In June, Williams was sent on an 11-city tour to promote the release of *The Sign of Zorro*. He appeared on stage at the theaters screening the movie and thrilled audiences by performing a sword fight with stuntman Buddy Van Horn, who had doubled for Williams on the TV series and often appeared with him dueling atop the riverboat Mark Twain, at Disneyland. The *El Paso Herald Post*'s Barbara Causey attended one of these appearances. She reported in the June 11, 1960 edition:

More than 1,000 children from El Paso and Juarez greeted Zorro when he arrived at International Airport yesterday afternoon. The hero of the Walt Disney production *The Sign of Zorro* was scheduled for three personal appearances on the Plaza Theater stage today, at 2:45, 4:50 and 8:40 p.m. In real life, Zorro is Guy Williams, a tall, handsome fellow with a debonair personality. Last night he and Buddy Van Horn, his rival in a duel on the Plaza stage, were guests at a dinner for press, TV and radio people. Children who didn't make it to the airport also came to the Hilton Hotel to get a special Zorro handshake. He greeted them with a big smile and displaying his versatility by discussing baseball as well as fencing with the young fry…. El Paso was chosen as the initial site for the introduction due to being a border city. The heroics of Zorro stem from a Mexican legend, a tale which belongs to the good neighbors of the South-Mexico and the United States. Mr. Williams is charming to youngsters and ladies alike. While the kids are getting an autographed photo, ladies get their hands kissed.

A couple of days later, Williams and Van Horn were putting on three performances at the Paramount Theater in Austin, trading swordplay and greeting the fans before each screening of the movie. One day later, they took their act to the Majestic Theater in San Antonio, and then jetted off to other locations.

Business was brisk in the theaters where Williams made public appearances, but sluggish elsewhere. Exhibitors reported that the take was only "okay" at the 1,536-seat Orpheum in Portland, Oregon; "weak" in Denver at a 2,432-seat theater named after its city; "bad" at the 2,200-seat Music Hall in Seattle; "modest" at the 2,043-seat Uptown in Kansas City; "fair" in the same city at the 1,217-seat Granada; "dim" at the SW Downtown and Hawaii theaters, in Los Angeles; "drab" at the 3,000-seat Rialto in Louisville; "slow," at 2,800-seat Circle in downtown Indianapolis; and "average" at the 3,500-seat Broadway-Capitol in Detroit. At the Twin Drive-In, located in Cincinnati, and able to accommodate 1,200 cars, business was reported as merely "okay."

In July, and continuing into early 1961, *The Sign of Zorro* played in neighborhood houses in cities across America, always to mixed results. Television was clearly where *Zorro* belonged. To this end, during the summer of 1960, Williams filmed one two-hour episode and three additional one-hour episodes of *Zorro*, all to be aired the following season on *Walt Disney Presents* (to be given a new title by its new network, NBC, as *Walt Disney's Wonderful World of Color*).

The return began October, 30, 1960, with the two-hour color telecast of "El Bandido." One week later, on November 6, "Adios, El Cuchillo," the first of the three one-hour color programs, aired. Seven weeks later, on January 1, 1961, "The Postponed Wedding" had its broadcast. Eleven weeks after that, on April 2, the fourth and final installment, "Auld Acquaintance," was televised.

A year passed before Williams was seen on the screen again. He remained on salary with Disney – paid to do nothing. Williams told Michael Fessier, Jr., of *TV Guide*, "Maybe I'd go on an eight-day rodeo tour and then go off for three, four weeks sailing." (GW-TVG66)

Williams with Sean Scully and unknown actor in *The Prince and the Pauper* (Walt Disney Productions, 1962).

In May 1962, Williams starred in *The Prince and the Pauper*, a Disney movie based on the Mark Twain story, which was aired in three segments on *Walt Disney's Wonderful World of Color*. He took over the role that Errol Flynn had played for the 1937 film of the same title.

Cecil Smith, covering the TV "event" for the *Los Angeles Times*, called it "Disney's most ambitious project of the year," and revealed the budget to be $900,000, a hefty chunk of change for a TV movie, even one presented in three installments. Smith said:

> I saw the work print of the film when it arrived from England recently and it's a superb retelling of the swashbuckling old legend with Guy (Zorro) Williams as the principal swashbuckler, Miles Herndon, and an enormously appealing Australian lad named Sean Scully in the twin roles of Prince and Pauper…. Color adds immeasurably to the rich and regal trappings of the court of Henry VIII and to the twisting streets of 16th-century London, but even in black-and-white this is a remarkable show. It's long been the belief of many that the world of color in television is wonderful. But it really took Disney to make it so.

After the three-part movie aired, Williams was freed from his contract with Disney and went to work on two back-to-back adventure films in Europe. The first, already in the can and due to be released in America by MGM, was *Damon and Pythias*.

Interviewed by Bob Thomas for a syndicated newspaper article making the rounds in March 1962, Williams said, "We made two versions of some sequences, one for America, one for Europe. I did one scene that was quite explicit. In the European version, we were, uh, prone. In the American version, we were not quite so prone. Actually, I think the European version was less suggestive. There could be no doubt about what was going on. But the American version, things were hinted to as what might have taken place. The imagination has more chance to run rampant.... All of this is about 500,000 miles removed from Disney." (GW-IPT62)

Don Burnett and Guy Williams in *Damon and Pythias* (MGM, 1962).

Daily Variety reviewed the film on September 10, 1962, saying:

> Although *Damon and Pythias* measures a cut or two above the run of spear-and-sandal spectacles, its virtues should not alienate the seemingly resilient audience for this kind of escapist mummery... The dialogue maintains a relatively intelligent and persuasive level, the acting is good or better, and Curtis Bernhardt's direction is smooth and even rather thoughtful.... As Damon, a sort of rascally bohemian in ancient Syracuse, Guy Williams etches a simpatico performance.

Guy Williams as Captain Sindbad (MGM, 1963).

Next up for Williams was the second splashy sword-and-sorcerer piece filmed in Europe – *Captain Sindbad*. Interviewed by Erskine Johnson for a syndicated newspaper article, Williams said, "I turned all of them into huge vacations for my whole family (wife Janice and two children). It took us three months just to get home from one location. We saw the world. Now I'm settling down again." (GW-NP65)

Reviewing the movie for the *Los Angeles Times*, Margaret Harford said:

> *Captain Sindbad*, a King Brothers Arabian Nights fantasy filmed in Bavaria, makes those Italian spectacles that have been coming our way for too many years, look terrible. Veteran

director Byron Haskin gives a professional touch to the imaginative proceedings in the adventures of the legendary sailor…. Guy Williams may not be a swashbuckler in the old Errol Flynn manner but TV's popular Zorro seems an ideal choice for the kids. He has the muscles to dodge all kinds of death-dealing traps, outwitting a fiendish dictator and a sly magician who is under the tyrant's spell…. Good triumphs over Evil and the film's special effects are a triumph all by themselves.

Above: Lorne Greene with Guy Williams. Below: Williams as he appeared in the opening title sequence for five episodes of *Bonanza*, the most-watched television series in America during 1964 (NBC-TV, 1964).

As a result of being in Europe for two years filming *The Prince and the Pauper*, *Damon and Pythias*, and *Captain Sindbad*, the man who had played Zorro missed out on work in the U.S., and three years' worth of "pilot season," when the TV properties are developed. Williams told Hollywood Correspondent Dick Kleiner that he had planned to only take three years off between *Zorro* and whatever would be his next series, but that he had miscalculated. After filming the last of his three costume movies in Europe, he and his family took the long way home. Williams told Kleiner, "We were halfway across the Atlantic when it hit me. My God, I said, I've missed the pilot season. And I had. I had to wait an extra year." (GW-NP65)

Arriving home in mid-1963, too late to be considered for a series in the fall, Williams took the next best thing – a six-episode story arc on NBC's top-rated *Bonanza*. He played Will Cartwright, nephew of Ponderosa owner Ben.

A new Cartwright was being introduced in response to co-star Pernell Roberts' demands for a raise. With a new young Cartwright available, NBC hoped that Roberts would back down. The plan devised by the producers and NBC: If all went wrong in negotiations with Roberts, Williams would stay with the series and receive second billing, as Roberts had, under Lorne Greene. Williams said, "I needed a job, to get into something highly visible, and *Bonanza* did just that." (GW-SL87)

The experience turned out to be anything but pleasant.

Kathie Browne and Guy Williams, new additions to the cast of *Bonanza* in the spring of 1964, and intended to return in the fall (NBC-TV, 1964).

Roberts suspected that the producers had brought Williams in to throw a scare into him. And Landon and Blocker saw the new kid (or man) on the show as anything but a welcome guest, since he stood to have a bigger place in the series than they did. Williams said, "I realized I was being used, and I didn't get any help from the other actors, because if Roberts left, they would take up the slack. The whole session was very negative for me." (GW-SL87)

Roberts signed on for another year of *Bonanza* and Williams' character got married and hit the road, riding off into the sunset with guest star Kathie Browne.

Then Irwin Allen's office called. Interviewed by Joan E. Vadeboncoeur in 1965, Williams said that his youthful looks almost prevented him from being cast in *Lost in Space*. He explained, "I don't look 45 and the character was, and I didn't want to use age makeup. I told them I'll get there soon enough without it." (GW-SHA65)

At this time, Williams was thirty-nine. But age was not the only concern voiced by CBS regarding the casting of Williams as John Robinson.

Kevin Burns said, "Only Guy Williams had to do a screen test. At least, we've found no evidence that any of the others did. I did find a memo and remember reading that CBS did not want Guy Williams because they didn't think he looked like an astronaut – because astronauts up to that point were all Anglo-Saxon, blonde jet pilots who looked like Neil Armstrong and John Glenn. And they wanted somebody with that look. That's why they were thinking Eddie Albert, with the brush cut. They wanted someone kind of Nordic. So when Irwin wanted Guy Williams, they thought of him as Zorro. 'He's a Latino, isn't he?' They didn't think of him as Italian. Regarding his look, they literally used the word 'swarthy.' And they used as an excuse, 'He's too young.' Well, he wasn't really too young." (KB-AI16)

This brought about the notorious screen test of Williams, directed by Allen, who, off camera, conversed with the actor. Two versions of the test can be seen as bonus features on the 50th Anniversary Blu-ray release of *Lost in Space*. At least one of these can also be viewed online. The third take has never been located. That was the "keeper" – the one sent to CBS.

Viewing the two versions that have survived, one might think them curiously odd. Williams wears makeup so to appear slightly older, and the banter between him and

Allen feels artificial. Allen appeared to be fishing for just the right answers and reactions to the questions he asked and observations he made. He was actually coaching Williams.

Kevin Burns explained, "So Irwin does this test, literally days before they started shooting the pilot, because CBS probably required that he do it. And they put this kind of white stuff in Guy's hair. And they have him smoking, because at that time they didn't know they were going to be on at 7:30 and were probably thinking that the big network sponsors were cigarette companies. So, in each of the two takes they did that we have found, Irwin says to Guy, 'By the way, you can smoke if you want.' Well, that was all deliberate. And even Irwin saying, 'By the way, there's Richard Basehart. Oh, Richard, hello. Oh, and over there's David Hedison. Hello, David.' Well, that was all contrived, because they weren't there. But June is there. So when Irwin says, 'Have you ever worked with June Lockhart?,' Guy smiles and says, 'No.' But judging from the giggles in the room, everyone else acts like this fix is in. Guy Williams *will* play John Robinson.

"Also, Irwin was so clever. He knew how to play the CBS execs. After he deliberately drops the names of Richard Basehart and David Hedison, he mentions that it had been a 'Merry Christmas' for them – because it was right after Christmastime; this was done in the first days of January, and what he's basically telling CBS is, 'I have a hit show on, starring Richard Basehart and David Hedison, so I know what I'm doing.' And also he's getting in the profile – getting Guy to look this way to say hello to Richard, who of course isn't there, and then the other way, to say hello to David, who of course also isn't there. So he's doing a screen test but also getting a subtle dig at CBS by plugging his ABC show.

"By the way, the third take is missing from the vault, and that would be the one they shipped to CBS. So we see the two false takes – rehearsals, if you will.

"The other funny thing about this – and I did not know this until Mancow Muller in Chicago told me – but Irwin saying, 'Have you read any good books lately?,' and Guy answering, '*Only You, Dick Daring*,' followed by Irwin saying, 'You're not supposed to say that!' – was also an in-joke. *Only You, Dick Daring* was an infamous book at the time about how a writer got screwed over by CBS. And, by Guy saying that, it was such a dig. It's great stuff. That screen test has so much story in it, because it was Irwin's way of saying. 'I want Guy Williams' – which I give him credit for, for hiring somebody who didn't look like the prototypical astronaut, and to hire somebody who looked like, quote, unquote, 'an ethnic.' But he wanted Guy because of Guy's onscreen heroism. He wanted the dad to be a hero; to be a kid's hero. And that, I think, was a very smart choice, which went up against the networks' conventional casting from this era.

"But the grey in the hair, and the 'How old is your kid?,' to which Guy says, 'He's twelve,' and Irwin says, 'Can he be older?,' then 'Ah, he's fourteen,' then 'He's eighteen, isn't he?' 'Oh yes, he's eighteen' – I mean, it's hysterical. And it's all contrived." (KB-AI16)

The screen test was just a formality. Allen was going to have Williams in his pilot.

Interviewed in 1987 for *Starlog* magazine, Williams said, "I wasn't taken with the script; it was typical TV. If I had been asked to do *Richard III*, that would have been a surprise, but to go into *Lost in Space* after having done *Zorro*, it was just standard TV subject matter." (GW-SL87)

Nonetheless, Williams signed on the dotted line.

***

The deals with the cast were set one day before the pilot episode began filming. Cliff Gould wrote to Irwin Allen on January 5, 1965:

> Here is the information you requested regarding deals on the actors for your pilot LOST IN SPACE.
>
> GUY WILLIAMS: His salary for the pilot is to be $3,500 for 12 days services. When the series sells he will receive $2,000 per 7 day episode. He is guaranteed 13 out of 13 episodes produced. Mr. Williams' billing will be first position on a separate card.
>
> JUNE LOCKHART: She is to be paid $2,000 for 10 days work on the pilot, pro rata at 1/10th thereafter. When the series sells she will receive $1,500 per 7 day episode. She is guaranteed 13 out of 13 episodes produced. Miss Lockhart is to receive co-star billing in second position.
>
> MARK GODDARD: For the pilot, he is to receive $1,750 for 12 days services. When the series sells he will receive $1,250 per 7 day episode. He is guaranteed 13 out of 13 episodes produced. Mr. Goddard is to receive co-star billing in either 3rd position or last position as a separate card.
>
> MARTA KRISTEN: She will receive $1,500 for the pilot for 12 days services. When the series sells she will receive $850 per 7 day episode. She is guaranteed 13 out of 13 episodes produced. Miss Kristen is to receive co-star or also starring billing at our discretion.
>
> BILLY MUMY: His salary for the pilot is to be $1,500 for 12 days services. When the series sells he will receive $1,000 per 6 day episode. He is guaranteed 13 out of 13 episodes produced. Billy is to receive co-star billing in not less than fifth position; with the further provision that no other actor, with the exception of the star of the series or guest star, may receive larger size of type.
>
> ANGELA CARTWRIGHT: Her salary is to be $1,250 for 12 days services for the pilot. When the series sells she will receive $850 per 7 day episode, and is guaranteed 13 out of 13 episodes produced. Angela is to receive featured billing, the size and placement of which shall be in our discretion.

The following morning, Allen assembled his cast and introduced them to his distinctive ways of calling for "Action!" A hammer banging off a metal bucket; a pistol shot; and *Lost in Space* was launched.

Next stop: October 16, 1997.

7

"No Place to Hide"

Teleplay by Shimon Wincelberg and Irwin Allen; story by Irwin Allen.
Directed and produced by Irwin Allen.

THIRD REVISED
SHOOTING FINAL

LOST IN SPACE

SERIES

"NO PLACE TO HIDE"

SEGMENT NO. 7

AN IRWIN ALLEN PRODUCTION
IN ASSOCIATION WITH
VAN BERNARD PRODUCTIONS
AND
TWENTIETH CENTURY-FOX TELEVISION, INC.

DECEMBER 15, 1964

Script:

Shimon Wincelberg's 1st and 2nd draft teleplays: Early to mid-November 1964.
Irwin Allen's Shooting Final teleplay: November 11.
Allen's Revised Shooting Final teleplays: Late-November 1964.
Allen's 2nd Revised Shooting Final teleplay: Early December 1964.
Third Revised Shooting Final: December 15, 1964.
Fourth Revised Shooting Final: December 28, 1964.
Fifth Revised Shooting Final: January 6, 1965.
Page revisions, for post-production work (pink and blue paper): January 26, 1965.

Shimon Wincelberg was 39. He had written numerous short stories before moving to the West Coast to break into movies. His first job as a screenwriter was for the 1953 war film *Fighter Attack*, starring Sterling Hayden. In 1956, he did the final rewriting on the low-budget jet-age pseudo-sci-fi, *On the Threshold of Space* (primarily about jet test pilots). Next, he moved into writing for TV, including 24 episodes of *Have Gun – Will Travel*, and six for the gritty hour-long cop show *Naked City*. Then he was tapped by Allen to write the first and second draft teleplays for "Space Family Robinson."

When asked by Kevin Burns in 1995 to tell the story of being hired for the *Lost in Space* pilot, Wincelberg said, "I assume Irwin read my credits. Also, *The Best American Short Stories* [an anthology] came out that year, and that had something to do with it, with my story 'American Soldier in Japan.' But, mainly, I think he hired me based on his own intuition after meeting with me and talking to me about the so-called 'bible' he had prepared for the show."

Marta Kristen, Shimon Wincelberg and Guy Williams during filming of the pilot, January 1965 (photo courtesy Bryna Kranzler).

Memories play tricks. Wincelberg indeed had a story in this anthology, but it was in 1953, and was called "The Conqueror." A one-act play of the same name, by Wincelberg, was included in a 1954 book. In the 1959 *International Year Book*, "Kataki," by Shimon Wincelberg, was a two-character *tour de force* about a Japanese soldier and an American soldier on a Pacific island.

Regarding the material handed off to him by Allen, Wincelberg said, "I think a lot of thought had gone into it on Irwin's part, and he had written a great deal about the characters, about the background that he wanted, about the kind of feeling that he wanted the series to have. He had done a lot of research, and he had written a general outline, so my job mainly was just to get some kind of a human story going." (SW-KB95)

Irwin Allen ignored Guy della-Cioppa's suggestion that the pilot script be fashioned as if it were a typical episode, with a montage sequence establishing the backstory, showing how the Robinson family and Donald West were sent into space, then came to be shipwrecked on an alien world. From there, this sample story was to center around one adventure which could be the fifth, or tenth, or twentieth episode in the series.

Instead, after the crash landing, Allen had Shimon Wincelberg write a multifaceted journey highlighted with numerous high concept adventures, beginning with the castaways abandoning the spaceship and embarking on a journey in the Chariot, encountering a Cyclops giant, then the ruins of an ancient city, then crossing a stormy sea, and finally setting foot in a tropical forest where they were spied on by advanced alien beings. The scripted blueprint made for a massive undertaking in production and left the viewer with no real sense of what would follow, or whether the castaways would even return to their wrecked spaceship.

In the script, "Dr. Donald West" was described as "a brilliant, all-round scientist," serving as a young assistant for "Dr. John Robinson," an "American nuclear physicist." The wife now had a name – Dr. Maureen Robinson, and she was a "distinguished biochemist." The oldest daughter had been given a name, too – "Judith." She was 19. The younger children were "Billy" and Penny.

The real challenge for Wincelberg was to breathe life into the characters. He said, "Irwin had the Robinson family thoroughly worked out. He had written a bible listing the characters, their names and backgrounds. To me, the characters were very bland and very much alike, and there was *no* real source for conflict. If I had invented the whole thing from the beginning, I would have had much greater contrast among the characters… greater potential for conflict, inner doubts – all the stuff that writers work with. In a way, it didn't bother me, because action would carry the pilot through."

Among scenes to be removed from the script before filming, Wincelberg said, "You first saw them as characters the audience can identify with. I showed them getting the news that they had been selected for the space flight. I had a sequence where they trained like astronauts, using some stock footage of centrifuges and rocket sleds. Anyway, this was all in the early drafts and got lost in the shuffle." (SW-SL90)

Another cut had to do with a section of dialogue in the Fourth Revised Shooting Final teleplay which never found its way into the filmed pilot. During the campsite scene, after Penny points out to her parents that Don kissed Judy's hand, Maureen says to John: "I do find it hard to think of Judy as anything but a child. She's had so little experience with young men." John says: "Maureen, when we agreed to taking Don with us, we <u>knew</u> that, whether it was now, or a hundred years from now, he and Judy were going to wind up together … in point of plain fact, become the Adam and Eve of any future human race … *(smiles)* … We can't very well, at this stage of the game, ask Judy to look around some more. I'm afraid anyone <u>else</u> she met on this planet would hardly strike us as an improvement."

The giant hummingbird from Allen's original treatment had been replaced by something more affordable – a giant man. It was described as a "huge creature, half-Neanderthal man, half-carnivorous vegetable." Of this, Allen handwrote onto Wincelberg's script: "40 feet tall."

As for working with Allen, Wincelberg said, "He was always excited and enthused. And I vaguely remember that he told me about it as kind of a typical American family adapting to a totally alien environment, something where you know plants could talk to you, where you couldn't even be sure of the gravity under your feet, and I kind of found that exciting. Irwin had this wonderful charm, like a 12-year-old quality, this sense of fun. And he had this total dedication to whatever he was working on at the moment, which made him fun to work with. On the other hand, he also had a need to control everything – to control his writers – and that brought him into conflict with some of us. But the objective was to get the film made, and to get it made as closely to Irwin's vision as possible. And, naturally, he and I didn't always see things the same way, but we worked pretty harmoniously." (SW-KB95)

Wincelberg's daughter, Bryna Kranzler, who was six years old at the time, used to accompany her father to Allen home in Bel Air. She recalled, "My father was Orthodox; couldn't work on Saturdays, so people who wanted to work with him outside of business days had to do so on Sundays. So, for a while, while they were working on *Lost in Space* and probably *Voyage to the Bottom of the Sea*, my father used to go over to Irwin Allen's house on Sundays. What was really nice was Irwin Allen had a pool, and he was warm and friendly to me and allowed me to swim and hang out, and he made something in his home soda fountain for me. I mean, it was a nice set up for a kid, even though he didn't have kids. He was like a big kid, and that's probably why he had a soda fountain in this glass room that led out to the pool. I just thought it was so cool to be able to go somewhere and swim and have ice cream. He was very nice to kids, so it was it was just a very sweet time.

"I vaguely recall he once gave me a model of the submarine from *Voyage to the Bottom of the Sea*, and I have no idea what happened to it. I probably wasn't all that excited about a submarine, but if it had been the Jupiter 2 spaceship, I know I would have kept it!" (BK-AI16)

While Bryna played and ate ice cream, her father and Allen worked. Shimon Wincelberg said, "It was originally called 'Space Family Robinson,' and that was the basis on which he sold it. I had read the *Swiss Family Robinson*, about a family marooned on a desert island, and I assumed a similar structure. But then he couldn't use that title, so he had to come up with something else. And, at that time, I thought *Lost in Space* was not a great title, but, as usual, I turned out to be wrong."

Wincelberg admitted that he knew "very little" about science fiction. He said, "I was not a great reader of science fiction. I didn't see many science fiction movies. I had only two friends that were science fiction writers – Avram Davidson and Ward Moore. So I treated it pretty much like *Little House on the Prairie*. It was a tight family surrounded by a hostile environment. The emphasis was very much on making it a family story. I think the time slot [that CBS had in mind] had something to do with it. Well, I saw the designs that they brought along. What I didn't know how to do was give him dialogue in computer language, which was pretty new at the time. So, I guess other people filled that in for me." (SW-KB95)

Among the notes Irwin Allen sent to Wincelberg:

> P. 3: [I question] the advisability of using milky fluid as means of halting again process (electricity might be better).
>
> P. 3: Determination of Mars as unfit for human habitation is questionable.
>
> P. 4: Mention of dates should be avoided in all scripts, and series is to take place 15 or more years from now.
>
> P. 4: If transmitter is knocked out, are we to assume the computer in ship has been able to decide that Mars is new landing site. Passengers are presumably still "asleep."
>
> P. 4: What is reason for so shattering an impact on Mars?
>
> P. 7: Earth observation scene should come much earlier – perhaps 1st Act should open with Dr. Lessing receiving computer data as to meteor damage & charting course to Mars as best available planet for Rocket to land on. As this scene is now, it drops the whole play. I can't conceive of Dr. Lessing abandoning a chance for investigation, even if assumes the Robinsons are dead.

> P. 8: Bloop must be described.
>
> P. 8: Don's image is not good throughout whole script. Audience must like him. Plus, good "Father, son" type of relationship should be established.
>
> There must be no choice as to whether they can stay in ship for winter or go to equator.
>
> They should not encounter destination.

Wincelberg addressed Allen's notes in his rewrite. His contract required a minimum of two drafts before Allen could take over and do further rewriting. Wincelberg didn't expect many of his original words to survive that process. He said, "I think he just physically needed somebody to write what he considered the first draft, although for me [with all the rewriting] it was the fifth or the tenth draft. And what he didn't realize was that, if you know that you're going to be rewritten, it's very hard to put your best effort into the early drafts, because you know you're just furnishing raw material. But he had, for me, I guess, to feel that he had written the script or that he was at least legally the author of it. And, you know, if you liked the money, you went along with it."

"Going along with it" meant that Wincelberg knew going in that he would not be given a co-creator credit, even though he would be doing the lion's share of the writing. He said of Allen, "I think it was really a matter of his need of authorship. He had the power, and he used the power. And I can't blame him." (SW-KB95)

On December 4, 1964, after reading the Second Revised Shooting Final teleplay, Jesse K. Alexander, of CBS Program Practices Department, wrote to Guy della-Cioppa at Van Bernard Productions. Alexander told della-Cioppa:

> As a prospective early evening program, the following are suggested to lessen the horror-picture impact on young viewers:
>
> Page 3, Scene 10 and following: Please display the freezing process causing a body's sudden immobility with perhaps a clouding of the freezing chambers rather than having the actors assume a gruesome frozen attitude, suggestive of staring-eyed death. Perhaps freezing all or most of the characters with closed eyes would decrease the horror of the process.
>
> Page 7, Scene 24: The frozen bodies in the out-of-control spaceship should appear unknowing, rather than impotent. (Closed eyes would probably be the solution.)
>
> Page 14, Scene 56 and following: The GIANT, with horror implicit, should not depart too far from the human if it is to suggest a humanoid vegetable. Judgment or acceptability of the GIANT cannot be made until it is seen in scenes with humans.

Page 28, Scene 113: The FADEOUT should not occur as the child PENNY is menaced by a huge hummingbird. Suggest that ROBINSON appears to aim his laser gun at the animal, to lessen the cliff-hanging aspect of the FADEOUT. The bird itself should not be too horrible.

Page 36, Scene 149: Please delete two mentions of Crescent wrench. Suggest "Number five adjustable wrench" or "Number five socket wrench."

Page 57, Scene 230: Please use restraint in the level and duration of JUDY'S reverberating scream.

Page 59, Scene 246 and following: Restraint is suggested in the scene of the menacing GIANT.

Page 61, Scene 262: Restraint is suggested in the GIANT'S screams.

CBS was an old-school network, especially when it came to series intended for the family hour. Children should never be put in peril on the CBS Television Network. And no one on screen should ever say "Boo!" loud enough to frighten the small fries watching at home. Allen had encountered less waves from the ABC censors over *Voyage to the Bottom of the Sea*, but there were no children in that series. CBS, as Allen and his staff would soon learn, intended to hold the reins tighter on *Lost in Space*.

Pre-Production:

On December 2, 1964, with Allen's Shooting Final teleplay as a guide, the estimated budget for the *Lost in Space* pilot came in at $392,142. A collective gasp could be heard from various executive's offices across the 20th Century-Fox lot. This price equates to over three million dollars in 2015. Other than the pilot for *Voyage to the Bottom of the Sea* for ABC, no studio or network up to this time had ever paid as much. And the estimate would have been much higher, had the decision not been made to film in black and white.

Shimon Wincelberg told interviewer Flint Mitchell, "I was trying to persuade Irwin Allen to shoot it in color, and, in those days, you know, color TV seemed a long way into the future. And what it came down to was Irwin wanted to shoot it in color, but the studio said, 'If you want to do it, you have to pay for it yourself.' And it would have meant an extra $30,000-$40,000 out of his pocket." (SW-LISF6)

Allen decided he could do without color. Regardless, the footage filmed on location of the crash of the spaceship, and the journeys of the Chariot, would be lensed in color, just in case the series should sell, and these scenes could be used for stock footage.

William Self's office worked with Allen's people and the various Fox production departments to cut costs. By December 21, they'd chipped away enough to have a projected budget of $359,226. This, however, did not include the building of the interior and exterior of the full-size Gemini 12 spacecraft. That would cost almost as much as everything else combined, and therefore be amortized over the run of the series – provided there was a series.

For the pilot, Allen was joined by several longtime associates, including Art Director William Creber, who, at 33, had been serving as art director on *Voyage to the Bottom of the Sea*. He would work in the same capacity on the 1965 epic *The Greatest Story Ever Told*, a co-venture between United Artists and 20th Century-Fox, with UA taking North America release and Fox distributing overseas. Creber then returned to Allen's camp for *The Time Tunnel*. Creber also worked on 1968's *Planet of the Apes* and its sequels for Fox.

Paul Zastupnevich, Allen's assistant since 1959 (beginning with *The Big Circus*), would serve *Lost in Space* in the same capacity as he was doing on *Voyage to the Bottom of the Sea* – as costume/monster designer.

Norman Rockett, by surname alone, sounded a perfect choice for this project to serve as set decorator. He was a Fox man, having worked in the same capacity on the studio's TV series *Adventures in Paradise*. He'd decorated the sets on an Irwin Allen production before, with *Five Weeks in a Balloon*. Along with William Creber, as part of a team of six decorators, Rockett shared in an Academy Award nomination for 1965's *The Greatest Story Ever Told.*

Working with Rockett was Walter M. Scott, also assigned to the project by the studio. Scott had worked on all of the studio's TV series prior to this, as well as the first season of *Voyage*. He had other experience with otherworldly set decoration, or, at least, deep in the center of the world set decorating, with *Journey to the Center of the Earth*, and rocket interior sets, with the 1966 Jerry Lewis film *Way … Way Out* (filmed in 1965). He had also decorated sets on the feature film version of *Voyage to the Bottom of the Sea* and Allen's *The Lost World* and *Five Weeks in a Balloon.*

L.B. Abbott, head of 20th Century-Fox's special FX department, would be in charge of filming the spacecraft – its launch, its journey through space, and its crash landing on an alien world.

Oscar-winning Director of Photography Winton Hoch, taking a break from the *Voyage* series, would serve as cinematographer.

Gene Polito would be Hoch's camera operator. Since Hoch was busy working on *Voyage* during *Lost in Space*'s pre-production phase, Polito was also given the task of using his cameraman's eye in helping select locations for filming.

This was an immensely talented group of professionals. Bill Mumy later said, "I think Irwin was a great assembler, with all his projects. He was very, very talented at assembling initial teams – you know, his initial cast, the initial cinematographers, and, perhaps especially, his composers. He really chose well." (BM-AI15)

Earlier in December, the Art Department of 20th Century-Fox, under the direction of Bill Creber, began designing the sets. Jack Martin Smith, who was head of the department, would also be listed in the credits for the pilot.

The earliest drawings for "No Place to Hide" in the 20th Century-Fox archives, dated December 9, 1964, were for "The Enchanted Forest," where, among other sequences in the pilot film, Penny was seen riding a tortoise-like creature and then took a ride with her father and Debbie the chimp, on the back of the Rocket Belt. Also dated December 9 were the preliminary drawings for the Chariot. These were finalized on December 17, then the pressure was on to build the futuristic-looking vehicle in two weeks – to be available for Second Unit location filming in late December, prior to the start of principal photography in early January.

The full-scale Chariot was constructed from a 1964 Thiokol Snowcat "Spryte." 20th Century-Fox had acquired one or more for use in its film *Caprice*, starring Doris Day, which would be released in early 1967, and also benefitted from the services of art director Bill Creber. This model of the Snowcat was eight feet wide, and utilized rubber wheels that ran on the inside of a revolving track of metal cleats. The cab was removed and replaced by a custom structure with a frame of one-inch square steel tubing, designed to withstand the weight of a full-grown man (since the character of Major West would have to climb onto the roof of the vehicle). The frame was encased in clear acrylic sheeting.

Besides the full-size Chariot, two miniatures were constructed. The smallest was built at a one-inch scale, with each inch equal to a foot. This version was planned for long-distance shots of the Chariot caught in a whirlpool on the inland sea. The larger miniature was built at a scale of two-and-one-half-inches to the foot. This was intended for the shot in which the Chariot approaches and enters the water of the inland sea, as well as the scenes with the Giant. Construction of these was given top priority.

Meanwhile, a location for the alien world had to be chosen.

Gene Polito and Bill Creber were dispatched to accompany Second Unit Director Sobey Martin to scout locations for a suitable terrain within a couple hours' drive of Los Angeles. One area considered was Vasquez Rocks, which had been used for numerous westerns and even some science-fiction productions, including *The Outer Limits*' episode "The Zanti Misfits," and, in the near future, *Star Trek*'s "Arena," among others.

Another location the three men wanted to look over was a section of Red Rock Canyon, near Death Valley, on the state line of California and Nevada.

Polito told interviewer Flint Mitchell, "[W]hen we were up in the Mojave desert area, one night over dinner, Bill said, 'You know, I know a place that I scouted for [the movie] *The Greatest Story Ever Told* for [director] George Stevens that we never used, called the Trona Pinnacles.' And he said, 'Really a bizarre looking place; it almost looks like a lunar landscape.' … So, we took off and went to look at it, and when I saw it, I said, 'Wow, this is fantastic!'"

The Trona Pinnacles are ten miles south of the town of Trona, California, 170 miles northeast of Los Angeles. This was about a five-hour drive from the Fox studio in an era before freeways crisscrossed Southern California. Worse, the only way to access the Pinnacles was via a dirt road that would often be closed during winter months due to rain. Despite this, Creber and Polito felt the trip would be worth it. The unusual landscape consisted of more than 500 tufa spires, some as tall as 140 feet, rising from a dry lake bed.

Polito recalled, "[W]hen we got back to the motel, we told [Sobey Martin] – because the director at the time didn't particularly want to go out there – what a fantastic location it was. So, based on my recommendation and the art director's, we had a whole change of plans, which were really substantial, because it involved about a sixty-mile extra-long drive for the whole cast and crew to an area that the production people weren't prepared for. And they had to call Irwin Allen to get his permission. And Irwin said, 'Well, you know, if Gene recommended it and Bill Creber recommended it, I'll go along with it, But, by God, if it isn't everything that they say it is, I'm going to have their heads.'" (GP-LISF5)

On December 8, Allen and six others took a Western Airlines flight from Los Angeles to Las Vegas, Nevada, where they spent the night at the Tropicana Hotel. The following morning, using a pair of Hertz rent-a-cars, all in the party except for Allen drove to Death Valley, then out to the Trona Pinnacles. Among the six to make the journey by car were director Sobey Martin, Bill Creber, and, with a film camera for taking test shots, Gene Polito. Allen found a better way to get to the Trona Pinnacles.

Poltio remembered, "On the first morning we were out to this location, here comes a helicopter flying in, and, lo and behold, it was Irwin Allen. And he got out and came on over to where we had the camera set up. So, I said, 'Well, what do you think, Irwin?' And he said, 'Well, this is really fantastic. This is terrific.' So, he stuck around for a while, then he climbed back in the helicopter, wished us luck, and he took off." (GP-LISF5)

The decision was made to film the crash of the Gemini 12 at Red Rock Canyon, as well as sequences with doubles for Guy Williams and Mark Goddard, wearing Parkas with the hoods over their heads, scaling the side of a rocky formation; a double for Billy Mumy, with back to camera, firing a laser gun at the Cyclops giant; and footage of the Rocket Belt in use. The travels of the Chariot would be filmed in the expansive valley with the Trona Pinnacles, as well as spectacular aerial footage taken from a helicopter.

Later in the day, the group drove back to Las Vegas. That evening, rejoined by Allen, the seven took a TWA flight to Los Angeles.

At this location, Second Unit filming was scheduled to begin in eighteen days.

Production Diary:

(December 28-31, 1964, and January 6-27, 1965; total of 20 days)

On December 27, at six in the morning, a caravan of cars and trucks, with a company of thirty personnel, left 20th Century-Fox studios in West Los Angeles for the five-hour drive to Mojave, California. The vehicles included vans to carry camera equipment, grip equipment, props, wardrobe, and the needed miniatures (one of a G.I. Joe-sized male doll strapped to a mini rocket belt, as well as the four-foot model of the Gemini 12). Also among the convoy: a flatbed to carry the full-size Chariot, a truck designated entirely for the Rocket Belt and its hazardous fuel, a Honey Wagon, a bus, and a limo-like expanded car. Among the thirty in the party: Irwin Allen and Bill Creber (who would only stay for one day before returning to Fox to resume work on the *Voyage* series); Sobey Martin; Gene Polito; photo effects supervisor Howard Lydecker, as well as his brother and colleague, Theodore; former ball player turned actor/stuntman Lamar Lundy (to play the Giant); a group of six "photo doubles"; two Rocket Belt engineers and a Rocket Belt pilot; two camera operators; two assistant camera operators; a stills photographer; members of the lighting crew (a "Key Grip" and a "2nd Grip"); an electrician; two property masters; a wardrobe man and woman; a landscape man; two prop makers; two craft service men; a script supervisor; and a First Aid man.

The unit headquarters, as well as the accommodations for the twenty-eight who remained until December 31, were provided by White's One Stop Service Station, Café and Motor Inn, in Mojave, California. According to the inn's brochure at the time, the guests were treated to "ultra modern cabins, individual units, garages, carpeted floors," and dined where "good eats are our specialty!"

Gordon Yaeger and Bill Suitor were the two Bell Systems "Rocket Belt" pilots on location at the Trona Pinnacles.

The jet pack used in the pilot (both on location and later at the studio), was not a special effects prop. It was the real McCoy.

In 1959, Aerojet General Corporation won a U.S. Army contract to devise a jet pack. In 1960, the Bell "Rocket Belt" was introduced. To propel it and its sole operator upward, a jet of gas was provided by a hydrogen peroxide-powered rocket. In *Thunderball* (filmed in 1964, for 1965 release), James Bond used a jet pack in the pre-title sequence. That pack was piloted by Gordon Yaeger and, for additional shots, Bill Suitor. Now, the same pack was used for *Lost in Space*, this time withSuitor doing all the flying on location, standing in for Guy Williams.

Regarding the crash landing of the spaceship, L.B. Abbott recounted, "When we filmed the scene where the Jupiter 2 is in flight over the mountains, we took the four-foot miniature to the Red Rock Canyon and to Trona and flew it on a two-wire system which had two shivs forward and aft, and port and starboard. Gravity was the motivating force. The wires [were] painted to blend in with the background." (LBA-LISF)

Next came the giant Cyclops. Paul Zastupnevich said, "The most fabulous monster that I did was the one-eyed Cyclops in *Lost in Space*, and that was made out of palm tree bark! I was walking along the street at Fox and they were trimming the palm trees, and I happened to bend over and pick up part of the bark that had come off, and I played with it and I said. 'Gee, this looks so strange and so foreign; it would make a wonderful costume.' So, I went back to my office and I took a hammer and I pounded it, and made it very flexible, then I sprayed it with some fire retardant and found that it even got softer. I found out there were about three truckloads of palm leaves that they had just gathered up, so I had them take it down to the staff shop and just drop it off. I had the paint department process it and fire proof it, and then we got it back up to wardrobe and we sewed it over a diver's suit, and we made the cyclops outfit out of that." (PZ-KB95)

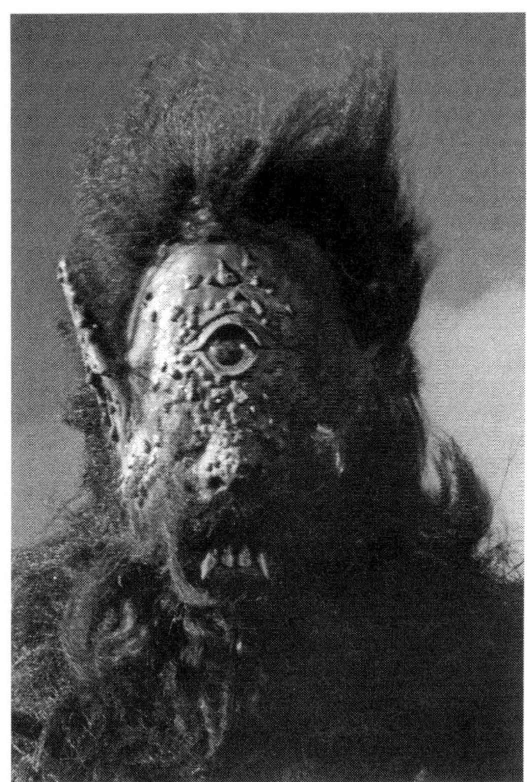

Two men took turns playing the giant Cyclops – Los Angeles Rams defensive end Lamar Lundy (above) and movie extra Robert "Big Buck" Maffei (below).

Zastupnevich told syndicated columnist Charles Witbeck, for an April 1966 article, "You can easily get carried away on some of these projects, but you have to think about the actor inside. He must be able to see and breathe.... [Lamar] Lundy was a splendid choice." (PZ-WDN66)

Lundy, standing six feet, six inches tall, was well-known as having been a member of the "Fearsome Foursome" defensive line for the Los Angeles Rams in the 1960s. The other three were Merlin Olsen, Deacon Jones and Roosevelt Grier. Each went on to have a successful acting career. Lundy tried too, but he had only this sequence, later included in the episode "There Were Giants in the Earth," to show for his efforts.

Irwin Allen told *New York Journal-American* writer Frank Judge, "We took the six-foot-six-inch Lundy, padded him all up, wrapped the bark of a couple dozen palm trees around him, and gave him a single huge eye. He made a fine giant. Just the sort of thing you'd expect to scare the wits out of you on some strange planet." (IA-NYJA65)

Lundy was actually one of two men who took turns wearing the costume for the giant Cyclopes. The other was Robert "Big Buck" Maffei. He revealed, "I did the scene where the Cyclops was throwing a rock at the chariot. The scenes on location were done with Lamar Lundy. What they had done was they stood me up high. But Lamar did most of the action scenes in a place in California where it was 130 degrees in the shade!"

For his turn in the suit, Maffei disclosed, "They installed a zipper in the back of [the costume], and I slipped into it from my neck down to where my buttocks starts. That's where the zipper was put. I had to stand there in the costume shop while they put this palm leaf stuff on me.... I did the original dress-up – all the makeup, body, the mask, and everything. I also did a couple scenes shot out on location. Then Lamar Lundy took my place. I wouldn't do the falls or the stunts. I'm a motion picture actor, not a stuntman.... [T]hey had to make a padded suit for Lamar because he wasn't as big as me. I'm huge! I am seven feet tall and weigh over four hundred pounds."

Maffei added bitterly, "I never got credit for the *Lost in Space*. It seems that Irwin Allen and I had a little 'talk' and we had a little problem. I think I was paid close to $1,000 for the part, but I'm not sure because of what they call day pay – that's how bit parts get paid. It was a pain in the neck!" (RM-LISF)

The Second Unit production days were Monday through Thursday, December 28, 29, 30 and 31. The company made the drive back to Los Angeles in the late afternoon and evening hours on New Year's Eve.

***

On January 4, 1965, Irwin Allen sent an open letter to his department heads:

> BLAST-OFF! All systems are Go-Go-Go! for the blasting off of the *Lost in Space* Pilot ... Wednesday, January 6, 1965.
>
> I thank you all most warmly for efforts above and beyond the call of duty for making this deep thrust into outer space possible.
>
> I urgently request that you carefully examine the attached shooting schedule and that you call me to-day to answer any questions or solve any problems that you and your department might have regarding the meeting of these dates.
>
> HOLD THE BUDGET LINE! See you in outer space!

Allen joyfully directed the pilot with the support of a company of seasoned Fox artists and technicians, and a dream cast.

Dream cast member June Lockhart said, "Preparation for the pilot was a joy. I had met Paul Zastupnevich, our costume designer, on *Voyage*, of course. He was Irwin's right hand man. Paul was largely responsible for the overall look of the show – the color, the silver look, all the costume designs, the wardrobe of villains and the heroes, the aliens and monsters. He was one of Irwin's greatest assets and was never lauded as he should have been." (JL-LISM)

Mark Goddard admitted, "The day that I went to wardrobe and they put the silver lamé spacesuit on me, I think I cried. … My then-wife put her head on my shoulder and said, 'It's gonna be OK,' but I said, 'I don't know if I can do this!' She said, 'Yes, you can; yes you can!' So, I said to myself, 'Yes, I can; yes, I can!' I had realized that it was *not* going to be an acting challenge. It would be physical, and I wouldn't be getting the kind of direction that I wanted. I wouldn't be getting my teeth into the material that had to do with [real] things, into the reality of emotional stuff. I just knew it had to do with outer space and things that would be hard for me to relate to." (MG-SL93)

January 6, 1965: The first day of principal photography, outside the shipwrecked Gemini 12. Above: Billy Mumy chases an ostrich toward June Lockhart and Marta Kristen. Below: Mark Goddard and Guy Williams with Mumy, Kristen, Lockhart and unnamed crew member.

Day 1, Wednesday, January 6. The first day location was Fox Stage 15, for the "Ext. Spaceship & Camp" set, as well as "Int. Spaceship at Camp."

Concerning that spaceship, the Robinsons' flying saucer-like craft was called "Gemini 12" in this unaired pilot. When the show went to series, the ship was renamed Jupiter 2, partly to avoid any confusion with NASA's actual Gemini space program.

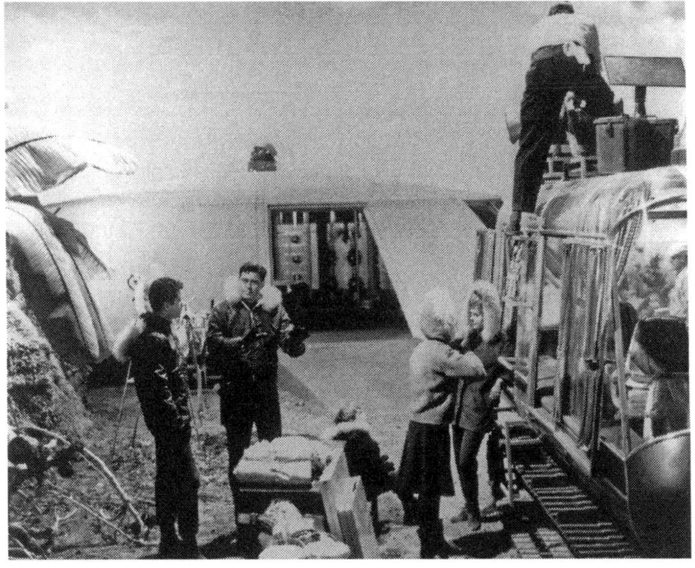

Gemini 12 was a single-deck flying saucer spacecraft. There were no seats for the pilot, very few controls at the front of the craft, and no elevator. The crew of six rode out the journey in suspended animation freezing tubes.

All six principals – Williams, Lockhart,

Above: Work continues on first day of principal photography. Below: Allen (left) gives direction to Cartwright, with Debbie the Bloop on a mechanical tortoise.

Goddard, Kristen, Mumy and Cartwright – were present, along with four ostriches, a chimp named Debbie, and the Chariot.

Marta Kristen confessed, "When I first walked on that set – the spaceship – it just blew my socks off. I couldn't believe that I was part of this. I think it was an experiment in television, because it hadn't been done before. It was an amazing set for a TV show. Apparently, we borrowed from all over the studio. And the cast was so impressive. I think I was awestruck. And starstruck, too, because of June and Guy. Guy Williams! *Zorro* was my favorite show. And Angela from *The Danny Thomas Show*, and she had done *Sound of Music*. And I'd worked with Billy in *Alfred Hitchcock Presents*. I would drive to the studio and I would think to myself, 'I'm a girl from the orphanage, and I am driving to 20th Century-Fox and I'm doing a television series!" (MK-AI15)

Also awestruck over being in the company with the man who had played Zorro, Billy Mumy said, "At first it was a thrill. But then, it was just a pleasure working with Guy.... I loved [the scenes featuring] the father and son talks we would have. He was so good at it." (BM-LISBR15)

Mark Goddard was also impressed, later saying, "Guy was great. He was a

star." (MG-LISBR15)

Day 3: Friday, January 8, 1965. Above: June Williams with Irwin Allen on Stage 15. Below: filming inside the Gemini 12.

Guy Williams understood from the first day what the greatest challenge would be in filming *Lost in Space*. He said, "The main idea of *Lost in Space* was the special effects. Irwin is great at them, and our struggle was to stay away from all the flashing equipment when we were doing our scenes. They would stick us in front of equipment that was whizzing or whirring, and I knew that the audience would watch the machine. So, we moved to the left or the right, and the camera would hopefully follow, and we would get away from the machine." (GW-SL87)

The plan was to finish the pilot in twelve days. The late start, however, gave indication that the goal was not likely to be achieved. Allen took his first shot at 8:05 a.m. on this day, and completed his last at 6:45 p.m., a half-day behind schedule.

Day 2, Thursday, January 7. It was another full day on Stage 15 and the "Int./Ext. Spaceship at Camp" set, with all principals and animals returning.

Allen's secretary, Lili Glinski Woodfield, said, "I remember when we were shooting the pilot, and it was early on, and there was this scene where Billy Mumy is supposed to be chasing this ostrich. Now, this ostrich was a big, mean, wild bird, and I said either to Billy Mumy or his mother, 'My God, I wouldn't get anywhere near that bird.' The next thing you know, Irwin is screaming, 'What do you mean Billy refuses to do the scene with the bird?! Who the hell was it who scared Billy Mumy?!' So, I had to just stand there with this expression on my face of, 'Who would do such a thing?!'" (LGW-LISF)

Mumy concurred, "The ostriches were awful… and they were just kicking and spitting at everybody. I hated them!... Don't ever work with ostriches!" (BM-LISW)

Allen shot from half-past-eight in the morning until half-past-six in the evening with

Day 4, January 11: Alpha Control Communications Center.

ostriches kicking and spitting. Most of the footage ended up being cut. When Allen stopped, he was three-quarters of a day behind. They blamed it on the ostriches, which is one reason why the big birds didn't carry over to the series.

Day 3, Friday, January 8. Filming started at 8:05, still outside the spaceship in the campsite area, with all principals and animals. By midday, Allen had taken his last shot outside the spaceship and moved inside for the scenes that show the launch pad through the front windows, then shots of the frozen principals as the spaceship dove into the atmosphere of an alien world. Wrap time came at 7 p.m.

Day 4, Monday, January 11. The location was the "Int. Underground Communications Center" set. It was not on a soundstage but was instead inside the Construction Department building on the Fox lot, in a large storage area with stairs leading up to a mezzanine level. The storage in this area was cleared out; the area then draped and outfitted with state-of-the-art computer equipment and three large view-screens.

Regarding the impressive Alpha Control set, Shimon Wincelberg revealed, "That [scene] was added later. I didn't write that. It may have been CBS' idea, to add scope. I think JPL [Jet Propulsion Laboratory] had this type of control room. Irwin also added some narration, which I wasn't too happy with." (SW-SL90)

Wincelberg had written a montage of scenes intended to give color to the characters, and assigned them distinctive personality traits. Allen replaced all of that with a page-and-a-half of narration for Dick Tufeld to read, including:

> The "space family" selected from more than two million volunteers for its unique balance of scientific achievement, emotional stability, and pioneer resourcefulness, will spend the ninety-eight years of their voyage frozen into a state of suspended animation, due to terminate automatically as the space craft enters the atmosphere of another planet.... Heading the expedition will be Doctor John Robinson, Professor of Astrophysics at the University of Stellar Dynamics, now seen on your screen. With him, marking the first time in history that anyone but an adult male has passed the International Space Administration's grueling

physical and emotional screening for intergalactic flight, will be his wife, Doctor Maureen Robinson, the distinguished biochemist of the New Mexico College of Space Medicine; their daughter, Judith, age nineteen, who has rather heroically postponed all hope for a career in the musical comedy field for the next two centuries, at least. Their son, Will, who recently was graduated from the Camdoe Canyon School of Science at the age of nine, with the highest average in the school's history. And their daughter Penny, age eleven: I.Q., 147; hobby, zoology. Their assistant, Doctor Donald West, graduate student at the Center for Radio Astronomy, is the same young man who, last year, rocked the scientific world with his theory regarding other planets' fitness for human habitation.

Costume designer Paul Zastupnevich (second from right) has a cameo.

To Allen's thinking, this was enough background information on the characters. They were highly educated, immensely qualified, and admirably heroic. What more could anyone want to know?

All principals, whose characters were written more for posing than emoting, were present, as well as seven other actors, including Allen's old friend, Don Forbes, as the TV commentator, and numerous extras.

Forbes was 53. He was an actor who often portrayed announcers in movies, probably because he was an announcer who also acted … or, at least, acted like an announcer. He played the part of an "Assistant Announcer" in a movie in which Irwin Allen served as associate producer, *A Girl in Every Port*. Allen had him do similar roles for *The Big Circus*, *The Lost World* and *Voyage to the Bottom of the Sea*.

Although the call time was 7 a.m., it took a great deal of effort to get everyone in place and block the first shot. The camera began its roll at 9:30 a.m., establishing the giant room filled with technicians, military personnel, and members of the press. One of those representatives of the press – the goateed man who is the third in the line of foreign reporters seated at the long table, speaking in numerous languages as they call in their reports – was Paul Zastupnevich.

Allen took his last shot at 7:15 p.m., finishing all the work needed for this location. Alpha Control was dismantled and turned back into a storage facility the following morning.

Day 5, Tuesday, January 12. It started at the outdoor moat location, for the "Enchanted Forest and Beach" set. This area of the Fox backlot was an 18-acre parcel (later to become part of Century City when, after massively overspending on the feature film *Cleopatra*, the studio was forced to sell most of its property).

Day 5: At the outdoor "Moat" location, Debbie the Bloop and Angela Cartwright piggyback on Guy Williams and his rocket belt. Note that Williams stands on a crane which will lift all three into the air. Below: footprints of a giant.

The moat and the surrounding cliff areas had been seen in the 1959 film *Journey to the Center of the Earth.* The cliffs could be tarped over, allowing the lighting to be controlled. This allowed the rock walls to appear deep underground when necessary. The giant mushrooms seen in the pilot, along with stalactites and stalagmites, had been created for *Journey to the Center of the Earth*. The moat was also often featured in *Voyage to the Bottom of the Sea*.

Filmed here: the Chariot approaching and exiting the inland sea (accomplished with the 24-inch miniature); Penny's ride on the tortoise (which was mechanical, not alive); and John Robinson, strapped into the Rocket Belt, landing in the area, then having Penny and the Bloop climb onto his back for the aerial trip back to the Gemini 12. This liftoff sequence was accomplished by having Guy Williams, Angela Cartwright, and Debbie the chimp stand on a camera crane, and then be lifted into the air. The wider shots, with Bill Suitor flying the Rocket Belt, with lightweight dummies representing Penny and the chimp, had been filmed earlier at Trona Pinnacles and Red Rock Canyon.

Day 6, Wednesday, January 13. A different part of Stage 15 was used on this day, providing for the "Ext. Plateau" and "Ext Foothills" sets.

The top of the plateau where John and Don discover the giant footprint near their weather station was actually just alongside the Gemini 12. Careful positioning of the camera, and set dressing, including repositioning of the large rocks, helped create the illusion of a far-off region.

Above: Allen with Lockhart and Williams. The large Ritter fan on the platform behind them is used to create wind effects during filming. Below: A "Ladies Wardrobe" test for Debbie.

All principals were present on this day, as with all the days of Main Unit production. After blocking and rehearsal, Allen started the camera roll at 9:10 a.m. In the late morning, even though there was still more work to complete on the existing sets, the company moved a short distance on Stage 15 to film the "Von Trump Villa," with Ford Rainey as the President of the United States.

Rainey was 57. He had also played a future President of the United States for Irwin Allen in a pair of episodes from *Voyage to the Bottom of the Sea* ("Hot Line" and "Doomsday"). Allen would have him play a different President of the U.S., Abraham Lincoln, in *The Time Tunnel*. Rainey appeared close to 200 times on TV and in films, and had a recurring role (as a character named Jim Elgin) in various episodes of *The Six Million Dollar Man* and *The Bionic Woman*. Now he was here to act presidential again on *Lost in Space*.

Stage 15 was an immense area – big enough to house the Gemini 12 (interior and exterior, surrounded by the campsite area, and enough sandy floor space to pass for other areas on the planet), then, immediately to the right, the stage also contained the interior of the von Trapp Villa. It had been built the previous year for filming of *The Sound of Music*, and was also where Guy Williams had posed for his *Lost in Space* costume tests. At this time, in early January 1965, the set was being used as a hotel interior for the Doris Day movie *Do Not Disturb*. Later, Allen would use it as the grand hall of the Titanic in the pilot for *The Time Tunnel*.

Next to this enclosed set, on the left side of the stage, was another large set – the Cave Tomb & Corridors, used for the underground ruins of an alien city in the pilot. This set was originally built for *Cleopatra*, although the serpent head columns date back further, originally designed for the 1953 film, *Treasure of*

the Golden Condor.

It was inconvenient for Allen to interrupt filming on the right side of the stage with the sequences needed on the "Ext. Plateau" and "Ext Foothills" sets. But, based on the always changeable shooting schedule, Rainey had been booked today with a 7 a.m. call. He had since cleared makeup and was patiently waiting. Allen moved the camera crew to the von Trapp Villa, which had been pre-lit for "President Rainey" to give a televised speech from the White House. It took three-and-a-half hours to shoot the short sequence. Then, Rainey was released, and the company rolled the camera back stage left, to pick up where they had left off on the "Ext. Plateau/Ext. Foothills" set. Allen completed his final shot at 7 p.m. The production was now one-and-a-half days behind schedule.

Day 8: The "Int. Tomb – Cave" set on Stage 15. Above: Allen demonstrates the high-tech "futuristic" flashlight for Angela Cartwright and Billy Mumy. Below: Movie magic allows the flashlight beam to read as bright. It had to be in order to shine through the hot stage lamps which bathed the set in light.

Day 7, Thursday, January 14. Work resumed on Stage 15, now for the "Int. Crevice on Plateau" and "Int. Courtyard – Cave," as John and Don take sanctuary in a cave and avoid the hand of the Giant. The camera began its roll at 8:30 a.m. Following this, more filming at the "Ext. Spaceship & Campsite" set, with the rest of the principals and the chimp. Allen took his last shot at 6:55 p.m., at which time it was calculated that the production was two full days behind.

Day 8, Friday, January 15. The left third of Stage 15 now provided the underground city ruins, with sets identified as "Int. Corridor – Cave," "Int. Storeroom – Cave," and "Int. Tomb – Cave." All principals were present, including Debbie the chimp. The camera began rolling at 7:40 a.m. Later, with a move back to the "Int./Ext. Crevice on Plateau" set, Allen took some pickup shots. He finished at 6:40 p.m., holding at two days behind.

Day 9, Monday, January 18. Work continued in the underground city, with the interior corridor, storeroom and tomb. Even with a 7 a.m. call time, Allen didn't begin his first shot until 10:05 a.m.

Guy Williams children, son Steven, who had just turned twelve, and daughter Terri, only six at the time, were visiting the set on this day. Steve said, "I remember they were setting up an earthquake scene. They had these neat flashlights, and I think the Chariot was off to the right, so we got to explore the Chariot. They were dropping rocks on people from above – these fake rocks – and people were shaking the walls, and stuff was falling, and it was pretty neat." (GWJ-LISBR15)

Mark Goddard said, "I remember when we had an earthquake scene, which took about five hours to set up. There were phony rocks falling down and cobwebs were in this cave and they had set all this up. We filmed the scene and the camera wasn't going. So they had to start over with the cobwebs and it took about another half day to get that all set up again." (MG-LISF)

Billy Mumy believed the reason the scene had to be staged again was that Guy

Above: The light on the laser gun that caused a second take of the earthquake scene. Below: Director Allen confers with his cast. The woman between Allen and Billy Mumy is likely the social worker assigned by the studio, required on set whenever minors were working.

Williams forgot to turn the light off his laser gun. Therefore, as he was waving it around, he was, in a sense, killing his family. Either way, it resulted in the expenditure of time and money … and patience.

Above: The scream that frightened the CBS censors so much that it never made it onto the air. Below: Allen gives direction to Cartwright, Goddard and Kristen.

June Lockhart recalled, "[W]e were doing an earthquake scene in a cave and we were supposed to be rocking and bouncing left to right all the time, with dust and earth falling on us. Irwin went up to the catwalk with a big metal wastepaper basket and a hammer and every time he wanted us to be jolted, he would bang his hammer on the top of the can. Finally, I made some comment about it to one of the men in the crew, and he turned to me and said, 'This is nothing … he used to use a shotgun!' [sic; it was a starter's pistol]. I also remember that in this scene we were all in there acting our hearts out and finally Irwin yelled 'cut' when the scene was over. Not one word was said about our acting. He got up and shouted, 'The debris was beautiful!'" (JL-LISM)

Allen took his last shot of the beautiful debris at 6:40 p.m. He seemed over the moon, even though he had fallen further behind – now by two-and-a-half days.

Day 10, Tuesday, January 19. The morning hours were spent taking pickup shots at the moat location, and the "Ext. Enchanted Forest" set, plus a new scene – the "Ext. Equatorial Jungle" set (a redress of the enchanted forest). Filming began at 8:10 a.m. They then moved back onto Stage 15 to finish in the "Int. Cave Sets," then over to the "Ext. Night Camp." It was during the set up of this last scene when Allen noticed that Billy Mumy was entertaining himself by playing guitar and singing. Allen suggested that it would be nice if Will Robinson were to serenade his family with a song.

Lockhart said, "He was only just beginning to play the guitar when we made the *Lost in Space* pilot. He could only play one number, and, naturally, it was the theme song from *Lassie*. I thought, 'Oh my God. It's even followed me here." (JL-SL83)

Actually it wasn't the theme to *Lassie*, although the two melodies are similar. "Lassie Main & End Title," as the music was copyrighted by its composer, Les Baxter, was the best known *Lassie* theme and used during the years that Lockhart was a cast member. "Greensleeves," however, is an English folksong dating back to the late 1500s. Since "Greensleeves" was a song in the public domain, it wouldn't cost Allen any money to have it included in his pilot.

Above: Billy Mumy amuses himself on set by playing guitar and singing "Greensleeves" … which would give his director an idea – "Billy, let's put it in the picture!" Below: On Day 10, Mumy makes his singing debut on national television.

Of his performance, Mumy groaned, "I cringe whenever I hear that. I just learned to play the guitar about three months before we did that. [Irwin said], 'Well, we need something in this kind of picnic scene. Billy, why don't you play your guitar?' 'Un, okay.'" (BM-LISW)

Mumy sang his song and Allen took his last shot at 6:50 p.m.

Days 11 and 12, Wednesday, January 20, and Thursday, January 21. Something new on Stage 15: "Ext. Chariot at Giant's Pass," "Ext. Edge of Plateau," "Ext. Country Near Space Camp," "Ext. Scooter in Sky," "Ext. Near Enchanted Forrest," and "Ext. Plateau Near Cave." As usual, all principals were needed, as well as the chimp, the Chariot, and the "scooter." The scooter was actually the rocket pack, worn by Guy

Williams, with him standing on a camera dolly lift which could elevate him up and down, and back and forth, in front of a process screen. The production was three days behind.

Days 13 and 14, Friday, January 22, and Monday, January 25. The company was on Fox Stage 5, for "Int. Chariot on Inland Sea" and "Ext. Chariot on Inland Sea – Roof." All principals and the chimp were present.

The full-size Chariot was positioned in front of a process screen, for rear-view projections. It sat on top of an elaborate rocking device built to safely accommodate the weight of the Chariot and its occupants and move in multiple directions, while being subjected to buckets full of water.

Marta Kristen maintained, "We had a great time filming the pilot. We would laugh and joke. Guy and June were so funny and had great jokes. Mark was a real cut-up; he would tell stories that would make you blush. It was fun, and we would often start giggling because of the long hours and tension of getting it done. 'Time is money, time is money!,' Irwin would say. You can probably see, if you look for it, we'll be holding our lips tight to keep from laughing. One of us will probably bounce a little to hold in the laugh. When we were in the Chariot for the first time, I had to say, 'Don't start the engine, Don!' Every time I would start the line, we would begin giggling, and Irwin would get so upset." (MK-SL88)

Billy Mumy said, "We had so much fun in that Chariot. We were in it for days, as the crew rocked it back and forth. We had a blast!" (BM-AI15)

June Lockhart related, "Shooting the pilot was a treat for the child in me. It was like being in kindergarten and going out in the backyard, playing Space in the sand. We actors enjoyed each other and looked forward to working together for the next few years." (JL-LISM)

Above: Irwin Allen prepares "his stars!" for a spectacular water effect. Below: "Cue the effect!" ... after which Allen's stars demonstrate that they are all good sports.

Mark Goddard said, "Allen was a good director when it came to 'vision,' and he knew what he wanted as an editor; he probably knew editing; he probably could envision things. But he wasn't a good director as far as actors were concerned, because he didn't like actors. And a director has *gotta* like actors; he has gotta *want* to work with them in some way!" (MG-SL93)

For the second full day on this set, and on the rocker, the water dumping began.

Angela Cartwright remembered, "As kids, we loved what was about to happen. And we tried to get as wet as possible. Oh my God, every time it came through the top, we would lean over to get as wet as possible." (AC-LISBR15)

Allen's co-writer Shimon Wincelberg visited the set during the filming of these inundations. He recalled, "One of the female cast members asked what she had to do to, uh ... get off the show." (SW-SL90)

Lockhart explained, "We had a scene in the chariot where we were supposed to be in a whirlpool. We were all just sitting in the chariot and several huge, 50-gallon drums of water were dumped on us. It was like being in a big bathtub with the water rising up around us. We shot it several times – so, by the time the scene was over, we were all absolutely drenched! So, I jokingly leaned over the front of the chariot and called to Irwin, 'Who do I have to [blank] to get off this show?" (JL-LISM)

Guy Williams, having experienced his share of action/adventure, wasn't feeling a desire to blank anyone to get out of the production, or the Chariot. He contently said, "Nothing is uncomfortable if you're doing it for a lot of money. In *Captain Sindbad*, they had boxcars full of water releasing on us. The wave would hit you and *Wham!* The Chariot sequence was a piece of cake." (GW-SL87)

Lamar Lundy returned on January 27th – the fifteenth day of principal photography – to film additional sequences on stage in which the giant Cyclops catches a miniature John Robinson. Here we see "Paul Z." holding the doll.

The piece-of-cake job continued until 8:10 p.m. on Monday. When "wrap" was finally called, the production was four days behind.

Day 15, Tuesday, January 26. Stage 5 now provided for the "Int./Ext. Chariot Before Nite Camp" set, as well as those for "Int./Ext. Chariot Near Cave" and "Int. Chariot at Giant's Pass." Along with all the principal players, and the chimp, Lamar Lundy returned for additional process shots. The company filmed from 8:05 a.m. to 7:30 p.m. Allen held at four days behind.

Day 16, Wednesday, January 27. Back on Stage 15, they now filmed on the "Ext. Basin Nite Camp" set. The first shot was taken at 9:40 a.m. Allen also took pickup shots of the ostriches, who continued to kick and spit. At midday, the company moved back to Stage 5 for process shots for "Int. Chariot in Basin Near Cave." The wrap was called at 7:35 p.m. The production was finally completed, over budget and four-and-a-half days behind schedule.

Mark Goddard stressed, "It took about 21 days to shoot the pilot [between the Second and the Main Units, and a further day of photo effects]. That's a l-o-n-g time to shoot a pilot. It was a lot of earthquakes and water stuff, all physical – there wasn't really much acting to do. I've always been athletic, so I enjoyed that part of it. *And they sold it.* So, I went to find David Gerber, 'cause he had said, 'I promise I can get you out of this if you don't like it.' But he wasn't around anymore! About six months had passed and he had become a producer over at 20th Century-Fox, where Irwin was. So, I just said to

Day 15: Lamar Lundy, and scenes filmed but never aired on *Lost in Space* in which the giant Cyclops catches an airborne John Robinson in his clawed hand.

myself, 'Well, this is meant for me to do, so I'll just do it, and do the best job I can.'" (MG-SL93)

Shimon Wincelberg noted, "The production values were terrific, and I was amazed with what they accomplished given the limited amount of time and money. It also gives you such a feeling of power that your lines are being spoken. You see it treated respectfully by the actors and technicians. In those days, they assumed that the writer was a *necessary* part of the team." (SW-SL90)

Billy Mumy opined, "I think Irwin was a good director. I think the pilot is arguably the best of what we ever did on that series. And Irwin directed all of that himself. And I think Irwin was good in his profession, especially as a producer. But I also think he was a fine director, as well, although he only directed the pilot. It holds up very well." (BM-AI15)

Marta Kristen said, "That was a spectacular pilot, and the most expensive pilot ever made. And it was a beautiful, beautiful show. That pilot to me looked very Fritz Lang. It was dark, with, you know, the shadows, the black and white, the way we were lit, and the way the shots were all done." (MK-AI15)

Kristen's comparison of Allen with Fritz Lang was high praise indeed. Lang, an Austrian-German director, had directed the 1927 classic *Metropolis*, the most expensive film made until that time. He also specialized in *film noir*. And he nearly bankrupted his studio Ufa, a practice that some feared Allen might also emulate at Fox, whether intentionally or not.

Post-Production:

Even after the completion of principal photography, the Gemini 12 launch sequence and flight through space still remained.

There were two Gemini 12 miniatures. The smaller of the two had a diameter of twelve and a half inches and was used for long-distance flying scenes, such as when the spaceship approached a planet. The second was the four-foot version, with a scale of one inch equal to one foot (representing a spaceship 48 feet in diameter). This was used for the crash landing seen filmed at Red Rock Canyon.

L.B. Abbott told interviewers Joel Eisner and Barry Magen, "The miniature Jupiter 2 [called the Gemini 12 in the pilot] was shot flying in front of a starry sky and then the meteors were animated and optically added later, creating the illusion the ship was being hit by the meteors. The Jupiter 2 miniature was also flown hanging on three wires and suspended from a sound boom. The power for the ship's lights was supplied through the suspension wires. The starry sky backgrounds were created by hanging a black [Duvetyne] cloth on the back wall of the stage and spraying it with a sticky spray, then throwing colored [Christmas decoration] 'flitters' on it…. Five feet in front of the back wall we hung a bobbinet and treated it with the same flitters. This separation between the two star planes allowed us to get a third dimension in the sky background when we moved the camera." (LBA-LISF)

The five-foot distance between the black drape and the bobbinet netting with additional Christmas "flitters" helped create a sense of depth, giving the star background perhaps the most realistic perspective seen so far on screen. It would remain the high watermark for one year, until the premiere of *Star Trek*, with its moving star patterns, which were actualized by filming through three separate animation plates as they traveled toward the camera at differing velocities.

The score heard in the pilot was not the one 20th Century-Fox music department head Lionel Newman had original arranged for.

Kevin Burns said, "There is a complete score we have found in the vault which matches all scenes, and you can tell where they would have used each of these music cues, but it doesn't feel epic enough; it doesn't feel big. And it was confusing to us, because we knew it was not the score that was used, and we wondered, 'Where'd they get this?'" (KB-AI16)

Lew Hunter, assigned as ABC production manager on *Voyage to the Bottom of the Sea*, was a frequent visitor to the Irwin Allen production offices, and had the inside track. Interviewed for this book, Hunter said, "Hollywood was like a small town back then, and TV and motion pictures were much more joined together. At that time, we used to say, 'It's not a small town, it's a *closet*!,' because everyone knew *everything* that was going on in all of the studios. And then, of course, you only had three networks. So, [*Lost in Space* story editor] Tony Wilson told me how Irwin was trying to get music for *Lost in Space*, and he rejected many suggestions by Lionel Newman, who, by the way, was a wonderful musician. And Irwin would say, 'No, that's not outer space!' And then Max Steiner tried, and he composed a score. And Irwin said, 'No, that's not outer space!' And then, finally, whoever ended up having the credit on the show came in, and played something, and Irwin said, 'Now *that's* outer space!' And you have to wonder, 'What in God's name made him say that *this* was outer space and *that* was not?' So we would all laugh when we heard that." (LH-AI15)

One can only imagine Lionel Newman's reaction to Irwin Allen saying 'no" to Max Steiner. After all, Steiner had won three Academy Awards for his film music – with 1935's *The Informer*, 1943's *Now Voyager* and 1944's *Since You Went Away*. Steiner had also been nominated for an additional twenty-one Oscars! Among these: his scores for 1939's *Gone with the Wind* and 1942's *Casablanca*.

But Steiner had never written a score for a science fiction film or TV series.

According to Kevin Burns, "Irwin said, 'It doesn't sound like what I want. I want it to sound like Bernard Hermann in *The Day the Earth Stood Still*!' So then, Fox went through the library and took everything they had that was Bernard Hermann – and other cues, too; there's more than Bernard Hermann in there; in fact, a lot of Fox music cues are in that pilot – but it's principally Bernard Hermann from three different movies: *Journey to the Center of the Earth*, *The Day the Earth Stood Still* and *Beneath the 12-Mile Reef*. And I think that's why the score to the pilot is 'needle dropped' and not original, because Irwin did not like what had been composed." (KB-AI16)

Bernard Herrmann was no stranger to the Academy Awards, either. He had been Oscar nominated for his first film score, the somber music heard in Orson Welles' 1941 masterpiece, *Citizen Kane*. Welles had employed Herrmann for his radio shows, including the 1938 Halloween Eve broadcast of *The War of the Worlds*, and then brought the composer along for his move into motion pictures. Following *Citizen Kane*, Herrmann composed other scores for Welles, including 1942's *The Magnificent Ambersons* and 1944's *Jane Eyre*. Herrmann was also a favorite of Alfred Hitchcock, scoring many of his films, including 1956's *The Man Who Knew Too Much*, 1958's *Vertigo*, 1959's *North by Northwest,* and 1960's *Psycho*. Along with 1951's *The Day the Earth Stood Still*, other notable sci-fi, horror or fantasy films scored by Herrmann included 1959's *Journey to the Center of the Earth*, 1961's *Mysterious Island*, and 1963's *Jason and the Argonauts*, as well as numerous episodes of *The Twilight Zone*. Herrmann won an Oscar in 1942 for his score heard in the film *All That Money Can Buy*.

Someone who didn't make it onto the CBS broadcast version of the series was this curious "lady." However, you do see him at the end of the original unaired pilot film.

***

More work was required before CBS would accept the pilot and screen for its affiliates and advertisers. The network ordered cuts, including Angela Cartwright's bloodcurdling scream, which had been heard when Penny and Will were trapped in the underground tomb. (The scream, among other previous cuts, were added back in and first seen by the public in the 1980s for a broadcast of Allen's original pilot film on the Sci-Fi Channel, and can also now be watched as part of the bonus material on the 50th Anniversary Blu-ray release of the series).

According to Kevin Burns, "When I told Angela I was restoring her scream from the un-aired pilot to both 'There Were Giants in the Earth' and 'The Hungry Sea' episodes, she was thrilled and told me that she was famous for her scream. She used to scream bloody murder on *Make Room For Daddy* when Danny Thomas chased her around the coffee table. It always got a big laugh. Later, I spoke with June Lockhart about it. She told me how Angela screamed and screamed all during the whirlpool scenes, too – that is until June said to her, 'Save it, honey. CBS will never let us use it.'" (KB-AI16)

The final cost of the 90-minute pilot came to $339,545, which included script, wardrobe, props, making the miniatures, filming, editing, rerecording, opticals and titles. This budget did not provide for the making the full-size Gemini 12, inside and out. In the final budget, the money allocated for sets was only $26,435; Labor and Materials was an additional $8,633; Art Costs added on $8,669; Set Dressing accounted for $8,404. However, according to *TV Guide* writer, Melvin Durslag, for a November 1965 article on *Lost in Space*, the Gemini12/Jupiter 2 set (for the pilot and then redesigned for the series) reportedly cost $350,000.

With the $339,545 spent during production and post-production added to the ballpark figure of $350,000 for the spaceship, the pilot film's total cost came to roughly $689,545. Adjusted for inflation, this amount in 2015 would be the equivalent to a staggering $5,189,533.

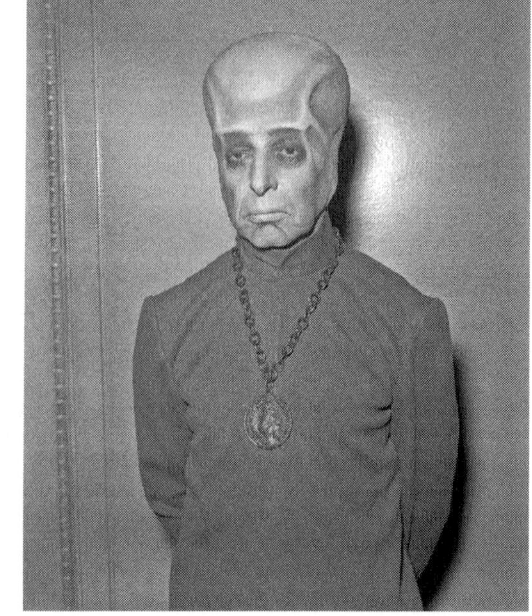

In the September 1, 1965 issue of *Variety*, it was reported that the *Lost in Space* pilot cost in the neighborhood of $600,000. Even if only this high, it nonetheless was the second most expensive pilot made up to this time. Third place was a tie, going to *Voyage to the Bottom of the Sea* and *The Big Valley*, costing $550,000 each. Top honors, threatening to bankrupt its studio (Desilu), went to *Star Trek*, at $700,000.

After divulging the sky-high cost of constructing the full-size spaceship, Irwin Allen told Melvin Durslag, "In other words, if this show doesn't stay on the air three years, everyone is bankrupt." (IA-TVG65)

8

T-Minus Eight Months to Launch and Counting

On February 5, 1965, *Daily Variety* reported that *Lost in Space* was on the CBS schedule for the fall, "as of now."

Shimon Wincelberg said, "I don't know about CBS' reaction to the pilot, but at 20th Century-Fox they were ecstatic at last to have sold a series to CBS, which was then the class network." (SW-LISF6)

On February 10, *Variety* printed a "checkerboard" graph showing the network's "first draft" schedule for the fall TV season. *Lost in Space* was penciled in to air between 7:30 and 8:30 on Tuesday nights, opposite ABC's hit World War II drama, *Combat!*, and the NBC western series, *Laredo*. Another new CBS series aimed toward the younger crowd, *The Wild, Wild West* – a unique blend of western, espionage and a sprinkling of science fiction – was planned to go head to head against a new sci-fi show on NBC, *Star Trek*.

The following day, February 11, *Daily Variety* reported that CBS had been rearranging the schedule. Now *The Wild, Wild West* had the better Tuesday 7:30 to 8:30 p.m. slot. *Lost in Space* was pushed to Friday nights. NBC had been rethinking its fall schedule, too. *Star Trek* was gone, the result of the first pilot's rejection; an unprecedented second pilot was under order. Two half-hour shows filled its place. The first, *My Mother the Car*, was as silly and simplistic as its title: a sitcom about a fellow who buys an antique car only to find out his mother's ghost has possessed it. Following was *Hawk*, a lawman show with a twist: Burt Reynolds starred as a full-blooded Iroquois, working a night beat for the New York DA's office. Opposing *Lost in Space* on ABC were *The Flintstones* and *Gidget*.

Come February 24, when the trade reported the network's "Semi-Final" primetime schedule, the game of musical chairs continued, with *Lost and Space* back on Tuesday nights, and *The Wild, Wild West* delegated to Fridays.

Days later, after a top brass shakeup at the network which saw the firing of CBS Programming President Jim Aubrey, *Lost in Space* was off the schedule.

This didn't last long. On March 4, *Daily Variety* led with the headline, "*Lost in Space* Refound by CBS." The trade reported:

> *Lost in Space*, the hour-long sci-fi series produced by CBS-TV in association with 20th-Fox TV and Irwin Allen for next season, and considered dead on the departure of network prexy Jim Aubrey early this week, has been firmed up for next season's sked, it was reliably reported yesterday. Show will be on either at 7:30 p.m. Tuesdays or 7:30 p.m. Wednesdays. While [West] Coast program veepee Hunt Stromberg, Jr., now in N.Y. for program confabs with new prexy Jack Schneider, couldn't be reached for comment, it was learned that it was Stromberg's personal intervention with Schneider that secured for the series its firm start for next fall. Schneider, it's understood, agreed with Stromberg that *Space* has a strong, great potential program-wise.

In the days to come, *Lost in Space* was back on the "iffy" list when its staunch supporter, Hunt Stromberg, found that his job was also on the line.

On March 10, *Variety* reported:

> CBS-TV's "housecleaning" period is over, and there will be no further exodus of execs from the network, it was indicated yesterday (Mon.) by web program chief Michael H. Dann.... Network prexy James T. Aubrey exited his post 10 days ago, with [West] Coast program chief Hunt Stromberg, Jr. departing last week.

In the same issue, for a different article, staff writer Les Brown reported:

> Who is manipulating the CBS-TV program strings? All evidence points to Bill Paley, the corporate papa, himself. The CBS board chairman, who had been absent from network operations for several years, has been more at liberty while CBS Inc. prexy Frank Stanton has become ever more so deeply enmeshed in corporate activities. So it is he who has remained free to once again guide the course of "Paley's Comet," and it figures to be a somewhat different course from that which Jim Aubrey had plotted. Paley's reemergence as a very interested party in his network's program affairs manifested itself initially in his conspicuous front row presence for the first time in several years when Hollywood packagers were pitching their new wares to CBS brass and, second, in a series of skirmishes with Aubrey over program policy in the latter months. Doubtless his faith in the past network prexy's ability to pick the winners had been shaken by Aubrey's fumble of *Bewitched* [lost to ABC] and near disposal of the *Gomer Pyle* pilot (rescued by General Foods), if not by the way the numbers have dropped for Columbia this term.

Curiously, CBS was still top dog in the ratings. The drop had been a minor one.

On the same day, a third *Variety* article reported:

> CBS-TV's 1965-66 schedule got another shakeup last week as the Jim Aubrey-Hunt Stromberg Inc. tandem was dissolved and the troika of Bill Paley, Jack Schneider and Mike Dann took over. From all appearances, a good deal of agitation was given from the CBS architectural forum of programming as the eye-to-eye trio (and associates) carried out what was mostly a design of restoration. Saved by the more traditional philosophies now extant were such sturdy video "classics" [which previous management had canceled] as *Hazel*, *Password* and *Rawhide*.

Also saved from the axe that had been sharpened by the previous management of Aubrey and Stromberg, was *Perry Mason*.

Aubrey and Stromberg had been loading the schedule with series that didn't appeal to the network's founder, such as *My Favorite Martian*, *Mr. Ed*, *The Beverly Hillbillies*, *The Munsters*, *My Living Doll*, *Gilligan's Island* and, new for the fall, *Green Acres*, *Hogan's Heroes*, *Lost in Space* and *The Wild, Wild West*.

Jim Aubrey said, "I'd gone to CBS, and I'd become convinced *Beverly Hillbillies* was going to work. Bill Paley wasn't convinced.... And he genuinely disliked *Beverly Hillbillies*. I put it on the schedule anyway." (JA-LAT86)

The Beverly Hillbillies was a hit. For that matter, so were *My Favorite Martian*, *Gilligan's Island* and *The Munsters*. Even *Mr. Ed* won an audience. In later years, CBS would look down on these "corn belt shows" as lacking in sophistication. Several were cancelled despite strong ratings.

CBS founder William Paley was fond of courtroom dramas, such as *Perry Mason* and *The Defenders*; variety shows like those hosted by Ed Sullivan, Jackie Gleason, Red Skelton, and Danny Kaye; primetime panel shows like *What's My Line?* and *Password*; wholesome sitcoms, such as *The Danny Thomas Show*, *Hazel*, *The Andy Griffith Show*, *The Dick Van Dyke Show*, *My Three Sons*, and *The Lucy Show*; and traditional adult westerns, such as *Rawhide* and *Gunsmoke*. In other words, the shows CBS had been airing for years. He wouldn't have liked *Bewitched*, which Aubrey and Stromberg had passed over, but he was envious when it became ABC's top-performing series, giving the CBS panel show *Password* a bloody nose.

While *Lost in Space* seemed destined for the same fate as *Star Trek* had encountered weeks earlier – on the schedule one minute and off the next, perhaps with a consolation prize of an order for a second pilot film, provided its studio would put up half the money. Unlike *Star Trek*, which was never seen beyond the network screening room, *Space* had sponsors that were already lining up.

A third article in the March 10 issue of *Variety* reported.

> [T]he pilot for *Lost and Space* came in and everyone flipped with high hopes of a hit (there were five prints of the 20th-Fox family space adventure delivered to 485 Madison Ave., and late last week film cans were making the ad agency circuit like as many flying saucers.

On March 31, with sponsor interest, *Lost in Space* was locked into the fall schedule for Wednesday nights. The other networks had solidified their schedules, as well. On ABC, *The Adventures of Ozzie & Harriet* was entering its thirteenth season. Helping to maintain its popularity with teens was Ozzie and Harriet's son, Ricky Nelson, who had been the second most successful recording star of the late 1950s and early '60s, just under Elvis Presley. Following Ricky Nelson and family, and beginning its third season on ABC, *The Patty Duke Show*. The sitcom with juvenile appeal featured Duke, fresh from her Academy Award-winning performance in *The Miracle Worker*, as teenage twin sisters Patty and Cathy Lane. During its first season, *The Patty Duke Show* had been ranked by A.C. Nielsen as the eighteenth most popular series in primetime. On NBC, *The Virginian* would be starting its third year, having finished the previous season as the twenty-second most popular show in primetime, according to Nielsen. *Variety*, for its in-house ratings surveys, in collaboration with Arbitron ratings service, saw all three shows as being even more popular. A *Variety*/ARB regional report from November 1964 placed each series in the primetime Top 10. *Patty Duke* was at No. 5, *The Virginian* at No. 7, and *Ozzie and Harriet* at No 8. A second round of *Variety*/ARB regional reports, this time from early March, 1965, and conducted in six major markets, placed *The Virginian* at No. 7, *The Patty Duke Show* at No 9, and *Ozzie & Harriet* at No. 10. The competition for Irwin Allen's new series would be formidable.

Lost in Space now had a firm time slot, and an order for 16 episodes. But many changes were still ahead before the first of those episodes filmed.

Irwin Allen would not be given *carte blanche*. The pilot film had been the second most expensive made to this date. The prize for being the mostly costly went to Desilu's first *Star Trek* pilot, "The Cage," which had filmed in December 1964. Prior to that, the most money spent to film a pilot had been with Allen's own *Voyage to the Bottom of the Sea*. Science fiction did not come cheap. And CBS would only pay around $100,000 for the licensing of each new episode (plus roughly an additional $50,000 for any episodes the network chose to repeat). This meant 20th Century-Fox would be conducting deficit financing with every episode, hoping for the possibility of repeat airings and foreign sales.

Beyond the studio's concern over the price tag was a lack of soundstage space. Fox was suddenly one of the busiest studios in town, with seven series in production, or soon to be: *Peyton Place*, *Daniel Boone*, *12 O'Clock High*, *Valentine's Day*, *Voyage to the Bottom of the Sea*, and added to that, *The Loner* and *Lost in Space*. Filming pilots or planned for mid-season pickups: *The Long Hot Summer*, *The Legend of Jesse James*, *Blue Light*, and *Batman*. Films shooting on the lot included *Stagecoach*, *Do Not Disturb* and *Fantastic Voyage*.

Illustrating the difficulty ahead was a memo from April 8, 1965, sent by Irwin Allen to production manager Gaston Glass. Allen said, in part.

> Dear Gaston: This memo will alert you to the stage space requirements and permanent sets needed as tentatively planned by us for "LOST IN SPACE." Attached herewith you will find diagrams and lists naming these sets and a description of how they would be laid out....
>
> The basic sets are described as follows:

> 1) INT. SPACE CONTROL CENTER. The spaceship used in the pilot will become our Interior Control Center and since we will be shooting with process, it will thus necessitate a large stage to contain the machine and crew for sixteen-foot process and picture.
>
> 2) INT. SPACESHIP LOWER DECK. We plan to design a lower deck set which will contain living quarters, galley, laboratory, power compartment, escape hatch and storage area for our chariot.
>
> 3) INT. & EXT. CHARIOT – PROCESS. The present chariot would remain intact as a tracked vehicle for use in exterior scenes on stage. We would construct a process mock-up chariot which would be mounted on a rocking gimbal. The shooting of this requires a sixteen-foot process picture.
>
> 4) EXT. SPACESHIP. We will build an exterior set on stage adjacent to a large blue screen backing to develop travelling mattes with people outside the spaceship on wires. This set would also be laid out in conjunction with a basic cyclorama exterior set in a typical landing position. The stage would also be used to develop other exterior areas to meet story requirements. We presently contemplate at least nine different change-overs in the first five segments. This area also could be used for miniature shooting with spaceship landings and chariot run-throughs and other large scale miniature sets. However, when time and schedule prevail, a smaller stage such as [Fox Stages] 7 or 12 could contain these miniatures.

After describing the sets, Allen proposed two possible and very different means of finding stage space. The first, "Scheme A," as it was called, was the one Allen most preferred. He told Gaston Glass:

> This is the preferred set-up for functional operation planning and economical shooting.
>
> 1. Stage 5 will be the basic exterior cyclorama set for all campsites and also changes of landscape and planets.
>   a. This cyclorama set [which includes the exterior of the spaceship] will also be used for all "FLYING" sequences of the crew in outer space.
>   b. Other spaceship sets which will be required for various stories will be shot against this background.
>
> 2. Both interiors of the spaceship, "CONTROL ROOM" and "LOWER DECK," can be shot with ease on this stage, with process or without process [rear screen projection]. These interiors can also be shot with the broad scope of the cyclorama set in the background.

3. The one handicap of containing ourselves on this one stage is the need of another stage for the interiors of the spaceship when any extensive change-over of the exterior cyclorama set might interfere with the shooting of these interiors on Stage 5.

Allen's alternate proposal was identified as "Scheme B." His memo continued:

> This is a "make do" unacceptable compromise plan. It is submitted merely to indicate the overwhelming difficulty if Stage 5 plus a small swing stage were not made available for our LOST IN SPACE. It also presents the additional problem having to do with the fact that VOYAGE TO THE BOTTOM OF THE SEA desperately needs Stage 6.
>
> 1. Stage 11 will be the basic exterior cyclorama set.
>   a. The diagram shows it to be a very crowded set-up.
>   b. Difficult to set up the interiors of the spaceship to shoot the exterior background.
>   c. Changeover of the basic exterior set will be difficult to do due to the lack of "elbow room."
>   2. Stage 10 will be used for the set-ups for process and interiors of the spaceship.
>   a. New SOUNDPROOF sheds must be built for process shooting if color film is considered.
>   b. Process projection with a mirror will be necessary for black and white film. No shed will be required.

As it turned out, Stage 11 would indeed house the interior of the upper deck of the Jupiter 2, as well as the exterior of the spaceship and the campsite outside. Stage 6 would house the lower deck of the Jupiter 2, and the Chariot. When the Jupiter 2 was seen in space, a rear-projection process screen was positioned in front of the windows and portals, for both the upper deck on Stage 11 and the lower deck on Stage 6. This was used to display star fields. Both stages would allow for some of the surrounding planet areas. In addition, Allen would have access to the studios backlot area, primarily "The Moat," where many scenes for *Voyage to the Bottom of the Sea* were also being filmed.

Enter Buck Houghton, Tony Wilson … and Dr. Smith

CBS and 20th Century-Fox felt Irwin Allen needed a producer. Allen, after all, already had an ABC series he was making at Fox. Also, he had never worked for CBS. After discussing the matter, the three parties with a vote – CBS, Fox, and Space Productions (Allen and Guy della-Cioppa) – agreed that Buck Houghton was the producer most qualified for this series which was unlike anything made before.

In 1954, Houghton had served as associate producer on the syndicated series *The New Adventures of China Smith*. In 1958, for ABC-TV, he moved up to the producer's chair for *Man with a Camera*, starring Charles Bronson. The series ran for two seasons, but Houghton excused himself after only one and took the less prestigious and less demanding job of associate producer for the western series *Yancy Derringer*, produced by Desilu for CBS. That job lasted for a year. From 1959 through 1962, Houghton was the producer for the first three seasons of *The Twilight Zone* for CBS. Immediately after leaving *The Twilight Zone*, Houghton produced a pilot for Universal and CBS. It didn't sell, but it did air on the network in 1962 as an episode of *General Electric Theater*. For the 1963-64 TV season, Houghton moved over to NBC and produced the short-lived *The Richard Boone Show*. In the summer of 1964, 20th Century Fox brought Houghton in to develop TV pilots. The first was *The Long Hot Summer* (which would become a series in 1966 on ABC, but without Houghton's further involvement). It was at this time that Fox and CBS, with the consent of Allen and della-Cioppa, assigned Houghton to *Lost in Space*.

Producer Buck Houghton.

On April 7, 1965, the Hollywood trades made it official, saying Houghton had been named producer of *Space*.

Three weeks later, it was announced that Anthony "Tony" Wilson had been named story editor.

Wilson had been writing and producing for television since 1959, with the anthology series *Alcoa Theatre*, then, in 1960, *Goodyear Theatre*. During the 1961-62 television season, he served as producer for *Follow the Sun*, a 20th Century-Fox half-hour adventure show about a pair of freelance journalist working the news beat in Hawaii. It lasted one season. Even while serving as a show-runner, Wilson found time to moonlight and sell two scripts to the western *Have Gun – Will Travel*. He even directed the second of these. For the 1962-63 TV season, Wilson served as associate producer on the contemporary western *Empire*, a series dealing with life on a wealthy cattle ranch. Working both sides of the street again, he sold a story to the cop show *Naked City*. During the 1963-64 season, Wilson was a temporary story editor at *Bonanza*, where he also originated one script, and then he served in the same capacity on the western *The Travels of Jaimie McPheeters*, which starred Dan O'Herlihy and a young Kurt Russell (the latter to appear in *Lost in Space*). But mostly that year, he freelanced, with one script each for *Combat!*, *Mr. Novak* and *The Twilight Zone* ("Come Wander with Me," starring Gary Crosby as a rockabilly singer who searches the backwoods for new songs). In 1964, Wilson wrote one script each for *The Lieutenant* (producer Gene Roddenberry's first series) and *Voyage to the Bottom of the Sea* (the excellent "The Fear-Makers). Irwin Allen was impressed with Wilson's writing, as was Houghton with Wilson's script for *The Twilight Zone*. Both agreed he would make a good story editor for *Lost in Space*.

Also during the 1964-65 season, Wilson wrote two more scripts for *Combat!*, and sold one story each to *Bewitched* and *The Addams Family*. Even after going to work for *Lost in Space*, and in charge of polishing every script to be filmed, the prolific Wilson somehow found time to moonlight, selling one script each to *The F.B.I.* and *Gidget*, and writing a two-parter for *The Fugitive*. During *Lost in Space*'s second year, he would moonlight again, writing an episode of *The Invaders* on his days off.

***

By mid-June, 1965, most series scheduled for broadcast in the fall were already in production. *Voyage to the Bottom of the Sea* had begun production of its first episode (following the pilot film) on June 15, 1964. The first episode for that series' Second Season began filming on June 24, 1965. But *Lost in Space* was bogged down in pre-production development, and retooling, and, soon, additional casting.

First order of business: reinvent the space wheel. June Lockhart said, "It happened that the pilot had too many climaxes in it. We crash landed, we were caught in a whirlpool and frozen, then we saw a one-eyed giant, and more. The plight of the family lost credibility. So, these sequences were cut up and became climaxes of the first five episodes. We had to shoot new scenes leading up to these climaxes which we had already shot." (JL-LISM)

But the problem was bigger than too many climaxes in the pilot.

Shimon Wincelberg said, "Tony, Buck and I went out to lunch one day and discussed what was lacking in the show." (SW-SL90)

In another interview, Wincelberg said, "[T]he role of Dr. Smith was only an afterthought altogether. It wasn't in my original script; it wasn't in Irwin Allen's original prospectus. It was only when we brought in a story editor. I think it was the late Tony Wilson who suddenly came up with the idea about, 'Yeah, how are we going to get stories week after week?' And we all realized what we needed was an irritant, a colorful character like Long John Silver in *Treasure Island* – somebody who would relate well to the boy but who would still be basically a troublemaker. And that's how Dr. Smith was created, and I wrote him into my script [for 'The Reluctant Stowaway']." (SW-LISF6)

Wincelberg added, "The original actor we thought of for it was Carroll O'Connor [who had been featured in an episode of *Voyage to the Bottom of the Sea*], but he eventually turned it down, and then we got Jonathan Harris, who I think was a much better choice. He actually *became* Dr. Smith." (SW-SL90)

Actor Roger C. Carmel said, "That was actually offered to me before they thought of Jonathan Harris. I decided to turn the offer down. If it had been a comedic part, I might have done it. Comedy appealed to me more, and suited me. And I couldn't really see how that character would have survived for very long. He was a real villain at that time. Even if the show clicked and they decided not to kill off the character, I wasn't inclined to tie myself down for that type role, not with the deal they were offering me. I was working a great deal, making guest appearances in every show you can imagine, and enjoying the variety of roles coming my way. Now, Jonathan was a friend of mine, and I never told him this story. I didn't want to hurt his feelings. He has a vulnerable side to him and it might have bothered him at that time to know he was second choice … or third, for that matter." (RCC-AI-82)

Werner Klemperer (who would guest star in a first season episode of *Space*), Jack Elam and Victor Buono (whom Allen cast in a 1965 episode of *Voyage to the Bottom of the Sea*) were also considered, although never offered the role.

Writing the retooled series opener, combining new scenes with those to be harvested from the pilot, Wincelberg said, "I did several versions. In one, Smith is *really* a bad guy. You see him in a car outside the invisible force field that's protecting the spacecraft. He wants to get on board, but doesn't know how to get through. He has a young woman with him, so he cons her into going over there and picking a flower for him – and she runs right into the force field and gets incinerated! Smith realizes he can't go that route, and casually drives off. I had a note in the script that he wore a ring with a big heart on it, and said 'Mother.' Both of these things Irwin made me take out. And I think he was absolutely right. I was delighted to add Smith, since there was something lacking. All the adults were uninteresting, and Smith was interesting because he was a child. He had the willfulness of a *child*, a weak sense of consequence. He had this feeling of 'I want it and I want it *now*!' That made him fun." (SW-SL90)

It would never be established which foreign power Dr. Smith worked for. The easy assumption was the Soviet Union, considering its midcentury rivalry with the U.S.A. in all things space related. Would the Soviet Union still be America's greatest threat in 1997? Wincelberg said, "In those days, we weren't too specific who the enemy was going to be. After all, the show was set 30 years in the future and we didn't want to say the Russian or Chinese were going to be the bad guys. Besides, television at that time was very, very apolitical." (SW-SL90)

Allen had already learned how apolitical network entertainment television could be from his experience of filming the first season of *Voyage to the Bottom of the Sea*.

To avoid controversy, network television of the 1960s tried to present a world without conflict between real or specifically named nations. A producer whose show's original story included references to real-life issues was immediately warned to make these terms vague or generic. This afraid-to-offend attitude was behind Gene Roddenberry's use of *Star Trek* as a venue for commentary on the modern world. (See this author's books about *Voyage to the Bottom of the Sea* and *Star Trek* for in-depth coverage of these topics.)

Colonel Zachary Smith, then, would never disclose the identity of his employers. He merely worked for "the other side."

Now that the character of Smith had been added into Shimon Wincelberg's new script, other writing assignments could he given out. Wincelberg quickly wrote a "bible" for the first several episodes, creating a blueprint of how the various action sequences from the pilot could be built into a five-episode story arc.

On June 15, it was announced that six writers had been placed under contract to prepare the first six episodes of *Lost in Space*. They were Wincelberg, scripting "The Reluctant Stowaway"; Peter Packer, with "The Derelict"; Norman Lessing, with "Brave New World" (later to be given the title "Island in the Sky"); Carey Wilber, with "Giants in the Earth" (with title to be expanded to "There Were Giants in the Earth"); and Edward J. Lakso, with "The Sea Is Boiling Hot" (destined to be cancelled and replaced with "The

Hungry Sea," by William Welch); and then what was planned as the first stand-alone episode – Herman Groves, with "Refuge" (later to be rewritten by Barney Slater as "The Sky Is Falling").

With the writers hard at work, and being pushed to deliver their scripts quickly, the next urgent task was to find the actor who would play the traitorous Dr. Smith.

From *Daily Variety*, June 23, 1965:

> Producer Irwin Allen of *Lost in Space* [is] casting for a new regular in the CBS-TV-20th-Fox TV series debuting next fall. Would be a doctor who is a "real con man, our Long John Silver, a benevolent villain," explains Allen.

In Search of Dr. Zachary Smith

Jonathan Harris was born in New York City on November 6, 1914, the second of three children, raised in a six-story tenement building in the Bronx. His parents were Jewish Russian immigrants with a name so long that Harris later joked to interviewers that he couldn't always remember it – Charasuchin. Interviewed in 1985 for *Starlog* magazine, he said, "A neighbor found a way to pronounce our name beginning with 'Harris.' We prevailed upon our father to change our name, and it has been Harris ever since." (JH-SL85)

For the first eighteen years of his life, the pronunciation of Charasuchin was "Harris-suchin." The actual change of the name to Harris took place in 1932.

Harris enjoyed the company of his father, Sam Charasuchin, who introduced his son to music and other aspects of entertainment. Harris said, "My father and I sat in the dining room where the radio was and listened to the opera. I fell in love!"

The relationship with Harris's mother, Jenny, was not as close. He admitted, "My mother was a strange lady. We never got to the bottom of here. It seemed to me in retrospect she did not take joy in her children."

The family was working class. Harris said, "My mother took in borders and I was horrified with that, because the borders slept in my bed, in my room. And I slept on the dining room chairs." (JH-A&EB02)

Agent Rith Vennari said, "He hated it. But he knew that they had to take in borders at that time for them to survive and for them to eat." (RV-A&EB02)

Harris remembered how by the time each of the children turned twelve, he and his two sisters were expected to learn a trade, then work part-time in order to help support the family.

After spending much of his spare time in the drugstore below the family's apartment, Harris decided to become a pharmacist. He studied his new trade daily from 9 a.m. to 3 p.m. at Fordham University in New York City, and then took the subway downtown where he worked in another drugstore until midnight. Decades later, Harris said, "I'm glad I did it. It gave me a work discipline that I retain to this day." (JH-SL85)

Despite his busy schedule of work and study, Harris found time to make frequent visits to the movie and playhouses. He was an avid fan of both films and stage productions, with a level of interest that was far beyond what his meager earnings could provide. Therefore, Harris did what Dr. Zachary Smith might have – he'd sneak into the theaters through the side doors when patrons exited, catching the second part of a double movie bill or a play only from the halfway point. He said, "I never saw the *first act* of a play for years." (JH-SL85)

Childhood sweethearts Jonathan and Gertrude, circa 1926, when Harris was 12 and Gertrude 13.

In 1938, Harris married Gertrude Bregman, his high school sweetheart.

Kevin Burns said, "They met when she was thirteen and he was twelve. He used to say that she robbed the cradle! And they were totally self-invented – both of them. She had the same British accent as Jonathan, yet they were both from the Bronx! Jonathan hated his Bronx accent, so he would go to British movies and copy what he heard. He'd say, 'I figured, *that's* the way to talk.' Apparently, Gertrude picked it up from him. They were a fascinating couple. I adored them." (KB-AI16)

One year after marrying, Gertrude enabled Harris to begin pursuing his true dream career.

Kevin Burns shared: "While Jonathan was working for this pharmacy in the Bronx, his wife was working as an entry-level executive in ladies' hair care. She had been the secretary for Lawrence Gelb, who, along with his wife, Joan, had created Clairol. Then, as Clairol became bigger and bigger, Gertrude rose in the ranks and became one of the first female executives working as a brand manager. She was a tremendously interesting woman, and she said, 'I was one of the first female executives anywhere! You went into the room and it was all men, except for me! And they would say, 'Good morning, gentlemen … and Mrs. Harris.' So, she was making good money. Then, one day, this woman came into the pharmacy where Jonathan worked and asked, 'Do you have mineral oil?" He said in his very proper British accent, 'Yes, we do.' 'How much is it?' He said, 'It's thirty-eight cents.' And she said, 'Well, it's only thirty-two cents across the street!' So he said, 'Well then, why don't you go *there* and buy it.' And his boss heard this, and came over and fired him. So, Jonathan came home that night and said, 'I just lost my job.' And Gertrude said, 'Look, you always wanted to be an actor. I'm making good money. Why don't you do it. I'll support you.' And that's how he became an actor." (KB-AI16)

Harris doctored up a phony acting resume and tried out for a repertory company in Roslyn, Long Island. The ruse worked and over the next couple years he had supporting roles in sixteen of the company's plays.

In late 1941, at the age of 27, and as his interest in the theater and movies sparked, Harris took a bold step away from the life of a druggist and toward show business. He recalled, "I picked up *The New York Times* and an article said a Mr. Gilbert Miller was going to do a play called *Heart of the City*. And I said, 'I'm going to be in that one.' I decided that. I went to his office and I hounded that secretary to death. There was just no getting rid of me. I was young and strong and ambitious." (JH-IASB2)

In another interview Harris said, "The brashness of youth! I had to make up a whole resume of prior experience, but none of it could be in New York where it might be traced.... One might say I lied my way into show business." (JH-SL85)

The imaginary credits didn't get Harris the immediate response he was seeking. Yet he wasn't about to accept the standard "Don't call us; we'll call you" line.

Harris said of Gilbert Miller's secretary: "She threw me out and I came back every time, and finally, in desperation I suppose, she said, 'All right, if you wait, I'll let you see him.' So I waited, two or three hours, and finally I was allowed in the sanctum to meet the great man, Mr. Miller... and I said, 'Mr. Miller, I've been waiting for hours to see you and I just know that there is a part in your play for me.' He said, 'As a matter of fact, there's a small part of a Polish flyer in the third act. You got a Polish accent?' I said, 'Oh yes!' 'Well,' he said, 'you can have the part. Go outside and tell her.'

"Well, of course, I was hysterical. I went outside and told her and she said 'Fill out the papers.' And then it hit me: 'Polish accent?! What is that? I mean, what does it sound like? I don't have a clue.' But I was very smart. I said [to myself], 'There's a Polish consulate in New York; everybody in the consulate will be Polish. And they will speak English with a Polish accent, right?' So I looked in the telephone book and on 57th Street there was the Polish consul. I went down there and there was the most charming girl behind the reception desk, and I said, 'You'll never believe this, but I am about to make my Broadway debut.' She said, 'Oh?' I said, 'I must meet all the people who speak English with a Polish accent.' And she said, 'Monsieur, of course...,' and I said, 'Just a minute! You're a French lady!' And she said, 'No, no, no, I am Polish!' Well, it didn't make too much sense like that, but she introduced me to about ten people, all of whom spoke English with an accent – but all the accents were totally different! I was beside myself. And I said to this dear young lady, 'Where is the Polish accent? They all sound different!' She said, 'Of course they do. It depends on which border they were born near, their travel, their education.' I said, 'Are you telling me there is no such thing as an authentic Polish accent?' She said, 'Of course not!' Well, I went home, in a dreadful state. I put all the accents together and came out [with] 'THE accent.'

"Then came the fateful day – the first day's rehearsal on a Broadway play.... [I]t is the most terrifying experience any actor has ever had.... And Mr. Miller says, 'Good morning, ladies and gentleman. Shall we read the play?' And so we begin to read the play. It came to my part and I had ten lines, and I said them out loud and clear in my Polish accent. I was so proud – I didn't stumble or anything. We finished the play and Mr. Miller said, 'Thank you, ladies and gentlemen,' and pointed to me and said, 'You come here!' I thought, 'Oh my God! Fired already! My first time on the stage? Why would he do that to me?' So, I went over and said, 'Yes, Mr. Miller?' He said, 'Where did you get that accent?' And I lied. I said, 'Why, Mr. Miller, I came by it naturally. My parents are Polish. They speak that way.' And he turned to his assistant and said, 'All right, five dollars. I told you I could spot a real one.'"

Harris concluded, "That was my Broadway debut. Lied my way into show business and never stopped. I must also say, that accent I have also used playing Chinese, Hindustani, Jewish, Italian, Romanian, Baltic, Russian, Arab, Finnish, Swedish, and Norwegian. It always works. It's called 'THE accent.'" (JH-IASB2)

When the United States entered World War II, Harris, in his best Dr. Smith fashion, found a way to serve his country and himself at the same time. He enlisted in the USO and performed overseas to soldiers eager for any kind of entertainment.

1946 Broadway production of *A Flag is Born*, with Marlon Brando (far left) and Jonathan Harris (second from left).

After the war, Harris returned to New York, and to the stage. By this time he had created a persona for himself. He said, "[F]or the first years of my life, I spoke pure New Yorkese. I hated it! I thought, 'Oh dear, I want to be an actor. I cannot have this kind of speech.' So I went to all the English movies I could find. I thought they spoke so lovely. I listened to them carefully, and what I did was, I will admit it, I decided what kind of an actor I was going to be. I was going to have style and manners, which indeed I do. And that I was going to talk the way that you hear. This is what I was going to sell, if I was lucky.... I developed this sound and this style and I toned it to a very sharp point, so that it became a 'Jonathan Harris' part and I was hired to play a 'Jonathan Harris' part. It all came together and it worked fine." (JH-IASB2)

Within a few years following the end of World War II, the Golden Age of Television arrived. Nearly all the programming at that time originated from New York City, where it was broadcast live from the East Coast and then filmed off a TV monitor on the West Coast, rushed to the development lab, then televised three hours later for the Pacific Time zone. The crude process was called kinescope.

To Harris' recollection, he appeared in hundreds of East Coast telecasts spanning a six-year period before deciding to make the move west in the mid-1950s, following the migration of the TV production companies to Hollywood.

Harris was very welcome in the new TV capital of the world. He had developed his own "niche," which, in 1985, *Starlog* writer Mike Clark described as "the somewhat eccentric, sometimes prim, usually haughty person whose inner tension pulsed just below the surface."

Harris told Clark, "We are all put into certain categories in Hollywood, and I developed a style – a manner of speech – because no one else, outside of Clifton Webb, was doing it. And it worked." (JH-SL85)

By 1958, Harris was getting guest-starring roles, as well as an occasional lead, in anthology series' segments, such as "Man of the People" on Bell's *Telephone Time*, where he played Archimedes of Syracuse, the ancient Greek mathematician, physicist, engineer, astronomer, and inventor. Later that same year, Harris had second billing to Lou Costello in "Blaze of Glory," an episode of the *General Electric Theatre*. It was a comedy, and Harris' performance was deemed by *Daily Variety*'s TV critic as being "broadly-played."

In 1958 (for airing in 1959), Harris made three appearances on Guy Williams' *Zorro* series as Don Carlos Fernandez, a cold-hearted land baron. Interviewed in 1998 by Kevin Burns, Harris was dismissive of the experience, only saying, "I remember there was something about a horse that I refused to ride because I didn't ride horses and I'm terrified of them. And I remember I insisted they use a double for the ride-in. I remember that. But that's about it." (JH-KB98)

Harris, as Don Carlos Fernandez, in one of three appearances with Guy William on *Zorro* (ABC-TV, 1959).

Also in 1958, Harris landed his first series, *The Third Man*, giving support to star Michael Rennie (from *The Day the Earth Stood Still*, and later to play "The Keeper" in a two-part *Lost in Space*).

Harris said, "Ah! *The Third Man* – a wonderful show. I'm sure you'll agree. Much before its time. It was glistening, sharp and sophisticated. Oh, just wonderful. The part was written for me, by the way, by the producer. My part, Bradford Webster, had not appeared in the movie at all. I got that call one day after the deal was made to come to 20th Century-Fox and start shooting *The Third Man*. Now, I had never worked with Michael Rennie. It had never occurred to them [the studio] to have a little party for Michael and I to get to know each other. We were going to spend 39 weeks together, but it never occurred to them. So I went to Fox, where I was introduced to this tall, strikingly handsome man. I said, 'How do you do?' And he said [in a very serious English accent], 'How do you do?' And I said [to myself], 'Jesus Christ, 39 weeks with *this one*? What am I going to do?' I thought, 'It's out of the question. With all the work I've done, I've got to have a giggle or two or I'll go quite mad.' … I [thought], 'I wonder if there's anybody there, behind all that?' I decided to find out. *And there was*. There was a wonderfully wicked, vicious, marvelous man named Michael Rennie. We became fast friends and we laughed our way through *The Third Man*. We really did." (JH-IASB2)

It has been said that Harris created his first incarnation of Zachary Smith with the character of Bradford Webster. Harris said, "I decided he was a true eccentric. He always wore the same suit and kept his watch only on New York time. It was not unusual for him to have breakfast in Afghanistan at 5 p.m. because his watch said 7 a.m. I found him tremendously interesting and exciting." (JH-LIS25A)

Above: Harris with Michael Rennie in *The Third Man* (National Telefilm Associates, 1959); Below: as persnickety Mr Phillips on *The Bill Dana Show* (NBC-TV, 1963).

Arthur Hiller directed seven episodes of *The Third Man*. He recalled, "Jonathan, even though he was playing a role that was the same each week, *wasn't* the same each week. He would bring little things to it that were a little different; a little twist; a little turn." (AH-A&EB02)

The Third Man stayed in production for two years, amassing 77 episodes which were slowly released into syndication over a six year period from the fall of 1959 into early 1965. "Otta," a critic for *Variety*, reviewing the series on April 17, 1963, said that Rennie delivered a "well-tailored Lime, languid and expressionless" and that "Jonathan Harris provided some pop-eyed gags as his sidekick."

In 1960, Harris made his first visit to *The Twilight Zone*, as a psychologist, for "Twenty-Two." He returned for a 1961 episode, "The Silence," as the confidant of a young gambler played by Liam Sullivan (who would later guest-star on an episode of *Lost in Space*).

In 1961, Harris was topped-billed as a guest star in "Outrage at Pawnee Bend," a comical episode of *Outlaws*, playing a train conductor who decided to turn train robber.

Harris said, "I make it a point to take joy in what I play or I won't play it at all. I think it shows up on the screen and I don't like apologies on the screen: 'Well, I took this part for the money.' Of course, we all work for the money, but I really do try and, for the most part, to succeed in having a good time whenever I'm acting. I like playing strange, eccentric characters – they are so interesting! I love doing villains; heavies. It is true, that in these parts you don't get the girl, because you already killed the girl in the previous scene. And what a scene it was!" (JH-LIS25A)

Bill Dana and Jonathon Harris, pleasing TV critics for two years on The Bill Dana Show (NBC-TV, 1964)

In 1963, Harris began two years on *The Bill Dana Show*. For its September 25 issue, *Variety* said:

> "Jose Jiminez," character created by Bill Dana for the old Steve Allen show and carried over into the disk arena with click results, is turning up an appealing comic figure in this new early Sunday night NBC-TV entry. There may not be much subtlety in this show, but it's salted with enough yocks to carry it through the half-hour. Dana plays a Mexican-accented bellhop in a swank hotel. Premise for the humor is Jiminez's effort to add an extra touch of human warmth to the regulation hotel service. He spends the hotel's coin on birthday flowers, plays checkers with the guests and generally befriends the lonely residents of the hotel. This philanthropic tendency on the preem got Jiminez into and out of trouble with the hotel manager. Backing up Dana are Gary Crosby, who plays a fellow bellhop with the flip casualness that is characteristic of his father, Bingo Crosby. Jonathan Harris, as the manager, also handled his assignment in fine style.

The series also featured Don Adams (later to become famous as secret Agent Maxwell Smart), as the inept house dick.

A syndicated newspaper article carried in the January 10, 1964 edition of *The Manhattan Mercury*, said:

> A delightful comedy entry based on Dana's successful character created for *The Steve Allen Show* and later used for hit records. Slanted for the kids, the character of Jose Jiminez is appealing, the show is cute, and the supporting cast, headed by Jonathan Harris and Gary Crosby, is fine. The principal problem here is the bad time slot caused by producer Sheldon Leonard's anxiety to get the show on this season instead of next and the fact that Jose is Cuban, a consideration which supposedly alienates some of the Midwestern audience.

Sunday nights from 7 to 7:30 p.m. was the *Lassie* time slot, and according to the various TV ratings services, it was little else. Fortunately, the third network and rival, ABC, was falling down on the job, or so said the first A.C. Nielsen report, which gave

Lassie a 35.6% audience share, to *The Bill Dana Show*'s 31.9%. ABC settled on 7.6% for a pro football game in the days before pro football games were a national obsession.

A week later, to the surprise of the industry, *Lassie* had dropped to 24.3% of the viewing audience, and *Bill Dana* was up to 37.7. ABC, with a movie now opposite the two early Sunday half-hour shows, had 18.4%. This would not be the norm; *Lassie* was the winner most Sunday nights, but Dana's show did well enough to survive through the season.

Harris guest starring on *Bonanza*, as Charles Dickens, (NBC-TV, 1963)

Within weeks of the premiere, on September 29, 1963, Harris had double-duty on the NBC primetime schedule, seen first in an episode of *The Bill Dana Show*, then as the guest star in an episode of *Bonanza*, as writer Charles Dickens.

Reviewed by the syndicated entertainment column, "TV Time Previews," and carried in the September 28th edition of *The Gettysburg Times*, the critic said:

> A unique script features a characterization of novelist Charles Dickens. You'll recognize Dickens as Jonathan Harris, who plays the impeccable hotel manager on *The Bill Dana Show*. He is haughty to the point of arrogance, especially when accused of a crime of which he is innocent. Harris is perfect in the part. Only our respect for Dickens and the script's harping on his unshakable honesty keeps us from disliking him as much as the people of Virginia City.

Harris said, "[I]t was a great pleasure doing him. He was really a full blown, well rounded character, and was well written." (JH-LIS25A)

For the fall of 1964, *The Bill Dana Show* was picked up for a second year and pushed back to 8:30 p.m., opposite the last half of *The Ed Sullivan Show* (on CBS) and a military sitcom called *Broadside* on ABC. Shortly after its fall premiere, Harris was featured in a syndicated newspaper article, carried in the November 14, 1964 edition of Maine's *Biddeford Journal*, which said, in part:

> When it comes to delivering a dressing-down to an incompetent employee, to assuming a martyred put-upon expression, and to acting in obsequious and yet amusing fashion to the guests in his fictional hotel, Jonathan Harris, who plays Mr. Phillips in NBC-TV's *The Bill Dana Show* is a veteran master. The terribly correct manager of the fictional Park Central Hotel must minister to the needs of his guests, despite the interfering "attention and favors" of his Latin American bellhop, Jose Jiminez (Bill Dana).

> It is no easy chore to do Mr. Phillips' job, and it is even more difficult for the role to be played with conviction without diminishing its comic effect. So successful has Jonathan Harris been in walking this tightrope, that the instances in which he calls Jose upon the carpet have become one of the most delightful hallmarks of the comedy series. He has been equally successful in the past in the roles of an English bon vivant, a Chinese man of mystery, a Hindustani diamond thief, a Polish pilot for the RAF and dozens of other fictional characters which required that he submerge himself in the role.

With two popular series under his belt airing simultaneously in many cities across America, Harris was becoming not only a gainfully employed actor, but a celebrity. At this time, he lived on a hilltop in Encino, in a contemporary home with a view of the San Fernando Valley, with his wife of 26 years, Gertrude Bergman. Harris was very proud to tell visitors how the house had been built by Walt Disney for his daughter to live in. Harris was also extremely proud of his loving and supportive wife.

For a 1967 newspaper interview, when asked what he thought of actors marrying actresses, Harris said, "Good heavens, no! What a crushing bore. What is there to talk about when you're doing the same thing? My wife is in real estate. When we get home we like to exchange experiences." (JH-EPHP-67)

According to Kevin Burns, who knew both Jonathan and Gertrude Harris well, Gertrude had never worked in real estate. Why the ruse found in this one particular newspaper story? Burns speculates that Harris was protective of his wife's privacy. What she really did for a living – and, as we know, she had been gainfully employed by Clairol – was no one's business except for those whom Gertrude chose to share the information with.

Also of no business of the press was Jonathan and Gertrude's son, Richard, who in the mid 1960s was a graduate student in business administration at UCLA.

Regarding his being contacted regarding the role of Dr. Smith, Harris told interview Kevin Burns, "My then agent, whose name escapes me at the moment, called up to say that Irwin Allen was doing a series at 20th Century-Fox called *Lost in Space*. By the way, I'd never heard of Irwin Allen at that time. And he wanted to see film on me?! Producers like to see film on you – it makes them feel a sense of security to know that somebody else hired you and that you can walk and talk and chew gum all at the same time, and not fall down or trip over the camera cables. And I, in my career, have been very loathe to show film unless I was absolutely sure that I had in stock some film that resembled the part that they were looking for. Otherwise, you could blow the whole thing. So, I said to the agent, 'What's the part?' 'Oh, I don't know,' said Mr. Ten

Percent.' I said, 'Well, you tell Mr. Allen that I hesitate to show him the wrong film. I prefer to show him the real thing – *me*!' And he said, 'Well, he's not going to like that.' Well, 20 minutes later he called up again and he said, 'Allen wants to know who the hell you think you are? And he'll see you at four o'clock.'

"I went to 20th Century-Fox – my favorite movie studio, because that's where I started my Hollywood television career in my first series – and I found my way to Irwin Allen's office. I was nervous, you know. An actor is always nervous when he's asked to audition or to make his first appearance. And I was ushered into the presence of Irwin Allen. There he was, sitting behind a huge desk surrounded by his coterie of 'yes men' – about 12, I think. So, I said, 'Good afternoon, gentlemen.' And Irwin pointed his finger at me and said, 'Who the hell do you think you are – *no film*?!' Well, that sort of staggered me for a moment. And I said, 'Well, Mr. Allen, I-I-I-I hesitate to show you the wrong film – you wouldn't want that. I prefer to show you the real thing – me.' And he turned his head to a 'yes man' named Frank La Tourette – who turned out to be a very nice man – and he said, 'What did he say, La Tourette?' I thought, 'Oh, this is strange.' And La Tourette said, 'He doesn't want to show you the wrong film.' 'Oh,' he said. 'Do you want to be in the series?' I said, 'Well, Mr. Allen, I haven't seen the script.' He says, 'What is he saying, La Tourette?' And La Toorette says, 'He hasn't seen a script.' I began to shiver a little bit. It was very strange, I must tell you.

"By the way, I have total recall for things like that, and sentences and conversations. Anyway, Irwin said, 'Somebody give him a script!' And somebody gave me a script. Then he turned to the casting man, who was also in the office, to whom I had not been introduced, and he said, 'Sign him up and don't pay him too much money!' Hmm. Then he said, 'I suppose you want billing!'

"I found all of this very, very strange, I must tell you. It never happened to me before. And I said, 'Oh, Mr. Allen, it's customary for an actor of my stature to receive proper billing on screen.' He said, 'What did he say, La Tourette?' La Tourette says, 'He wants billing.' Then Mr. Allen said, 'Let me tell you, your character was not in the pilot. I've already shot the pilot. And I've already signed all the other actors. You'll have to be last.' And I said, 'Oh? Er – would you mind telling me who the other actors are?' And he told me. I said, 'Oh, very nice, I'm sure, but I don't believe I would be comfortable in last position.' 'What did he say, La Tourette?' 'He doesn't want to be last.' 'Well,' he said, 'you listen to me. You go home and you think it over. And then you call me up with a solution. And now get outta here, because I'm busy!' I backed out of the there, tripping over my feet – it was ghastly. I can't remember such a dreadful experience in my whole life.

"Well, I went home and read the script. I've got rather good instincts about things like that, gleaned through the years of experience, and I said, 'Hmm, this is a good one, I think. But last position? But I think I want to do this show. But I cannot tamper with other people's contractual agreements for billing. Hmm. I'd have to be last? Last?!' What about some sort of special 'last,' I wondered? So I called a friend of mine who was head of casting at NBC at the time. I said, 'Have you ever given 'special guest star' billing to a running member of the cast; a recurring part in a television series?' And he said, 'Absolutely not. It's never been done. I would never give billing like that. It's crazy.' And I said, 'Thank you, that's all I need to know.'

"So, I called Mr. Allen and I said, 'I have solved the billing problem.' 'Yeah? What?' I said, 'I will accept last position if it says "special guest star Jonathan Harris" on a separate card every week. Well, the proverbial blank hit the fan – a screaming, 'What?! I never heard of anything… You actors, you're all crazy! None of you can act anyway! I hate you all!' Twenty minutes of this nonsense. And I just sat through it and listened, and, finally, he said 'okay' and hung up the phone.

"And that was it. That was the first time that billing had ever happened in television. I'm full of firsts, as you can see. From that day to this, billing has now become the most ridiculous thing you've ever seen in your life. It's a very important thing for actors, of course, because the industry makes a very important thing of billing. Now you see 'with the special appearance of,' 'with a cameo appearance of,' with somebody in a box and somebody in a double box, and it's just madness. And I started it, the whole thing. Isn't that nice to have started something like that? And that's how I got into *Lost in Space* – happily." (JH-KB98)

What Harris didn't know was that he had the job before he ever entered Irwin Allen's office.

Gilbert Mandelik, one of the series' assistant directors, said, "Jonathan Harris was hired for the part of Doctor Smith on the recommendation of Tony Wilson, the story editor. He told the people from the network at the showing of the pilot that they were going to add a comedy character which we are pretty sure will be played by Jonathan Harris. He had met Jonathan recently before and knew he was available. So he mentioned that, even though he wasn't sure he could get him. The network people got excited and said, 'Are you sure you can get Jonathan Harris? Because, if you can, we will buy the show.' So, it was on the basis of Jonathan that *Lost in Space* was sold to CBS." (GM-LISF)

Harris eventually found this out. He said, "I got this from CBS: They went to see the pilot, which was one flood after one earthquake after one explosion, and they laughed. Irwin was furious. They said, 'Go get Jonathan Harris.' That's what I heard happened. That's why – if the CBS story is true – Irwin hired me that minute in his office, without seeing any of my film." (JH-SL98)

Harris would be the second-highest paid actor on *Lost in Space*, under Guy Williams. By the time the series entered its second season, he was the highest paid. And a "special guest star" all the way.

On July 7, Irwin Allen announced that Jonathan Harris had been cast as Dr. Zachary Smith.

There was still one other character to cast – a character unlike any seen before on television, and one which would take two performers working together to bring to life.

In Search of the Robot

Shimon Wincelberg said, "In an early redraft of the first episode, the Robot was there, but he wasn't all that important. He was only there for emergencies. Since I was working on storylines for the first six episodes. I don't remember when the Robot became important." (SW-SL90)

In Wincelberg's script for "The Reluctant Stowaway," the Robot served only one purpose – to pose a threat. It would remain one-dimensional for the next four episodes, with stories by Wincelberg, but being rushed through the scripting process by four different writers. These writers were working off a design they had seen – a blueprint of a sort – as the actual Robot had yet to be built. That task fell onto the shoulders of the man who was perhaps the most qualified person in the entertainment industry to meet such a challenge.

Above: Robby the Robot, in 1956's *Forbidden Planet*; Below: Robbie's maker, Bob Kinoshita, with his wife and daughter, visiting the set of Lost in Space.

Bob Kinoshita was 51. He had served as set designer for numerous TV series, including *Highway Patrol*, *Sea Hunt*, *Bat Masterson*, and *Science Fiction Theatre*. He served as art director on the 1959-60 series *Men into Space*, and production designer on the 1961 science fiction film *The Phantom Planet*. His greatest claim to fame was for designing three of the most famous robots in science fiction: Tobor from the 1954 film *Tobor the Great* (also featured in the 1957 TV pilot, "Here Comes Tobor"); Robby the Robot from the 1956 film *Forbidden Planet* (which was resurrected for the 1957 film *The Invisible Boy*); and, lastly, the robot for *Lost in Space*.

In the late spring of 1965, Kinoshita was hired by Irwin Allen to serve as art director on *Lost in Space*, a title he shared with art department head Jack Martin Smith. Two of the first tasks for Kinoshita were to work with Smith in redesigning the Gemini 12 from the pilot film (soon to be renamed Jupiter 2), giving it a lower deck, and then come up with the series' Robot.

Kinoshita said, "It took about six designs... a bunch of little rough sketches and ideas. You're laying in bed, and something comes to you, until finally you get to a point where you say 'This could work! Okay, let's see what the boss man says.' And you present it to him. I think it only took me six weeks [to finish building the Robot], because I had a bunch of people [helping]…. At one time I had 14 people working for me."

During those six weeks, the Robot went through various incarnations. Kinoshita said, "First we were trying to do it without anyone in there because we knew it was dangerous. At any moment it could stop or trip… and inside there is all kinds of stuff that he could get hurt on. There was a yellow cord running up the back of the Robot that held 2,000 volts. There was more talk about not having a Robot operator, because that would save the cost of another actor. But it was harder to manipulate the Robot on command if there wasn't a human operator. Plus the idea was the guy inside operating would give it personality." (BK-ICONS-08)

According to a 1965 press release from 20th Century-Fox TV, the robot cost $36,000 to make, weighed in at 275 pounds, and stood seven feet tall on its web-track feet. And then, of course, there was 2,000-volt wire that had to connect to various lights and electronically operated mechanisms. Who in the world would want to spend five days a week inside of that?

Bob May's grandfather, Chic Johnson (above; right); and May with Jonathan Harris on the set of *Lost in Space* (below). Note the dark makeup on May's face, as well as dark clothing, so he would not be visible when inside the Robot.

Bob May was born in 1939 and was third-generation show business. His father, Marty May, had performed on Broadway, and was a song-and-dance comedian in Vegas. Bob May's grandfather was Chic Johnson, who was one half of the performing team of Olsen and Johnson, famous for their 1938 revue, *Hellzapoppin'* (turned into a movie starring the team in 1941).

May said, "Olsen and Johnson shows were like big parties; they were just a few years ahead of their time. People who came to the show became part of the cast, and Olsen and Johnson had fun with everybody in the theater as well as everyone in the show." (BM-SL94)

Young Bob May was often part of that show. Starting at 13, he performed with his grandfather and his partner, Olsen, as a singer and dancer. By the time he was 16, May was also helping in directing and producing many of the team's road shows. He said, "We not only did stage, but TV, as well. They had their own TV show [*Fireball Fun-for-All*, 1949], and we also did *All-Star Revue* and *The Colgate Comedy Hour*. The only [medium] I didn't work with them in was film. All the television was live in those days, done out of New York." (BM-SL94)

Throughout the 1950s, May continued to work with Olsen and Johnson. He got his start at acting thanks to Jerry Lewis.

Kevin Burns said, "Jerry had worked with Olsen and Johnson, so he was fond of them and had a soft spot for Bob. And he did put Bobby in *The Nutty Professor*, in a part where he was a short guy dancing with a tall woman in a nightclub, and his head is on her breasts. Even after *Lost in Space*, Bobby would get walk-ons and bit parts in Jerry Lewis movies because Jerry would do him a favor." (KB-AI16)

May also appeared as an extra in numerous episodes of producer Gene Roddenberry's 1963-64 series, *The Lieutenant*, as one of the Marines serving under star Gary Lockwood.

In mid-1965, as *Lost in Space* was being retooled, May, hoping to get a job – *any job* – visited the set where a TV remake of *Stagecoach* was being filmed.

Kevin Burns said, "They were shooting *Stagecoach* on what was kind of a makeshift backlot, since Fox was tearing down their backlot at that time, having sold the property. What they did was use portions of the main lot and dress areas to look like a backlot. So, they had built a western street and they were shooting *Stagecoach* and Bob showed up trying to get work as an extra. He went up to Red Buttons, who he was acquainted with, and said, 'Is there any work on this picture; anything for me?' And Red said, 'I don't think so, Bob, I don't think there's anything. But Irwin Allen is a friend of mine, and he's doing a TV show on the other side of the lot. Mention my name and maybe there's some work for you on that.' So, Bob goes to Irwin's office and knocks on the door – and Irwin is a big producer, he's fairly formable – but Bob was determined. And he says, 'Hi, Mr. Allen, I spoke to Red Buttons, he thought maybe there would be something for me on your TV show.'" (KB-AI16)

May recalled, "Irwin looked at me and he said, 'Wait a minute. Didn't you work for me once before?' And I said, 'Yes, I worked on *Voyage to the Bottom of the Sea*. It was a small, little part.' But he remembered me, and he said, 'How would you like to work on this new television show of mine called *Lost in Space*?' I said, 'Fine.' He said, ''Don't you want to know what you're doing?' I said, 'That doesn't matter." (BM-KB95)

May was not in a position to be particular.

Kevin Burns, who knew and interviewed May, along with many others who worked with Irwin Allen, added, "Irwin said, 'How tall are you?' – because they were looking for somebody to be in the Robot. And they never thought it was a part worth anything; they just thought, 'We need somebody to fit the suit.' The suit was built, so he just said, 'How tall are you?' I don't know Bob's exact answer, but let's say that he said, 'Five-seven.' And Irwin said, 'Can you be five-*five*?' 'Yes, sir, Mr. Allen, I can be five-five.' And Irwin said, 'If you fit the suit, you get the part.'" (KB-AI16)

May said, "They took me down to the prop shop to see if I could fit into it. And this was not only a part for an actor, but the guy almost had to be a stuntman, too, and withstand the weight of the whole costume when carrying it on 'cut offs' [where the bottom half was not on camera], and be able to not have claustrophobia." (BM-KB95)

Burns clarified, "So far as I know, Bobby was not a stuntman. But he was an ingenious guy. That suit was a little too short for him, but Bobby scrunched down so that he could get in it." (KB-AI16)

May said, "You know, a series is what every actor wants and begs for, and there are thousands of actors wanting a job like this. So I squeezed into it, and then spent three years in the bucket – and was very happy about it." (BM-KB95)

Burns said, "Everyone treated it just like, you know, 'It's a grip's job.' He never got screen credit. He was never intended to be the voice, as they would never have miked him, because he was in a costume. He did have to memorize all the lines, because he had to feed the other actors, and he might have *thought* they were miking him. But I don't think they ever had any intention of using his voice. He literally fit the suit, and that's how he got the part. But however it happened, Bobby was perfect for it. Really perfect. He had to be an actor, a puppeteer, a mime, and a stuntman all in one. He did amazing things with that suit. People believed it was real. In fact, many people I talk to are still surprised there was a man inside. That's a real tribute to Bobby's passion and his talent." (KB-AI16)

That he was not allowed to provide the voice for the Robot was always a sore subject for May. Post production supervisor George Swink said, "The fellow inside the Robot always wanted to use his own voice. We tried it once, and it just didn't fit for a Robot voice." (GS-LISF)

Therefore, to May's dismay, the search for the other half of the Robot was on. Coincidentally, although no one knew it at the time, the man meant to become the voice of the Robot was already scheduled to work on the series.

Irwin Allen knew Dick Tufeld from *Hollywood Merry-Go-Round*, where he had served as the announcer. Tufeld recalled, "When I was 19 years old, I was going to school at northwestern University, and during the summer I'd come home to Los Angeles and work at KLAC radio as an announcer. There was at that time a guy who was a Hollywood agent who had a Hollywood gossip radio show. The guy's name was Irwin Allen. Irwin would come in once a week to do his show. He would nod to me; I would nod to him. I would spin his theme music and then say, 'Now it's time for Irwin Allen and Hollywood Chatter [sic]. And here's Irwin.' When the show was over, he nodded to me, and I nodded to him, and that was it. That was the extent of our relationship." (DT-KB95)

And that was the end of the relationship … at least for the better part of two decades.

During the interim years, Tufeld was an announcer in Hollywood for ABC, which included narrating *Space Patrol*, *Men in Space*, *Disneyland* (as *Walt Disney Presents* was called when on ABC), and other Disney/ABC co-ventures, including Guy Williams' series, *Zorro*. Other ABC series he served as narrator for were *Surfside 6* and *The Gallant Men* (both produced by Warner Brothers). In the 1960s, Tufeld also served as the voice of ABC's primetime variety series *Hollywood Palace*. In 1963, Tufeld spent an hour or so in the looping room contributing narration for an ABC pilot – *Voyage to the Bottom of the Sea*. He was not aware that this pilot was the work of Irwin Allen, after a 15-year absence from television. In fact, it had been close to two decades since Tufeld and Allen had last seen one another, and exchanging nods.

Tufeld said, "Fifteen or twenty years later [since last seeing Irwin], a friend of mine named Emmet Lavery, Jr., who was working in Business Affairs at 20th Century-Fox, was walking out of the commissary one day. Irwin happened to be walking next to him. Irwin turns to Emmet and said, 'We have a show called *Lost in Space*; do you know anyone who would be good as the narrator for the show? Emmet said, 'How about Dick Tufeld?' Irwin said – and Emmet told me this – 'Dick Tufeld, my oldest and dearest friend! What a great idea!'"

Tufeld was immediately hired for the job. Soon after, it was decided there was a need for a second voiceover artist on *Lost in Space*.

Tufeld said, "About two weeks [after getting the job as narrator], I got a call from my agent, who said to me, 'Could you be at the looping room at 20th Century-Fox Tuesday at four o'clock? Irwin thinks you could be the voice of the Robot.' I showed up and Irwin says, 'Okay, we have a Robot character here.' I said, 'I presume, Irwin, what you want is a mechanical, robotian kind of sound.' Irwin patted me on the head and said, 'My dear boy, that is exactly what I do *not* want. This is a highly advanced civilization. What I want is a cultured, low key, Alexander Scourby kind of approach' – referring of course to the marvelous New York narrator and actor. So now I'm doing the lines in my best Alexander Scourby imitation. I'm saying, 'Warning! Warning! It will not compute!,' and 'Danger, Will Robinson, aliens approaching!' And he said, 'No, that's not it. Try it again.' And I tried it again. He said, 'That's not it. Try it one more time.' Finally, after ten minutes, Irwin says to me, 'Dick, I appreciate you coming in. We're just not getting this. You're not right for the Robot, but you're still the narrator in the show.' I said, 'Irwin, before I go, let me try one more thing for you.' And now in my best mechanical, robotian kind of sound, I say, 'Warning! Warning! It will not compute! Danger, Will Robinson!' Irwin looks up, and his eyes get wide, and he says, 'My God, that's the Alexander Scourby approach I wanted! What the hell took you so long?!' And, I swear, I had to turn my back to him so as not to laugh in his face, because I thought it was so humorous." (DT-KB95)

Finally, all systems were go. With the first batch of scripts now coming in, the series could begin filming.

9

Fall 1965

***Lost in Space* sells to CBS!**

In March 1965, Irwin Allen learned that *Lost in Space* was a definite "go" for CBS's fall schedule. The knowledge freed him to embark on one of his most joyous tasks: promotion. One of Hollywood's masters of ballyhoo went to work.

On March 23, 1965, Allen was creating a little buzz when Army Archerd reported for his "Just for Variety" column in *Daily Variety*:

> Irwin Allen, readying his *Lost in Space* series, notes, "The Russians just did our segment 7!... Every time someone reads one of our scripts and says, 'Aw, c'mon,' the next day it's on the front pages. It's tough to keep up with fantasy."

It wasn't true. *Lost in Space* didn't have a script for Episode 7 yet, much less Episodes 1 through 6. Those assignments wouldn't be given out until late April and early May.

On June 1, 1965, Dave Kaufman printed perhaps the first detailed interview with Allen about his new series, *Lost in Space*. The coverage appeared in Kaufman's "On All Channels" column in *Daily Variety*:

> Irwin Allen is a television producer who just can't keep his feet on the ground, and 20th-Fox TV couldn't be happier. Allen last season came up with *Voyage to the Bottom of the Sea*, a series which deals with underwater adventures of a sub-of-the-future and its crew. Next season, he launches *Lost in Space*, which takes place on another planet in the year 1997. Quipped Groucho Marx, a pal, to Allen recently: "When you're ready to make a series on land, I'd like to do one with you." However, Allen's predilection for the offbeat has paid off, because whereas a year ago he was new to TV, today he's quite a going concern, with 225 on his payroll, and occupying six of 20th's stages with his two series.

> ...*Space* has been tabbed "*Swiss Family Robinson* in Outer Space," and the producer acknowledges that's an accurate description of his new show. He calls it "science-fact science-fiction," as distinguished from sci-fi, explaining "science-fact is actually possible today, but is not commonly known. Science-fiction may or may not occur. What we do will strain your credulity, but not beyond the point of belief." He adds, unnecessarily: "There is nothing like this show on TV."

Allen told Kaufman, "*Space* will be the first primetime cliffhanger in the history of TV. The whole series is a cliffhanger! We will leave them – our series family – hanging in space, and resolve it the next week, then get them in worse difficulties that week."

Kaufman wrote:

> Allen plans stories which are bigger than life, and even exaggerated. There will be humor, but those involved will play it straight.

Allen said, "This is a show designed for adults. You couldn't keep the kids away with a baseball bat. So we had damned well better write adult stories to get maximum appeal. You must appeal to all types. No one type of audience is good enough for pictures or TV." (IA-DV65)

Kaufman said,

> There will be use of some guest stars, although Allen declines to say how they'll be worked in story-wise in outer space. A good guess: That unknown planet [the space family Robinson will land on] is inhabited.

Three days later, for his *Daily Variety* column, Army Archerd wrote:

> While U.S. astronauts are off today to set this old Earth on its ear via their "Gemini 4" [historic first space walk], Hollywood is going to keep ahead of fact with its fiction: at 20th, a script for *Lost in Space* calls for June Lockhart to take a "space walk" with her pet chimp on a leash. Irwin Allen's TV space ship is "Gemini 12."

Allen was being truthful. There really was a script in development featuring a space walk – in fact, two scripts ("The Reluctant Stowaway" and "The Derelict"). Lockhart would be part of that spacewalk. And there would be a chimp in the series. But the chimp would not be walking in space. Also, before the cameras could roll, the Gemini 12 would be renamed the Jupiter 2.

On July 22, 1965, a UPI syndicated story was carried in, among other newspapers, the *New Castle News*, in New Castle, Pennsylvania. Hollywood columnist Vernon Scott wrote:

> June Lockhart, Lassie's "mother" for six years, returns to television this fall in another maternal role in a new series titled *Lost in Space*. Unencumbered by tacky farmwife dresses and aprons, the sprightly Miss Lockhart happily reveals a dazzling figure in 1997 space suits. "It's a real boost for my morale," she said during a luncheon interview near her home.

Lockhart told Scott, "I play the wife of Guy Williams, and we're the parents of Marta Kristen, 19; Angela Cartwright, 11; and Billy Mumy, 9. We're selected as the ideal family to colonize a new planet because all of us are scientists – even Billy – and because we are supposed to be emotionally stable.... I've been playing character roles since I was 12 years old. I'm happy to get away from the drab housewife in *Lassie*. And when people see me in my fitted space suit I hope they'll be happy, too."

It appeared that *Lost in Space* would be offering wholesome characters, family values, and a little sex appeal, too.

Lockhart added, "I hope my new series runs as long as *Lassie* has. We all share the burden of the story lines in the space show. I have no desire to carry a program by myself. It's too much work. This way I'll only be working two or three days a week with the rest of the time off to devote to *my* family." (JL-NCN65)

Lockhart would soon learn: She'd have more time to devote to her family than she could have possibly imagined.

On August 7th, syndicated columnist Don Royal, under the title "*Lost in Space*: Fun and Fantasy – an Out-Of-This-World Interplanetary Cliff-Hanger," wrote:

> The year is 1997. On an uncharted planet somewhere in the infinite reaches of the universe, an American family is marooned while on a voyage to colonize a new world.... Fantastic? Perhaps, but not nearly so much a strain on the imagination in today's space age as it would have been a few decades ago, before science fiction became fact. The space race of the 1960s has enlarged the horizons of man's dreams of finding new life among the stars. Irwin Allen, a producer who keeps his feet on the ground and his head in the clouds, is leading the race to adapt these dreams for television entertainment. In *Lost in Space* he has taken science fact, put together with nuts and bolts a space vehicle of science fiction, and launched a space spectacle which he describes as "bigger than life." This is an apt description of his fantasies of the future. The thrills of interplanetary travel, the exotic environment of an unknown planet and the discovery of strange space creatures lead to high adventure for the world's first space colonists.

On August 29, 1965, the cover of *The Nevadan TV Week*, a television supplement in the *Las Vegas Review-Journal*, was a striking picture of the one-eyed giant attacking the Chariot, from the pilot film (and to be featured in Episode 4, "There Are Giants in the Earth"). The Cyclops was an eye-opener. *Lost in Space* apparently would be, too.

On September 5, 1966, entertainment correspondent Joan E. Vadeboncoeur, for a syndicated newspaper article carried in the *Syracuse Herald-American*, among other newspapers, wrote:

> Cliffhangers which first gained popularity in entertainment with *The Perils of Pauline* are in vogue on television this season. The principle exponent of the premise is CBS-TV's *Lost in Space* series and its star Guy Williams doesn't hesitate to term his show precisely that. Says the actor, "It's so old, it's *new*." He also calls his program "a visual feast" and refers to it as "not tongue in cheek," unlike many other entries of the season in the larger-than-life category.

Williams was confident he was part of a winner. He told Vadeboncoeur, "It's like when I started to do *Zorro*. I can just smell that it will be a hit."

Mark Goddard was banking on a hit, too. For a syndicated article carried in the September 27, 1965 edition of the *Eureka Humboldt Standard*, Goddard told Hollywood columnist Dick Kleiner that *Lost in Space* was more than just a series, but part of a seven-year plan. Goddard had begun the plan four years earlier. He had been a regular in three other series during that time – a western (*Johnny Ringo*), a crime show (*The Detectives*), and a situation comedy (*Many Happy Returns*). Now he was part of an action/adventure show. By 1968, at the end of his seven-year plan, he wanted to be well on his way to producing.

"I want a hit show," Goddard told Kleiner, "and I hope this is it. If it is, I can spend the time watching and learning. And perhaps, in a year or so, get a crack at directing an episode."

Williams, in his interview with Joan E. Vadeboncoeur, said he felt differently than Goddard. He wanted no part of directing for *Lost in Space*, or any other TV show. He said, "Television directing is torturous. You're blocked and frustrated by costs and time and at best you can only help the actors. It's more like directing traffic." (GW-SH-65)

Williams was happy to leave his work at work, and go home to enjoy his classical music collection, and books, and his family. In contrast, Goddard left the studio four times a week to take directing classes, and study his profession-elect.

For its September 11, 1965 issue, hitting the newsstands just days before liftoff, *TV Guide* said:

> *Lost in Space* is, according to the advance publicity, about "an average American family pioneering the frontiers of the future on strange, distant planets." This "average" family is composed of a handsome astrophysicist (Guy Williams); his stunning wife (June Lockhart), who is a biochemist; and their three children, two of whom are precocious (Billy Mumy, Angela Cartwright) and the other voluptuous (Marta Kristen). The year is 1997, and the Robinson family blasts off – nattily attired in silver-lamé space suits – to become the first family to put down stakes up yonder. They are accompanied by a dashing young geologist (Mark Goddard) and by a stowaway who, clearly, is up to no good. Visual effects abound (monsters, storms, ray guns, futuristic machines, etc.) and each episode ends with a cliff-hanger – or crater-hanger, as the case may be – out there.

For September 15 – blast-off day – CBS bought ads in newspapers across America that featured Guy Williams with a laser gun in one hand and holding June Lockhart close to him with the other.

> If you're one of the younger generation you may be traveling to a distant planet sometime in the not-too-distant-future. You may even choose to live there. But right now the world of television fiction is about to depict the first space colonists' blast-off to open a new frontier among the stars. That's what happens in *Lost in Space*, a new series beginning Wednesday at 7:30 p.m. on Channel 8. *Lost in Space* is set in the year 1997, when the world's population explosion prompts an exploratory colonial voyage.

Also on the 15th, the *Times Herald-Record* of Middletown, New York ran a panoramic view of the Jupiter 2's upper deck, with the family and Goddard in their freezing tubes. It related:

> New family space series is just like the old movie serial, decked out in modern gadgets with pseudo scientific nonsense for dialogue. Kids can hiss the villain, listen to space jargon, face a crisis every three minutes, and watch the weightless family fly about like Peter Pan. It's great for 8-year olds.

Also on this day, Richard K. Doan, in a syndicated newspaper article carried in the *Emporia Gazette*, among other newspapers, and led by the downbeat heading, "A Season of Duds," opined:

> The network television season will be the worst dog since pre-Moscow days, saved from almost total critical ignominy only by a massive infusion of entertainment, news, and cultural specials evidently ordered up by TV's programmers in an attempt to cover up an embarrassment of dullness. It is not necessary to have previewed any of the 35 new weekly series to know this. Never before in the memory of this writer (who has pre-screened not one of the new shows) have there been so many private confessions in high TV circles that the season which is upon us, as far as weekly fare is concerned, will be a

dud artistically and creatively.

Doan complained that true stars such as Danny Thomas, Judy Garland, and Bing Crosby, were sitting the new season out. In their place, the American and Canadian public were being handed pseudo-stars and pseudo-talent, such as Barbara Stanwyck, Efrem Zimbalist, Jr., Lloyd Bridges, Robert Horton, Ben Gazzarra, and John Forsythe. He didn't even bother to mention Guy Williams, June Lockhart, Robert Conrad, Don Adams, and Robert Culp, all having been prominently involved with hit television series in the past.

Doan grumbled that the new season couldn't meet the innovative standards of the previous year, which included *That Was the Week That Was*, *Peyton Place, Bewitched*, and *The Man from U.N.C.L.E.* He arrogantly dismissed such future classics as *I Spy*, *Get Smart*, *Hogan's Heroes, The Wild, Wild West*, *I Dream of Jeannie*, *Gilligan's Island*, *F-Troop*, and, of course, *Lost in Space*. Doan somehow saw *I Spy* and *Get Smart*, and even *The Wild, Wild West*, as merely being retreads of *The Man from U.N.C.L.E.*, and he was certain that *I Dream of Jeannie* would weigh in as nothing more than a wannabe *Bewitched*. *The Big Valley*, he said, with Barbara Stanwyck, was a matriarchal *Bonanza*. He sniffed that *Laredo* was a spinoff from *The Virginian*, and *Green Acres* had been spun from *Petticoat Junction*. Heaven knows how he could describe *Gilligan's Island* or *Hogan's Heroes* as derivative. Perhaps his real beef was that the schedule felt predominantly juvenile.

Then Doan cast his critical gaze toward the sole sci-fi entry on the list of new shows. He said:

> Now let's get down to serious things: CBS sources suggest that the season's real departure will be *Lost in Space*. Nobody, you see, has launched a drama into interplanetary travel – not, that is, since *Buck Rogers*. The travelers aboard in this outing will be a space-age Swiss Family Robinson, giving the show a wholesome all-family appeal.

Buck Rogers had lasted less than a year, from middle 1950 to early 1951, on ABC. And of course it was a TV version of the comic books, radio, and movie serials. Doan didn't consider the fusion of *Swiss*

TV gone wild in 1965. Photos (previous page): Cast of CBS's *Hogan's Heroes*, starring Bob Crane, Werner Klemperer and John Banner; CBS's *Gilligan's Island*, with Alan Hale, Jr, Russell Johnson and Bob Denver; NBC's *Get Smart!*, starring Barbara Feldon and Don Adams; (This page): Robert Conrad in CBS's *The Wild, Wild West*; Robert Vaughn in NBC's *The Man from U.N.C.L.E.*; Robert Culp and Bill Cosby in NBC's *I Spy*.

Family Robinson into *Buck Rogers* as constituting originality. He would have been appalled to see what passed for creativity on television in the twenty-first century.

Perhaps because we weren't TV critics, we Baby Boomers (and our parents) didn't know better than to be entertained in blissful ignorance. We were set to enjoy what would prove to be one of TV's most creative, imaginative periods.

10

Episode 1: "The Reluctant Stowaway"

Written by Shimon Wincelberg (as S.Bar-David)
(Script polishing by Anthony Wilson)
Directed by Anton M. Leader (as Tony Leader)
Produced by Buck Houghton (uncredited), with Jerry Briskin;
Executive Producer: Irwin Allen

Plot outline from *Lost in Space* show files (Irwin Allen Papers Collection):

> In 1997, from the now desperately overcrowded Earth, the Robinson family and their pilot set off in the Jupiter 2 spaceship, as pioneers to colonize a distant planet circling Alpha Centauri. At blast-off, Smith, agent of an enemy power, who has programmed the Jupiter 2's Robot to destroy the ship, is trapped aboard. The Robot is de-activated before completely carrying out his orders, but the ship is damaged and now far off-course, lost in another galaxy. Robinson is outside trying to mend the damaged scanner when his tether breaks, leaving him floating helplessly in space.

(Episode numbering and the order in which they are presented in this book are by air date. For Seasons One and Two it is also the order in which the episodes were produced. *Lost in Space* was unique in that it is one of the few filmed primetime series which – until the third season – aired its episodes in the order they were produced. This was done because each episode during the first two seasons was linked to the one which followed by means of the cliffhanger, and each cliffhanger had to be factored in to the overall running time of the episode.)

From the Script:

(Rev. Shooting Final draft teleplay, July 22, 1965 draft)

– *Smith:* "Aeolis 14 Umbra, come in please. Do you read me? Mission accomplished. *(a short, dry laugh)* "Mission accomplished!" What do I do now? *(bitterly)* What clever instructions do you have for me now? How much more money are you going to pay me for this excursion? Aeolis 14 Umbra, do you know where I am? Do you know? Do you know?"

– *Will:* "My dad said you were left aboard when you came down here to adjust the helium-nitrogen intake…" *Smith (vaguely):* "That's right." *Will:* "But the helium-nitrogen intake valve is on the upper level." *Smith:* "Oh? Well, who said anything about the intake valve? … It's the emergency supply I was concerned about." *Will:* "Then I'd better go up and tell them they were wrong about you." *Smith:* "'Wrong?' Why, what did they say?" *Will:* "Oh, Major West said, when he went to cadet school, an excuse like that wouldn't have got him out of Sunday chapel." *Smith (glancing up balefully):* "He said that, did he? Well, that's the military mind for you … 'Kill or be killed,' that's all they understand."

– *Smith (aghast):* "I must have been blind not to spot it before take-off." *Will:* "I thought freezing kills any virus." *Smith (tolerantly):* "You 'thought'. A good thing I'm the doctor and not you. You know what that virus would have done, while the rest of your body was in a state of metabolic de-animation? Just taken it over, bit by bit! After five years, there'd be nothing left of you but the metal on your space suit. All the rest of you would be one big raging mass of virus."

– *Maureen (to Robinson):* "Don't you have an opinion?" *Robinson:* "I do not. Not until we've checked every component, inside and out, and know just where we stand." *Maureen (challengingly):* "And then…?" *Robinson:* "Then I'd let the computer make the final decision." *Maureen:* "And will the computer also take into consideration a man's love and concern for his family? Or has that all been put into cold storage for the duration?" *Robinson (sternly):* "Maureen, you knew perfectly well what you were getting into." *Maureen (to Smith):* "Colonel Smith, could it be that certain parts of the body don't reanimate as quickly as the rest? The heart, for instance?"

Assessment:

We hadn't seen anything like it on television. In the early and mid-1950s, there had been several ultra-cheap sci-fi kiddie shows, usually televised in the late afternoons, such as *Space Patrol* (1950-55); *Buck Rogers* (1950); *Tom Corbett, Space Cadet* (1950-

55); *Commander Cody: Sky Marshall of the Universe* (1953); *Flash Gordon* (1954-55); *Rocky Jones, Space Ranger* (1954); and the "Supermarionation" process of Gary and Sylvia Anderson, commencing with 1962's *Fireball XL5*. In primetime, there were a handful of episodes of *The Twilight Zone* and *The Outer Limits* that depicted astronauts traveling the cosmos. But no one had attempted on a weekly basis in the 1960s to depict men in space, or on alien worlds, on the scale of Irwin Allen with *Lost in Space*.

On Wednesday, September 15, 1965, we witnessed the lift off. For those of us in front of our television sets that night, it was a treat we wouldn't soon forget. The concept to take *Swiss Family Robinson* into outer space was a brilliant one. The idea of a family with young children facing this adventure together seemed too good to be true for the Baby Boomers among the television audience. Throw in a claw-handed robot, and a villainous saboteur, and there was no other show on TV that was going to please the kids as much as this. *Star Trek* was still a year away. Who, other than Gene Roddenberry, could even imagine that? For the time being, we were happy to be lost in space.

This first episode had it all: parents and children encased in freezing tubes; a robot gone berserk; a flying saucer battered by meteorites; and, at the end, the father of the intrepid family helplessly drifting away into space. The production values and the special effects were first rate. By the time the picture froze, and the words flew onto the screen telling the audience to tune in the following week, same time, same channel, we were hooked. An hour had rarely sped by faster.

Script:

Story Assignment 8541 (Production #8501)
Shimon Wincelberg's treatment, and 1st and 2nd draft teleplays: May 1965.
Reformatted Mimeo Department Shooting Final teleplay: June 1965.
Tony Wilson's script polish (Rev. Shooting Final teleplay): Late June 1965.
Wilson's further polish (2nd Revised Shooting Final, on blue paper): July 8, 1965.
Page revisions by Wilson (pink page inserts): July 14.
Additional revisions by Wilson (yellow page inserts): July 15.
Additional revisions by Wilson (green page inserts): July 16.
Additional revisions by Wilson (gold page inserts): July 22.

When Shimon Wincelberg returned to convert his pilot script into the series opener, his assignment was to break up the original action sequences so they could be spread over several episodes. It was only after he began rewriting that it was decided to introduce two new characters – Colonel Smith and the Robot.

Wincelberg recalled, "Tony Wilson had the idea: 'Why don't we bring in a character somewhat like Long John Silver, who would be kind of a treacherous, hitchhiking fellow traveler whom they couldn't get rid of, and who was full of ideas for mischief, and who also would form a relationship where he was more of a father figure for the little boy than the father was, who was pretty straight. And I immediately saw the value of this, and wrote another draft of the script. At first, I had kind of an exotic name for Dr. Smith – something like Asgard; a name out of Nordic mythology. I was always doing research in books like that. And again, Irwin said, 'No. Call him a straightforward American name.' So, I called him Dr. Smith. And I think he was right about that." (SW-KB95)

With his choice for the character's first name, Wincelberg snuck in a bit of the exotic nonetheless. He would be Zachary Smith.

As for the Robot, that idea went back to the pilot, although due to time restraints and mounting costs it was dropped. Wincelberg divulged, "The Robot was in there to begin with. It was part of the original concept that Irwin gave me." (SW-KB95)

Wincelberg's story and script was a vast improvement over the pilot script he had written with Allen from the latter's story, which presented characters lacking in dimension. There is more warmth between the family here, and a sense of fun in scenes such as when the gravity is turned off and the children experience weightlessness. Also, there is more emotion from the characters, such as when John Robinson and the children react to Maureen collapsing after exiting the freezing tube. Also added: conflict, as played between Major West, along with the entire Robinson family, and Smith. The antagonist Zachary Smith and his Frankenstein's monster – the Robot – added greatly to the drama, even serving as the catalyst for turning Robinson against Robinson, as Maureen asks the not-so-good doctor if some parts of the human body are slower to be reanimated after freezing, such as her husband's heart. Betrayal, always a good ingredient in drama, is provided by Smith, an Air Force Colonel and doctor who has sold out his country, as well as the space travelers. Another excellent dramatic device added into the episode is the irony of a traitor's entrapment on the very ship he has sabotaged.

Situational comedy is present too, as the characters struggled against weightlessness, and in a scene masterfully played between Harris and Mumy as the doctor claims to spot a bit of virus on the boy's tongue. The setup for future comedy with Smith was already in place.

If one were to miss the tongue-in-cheek tone with some of the scenes involving Smith, the producers did their best to show their hand to the audience with the opening title sequence. The theme music for this futuristic series began with bubbling, popping sounds, but soon resolved into a hummable melody with good-natured trumpet stings and riffs. While the jovial music played, animated representations of the cast drifted onscreen and off, with Dr. Smith's figure trailing in perpetual pursuit.

After Wincelberg completed his second draft, the staff took over. Much of the rewriting was done by Tony Wilson, under the supervision of Allen and Houghton, often to appease CBS. Among the script changes requested by an unidentified executive at the network:

A) Don't have Smith kill the guard.
B) Establish the robot, its function and its importance before the entrance of Smith (this might be accomplished in off-stage TV

Commentator lines, "and the final member of the family is," etc, etc.).

C) Clarify Smith's mission and its purpose (make him a citizen of the world working for the highest bidder). His villainy does not express a personal viewpoint but is rather done for money.
D) There is too much sweetness and light on the part of the family, too many smiles, too much tenderness (there should be more toughness and humor as between and amongst themselves).
E) The Judy and Don relationship should be built toward – not immediately lain on the line.
F) Keep the clock alive so as to build up the time lock.

In another report, dated May 28, 1965, and this time from Sam Taylor, Jr., from CBS Program Practices in Hollywood, the producers were told:

> As discussed with Mr. Houghton:
>
> Page 15: Given the circumstances described in the synopsis, we do not feel it should be developed that [John] Robinson might become an "executioner of a fellow human being" [Dr. Smith].

On June 11, Taylor added:

> Page 10, Scene 30: In the scene where Smith disposes of the Guard's body, we request directorial care in order to avoid gruesomeness which might disturb the program's youthful audience.

It was a sign of things to come, and led to a final rewrite by Wilson that would prompt Wincelberg to use the pseudonym S. Bar-David as a screen credit.

He balked, "A lot of my dialogue got homogenized. In those days, I was very stuffy about that sort of thing. I had plays on Broadway and didn't want my name contaminated by association with lines of dialogue I wouldn't have written. I would be eternally linked with some crummy lines of dialogue." (SW-SL90)

Regarding the *nom de plume* of S. Bar-David, the name was derived from Wincelberg's Jewish background. He explained, "Bar-David means 'son of David,' which I am, and the 'S' stands for 'Shimon.'" (SW-SL90)

Pre-Production:

Tony Leader was chosen to direct the premiere episode, incorporating footage from the pilot, but primarily comprised of new material. He was 51 and had directed a pair of episodes for *The Twilight Zone,* as well as the 1964 cult horror film *Children of the Damned* (under the name of Anton Leader). These credits alone may have won him a directing job on *Lost in Space*, but, in addition, Leader had also proven himself good with child actors, having helmed episodes of *Leave It to Beaver* and *National Velvet*. He had also directed action series, such as *Sea Hunt* and *Rawhide*.

Leader told authors Joel Esner and Barry Magen, "I was chosen to direct *Lost in Space* because I had done some science fiction and I also had a good reputation. I learned later that someone had told Irwin that he had spent too much time [in the pilot] on the mechanics of his show... and suggested that someone might be brought in to give a new dimension to the people and the characters involved. And that is where I came in." (TL-LISF)

Leader would return to direct a second installment for the first season – Episode #3: "Island in the Sky."

Jerry Briskin served as associate producer during the first season. He had done likewise for the 1961-62 series *Shannon*, and, one year before *Lost in Space*, the 1964-65 season of *Bewitched.* With Allen as executive producer, and Houghton as show runner, Briskin was the nuts-and-bolts producer, arranging to realize on set whatever fantastic concepts were introduced in the scripts. His good right-hand men were Gaston Glass, as production manager, and Les Warner, as unit production coordinator.

Gaston Glass had been a production manager since 1936 for numerous movies, and had also served in this capacity for several 20th Century-Fox series from the early 1960s: *Hong Kong*, *Adventures in Paradise*, *Bus Stop*, and *Follow the Sun.* He was also production manager on the first season of *Voyage to the Bottom of the Sea.*

Les Warner had also been serving Irwin Allen, as production coordinator on *Voyage.* Prior to that, he worked at Fox as an assistant director.

Gene Polito was promoted from camera operator to director of photography, beginning with this episode. He continued to serve as the cinematographer on 24 of the first 25 episodes (excluding "Magic Mirror," which was filmed by a different D.P. while Polito ran the camera crew on "War of the Robots"). His father, Saul Polito, was one of Hollywood's top cameramen, having filmed numerous Busby Berkeley musicals. Son Gene was a chip off the old block and worked his way up, starting as a film loader, then, after finishing college with a major in engineering, apprenticing under cameraman Norbert Brodine on the television series *The Loretta Young Show.* When Brodine decided to retire, he and Young promoted Polito to cameraman. This led to work as director of photography in 1960 on a Jeff Chandler film, *The Plunderers*, working under director Joseph Pevney. He stayed with Pevney for 1961's *Portrait of a Mobster*, starring Vic Morrow and Leslie Parrish. In early 1965, besides working as director of photography on television's *Twelve O'Clock High*, Polito served as camera operator on the *Lost in Space* pilot film "No Place to Hide," under Winton Hoch. With Hoch busy as the director of photography on *Voyage to the Bottom of the Sea*, Polito was given the first season of *Lost in Space*, bringing to the series a striking black-and-white *film noir* look.

Back from "No Place to Hide" was set decorator Walter M. Scott. Working with Scott was Sven Wickman, having taken over for Norman Rockett. Wickman had been working alongside Scott on the *Voyage* TV series.

Johnny Borgese joined the company here, assigned by Fox to serve as special effects supervisor. He was in charge of all the smoke, sparks, and other on-set effects needed for *Space.* He had worked as a member of the special effects team on the studio's *Journey to the Center of the Earth*, as well as the feature film version of *Voyage to the Bottom of the Sea* and Irwin Allen's follow-up, *Five Weeks in a Balloon.* A key member of Borgese's team was Stuart Moody, who rigged many of the flashes, smoke screens and explosions. Moody was missing a finger as a result of an effect gone wrong earlier in his career.

Clyde Taylor was selected as the series lighting director, also known as a gaffer. He would remain through the end of the first season, working closely with Polito in giving the black-and-white episodes their dark, ominous look. Taylor had worked as an assistant gaffer on Fox films such as *The Robe* and *The King and I.*

Joe D'Agosta remained as casting director. Also on board was the ever-reliable Paul Zastupnevich, as wardrobe designer, in addition to the many other functions he provided on this series and *Voyage to the Bottom of the Sea*. His duties were so varied that he was given the credit of assistant to the producer.

Brett Parker, cast as the Security Guard, was a bit actor who also appeared in an episode of *The Time Tunnel*. He would return briefly for the "Reluctant Stowaway" sequel, "Time Merchant."

Chuck Couch was Guy Williams' stunt double for some of the space walk sequences.

Also appearing – as they had in the pilot – were Don Forbes as the TV Commentator and Ford Rainy as the President.

The launch date established in the pilot was 1997. While this was 32 years away during filming, most of the cast members felt it was entirely possible that man might reach into the stars by then, and that they would likely live to witness this.

Angela Cartwright said, "As a teenager, the idea of space travel in 1997 didn't seem at all bizarre." (AC-TVG97)

Marta Kristen marveled, "The whole idea of the space program had started, and Kennedy had put so much emphasis and created attention to it. And, all of a sudden, I felt like I'm part of it, in a strange way." (MK-AI15)

June Lockhart said, "I fully thought we'd be up there by 1997, and we *are*. People are living in space right now. Not a family, *per se*, but I bet they get to be very family-like after a few months of togetherness." (JL-TVG97)

Billy Mumy quipped, "Crawling inside Irwin Allen's id is the weirdest sci-fi plot I can imagine, but I have the courage to go there. I think he believed the concept to be quite possible, because Kennedy wanted a man on the moon by the end of the '60s, so families on other planets by the '90s certainly seemed within our grasp." (BM-TVG97)

Production Diary:

Filmed July 19-28, 1965 (8 days)

Coincidentally, the retooled first episode of *Lost in Space* began filming on the same day that "Where No Man Has Gone Before," the second pilot for *Star Trek*, had its first day of production a short distance from 20th Century-Fox, at the Desilu-Culver City Studio.

Guy Williams was paid $2,000 per week. Jonathan Harris may have been seventh billed, but he was the second-highest paid, with $1,750 per episode. June Lockhart was given $1,500. Mark Goddard got $1,250; Billy Mumy received $1,000; Marta Kristen and Angela Cartwright were paid $850 each; and Bob May took home $350. To have a better perspective on these earnings, at this time you could buy a new home in Los

Veronica Cartwright, a regular cast member on NBC's *Daniel Boone*, also filmed on the Fox lot, poses for a studio publicity picture with younger sister Angela.

Angeles for $21,500; a McDonald's hamburger for 18 cents; and a gallon of regular gasoline for 31 cents (with the service station attendant also washing your car's windows, putting air in your tires, checking your oil, and handing you a sheet of Green Stamps, with a smile).

Footage utilized from the pilot included most of the sequences from the Alpha Control Center communications room, plus shots of the freezing tubes being activated, and the optical effect which accompanied them; the lift off, also saving the cost of an optical effect for this episode; and the meteor storm.

Day 1: Monday. Billy Mumy said, "[We] started filming on my mom's birthday, July 19, 1965.... It was great to be reunited with everyone from the pilot, knowing we were making a cool sci-fi television series.... Mark Goddard had Irwin Allen and others really worried because he had a motorcycle accident right before we started to film." (BM-LISM)

In a different interview, Mumy clarified, "He scraped his leg up very badly and he was bandaged for the course of the first couple episodes." (BM-KB95)

Filming began on Stage 16 at 8 a.m. with "Int. Section of Control Center – T.V. Commentator's Desk," where Don Forbes reprised the role he had played in the pilot, now with a few new lines of dialogue commenting on the plight of the Robinson family. While the sequence in the pilot featured Forbes delivering his lines to camera, here we see him only in profile, with a curtain in the background. The reason: This pickup shot was taken on Stage 16, not the mezzanine of the Fox studio's Construction Department's storage facility, where the Alpha Control scenes in the pilot had been filmed.

Next, they filmed on the "Int. Another Section of Control Room" set, where actor Fred Crane played an Alpha Control administrator who calls the President to inform him that the Robinson family are hopelessly "lost in space."

The next set had a curious name: "Int. Torture Chamber." This is where Will Robinson received his final medical exam from Dr. Smith, and then was joined by the rest of the family.

Billy Mumy said, "Meeting and working with Jonathan was wonderful. He was great in it." (BM-LISM)

The "Int. Ready Room" set came next, as the family walked toward the "torture chamber" through a room crowded with military personnel and members of the press.

After these scenes were shot, the company moved to Stage 5, which was to be a regular *Lost in Space* location. This was where the Jupiter 2 had been built, both upper and lower decks (although the upper deck would be relocated to Stage 11 by Episode 4). Filmed on this day were the scenes in which Don and the technicians checked over the ship as the Robinsons board, as well as them listening to the President's message, and then taking their places in the freezing tubes. For every scene in the episode, the recurring cast (other than Jonathan Harris) wore their silver space suits.

Costume designer Paul Zastupnevich said, "In the very beginning, we used what had originally been a fire retardant suit and cut it apart and made a flying suit out of it. I had 'leaning boards' for June and Angela and Marta because the silver suits were so stiff and so uncomfortable to sit in. And they were hot, too." (PZ-KB95)

June Lockhart revealed, "Mine was cut down to fit so tightly that I could not bend my legs – or sit in the suit. I reclined on a cot when I needed to get off my feet." (JL-LISM)

Angela Cartwright said, "As a kid I remember having to stand very still in my freezing tube… creating the rocking and rolling as the Jupiter 2 went off course … and having to suffer through wearing those dreadful spacesuits. They were so stiff and hot." (AC-LISM)

Zastupnevich related, "[O]nce they got those on, and if they were zipped in, it was like being in a sauna inside…. [T]he fabric didn't breathe. When they wore their silver spacesuits, they sometimes lost two and three pounds" (PZ-LISF6)

The final shot of the day was taken after the cast was dismissed – the tricky elevator shot designed to seamlessly connect the upper and lower deck.

June Lockhart remembered, "The elevator from the top deck actually went right down into the ground. Guy joked that it would be a good place for a wine cellar, so I had our special-effects man build some shelves down there. We convinced Guy to go down and have a look, and he found a couple bottles of wine we had placed on a shelf next to a sign reading 'John Robinson.'" (JL-SL83)

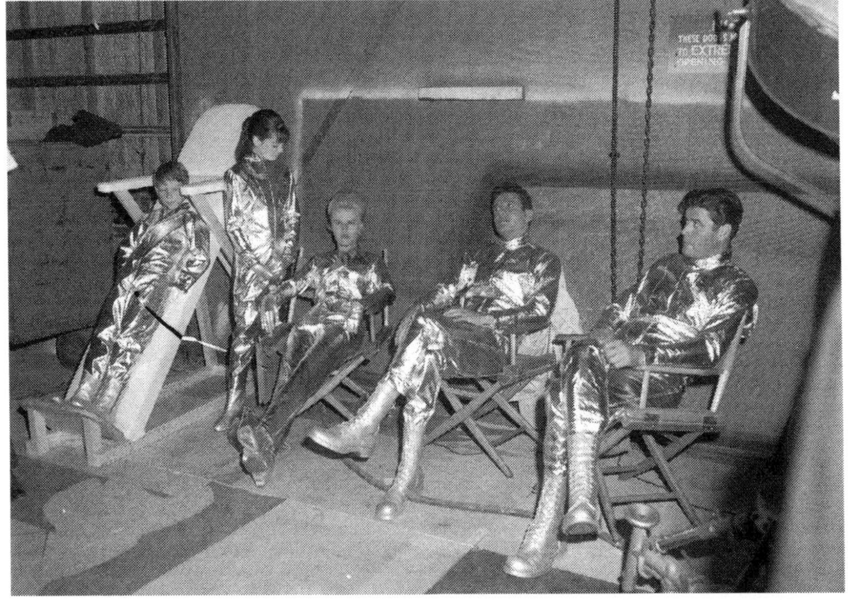

Paul Zastupnevich said of the suffering cast members in spacesuits, "If they were zipped in, it was like being in a sauna inside."

The camera stopped rolling at 7:15 p.m. The production was on schedule. That would soon change.

Day 2: Cast and crew move to the upper deck of the Jupiter 2.

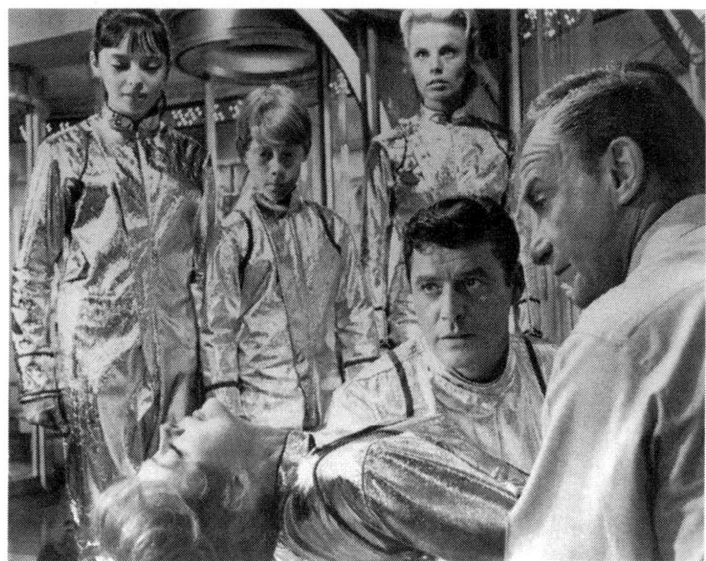

Day 2: Tuesday, July 20. The remainder of the production was lensed on Stage 5 and the interior Jupiter 2 sets. Filming started at 8 a.m., with Smith dashing to the upper deck and trying to get off the ship. After being trapped inside, he hurled the extinguisher at the window, and then left the deck to secure himself below. Next, a long sequence was started, as Smith returned to the upper deck after the Jupiter 2 was in flight, saw the coming meteor storm, and revived Major West.

Mark Goddard admitted, "I was curious about the changes that Irwin Allen and CBS made in regard to cast additions. I was impressed with the evilness of Dr. Smith's character, and I agreed with the element of conflict that was needed in a dramatic series." (MG-LISM)

Marta Kristen echoed, "I thought 'The Reluctant Stowaway' was very well done, and bringing Jonathan Harris in as the villain was a very good idea. The special effects were wonderful, and a lot of money went into producing this episode. It was filmed in black and white, which gave the episode a darker feeling and a different look, as was the first season of *Lost in Space*." (MK-LISM)

Interviewed for this book, Kristen added, "Irwin really was a genius to be able to put all of this together, and for him to do this pilot in the way that he did. When I saw all that was going on, I was just thrilled to be there." (MK-AI15)

Director Tony Leader said, "I found *Lost in Space* a very interesting experience for myself. I enjoyed working with the cast very much. They were responsive to me; they were attentive."

However, not all was good. Leader added, "The conditions under which we worked were not the best because they were still building the set while we were shooting it. Many of the things did not work." (TL-LISF)

The main thing that didn't work was the overly ambitious production schedule. Leader only managed to get the scene in which Smith revives West partially shot before being asked to stop at 6:48 p.m. He was one-half of a day behind.

Day 3: Wednesday, July 21. Leader filmed from 8 a.m. to 6:35 p.m., resuming work on the long sequence with Smith and West, then continuing as West piloted the ship out of danger. Leader held at one-half day behind.

Above: Bob May gives Angela Cartwright an affectionate lift, showing her that the Robot isn't so bad after all. Below: Despite discomfort from the spacesuits and flying harnesses, Cartwright and Mumy recalled the anti-gravity sequence of "The Reluctant Stowaway" as great fun to film.

Day 4: Thursday, July 22. Filming began at 8 a.m., covering the scene in which the gravity in the ship was shut off and the children floated around the upper deck.

The director took creative license with Judy's and Penny's ponytails rising when the gravity is shut off in the Jupiter 2, as if gravity had been reversed rather than merely eliminated. Also, when John Robinson, attempting his space walk, slides and tumbles down the exterior of the Jupiter 2 in what should have been the weightlessness of space, and his tether line snaps as if subjected to great stress in a situation where, due to lack of gravity, there would have been none.

When work stopped at 6:30 p.m., Leader had fallen further behind, now by one-and-a-half-days.

Day 5: Friday, July 23. It was a long day, filming from 8 a.m. to 7:40 p.m., with the scene when the Robot tried to "destroy" the ship, which included the fight to disable the mechanical man. This was the first day of the production to feature the Robot.

The only blood that was spilled during the fight with the Robot came from the man *inside* the Robot – Bob May's feet were "shredded" from walking while in the heavy metal boots.

Bob May admitted, "As we began filming 'The Reluctant Stowaway,' when I walked onto the set for the first time, I was amazed. There were the likes of Jonathan Harris, June Lockhart, and all the rest of the *Lost in Space* cast." (BM-LISM)

Mumy beamed, "Seeing the Robot for the first time was very cool. A fantastic piece of work. Bobby May was 'finding his groove' inside it, and so were the stunt team that pulled him around. It took some time to get it right, but it sure did get there." (BM-LISM)

Mark Goddard noted, "What I most remembered about the episode was the so-called fight scene between the Robot and West. All I had to do was disconnect his power pack. But darn, I kept breaking my fingernails on the Robot's lobster claws. He was tough, but the Major prevailed." (MG-LISM)

Tony Leader complained, "One of the trying problems was with the Robot. The little man who was in the Robot tried most earnestly and desperately to do all of the things he was asked to do, [but] it was a little bit like working with children. When you work with children, you are permitted to use them only so many minutes out of an hour, or so many hours out of the day. His physical set-up inside that metal suit was so desperate as to require rest periods, otherwise he would collapse or become near to it." (TL-LISF)

Bob May said, "In the first scene where the Robot wreaks havoc on the Jupiter 2, I had to walk the Robot. After doing the scene, I got out of the Robot, and my legs were completely bloody." (BM-LISM)

Kevin Burns said, "The outfit was originally designed for the actor in it to walk in the heavy shoes. It would either be pulled forward or back by wire, or they could decouple the legs and let him walk independently. But after the fight in 'The Reluctant Stowaway,' when they took those shoes off of Bobby, his legs were shredded – *covered in blood* – because the feet were so heavy and the insides were literally raw metal. What wasn't rubber was metal! And his legs were just chewed up. And they said, 'Well, this isn't going to work.' Plus, it took him too long. It just took forever for him to walk from here to there, and you can imagine how torturous that was for Bobby. So, after that episode, they rarely showed the feet again when he walked, which allowed Bobby to wear the Bermudas – which was the rubber pants with the wood waste band. And then he had this parachute harness which enabled him to carry the upper torso of the Robot and the bubble on top of him, on his shoulders. So the weight of it – which was only about eighty-five pounds – was still very heavy to have resting on his shoulders. He was only good to walk in it for about eight or nine minutes before they'd have to take it off. And eight or nine minutes probably seemed like an eternity. So he worked like a dog." (KB-AI16)

Irwin Allen was on set during the filming of the fight with the Robot, as the ship rocked and the crew had to fall in one direction, and then the next.

Marta Kristen remembered, "Irwin had a bucket and a hammer. Whenever an explosion happened, or whenever we had to move this way or that way when the ship was going out of control, he'd hit that bucket with that hammer to cue us. He was like a kid. He loved explosions, he loved all the crazy monsters." (MK-AI15)

Billy Mumy stated, "I never saw Irwin as a funny guy, but he was pretty funny when he was banging on a bucket with a hammer to get us all to lurch and have things explode." (BM-AI15)

At the end of the day, the bucket and hammer were returned to the set of *Voyage to the Bottom of the Sea*. Leader was now one and three-quarters days behind schedule.

Day 6: Monday, July 26. Filming went from 8 a.m. to 6:50 p.m., including John Robinson preparing for his space walk, and then leaving the ship. Leader was two full days behind at the finish. This was the last day that had been planned for the filming of "The Reluctant Stowaway," but it still had a ways to go. The next episode to film, "The Derelict," was pushed back.

Day 7: Tuesday, July 27. They worked on the lower deck this day, as stowaway Smith made his entrance into the episode.

Jonathan Harris said, "Of course, when I joined the cast, who had already shot the pilot, I was the 'new boy.' Always a bit nerve wracking. However, all went well until I had a run in with Tony Leader, the director." (JH-LISM)

Harris was not comfortable getting into the enclosed compartment containing the hidden acceleration couch. The script identified it as a "womb couch." Harris insisted that a stand-in do the "stunt." He later related, "There was one scene where I had to be in a coffin-like structure under a counter, and then be pulled out. Well, I'm terribly claustrophobic, and I just wouldn't do that. I would have *walked* before I did that. And the director said, 'You have to be in the coffin.' Well, there's time for that later on, right? So, of course he called Irwin on the

When the set designer sketched the concept for the "womb couch," by which Smith would make his entrance into the episode, no one knew about Jonathan Harris's acute claustrophobia.

phone. Irwin came down to the set, and said, 'What's the problem?' I said, 'He wants me to do that, and I cannot do that. I cannot!' And he said, 'You have claustrophobia about that?' I said, 'Yes.' He said, 'I understand,' and he patted me on my shoulder. So, there's another facet of Irwin Allen, you see. He was very kind about that sort of thing. He understood. The director and I did not remain good friends for the rest of that episode, but screw him. The point is, I'm not about to get into a coffin. It had nothing to do with any airs or graces; it had to do with I couldn't stand the idea. And Irwin understood that. So that's something else about Irwin that we now know." (JH-KB95)

A double for Harris, wearing a mask to better resemble the actor, was put into the crash seat that retracted into the cabinet. It is this double who is first seen when the Smith character emerges from his hiding place. A simple shift in the camera angle then allows Harris to sit up into frame for his first close up.

During that visit to the set, and while watching Dr. Smith make his entrance into the episode, Allen was particularly impressed. Harris said, "I remember a close headshot that I did, quite calm and deadly, as indicated in the script. Irwin applauded and said, 'That face! What a great face! Hah!" (JH-LISM)

Because of the compliment, Harris immediately saw that there was a downside to his wonderfully sinister face. He stated, "It occurred to me that this wicked, deadly Dr. Smith was without any redeemable features, and would surely be killed off and written out after 5-6 episodes." (JH-LISM)

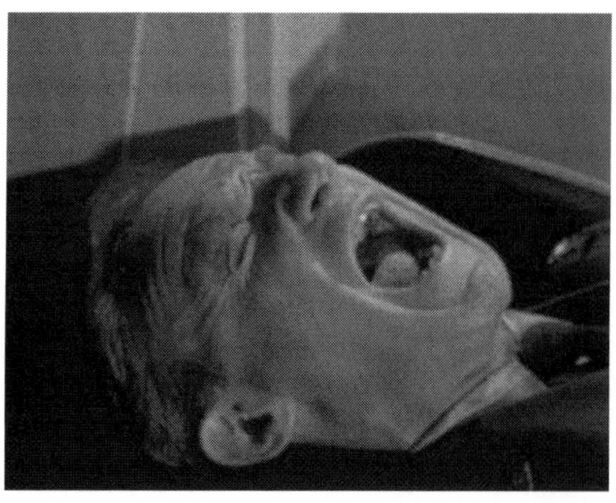

Harris was already thinking about how to protect his job. Bit by bit over the next several episodes, he would make subtle acting choices to take some of the bite out of Dr. Smith.

Also shot this day: the scenes in which Smith suffered the liftoff, the, later, when the not-so-good doctor programmed the Robot to destroy the ship.

The backslide finally stopped. Tony Leader, filming from 8 a.m. to

7:35 p.m., held at two days behind schedule.

Day 8: Wednesday, July 28. Another long day – 8 a.m. to 7:45 p.m. They continued filming on the lower deck, including Smith's anti-gravity experience. This scene was a rare occurrence when Jonathon Harris agreed to do his own stunt – hanging in the air, supported by thin wires. He saw the potential of comedy in the scene, which he felt could mean life or death for his character. He therefore chose to fly on wires.

The final shots taken on this last day of production were of John and Maureen Robinson outside the Jupiter 2. And that was finally a wrap … and the first cliffhanger.

Author's note: In September 1965, I was 10, and my entire family was watching the launch of the Jupiter 2. My father – a patriotic American who had fought for his country in World War II, and was very caught up in the space race between the U.S. and the U.S.S.R. – seemed as enthralled with the adventure as his four children were – until that tether line snapped, at which point he exclaimed "That line was *not* made in America!" A.

Post-Production:

Regarding the looping sessions for the Robot's voice, Dick Tufeld recounted, "I was never on the set. They made loops of Bobby May's voice tracks. They brought me into the dubbing stage, and I had to sync to his voice tracks. He was inside the robot suit pressing a button which activated a light in the robot's head. He would press the button for every syllable, so when I was in sync with him, I was in sync with the light." (DT-LIS4)

Bob May remembered how he felt when he first realized that his voice would not be heard in the series as the Robot. Remarkably, even though he had never been properly miked on the set to be clearly heard doing his lines, nor had he been brought in to loop the lines in during post-production, he nonetheless expected to hear his voice emit from the Robot in the broadcast episodes. Reality sunk in as he watched "The Reluctant Stowaway."

May said, "I'm, like, 'Whoa, what's this?!' Irwin had not said anything to me…. And it was almost like, 'You weren't good enough.' And then I started to think of people like Natalie Wood, who, when she did *West Side Story,* had two different voices singing for her. And you go down through the history of motion pictures and you realize this is not a bad thing. So, when I pulled myself together, and my wife stuck a few pins in me, I realized, 'Hey, that's okay. Do your job. Develop it as high as you possibly can, and feel fortunate that they brought in somebody as good as Dick Tufeld.' Dick was *the* man, and he was great, and he added to the character." (BM-KB95)

Composer/conductor John "Johnny" Williams.

Composer "Johnny" Williams was only 33 when he wrote and conducted the orchestra for the *Lost in Space* theme, as well as the formative score for this first episode. He had already composed the theme music for *Alcoa Premiere* (1961-63) and *Kraft Suspense Theatre* (1963-65). His association with Irwin began here, and Williams would return to compose the title themes for *The Time Tunnel*, *Land of the Giants*, and the second main title theme for *Lost in Space* (for its third season). He also scored Allen's 1970s feature films *The Poseidon Adventure* and *The Towering Inferno.*

Billy Mumy said, "The music is fantastic. Yay, Johnny Williams! And, 'Yay, Irwin,' for giving him the gig." (BM-LISM)

Williams had already achieved great success at a young age, but working for Allen proved to be the luckiest of breaks, for it was fans of Allen's 1960s sci-fi series, such as Steven Spielberg and George Lucas, who gave Williams the opportunity to achieve even greater fame. On the horizon for Williams: the scores for *Close Encounters of the Third Kind*; *Superman*; *The Empire Strikes Back*; *Raiders of the Lost Ark*; *Return of the Jedi*; *Indiana Jones and the Temple of Doom*; *Jurassic Park*, and countless other sci-fi and action/adventure classics. Williams had many awards in his future, as well, including Oscars for his work on *Fiddler on the Roof*, *Jaws*, *Star Wars*, *E.T.: the Extra-Terrestrial*, and *Schindler's List.*

Reviewing the score for "The Reluctant Stowaway" in the March/April 2015 issue of *Famous Monsters*, pop culture/music enthusiast Jeff Bond wrote: "Williams' puling, white-knuckle 'countdown' music for the spaceship's launch, his brilliant scoring of the asteroid storm (a teaser of his famous asteroid sequence music for *The Empire Strikes Back*), and his dire prelude to a spacewalk undertaken by paterfamilias John Robinson (Guy Williams) established the series' exciting sound – one that immediately gripped the imagination of children in the 1960s."

Roland Gross headed *Lost in Space* Film Editing Team No. 1, starting with this episode and cutting 27 more during the three-year run of the series. There were three teams, each given three weeks per episode. Gross had been nominated for an Oscar in 1945 for editing the film *None But the Lonely Heart.*

Don Hall, Jr. was the sound effects editor for *Lost in Space* and, starting with its second season, *Voyage to the Bottom of the Sea.* It is a key position, especially in the genre of science fiction, where layers of sound are often needed to create the atmosphere of the interior of a futuristic submarine or a spaceship, along with the sound of laser guns and the numerous strange noises made by alien devices. Hall would share an Emmy nomination with his sound effects team from *Voyage* in 1966, and then, for the same series, win the award in 1967. In 1970, he and his team would be nominated again, for *Land of the Giants*.

"The Reluctant Stowaway" was supposed to cost $136,325. When all the shooting had finally stopped, and post production had been completed, the price tag climbed to $199,372. This equates to 1.5 million dollars in 2015, no small chunk of change considering that some sequences, and nearly all the photographic effects, had already been paid for out of the budget for the series' pilot film.

Studios expect to experience deficit financing with television series, but not to this degree. The concern at 20th Century-Fox was whether a sci-fi space show of this type could truly be made within the confines of a television production schedule and budgeting. CBS would only pay a licensing fee of approximately $100,000 for each new episode of *Lost in Space*. For the episodes chosen to receive a summer repeat broadcast, the network would pay an additional sum (generally, about one-half of the initial fee). "The Reluctant Stowaway," however, would not air again on CBS, so the studio was in the red by roughly $99,000 on this one episode. The loss would have to be made up for in foreign sales or, much later, in syndicated reruns – and then only if there were enough episodes produced to warrant a rerun package. (In this era, the goal was to stay in production for a minimum of three seasons, with eighty or more episodes available for "stripping" – Monday-Friday rerunning). *Lost in Space* had a long way to go. If each episode added to the studio deficit by $99,000, 20th Century-Fox would have to pull the plug on this risky venture.

Despite the cost, Irwin Allen felt *Lost in Space* had an excellent kickoff episode. Now, if only he could get Shimon Wincelberg to see it that way.

Wincelberg recalled, "To persuade me to leave my name on the episode, he arranged a screening for me. After it was over, he said, 'Well, what do you think?' I said, 'I think it's a terrific show, but I still don't want my name on it.'" (SW-KB95)

Release / Reaction:

(Only CBS broadcast: Wednesday, September 15, 1965)

In the days before *Lost in Space* premiered on CBS-TV, the news was filled with drama. The known death toll from Hurricane Betsy stood at 63 in Louisiana, with 12 others in areas of the Bahamas, Florida and Mississippi. The First Cavalry Division of the U.S. Army arrived in Vietnam, bringing the total of American troops there to 125,000.

At the movies during this week: *The Sound of Music,* starring Julie Andrews and Christopher Plummer, and featuring young Angela Cartwright, was the top money maker, followed by *My Fair Lady*, starring Audrey Hepburn and Rex Harrison. Also a hit in the movie houses: *Help!*, starring the Beatles.

On TV, the other new series premiering this week were *A Man Called Shenandoah*; *Run for Your Life*; *My Mother the Car*; *F Troop*; *Gidget*; *The Big Valley*; *Green Acres*; *I Spy*; *Hogan's Heroes*; *Honey West*; *The Wild, Wild West*; *The Trials of O'Brien*; *Get Smart*; *I Dream of Jeannie*; Rod Serling's *The Loner*; *The F.B.I.*; *The Wackiest Ship in the Army*; *The Smothers Brothers* (the half-hour sitcom); and *The Dean Martin Show*.

Returning series, switching from black and white to color, included *Voyage to the Bottom of the Sea*; *My Favorite Martian*; *The Lucy Show*; *The Andy Griffith Show*; *Dr. Kildare*; *The Beverly Hillbillies*; *Gomer Pyle, U.S.M.C.*; and *The Man from U.N.C.L.E.*

Also on TV this week, the Emmy Awards were handed out. *The Dick Van Dyke Show* was voted Best Comedy, and Van Dyke won an Emmy for himself, as Best Lead in a Comedy. *The Ed Sullivan Show* didn't receive any Emmys, but Ed had the Beatles on his Sunday night show, performing "I Feel Fine," "I'm Down," "Ticket to Ride," "Help!," and a couple of songs you couldn't even buy or hear on the radio yet – "Act Naturally" and "Yesterday."

More Beatles news: The Fab Four had the top song on the radio, with "Help!," and also the top-selling album in record and department stores, with – you guessed it – *Help!*

After removing his name from the premiere episode, Shimon Wincelberg said, "Irwin got his revenge in a wonderful way. When the show aired, it got a rave review in *The New York Times*, which nobody expected. And they also had a particular praise for the writer, under the pseudonym of S. Bar-David, which nobody knew. So he took that review and published full-page ads in the trade papers, praising S. Bar-David. And I thought that was a very elegant way to get revenge." (SW-KB95)

Jack Gould's review in *The New York Times* came out on September 16, the morning after the premiere. His critique was also syndicated to other newspapers, including West Virginia's *Morgantown Post*. Gould wrote, in part:

> *The Perils of Pauline* have been put into a split-level space saucer and *Lost in Space* is a surefire winner for young viewers and probably will amuse senior devotees of science fiction. Allen has developed fantastically super duper settings and a wonderful futuristic environment to rocket the entire Space Family Robinson – the parents and their three children – to another planet.... Gleaming spacesuits, chambers to freeze astronauts into a state of limbo for five-and-a-half years, and mysterious electronic doodads are part of the exotic gear.
>
> The show essentially is a *tour de force* of versatile hardware but there's also a stowaway villain from that enemy country who fouls up the environmental control robot and sends the craft off course. First it is dad who must take a walk into space to repair the saucer, next mother goes out to rescue dad, and then C.B.S. says tune in next Wednesday. The trick photography of L.B. Abbott and Howard Lydecker is superb.

The rest of the reviews were mixed. One could wonder if the various critics had watched the same show.

On the day after the premiere, Clay Gowran of the *Chicago Tribune* hissed:

> ...This science fiction misadventure must be seen to be disbelieved. The nasty robot who spent his time wrecking the spaceship must have written the script. The first episode ended with one of the crew hanging upside down in space or whatever. And why is it that spacecrafts concocted for TV are always as big inside as the Aragon ballroom, while our real astronauts have to orbit in interiors that are the size of a flying broom closet? Our final word on the subject is that *Lost in Space* may find itself lost in the ratings.

That same day, Jerry Coffey had his thumbs up. Writing for the *Fort Worth Star-Telegram*, he said:

> Zorro and Lassie's master's mother turned up Wednesday evening in an adventure series that makes *Buck Rogers* and *Flash Gordon* seem about as far out as *Ozzie and Harriet*. *Lost in Space* is a lead-off entry by CBS, and I suspect that a sizable portion of the TV audience – young and old – will find it irresistible.
>
> The show is the first original television serial in the cliff-hanger style of the old movie continued pieces, except that there are no cliffs to hang from millions of miles out in a runaway spaceship.
>
> ...Jonathan Harris as the snickering, cowering villain, and the robot practically stole the first show, but the real star of *Lost in Space* is producer Irwin Allen, the special effects master, who also is responsible for *Voyage to the Bottom of the Sea*. The space gadgetry and visual effects are something to behold.

Also weighing in on September 16, but taking the counterpoint with his thumb way down, was Jack O'Brian of the *New York Journal-American*. He groaned:

> *Lost in Space* should be. Its premiere plot (out of *Perils of Pauline* by *Swiss Family Robinson*) was about a family sent to colonize a planet 'way out there someplace by Gemini.' An enemy agent (played by Jonathan Harris, using the suspiciously foreign name of "Smith") sabotages the spacecraft, but not enough to stop the show. The authors, directors and producer accomplished that little thing. And what's a nice girl like June Lockhart doing in a space-bomb like this?

On the same day, Al Salerno, of *The New York Telegram*, declared:

> If the stories, action and acting half measure up to the fantastic sets, gadgets and costumes, this hour will attract more than the young folks it is aimed at in early evening. I'll watch it, too, just to see that robot in action and those electronic panels go tilt.... Will the show garner a rating? I think it will. Even if it doesn't, getting there is half the fun.

On September 17, "Daku," writing for *Daily Variety*, had his thumb down, sneered:

> *Lost in Space* is going to be lost in television if they don't get back into orbit.... Unwittingly, it's more comedy than anything else. Producer Irwin Allen, who brought the successful *Voyage to the Bottom of the Sea* to TV last season, apparently tried to emulate this with a futuristic drama in outer space. Not a bad idea; in fact, a very good one. But the execution was something else. *Space* relies heavily on its flashy display of space gadgets and gimmicks, with superficial story reducing the humans involved to the roles of bystanders, not having as much to do as a robot in the film. While this all may be designed to appeal to the little ones, they will have to be very little. Adults, for whom the series is also aimed, are apt to find the whole thing an unbelievable mish-mash. And sci-fi buffs will just forget it, as an insult to their intelligence.... Only character the story delved into at length was the heavy, and this leering, sneering heavy was right out of "The Drunkard," lacking only a neon sign stating "Villain." This hot and cold running spy occupied most of the footage, with the robot a close second.... If the viewer has courage, he'll tune in next week to see what happens.

That same day, with thumb up, was Frank Baron, writing for *The Hollywood Reporter*. He stressed:

> *The Perils of Pauline* were mere snickers compared to dangers encountered in CBS-TV's new sci-fi cliff-hanger *Lost in Space*,

> which debuted Wednesday night at 7:30. Weekly serial, great tongue-in-cheek spoofer, should lure kids like old Saturday matinees, while adults will watch just to hiss the villain or make snide remarks. Producer-creator Irwin Allen has a sure-fire hit in this one, with director Tony Leader using cameras to great advantage, especially with special effects.

The character who made the greatest impression on Baron was Dr. Smith. After paying lip-service to the top-billed stars, he wrote:

> But the villain of the piece is Jonathan Harris, who though billed as special guest star will continue to harass every week. He sneered, scoffed, scowled and menaced, doing all but twirl mustache. His weekly scenery chewing, emoted so facetiously, is to be awaited.

Two days after the premiere, on September 18, A.C. Beckler, Jr., writing for the *Galveston Daily News*, said:

> *Lost in Space* got off the ground Wednesday night. The initial episode was too juvenile for even the younger set. Unless following chapters pick up, the show is doomed to remain … *Lost in Space*.

On September 20, *Broadcasting* magazine sampled other reviews from around the country.

Percy Shain, of the *Boston Globe*, said: "[*Lost in Space*] got lost in its own hyperbole…"

Louis R. Cedrone, Jr., of the *Baltimore Evening Sun*, said: "[*Lost in Space*] looked like the poor man's *Outer Limits* …"

John Horn, of the *New York Herald Tribune*, said: "[*Lost in Space* is] pure grade B hokum…"

Also on September 20, syndicated entertainment critic Allen Rich, carried by the Hollywood *Citizen-News*, tried to sum matters up, writing:

> *Lost in Space*, despite the fact that some among reviewers have deemed it juvenile, is regarded by this column as a sure-fire hit…. This is a big production which got off to a fast start when "The President of the United States" wished all hands well at blast-off time and from there to the cliff-hanger closing with the father of the family dangling outside the ship in an attempt to repair trouble, one crisis followed another and there were no lulls. Before our real-life astronauts blazed new trails the whole thing might have seemed incredible and childish. But not now. It's right on the beam, even allowing for the dramatic license it takes with true space measures.
>
> Tremendous attention has been paid to special effects and this paid off handsomely on the opener.

> Jonathan Harris, once seen as a comedian on *The Bill Dana Show*, turns up as a delightful, tongue-in-cheek villain who seeks to sabotage the venture in this one. There's also an ingenious robot aboard and he, or 'it,' bodes ill for the safety of the family....
>
> With the kids controlling the TV dial at 7:30 and the current interest in space matters, *Lost in Space* has to be a big winner.

On September 22, the critic known as "Horo," reviewing the series for the weekly edition of *Variety*, disagreed with the TV critic at sister trade *Daily Variety*, who had loathed the show. Horo countered:

> For the young set, and those who like their science fiction no matter how simple the characters and plot lines, *Lost in Space* looks like a winner. The opener was as up to date as the last space shot and then some. Created and produced by Irwin Allen, under the banner of 20th Century-Fox, the big credit in this hour-long space series goes to L.B. Abbott and Howard Lydecker, who did the special photographic effects. These effects included a walk in space, a rain of meteors striking a space craft, an up to date Frankenstein in the form of a robot, and a man lost in the wild expanse of yet to be explored universe. In the preem episode, the plot was sheer space corn, but the viewer was offered so much in space hardware and imagination, that the corn was quite digestible. The preem unreeled as if scripter S. Bar-David took an old serial movie and put it into tomorrow's space setting. The villain, of course, had the biggest role and Jonathan Harris played a turncoat American colonel as if he wanted to put Vincent Price out of business.... The production values were lavish. It must have cost a fortune to simulate the space center. Ditto the hardware of the space ship and all those special effects.

On September 23, Milton R. Bass, writing for Massachusetts' *Berkshire Eagle*, rejoiced:

> ...Producer Irwin Allen didn't let us down and I consider *Lost in Space* a must program for kiddies and science-fiction bugs. The program has settings and electronic marvels enough to keep everybody hanging on the edge of his seat as well as space.... They have a zinger of a space ship, a zowie of a robot and a gee-whiz of a villain to go with their own goodies. It is obvious that we are going to be left with a cliff-hanger each week in the classic style of the old movie serials, and the trick photography ensures they will be lulus. The series is a corker, by Gemini.

Also that day, William E. Sarmento filed his assessment, writing for the syndicated "Show Time" column, with the heading, "Nominees for Quick Cancellation." He grumbled:

> *Lost in Space* is as awful as an hour as you could imagine. It has a typical American family launched into space to explore another planet. The family is headed by June Lockhart who has given up her playing second fiddle to a dog, and exposing her children's teeth for fun and profit, to play the wife. Her spouse is another TV castoff, Guy Williams, who has forsaken his black hat, mask and cape of Zorro to do this terrible show. They are supported by three talentless children, which is not surprising when you consider their roots. When last I saw Miss Lockhart and Mr. Williams, they were floating in space to try to get back into their space capsule. Let's hope they don't make it.

The reviews were 50/50 good and bad. Regarding those against, Irwin Allen's cousin and longtime collaborator Al Gail rationalized, "As you may know, critics are very snobbish. And they felt, possibly, it was below them to praise these type of shows, which were aimed at the family and at the youngsters, and at that level of entertainment. And I don't think they praised any shows of this type. I think [Gene] Roddenberry had the same problem [with *Star Trek*]. Well, Gene Roddenberry said he enjoyed what Irwin was doing, and he gave Irwin a lot of credit for the things that Gene did himself. And Gene himself said the critics never gave him a fair shake. So, it was a problem. I don't think it was a problem with the show, or with the people, I think it was a problem with the critics who felt it was beneath them." (AG-KB95)

The critics had spoken. But what about the people?

The competition for *Lost in Space* on NBC was *The Virginian*, beginning its fourth season with series regular Clu Gulager (as Ryker) setting out to capture his close friend, Matt Denning (Robert Lansing), who had broken his brother out of an Army stockade. On ABC: *Ozzie and Harriet*, starting its fourteenth TV season, presented a story in which a neighbor's wife talks a bewildered Ozzie into posing as her husband (don't ask), and with Rick singing "Try to Remember." Next, on *The Patty Duke Show*, embarking on its third season, Frankie Avalon was the special guest.

A.C. Nielsen's 26-City Trendex Survey from September 15, 1965 ranked the early Wednesday night shows as follows:

7:30 – 8 pm:	Rating:	Share:
ABC: *The Adventures of Ozzie & Harriet*	10.0	21.7%
CBS: *Lost in Space*	**17.2**	**37.1%**
NBC: *The Virginian*	15.9	34.6%

8 – 8:30 pm:	Rating:	Share:
ABC: *The Patty Duke Show*	14.1	29.3%
CBS: *Lost in Space*	**17.8**	**36.9%**
NBC: *The Virginian*	12.4	25.8

Looking at the entire week (September 13-19, 1965), as reported in September 27, 1965 issue of *Broadcasting* magazine, A.C. Nielsen 30-Market survey ranked the Top-40 primetime shows (from more than 80 programs) this way:

1.	*A Man Called Shenandoah*	ABC
2.	*Bewitched*	ABC
	Run for Your Life	NBC
4.	*Bonanza*	NBC
	The Fugitive	ABC
6.	*Get Smart*	NBC
7.	*The Man from U.N.C.L.E.*	NBC
8.	*The Smothers Brothers*	CBS
9.	*The FBI*	ABC
	The Dick Van Dyke Show	CBS
11.	*F Troop*	ABC
12.	*The Dean Martin Show*	NBC
13.	*The Legend of Jesse James*	ABC
14.	*Green Acres*	CBS
15.	*Don't Eat the Daisies!*	NBC
16.	*Peyton Place 1*	ABC
	I Dream of Jeannie	NBC
18.	*McHale's Navy*	ABC
19.	*Honey West*	ABC
20.	*I Spy*	NBC
21.	The Saturday Night Movie	NBC
	Hogan's Heroes	CBS
	The Tuesday Night Movie	NBC
24.	The Sunday Night Movie	ABC
	Peyton Place 2	ABC
26.	*12 O'Clock High*	ABC
	My Mother the Car	NBC
28.	*Gidget*	ABC
29.	*O.K. Crackerby!*	ABC
30.	*My Three Sons*	CBS
31.	*Gomer Pyle, U.S.M.C.*	CBS
	The Lucy Show	CBS
32.	*The Farmer's Daughter*	ABC
34.	*The Wackiest Ship in the Army*	NBC
35.	*Hazel*	CBS
36.	*Gilligan's Island*	CBS
	The Andy Griffith Show	CBS
38.	***Lost in Space***	**CBS**
39,	*The Big Valley*	ABC
40.	The Thursday Night Movie	CBS

Among those watching was Shimon Wincelberg and his family. Daughter Bryan, six years old at the time, later said, "I remember very specifically that my father didn't let us watch the programs he wrote for quite a while, but I do remember us seeing the pilot, and it scared me. And I remember kind of leaving the room and sort of peeking from around a patrician from where the room split into another. So, I was peeking around to watch it but also being scared. Zachary Smith was really menacing." (BK-AI16)

11

Episode 2: "The Derelict"

Teleplay by Peter Packer; story by Shimon Wincelberg
(with script polishing by Anthony Wilson)
Directed by Alexander Singer
Produced by Buck Houghton (uncredited), with Jerry Briskin
Executive Producer: Irwin Allen

From the *Lost in Space* show files (Irwin Allen Papers collection):

> Robinson, outside the spaceship when the tether broke, is rescued by his wife. Next, they see an enormously large alien spaceship, seemingly adrift. It bears down on them and engulfs their whole vessel inside it. While John and Don are studying its navigational system for clues to their whereabouts, Will, exploring, finds a huge chamber full of strange, frozen forms. Unwittingly he presses the button that defrosts them. Smith, finding Will and terrified by these strange-looking creatures, fires at them. The angry aliens mass to attack...

From the Script:

(Shooting Final teleplay, July 29 draft)

– *Maureen (into mike):* "Don's suiting up now. He's going to shoot another line out with the rocket gun…" *Robinson's Voice (urgent):* "No! Not Don! He's got to stay with the ship!" *Smith:* "A brave man. Words like that are worthy of an epitaph." *Don:* "There is something useful you can do, Doctor. Suit up!" *Smith:* "I? In the airlock? My dear man, in the first place, I am not an official member of this expedition, and, in the second, I'm simply not conditioned for it – the heart … at my age … *(snaps his fingers)* … out like a light!"

– *Robinson (to Smith):* "You realize, of course, that we seem to be imprisoned here." *Smith (with mock concern):* "Yes, yes, quite a predicament. Have they, uh – communicated with you yet?" *Don:* "Not by any signal we can read." *Smith (sure that the unseen occupants are his friends):* "Well – they're not in any hurry – I don't suppose." *Maureen:* "How can you possibly know that, Dr. Smith – when we're almost certain this ship can't be from our planet." *Smith:* "Is that what you think?" *Don:* "Don't you?" *Smith:* "Well – uh – if you're all agreed, I – guess I must go along with you."

Assessment:

"The Reluctant Stowaway" had been a thrill ride hard to beat, but "The Derelict" seemed to top it. Over a year before a television audience would see the U.S.S. Enterprise encounter the giant spaceship Fesarius in the first-season *Star Trek* episode "The Corbomite Maneuver," we were treated to the sight of the Jupiter 2 encountering a ship better than ten times its own size. And then Goliath actually swallowed David! As the hangar doors closed, the mouths of the kids watching from home dropped open. We in the viewing audience sat in awe as John and Don, with the not-to-be-trusted Dr. Smith tagging along, left the ship and journeyed into the dark and eerily alien surroundings of the gargantuan spaceship. With crystalline elements hanging like cobwebs, and the membrane-like material on walls and sometimes even floors, the sights and sounds were truly out-of-this-world. Next came the bubble creatures, crackling and buzzing, seeming to speak with electrical charges.

The FX are the guest stars of this episode – that giant alien spaceship, the miniature Jupiter 2 moving through the interior of the ship, then rotating and landing, and those curious bubble creatures. Kudos to the seven principal actors; writers Peter Packer and Tony Wilson; director Alexander Singer; wardrobe designer and all-around helper Paul Zastupnevich; art director Robert Kinoshita; set decorators Walter M. Scott and Sven Wickman; photographic effects wizards L.B. Abbott and Howard Lydecker; special effects supervisor Johnny Borgese; composer Herman Stein; and producers Houghton, Briskin and Allen. Their combined talents made for a very memorable adventure.

Script:

Story Assignment 8542 (Production #8502)

Story outline by Peter Packer received May 25, 1965.

Peter Packer 1st draft teleplay, also delivered on May 25, 1965.

Packer's 2nd draft teleplay: Early June 1965.
Reformatted Mimeo Department Shooting Final teleplay: Early June 1965.
Tony Wilson's script polish (Revised Shooting Final teleplay): July 1965.
Wilson's additional polishing (2nd Rev. Shooting Final teleplay, with beige page inserts): July 27, 1965.
Page revisions by Wilson (blue insert pages): July 28.
Additional revisions by Wilson (pink insert pages): July 29.

Writer Peter Packer.

Tony Wilson brought Peter Packer to *Lost in Space*. They knew one another from *Bonanza*, where Wilson had worked as a story consultant, and consulted on a scripts written by Packer.

Packer was 59. Despite being born in London, England, he loved westerns and mostly stayed with that genre in a screenwriting career that began in 1955. Prior to that, he wrote novels, such as *White Crocus* and *The Love Thieves*. Later, he wrote the screenplay to the 1956 western, *7th Cavalry*, with Randolph Scott as one of the few survivors of the Battle of Little Big Horn, sent to bring back the body of General Custer. On TV, Packer had multiple script assignments for *Bonanza* and *The Big Valley*, and also wrote one script each for other TV westerns, such as *Stoney Burke* and *The Virginian*. He created *Man Without a Gun*, a half-hour western series in the late 1950s, which ran for one season. He produced *Law of the Plainsman*, another western series, which also ran for only one season (1959-1960). It starred Michael Ansara, who would later be a *Lost in Space* guest star in "The Challenge." In addition, Packer served as a producer on two other series: *My Friend Flicka* and *The 20th Century-Fox Hour*. After meeting Irwin Allen, he wrote one script for *Voyage to the Bottom of the Sea*, and would later contribute one to *Land of the Giants*. But his real claim to fame was for writing 25 episodes for *Lost in Space* – more than any other writer. This was his first.

Peter Packer turned in his first draft teleplay on May 25, 1965. Included in the script:

> 194. INT. PASSAGEWAY VAULT – NIGHT
>
> MED. SHOT
> ON Will and Smith – staring apprehensively toward the o.s. bubble creatures – backing away – searching for the exit as a membrane-like section appears to block their progress.
>
> 195. THE BUBBLE CREATURES
> Buzzing and crackling angrily. There is a general stirring among them as though they are preparing to advance.
>
> 196. CLOSE – SMITH
>
> desperate now – he raises his gun – discharges it again.

> as one of them bursts apart in a vivid explosion of light – and the crackling and buzzing of the others goes to a crescendo. They begin to advance.

Up to this point in the development of Packer's script, Smith was seen blasting a couple of the bubble creatures out of existence with a laser gun, and John and Don had to destroy the alien spaceship in order for the Jupiter 2 to escape.

Three days after receiving the script, Sam Taylor, Jr., of CBS Program Practices, Hollywood, sent request for changes, including:

> Page 14: As discussed with Mr. Houghton, you may decide not to show the "creatures" from the Derelict being killed as this synopsis indicates. If they are killed, the action, even though taken by Smith, a heavy, will be defensive. The same philosophy should govern the possible "explosion" of the Derelict (with its inhabitants). It should only occur if necessary to save the life of the Robinsons.

After Packer's second draft script was submitted, Taylor sent a request for additional changes:

a) Re-establish Smith's function and mission and the fact that he was an interloper.
b) Carefully review and eliminate all the sweetness and light. Also, double check objectionable lines indicated in marked script (Especially watch stage direction indicating such attitudes in order that director not be misled).
c) Smith's speech in the middle of Page 22 should have the addition "and get back to Earth."
d) John's voice – Scene 101 – speech should comment on the presence of Smith and the annoyance he has caused the family.
e) Re: the "bubble people" – sound effects will play an important part here – use echo chamber – to get humanlike aspect to a non-human looking apparition. Have Will remark: "They are not like us but maybe they are."
f) Page 58 – Scene 234 – John's first speech, change the word "alien" to "inhuman."

CBS also had issues over Maureen Robinson being placed in danger during the space walk scenes outside the Jupiter 2, and her children's reactions as they watched in alarm from inside the ship.

Paul Zastupnevich said, "The mother should never be in jeopardy. That's why poor June never could do anything. Even when we put her out in space at the one time, to try to help Guy back into the spaceship, there was quite a bit of flack about that." (PZ-KB95)

A clever trick, begun by Packer and Wilson and honed to perfection by director Singer and Jonathan Harris, was presenting Smith as a dastardly villain who we nevertheless couldn't help but like. The comical exchanges between Smith and Robot, while guardedly subtle at this early stage in the series, nevertheless raised a smile on the faces of those watching.

Pre-Production:

Alexander Singer was hired to direct. He was 37 and, after directing a 1961 indie called *A Cold Wind in August*, Singer started picking up TV assignments, such as one episode each for *Ripcord*, *Dr. Kildare*, *Profiles in Courage*, and two for *Checkmate*, then several for *The Fugitive. Psyche 59*, a 1964 feature film, did well enough to make him a sought-after director for about a year, and that brought him to *Lost in Space* for his one and only assignment.

Stuntman Dawson Palmer was the man hired to get inside the Bubble Creature suit, making his first of sixteen known *Lost in Space* "appearances."

Production Diary:

Filmed July 29 through August 9, 1965 (8 days).

The entire episode was filmed on Stage 5, which included the upper and lower decks for the Jupiter 2, and the wonderland interior of the alien ship, which included the landing bay area where the full-sized prop of the entire Jupiter 2 was placed. It was a massive undertaking, helped somewhat by materials used in the 20th Century-Fox film *Fantastic Voyage*, currently shooting on the lot.

New York's *Daily News* writer Kay Gardella visited the set and the offices of Irwin Allen while this episode filmed. She filed a story with her newspaper on August 3, reporting:

> Oh, it's big-budgeted all right. In fact, as Allen himself admits, no show in TV has ever spent more in pre-production -- $650,000 -- with each episode budgeted around $200,000. A robot, one of the cast of characters, cost $32,000 to construct…. For the show, a 60-ft., two-story space ship, replete with castoffs and obsolete equipment from our nation's space programs, has been constructed.

There's no specific technical advisor on the show. However, Elizabeth Manuel, head of the research department, keeps a hot-line between here and Washington for final checks on scientific detail and accurate dialogue provided by story editor Tony Wilson and his stable of writers. Where this isn't necessary is in the area of pure fantasy. For instance, when the world's first space colonists are confronted with weird space creatures. We were introduced to just such people on Stage 8. They were plastic-like mobiles heavily populating a ceiling-to-floor sea of what appeared to be cotton candy. "These," said our gallant guide, [Guy] Williams, "are some of the people we meet in space. They're called 'Bubble People.' And all the time we thought they were all here in Hollywood.

Irwin Allen's intention was that *Lost in Space* would have some sex appeal. Before CBS objected, John and Maureen Robinson were meant to openly display affection, as these unreleased promotional pictures from "The Derelict" reveal.

Not verbalized to reporter Gardella, but on everyone's mind: the series was rapidly falling further behind schedule. The show had gotten a late start in production due to the changes in the format – having to build the robot and add two new cast members. And, already, it was not keeping up with the six-day production schedule assigned to each episode by 20th Century-Fox.

"The Reluctant Stowaway" had taken director Tony Leader eight days of filming to complete, despite the use of some footage from the pilot film. This was a full two days late in finishing. Alexander Singer had been waiting in the wings on Tuesday and Wednesday, and now, on Thursday morning, he finally got started. The pressure from the front office was on him to make up for Leader's lost time. The shooting schedule for this second episode was also planned for six days.

Day 1: Thursday, July 29, 1965. Filming began at 8 a.m. and continued until 6:40 p.m. First up: the children watching helplessly through the porthole as their parents faced danger outside the ship; Don suiting up and going into the airlock in an attempt to rescue John and Maureen; Smith bringing up the fire extinguisher from the lower deck; Don trying to open the hatch, and using the fire extinguisher to cool the expanded metal bulkhead. When production suspended, Singer was one-quarter of a day behind.

Day 2: Friday, July 30. Filming lasted from 8 a.m. to 6:50 p.m. They began with the scenes Singer had missed getting the day before, including Don pulling John and Maureen into the ship, then Maureen having trouble recovering. Next, the encounter with the giant alien ship in space. The cast didn't have to pretend they saw The Derelict; rear projection was used and they could actually see what was pulling them in. Locked-off mattes were used for POV shots through the Jupiter 2's view ports.

As for learning to react to off-screen menaces that would only be added in post, June Lockhart observed: "You could pretend *anything* while doing such a scene. You just dip into your little bag of reactions and pretend you're in peril. When I was doing *Lassie*, for example, I knew there actually *wasn't* a bear in the tree, but I did have to protect the kid and the dog. It's really just a game. If you go overboard with your own reaction, the audience has nothing to be frightened about seeing. If you carry on too much, you remove their involvement. I don't follow any formula for filming reaction shots, other than, 'Don't smile until the director yells *Cut*!'" (JL-SL83)

A rear projection screen was used outside the main viewport of the upper deck in order to allow cast members to see what their characters were reacting to.

More drama as the Jupiter 2 was sucked into the huge alien spaceship, followed by John and Don's decision to go outside to investigate, with Smith, while the rest watched in suspense.

When all had been filmed, Singer was a half of a day behind schedule.

Day 3: Monday, August 2. They filmed from 8 a.m. to 6:48 p.m., still on the upper deck of the

Jupiter 2, as Don returned, then prepared to lift off and pilot the ship out of the giant alien vessel. When Singer called for a "wrap," he was a full day behind.

Day 4: Tuesday, August 3. Filming from 8 a.m. to 6:48 p.m., again on the upper deck set. Only two-and-four-eighths pages of script were covered. Among these: the action onboard the Jupiter 2 as the ship escapes from the giant spaceship, and then the decision whether to investigate the alien planet. Singer was now one-and-a-quarter days behind.

Day 5: Wednesday, August 4. It was a longer day – 8 a.m. to 7:17 p.m. Singer shot eleven pages from the script on the lower deck of the Jupiter 2, including the scene where Smith tampered with the Robot; the later scene where John confronted Smith in his cabin; John visiting Will in his cabin; and then into Penny's cabin. The voice reading Shakespeare on tape played by Penny was an uncredited Richard Basehart, then starring in Allen's other current series *Voyage to the Bottom of the Sea*.

To get the above shot, Jonathan Harris had to stand on an "apple box" (below image).

Also filmed, Will outsmarting the Robot by mimicking Dr. Smith. Bob May was again called upon to injure his legs by "walking the Robot," although this time he only had to only go a few steps.

Singer finished one-and-a-half days behind.

Day 6: Thursday, August 5. This was supposed to be the last day of filming. Everyone knew it wouldn't be, and the next episode scheduled to film, "Island in the Sky," was pushed back. Filming began at 8 a.m. in the hangar deck of the alien ship, outside the Jupiter 2.

The full-size Jupiter 2 allowed the cast to stand inside on a platform and be visible through the main viewport. Of course it wasn't as big as the ship would have been to contain the interior sets we saw, but it was nonetheless a marvel to see … and yet we would only see it a few times (most notably in this episode and Season Three's "A Visit to a Hostile Planet") due to the time it took to ready the "prop."

Billy Mumy said, "The full-sized Jupiter 2 prop, which resided on the back lot near the carpenters' shop, was made of wood and steel. It looked great … until you walked up the landing gear and tried to fit inside its empty husk, with four-by-four nails everywhere… It was very cool, though. But we only used it a couple of times." (BM-LISM)

The other two times were for Season Two's "The Ghost Planet" and Season Three's "Visit to a Hostile Planet."

Work continued in different areas of the derelict ship, including Will and Smith's encounter with the "Bubble Boys" (as the shooting schedule referred to them).

Among the portions of the script shot this day:

177 INT. PASSENGER VAULT

ANGLE ON SMITH
entering – his smile becoming fixed and grotesque as:

178 SMITH'S P.O.V. – BUBBLE CREATURE
floating – buzzing – crackling – the inner ultra-violet light almost dazzling in its intensity.

179 ANGLE ON SMITH
A blob of terror – fumbling for the electron gun – producing it – aiming it –

WILL'S VOICE
(yelling out)
No - ! Don't shoot!

Smith reacts – staring around in shock as Will runs toward him.

WILL
They were in those walls. I disturbed 'em...
(indicating)
That one – he – I think I can communicate with him –

SMITH
(staring incredulously –
half dismayed –
shaking his head)
Not human – nothing ... and I was so sure –

WILL
Human? Out here? Billions of miles from Earth?

Smith stares hopelessly – then with a kind of malevolent fury at being frustrated, again raises his electron gun. Will grabs it.

WILL
No! Maybe they can help us!
(beat)
I mean, they're not like us but maybe they are...

Smith stares at him – he looks toward the bubble creatures.

180 THE BUBBLE CREATURES

at a distance – hovering – almost still as they seem to be watching Smith ... the leader just as still – in front of them.

181 TWO SHOT – SMITH, WILL

SMITH
(silkily)
All right, my boy – see what you can do.

While Jonathan Harris and Billy Mumy filmed their scenes with the "Bubble Boys," Guy Williams was interviewed by a Hollywood correspondent for a syndicated article, carried in the September 3, 1965 edition of the *Galveston Daily News*. The writer told us:

> Guy Williams is a bit more relaxed, now that his new CBS-TV series, *Lost in Space*, has actually gone into production. After the pilot was made and sold, many months went by before shooting began on the series, leading Guy to say that if they delayed much more, "by the time we get in our sixth show, we may be doing it live. Actually, anybody can start filming early. This is just another challenge in a business that thrives on challenges."

They didn't wrap until 6:55 p.m. Singer was now a full two days behind.

Day 7: Friday, August 6. Another long day – 8 a.m. to 7:13 p.m., filming in the "Hall of Controls" area of the alien ship. The images of star clusters and distant galaxies were provided by The California Institute of Technology, also known as CalTech. The private research university located in Pasadena, California, managed JPL (Jet Propulsion Laboratories) for NASA. The pictures were taken from CalTech's 200-inch telescope, located on nearby Palomar Mountain. Beginning in 1948, and for more than 40 years, it was acknowledged to be the world's most powerful optical telescope. The picture provided to *Lost in Space* had been taken in 1959, as acknowledged in the end credits of every episode from the series.

At the end of the seventh day of production, Singer held at two days behind.

Above: Guy Williams standing outside the full-size Jupiter 2 "prop." Below: June Lockhart resting between scenes on a slant board. The stiff spacesuit did not allow for her to sit.

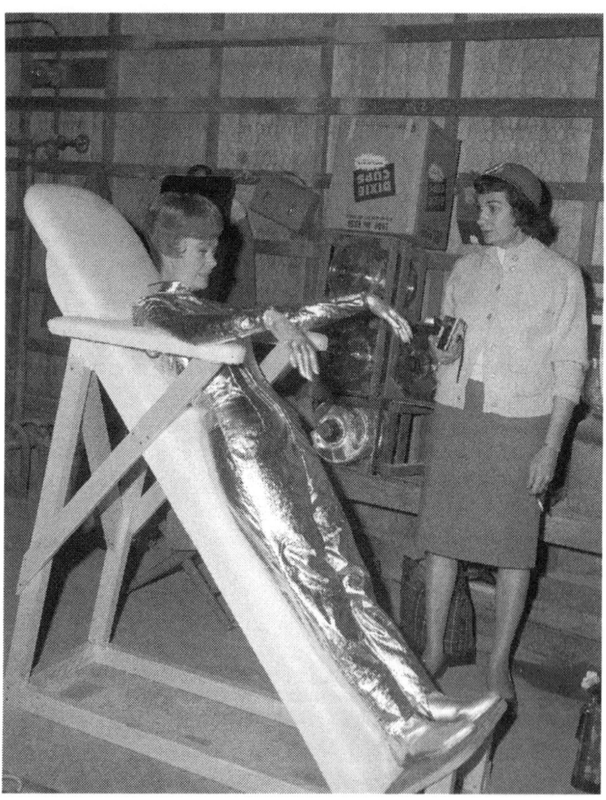

Day 8: Monday, August 9. The longest day yet, with Singer being pushed to finish. They filmed from 8 a.m. to 7:55 p.m. It took all of that to cover the remaining eight-and-three-eighths pages from the script in and around the "Hangar" of the alien spaceship.

Also filmed: the exterior shots of the Jupiter 2 in space, as John tried to repair the ship, then drifted off into space, and then was rescued by Maureen.

June Lockhart told interviewer Steve Swires of *Starlog*, "That was very complicated. I had to wear a special flying suit with a harness around my pelvis. There were bolts which stuck out at the hip and were attached to wires outside the suit. When I was lifted up, the wires supported me by my crotch, and I had to balance myself so I was flat. Because the harness was so tight around the femoral artery, it shut off the flow of blood to my brain, so I could only stay up there for a short while. It was a very difficult stunt to do, but I got a kick out of it. It helped to be athletic, which I am." (JL-ST83)

Interviewed by syndicated entertainment columnist Erskine Johnson while filming this episode, Guy Williams admitted that he kept telling the production people that he weighed ten pounds more than he actually did. He said, "They keep asking me to fly on wires, and they look worried, like maybe they are not sure of the wire's strength. I'm wired like a puppet, but those wires have to be thin enough so they won't photograph."

Johnson wrote:

> For his space walking in the show he is dangled from wires attached to a trolley-like affair on the high ceiling of the biggest sound stage at the 20th Century-Fox studio. The trolley is operated by a technician seated at an electronically operated console who, explains Guy, "can reel me in and out [from] our space craft just by pressing buttons. Really, it's amazing."

In a different interview, with Joan E. Vadeboncoeur, and published in the September 5, 1965 edition of the *Syracuse Herald-American*, Williams told how the producer's efforts to make *Lost in Space* a visual feast had caused giant problems. One month before the series' scheduled premiere on CBS, he said, "We haven't filmed the third show yet." The on-set effects, he said, were "a good part of the reason we're behind."

The production ended as it had been for three days now – two days late.

Alexander Singer chose not to return to the series or to direct any other one-hour episodes for Irwin Allen.

June Lockhart said, "We had some very good directors on *Lost in Space* that first season, but they probably only did one or two shows, and then probably went to a halfway house!" (JL-SL94)

It was likely Irwin Allen would not have invited Singer back. Allen kept a record of how many "camera hours" each director took to complete his episode(s). Singer used up 80.6 camera hours to finish his. Only two First Season episodes took longer, and, after getting a second chance, the director of those was not asked to return either (see "Island in the Sky").

Singer was in demand elsewhere and kept busy on less problematic series, including directing nine episodes of *The Fugitive*; eighteen for *Lou Grant*; fourteen for *Knot's Landing*; and sixteen for *Cagney & Lacey*. Returning to the sci-fi genre, Singer directed six episodes of *Star Trek: The Next Generation*, six for *Star Trek: Deep Space Nine*, and ten for *Star Trek: Voyager*. Proving there was no residual bad blood between himself and Irwin Allen, Singer also directed a 1976 TV movie and back-door pilot for Allen – *Time Travelers*.

Of the Jupiter 2 miniature seen inside the derelict ship, L.B. Abbott said, "We had a two-foot diameter Jupiter 2 with the mechanical sophistication capable of physically performing the lowering and recovery." (LBA-LISF1)

Lost in Space fan and magazine writer Mike Clark was more specific, saying, "The interior of the Derelict starts off with the 15" Jupiter II miniature on horizontal Lydecker-style guide wires that tangled as the jaws of the Derelict closed, causing the model to shake. The live-action team neatly carried the shake through to the shot of the Robinsons inside the Jupiter, and it cut beautifully.

"However, once fully within the Derelict, the 48" model was flown by vertical wires and took over for the hovering and landing." (MC-AI15)

What appears to be a matte shot placing June Lockhart and the children in the Jupiter 2 when the ship was stationary inside the belly of the giant alien ship was actually something much more impressive than a matte process. Clark revealed, "This is not a miniature or a matte shot. It's a live action shot of the full-scale Jupiter 2 with the actors at the window." (MC-AI15)

In other shots, when the Jupiter 2 is in motion, turning and making its way through the interior of the alien craft, the motionless crew members seen through the main viewport are miniature figures. On the smaller television screens of the 1960s, the stick figures almost looked good enough.

Frederick Baratta was the head of the second film editing team on *Lost in Space*. "The Derelict" was his first of 27 episodes. He had already cut three episodes of *Voyage to the Bottom of the Sea* during its first season. Prior to that, he'd been the lead film editor on twelve episodes of *The Outer Limits*.

Composer Herman Stein.

Herman Stein wrote the music score for this episode. Stein was a child prodigy who reportedly played piano at age three, and was a concert performer by six. Starting in 1951, he spent ten years on the staff of the Universal-International music department where he composed themes and scores for many of the studio's science-fiction and horror films, including, from 1953, *It Came from Outer Space* and *Abbott and Costello Go to Mars*; from 1955, *This Island Earth* and *Revenge of the Creature*; from 1956, *Francis in the Haunted House* and *The Mole People*; and from 1957, *The Incredible Shrinking Man* and *The Monolith Monsters*. Stein did his share of westerns and comedies, as well. In this episode of *Lost in Space*, with certain scenes featuring Smith and/or the Robot, Stein's sense of humor comes through. He was 50, and would contribute music to three more episodes of *Space*, one of *Voyage to the Bottom of the Sea*, and eighteen of *The Time Tunnel*.

As for replacing Bob May's voice with his own as the Robot, Dick Tufeld said, "The dubbing was done rather imperfectly. They used to dub one reel at a time. There were a couple to the show, and we would sometimes have a different mixer in the second part of the show. The sound mixer would not always use the same equalization for looping. One mixer might give a tinny/metallic sound, while another might push the lower register. Consequently, you would have the robot sounding one way before the commercial break, and sounding another way for the last part of the show sometimes." (DT-LISF4)

Total cost for "The Derelict": $189,915, far above 20th Century-Fox's target of $130,000 per episode.

Release / Reaction:

(Only CBS broadcast: Wednesday, September 22, 1965)

The Beatles, with *Help!*, still had the top-selling album at Sears and Montgomery Ward, as well as other stores that sold records. The title track was the most requested song on America's radio stations. On TV, the new Beatles cartoon series began on ABC's Saturday morning schedule. It would run for three years. The most popular movies playing across the country were *The Sound of Music*, *My Fair Lady*, and *Those Magnificent Men in Their Flying Machines*.

As for "The Derelict," the syndicated newspaper column "TV Scout," carried in the September 21, 1965 edition of *The Edwardsville Intelligencer*, said:

> Series has more cliff-hanging thrills for the younger set. The Robinsons are still floating around in space from tether to tether. Some of their new problems include a huge, mysterious space craft which gobbles up their ship, and Dr. Smith, who keeps teaching his robot mean tricks. Also, there's the chance to land on a planet, which glows like a rotten tomato.

On September 23, after watching two episodes of *Lost in Space*, Bob MacKenzie, writing for the *Oakland Tribune*, reviewed the series, and, especially, "The Derelict," saying:

> When my brain has become numb and paralyzed by the strained and labored doings of the half-hour comedies, when I am weary and heavy laden with the pathetic antics of Ivy-League Frankensteins [*The Munsters*] and affluent hillbillies [*The Beverly Hillbillies*], when the hollow reverberations of the laugh-track have sunk me into despair – then I turn to a program where innocence reigns; where the comedy is pure and unintentional, unaccompanied by electronic guffaws. *Lost in Space* is its name, and its charms are boundless. Not that it is so radical. Its thesis is no less preposterous, nor its plots more ungainly, than those of the more unlikely comedies. Its delicious appeal lies in the fact that it is apparently meant to be serious. In all seeming solemnity and good will, it puts forth the notion of a wholesome American family, clad in fetching Saran wrap, meandering through the stratosphere in a flying saucer without the least idea of where they are, with nobody for company but an irritable robot and a sinister foreign spy.
>
> If the actors have any inkling that the situations are ridiculous, the dialogue side-splitting and the whole series irresistibly comic, they don't betray it by the quiver of a lip. They play it with all the solemn earnestness of a ladies club meeting to discuss the Viet Nam question. Most charming is the beautiful naiveté with which the program ignores the elemental scientific facts known by every literate six year old in this, the age of space. In last night's

> episode, John and Maureen were outside the ship fixing something when the door stuck shut, trapping them outside temporarily. There was a comet on the way, and John and Maureen bravely told the others to drive on and leave them in space, to save themselves from the comet. Of course, all they would have had to do is hang on to the ship by their guide-wires, and they could have ridden right along without the least discomfort. But, if the writers knew that, they weren't letting on. Later, Don came out and laboriously lifted their unconscious bodies back into the ship, straining noticeably under their weight. A cynic would object here that people in space don't weigh anything, and Don could have thrown them both in with one hand. Anyone who would bring up an objection like that is ill-tempered and reactionary. Later on, they are trapped inside a giant space ship by a large creature resembling a caterpillar. Little Billy Mumy struck up a promising friendship with the caterpillar, who apparently had no trouble understanding English. But, before we could learn if the caterpillar was a former Rhodes Scholar, the spy shot it and the group had to make a fast exit.
>
> The character with the most verve is Jonathan Harris, smirking diabolically as "the spy of a foreign power." It is not stated what foreign power he represents, but he has a decided British accent. Does this mean we will be at war with the British in 1997? Come to think of it, those British have been getting rather uppity lately.

On September 26, Ginny Fisher, writing for the *Sunday Journal and Star*, out of Lincoln, Nebraska, said:

> The new series, which airs in the 6:30 p.m. [Central Time] Wednesday timeslot is, naturally, geared towards the younger crowd. The trouble is that it isn't so much a top effort for children as it is just a childish effort – and there is a big difference. Any weekly show that feels, after an hour's worth of programming, the need to stop suddenly in the midst of a harrowing adventure and briskly announce "continued next week" is slightly immature. Cliff hangers were bad enough, but space hangers, come now!
>
> What's really irritating is that "space hangers" and rough robots that go around mumbling "destroy, destroy" are not needed. Basically, the show is good enough entertainment, especially for the young or for Flash Gordon diehards. The stars are capable, the topic is timely and the stage is set for multiple adventures. Monsters they should have, sure, it's that type of show. But gimmicky monsters, never! ...
>
> The show is somewhat akin to *Gilligan's Island*, which proved such a successful sleeper last year, and, naturally, to the novel *Swiss Family Robinson*, which is ever popular.... Therefore, the series should have some audience potential, but it may have to

> straighten out and fly right a bit first. Erase the comic strip gimmicks and techniques and the show may have a chance.
>
> This will never be a great or critically acclaimed show, but as a possible adventure series it could eventually become good escapism fare. However, if the show continues to have space hangers and such, it could turn out that unlike "Trix," this serial is for rabbits – kids are too smart.

On September 29, *Los Angeles Times*' entertainment correspondent/critic Hal Humphrey had one of his articles syndicated across America, picked up by newspapers such as the *Steubenville Herald-Star*. Humphrey wrote:

> In a flush of disgust after witnessing the first scenery-chewing episodes of the new CBS-TV series *Lost in Space*, I tagged off my review by commenting that "Your 5-year-old will eat this up." I have since been upbraided thoroughly for my remark, and with considerably justification on the part of my upbraided, who is Mrs. Orman Longstreet, a former chairman of the Los Angeles 10th District PTA's TV-radio committee.
>
> "The time and format of *Lost in Space* suggest that it is indeed aimed at families, and that there are probably a number of 5-year-olds who are its actual or potential audience, but a 5-year-old won't eat it up, he'll hate it," writes Mrs. Longstreet.
>
> "In an age of space and space technology," she continues, "a 5-year-old would not understand this show as fantasy, and my main objection to it is that, having hurried a family into orbit without even minimal safety or security precautions, the plot first puts the mother into considerable peril and shows her family being worried about her, and then goes on to put the father into mortal danger and leaves him there until the next week!"
>
> ...Mrs. Longstreet's letter closed with this provoking thought: "Unless children are provided with material of quality, they will grow up not knowing what quality is. If they are exploited, and frightened, and condescended to in the name of entertainment or anything else, they will grow up to exploit and frighten and look down on other people, and to some extent we will all be the poorer."
>
> I do not intend to cop a plea here, although I did not mean to imply that simply because the *Lost in Space* series obviously was geared for kids it necessarily would be good for them to watch.... So, if I in any way implied a recommendation of *Lost in Space* for 5-year-olds, I hereby take it back.

One day later, United Press International writer Rick Du Brow took assessment of the new season. His syndicated commentary was carried by newspapers across the

U.S., including the *Bristol Daily Courier*, of Bristol County, Pennsylvania. Du Brow raved over NBC's *I Spy*, which he found "delightful," and liked ABC's *The Big Valley*, with characters that struck him as "straight and unpretentious." Then, Du Brow turned his attention, and his sharpened pencil, toward "the tiffany network," writing, in part:

> Meanwhile, back at the launching pad, CBS-TV offered a new hour series called *Lost in Space*, a science-fiction concoction of depressing cleverness and comic-strip juvenility concerning a family of the future that is sent to another planet for colonizing purposes. Unfortunately, a spy aboard throws the spaceship out of whack, and while we left the family lost in space Wednesday night, we are assured they crash on an unknown planet.... I understand, by the way, that this show is also supposed to be tongue-in-cheek at times, but the acting indicates that is just an excuse. In short, it's like a live-action cartoon.

Irwin Allen's agent Herman Rush, said, "It was a frustration for him when the critics were negative. The critics were always looking at things like they should be classics, they should be *Playhouse 90*; they should be that type of product. They always were critical of adventure, children's shows, that type of thing. Irwin understood that, he accepted it. It was frustrating, but that was the world he lived in. And he paid attention to those reviews. He may have been unhappy with them, but he'd say, 'Maybe they have something here; let's analyze it.' He faced it. A lot of those weekends [at his Bel Air home] were spent reading reviews. He had a clip service that gave him the reviews from all over the country, so he had a lot of local paper reviews, as well, not just the national ones from the various TV guides." (HR-AI15)

Despite receiving mostly bad reviews, *Lost in Space* was winning where it most countered – in the TV ratings.

According to the A.C. Nielsen 30-City Ratings survey for September 22, 1965, the 7:30 to 8:30 p.m. network race played out this way:

Network / Program:	Rating	Audience Share:
7:30 – 8 p.m.:		
ABC: *Ozzie and Harriet*	9.9	19.0%
CBS: *Lost in Space*	**19.1**	**36.7%**
NBC: *The Virginian*	15.8	30.4%
8 – 8:30 p.m.:		
ABC: *The Patty Duke Show*	13.7	24.6%
CBS: *Lost in Space*	**20.2**	**36.3%**
NBC: *The Virginian*	16.0	28.7%

12

Episode 3: "Island in the Sky"

Teleplay by Norman Lessing; story by Shimon Wincelberg
(Additional scenes written by Wincelberg and Irwin Allen; uncredited, with script polishing by Anthony Wilson)
Directed by Anton M. Leader
Produced by Buck Houghton (uncredited), with Jerry Briskin;
Executive Producer: Irwin Allen

From *Lost in Space* show files (Irwin Allen Papers Collection):

> In the alien ship's control room, John locates a neighboring planet with a mass nearly equivalent with that of Earth. They decide to land there to make necessary repairs. While they orbit round the planet, Robinson leaves the ship to land and investigate further. Smith, who programmed the Robot to respond only to his commands, tries to take over and return to Earth. Don foils him but, in the process, the ship crash-lands. No one is hurt and the family sets out to find John, whom they rescue unhurt from the edge of a crater. They also find a monkey-like creature that Penny adopts as a pet and calls Debbie. Meanwhile, Smith programs the Robot to destroy anyone he finds alone excepting Don, whom Smith needs to pilot the ship. The Robot finds Will alone and prepares to destroy him.

From the Script:

(2nd Revised Shooting Final teleplay, August 10, 1965 draft)

– *Smith:* "What was it they said about the fallen sparrow?" *Robot:* "William Shakespeare, 1564-1616, 'There is a special providence in the fall of a sparrow…'" *Smith (admiringly):* "My, you have a many splendored thing. They even programmed you with Shakespeare … *(distracted by the Robot's quick counter-move in their chess game)* … Don't you ever stop to think? This is a complex game. One must look before one leaps." *Robot (metallically):* "Samuel Butler, 1600-1680. 'And look before you leap, for as you sow, ye are like to reap.'" *Smith:* "Sometimes I wonder about you. If I didn't know better, I'd think some form of morality was accidentally programmed into you."

– *Smith:* "With the loss of this excess weight, we now have a reasonably good chance of making our way back to the green hills of Earth … *(off their silence)* … I think at least we should discuss it." *Don:* "I'm going to have a lot of things to discuss with you once we set down. … *(to Maureen)* … Keep an eye on the gauge. If it passes into the red zone on the approach, call out." *Smith:* "Perhaps in the true democratic process, we should put it to a vote." *Don (to Maureen):* "Give me an ETA reading." *Maureen (reading):* "Four-fifty to touchdown." *Smith (more urgently):* "I demand that this be put to a vote while we can still get away." *Don:* "All right. I vote 'no.' … *(off Maureen's look, then to Smith)* … You're out-voted." *Smith:* "Not quite yet. I have a proxy. … *(to Robot)* … Come here."

– *Smith:* "Excellent! Now where were we when we were so rudely interrupted? … I believe we had just taken a vote to leave this dreadful place. I think it's safe to say that the two of us now constitute a voting majority." *Robot:* "I do not vote. I am not programmed for free choice." *Smith:* "Don't worry about it. It's vastly overrated."

– *Smith:* "You tin-plated fraud! You're a worthless electronic scrap heap! You've got to know how to fly this ship!" *Robot (stolidly):* "Space flight is not a function of environmental control Robots." *Smith (raging):* "Function? I'll function you right down to a bunch of melted transistors! Where's that laser gun?" *Robot (klaxon-like):* "Warning! Warning! Warning!" *Smith:* "Warning? What warning?" *Robot (ignoring this):* "Emergency protection circuit activated. Warning! Forty thousand volts now in circuit! Warning!" *Smith (choking a little):* "Temper … temper … temper!" *Robot (repeating):* "Emergency protective circuit activated. Warning ! Warning!" *Smith (quickly):* "But you misunderstood me, my impetuous friend. I'm your trusted master. Would I want to hurt you? … *(comforting)* … There, there – It's all over now. Naturally, I couldn't expect you to fly this ship. You have far too many more fascinating talents." *Robot:* "Emergency protective circuit de-activated." *Smith:* "Who wouldn't love you?"

Assessment:

Looking for logic and scientific accuracy? Don't crash land into this episode! But if you're looking for thrill-packed escapism, *Lost in Space* is the place, especially the first batch of black-and-white episodes. One can easily imagine a young Steven Spielberg or George Lucas sitting with their eyes glued to the TV screens, devouring every minute of these classic early episodes and using *Lost in Space* as a springboard into their own flights of fancy.

We who were there in the fall of 1965 continued to watch in wonderment. With Episode 3, as John Robinson, his retro-jets sabotaged by Dr. Smith, freefalls toward a strange alien world, then the Jupiter 2 dives into the atmosphere, out of control to a crash landing, we were awe-inspired. The landscape of the alien world was as foreign and uninviting as anything one could imagine – even though it existed right here on Earth, hidden away in a no man's land in Southern California. Next, we were given our first look at the Chariot – another marvel that, like the Jupiter 2, seemed as real and functional as the big knobs on the front of our TV sets. We were also introduced to the Bloop and an electrically charged tumbleweed. This wild ride was getting more amazing by the week.

When judging television on a purely imaginative level, along with technical prowess and sheer entertainment value, "Island in the Sky" was up there with the best of *The Twilight Zone* and *The Outer Limits*. Even with its faulty science, the magic of *Lost in Space* is on grand display with this 50 minutes of guiltless pleasure.

Script:

Story assignment 8543 (Production #8503)
Story title: "O Brave New World," assigned May 25, 1965.
Norman Lessing's treatment, and 1st and 2nd draft teleplays: June 1965.
Reformatted Mimeo Department Shooting Final teleplay: July 1965.
Tony Wilson's script polish (Revised Shooting Final teleplay): Late July 1965.
Wilson's 2nd Revised Shooting Final (green insert pages): August 5, 1965.
Additional page revisions by Wilson (pink insert pages): August 10.

Shimon Wincelberg, who came up with the story for this episode but did not write the teleplay, told interviewer Flint Mitchell, "For Lost in Space, I think they had a staff writer who would occasionally do some rewriting. And, at first, I was going to be involved in that capacity, too, but then I was offered a feature film, so I couldn't stay with the show much longer. In fact, I didn't write the first five or six scripts; I only wrote outlines, and then I wrote one more script that was called 'Invaders from the Fifth Dimension,' of which I remember absolutely nothing." (SW-LISF6)

Norman Lessing was hired to write a script based on Wincelberg's outline. Lessing was 54. He had been writing for TV since 1949, making stops at popular series such as [Bell] Telephone Time, The U.S. Steel Hour, Shirley Temple's Storybook (where he also served as story editor/associate producer), Bonanza, and The Fugitive. Still to come: numerous assignments on The F.B.I. and Hawaii Five-O, among others. This, however, would be Lessing's only job working for Irwin Allen.

The title was "O Brave New World" when Lessing did his part of the writing. Buck Houghton later changed this to "Island in the Sky."

On August 2, 1965, Houghton's office sent a memo to the effects and prop department, saying:

> Scene 6, Page 2: Obtain new chessboard and pieces for futuristic look and for maneuverability by robot's claw.
> Scene 6-9, Pages 2-4 (and elsewhere): Wherever Robot appears and functions, it is recognized that his accompanying noise will

> interfere with dialogue. Consult Electrical Department to see if his body and brain lights can be activated silently.
> Scene 72, Page 76: Contrive way for Judy to unzip uniform enough to slip out handkerchief for wiping blood away from Don's forehead. He will wear a small tape over slight wound for balance of episode.
> Scene 87, Page 32: Determine in advance whether Robot's apparatus can function without bottom half while he sits in Chariot. Is Chariot high enough to accommodate his top half?
> Scene 104 on: Can Bloop (monkey) do all he's required in the script?

Houghton wrote to Tony Wilson:

> Note: How are we going to justify parkas to match all PILOT chariot run-throughs in Episode #3 and #4? They do not talk about the cold until Sc. 129 in Ep #4?
> 163: Smith topples forward from tube into Robot's arms? Robot slaps Smith on backside? Lifts Smith up like a doll and shakes him violently? Drops him to the floor?

Houghton knew that great care would need to be taken in having Jonathan Harris, stiff as a board, topple from the freezing tube into the Robot's arms. And there was no way Harris was going to allow Bob May to "smack him on the backside." Or lift him up like a doll and shake him violently. Or drop him to the floor. The script would have to be changed.

Meanwhile, CBS Program Practices was also finding things that would need changing. Sam Taylor, Jr. wrote:

> Page 3: As discussed, Robinson will probably *not* be heard to give a "dying scream."

Jesse K. Alexander wrote next, on June 24, saying:

> Scene 209, in which ends the episode with an unresolved horror situation (a teenager at the mercy of a murderous robot), is unacceptable.

The concern had to do with the nighttime scene in which the Robot confronts young Will at the Chariot, with electrical bolts flying, and saying in a cold, mechanical voice, "Kill."

Sam Taylor, Jr. tried to be a little less inflexible on the cliffhanger, writing to the producers on August 2:

> Page 68, Scene 208: The changing of the word "kill" in the ROBOT's line to the word "destroy," and the deletion of Scene 209, lessons the frightening aspect of the tag sequence. However,

our concern is not entirely eliminated and we must reserve final judgment until the film has been viewed.

The producers would have to fight to keep this exciting cliffhanger in the episode. Even then, judicious editing was used to lessen the shock value.

Debbie the Bloop had appeared in the pilot film, and now returned for the third broadcast episode. The affection between Billy Mumy, Angela Cartwright and Debbie was undeniable (photos from Season Two).

Pre-Production:

Anton M. Leader, aka Tony Leader, returned for his second and final *Lost in Space*.

Debbie the Bloop, making her first *Lost in Space* appearance since the pilot, was a seasoned Hollywood pro. She had been seen frequently in another CBS series – *The Beverly Hillbillies* – as a pet of Ellie May Clampett's, who the family named "Cousin Bessie." In 1965, Debbie also had a prominent role in the Disney feature film *The Monkey's Uncle*, starring Tommy Kirk and Annette Funicello. Among other scenes in the movie, Debbie, on tambourine, accompanied Funicello and the Beach Boys on the movie's title song. Also in 1965, she was featured in *Clarence the Cross-Eyed Lion*, which led to a TV spinoff and regular work on *Daktari*, as "Judy the Chimpanzee." Debbie would later be featured in *Lancelot Link, Secret Chimp*, as Mata Hairi.

Billy Mumy said, "[It was] a cute, nice chimpanzee named Debbie. Lou Shoemaker was its trainer, and Angela really liked working with it; a little more than I did. Well, it was more her thing. Penny was supposed to be more of a zoologist type of a character, and Will was more of an engineer, electronics type. Originally, we all had these clear-cut characters, you know." (BM-LISW)

Angela Cartwright fondly remembered, "I loved having Debbie on the set. It was an uncomfortable apparatus that she had to wear on her head. That was a drag for her. But I love animals, so it was great having her, and I loved that Penny was involved in zoology and stuff like that." (AC-SCO14)

Production Diary:

Filmed August 10 – 19, 1965 (8 days).

Tony Leader had taken eight days to film "The Reluctant Stowaway," pushing director Alexander Singer and "The Derelict" back by two days. Then Singer took eight days to film his episode, delaying Leader by two days for the start of his second assignment. If Leader hoped to get a third assignment, he would have to finish this one in six days.

Day 1: Tuesday, August 10. They filmed from 8 a.m. to 7:20 p.m. on Stage 5, on the upper deck of the Jupiter 2, as the decision was made for John to suit up and go outside the ship; the family reaction to John's ordeal in space; Smith's attempt to coerce Don to return to Earth; Don appearing to give in to Smith's demands, then making the ship lurch and putting Smith into the freezing tube; and the post-crash, with the damage to the interior of the ship revealed.

Among the pages shot was this portion of a scene with Don, Maureen, Smith and the Robot:

SMITH
(holds up helmet)
Marvelous piece of work! Constructed, I believe, to withstand a pressure of ten thousand pounds per square inch.
(turns to Robot)
Tell me, my friend, do you think you're robot enough to crush this helmet?

ROBOT

Affirm-a-tive.

SMITH

You have my permission to do so.

54 INSERT

A set of long, steel claws emerges from the Robot's arms. He takes the helmet and crushes it like an eggshell.

55 CLOSEUP – SMITH

He nods in satisfaction.

SMITH

Much as I detest violence, it can be done just as easily with your head inside.

(sternly)

Now you will fire all rockets and we shall leave this vale of tears and head back to Earth!

Mark Goddard said, "I remember one time when Bobby was inside the Robot suit and the robot was supposed to be able to do anything. He was powerful and strong and Smith was trying to get the Robot to do something to show us he had the Robot in his control and that he could take over control of the ship. He took one of those astronaut helmets – they had one real one and a phony one made of eggshell. Smith puts the eggshell into the Robot's arms and he said 'I will show you how powerful he is. He will crush the helmet.' The next thing you hear is a loud squeezing sound coming from inside the Robot.... Bob didn't have the strength to crush it, and that broke everybody up." (MG-LISF)

The premiere of *Lost in Space* was still a month away when "Island in the Sky" filmed, but the buzz in the Hollywood trade magazines was that this unique series would be a hit.

Above: Day 2 and 3 of filming were spent on the upper deck of the Jupiter 2, with the planet set visible through the main viewport. Below: On Day 4, the company filmed outside the crashed Jupiter 2.

Leader was an hour late on wrapping, but otherwise ended Day 1 on schedule.

Day 2: Wednesday, August 11. A second day on Stage 5, this time with the filming of the scenes on the upper deck of the Jupiter 2 when the Robot returned to the ship and freed Smith from the freezing tube. Next, Smith getting angry and threatening the Robot when he discovered it couldn't pilot the ship. Filming began at 8 and concluded at 6:40 p.m. Leader was now one-half of a day behind.

Day 3: Thursday, August 12. They filmed from 8 a.m. to 7:04 p.m. Again, the location was Stage 5, as Leader covered scenes that had been planned for the previous day, including when John and Don returned to the Jupiter 2 and reacted to Smith being free; and Don repairing equipment while Judy watched. When they wrapped, the production had fallen to three-quarters of a day behind.

Day 4: Friday, August 13. They were supposed to be on Stage 11 this day, but Leader had unfinished business on Stage 5 from the evening before. Valuable filming time was then lost as the company made a midday move to Stage 11, for "Ext. Jupiter 2 and Crash Site," as well as sequences involving the Chariot. Filming lasted from 8 a.m. to 6:55 p.m.

Day 5: Monday, August 16. The entire day was supposed to be spent on the outdoor moat set, but the company spent the first half of the day on Stage 11, finishing the work from the previous day. Next, they moved to the backlot for the scene where Don

Irwin Allen's vision for Dr. Smith was as a classic movie villain (as indicated by the above publicity photo). Jonathan Harris (below, talking with Lockhart and Williams on set) had other ideas and found ways to sneak comedy in during filming – all to the liking of CBS.

found the Bloop and the camera panned to reveal John in the electrified pit. When Leader called for a wrap, he was one-and-a-half days behind.

Day 6: Tuesday, August 17. The production was supposed to end this day, but Leader still had more than a third of the episode to film. The entire day was spent outdoors at the moat, as John was rescued. When they finished, Leader was two days behind. The next episode to film, "There Were Giants in the Earth," was pushed back.

Day 7: Wednesday, August 18. It was another long day – 8 a.m. to 7:10 p.m. – complicated by the fact that the company started shooting outdoors by the moat, finishing scenes started the day before, then having to make a move indoors, onto Stage 5. Here, they filmed scenes on the Jupiter 2's lower deck. These included Smith and the Robot playing chess, and John making journal entries.

Regarding Smith's first game of chess with the Robot: A syndicated newspaper piece, carried in the September 18, 1965 edition of the *Biddeford Journal*, revealed:

> Guy Williams, once a ranking tournament chess player, has found an unexpected use for his skill at the game behind the scenes of *Lost in Space*, science fiction series in which he stars, beginning on the CBS Television Network. He helps figure out the on-camera moves for a chess-playing robot.

Jonathan Harris snuck in more comedy, in his nonplussed reactions to the Robot's evident mastery of both chess playing and literature. It helped counter against the despicable actions taken by Smith in this episode, sabotaging John Robinson's retro jets, and instructing the Robot to crush the space helmet, before ruthlessly trying to commandeer the Jupiter 2. The writers threw Harris a bone in his efforts to make Smith

Above: Irwin Allen talks with his stars, who are clearly suffering in their hot and stiff spacesuits. Below: There were always cakes to celebrate every cast member's birthday on the set of *Lost in Space* – even Debbie's – as Allen, Mumy and Cartwright surprise the chimp with a cake. Banana flavored perhaps?

less heartless, giving him the line about regretting that Will didn't have to be abandoned on the planet along with the rest of the family. Smith saw something in the boy that he liked, and that helped us to see something in Smith that we liked.

At the end of the filming, they were still two days behind.

Day 8: Thursday, August 19. Work started at 8 in the morning and didn't end until 8:32 at night. Despite the late hour, production records reveal that no one was served dinner. The producer on the set was pushing Leader to finish, and this meant shooting twelve pages from the script. Covered on this day: more scenes on the lower deck of the Jupiter 2, including Will demonstrating how he had learned to mimic Smith's voice and get the Robot to obey, and Maureen waking the children after the ship crash-landed.

June Lockhart said, "The costumes were *unbearably* hot. They were really racing car drivers' fireproof

Jonathan Harris with director of photography Gene Polito.

aluminum suits. We had to wear them because there was no fabric which had the same look.... Underneath, we wore body stockings, so we could drop the tops down and be comfortable -- at least from the waist up.... And they were so tight, we couldn't sit down in them. When we moved, we were all *very* stiff-legged. In order to rest between shots, I had to hold somebody's hand and be lowered back onto a cot, and then be helped to stand up. Otherwise, I couldn't get my legs under me." (JL-SL83)

You can see how stiff the costumes were—watch Lockhart assist Kristen out of her crash-seat after the Jupiter 2 crashes.

Also filmed this day, on a different area of the stage: the process shots involving the Chariot. With this, the episode was finally complete.

Director Tony Leader would not return. Jonathan Harris believed it was because of the falling-out he and Leader had while filming "The Reluctant Stowaway," when Harris refused to get into the "coffin-like" cabinet for Dr. Smith's entrance into the episode. He said, "Tony Leader was... a bit of a shit, really.... Well, Tony and I never spoke again, and he never returned to do another show. Because that's the way it is, and that's the way it has to be." (JH-IASB2)

Leader believed the reason had more to do with the relationship between himself and Allen. He said, "Working for Irwin Allen was not a pleasure. He was a bright, imaginative man whose values were not the same as mine. So, we did not enjoy each other particularly, which is why I never did more than two episodes." (TL-LISF)

The greatest factor in Leader not returning to *Lost in Space* was that "Island in the Sky" took 83.7 "camera hours" to complete. No other First Season episode required as many. One came close, at 81.1 camera hours – Leader's other *Space* directing assignment, "The Reluctant Stowaway." The season average – and Irwin Allen tracked these things – was 68.3 camera hours.

Leader went on to have great success in television, a galaxy or two away from Jonathan Harris and Irwin Allen. *Gilligan's Island* was happy to have him, for six episodes. He also did three episodes of *Tarzan* for the following season. The season after that, one for *Star Trek* ("For the World Is Hollow and I Have Touched the Sky"). It would run late too, and also take eight days to film. The director had a better time at *Ironside*, where he took eight assignments, and on *The Virginian*, where he directed fourteen. He did three for *Hawaii Five-O*, and retired shortly thereafter.

Post-Production:

"Island in the Sky" was the second episode to be scored by John Williams, following "The Reluctant Stowaway." Jeff Bond, writing for the March 2015 issue of *Famous Monsters*, said, "Williams created a brilliant, shrill accompaniment to the crash landing sequence engineered by miniature-effects specialists Howard and Theodore Lydecker. Williams also created some bouncing music for the Robinson's treaded Chariot vehicle that he would continue to develop with an epic brass theme in 'The Hungry Sea,' with its spectacular sequence of the Chariot negotiating desert terrain and operating amphibiously in an inland sea."

It was always during the post-production phase when Dick Tufeld made his contribution. He enjoyed working on *Lost in Space*, telling interviewer Barry Magen, "But as much fun as the robot character was, I was absolutely locked into Bobby May's talking. If my timing was exact, then I [was] in sync with the flashing light on the Robot's head. It really became less of a creative job for me, and more of a technical job." (DT-LISF4)

But then, isn't that how it should be for a robot?

Release / Reaction:

(Only CBS broadcast: Wednesday, September 29, 1965)

Promotional pictures from this time were depicting the Robot as a true "heavy." But before these early episodes even aired, CBS was putting the pressure on Irwin Allen to either lighten up on Dr. Smith and the Robot or let them be permanently "lost in space."

During this week, President Johnson was in the hospital getting his gall bladder removed, and, for the first time in U.S. history, the functions of a living President were deliberately transferred to the Vice President. Hubert H. Humphrey was briefly in charge.

Jackie Gleason had the cover of *TV Guide*. People were still flocking to the movie houses to see *The Sound of Music*, *My Fair Lady*, *Those Magnificent Men in Their Flying Machines*, and *What's New Pussycat?* "Eve of Destruction," by Barry McGuire, was the song getting the most spins on radio station turntables. The Beatles still had the best-selling long-player in stores, with *Help!*, and many of its tracks were getting radio play, as was customary for Beatles albums. The LP's non-single cuts getting the most attention: "The Night Before," "You've Got to Hide Your Love Away," and "You're Going to Lose That Girl."

Syndicated "TV Keynotes," in the September 29 edition of the *Galveston Daily News*, among other newspapers, picked *Lost in Space* as among the night's "Top Television shows," saying:

> Enjoyable episode for the children. The Robinson family makes a crash landing on an unknown planet where frightful pitfalls await, along with some friendly and unfriendly outer space creatures. The latter may turn out to be the stars of the series, and the kids will particularly like an animal named a "bloop" tonight.

Also from September 29, syndicated "TV Scout," carried in Appleton Wisconsin's *Post-Crescent*, said:

> *Lost in Space* gets down to settling on an unknown planet with the Robinsons regarding their new "home" with the same awe the Pilgrims did theirs in 1620. There are no redskins around but plenty of diverting and scary things like electrical-volcanic pits and space creatures that go "bloop, bloop." Also watch Dr. Smith go berserk and kick his robot pal's metallic shins.

The audience estimates were down slightly for the third broadcast episode of *Space*. A.C. Nielsen 30-City Ratings survey for September 29, 1965, reported:

Network / Program:	Rating	Audience Share:
7:30 – 8 p.m.:		
ABC: *Ozzie and Harriet*	11.7	21.3%
CBS: *Lost in Space*	15.7	28.6%
NBC: *The Virginian*	**18.1**	**33.0%**
8 – 8:30 p.m.:		
ABC: *The Patty Duke Show*	15.4	25.0%
CBS: *Lost in Space*	18.0	29.2%
NBC: *The Virginian*	**19.6**	**31.8%**

Those who missed out would have to wait to see "Island in the Sky" until the fall of 1968, when *Lost in Space* entered into syndicated reruns. Despite its excellent production values, "Island," as with the entire five-episode story arc that opened the series, was passed over by CBS for a network repeat.

13

Episode 4: "There Were Giants in the Earth"

Teleplay by Carey Wilber; story by Shimon Wincelberg
(additional scenes written by Wincelberg and Irwin Allen, uncredited; with script polishing by Anthony Wilson)
Directed by Leo Penn
Produced by Buck Houghton (uncredited), with Jerry Briskin;
Executive Producer: Irwin Allen

From the *Lost in Space* show files (Irwin Allen Papers collection):

> The Robinsons find Will in time to save him from the Robot, who is temporarily de-activated. The family are beginning to settle down on the strange planet when they become aware that a giant is prowling the valley. That, and the discovery that the temperature is dropping rapidly, causes them to decide to move south. They pack up the chariot and all start off, except Smith, who refuses to leave the safety of the spaceship. They escape the giant, who tries to block their way out of the valley, but running into a heavy storm they seek shelter in what appears to be a cave in the mountainside. Once inside, they find themselves in a huge corridor with stone walls carved with a form of hieroglyphics.

From the Script:

(Revised Shooting Final teleplay, August 13, 1965 draft)

– *Will:* "About the Robot." *John:* "You'll leave it alone. That's an order. Understand?" *Will (reluctantly):* "Yes, sir, but..." *John:* "That's enough, William." *Then after Robinson exits, Penny says to Will:* "You didn't offer much of an argument, did you?" *Will (glum):* "You heard what he called me, didn't you? When Dad calls me William in that tone of voice it's no use arguing."

– *Don:* "Abandon the spaceship? Well, what if it's finally spotted by some passing rocket?" *John:* "They'll televise a picture back to Earth." *Don:* "Oh, that's great. A picture showing no signs of life. No survivors." *John:* "Well, Don, I'd rather not be found at all, than to have to be picked up by a pair of ice tongs."

Assessment:

For us who grew up to *Lost in Space*, whether we were watching in the fall of 1965 or catching up with the series later in syndicated repeats, the first five episodes made for an exhilarating launch. Each seemed to top the one before, and that can certainly be argued with "There Were Giants in the Earth." The title character – as good as this one-eyed, boulder-throwing wonder was – didn't provide the only thrills. We were also given mutated giant peapods with a "black tentacle" (as the script described it) which "emerges from the slit [cut by Smith] and gropes blindly"; sudden climate change and the ensuing threat of a deep freeze that even the sanctuary of the Jupiter 2 could not offer protection; a journey across the strange desolate alien world in the futuristic Chariot; the discovery of an ancient underground city with entombed mummies; and an earthquake threatening to bury our wandering travelers in the catacomb ruins. All of this in just 50 minutes, along with a fair amount of comedy from the work-phobic Dr. Smith, and a Robot suffering a nervous breakdown after seeing a humanoid so big that it could not possibly compute.

There isn't a dull moment in "There Were Giants in the Earth," the fourth excellent episode in a row, and perhaps the best yet.

Script:

Story Assignment 8545 (Production #8504)
Carey Wilber's 1st draft teleplay: Late June/early July 1965.
Wilber's 2nd draft teleplay: July 13, 1965.
Reformatted Mimeo Department Shooting Final teleplay: Late July 1965.
Tony Wilson's script polish (Rev. Shooting Final, on yellow paper): August 10, 1965.
Page revisions by Wilson (blue insert pages): August 12.
Additional page revisions by Wilson (pink insert pages): August 13.

Carey Wilber said, "Tony Wilson, the story editor, called me in on a script because for some reason Shimon Wincelberg couldn't do the teleplay, so I was given the assignment, and, from there, we went on to others." (CW-LIS25)

Wilber seemed a natural for *Lost in Space*. He had cut his teeth writing for TV's *Captain Video* in the mid-1950s. It was hard to nail Wilber down to a specific style or genre. He wrote for the anthologies, including *Lux Video Theater* and *Armstrong Circle Theatre*, and the westerns *Daniel Boone*, *Rawhide* and *The Virginian*. He did war drama with assignments on *Twelve O'Clock High*, and crime drama with *The Untouchables*. Then he met Irwin Allen, who put him to work on both *Lost in Space* and *The Time Tunnel*. Over the next two years, Wilber would write seven *Space* episodes. He also wrote one for *Star Trek* – the classic "Space Seed," which introduced the character of Khan Noonien Singh.

This episode's title is from Genesis 6:4. "There were giants in the earth in those days; and also after that, when the sons of God came in unto the daughters of men, and they bare children to them, the same became mighty men which were of old, men of renown."

The first few verses of the sixth chapter mention "the sons of God," their pride, and their habit of taking up with "the daughters of men." This behavior is part of the evil world that Noah's flood would soon wash away.

The oversized monster's appearance in this episode is a harking-back to the Polyphemus, one of a race of one-eyed Cyclops encountered by Odysseus in his travels back home after the Trojan wars, in Homer's *Odyssey*. In fact, the term *Cyclops* is from the Greek for "round eye."

CBS had their own bible to consult – that of Broadcast Standards. The network had issues with the cliffhanger for the previous episode, "Island in the Sky," when Will is accosted by the Robot, which has instructions to "kill," then fires electrical charges in his direction. It was against CBS policy to depict children in great peril during the network's family hour. The cliffhanger was allowed to stay when the word "kill" was changed to "destroy," and the electrical charges were not aimed in the direction of Will. Only then would the network allow the picture to freeze and the words "TO BE CONTINUED NEXT WEEK! SAME TIME, SAME CHANNEL" appear on screen. A greater compromise had to be made for the Teaser of "There Were Giants in the Earth." The network insisted that something be introduced to decrease the level of peril facing Will. The solution: Having Will mimic Dr. Smith, saying, "Stop, my mechanical friend! … Before you continue, my metallic cohort, we must put you through a routine check." The script specified that the Robot comes to a stop and says, "Temporary delay allowed. Circuits open for routine check." While the element of danger was still present, the boy was out of immediate danger.

Script editor Wilson was also inserting comedy to help soften the character of Smith. After all, the not-so-good doctor had given the Robot instructions to "liquidate" the other members of the expedition, with the exception of Major West, whom he needed to pilot the ship back to Earth. Now, in Act I of this script, Wilson polished a scene written by Carey Wilber, giving Jonathan Harris the wiggle room needed to add other dimensions to Smith – culinary skills, harmless eccentricity, and cowardice. The July 9, 1965 Shooting Final teleplay read:

21. INT. LOWER DECK – NIGHT

SMITH happily moving about the ship's galley, carefully seasoning a steaming pot as Don enters. Smith turns and beams a welcome.

SMITH

Ah, Major West. Just in time to test a culinary marvel. A *crepe suzette Henri Carpentier de Paris* which I learned at the feet of the master.

He backs away nervously as Don closes in on him.

DON

Get outside and stop that tin monster or I'll wring your neck.

Smith leaps back, flourishing his ladle in a *pas des armes*.

SMITH

Threaten violence, will you! If you don't stand back I'll drum on your noodle until it rings like the Canterbury chimes.

22. ANOTHER ANGLE

As Don steps in, Smith makes an abortive pass at him with the ladle which Don blocks, then gets ready to throw a punch. Smith steps back, lays the ladle over arm in manner of surrendering a sword.

SMITH

I surrender.

Harris milked it for all it was worth, as well as choosing to ignore the instructions in the script to make "an abortive pass" at striking Don with the ladle.

Wilber and Wilson added another layer to the Smith character – his indolence. We see Smith cleverly avoid doing any work, as the rest in the party labor away. The crowning moment comes when Maureen catches him on the lower deck, pouring a cup of coffee. She crossly asks him why he is there. Smith tells her: "My dear madam, there are limits to the endurance of mere bone and sinew. I have been going at top speed all day and I have reached the point of exhaustion. I am happy to say that I not only solved our hydroponic farming problems but also we shall shortly be enjoying the fruits of my labors behind an impregnable defense system to which I also contributed."

Wilber and/or Wilson then wrote: "ANGLE ON MAUREEN. And if looks could kill, Smith would be dead on the spot. But he pays no attention as he pleasantly sips his coffee."

This problem – how to retain a traitor, saboteur and potential killer as a recurring character in a CBS series, especially one with children in the cast – was already being worked out.

The next challenge for the writers: How to take some of the threat out of Smith's mechanical henchman? When Will repairs the Robot, Wilber and/or Wilson described how the Robot is activated by Will, then, for a brief moment, appears to be bearing down on the boy. The script read:

Then, the Robot, like a cumbersome puppy, reverses course and tracks off, spins around, sidles from side to side like a person trying his muscles.

ANGLE ON WILL as he stares in astonishment, then in relief.

ANOTHER ANGLE on the Robot as it moves forward, everything going at once. Will laughs.

WILL

Stop that. You look silly.

If a ten-year-old boy on the TV screen could stop fearing the Robot, then the ten-year-olds watching at home would likely stop fearing it as well.

Another scene designed to lean the Robot away from menace and toward comedy relief was its "nervous breakdown" after encountering the giant.

A final touch: Will's goodbye scene with the Robot. Wilber and/or Wilson wrote:

Will is saddened at leaving the Robot behind.

WILL

I guess this is goodbye ... Robot.

ROBOT

Goodbye ...

(he clicks)

... Good-bye: a sentimental phrase to indicate a separation or parting of emotional beings...

WILL

Never mind that. It means I won't be seeing you for a while.

ROBOT

... derived from an early English expression...

WILL

That's enough! Now try to show a little decent sentiment. We won't be together anymore.

ROBOT

That does not compute.

Will reaches out angrily and snaps out the Robot's power-pak [sic].

It was a well-devised scene in more ways than one. First, it showed the growing affection Will had for the Robot. After all, who could a ten-year-old boy have as a friend when isolated from peers of his own age and sex? His father was certainly caring, but also a serious-thinking and all-work-no-play disciplinarian. Will's mother and sisters were, well, just women and girls. Smith was not yet to be trusted, although affection between him and Will would soon be established in the series. But there was also the Robot, early in his "life" and, in a sense, growing up just like Will, as he learns more about humans in each episode. In time, the Robot would even begin to emulate human emotional traits. Lesson No. 1: Don't get these humans angry. Will states it well when, after pulling the plug, he says, "Maybe that will teach you something about sentiment."

The architectural work on *Lost in Space*, retooling it from pilot to series, and ensuring that Dr. Smith and the Robot could remain on the show, was already making itself evident.

Pre-Production:

Director Leo Penn.

Leo Penn was both an actor and a director. In the latter capacity, he worked the most for *Ben Casey* (with nineteen episodes) and its medical drama counterpart *Dr. Kildare* (with nine). At this time, he was also well-liked at *I Spy*, where he directed four. Irwin Allen hired Penn to do one episode each for *Voyage to the Bottom of the Sea* and *Lost in Space*.

Penn told *Starlog*'s Pat Jankiewicz, "I liked Irwin. There are many things I didn't share with him in relation to a point-of-view, but Irwin was one of the last of a vanishing breed – a genuine showman. He had a lot of passion and enthusiasm for his work; he was a good guy." (LP-SL92)

Lamar Lundy, the former Los Angeles Rams defensive lineman, now decked out as a Cyclops giant, with a suit made of treated palm tree bark, appeared courtesy of stock footage from the pilot.

Production Diary:

Filmed August 23 – 27, 1965 (6 days).

The start date for "There Are Giants in the Earth" had been pushed back three times since originally set. All three episodes filmed thus far – "The Reluctant Stowaway," "The Derelict" and "Island in the Sky" – had been planned as six-day productions, yet each had run eight. Anton "Tony" Leader had failed twice to keep up with the production schedule, and Alex Singer had failed once. Now, after having to rearrange his schedule a few times, Leo Penn would have his shot. But he was being given less time from the outset. Taking into account that a great deal of footage was being harvested from "No Place to Hide," constituting nearly half of the script pages and screen time, Penn was still expected to shoot his portion of the episode in only five days.

Above: The cast enjoyed being in the Chariot when it was placed on a "rocker" in front of a process screen. The scripts may have called for "grim," but there was also plenty of levity between the players. Below: The second half of Day 1 and all of Day 2 were spent on the lower deck set of the Jupiter 2.

Day 1: Friday, August 20, 1965. Production started on schedule at 8 a.m. Filming took place on Stage 5 for the Int. Chariot process shots, with the cast in the Chariot, acting out their dialogue and reactions while images were projected onto a screen behind them. Included: the encounter with the giant; the Chariot hitting bumps in the road (a giant's footprints); and the Chariot being rammed by an electrified tumbleweed.

The cast were in good spirits. Penn was an excellent director, and, since he was a former actor, he related to actors far better than Irwin Allen. Also helping morale – the cast members were now out of those uncomfortably stiff and hot silver-lamé spacesuits.

Filmed next: the scenes taking place on the lower deck of the Jupiter 2: John telling his family and fellow castaways that they would have to work together to be self-sufficient; Will not able to sleep as he worried about the Robot, then leaving his cabin; the family discovering that Will is missing; Maureen and Penny preparing dinner; Smith cooking *crêpe suzettes*, and defending himself with a ladle against Don; Smith refusing to leave the ship when John and Don tell him their plans to travel south; and John writing notes in his journal. At least, all of that was on the schedule. Penn only covered a fraction of it. Work lasted until 7:03 p.m. Penn was only able to shoot three and two-eighths pages from the script (out of the ten per day that the TV production schedule mandated). He finished one-quarter of a day behind, just as had

happened when he worked for Allen during his one directing assignment on *Voyage to the Bottom of the Sea*.

Penn later said, "We had this enormous set – it was really a whole stage – and, I think, by 10 a.m., we didn't have a shot in the can yet. There were a lot of technical reasons why. I remember the producer coming on the set and telling me how, in one day, I had succeeded in ruining his career!" (LP-SL92)

That producer was likely Jerry Briskin, but could also have been Buck Houghton, who would soon be leaving the series.

Day 2: Monday, August 23. An even longer day on Stage 5 as Penn worked to catch up and cover the remaining scenes in the lower deck of the Jupiter 2. Included, this page from the script:

225. INT. LOWER DECK – DAY

CLOSE SHOT on Smith, the picture of righteous indignation.

SMITH

Leave the ship? Are you out of your collective minds?

CAMERA DRAWS BACK and we see Smith confronting Robinson and Don.

SMITH

Here we have simple comforts, an adequate cuisine and more than ample protection from the perils of the planet and you want me to leave.

ROBINSON

It's either that or freeze.

SMITH

My dear sir, Zachary Smith would rather freeze to death intact than provide a few morsels for some carnivorous giant. Do as you please but I shall stay here.

DON

It's your funeral, Smith.

SMITH

Just leave me a few necessities and I feel confident that I shall survive.

ROBINSON

We'll leave you all we can spare. Let's see about getting underway, Don.

(to Smith)

Good luck. You'll need it.

They move off as Smith calls after them.

SMITH

(unnerved)

You'll be back! Never fear! And I'll be here snug as can be! You'll see!

As they disappear, his bravado collapses into doubt.

The cast was in makeup starting at 6:30 a.m., ready to start filming by 8. Other than a one-hour lunch break, work continued until 7:05 p.m. In all that time, only five and five-eighths pages of script were put to film, and the production was now one-half of a day behind schedule.

Day 3: Tuesday, August 24. Stage 11 was the location for the remainder of the production. Up first: the scenes on the upper deck of the Jupiter 2, including Smith getting out of more work, this time while talking to Will who is busy fixing equipment; and then John, Don and Maureen preparing to go out in search of Will, as they catch a guilty-looking Smith inching toward the elevator.

Paul Zastupnevich adjusts the wardrobe worn by June Lockhart, as she refers to her script while rehearsing with Marta Kristin.

Next: the scenes outside the Jupiter 2 in the hydroponic garden, with Smith getting out of more work, and planting seeds in the untested soil. An hour and a half of union overtime, known as "golden hours," was needed as the company filmed from 8 a.m. to 7:50 p.m. Penn covered four and five-eighths pages from the script, and fell to three-quarters of a day behind.

Day 4: Wednesday, August 25. On Stage 11, Penn started filming at 8 a.m., covering five and four-eighths pages of material, dealing with Will's encounter with the Robot at the Chariot; the family coming to Will's rescue; and the

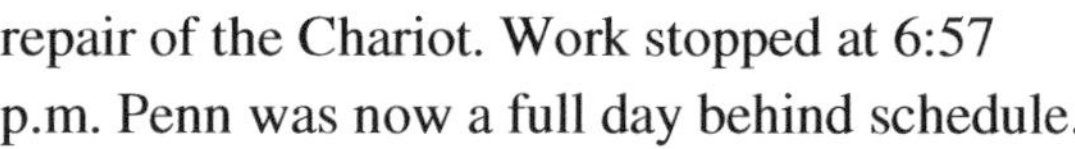

repair of the Chariot. Work stopped at 6:57 p.m. Penn was now a full day behind schedule.

Day 5: Thursday, August 26. It was meant to be the final day of production. To get back on schedule, Penn would have to do two day's worth of work in only one. Everyone knew he wouldn't make it, and the next episode, "The Hungry Sea," was pushed back.

Still on Stage 11, the overwhelmed director rolled camera on and off from 8 a.m. to 7:50 p.m., covering all the scenes at the campsite outside the Jupiter 2, including Smith ducking out of helping John and Don work; the men setting up the force field; John and Don leaving to fix the Chariot; Judy calling for help and then leading Maureen, Penny and Smith to the giant pea pod in the hydroponic garden. Also planned, but not covered due to lack of time, was a scene which did not make it into the episode, in which the Robot came across the gigantic footprints, then encountered the Giant, before making "a hasty retreat." By the end of the day, six and six-eighths pages from the script were filmed. The production held at one day behind.

Day 6: Friday, August 27. It was decided in the morning that this would be the final day of production, even if the company had to work until midnight. Fortunately, it didn't take that long. But they did film from 8 in the morning until 8 at night, covering scenes outside the Jupiter 2, as Will worried about the Robot, then received a lecture from his father; the Robot returning, in a state of shock; and Will trying to get the Robot to say goodbye.

This was only the second time that the Robot had had his power-pack yanked. Bob May told *Starlog*'s Tom Weaver:

"There were many different things that I figured out how to do, and some of it was tough – it was like patting your head and rubbing your stomach at the same time, that same principle. I had to press a button with each syllable of every word that I said, because the Robot's voice light had to be blinking right along with the voice. If the Robot was shot, I had to kill the switches and die, and I had to slump down if Dr. Smith pulled the power pack – which he did a lot! I had to raise the bubble up with my own head, turn 360 degrees (I won't tell you how I did that) – lots of different things that had to be done." (BM-SL94)

A scene that was planned but cut due to lack of time had Smith reactivating the Robot, then both seeing the Giant, at which point Smith had the Robot fire its electrical charges at the beast. Rumors have it that Irwin Allen tore pages from the script to ensure that the episode would not carry over into a seventh day of filming. The camera crew was paid for eleven hours, and the production finished, one day over schedule.

The producers and studio had wanted this episode to take five days, but it lasted for six. It was supposed to cost $130,455, but the tally at the end was $150,433. Leo Penn would not be asked to return. The same consequence would happen a year later when he ran a day late completing his first and only *Star Trek* assignment, the classic "The Enemy Within," in which a transporter malfunction divides Kirk in two.

In comparing *Star Trek* creator/producer Gene Roddenberry to Irwin Allen, Penn exclaimed, "Oh God! I think Gene Roddenberry was a very serious thinker. This isn't to take away from Irwin; it's another venue, a whole other focus. Gene would have been a great teacher. He wanted to say something. For him, it wasn't just for the singular purpose of entertaining. Irwin was a master at creating spectacle." (LP-SL92)

From here, Penn went on to direct often for other 1960s series such as *Run for Your Life*, *Judd for the Defense* and *Bonanza*. In the 1970s, he directed multiple episodes for *Marcus Welby, M.D.*, *Cannon*, *Barnaby Jones*, and *Kojak*, among others. In the 1980s, he was an often-employed director at *Hart to Hart*, *Trapper John, M.D.*, *Magnum, P.I.*, and *Columbo*. And Leo Penn was a proud dad, too, to musician Michael Penn, actor Chris Penn, and Academy Award-winning actor and director Sean Penn.

Post-Production:

Herman Stein again provided the musical score, which included the second use of the composer's hauntingly lovely melody called, "Family." It is played during the scene in which John Robinson has a heart-to-heart talk with Will about the boy disobeying his order to not work on the Robot. This composition was first heard in "The Derelict" and would find its way into a handful of other early episodes, usually during touching moments between father and son, or sentimental exchanges between husband and wife.

Bernard Herrmann's score was left in the scenes taken from the pilot, including the journey into the subterranean ruins of an ancient alien civilization.

Roland Gross and Editing Team No. 2 were given their second assignment with "There Were Giants in the Earth," having completed work on "The Reluctant Stowaway."

As it had been done in the pilot film CBS screened for its affiliates and sponsors, Angela Cartwright's piercing scream when Penny reacts to seeing the mummy in the underground tomb was again left out. This extraction was made at the insistence of CBS executives who felt it indicated Penny was in extreme distress. Only minor distress would be tolerated. The scream was later put back into the cliffhanger of this episode, as well as the Teaser for "The Hungry Sea," for the 2015 Blu-ray release of the series.

Release / Reaction:

(Only CBS broadcast: Wednesday, October 6, 1965)

The new movie to make the Top Five box office money-makers (alongside *The Sound of Music*, *My Fair Lady*, *Those Magnificent Men in Their Flying Machines*, and *The Ipcress File*) was *Marriage on the Rocks*, starring Frank Sinatra, Deborah Kerr and Dean Martin. Don Adams and Barbara Feldon, of *Get Smart*, had the cover of *TV Guide*. "Hang on Sloopy" by The McCoys was the song playing the most on radio station turntables. And the Beatles' *Help!* was still the top-selling album in America.

On Sunday, October 3, 1965, between the broadcasts of "Island in the Sky" and "There Were Giants in the Earth," Marta Kristen was featured in a *Los Angeles Times* TV magazine cover story. Entertainment correspondent Hal Humphrey wrote:

Publicity picture taken by the set photographer during filming of "There Were Giants in the Earth," still emphasizing Smith as the true "monster" in *Lost in Space* ... even more threatening than a giant Cyclops. CBS put a stop to this fairly quickly, and would never allow a moment such as this, with Smith physically assaulting a minor, to be aired.

> One of the reasons space-adventure shows generally are considered to be for male audiences is that wily producers of such fare always include in their casts girls like Marta Kristen (see cover). Grizzled veteran viewers of TV probably recall a series of more than a decade ago called *Space Patrol* which featured Nina Bara as Tonga, a reformed sultry brunette who kept daddy watching the series with junior. It's safe to say several daddies already have discovered the blue-eyed blonde Marta in the newest space series, *Lost in Space*, which streaked across TV's mass appeal spectrum several Wednesdays ago on CBS.... The dirtiest trick producer Allen and CBS have played on Marta is shooting the series in black-and-white.... [S]ays Marta, who seems ecstatic about

> everything…. "We have such a happy company, and we have a lot of fun. I'll be flying soon, too – you know, with a harness and wire. It's when I'm in my antigravity suit. You wouldn't believe all the special effects we have. There's a washing machine which one minute after you put the clothes in are washed, ironed and turned out in plastic bags." …
>
> Except for those "special effects" Marta finds so intriguing, the adventures of the Robinson family in *Lost in Space* (once they settle down to living on their unknown planet) aren't likely to sound much different from those found on ABC's *Ozzie and Harriet* or on NBC's new *Please Don't Eat the Daisies* family situation series. The big difference may turn out to be Marta herself in those blue tights and red sweater.

Also appearing in newspapers during this week was a blurb out of 20th Century-Fox:

> Producer Irwin Allen currently is filming his exciting science fact/science fiction adventure series, *Lost in Space*, at 20th Century-Fox Television and seen each Wednesday at 7:30 p.m. over CBS-TV. Representing the animal world in the series is Debbie, a two-year-old chimpanzee, who portrays the "space bloop," pet of young Angela Cartwright. In order not to tire the animal more than necessary, a second chimp is used to stand-in for Debbie during the tedious lighting session. When meal time rolls around, animal trainer Lou Schumacher has to feed Debbie first, else Dame Temperament will raise her ugly head.

For another studio-released wire story, Irwin Allen, in discussing Jonathan Harris's portrayal of Dr. Smith, said, "What the industry needed was a slick, sophisticated 'space-age' villain. The day of the boogey-man running around in a black slouch hat and opera cape is passé. Kids have become so familiar with this prototype from old movies that they tend to be amused by them rather than frightened." (IA-IAPC65)

"TV Previews," found in the October 6, 1965 edition of Ohio's *Dover Daily Reporter*, among other newspapers, said:

> The fourth episode of this space-hanger finds our castaways running into the jolly green giant, or his hideous family, and Mr. Big isn't their only problem. Their hydroponic garden shrivels, the temperature is about to drop to 150 degrees below zero, the robot can't be trusted, Smith is a sneak, and they find a mysterious castle. You may not be able to believe much of what happens, but it's sure a full hour.

"TV Tonight," syndicated to newspapers such as New York's *Syracuse Herald-Journal*, also on October 6th, leaned toward *The Patty Duke Show*, calling it "especially amusing," and gave a mixed reaction to *The Virginian* … and *Lost in Space*. The reviewer said:

> Tonight's episode whizzes along with a potpourri of thrills and chills that should only interest the youngsters. The Robinsons on their new planet run into a valley of Cyclops (so huge they even scare their robot) and end up in a cave as spooky as an ancient Egyptian mortuary. Least impressed is little Angela Cartwright who finds their new home as pleasant as Alice's Wonderland.

"TV Keynotes," syndicated to newspapers across America, including the October 6th edition of the *Galveston Daily News*, in Galveston, Texas, picked *Lost in Space* as the only 7:30 to 8:30 show worth watching. The critic said:

> New treats in store for the youngsters when the Robinson family encounters one-eyed giants on the unknown planet. The giants, part animal, part vegetable, provide the most excitement in this space show which continues to come up with a story climax every five minutes or so.

How did it fare in the ratings? A.C. Nielsen, from its 30-City Ratings survey for October 6, 1965, estimated the audience ranking as follows:

Network / Program:	Rating	Audience Share:
7:30 – 8 p.m.:		
ABC: *Ozzie and Harriet*	13.4	23.0%
CBS: *Lost in Space*	18.6	31.2%
NBC: *The Virginian*	**19.7**	**33.8%**
8 – 8:30 p.m.:		
ABC: *The Patty Duke Show*	15.3	22.1%
CBS: *Lost in Space*	**21.6**	**34.0%**
NBC: *The Virginian*	20.6	32.4%

From the Mailbag:

A letter sent to Irwin Allen from this time read:

> I am a professional flagpole sitter and hold the record in the State of Texas with 43 days continual sitting. I currently am working a State fair in Oklahoma and have a little portable TV set with me. My favorite show is *Lost in Space*. When I finish this assignment, I am going to try to break the underwater record in a diving bell. Naturally, I will watch *Voyage to the Bottom of the Sea*. Would you be interested in using my act in either of your series? I work cheap and have my own television set. My cheeks are rosey and I look great in color. Please advise.

Allen's reply:

> To date, we haven't had any script situations involving a man of your particular talents. However, if we ever need a sitter on the periscope of the submarine, Seaview, rest assured you're our man.

***

Shortly after the telecast of "There Were Giants in the Earth," the Aurora Plastics Company of West Hempstead, Long Island issued three styrene plastic do-it-yourself model kits. One featured the Robot and the other two each featured the Cyclops attacking the family – although if you wanted the one with the Chariot it was going to cost you $1.98 instead of the usual 98 cents. For decades, fans have long believed that famed illustrator (and Aurora monster model kit box artist) James Bama painted the now-iconic box art. But according to Kevin Burns, all three boxes were the work of the equally notable Mort Kůnstler, who later did the key art for Irwin Allen's 1972 film, *The Poseidon Adventure*. Kůnstler's depiction of the *Lost in Space* Cyclops towering above the Chariot became visual wallpaper for a generation of baby boomers when it graced full-color, full-page ads in comics books everywhere in the mid 1960s.

Artwork used for the packaging and promotion of the Aurora model kit based on this episode. Regardless of the tie-in, "There Were Giants in the Earth," along with the other early, formative episodes of *Lost in Space*, would not repeat on CBS. The network refused to rerun episodes in which Dr. Smith and the Robot posed a true threat to Will and Penny.

14

Episode 5: "The Hungry Sea"

Teleplay by William Welch; story by Shimon Wincelberg
(Additional scenes written by Wincelberg and Irwin Allen, uncredited; with script polishing by Anthony Wilson)
Directed by Sobey Martin
Produced by Buck Houghton (uncredited), with Jerry Briskin;
Executive Producer Irwin Allen

From *Lost in Space* show files (Irwin Allen Papers Collection):

> [The Robinson party] escape from the cave with its relics of an ancient civilization just as an earthquake topples the whole structure. Continuing their way to the tropics they discover that, owing to the planet's elliptical orbit, they are in danger of being roasted alive during the rapidly approaching moment when it comes closest to its sun. They manage to survive this ordeal but John decides they must get back to the comparative safety of the spaceship as soon as possible. To Don's anger, he won't allow him time to check their equipment first. John is proven wrong when, crossing the inland sea in a storm, the solar batteries give way and they cannot steer the chariot. Don climbs out to repair them and is nearly washed overboard. When the danger is over, the two men reconcile their differences and they all get back to the spaceship.

From the Script:

(Shooting Final teleplay, August 25, 1965 draft)

– *Robot:* "Artificial heat now at maximum. Power reserves failing. Recommended action – abandon ship and head south." *Smith (with haughty disdain):* "Listen, my pusillanimous puppet, I have no intention of chasing off after that family of lunatics. *(almost an afterthought)* Besides, it's too cold out there now to travel. *(begins to pace nervously)* This is a pretty mess you've let me get into. You're supposed to be an environmental control Robot. Control something! Do you realize that if I don't get some heat I'll freeze to death?" *Robot (with perfect aplomb):* "In precisely one hour, twelve minutes and fifty-eight seconds."

– *Smith:* "A pretty how-do-you-do this is! Stranded on an alien planet with no one to exchange intelligent ideas with – no one to talk to but this … this animated weather station! *(turns to notice the chessboard)* And I can't even beat him in chess!… Maybe they'll listen to you. *(looks him over critically)* You have the sort of open, idiotic expression people seem to trust. *(considers this)* Why not? My friend, how would you like to take a little walk … say, seventy or eighty miles? I have a message for the Robinsons – a special delivery message!"

– *Robinson:* "In a matter of hours – even less – we'll be in danger of roasting alive. There's no time to get back to the ship. We'll have to set up shelter right here." *Don:* "Do you mean to say you're going to pay attention to what that man Smith says, after all he's done?" *Robinson:* "What does it matter now what he's done? These are facts." *Don:* "Are they? The man's a pathological liar. What makes you think he's suddenly reformed? Do you think he'd lift a finger to save our lives? We started south; I say we keep going." *Robinson:* "You're in no position to give orders!" *Don:* "And you are. Too bad there isn't judgment to go with that self-confidence." *Robinson:* "That's enough, West! Like it or not, I'm going to try to save your life – along with everyone else's!"

Assessment:

One of *Lost in Space*'s best. As with the previous four episodes, "The Hungry Sea" has plenty of action, and – for its time – first-rate effects sequences. Watching the Chariot cross an icy inland sea, then the return trip, over storming waters and caught in the pull of a whirlpool, was as exciting as anything presented in the previous stories. Another plus is the way-out presentation of an actual phenomenon, the "flat elliptical orbit." A planet with such a noncircular orbit would swing widely in and out of its sun's life-giving warmth. For the sake of a good tale, such a world could bear life that was adapted to these extremes of ice and heat.

While the entertainment values were front and center, the story element that elevates this episode is the conflict between John Robinson and Don West. Guy Williams and Mark Goddard displayed their dramatic acting chops to good results as the two characters, burdened by the relentless strain of dealing with one crisis after another, butt heads.

The elements of Man against Man, and Man against Nature are well in place, but this story also benefits from Man against Himself. John and Don both take turns in realizing they have over-reacted and therefore must eat a little humble pie.

This is action/adventure, science-fiction spectacle at its best … or, at least, as good as possible for a television production from 1965. And it still delivers, half a century later.

Script:

Story Assignment 8447 (Production #8505)
Edward J. Lakso's treatment and 1st draft teleplay: June/July 1965.
William Welch's 1st and 2nd draft teleplays: Early/mid-July 1965.
Reformatted Mimeo Department Shooting Final teleplay: July 30, 1965.
Page revisions by Tony Wilson: August 23.
Additional revisions by Wilson (pink insert pages): August 25.

Freelancer Edward J. Lakso was originally given the assignment to turn the last of Shimon Wincelberg's five-story arc into a teleplay. Lakso had written a couple exploitation films in 1959 (*Roadracers* and *Operation Dames*) before finding he was well suited for TV. He was well liked at *Combat!* where, between 1963 and 1967, he wrote 33 scripts. *Ripcord* brought six from Lakso, and *Dr. Kildare* took seven. Things didn't work out as well at *Lost in Space*. After Lakso turned in his first draft script, the assignment was cut off, and then started anew with another writer. A few years later, Lakso would write one script for *Star Trek*'s final season, an episode many fans rank as the all-time worst – "And the Children Shall Lead."

William Welch was hurried in from his post on *Voyage to the Bottom of the Sea* to salvage Lakso's script.

Like Lakso, Welch was a TV hack. This doesn't mean he lacked talent (he had plenty, as this episode demonstrates), but he was quick to work for a fast buck. He could crank out a script in a matter of days, but his work often seemed rushed, with recycled ideas and little logic or theme.

Welch had cut his teeth on TV series which attempted to spook the viewer, such as *Lights Out* (from 1950 and '51), and those that appealed to youth, such as *Sky King* (in 1957 and '58). He wrote the screenplay for a 1963 low budget and somewhat trashy Jane Mansfield movie called *Promises, Promises*. He also tried his hand at being a playwright, with the 1960 way-off Broadway sci-fi *How to Make a Man*, starring Peter Marshall (later of *Hollywood Squares* fame) as a robot. Then Welch caught Irwin Allen's eye. Allen hired Welch to work as associate producer (in charge of rewriting scripts) for the first season of *Voyage to the Bottom of the Sea*. Once Allen saw how prolific Welch was, and with the series' need for first-draft scripts written quickly, he found someone else to do the rewriting and started giving Welch as many assignments as the workaholic writer could handle. By *Voyage*'s third and fourth seasons, Welch was averaging every other episode for the series. During the same period, he also wrote eight episodes for *The Time Tunnel* and four for *Lost in Space*.

Working from a solid story, and with about a quarter of his episode having already been written by Shimon Wincelberg and Irwin Allen (with the footage taken from the pilot), "The Hungry Sea" would be the best of Welch's four *Lost in Space* scripts.

Much credit must go to Wincelberg, for mapping out the nearly seamless linking of existing action sequences with a new story thread. Also, credit goes to Tony Wilson, the last to have his hands on the teleplay, smoothing the seams out with selected lines of dialogue connecting the dots in the plot.

Did you ever wonder why the family wear their parkas for the return trip across the inland sea, when we last saw them in t-shirts and sweating buckets? The parkas are there because these inland sea scenes came from the pilot, when the Robinsons and West only had to contend with dropping temperatures.

Another important change implemented by Wilson had to do with the Robot in the last quarter of the story. William Welch wrote the scenes where the Robinsons take refuge from the heat. As originally written, the Robot had been revived and was helping assemble the heat-resistant shielding. Wilson rewrote the scene and left the Robot knocked out from the laser blast. He then had Don dismantle the Robot in order to pack him away in the Chariot, properly secured for the rough voyage home across the stormy inland sea. Wilson did this because the stock footage of the Chariot on the water did not include the Robot.

Wilson took further care in making old footage and new fit together. He added a line of dialogue in which Don tells John he needs to realign the solar batteries on the Chariot, but John says there isn't time. In the following footage from the pilot, when Don goes outside the Chariot while on the stormy sea, he says that there must be a loose connection on the solar batteries. That line was from the pilot. To explain this away, Wilson added a new scene at the end of the episode, with Will asking Don if the real reason he had to go out onto the roof of the Chariot was because his Dad wouldn't allow the time needed to realign the batteries. Wilson wrote a white lie for Don to tell Will: "Where did you get an idea like that? It was just what I said – a loose connection."

However, one silly addition by Wilson gave the Robot a new talent: guitar playing. Anyone familiar with the instrument can tell you that the Robot's claw was not capable of forming chords on the guitar strings.

Despite this, as Buck Houghton was clearing out his desk and moving off the lot, *Lost in Space* appeared to be in good hands with Wilson polishing the scripts. Irwin Allen felt confident with Wilson at the typewriter and associate producer Jerry Briskin tending to the needs of the production. He didn't see the necessity for spending money or sharing credit with a new show runner. Houghton had served his purpose, calming the concerns of the CBS executives, as well as Guy della-Cioppa, during the making of the formative episodes. Now that the show was up and running, the series creator and executive producer determined that an Irwin Allen Production need only be run by one person – Irwin Allen. Also, one less producer drawing a salary would help the series stay on budget.

Pre-Production:

Director Sobey Martin was 56. In 1952, Martin directed about two dozen episodes of an early suspense and supernatural series called *The Unexpected*. The following season, he was cranking out cheap half-hour westerns with *The Cisco Kid*, and then, a year later, taking on the detective genre with more than a dozen episodes of *Boston Blackie*. He handled low-budget adventure with *Passport to Danger*, and wartime naval adventure (enhanced by stock war footage) in *The Silent Service*. In 1961, Martin advanced to the one-hour format with episodes of *Rawhide* and *Gunsmoke*. These last two series added a bit of prestige to his resume.

If writers who cranked out TV scripts designed to be shot to schedule and on budget were called "hacks," then perhaps Sobey could be called a hack director. He had a reputation for shooting cheap TV episodes within the allotted time and not causing headaches for the producers by attempting to do anything that could be construed as "artsy-fartsy." He also had a reputation on the set as a director who would take cat naps in his director's chair.

Marta Kristen said, "Dear Sobey, who would fall asleep in his director's chair in between takes. They would wake him and say, 'We're ready now,' and he would say, in his heavy accent, 'Choot it! Choot it!' You would ask him, 'Sobey, can I make a suggestion?' He would say, 'Chur, chur.' You would say, 'What if I stood on my head and wiggled my toes?' And he would say, 'Better, better! Choot it! Choot it!'" (MK-SL88)

With many critics accusing TV production as the equivalent of a "sausage factory," the German-born Martin was an adequate sausage-maker who kept the conveyor belts running on schedule.

Irwin Allen tapped Martin for several first season episodes of *Voyage to the Bottom of the Sea*, including "The Ghost of Moby Dick," which featured guest star June Lockhart. Allen then had Martin split his time between *Voyage* and *Lost in Space*, with *The Time Tunnel* and *Land of the Giants* in the near future. Martin would take his snooze breaks at various intervals while directing fourteen episodes of *Space* over the next three years, making him the series second-most-employed director, following Don Richardson.

Production Diary:

Filmed August 30 through September 3, 1965 (5 days).

No director had brought an episode of *Lost in Space* in on schedule or on budget – yet. Sobey Martin would be the fourth to try, and, like Leo Penn before him, Martin was only given five days to film his episode. With a fair amount of footage harvested from the pilot film, the studio figured that he should be able to do it.

Day 1: Monday, August 30. The cast members began arriving for makeup at 6:30 a.m. The call to the set was 8 a.m. Work began shortly after 8 for the first of two days on Stage 11 with the Ext. Jupiter 2 campsite. First up, the end of the story, as John and Don settled their differences and became friends again, then unloaded the Chariot. Next, the company moved to the inside of the Jupiter 2 for the upper deck scenes, beginning with the final scene from the episode – the cliffhanger that would tie "The Hungry Sea" to "Welcome Stranger." It was here that the Robot played "Home Sweet Home," and Will picked up a signal on the receiver, with the scanner showing an incoming "missile." Lastly, they filmed the scene in which Smith watched the movement of the Chariot on a scanner, and was given orbital information from the Robot.

One small step for changing a character and one giant leap for Jonathan Harris – Smith now dresses like the rest of the "family."

Jonathan Harris had a new costume for this episode, matching those worn by Major West and the Robinsons. He was now one of the family, dressed like a character the producers planned to keep around for a while. The problem in changing his attire at this point, and not in a later episode, is that it caused a continuity problem. At the end of the episode, we see the Robinsons and West return to the Jupiter 2 from their adventure in the Chariot. Smith looks out the porthole, then reacts and says, "Robinson alive? Impossible." For this line, Smith is wearing his previous wardrobe – the Air Force jumpsuit. The shot was recycled from Episode 3, "Island in the Sky," when Smith sees that John Robinson has been found alive. Since there was no footage showing Smith reacting to the return of all the Robinsons for "The Hungry Sea," the stock shot works here … except for that awkward wardrobe switcheroo. This is why characters in 1960s TV series – which were shot in a rush and with such small budgets – usually wore the same clothing week in and week out. It saved money on wardrobe, but, more importantly, allowed for pulling shots from past episodes to augment the new ones.

Work wrapped at 7 p.m. Sobey Marin covered seven pages from the script and had finished on schedule.

Day 2: Tuesday, August 31. It was another efficient day, with Martin filming from 8 a.m. to 6:45 p.m. They were again on the upper deck of the Jupiter 2, with only Jonathan Harris and Bob May needed, as Martin covered all the scenes involving this new comedy team.

One scene filmed – when the Robot warmed coffee for Dr. Smith – was a last-minute addition. The episode was timing out short and this new scene was added to make sure that there would be enough footage to fill out the 50 minutes needed for broadcast. It is not part of the July 30th Shooting Final teleplay, which includes Wilson's additional page revisions from August 23rd and 25th. Wilson may have written it as an afterthought, or the scene may have been improvised. Either way, this otherwise humorous scene creates a continuity glitch. In the scenes before and after this one, Smith's in fear of his life. Yet, for a few brief moments, he has a lighthearted exchange with the Robot.

Harris told interviewer Ian Spelling, "The original Smith was a deep, dark, scowling villain and I hated him. Quite honestly. I thought they might have to kill me off in five episodes because he was just so damn rotten. I didn't like the idea of being unemployed again, which is a dreadful state of affairs. I decided to take a chance – and I am a chance-taker – and sneak in the thing for which I am, at the risk of sounding immodest, justly famous. And the main thing I snuck in was comic villainy, which I adore." (JH-SL98)

Day 3: Among the new scenes filmed, to be mixed in with footage from the pilot, were all the sequences dealing with extreme heat.

A first for *Lost in Space* happened at the end of the day: the director had completed his second day of filming and was still on schedule. Not even Irwin Allen – who had directed the pilot – had managed this achievement. The remarkable thing was that Sobey Martin accomplished this between naps.

Day 3: Wednesday, September 1. This was the first of two days spent on Stage 6 with the "Chariot-Campfire" scenes, including when Don disabled the Robot with a laser blast; then the argument between John and Don; and, lastly, the family working together to assemble the sun-reflecting shields. Martin filmed from 8 a.m. to 7:25 p.m. Eight and five-eighths pages were covered – everything that had been on the schedule for that day. Martin was pushing the cast, but this did not prevent them from delivering excellent performances. The well-written scenes inspired equally good acting.

Day 4: Thursday, September 2. They began at 8 a.m. It was a difficult effects-driven sequence of shots, as the camp was savaged by extreme heat, bushes burst into flame, the Robot became charred, and then the perspiration-drenched castaways recovered after the heat blast.

Regarding the Robot approaching the party, and prompting Major West to take it out with a laser shot, Mark Goddard said, "When they started pulling him around the set on cables, up ramps, and around Styrofoam rocks, I knew the time between set-ups would be long and tedious…. Anyway, it seemed that I was always tripping over the cables or trying to stay out of the way when they moved the Robot in and out of the scene. I always thought the background music, whenever the robot moved around the set, should have been 'Beer Barrel Polka,' to a slow march beat." (MG-LISM)

Martin finished his allotted work at 8:32 p.m., breaching "golden hour" double-time pay rates, but otherwise was on schedule. The producers and the studio watchdogs were feeling encouraged. Perhaps *Lost in Space* could be shot close to budget.

Day 5: Friday, September 3. Since the crew and cast were kept so late the night before (most didn't leave the studio until after 9 p.m.), the call times were pushed back for this morning. Stage 5 was being used for the first time in this production, and had to be lit. That would take an hour, so the cast was told not to arrive for makeup until 8:30 a.m. Filming began at 10 a.m. The

actors spent the entire day in the Chariot, which sat on the rocker platform, and positioned in front of a process screen. Martin completed his final shot at 9:04 p.m. By the time the cast members had their makeup removed and changed into their civilian attire, and by the time the crew wrapped the set, it was 10 at night. But they could all sleep in on Saturday morning.

Even considering the overtime pay, this was the first episode to come in on schedule. To Sobey Martin's credit, and despite pushing to beat the clock, he had turned in a first-rate show.

Billy Mumy said, "I loved the first five episodes of *LIS*. They were largely … our original pilot. The pilot included many parts from those episodes. Of course, they were greatly expanded to include Jonathan and the Robot and much more plot, but those had the largest budget of any of our shows…. We were all very enthused to be making such a new type of show, and I for one was absolutely thrilled with it all. Those first five episodes make up wonderful memories for me and I think they're some of the very best shows we ever made." (BM-LISM)

Post-Production:

Even after efforts were made by the writers to play both Smith and the Robot as lighter "heavies," an additional push toward getting the audience to embrace both was made during the post production phase. For instance, in their first scene together in this episode, Smith gets a weather report from the Robot, who says, "Relative humidity, 47 percent. Outside temperature, minus one hundred and twenty degrees Fahrenheit and dropping…. Inside temperature, fifty-one degrees Fahrenheit and dropping rapidly." An alarmed Smith says, "Fifty-one in here? No wonder I'm chilly. And dropping, you say?" The Robot confirms, "Rapidly."

As printed, the lines are bare of direction or inflection. While recording the Robot's voice, and with the encouragement of the producers, Dick Tufeld rolled his "R's." His lines came out: "Rrrelative humidity? And "drrropping." The rolling "R's" rolled even further after Smith asked, "And dropping, you say?" Tufeld's reply: "Rrrrrapidly."

John Williams was given credit for the score. It was comprised mostly of music he had written for "The Reluctant Stowaway," interwoven in with library music by Bernard Herrmann that was originally featured in the pilot.

Jack Gleason was 47 when he started with *Lost in Space*, serving as the supervisor of Editing Team 3. This unit would now alternate episodes with Teams 1 and 2.

Gleason had been the supervising editor on the 1955-57 series *Navy Log*, then the 1959 series *Border Patrol*. He had worked as one of the editors on the 1958-59 series *Behind Closed Doors*. All were quickly forgotten. Then Gleason worked on a series that would make more of an impression, cutting 84 episodes of *Route 66* from 1960 through 1964. In 1963, with a team of four other editors, Gleason shared an Emmy nomination for Outstanding Achievement in Film Editing for Television, for an episode of *Naked City*.

Release / Reaction:

(Only CBS broadcast: Wednesday, October 13, 1965)

Early promo photo used by CBS had *Lost in Space* beating the hippie movement to "flower power" by more than a year.

On TV, the Los Angeles Dodgers faced the Minnesota Twins in the 62nd World Series game. Angela Cartwright was still in the top movie across America – *The Sound of Music* – now in its 31st week. "Yesterday," by the Beatles, was getting the most airplay on radio stations. It wasn't on their *Help!* album, but that record was still the top-selling LP across America. Anne Francis of *Honey West* had the cover of *TV Guide*.

From "TV Scout," syndicated to newspapers across America, including the October 13, 1965 edition of New York's *Syracuse Herald Tribune*:

> Tonight's episode is like the old Abbott and Costello sketch, "Who's on First?" For the first 20 minutes, the Robinsons wander around a spooky Egyptian-like cave, constantly losing one another and calling, "Will ... Penny ... Debbie ... Don ... Dad!" Before the evening is over they also meet up with an assortment of earthquakes, storms, and peculiar orbits. A routine evening.

"Routine" – compared to what? Had anything like this ever been seen on television before?

Rival syndicated review column, "TV Key-notes," carried in the October 13 edition of the *Galveston Daily News*, among other newspapers, found the episode to be better than routine. The critic wrote:

> The special effects which make the events of the series possible are quite marvelous in this children's series. Tonight, earthquakes, storms and a moving hot sun take turns attempting to destroy the brave and intrepid Robinson family on their strange planet. Gracious!

The critic known as "Horo," writing for *Variety*, reviewed "The Hungry Sea" on October 27 issue. He said, in part:

> In the hour span, the viewer witnessed life on a planet that soars close and far from the sun. For added eye-popping effects, there was a storm over the planet's inland sea. The special effects

almost were hypnotic, as the storyline took the leading characters from one cliff-hanging situation to another. There was some comic relief offered by the heavy, portrayed by Jonathan Harris, in his opening tilt with the robot. Harris, peeved at the robot, at one point said, "Oh, dry up." The robot responded by rendering a weather report. It was that kind of heavy space humor which occasionally scored in the opening few moments. As in the first script, Wednesday's outing was space corn, with the characters stereotypes, but what lifts this series aloft is the gee whiz special effects.

The critics seemed to be warming up to the series. More importantly, the ratings were solid. A.C. Nielsen, according to its 30-City ratings survey for October 13, 1965, reported:

Network / Program:	Rating	Audience Share:
7:30 – 8 p.m.:		
ABC: *Ozzie and Harriet*	11.4	20.7%
CBS: *Lost in Space*	**19.3**	**35.0%**
NBC: *The Virginian*	17.2	31.2%
8 – 8:30 p.m.:		
ABC: *The Patty Duke Show*	15.1	24.0%
CBS: *Lost in Space*	**21.6**	**34.3%**
NBC: *The Virginian*	19.6	31.0%

Nielsen also conducted a national survey, ranking the top half of the primetime series. The report was published in the November 9, 1965 issue of *Daily Variety*, and stacked the shows as follows (actual ratings may differ than above report, since the national survey took into account rural areas as well as large cities):

	Program/Network:	Rating:
1.	*Bonanza* (NBC)	32.2
2.	*The Beverly Hillbillies* (CBS)	26.9
3.	*Gomer Pyle, U.S.M.C.* (CBS)	26.9
4.	*The Lucy Show* (CBS)	25.9
5.	*The Red Skelton Show* (CBS)	25.7
6.	*The Andy Griffith Show* (CBS)	24.8
7.	*Get Smart* (NBC)	24.7
8.	Saturday Night Movie (NBC)	24.0
9.	*The Ed Sullivan Show* (CBS)	23.6
10.	*Petticoat Junction* (CBS)	23.6
11.	Thursday Night Movie (CBS)	23.5
12.	*Hogan's Heroes* (CBS)	23.5
13.	*My Three Sons* (CBS)	23.3
14.	*The Virginian* (NBC)	23.3
15.	The World Series (NBC)	23.1
16.	*Bewitched* (ABC)	23.1
17.	*Walt Disney* (NBC)	23.0
18.	*Daniel Boone* (NBC)	22.7
19.	*The Man from U.N.C.L.E.* (NBC)	22.6
20.	*The Dick Van Dyke Show* (CBS)	22.3

21.	*Flipper* (NBC)	22.3
22.	*Green Acres* (CBS)	22.2
23.	*F Troop* (ABC)	22.0
24.	*Gilligan's Island* (CBS)	22.0
25.	***Lost in Space* (CBS)**	**22.7**
26.	*Branded* (NBC)	21.3
27.	*I Dream of Jeannie* (NBC)	21.3
28.	*Bob Hope Chrysler Theater* (NBC)	21.2
29.	*Andy Williams Show* (NBC)	21.1
30.	*Lassie* (CBS)	21.0
31.	*The Wild, Wild West* (CBS)	21.0
32.	*McHale's Navy* (ABC)	20.9
33.	*The Fugitive* (ABC)	20.8
34.	*The Lawrence Welk Show* (ABC)	20.7
35.	*Combat!* (ABC)	20.5
36.	*The Munsters* (CBS)	20.5
37.	*Laredo* (NBC)	20.1
38.	*My Favorite Martian* (CBS)	20.1
39.	*Peyton Place* (ABC)	20.1
40.	*I Spy* (NBC)	19.8

On October 18, five days after "The Hungry Sea" aired on CBS, the results of a poll assessing the new TV season was published. Jack Boyle, of the Pasadena *Star-News* in California, had the results. He reported:

> Our questionnaire immediately following the premiere week of the 1965-66 television season asked for your reactions to the new series. And we got them – in overwhelming quantities.... In the case of some series, there was a wide discrepancy between the voices of men and women. *Green Acres* and *Lost in Space* scored heavily with men. *Trials of O'Brien* and *The Smothers Brothers* were heavily supported by women.... Comments attacking the *Lost in Space* series acknowledged that it was probably a good show for the kids, even though the adults thought it terrible.... As always happens, there were a substantial number of ballots hearing the comment that all the new shows were terrible.

Program:	Favorable:	Unfavorable:
Hogan's Heroes	63.8	19.3
The Loner	58.4	19.8
The Wild, Wild West	55.0	24.2
The Trials of O'Brien	50.7	22.4
Green Acres	43.0	26.0
Smothers Brothers	42.6	34.4
Lost in Space	**35.3**	**40.3**

This poll showed *Lost in Space* to be less liked than six other new series, four of which it routinely beat in the ratings. The conclusion: People who took time to participate in polls, especially ones in which they had to write letters, were more discerning than the average TV viewer. Not too many kids wrote letters, but they sure loved watching *Lost in Space*. And some of their parents, although perhaps not about to admit it, loved the show too.

15

"Refuge of the Damned"

The sixth episode planned for *Lost in Space* was based on a story "springboard" by Shimon Wincelberg. "Refuge of the Damned" was the final chapter in a six-part story arc mapped out by Wincelberg which took the Robinson expedition from the launch of the Jupiter 2 to the various conflicts with Smith and the Robot; the encounter with a massive alien spaceship; a crash landing on a strange new world; a battle with a giant Cyclops; the struggle to survive severe climate changes; a close encounter with a "hungry sea"; and finally being pitted against the "Damned."

Episode 5, "The Hungry Sea," was supposed to end as the pilot film had. We were to see the Robinsons and Major West achieving safe refuge in a tropical area, climbing out of the Chariot and kneeling to give thanks. Then would come the revelation that they were being spied on by two aliens with enlarged heads. The cliffhanger leading to the next episode would have the castaways discovering a wrecked spaceship from "an earlier decade."

For the setup to "Refuge of the Damned," Wincelberg wrote:

> Throughout all this, family remains unaware that their refuge is also occupied by scattered survivors of super-intelligent race, whose civilization has been destroyed by the giants.
>
> Living as fugitives, survivors of super-race have become cunning, malevolent, cowardly, treacherous, and clearly intend to deal with these intruders as soon as they can safely get away with it.

Later in his abbreviated treatment, Wincelberg wrote:

> Cautious exploration of crashed space-ship. Dead pilot's logbook suggests he had been forced to aid in escape of small band of international super-criminals, masterminded by "The Baron." No telling if any of them are still alive or at large.
>
> Logbook accounts for hostility and furtiveness of super-intelligent planetary race, whom the criminals' behavior had understandably soured on all Earth-men.
>
> Faced by the possibility of two separate groups of antagonists lurking in the jungle, Robinson puts his people on siege footing.
>
> One little skirmish involving danger to one of the youngsters ends happily, but impresses upon all that their antagonists will stop at nothing.

> Judy, after a lovers' quarrel with Don, has disappeared. Alone, she has a number of harrowing adventures, and winds up kidnaped by the Baron and his gang.
>
> Not being equipped with the new super-weapons carried by Don and Robinson, the Baron is forced to employ subterfuge, treachery, blackmail, and an assortment of traps, and his primary use for Judy is as bait for capturing the Chariot.
>
> Concerned for Judy's safety, the Robinsons nearly give in. But Don manages to effect a last-minute rescue.

Freelance writer Herman Groves was assigned to further develop "Refuge of the Damned."

Groves was 38 and in his fifth year as a TV writer, having written for westerns (*The Restless Gun*, *The Gallant Men*, *Bonanza*), crime shows (*Surfside 6*, *The Untouchables*, and, featuring Mark Goddard, *The Detectives*), as well as far-fetched sitcoms, such as *Bewitched*.

After the story treatment was turned in and assessed by Irwin Allen, Buck Houghton and Tony Wilson, the assignment was vacated and Groves was given a different story to develop ("The Sky Is Falling").

There were many good reasons for abandoning "Refuge of the Damned":

- There was no place in the story for Dr. Smith or the Robot. As the producers began receiving story treatments and first draft scripts for the other seven assignments that had been given out up to this point – "The Reluctant Stowaway," "The Derelict," "Island in the Sky," "There Were Giants in the Earth," "The Hungry Sea," "The Cyclamen" (to be given the new title of "Attack of the Monster Plants"), and "Welcome Stranger," and as Tony Wilson was busy doing his script polishing – it had become apparent that Smith and the Robot were too important to the series to be missing from an entire episode.
- "Refuge of the Damned" was likely to be an expensive production. It introduced numerous new characters, required a wrecked spaceship and an extensive jungle setting.
- CBS would be sure to tell them, you couldn't say "damned" on television in the 1960s.
- Lastly, it wasn't that good of a story anyway.

With "Refuge" cut, the next script to go before the camera brought a wayward Earth astronaut to the Robinson colony … with a delightful performance by a much in-demand TV guest star.

16

Episode 6: "Welcome Stranger"

Written by Peter Packer
(with script polishing by Anthony Wilson)
Directed by Alvin Ganzer
Producer: Buck Houghton (uncredited), with Jerry Briskin;
Executive Producer: Irwin Allen

CBS press release:

> Jimmy Hapgood is a happy-go-lucky space traveler who has been planet-hopping for 15 years after becoming lost on a mission to Saturn. When he drops in on the Robinsons, they try to help him repair his ship's guidance system in return for passage for their children back to Earth. Hapgood is not too keen on the idea until Penny's bout with a wild fungus growing from his spacecraft causes a change in heart. His sentiments are short-lived, however, when Dr. Zachary Smith presents another selfish scheme.

From the Script:

(Shooting Final teleplay, September 16, 1965 draft)

– *Will:* "I bet you were surprised to find us." *Hapgood:* "Finding people don't surprise me." *Will:* "What does?" *Hapgood:* "Finding things you know can't exist, but do. Happenings that put your heart in your mouth and your blood down to your toes. Living things that breathe in fire, and swim in ice. *(grins)* And you know something, sonny? I haven't seen more 'n a smidgen of it."

– *Robinson:* "Remember when we first discussed the plans for the space flight? There was a time when we couldn't decide whether or not we had any right to bring along Will and Penny." *Maureen (low):* Yes … I remember." *Robinson:* "Have you ever regretted the decision we made?" *Maureen (for a moment she finds it impossible to answer):* "The truth?" *Robinson:* "The truth. *(off her nod)* I thought you felt that way. It's possible to let them go. There'd be room on Hapgood's ship if we pulled out the ballast tanks." *Maureen (not willing to meet his eyes; quietly):* "Is that what you want?" *Robinson:* "They're so young. They have a right to something more than this – not knowing how much longer we can last here – or whether we can ever get the Jupiter in shape to fly." *Maureen:* "Yes … if anyone should go, it's the children."

– *Hapgood (furious):* "I said forget it! I'd be plumb crazy to take on anything like that. A couple of kids along with me in [Hapgood's ship] Travelin' Man? I'd be signing their death warrant sure as can be – well as my own! *(glares suspiciously at Robinson)* In fact, I'm kinda surprised it was in your mind at all – or that you'd expect me to go along with it!" *Robinson:* "I was thinking of them, Jim – of their future." *Hapgood (cuttingly):* "Too bad you didn't think of it before you found out that space don't take kindly to a family outing! *(angrily)* You're not out of gas on a highway back home, mister. You're way out yonder, and there is no highway out here – and far as I'm concerned, you're out o' luck! All of you!"

Assessment:

Nothing was going to match the excitement of the first five episodes of *Lost in Space*, each (with the exception of "The Derelict") augmented with big action sequences from the pilot film. This doesn't mean "Welcome Stranger" is substandard by any means, merely paced slower, with more emphasis on character and story than action and adventure.

"Welcome Stranger" is an engaging story, highlighted by a character-rich performance by the charismatic Warren Oates, who manages to combine the conflicting personality traits of good old boy rowdiness with those of homespun wisdom and guarded sensitivity.

Few *Lost in Space* writers other than Peter Packer could have pulled off a story and a character like Hapgood with such good results. Packer's background in westerns (in print and on screen) combined well with a fertile imagination that easily adapted to the "what if" worlds of science fiction. Texas-born Jimmy Hapgood is a rough-and-ready character reminiscent of America's Old West transplanted into the new frontier of space.

The focus in the story may be on Hapgood, but the real glue that holds this tale together, bringing a deeper resonance, is the guilt that John and Maureen Robinson feel over taking their children into space, and their difficult decision to entrust Will and Penny to the wild adventurer. The theme, then, is the true test of love – self-sacrifice.

With the inspired writing and direction, excellent characterizations are provided for all the regulars, as depicted in John and Maureen's struggle to give up their children, plus:

- John's attempts to manipulate Hapgood, then his frustration in failing to get his way;
- Don's conflicts with Hapgood, which go from verbal to physical;
- Judy's change of heart. She goes from fascination with the rugged stranger to feeling betrayed by him and protective of Don;
- Will and Penny's attraction to the tall-tale-spinning loner, then their trauma over the prospect of being separated from their family;
- And last but never least, Smith's obsessive self-serving drive, and his well-calculated conniving to eliminate his competition and secure himself safe passage back to the green hills of Earth.

Taking into account the down-and-dirty aspects of 1960s television special effects, the sci-fi aspects of the show are very good. The presentation of Hapgood's spacecraft and the alien spores is convincingly done. The fight between Don and Hapgood is another plus – a pleasant mix of spit and vinegar and slapstick comedy. But the emotional sparring throughout is what wins this episode its high grade.

While the pacing is slower than the preceding episodes, the emotional impact makes this a trip into space worth taking. At times, "moving pictures" can also move the viewer's emotions. This episode is one of those times.

Script:

Story Assignment 8546 (Production #8506)
Story assigned to Peter Packer on June 24, 1965.
Packer's treatment and 1st draft teleplay: July 1965.
Packer's 3rd draft teleplay: Early August, 1965.
Reformatted Mimeo Dept. Shooting Final teleplay (on pale green paper): August 11, 1965.
Tony Wilson's script polish (pink page inserts): August 23.
Additional page revisions by Wilson (yellow page inserts): August 31.
Further revisions by Wilson (green page inserts): September 2.
Further revisions by Wilson (beige page inserts) September 3.
Further revisions by Wilson (gold page inserts): September 7.
Further revisions by Wilson (blue page inserts): September 16.

Peter Packer was given this second assignment following his excellent handling of "The Derelict." Buck Houghton and Tony Wilson handed the story's springboard off to Packer, knowing it was tailor-made for a writer who had a knack for both westerns and science fiction.

Packer, born and raised in England but enamored by the American western genre, came up with Hapgoodisms such as:

"Then you're just like me – lost as a wood tick on Bald Mountain";

"Oo-whee! Ship was aswarm with outlandish bugs no bigger'n locusts – but a hundred times as fierce – eating their way through the hull";

"Ever see so many stars – so many places – all there for the taking … if a man could live forever";

And "I been more trouble to you folks than a goat in a paper mill."

Between the homespun humor and wisdom, Hapgood also revealed his inner soul, telling the Robinsons: "There's nothing in space ever gave me this kind of a welcome … 'n I guess it's been about the same for you. No matter where you go, they've got the place posted – enter at your own risk … and pretty soon you get to feel there's no difference between livin' and dyin'. That's the way it's been for me – 'til now. Well – meeting you all has changed all that. There's a mighty big difference between livin' and dyin' – that I'd just about forgotten."

We get more backstory on Smith, which helps to explain why he was assigned to give the Robinsons a medical exam before their launch, but was also involved to some degree in the atmospheric systems on the Jupiter 2 … and now, in this episode, can do cyber-surgery on the Robot. He tells Hapgood that he has degrees in both science and medicine. (Judging by Smith's character as shown in the previous episodes, he probably cheated his way to those degrees, too.)

On August 8, 1965, after reading Packer's third draft of the script, Irwin Allen sent notes to Buck Houghton and Tony Wilson. In a clear indication that Allen was supportive of the transformation of Smith from cold-blooded to lily-livered, he wrote:

> P. 6 – Sc. 13: The Robot & Smith should <u>not</u> be leading the column [to find Hapgood's ship], as they were in the rear in the two preceding scenes (Sc. 11-12). It would be funny if we saw the Robot striding at his usual pace, catching up to Don, Robinson & Will, who have now become more cautious. Smith, attempting to still use him as a shield, talks quietly to him, saying, "Slow Down, you idiot! What are you trying to do? Get me killed?" …
>
> Hapgood's speech about the Robot needing to be more nimble doesn't come off as funny. It should be remembered that in all probability, Hapgood has never seen a Robot before. He would naturally be alarmed at this monster approaching him. …
>
> Hapgood should say, "Howdy – Hapgood's the name." The others lower their guns as Hapgood starts to continue speaking – as though to ease the tension of the meeting…
>
> P. 9 – Sc. 23: After the introductions are over, Hapgood would logically ask if Robinson could tell him where he is. As the script is now, Hapgood assumes they are as lost as he has been. This is wrong.

The action and dialogue Allen asked for was put into the script by Tony Wilson for the August 23rd revised draft. The script would be revised four more times to address concerns from CBS and reduce spending.

Pre-Production:

Director Alvin Ganzer was 54. He came to *Lost in Space* with an impressive resume. He had directed four episodes for his friend Buck Houghton at *The Twilight Zone*, and had visited other early TV sci-fi series, such as *Science Fiction Theatre* (two episodes) and *Men into Space* (eight episodes). Also, around the same time as this *Lost in Space*, he directed the second episode of *The Wild, Wild West* that featured Dr. Miguelito Loveless. Ganzer was well-liked at *Hawaiian Eye*, *The Man from U.N.C.L.E.* and *Route 66*, for which he directed several episodes each. He also directed Mark Goddard in several episodes of *The Detectives*.

Ganzer only did one *Lost in Space*. He said, "I did not want to do this show, but I was romanced into doing it by my friend, producer Buck Houghton, who was the line producer. He called me and asked me to do it. I said I really did not want to do a space show, but he said, 'Please do it for me.' So, I agreed to do it. I came on to the set and asked where Buck was and they told me that he had resigned the day before. So here I was, trapped on this show that I really did not want, but I did it and it was all right." (AG-LISF)

Houghton had given notice but, contrary to Ganzer's recollections, had not yet exited the building. He would remain in his office on a reduced basis until the end of the first week in October – three episodes down the road.

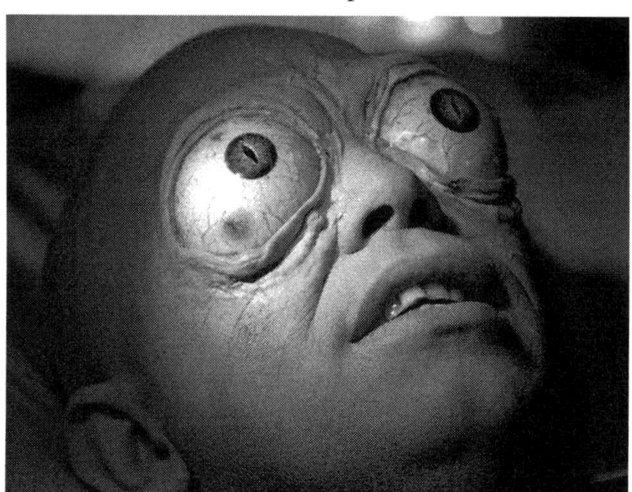

Warren Oates in "The Mutant," a 1964 episode of *The Outer Limits*.

Warren Oates played Jimmy Hapgood. He was 32 and, in the course of his career from 1956 until his untimely death in 1982, would amass close to 150 television and film appearances. Prior to *Lost in Space*, he had been a regular in thirty-two episodes of *Stoney Burke*, Jack Lord's one-hour drama set in and around the rodeo circuit. Oates was a natural for westerns, and not just in name. He had appeared in ten episodes of *Gunsmoke*, then four for *Wanted: Dead or Alive*, five for *The Rifleman*, three for *Trackdown*, and four for *Rawhide*. Oates also appeared once or twice each on *Wagon Train*, *Have Gun – Will Travel*, *Bonanza*, *The Virginian*, and even made a stopover at Mark Goddard's first series, *Johnny Ringo*. He was also featured in big-screen westerns, such as Sam Peckinpah's *Ride the High Country*, *Major Dundee* and *The Wild Bunch*. Peckinpah also gave Oates the lead in the offbeat 1973 drama *Bring Me the Head of Alfredo Garcia*. Oates had also done sci-fi, with a pair of *Twilight Zone* episodes, and a memorable guest spot as an astronaut turned into a mutant on *The Outer Limits*. Oates won a New York Film Critics award for playing the lead in the 1971 cult film *Two-Lane Blacktop*.

Production Diary:

Filmed September 8 – 17 (8 and ½ days).

There was a great deal of ping-ponging with the camera unit and cast for this episode. Above: It was a two-day surgery, filmed on September 7 and 9, 1965. Below and next page: Filming on and around "Travelin' Man" spaceship, on September 8 and 10.

The company had Monday, September 6th off in recognition of Labor Day.

Day 1: Tuesday, September 7. Filming began at 8 a.m. on Stage 5 for scenes in the lower deck of the Jupiter 2, including the one in which Smith planted seeds of doubt in Will's and Penny's minds about parting with their parents. Other scenes shot included Maureen telling John that Will and Penny were missing. Started but not finished: the surgery on the Robot. Filming lasted until 6:32 p.m. Alvin Ganzer covered eight pages of the script and finished on schedule.

Day 2: Wednesday, September 8. The company spent the day on Stage 11, filming the area around Hapgood's "Travelin' Man" spacecraft. Camera began rolling at 8 a.m., with the last shot completed at 6:54 p.m. Ganzer was only able to put five and six-eighths pages of the script to film, and ended one-half of a day behind schedule.

Day 3: Thursday, September 9. Back on Stage 5, they continued with the scenes left incomplete on Day 1, including the surgery on the Robot. The company filmed from 8 a.m. to 7:04 p.m., with Ganzer covering five and three-eighths script pages, and finishing a full day behind schedule.

Day 4: Friday, September 10. Filming took place on Stage 5 from 8 a.m. to 2:30 p.m., still trying to finish a scene from the day before. Next, a midday company move to Stage 11 to finish sequences needed in the area where Travelin' Man had landed. Ganzer had an ambitious shot in mind, requiring hauling a camera up into the rafters of the stage in order to shoot down at Jonathan Harris, as he shouted after the departing Travelin' Man. The problem with ambitious shots is that they require extra care and time. Ganzer ran out of both before even getting his shot started. The director only covered two and seven-eighths pages from the script on a schedule which called for roughly ten pages per day. They worked until 7:20 p.m., and were one-and-a-half days behind when production suspended.

Day 5: Monday, September 13. Ganzer filmed from 8 a.m. to 5:50 p.m. at the outdoor Moat location, as John, Don, Will, Smith and the Robot searched for the spacecraft that had landed nearby; then a second trip across the same terrain as Hapgood spun a tale for the amusement of Will and Penny; and the first meeting with Hapgood. Ganzer only covered six and six-eighths pages. By the time he finished, it was too late to keep the cast on hand as the company moved to Stage 6. The production was now a full two days behind.

Day 6: Tuesday, September 14. It was supposed to be the last day of filming, but the end was nowhere in sight. On the schedule for Stage 6: the cliffhanger (and tie-in to the next episode, "My Friend, Mr. Nobody"), and the scenes inside Travelin' Man. Ganzer filmed from 8 a.m. to 7:17 p.m., covering seven pages from the script. They were now two-and-a-half days behind. The next episode to film, "My Friend, Mr. Nobody," was pushed back. Irwin Allen was not happy, and his frequent visits to the set made that clear to everyone involved in the production. The director was trying too hard to create art. To Allen's thinking, the crew and the cast were behaving as co-conspirators.

Marta Kristen recounted, "When Irwin came to the set, you knew you were in trouble. He would come to the set if a director was running late. He would say, 'Time is money; time is money!' And he would get upset, and people would go, 'Oh no, Irwin is here.' And June and Guy, after a while, would just walk away." (MK-AI15)

Paul Zastupnevich concurred, "[Irwin] didn't know how to handle people. So, many times we would have situations and stress. Irwin would always tell people, 'Time is money; time is money.' And it would get to them. I would have to smooth things over with the people Irwin had ticked off. People always said I managed to calm the waters and keep people happy, especially women." (PZ-SL93)

Day 7: Wednesday, September 15. Work took place on Stage 11 from 8 a.m. to 6:31 p.m. They were finally filming the scenes at the campsite outside of the Jupiter. These sequences were originally scheduled for two days of production. Ganzer would take three. He covered eight and two-eighths pages from the script and slipped to two and a half days behind. Cast and crew got out of the studio with barely enough time to make it home, warm up their TV sets, and catch the series premiere of *Lost in Space* on CBS at 7:30 p.m.

Day 7. Note: the viewport window was removed for this shot, allowing the book mike to be mounted outside the ship.

Day 8: Thursday, September 16. The morning trades, as well as other Los Angeles newspapers, carried reviews of *Lost in Space*. Generally, the verdict was not positive. Morale had to be affected as cast and crew came to work. In a couple of days, however, the overnight ratings reports would arrive and the mood would pick up a bit. *Lost in Space* had won its time slot.

Work continued on Stage 11. They still had the fight between Hapgood and Don to film.

Mark Goddard fondly recalled, "I enjoyed working with Warren Oates. Warren and I had a fight written into his episode and we did the fight ourselves without the use of doubles." (MG-LISF)

Peter Packer, who had described his share of cowboy brawls in his many western novels, wrote:

DON

I think you owe him an apology, Hapgood.

Hapgood glares at [Don] for a moment – then pushes him aside, starts to move toward Robot's guidance system.

HAPGOOD

Out of my way, sonny.

Again he starts to pick it up, but Don grabs him by the arm and spins him around.

DON

I said you owe 'em an apology.

HAPGOOD

I owe 'em nothing – except a thank you for a meal that stopped giving me pleasure five minutes ago! Now get out of my way!

He gives Don a shove that staggers him – but Don comes right back and takes a swing at Hapgood. The blow connects with Hapgood's jaw – jars him – but instead of getting mad, he touches his face – and grins. This is something he is going to enjoy … and unexpectedly he sends a good hard jab at Don's head – and starts dancing around Don with his fists up.

HAPGOOD

(jovially)

Come on now – hit me again.

(points to his jaw)

Right here.

Hapgood is loving every minute of it as Don comes at him with a swing which he ducks, and sends a body blow at Don. Hapgood isn't hitting hard – just enjoying the pleasure of being in a fight. His violence is more of an inward delight than an outward show as he kicks a stool out of his way – shoves the table aside – dances around Don – while Don keeps swinging at him – connecting – Hapgood taking the punishment like water off a duck's back. Don sends a haymaker to Hapgood's jaw.

HAPGOOD
(roars with delight)

Oh-whee!

He lashes out at Don. They exchange maybe a half-dozen spine-shakers – then Hapgood dances out of range – leaps on the table – and as Don charges at him – he leaps down at him with a wild Texas yell and sends him flying backward to the ground by the sheer weight of his leap. He stands there grinning down at Don in great exhilaration.

HAPGOOD

C'mon! C'mon! You ain't finished yet – or are you?

Don starts to stagger to his feet. Hapgood is about to throw a haymaker when Judy comes up behind him and sends a frying pan crashing down on his head.

They filmed from 8 a.m. until the frying pan landed on Hapgood's head at 6:56 p.m. Ganzer held at two-and-a-half days behind.

Day 9: Friday, September 17. Work resumed at 8 a.m. on Stage 11, with Ganzer taking until 3:40 p.m. to film the last of the remaining script pages. It was finally a wrap.

Having taken eight and a half days to film what was supposed to be a six-day production, Alvin Ganzer was not asked to return for future assignments on *Lost in Space.* With his friend and colleague Buck Houghton preparing to exit the series, it isn't likely Ganzer would have asked for further work anyway. He moved on to *The Man from U.N.C.L.E.*, *Cimarron Strip*, *Ironside*, and *Hawaii Five-O*. Ganzer would also direct fourteen episodes of *Police Woman* in the late 1970s before retiring.

Release / Reaction:

(Only CBS broadcast: Wednesday, October 20, 1965)

On a Clear Day You Can See Forever opened on Broadway. There was finally a new top movie across America – *The Great Race*, starring Jack Lemmon, Tony Curtis, Natalie Wood, and Peter Falk. *The Sound of Music* moved down to second position. Red Skelton had the cover of *TV Guide*. "Yesterday" was the top song on the radio, and the Beatles also had the best-selling album in America, with *Help!*

Because it portrayed a child in terror, CBS passed on the promotional picture provided by the studio of Penny trapped in one of the plants outside the small spaceship. A picture of Warren Oates was used in its place.

In the weeks before *Lost in Space* premiered on CBS, Angela Cartwright, with sister Veronica, and Billy Mumy performed at the Hollywood Bowl.

Mumy recalled, "It was 'Scout Day.' We were both there in our silver spacesuits. And the Hollywood Bowl was packed with boy scouts, girl scouts, cub scouts, and brownies – fifteen thousand of them! Art Linkletter was the host of this thing, and a parade of entertainer/actors, mostly child actors from various television series and films, came out and kind of did a song or two. So, I came out and sang 'Tijuana Jail,' by the Kingston Trio, about going down to Mexico, gambling, getting drunk, and getting thrown in jail. And what always blows my mind about that is that neither Art Linkletter, no one at the Bowl during sound check, and neither my mother or my father, said, 'Hey, Billy, why don't you do "This Land is Your Land." Or how about 'Where Have All the Flowers Gone?' Nobody said a word to me about it. Nobody! So I went out there and sang *that* song. The first gig I ever had, playing a packed Hollywood Bowl, and it's been downhill ever since." (BM-AI15)

To promote the premiere of the series, Billy Mumy and Angelica Cartwright, with sister Veronica, performed at the Hollywood Bowl in July 1966.

From syndicated "TV Scout," featured in, among other newspapers, the October 20, 1965 issue of the *Abilene Reporter-News*:

> *Lost in Space* has a magnificent piece of inadvertent satire of television medical shows in a scene in which Dr. Smith must operate on his robot to remove the creature's spectroscope and navigation sensor. The operation is necessary because an astronaut, who has been lost for 15 years, lands near the Robinsons' space colony, and the instrument may be the thing needed to get him back to Earth. Warren Oates, who is the busiest guest actor on television this season, is good as the happy-go-lucky Texan who isn't too sure he wants to return home.

The A.C. Nielsen 30-City Ratings survey for October 20, 1965 reported:

Network / Program:	Rating	Audience Share:
7:30 – 8 p.m.:		
ABC: *Ozzie and Harriet*	18.2	30.0%
CBS: *Lost in Space*	**22.0**	**36.3%**
NBC: *The Virginian*	12.0	19.8%

8 – 8:30 p.m.:		
ABC: *The Patty Duke Show*	19.7	31.9%
CBS: *Lost in Space*	**24.1**	**39.0%**
NBC: *The Virginian*	15.9	9.8%

Nielsen's 30-Market survey for week ending October 24, 1965, as published in the November 1, 1965 issue of *Daily Variety*, told which of the 90 or so primetime TV programs had made it into the Top 15. *Lost in Space* was moving up.

1.	Saturday Night Movie	NBC	29.7
2.	Thursday Night Movie	CBS	27.3
3.	*Get Smart*	NBC	25.6
4.	*The Man from U.N.C.L.E.*	NBC	25.5
5.	*Bonanza*	NBC	24.9
6.	*The Beverly Hillbillies*	CBS	27.3
7.	*The Ed Sullivan Show*	CBS	23.2
8.	*Peyton Place 1*	ABC	22.8
9.	***Lost in Space***	**CBS**	**22.7**
10.	*Chrysler Presents Bob Hope*	NBC	22.6
11.	*I Dream of Jeannie*	NBC	22.5
12.	*Gomer Pyle, U.S.M.C.*	CBS	22.0
13.	Tuesday Night Movie	NBC	21.9
14.	*The Lucy Show*	CBS	21.8
15.	*My Three Sons*	CBS	21.8

Nielsen's nose-counting rival, Arbitron Ratings Service, ranked the Top 20 for October 16-22, 1966. The report, published in the October 31st issue of *Broadcasting* magazine, reporting:

1.	*The Jackie Gleason Show*	CBS	26.1
2.	*The Andy Griffith Show*	CBS	25.9
3.	*Chrysler Presents Bob Hope*	NBC	25.6
4.	*The Red Skelton Show*	CBS	24.2
5.	*Bonanza*	NBC	23.9
6.	*Peyton Place 1*	ABC	22.0
7.	*Green Acres*	CBS	21.7
8.	*The Ed Sullivan Show*	CBS	21.2
	Gunsmoke	CBS	21.2
10.	*The Lucy Show*	CBS	20.7
11.	The Thursday Night Movie	CBS	20.3
12.	The Friday Night Movie	CBS	20.2
13.	*I Spy*	NBC	19.6
14.	*Bewitched*	ABC	19.4
15.	*The Beverly Hillbillies*	CBS	19.2
16.	The Saturday Night Movie	NBC	19.2
17.	***Lost in Space***	**CBS**	**19.1**
18.	*Rat Patrol*	ABC	18.9
19.	*The Virginian*	NBC	18.7
	The Lawrence Welk Show	ABC	18.7
	Family Affair	CBS	18.7

Lost in Space was a certified hit.

17

Episode 7: "My Friend, Mr. Nobody"

Written by Jackson Gillis
(with script polishing by Anthony Wilson)
Directed by Paul Stanley
Produced by Buck Houghton (uncredited), with Jerry Briskin;
Executive Producer: Irwin Allen

From *Lost in Space* show files (Irwin Allen Papers Collection):

> Penny, exploring, finds a cave in a rocky area where a curious echo sounds as if it is trying to talk to her. The echo gradually forms intelligible words and Penny goes there every day to play with the mysterious, invisible friend, that Maureen believes is just a child's imaginary playmate. One day Smith discovers that the pebbles she brings back from the cave are diamonds. Greedy to get more without anyone else knowing what he is about, he tricks Don into blasting the cave wide open. Penny, guessing his purpose, flies back to protect her friend. She is knocked unconscious by the explosion and the Invisible Force, its home destroyed, its friend injured, erupts like a whirlwind, bent on the destruction of them all. Penny, recovering consciousness, runs after it, begging it not to destroy the people she loves. In response to this plea, the Cosmic Force disappears into the sky in the form of a thousand brilliant stars.

From the Script:

(2nd Revised Shooting Final teleplay, September 17, 1965 draft)

– *Penny (looking wildly around):* "I still can't see you – I can't even tell where you are." *Voice:* "I can see you!" *Penny (tearfully, plaintively):* "Please, don't you understand? I get scared! If you'd just once tell me who you are." *Voice:* "I… don't know who I am." *Penny (gasp):* "What?... Oh, but that must be awful! *(then, helpfully)* Maybe you've just been asleep – or growing up, maybe – or changing." *Voice:* "I… don't know yet." *Penny:* "Well, why don't you try and find out? Do you know what my brother calls you? He says you're Nobody, because I can't tell him you're somebody, but if you'd just…" *Voice (interrupting):* "Is that a name? Like Penny?" *Penny:* "Of course. But at least you could try to be Mr. Nobody, couldn't you? I mean, if you'd only just let me see a little bit of you!" *Voice:* "I don't… know how…" *Penny:* "But try! You can't just – just stay hiding down here until you die!" *Voice (beat):* "What is die?" *Penny (pause, softly):* "Oh… Well, I guess maybe I'm not exactly sure myself… But you know – when a person can't talk any more… or move anymore… Like it was before you can remember, maybe." *Voice (slowly):* "I… remember rocks… rocks bubbling…" *Penny (touching floor, incredulously):* "These? But this is granite! It takes millions and millions of years to… *(gasp)* You mean you're that old?"

– *Penny:* "Mother… Do you think maybe just a place could… think and talk and – well – like you, maybe?" *Maureen (smile):* "Maybe." *Penny (frown):* "I asked daddy if it's only people that can have brains. But he just said very few of them do."

– *Robinson (hushed):* "It's impossible! It's like a new Milky Way…" *Penny:* "Well, caterpillars can turn into butterflies, can't they?"

Assessment:

Notable cult TV historian Jon Abbott, in an article devoted to "My Friend, Mr. Nobody" for the February 1999 issue of *TV Zone*, wrote: "'My Friend, Mr. Nobody' is a beautiful elegiac fairy tale worthy of *The Outer Limits* or *The Twilight Zone*. The story also captures the day-to-day banality of the shipwrecked group's existence: John and Don laboring at the drill site for fuel; Maureen and Judy passing the time with 'women's interests' (styling hair and baking pies!); Smith and the Robot idling away their time at chess… and Penny, a lonely little girl until an alien life force, alone for centuries, gives her the attention and adventure she craves."

This tale presents *Lost in Space*'s first whimsical turn. It's a constrained little story that begins with the lonely Penny's first trip to the magical grotto (where we see a large section of the Fox Moat). Palm leafs beckon welcomingly, and bubbling water rises up to her lips. It's quite a contrast to the tumult that arises as "Mr. Nobody" gains awareness, with an emotion-driven wind and sand storm. More literal fireworks erupt as the Robot fires laser bolts skyward, and there's a final catharsis as Penny's friend figuratively transforms to cosmic butterfly.

"My Friend, Mr. Nobody" is a charming and magical story dealing with loneliness, and an underlining theme of how friendship and love can inspire growth, renewed life, and the realization of one's potential and purpose. The sensitivity and wonder of Jackson Gillis's storytelling, John Williams' beautiful and touching score, and Angela Cartwright's sincere performance, join together to make this a story for the ages.

Script:

Story Assignment 8451 (Production #8507)
Jackson Gillis's treatment: Mid-August 1965.
Gillis's 1st draft teleplay: August 17, 1965.
Gillis's 2nd draft teleplay: late August 1965.
Reformatted Mimeo Department Shooting Final teleplay: Early September 1965.
Tony Wilson's script polish (Revised Shooting Final teleplay): September 8.
Wilson's additional script polishing (2nd Revised Shooting Final teleplay): September 14.
Additional page revisions by Wilson (green insert pages): September 17.

Writer Jackson Gillis had one of the longer and more impressive resumes of Irwin Allen's stable of writers. Back in the early 1950s, Jackson was writing for *Racket Squad*, an early and very popular TV crime drama. He wrote thirteen episodes the following year for another cops and robbers program, *I'm the Law*, then, one year after that, he started writing scripts for *The Adventures of Superman*, with thirteen assignments spanning four years. At the same time, he cranked out twenty-six teleplays (in a single TV season!) for another series with juvenile appeal – *The Adventures of Spin and Marty*. It wasn't a big jump in 1956 for Jackson to turn out nineteen scripts for *The Hardy Boys*, another series for the youth market. He wrote a couple for Guy Williams' *Zorro*, plus close to a dozen for June Lockhart's series, *Lassie*. Gillis graduated to the one-hour format and was very popular with the producers of *Perry Mason*, where he wrote thirty-one teleplays from 1959 through 1966.

Gillis would write seven episodes of *Lost in Space*, and then return to work for Irwin Allen again with one episode of *Land of the Giants* in 1969. During this time, he also wrote for *The Wild, Wild West; Tarzan; I Spy; The Man from U.N.C.L.E.; The Fugitive; Mannix; The Mod Squad; Bonanza; Mission: Impossible; Hawaii Five-O;* and *Ironside*. Gillis was no hack, but prolific and versatile. Of his eleven scripts for *Columbo*, he received two Emmy nominations (in 1972 and 1974). One of his *Columbo* episodes, "Dagger of the Mind," featured Richard Basehart (*Voyage to the Bottom of the Sea*) and Honor Blackman (*The Avengers* and *Goldfinger*) as guest murderers. Irwin Allen would bring Gillis back to write a TV pilot (shown as a TV movie) – 1976's *Time Travelers*, and two episodes for Allen's 1981-82 series, *Code Red*.

With this episode, a further dash of cowardice (following the hint we saw in "Welcome Stranger") was added to Smith's character, along with his tendency to panic in situations that hardly call for such a dramatic reaction, as when he becomes stuck in the opening to the cavern and is afraid he may fall through. All Penny does is give a tug to his belt to help him back into a standing position in a situation that clearly poses no real threat. Smith is also further defined by his greed. This was the catalyst that brought him to the series in "The Reluctant Stowaway," but it is on better display here, as he obsesses over diamonds. When he first becomes aware of the precious gems, and the camera pushes in for a close up, his lust for wealth mimics the reaction we would expect to see from an addict. He loses all reason and will risk everything to get his fix.

Les Warner, a member of the production team, sent notes to producers Irwin Allen, Buck Houghton, Jerry Briskin, and story editor Tony Wilson on August 25, searching for ways to slash expenses.

> SUGGESTED CHANGES TO REDUCE PRODUCTION COSTS AND PROBLEMS: …
>
> 3. Change "tilting rock and hole" to "a pivoting rock that bars the entrance to the cavern." …
>
> 6. Delete Smith's falling into cavern, but keep Penny climbing out.
>
> 7. Modify the explosions in the cavern: Shake set, use dust and drop a little rubble and a few small rocks. Penny will be knocked to the ground and strikes her head against a rock.
>
> 8. Don and Smith running from the fissure drilling area (127 thru 136): Eliminate whirlwind, whirling brush, rolling and falling rocks, the POV of the "eruption." The earth will tremble and the men will fall, and we'll hear a sound effect of Mr. Nobody's anger.
>
> 9. Eliminate the whirlwind from the Space camp set and substitute some other visual gimmick that would be involved only with Photo Effects and/or a possible MINIATURE of the Spaceship and camp area … There could be a violent wind on the real set, but do not write in any whirling or moving objects; however, the business with Smith and the diamonds could be retained.

The ever prolific (and equally fast on the typewriter keys) story editor Tony Wilson handled the rewriting. Wilson had a passion for the whimsical, as well as fantasy. He also liked comedy bordering on the camp, but kept his tongue away from his cheek as he polished "My Friend, Mr. Nobody," retaining the serious tone, as producer Houghton wanted.

Among some of the Smithisms to find their way into the episode:

He calls the Robot a "blundering bag of bolts" and, for the first time in the series, says: "Oh, the pain, the pain." Neither of these lines were in the September 8th Revised Shooting Final script. Either Wilson added them at the last minute or Harris made them up on the set.

Pre-Production:

Director Paul Stanley was 44. He was very familiar with shooting action/adventure on a shoestring budget. He cut his teeth with fourteen assignments on the 1955-56 series *Appointment with Adventure*, then went on to helm five episodes in 1959 and '60 for *Adventures in Paradise*, as well as four episodes of *Combat!*, where he also stepped in to do some producing. He knew Jonathan Harris, directing ten episodes of *The Third Man* in 1959, and he had experience with science fiction, taking three trips into

The Outer Limits in 1964. He was well-qualified for *Lost in Space*, but this would be his only assignment on the series. Allen did bring Stanley back for a single episode of *Land of the Giants*. Other producers appreciated Stanley more, and he had a prolific career directing numerous episodes each for *Mission: Impossible; Medical Center; Hawaii Five-O; Charlie's Angels; Baretta;* and many others. In the sci-fi genres, he worked for *The Wild, Wild, West; The Six Million Dollar Man; Beyond Westworld;* and *Knight Rider*.

The cast seemed in agreement that Stanley along with directors such as Leo Penn were an asset to the series, and they would mourn the loss of these talented individuals. Billy Mumy, citing Stanley as among the directors he admired, said, "We had so many much more interesting directors during the first season." (BM-LISBB-15)

William Bramley provided the voice for Mr. Nobody. Among his on-screen appearances, Bramley played "Baldy" Baldwin in "The Premonition," an episode of *The Outer Limits*, and the leader of a group of modern-day Roman Empire centurions (policemen) in "Bread and Circuses" on *Star Trek*, as well as playing a pair of giants in *Land of the Giants* ("The Flight Plan" and "Giants and All That Jazz"). More notably, he played a cop in *West Side Story*, the subject of the song "Gee, Officer Krupke!" Bramley would return for Allen as the voice of the Robotoid in "War of the Robots."

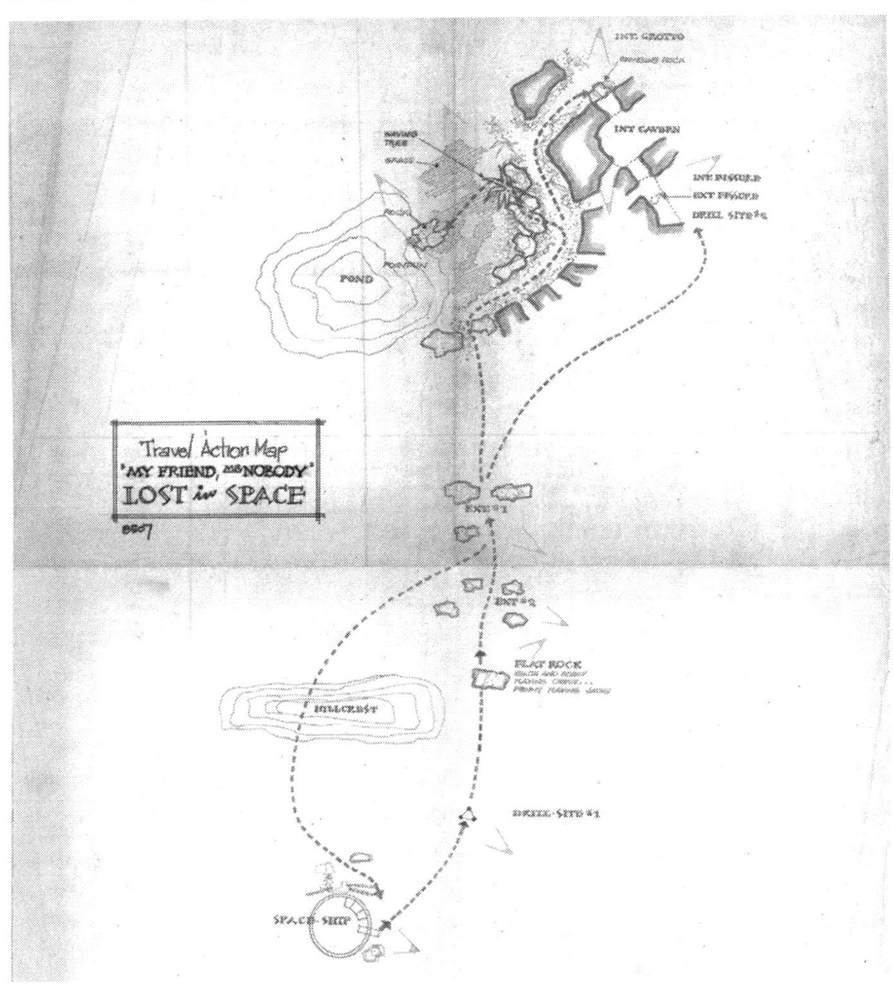

For most of the episodes of *Lost in Space*, Irwin Allen had the art department create a "Travel/Action Map," tracing the movement of the characters in the story.

A publicity photo taken during the production of "My Friend, Mr. Nobody" had little to do with the episode, but the set photographer couldn't figure out how else to illustrate excitement when the story involved a young girl's invisible secret friend. So, bring in the show's villain for a "photo opp." CBS sent this one out to newspapers, but pictures like this were about to be a thing of the past. The network objected to putting minors in peril, which is why this enchanting episode never repeated on CBS ... and why Dr. Smith either had to change or go.

Production Diary:
Filmed: September 17 – 28, 1965 (7 and ¼ days)

Day 1: Friday, September 17, 1965. The start of production on "My Friend, Mr. Nobody" was delayed until the late afternoon, while director Paul Stanley waited for Alvin Ganzer to finish his episode, "Welcome Stranger." The latter wrapped on Stage 11 at 3:40 p.m., and then the camera crew made a hasty move to Stage 6 where the set had been pre-lit. The scenes around the Ext. Drill Site for the Teaser were first up. Stanley filmed from 4 to 7 p.m. These few hours did not count as part of Stanley's allotted six-day shooting schedule. Jerry Briskin and Irwin Allen would start tracking his progress come Monday.

Day 2: Monday, September 20. Work continued on Stage 6, beginning at 8 a.m. Stanley finished filming the Teaser, with the explosion at the drill site and the dialogue that followed. Also shot: the scene when Will chided Penny, and a handful of diamonds landed on the chess board where Dr. Smith was playing against the Robot. Next came the scenes during which Smith leaned into the fissure, calling to Penny in the caverns below … and nearly fell in, requiring Penny to come around and help pull him free.

It read better in the script. Director Stanley wasn't able to find a way to photograph this scene properly with the set and time restrictions. It is silly, seeing Jonathan Harris lying on the rocks, his face in the opening, but clearly in no danger, as he cries out for Penny to save him. The script described it this way:

EXT. FISSURE OPENING – DAY

CLOSE SHOT as Smith clings to the edge of the fissure. His grip is slipping –

SMITH
Help! Help, somebody! Save me! Help!

INT. FISSURE – DAY

Smith continues to yell in terror – as Penny runs in.

PENNY
Dr. Smith! What are you doing here?

SMITH
Penny! Help me!

PENNY
Hang on – I'll be right there!

She runs out toward the cavern.

EXT. FISSURE – DAY

Smith hangs on for dear life as Penny runs in and grabs him. With much support and pulling from Penny:

SMITH
Easy now – Be careful…

PENNY
It's all right, I'm holding you – There!

SMITH
No, no, farther away – those rocks may give way again –
(finally sinking down)
Ahhhhh, thank you my child.

Part of the problem was the set. A bigger factor may have been Jonathan Harris's bad back. In an interview for the 2015 Blu-ray box set release of *Lost in Space*, Billy Mumy revealed that Harris always wore a back brace hidden under his costume.

This episode provided a plum role for Angela Cartwright – the first to put emphasis on Penny. At the time, the young Cartwright felt the pressure. She later admitted, "I remember looking at the script and just seeing tons of dialogue!" (AC-LISBB15)

Stanley filmed until 6:50 p.m. The production was on schedule.

Day 3: Tuesday, September 21. Technical problems delayed the start of filming until 8:30 a.m. The work included the scenes at the secondary drill site with Don and

Above: Giant fans called "Ritters" were used to kick up the sand and create windstorm effects. Middle image: Filming outdoors at what was left of the 20th Century-Fox backlot – an area known as "The Moat." Bottom: Filming inside the caverns at the Moat location.

Smith, and the bigger explosion. Also, the savage wind sequences, as Don and Smith fled, and Penny pled with Mr. Nobody to not hurt her loved ones.

Regarding the windstorm, Jonathan Harris said, "Irwin Allen, who was my boss in *Lost in Space*, knows only about earthquakes and floods. Doesn't know about actors, but he does know about earthquakes and floods, and he does them rather well. And he cares deeply about them. I don't, they're awfully wet. Plus, when they turn on that wind machine on the huge set with all the sand, it's rotten – it gets into your nose and ears. And all this under the general heading of 'art'." (JH-IASB2)

By 7:50 p.m., with everyone smarting from sand in their eyes, work stopped. Paul Stanley had fallen to one-quarter of a day behind.

Day 4: Wednesday, September 22. They worked outside at the Moat location, with the "Ext. Wooded Area," where Penny first heard the voice of Mr. Nobody; then Smith and the Robot followed her to the cave entrance; then a camera move into the "Int. Grotto" set for Penny's first encounter with Mr. Nobody. Production began at 8 a.m. and stopped at 6:15 p.m., allowing the cast time to change and strip off makeup, while the crew wrapped the set,

then giving everyone time to make it home for "The Derelict," the second episode of *Lost and Space* to air on CBS. Stanley had held at one-quarter day behind.

Day 5: Thursday, September 23. Even though the critics were still giving *Lost in Space* mixed reviews, the ratings from the night before were good, and cast and crew had much to be happy about as they came to work this day. Work began with renewed energy at 8 a.m. at the outdoor Moat location, which included the "Int. Cavern." This cavern, and the giant mushrooms, had been built for the Fox film *Journey to the Center of the Earth.* The sets were actually open at the top. In order to change the lighting to make the Styrofoam rock formations appear to be underground, the set was tarped-over.

Angela Cartwright said, "I remember when I did this, I did the dialogue with the script girl. I mean, that was not [Mr. Nobody's] voice – that was the script lady who was doing the dialogue of Mr. Nobody. And I had to look around the cave like I was hearing *the* voice." (AC-LISBR15)

Work lasted until 5:35 p.m. As the company moved the equipment to Stage 6, where filming would resume the following morning, the cast members were dismissed early. The production was holding at one-quarter of a day behind.

Day 6: Friday, September 24. Work began on Stage 6 at 8 a.m. for pickup shots needed from the drill site scenes. During the lunch break, the camera equipment was moved to Stage 11, and the upper deck of the Jupiter 2, which had been pre-lit during the morning hours. Filming would continue there until 7:08 p.m. Stanley was not able to catch up and, instead, had fallen to one-half of a day behind. The next episode to film, "Invaders from the Fifth Dimension," was pushed back.

Day 7: Monday, September 27. Work continued on Stage 11 (both this day and the next) with the daytime sequences on the Ext. Jupiter 2 campsite set. Work began at 8, as usual, but did not stop until 7:17 p.m. At that time, Stanley was a full day behind. "Invaders from the Fifth Dimension" was again delayed.

Day 8: Tuesday, September 28. While director Leonard Horn waited in the wings to begin filming "Invaders," Stanley struggled to finish his assignment, filming from 8 a.m. to 6:31 p.m. with the nighttime scenes on the Ext. Jupiter campsite set. This work included the furious wind storm, and that meant that the big fans were again brought out, blowing sand at the hapless cast. As eyes burned, the director called for a wrap.

The cast was subjected to a second sand storm to complete the filming of this episode – this time outside the Jupiter 2.

It had taken Stanley more than seven days to do the work planned for six.

William Self had hoped they could make this one for $132,304. It ended up costing $175,386, exceeding the desired studio budget by more than $40,000.

Stanley would not be asked back to *Lost in Space*, but did get a single assignment during the next TV season on Irwin Allen's *The Time Tunnel.*

Post-Production:

When this episode was screened for CBS, the self-appointed guardians of morality decided that John and Maureen Robinson were too affectionate. Never mind that the characters were married; never mind that supposedly their children had come into the world in the traditional way. No, this married couple showed too much passion in their two onscreen kisses. In an age when married couples on television were shown sleeping in separate twin beds, and one could only join the other in a single bed if one of his or her feet remained firmly planted on the floor, the mandate soon came down from the top: No more kissing. Irwin Allen has often been blamed for this, but many kisses where included when directing the pilot "No Place to Hide," and even a display of romantic and sexual interest between Don and Judy. It was not Allen who nixed the signs of physical affection, but CBS. After all, this was a series slotted in the family hour, targeting young viewers. Blasting monsters with laser guns was fine; smooching was not.

June Lockhart said, "In the pilot, the writers were developing a father-mother-husband-wife relationship for the Robinson parents. Then the edict came down from CBS that Guy Williams was not to touch me in any way ... not even to take my hand to help me down out of the spaceship. Someone at CBS thought that any demonstrative affection between the parents would embarrass the children watching at home. When our CBS representative came down to the set, I told him this and he said, 'That's ridiculous... I will go and check that.' Well, he came back and said, 'I can't believe it, but you're right. They don't want the parents showing any affection.' So, we had to show it with longing looks." (JL-LISM)

Something else that was bothering CBS: Dr. Smith was still coming off as too ruthless, and even a bit creepy in the scenes involving the children. Who would trust a man like this around their children? The executives at CBS wouldn't. More changes were needed if his character was to remain, or, at least, have any one-on-one scenes with the two youngest children. And CBS very much wanted the character of Smith to remain.

Roland Gross and Edit Team 1 were now on their third episode for the series, following "The Reluctant Stowaway" and "There Were Giants in the Earth."

John Williams returned to write his last score for a *Lost in Space* episode. Angela Cartwright said, "The 'Penny music' that was created by John Williams for this episode is one of the reasons it is such a special episode. When I hear those strains of music, it really does encompass Penny's deep feelings and wonderment, with a touch of mysterious alien planet mixed in. How cool is that!" (LISM.com)

Release / Reaction:

(Only CBS broadcast: Wednesday, October 27, 1965)

Billy Mumy named this episode one of his *Lost in Space* favorites.

Angela Cartwright said, "'My Friend, Mr. Nobody' is my all time favorite episode of *Lost in Space*. I love the look of it, the feel of the music, the message it sends. Playing the character of Penny has always been dear to my heart and in this episode she is very adventurous, very bold, and very curious. She really tries to understand what makes her new alien friend tick and has some soul-searching conversations with Mr. Nobody. I like Penny and like the fact that I was able to play her and feel so comfortable in her skin." (LISM.com)

See the bad man that a terrified child is pointing over his shoulder at? Well, as far as CBS was concerned, pictures like this would soon be a thing of that past. And this one was left unused altogether. Below: A safer way for the network to promote the series.

The week "My Friend, Mr. Nobody" had its only broadcast on CBS, the Beatles had the top song on the radio, with "Yesterday"; *The Cincinnati Kid*, starring Steve McQueen, was the top-grossing movie in America; and Chuck Connors of *Branded* had the cover of *TV Guide*.

"TV Scout," syndicated to newspapers across America, including the October 27, 1965 issue of the *Abilene Reporter-News*, said:

> *Lost in Space* has an adventure which is slightly reminiscent of "Alice in Wonderland." Penny, in her strange world, is fascinated by her echo in a cave studded with diamonds. Soon the echo, which she calls "Mr. Nobody," begins to have a voice of his own and the two become pals. The rest of the Robinsons only giggle at her escapades. But Dr. Smith and his robot decide to cash in on the

game only to meet some fierce cosmic powers. It's nonsense, but fun.

On the same day, rival critique column, "TV Key-notes," a regular in the *Galveston Daily News*, from Galveston, Texas, said:

> Part fairy tale, part science fiction, this is a yarn for the very young. The little Robinson girl makes friends with Mr. Nobody, an invisible cosmic being. Mr. Nobody's powers are strange and the storm he creates is impressive. Special effects, as usual, are outstanding.

The A.C. Nielsen 30-City Ratings survey for October 27, 1965 reported:

Network / Program:	Rating	Audience Share:
7:30 – 8 p.m.:		
ABC: *Ozzie and Harriet*	8.9	16.9%
CBS: *Lost in Space*	**17.8**	**33.8%**
NBC: *The Virginian*	17.5	33.3%
8 – 8:30 p.m.:		
ABC: *The Patty Duke Show*	13.1	22.1%
CBS: *Lost in Space*	18.7	31.6%
NBC: *The Virginian*	**20.3**	**34.3%**

Another nose-counting service, American Research Bureau's National Arbitron Ratings, with its own survey for the week of October 25-31, 1965, reported:

	Program/Network:	Rating:
1.	*Bonanza* (NBC)	27.8
2.	*The Andy Griffith Show* (CBS)	23.8
3.	*The Ed Sullivan Show* (CBS)	23.5
4.	*Peyton Place 1* (ABC)	22.9
5.	*The Dick Van Dyke Show* (CBS)	22.4
6.	*The Red Skelton Show* (CBS)	21.7
7.	*The Beverly Hillbillies* (CBS)	21.7
8.	*The Lucy Show* (CBS)	21.3
9.	*Daniel Boone* (NBC)	21.2
10.	*Hogan's Heroes* (CBS)	21.0
11.	*The Jackie Gleason Show* (CBS)	20.7
12.	*The Lawrence Welk Show* (ABC)	20.6
13.	***Lost in Space* (CBS)**	**20.6**
14.	*Gomer Pyle, U.S.M.C.* (CBS)	20.5
15.	*My Three Sons* (CBS)	20.4
16.	*I've Got a Secret* (CBS)	20.3
17.	*F Troop* (ABC)	20.3
18.	*Walt Disney* (NBC)	20.2
19.	*The Man from U.N.C.L.E.* (NBC)	20.1
20.	Miss Teenage America (CBS)	19.8
	Gilligan's Island (CBS)	19.8

Writer Dick DeBartolo and cartoonist Mort Drucker were among those watching, and “My Friend, Mr. Nobody” served as the basis for the July 1966 *MAD* magazine satire “Loused Up in Space” (with “Tonight’s Episode: ‘A Canyon of Precious Stones’ or ‘The Ruby Valley Story’).”

18

Episode 8: "Invaders from the Fifth Dimension"

Written by Shimon Wincelberg
(with script polishing by Anthony Wilson)
Directed by Leonard Horn
Produced by Buck Houghton (uncredited), with Jerry Briskin;
Executive Producer: Irwin Allen

From *Lost in Space* show files (Irwin Allen Papers Collection):

> A spaceship from another galaxy lands on the planet. One of its necessary computer parts has worn out and it cannot get back to its own solar system without a replacement. A human brain will do to replace the missing part, the aliens tell Smith, who discovers them. They will take him, shrinking his body to fit into the required space. Smith, terrified, offers them Will in his place, as being a better fit. He cons the boy into going with him to the spaceship, telling him he has a plan by which, together, they will save the others. Will is fitted into the space but he is so grief-stricken at the thought of leaving his family that he is unable to do the necessary computation; his emotion causing the computer to burn-out.

From the Script:

(4th Revised Shooting Final teleplay, September 30, 1965 draft)

– *Smith (terrified, sweating):* "Well, then, what do you want from me?" *Alien Voice:* "Only one type of 'computer' will serve our needs." *Smith:* "What's that?" *Alien Voice:* "A humanoid brain." *Smith:* "A what?" *Alien Voice:* "Even such a primitive one as yours." *Smith:* "Mine!" *Alien Voice:* "Only a portion of it." *Smith:* "Now wait a minute... Wait, wait... You don't want my brain. Why, I'm so ignorant, I'm almost feeble-minded. Try me. Ask me a question." *Alien Voice:* "We can remedy that. We may have to reduce your size somewhat to fit the available space." *Smith:* "That's impossible! You can't!" *Alien Voice:* "Why do you say that?" *Smith:* "I'm a medical man. I'm telling you. The human body isn't a grab bag. It's either all, or nothing."

– *Alien Voice:* "You show treachery and cunning. Noble qualities on your native planet, no doubt, but indicating defective relays in your reasoning circuits." *Smith:* "That's it, exactly! I'm a scoundrel. A thoroughly bad sort. Hopelessly unreliable. I'm doing you the greatest favor by furnishing a substitute for my morbid, villainous brain."

– *Don:* "Exactly what are you up to, Smith?" *Smith:* "You have an evil, suspicious mind, Major. I just happen to be off for a stroll... *(looks around)* You didn't happen to see Will, by any chance?" *Penny:* "He went over by the lava bed to go rock hunting..." *Don:* "You stay away from that boy, Smith." *Smith:* "Not much concerned about his higher education, are you?" *Don (moving toward him menacingly):* "I am concerned. Every time I see him with you."

– *Robot:* "I detect an alien presence." *Maureen (surprised):* "Alien?" *Robot:* "On this planet, we are all aliens." *Maureen:* "Touché."

–*Luminary's Voice (exasperated):* "Love... What is it? Can you eat it? What does it do, except befog the clarity of your brain?... *(seeing Maureen on monitor, as she's trying bravely to bite back her tears)* Extraordinary!... It seems to be a form of madness, common to all of them." *Will (defiantly):* "I can't help feeling the way I do..." *Luminary's Voice:* "What primitive, barbaric little creatures you are! On your own planet, you slaughter each other unceasingly. All in the name of love." *Will:* "At least we keep trying to be better!... We don't turn people into machines."

Assessment:

"Invaders from the Fifth Dimension" set the mode for the often recurring storylines in which Smith offers up one of the Robinsons – or West or the Robot – to save his own skin. Beyond that, this is a simplistic straight forward story that is stylistically macabre and contains many memorable scenes. The aliens, both in their appearance and that of their intriguing spacecraft, spike the "out-of-this-world" meter and provoke effective moments of mystery, suspense, as well as horror. The photography and music are extremely effective.

"Invaders" makes good use of footage from the pilot, including aerial shots of the Trona Pinnacles, Bill Suitor (as Don) flying in the Rocket Belt, and numerous views of the Chariot traveling through this strange terrain that seemed as if it could only be found on another world.

The pain-inducing ring placed around Smith's neck by the aliens may have inspired the collars of obedience in the 1967 *Star Trek* episode "The Gamesters of Triskelion," which in turn inspired the pain-inducing belts in that series' 1968 episode "Spock's Brain."

As became common in later stories, Dr. Smith displays a rather cavalier attitude regarding the life of Will, who generally trusts him. Major West catches on and threatens to wring Smith's neck if the other doesn't stop endangering Will.

"Invaders from the Fifth Dimension" may drag in a few spots, but this is nonetheless an episode with a high wow factor, and among the series' best.

Script:

Story Assignment 8453 (Production #8508)
Shimon Wincelberg's treatment and 1st draft teleplay, "Alas, Regardless of Their Doom": August 1965.
Wincelberg's 2nd draft teleplay, approved by Irwin Allen on August 31, 1965.
Reformatted Mimeo Department Shooting Final teleplay, sent to CBS on September 3, 1965.
Tony Wilson's script polish (Revised Shooting Final, plus 2nd and 3rd Rev. Shooting Final teleplays): mid-September 1965.
Wilson's additional polishing (4th Revised Shooting Final teleplay, on gold paper): September 24.
Additional page revisions by Wilson (blue page inserts): September 28.
Additional revisions by Wilson (green page inserts): September 30.

Shimon Wincelberg returned to the series one last time, after "The Reluctant Stowaway," and the story treatments for "The Derelict," "Island in the Sky," "There Were Giants in the Earth," and "The Hungry Sea." As writer for the first episodes and the unaired pilot, Wincelberg was uniquely qualified to construct situations that could take advantage of this early footage, such as the sequences at Red Rock Canyon and the Trona Pinnacles.

Resurrecting the conflict between John and Don over the leadership responsibilities that he had written into his story guidelines for the first five episodes, Wincelberg touched on the character conflicts again in a scene for this new script. Having returned from an exploratory trip in the Rocket Belt, with its fuel now depleted, and told that the family is concerned over Smith having asked about the whereabouts of Will, John finds out from the Robot that Will went rock hunting near the lava beds. The scene continues:

Robinson: "The lava beds! I told him never to go that way. Why didn't you stop him?" *Robot (aloofly):* "I have not been programmed for babysitting…" *Robinson (disgusted, then turns to Don):* "Is the other rocket belt ready to go?" *Don:* "No. You forgot to check it out last night." *Robinson:* "Then why didn't you do it?" *Don (bristling but controlled):* "Now look, Professor, I don't mind taking orders, but I draw the line at being bossed around like a field hand." *Judy:* "Don!" *Maureen:* "Both of you! Quit acting like barnyard roosters. Let's go find Will."

Maureen's line was later cut when it was decided she was sounding too critical of her husband, and downright bossy.

With "The Reluctant Stowaway," due to not liking the changes made by Irwin Allen, Buck Houghton and Tony Wilson, Wincelberg used the pseudonym S.Bar-David as his screen credit. For this episode, which was rewritten by Wilson in order to placate the CBS censors, Wincelberg was less critical and allowed his true name to appear. He would not be invited back to the series as a writer. He did do one script each for Allen's *Voyage to the Bottom of the Sea* (the second season kickoff, "Jonah and the Whale") and *The Time Tunnel* ("Rendezvous with Yesterday"), but the series Wincelberg had helped to develop was no longer accepting stories and scripts from him.

Wincelberg lamented, "I wanted to return, but there was still a bad feeling between Irwin and me because I had taken my name off the *Lost in Space* pilot [sic]. I had a meeting with one of Irwin's story editors, who was informed that I was *persona non grata*." (SW-SL90)

From here, Wincelberg went on to write for *Star Trek*'s first season ("Dagger of the Mind" and "The Galileo Seven"), but had similar problems with Gene Roddenberry, who also rewrote his material heavily and in a manner which offended its author. Wincelberg and Roddenberry had a falling-out, resulting in the S. Bar-David *nom de plume* again being evoked.

Next, in the pseudo sci-fi genre, Wincelberg did two scripts for *The Wild, Wild West*, then pure science fiction with three scripts for the 1970 series *The Immortal*, and one for Harlan Ellison's 1973 series *The Starlost*. In 1974, Wincelberg wrote an episode of the TV version of *Planet of the Apes*, using the name of S. Bar-David, then under his own name, for 1978's flash-in-the-pan *Man from Atlantis* (starring Patrick Duffy). Mostly he did medical drama (five scripts for *Medical Center* and a couple more for *Trapper John, M.D.*), detective shows (six for *Mannix* and four for *Police Woman*) and westerns (four for *Gunsmoke* and three for James Garner's 1971 series *Nichols*). He retired in 1997 after writing an episode of *Law & Order*.

Wincelberg admitted that he enjoyed working with Allen, saying, "He brings a wonderful sense of childlike fun and joy to a story. Irwin really knows how to have fun, something that is lacking in much of the youth-oriented TV today." (IA-SL85)

Wincelberg's script for "Invaders from the Fifth Dimension" was originally called "Alas, Regardless of Their Doom." The title was only changed after he completed his portion of the work – a story treatment, and a first and second draft script.

On August 27, Irwin Allen wrote to Buck Houghton and Tony Wilson about certain plot points that bothered him, including the first in a series of scenes where, after a confrontation with Major West, Dr. Smith moves out of the Jupiter 2. Allen said:

> P. 18-19: Don's decision to order Smith off the ship comes too suddenly; seemingly without enough cause for such a drastic step. Smith should say something more insulting than "He is a little tyrant, isn't he?"
>
> P. 23: Robinson says, "Come on. Let's take the Chariot." – He has just been talking to Don & it would seem he means for Don to go with him. Yet Don is not in any of the scenes of the Chariot searching for Will. Don is not heard from again until P. 45 in which we see him in the flying belt.... Before leaving, Robinson

should tell Don to reactivate the flying belt & start a search as soon as possible.

Summing up, Allen told Houghton and Wilson:

The script is overlong. Needs a good deal of cutting. Where is the Tag?

As a result of Allen's notes, Wincelberg wrote the conflict scene between John and Don.

The easy solution for an overly-long script would have been to pull out the subplot of Smith being evicted from the Jupiter 2, and save it for another episode. That decision would come later. The more urgent matter at hand was getting the episode produced at all.

The reformatted Mimeo Department version of Wincelberg's script – the September 3rd Shooting Final – was sent to CBS. On September 9th, Sam Taylor, Jr., of the network's Broadcast Standards department, wrote to Margaret Venetis of Van Bernard Productions:

As discussed briefly with Mr. Allen and at length with Mr. Wilson:

The physical perils and emotional duress to which WILL is subjected make this script, as written, unacceptable. We feel that the vivid portrayal of a child in such dangers would be highly disturbing to a very large portion of your youthful audience and a substantial portion of your adult audience. Our discussion with Mr. Wilson indicates that he feels the script may be made acceptable by extensive rewriting. To aid in your decision as to whether or not the script will be rewritten with WILL as the focal point of the storyline, we offer our point-by-point comments:

Page 1, Scene 2: We would request that the hand of the ALIEN CREATURE not be grossly repugnant.

Page 9: We object to most of the dialogue on this page: where ALIEN VOICE says, "Only a portion of it"; where SMITH says, "If you take out my brain, I'll die"; the speech of ALIEN VOICE which follows in Scene 30 is considered repugnant, as the audience will relate it to a later fate for WILL; the speech by ALIEN VOICE which refers to the shortening of SMITH's body.

Page 10, Scene 31: SMITH's line which includes words, "whom you won't have to cut down" is objectionable.

Page 31, Scene 82: WILL should <u>not</u> have tears in his eyes or speak in an agonized whisper.

Page 31, Scene 84: WILL's face should <u>not</u> be teary and strained.

> Page 39, Scene 116: SMITH's attitude should not be "nakedly sinister" as shown in your stage direction.
>
> Page 46, Scene 139: For a youthful audience, the words "human specimen" in SMITH's line are considered unsavory and objectionable.
>
> Page 47 & 48, Scene 144 through 126: WILL's attitude should not be one of terror but rather of bravado. If he is to enter the alien spaceship, he should do so willingly....
>
> Page 54, Scene 168: The stage direction which calls for WILL's head to be connected to a computer by wires and coils, his glazed, vacant expression ... described a situation which is unacceptable....
>
> Page 59, Scene 187: We object to MAUREEN's line, "If they're using his brain?"...
>
> Page 62, Scene 202: We feel that WILL's human emotions are already well known to the alien creatures (Page 60); this should be sufficient reason for them to reject the use of his brain. We believe, therefore, it is not necessary for WILL to be tearful in this scene. Consequently, we object to the first five speeches in the scene.
>
> Page 63, Scene 204: Under the circumstances which we have been discussing, we object to WILL's line, "Could I at least take one last look at them?"...
>
> A revised script, accommodating the objections offered above, would not necessarily be acceptable. A child might still be in serious jeopardy throughout the teleplay. We hold to the opinion, expressed to Mr. Allen, that such hazards should be inflicted, if at all, upon one of the adult members of your space group.

Allen's TV agent, Herman Rush, said, "Irwin was always concerned over putting children into peril and dangerous spots. That was a major concern of his in everything that he did. But he has a show with a premise that requires action and adventure and peril, so a great deal of thought and judgment has to come into play as to what is necessary peril for the sake of the story and what is not. And that was a debate that would always go on between the producer and the networks. That was very common." (HR-AI-15)

Regardless, it was becoming very clear to both Irwin Allen and Tony Wilson that they were not going to be able to make a science fiction space show with any sense of realism or the deadly possibilities of the genre ... at least, not when the Robinson kids were anywhere in sight.

Another problem still remained – what to do about Smith? The network was not going to tolerate him in the company of the children for very much longer if he continually posed a threat to them.

More notes from Irwin Allen followed a September 18th staff meeting as Tony Wilson prepared to rewrite the script:

> P. 18: Smith: "Goodbye, my dear" and: P. 19-20 – Scene 52, Smith: "Good bye, Major." These lines are carryovers from previous editions in which Don actually ordered Smith to leave the ship for good. In this version, Don merely says, "If ever I catch you telling Will stories again, so help me…" Don now says nothing about Smith going elsewhere to live. On Page 22, Scene 60, Judy relates to Robinson that Don told Smith to stay away from us. This still doesn't mean he's to live elsewhere. If it is brought out further on in the story that Smith is definitely to stay away from the ship for good, then it would be better for all concerned if Smith himself (in a huff) said to Don, "If that's the way you feel about me, I refuse to stay on this ship one moment longer." – (Smith would say this thinking that he would not be taken up on his offer, of course). Don's answer, in anger, would be "That suits me just fine." After this, there would be a moment of awkward silence in which Smith would realize that Don has no intention of relenting or persuading him to change his mind. Judy would have a chance to say, "Dr. Smith, Don doesn't really mean that. Do you, Don?" … (No reply from Don) … Smith is forced to recover his composure and continue with his Good-byes as proudly as possible.

It was a wonderful idea, but one that would be saved for "Wish Upon a Star," when the Smith-moves-out-of-the-Jupiter 2 subplot served the story well. So well in fact, it would be repeated in "Attack of the Monster Plants."

Despite the removal of the eviction-of-Smith story element, Smith was still very much the villain in this particular story. In an ongoing effort to render the character less offensive to media watchdogs, minor incidents of humor were added by Wilson. The bigger shift, however, came with Jonathan Harris's interpretation of the written word. The one silly scene in the episode is when Smith throws himself to the ground to draw Will's attention and concern. It is present in the script, and is certainly slanted toward comedy, but note the difference in tone here than in the way played on the screen:

> 69. EXT BED OF LAVA – DAY
>
> WILL, engrossed over his ore samples.
>
> 70. CLOSE – SMITH.
>
> Like a spider watching a fly. Again, he's painfully conscious of the glowing line around his neck, hides it under his color, and goes into action, by lying down. As he lowers himself out of FRAME, we hear a heartrending MOAN.
>
> 71. CLOSE – WILL
>
> STARTLED, FRIGHTENED, TURNS TOWARD Smith's hiding place. Another piteous MOAN.

72. ANOTHER ANGLE – WILL

Gets up and cautiously approaches, CAMERA TRUCKING in front of him. He suddenly stops, at the sight of:

73. P.O.V. SHOT – ANGLE DOWN AT SMITH

Lying on the ground, horribly contorted, panting, moaning, clearly in extremis.

74. CLOSE – ANGLE UP AT WILL

Shocked, he hurries over to:

WILL

Dr. Smith!

75. CLOSE – SMITH'S FACE

Looking up at Will, through blurred, unfocused eyes. A man at death's door and about to cross the threshold, taking a final glance over his shoulder as it were. His lips and vocal cords try painfully to formulate Will's name. Will kneels down beside him, in an agony of concern.

WILL

What happened? Are you all right?

Smith slips out of character just long enough to roll back his eyes in a look of disgust, as though to say: "Idiot, if I was all right, would I be lying here like this?" Instead, he feebly puts a quaking hand on Will's arm.

SMITH

(painfully)

Don't trouble about me, lad. ... Just save yourself ... and your loved ones.

Jonathan Harris chose to amplify the humor that had been merely hinted at in the script. Smith was still an unforgivable scoundrel, leading Will to God-knows-what in order to save his own slippery skin, but the humor added here, and the temporary redemption of the character in the end of the story, started the trend toward the Smith we would come to know and sometimes love.

Harris told interviewer Ian spelling, "I knew that playing Smith as that awful man, that dreadful spy, that they would have to get rid of me. It just wasn't working. It was not palatable. And that's when I started my little tricks. You see, Smith adored Will, but he was a nefarious sort that he was not above selling Will to the aliens. 'Take the boy! Take the boy!' But, of course, I always redeemed myself and got him back. Very clever. I think Smith loved Will as a dear young man, you see." (JH-SL98)

Irwin Allen said, "Jonathan can do anything. Smith in *Space* is a pivotal role. Without it, the series would be just another soap opera. Remember Ming the Merciless in the old *Flash Gordon* serials?... The kids would boo and hiss him at the Saturday matinees, but he would bring them back week after week, if only to see if he would get the better of Flash. Well, Jonathan is going to affect just such an image. He complements beautifully the charming appeal of the Robinson family." (IA-LISFI)

Tony Wilson also added a scene to further diminish the threat of the Robot. Here, we see "him" assigned the demeaning task of serving as a scarecrow. Later, he comes off as a reluctantly obedient hero, jeopardizing his own safety when ordered to advance and fire on the alien spacecraft.

Pre-Production:

This was the last episode produced by Buck Houghton. According to *Daily Variety,* he vacated his office sometime between October 8th and 14th. Houghton left by his own choice. He wasn't going to be a puppet producer answering to Irwin Allen, a boss who believed that a series was not big enough for two top dogs. Allen later said, "I believe there can only be one producer, and he should be the line producer and do the job." (IA-SL92)

After co-producing the first five classic episodes with Allen, and developing the next three to film, and even having a hand in story and script development for a few more to follow, Houghton decided to exit *Lost in Space*. He was gone, in fact, before the first episode aired on CBS, and his name was not included in the credits.

Houghton stayed on with 20th Century-Fox to produce the 1966 series *Blue Light*, then, for other studios, he served as a producer for short stints on *The High Chaparral*, *Harry O* and *Hawaii Five-O*.

Leonard Horn was hired to direct. He was 39, and had started directing for television in 1961 after trying for a career as an actor. At this time, he had directed three episodes for Alfred Hitchcock's TV series, an episode for Gene Roddenberry's *The Lieutenant*, and three standout episodes for *The Outer Limits* ("The Man Who Was Never Born," "The Zanti Misfits" and "The Children of Spider County"). He had worked for Irwin Allen already, directing six episodes for the first season of *Voyage to the Bottom of the Sea*, and three more for the second season (filming around the same time as this *Lost in Space*). But, after this *Lost in Space*, Horn had enough of sci-fi and moved on to series that catered to a more adult audience – directing numerous episodes of *Mission: Impossible* and *Mannix*, plus both directing and producing several episodes for *It Takes a Thief.* In 1975, however, he returned to the world of fantastic TV, with an episode of *Wonder Woman*. It was his last job. Horn died suddenly that year, at age 48.

Theodore "Ted" Lehmann was cast as the first "Alien." He was 42 and worked for 50 years as a voiceover performer and bit actor. He had appeared in an episode of *Johnny Ringo* with Mark Goddard, and would provide the voice of the "Disk" in another first season *Lost in Space* episode, "All That Glitters." Later, he played Hitler in the offbeat 1981 Chevy Chase movie *Under the Rainbow*.

Joseph "Joe" Ryan was the second alien, identified in the script as "Luminary." His career as a "day player" was brief, as were his roles. Among his bit parts, one episode each for Allen's *The Time Tunnel* ("Chase Through Time") and *Land of the Giants* ("Double Cross").

Ted Lehmann told authors Joel Eisner and Barry Magen, "I wore a mouthless headpiece which took nearly two hours to apply and caused the makeup people great consternation when lunch was called. They objected vehemently to the idea of removing it just so a mere actor could eat. A compromise was finally worked out with the producer whereby the makeup people would make a sort of flap incision through which I might shovel nourishment. I was sternly admonished not to get tuna salad on the precious appliance." (TL-LISF)

With this episode, Marta Kristen was given a new hairdo. She was delighted, never liking the hair style from the pilot which, she felt, showed too much forehead, but which she was required to keep through the first several episodes in order to match footage taken from "No Place to Hide." In a nice instance of series continuity, the new "do" was introduced on camera, as Maureen and Judy use a hair styling machine inspired by the one seen in the 1962-63 animated series *The Jetsons*.

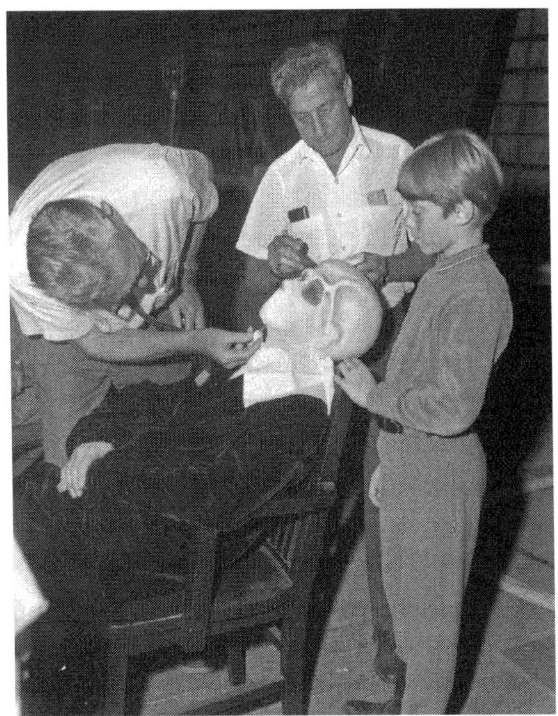

Above: Is it Ted Lehmann or Joe Ryan in the chair? He would have to stand up for anyone to know for sure. Below: Identical in all ways but height. Since this episode was planned to air close to Halloween, the set photographer had Billy Mumy hold a "Trick or Treat" bag.

While the portable hair styling device makes for a cheesy prop, art director Robert Kinoshita excelled when it came to the design of the alien spaceship, which the script described as "an irregular GLOBE-SHAPE, not much larger than a diving bell resting on prehensile stilts." It is arguably the most otherworldly looking craft featured in the series.

The interior of the ship is also visually effective, although clearly designed to save money. The script detailed this as "a huge limbo-like void in which weird instruments hang as if suspended in the air."

The aliens themselves are both startling and, from a production perspective, economical. As for the first alien to be seen, the script described him as "a bland, almost featureless 'human' face" which would appear against the black background, with no perceivable body.

The desired budget by 20th Century-Fox for each first season episode was $130,980. On September 30, 1965, William Self, approved a budget for this episode of $143,129. This was $12,149 over the targeted per-episode costs. Some of the big expenses: $13,191 for the new sets required, most notably the interior of the alien ship; $7,309 for the miniature of the alien spacecraft; and $1,473 for optical effects to animate the tractor beam that emits from the ship and freezes Smith in his tracks, as well as the face that appears in the eye of the ship, the Robot firing laser bolts at the alien space craft, and the disintegration of that ship.

20th Century-Fox's schoolteacher Frances Klampt with one of those mischievous invaders from the fifth dimension. Angela Cartwright said Frances had taught all the child actors at Fox from the 1930s through the 1970s, including Shirley Temple … and, of course, Angela Cartwright and Billy Mumy.

Production Diary:

Filmed September 29 through October 7, 1965 (7 days).

Day 1, Wednesday, September 29. The company worked from 8 a.m. to 5:30 p.m. on Stage 6. On the schedule: "Ext. Lava Bed," where, as the shooting schedule described it: 'Will [is] engrossed in rock samples – Pan over & discover Smith watching him." Next: "Smith fakes illness – gets Will to cure him with flashlite – tells Will of alien ship, etc. Neck band gives Smith a twinge – Will hears Maureen & John – Smith gets him to hide in rocks, etc." Then: "John, Maureen & Robot find some of Will's rock samples & see both his & Smith's footprints."

The last scene was the only work Guy Williams was needed for on this first day.

Shimon Wincelberg said, "Guy Williams was a very nice fellow and easy to get along with. He was a person who realized he was lucky because of the way he looked. He got a break, became famous and didn't have any illusions about what it took to be a TV star. And not to take away from any of the actors, who were fine people, but their characters were just not worked out to the extent that you could have real inner conflicts in them or between them." (SW-SL90)

Nine and six-eighths pages of script were filmed. Director Horn finished early, and on schedule. With a 5:30 wrap, everyone had time to make it home, have dinner and then settle down in front of their TV sets for the CBS airing of Episode No. 3, "Island in the Sky," and the dramatic crash landing of the Jupiter 2 on a desolate alien world.

Above: From Day 3, moments like the one above never pleased CBS, as Dr. Smith dares Will to put his hands in water ... or is it acid? Below: From Day 5, Smith's encounter with one of the more inventive and strangely alien spaceships seen on *Lost in Space*.

Day 2, Thursday. This was a standard day, 8 a.m. to 6:20 p.m. The locations were on Stage 6 and then the company moved to the outdoor moat/cliffs. Eight and seven-eighths pages were covered. Horn, having had experience working on Allen's *Voyage to the Bottom of the Sea*, was still on schedule.

Day 3, Friday, October 1. Work took place on Stage 5, from 8 a.m. to 4:20 p.m. On the schedule: the sequences inside the alien spaceship.

Only three and two-eighths pages from the "Invaders from the Fifth Dimension" were covered before a company move to Stage 6 was called to pick up urgently needed shots for Production #8507, "My Friend, Mr. Nobody." Horn had fallen to a quarter of a day behind before the move, and therefore was half a day behind by the time filming stopped at 6:20 p.m.

Day 4, Monday, October 4. Back on Stage 5, filming the Chariot on the rocker in front of the process screen, as John and Maureen, with the Robot, searched for Will. Process shots were also filmed with Mark Goddard wearing the Rocket Belt. They worked from 8 a.m. to 6:16 p.m., but only four pages from the script were filmed, keeping Horn at one-half of a day behind.

Day 5, Tuesday. Standard hours again – 8 a.m. to 6:26 p.m. The schedule called for this time to be spent on Stage 6, but Horn and the company didn't make it there until midday due to being a half-day behind and playing catch-up on Stage 5. Once on Stage 6, they began filming the scenes outside the alien spacecraft, starting with Smith's first

Exterior shots of the Chariot, as John and Maureen searched for Will, were shot in December 1964 in at Trona Pinnacles for the pilot.

encounter with the aliens, then Smith leading Will like a lamb to slaughter. More was planned, but they didn't get to it. Eight and four-eighths pages were covered from the script, during 12.2 work hours. By the time filming stopped, the production was a full day behind.

Day 6, Wednesday. The entire day was spent on Stage 6, with filming commencing at 8 a.m. Scenes filmed were of John, Maureen, Don, Smith, and the Robot outside the alien ship.

During the climactic fourth act, when the group took cover behind boulders near the alien ship, and the Robot followed, we catch a glimpse of Bob May's legs below the line of the "Bermuda shorts" rubber section of the Robot's lower mechanical extremities. It was the only time this happens in the series. The mistake was left in because there were no alternative shots to use, and it is not noticeable if one is not looking for it. But now that you know, you will never miss seeing it again.

Bob May bemoaned "It was very difficult to [lift the feet] – the Robot wasn't designed to 'walk.' That's when we started doing it with cables. The Robot was pulled around on cables, and then sometimes I carried it. We had cut-off versions of the Robot's legs and connected the outfit's top section to that, and I carried the whole thing on a parachute-style harness. We called that 'the Bermuda shorts.' It was about 250 pounds that I was luggin' around." (BM-SL94)

May continued to lug the weight around as they worked until 6:15 p.m. Eight and two-eighths script pages were committed to film. The crew clocked in 12.2 hours. And Horn was still a day behind schedule.

An hour and fifteen minutes later, "There Were Giants in the Earth" had its only CBS broadcast.

Day 7, Thursday, October 7. The next episode, "The Oasis," was supposed to start filming, but had to be pushed back. Horn was pushed as well, to film all remaining pages from the script, totaling fourteen and one-eighth. The location was Stage 11, for the scene outside the Jupiter 2, including the hydroponic garden, then onto the upper deck of the ship. The final sequence filmed was the cliffhanger, as Don worked on the water conversion unit with Judy, then both being subjected to an earthquake, resulting in Don being pinned by a giant boulder. The crew worked for 13.1 hours. The production ended a day behind … with pickup shots still needing to be taken on October 11.

Post-Production:

This was the second episode on which Jack Gleason and Edit Team 3 did the cutting, following their work on "The Hungry Sea."

As the first edit of the episode presented it, for the dramatic climax of Act IV, we don't know that Will might make it out of the alien ship before it disintegrates. John and Maureen Robinson didn't know either, causing them great distress. It would only be after the commercial break, for the Tag scene, when they would see that Will was lying on the ground in front of where the ship had been, shaken but otherwise unharmed.

Sam Taylor, Jr., of CBS Program Practices, watched the first cut on October 18th, then wrote to Margaret Venetis at Van Bernard Productions the following day, telling her:

> As discussed with Mr. Allen on October 18, the footage viewed by this editor is acceptable for broadcast. However, so as to avoid alarming a large portion of your youthful audience we would request the concluding scene in Act IV show WILL as having survived the disintegration of the alien spaceship.
>
> As discussed with Mr. Wilson on October 19th, you will re-edit this film so as to conclude Act IV with the disintegration of the alien spaceship and the unmistakable survival of WILL; we will see the boy begin to get up.

This episode did not feature an original score, instead utilizing "tracked" music (sampled from previous episodes), including elements composed by Herman Stein, John Williams and Bernard Herrmann. To the credit of supervising music editor Leonard A. Engel and music editor Joe Ruby, the choices were inspired and the patched-together score helps set the foreboding mood for this episode. The two men, along with sound editor Don Hall, can also be credited with introducing many of the eerie sounds heard in the episode, including the ominous chords that signal the appearance of the alien ship, and – for the first time in the series – the sonic "bong" note which would accompany the sudden appearance and disappearance of a person of thing (being popped in or out of a scene).

As for that budget of $143,129 that William Self had approved for this episode, by the time post-production had been completed, the final cost was $161,422.75.

Release / Reaction:

(CBS premiere broadcast: Wednesday, November 3, 1965)

(Network repeat air date: Wednesday, August 31, 1966)

Above: One of the last times the set photographer took a picture in which Smith was depicted as more the villain than the guest alien or monster of the week. Below: CBS much preferred to see Smith depicted as a victim

The Beatles still controlled the music charts in America, with their *Help!* album locking down the No. 1 slot, and "Yesterday" being the most-played song on the radio. Meanwhile, it was all about Steve McQueen at the movie houses, as *The Cincinnati Kid* held at the pole position for the third straight week. As for *TV Guide*, American's No. 1 magazine, John Astin and Carolynn Jones of *The Addams Family* had the cover.

During the week between the airing of "My Friend, Mr. Nobody" and "Invaders from the Fifth Dimension," *Lost in Space* had the cover of the October 31, 1965 *New York Journal-American* TV Magazine. To be specific, the women of *Lost in Space* had the cover. Angela Cartwright, Marta Kristen and June Lockhart, wearing their silver lamé spacesuits, posed on the metal-girder stairway leading up to the semi-full-sized Jupiter 2 mock up (as seen in portions of "The Derelict"). For the story within, Frank Judge wrote, in part:

> Women have been rebuffed in their attempts to become astronauts, but in the fantasyland of television all things are possible. Women go flying around with their husbands and kids. At least they do on CBS' *Lost in Space*, a creation of executive producer Irwin Allen's imagination.

From the San Antonio *Light*, November 3, 1965, syndicated "TV Key" column said:

> A spooky lot of strange new creatures from the fifth dimension will intrigue the kiddies and even the grownups tonight. These imaginative characters are a cultured group in need of a human brain to replace a computer, and they consider one of the Robinson children as a source.

Also on November 3rd, the TV Editor for the *Scottsdale Daily Progress*, in Scottsdale, Arizona, didn't sound like he liked it, but he nonetheless picked *Lost in Space* as one of only two Wednesday night "highlights" (with the other being a Jack Benny special). The TV editor said:

> Today, kiddies, we have some new villains. They are luminous pilots of an alien spaceship, who invade the Robinson's space colony from the fifth dimension. They need a "humanoid" brain to replace a guidance-control computer. When they capture the evil Dr. Smith (Jonathan Harris), he talks them into taking little Will (Billy Mumy).

The week "Invaders from the Fifth Dimension" first aired, Angela Cartwright, June Lockhart and Marta Kristen had the cover of the New York *Journal American* TV Magazine.

The November 3rd edition of Hagerstown, Maryland's *The Daily Mail*, carrying the syndicated "TV Scout" review column, said:

> *Lost in Space* continues to be lost in the outrageous. The Robinsons and pals have a visit from another spaceship (operated by luminous pilots) who need a "humanoid" brain to run their guidance-control computer which is all pooped out. Guess whom they select? None other than little Will whom captured Dr. Smith is willing to turn over to them. Spooky, but silly business.

Silly business or not, it was a first-rate episode. But *The Virginian* had one that appealed to more people on this night, resulting in the first time *Lost in Space* didn't win its time slot. An NBC press release for the western teased the potential audience: "James MacArthur guest-stars and the series' new feminine co-star, Diane Roter, is introduced in a story about a young girl's misplaced trust in a deceptively appealing killer."

The A.C. Nielsen 30-City Ratings survey for November 3, 1965 reported:

Network / Program:	Rating	Audience Share:
7:30 – 8 p.m.:		
ABC: *Ozzie and Harriet*	13.7	22.8%
CBS: *Lost in Space*	16.7	27.8%
NBC: *The Virginian*	**20.7**	**34.5%**
8 – 8:30 p.m.:		
ABC: *The Patty Duke Show*	15.2	24.9%
CBS: *Lost in Space*	17.4	28.5%
NBC: *The Virginian*	**21.9**	**35.8%**

19

Episode 9: "The Oasis"

Written by Peter Packer
(with script polishing by Anthony Wilson)
Directed by Sutton Roley
Produced by Irwin Allen, with Jerry Briskin

From *Lost in Space* show files (Irwin Allen Papers Collection):

> The sources of water on the planet are drying up. The Robinsons have rigged up a water-conversion unit but it doesn't supply enough for their needs. It becomes vital to find a new source. They set off in search and find an oasis. The water isn't drinkable but there is a lot of fruit growing there. They bring some back with them to test if it is safe to eat. Smith sees the fruit and eats some, not knowing that it has not yet been tested. The result is that he, and the pet bloop Debbie, who has also had some, start to grow at such a rate that they become giants overnight. Smith thinks the Robinsons have done this to him purposely because earlier he had taken more than his share of the water for a shower. He plans revenge and leaves the camp taking a fuel cell from the water-converter with him. Maureen goes after him and induces him to return to the ship with her and bring the fuel cell back with him.

From the Script:

(Shooting Final teleplay, October 6, 1965 draft)

– *Robinson's voiceover (writing in his journal):* "Although we have survived the earthquake and Major West's injuries have fortunately proved to be minor, the eccentric orbit of this hostile planet has now confirmed our fears that its sun would soon be a pitiless enemy. The land shrivels under its blinding heat, and the conservation of water has become our greatest problem."

– *Maureen (suddenly):* "Oh dear – we forgot all about Dr. Smith." *Judy:* "Yes – isn't it a relief?" *Maureen:* "What do you mean, Judy?" *Judy:* "To be able to forget about him."

– *Smith (into tape recorder):* "I must be quick before it overtakes me… let you judge for yourselves whether my death was natural – or murder most foul. I name them as my destroyers – Robinson, West – murderers both! I, who showed them how to survive on this alien planet; I, who brought happiness and intelligence into their bleak and despairing lives; I, who brought joy to their children's hearts – showed them courage in place of fear, hope in place of despair. And they have shown their gratitude – by poisoning me."

– *Don (a little irritably):* "Why did he have to take off? What did he expect to find out there – an emergency hospital?" *Robinson:* "The bull elephant takes off when he feels he's going to die. Leaves the herd and goes off by himself. *(wryly)* Smith was kind of a bull." *Don:* "I think you really like the old buzzard." *Robinson:* "Don't you?

– *Smith (babbling):* "Made me grow, did you say? Tall as a tree? Oh mercy no – it can't be. It isn't true! *(he falls to his knee)* Tell me it isn't true." *Will:* "It's not that bad to be big. Think of all the marvelous things you'll be able to do – gosh, you could get birds' eggs out of a nest without even climbing." *Smith (groans):* "Is that marvelous? Marvelous to be three times as tall as everyone else? It's horrifying! *(helplessly)* I'll never be able to go back to Earth now. They'll laugh at me – put me in a circus sideshow with the freaks!"

Assessment:

Irwin Allen's first excursion into a land of giants … a test run for the series he would produce three years later. In this regard, "The Oasis" gets an A-plus. The technical aspects are fine.

Other than offering us the absurd notion that Dr. Smith would be so foolish to take a shower in the middle of a heat wave that has brought about water rationing, the first two-thirds of the episode is quite effective. It capitalizes well on the "Swiss Family Robinson in Space" premise, with the shipwrecked pioneers struggling to survive nature's wrath. In addition, the drama inherent in Smith's plight – the possibility of him having been poisoned, and his fear that this was done intentionally so that the castaways can rid themselves of him – is handled well by writer Packer, director Sutton Roley, and the entire cast. The characters are played with sincerity and it is easy for the viewing audience to get swept away and find ourselves feeling empathy for Dr. Smith. He not only faces death, but the burden of believing he does so as an unloved man. Two-thirds of the way into this story, "The Oasis" ranks among the series' finest.

There is much to appreciate up to this point, including the tie-in with Episodes 4 and 5, which revealed that the planet's elliptical orbit would bring about regular hot and cold spells. And writer Peter Packer provided an explanation as to why the drought is worse and longer lasting this time around. Don says, "Until we know for sure which way this crazy planet's going to jump, I recommend we cut water rations – now." During his script polishing, Tony Wilson reassigned the line to John Robinson, with some mortification, but the explanation was retained – the orbit is constantly changing. This also explains how a large body of water – as established in "My Friend, Mr. Nobody" – could dry up to the point of being the small contaminated pond seen here.

Sutton Roley put in extra care, sprinkling in excellent directorial touches such as the camera traveling along with Maureen on her elevator ride from the lower to upper deck. The script did not call for this – it was Roley's idea, including the risk of falling behind schedule by undertaking such ambitious shots as these. Note how, after the sleight-of-hand trick connects the lower and upper decks (with a hidden edit), the camera rides along with June Lockhart, and then, without an additional cut, brings into view the upper deck's front viewing portals, as we catch sight of Dr. Smith outside the Jupiter 2, feasting on the untested fruit.

Roley also excelled in working with the cast – all of whom were provided with good roles in Packer's script. The scene with Angela Cartwright is one such example, staged in the campsite area outside the Jupiter 2, as she tries to comfort Debbie, then looks up toward the sky, saying, "You look so beautiful up there, sky. But you'd look more beautiful if you were all dark with rain clouds ... and the rain was falling – and filling the rivers and the streams and the lakes ... but not until we find Dr. Smith."

Kudos also go to the set designers and decorators for creating the sand dunes on Stage 6 where the Robinsons and West search for Smith in the dark of night, as well as the mound where Smith buries his tape recording and plants his flag. The work of hauling in extra sand and creating the mounds was done for this episode alone.

"The Oasis" provoked an immediate reaction from many watching in early November 1965 – those of us who had been wondering why Jonathan Harris was listed in the screen credits as "special guest star." Was he about to be killed off?

Toward the end of Act III, this excellent story about the fight to survive, the sadness over the impending loss of a member of the "family," and the bitterness or perceived betrayal, turns into something far less satisfying. Once the giant Smith is introduced, we have an entirely different type of story, with greatly diminished results.

We all know that *Lost in Space* never did let scientific accuracy or logic get in the way of spinning a tall yarn. Even so, should an audience – even a young one – be expected to suspend belief to the point of accepting that Dr. Smith's clothes will grow and then shrink along with the changes in his body size? Apparently Irwin Allen, Tony Wilson, Peter Packer, and CBS felt that we should, since no effort was made to find a reasonable solution to this immense story problem. They may have discussed it, and had a laugh over it, but there are no memos in the show files stored in the UCLA Special Collections Library, or in the privately maintained Irwin Allen Papers Collection, that give evidence to any concerns over this troublesome plot point. As a result, Irwin Allen lost credibility. After all, it was only months earlier when he was telling the entertainment press that his new series would be as much "science-fact" as science fiction.

Another disappointing aspect in this episode is its introduction of low comedy into a previously dramatic situation. Case in point: Smith's hot shower in the middle of a heat spell, with him and the Robot singing "Largo al factotum," from Gioachino Rossini's Italian opera *The Barber of Seville*. Did this even resemble the Dr. Smith we had seen in the previous eight episodes? Or the Robot? The network's desire to take the menace out of these characters can be understood, considering the restrictions of family hour TV in the 1960s, but turning Smith into a buffoon was unwise. In the final act, the previously cunning character of Dr. Smith is reduced to little more than a whimpering, whining, sneezing, foot-stomping, tantrum-throwing 20-foot tall child.

Peter Packer tried to explain away Smith's adolescent behavior with a line of dialogue given to John Robinson: "Smith the doctor probably knows more about the action of that fruit on the pituitary gland than any of us… *(shakes his head)* … but Smith, the victim, is in a state of shock and couldn't help himself even if he wanted to."

The line helped … a little. Nonetheless, the integrity of the character and the series took their first hit in the final 15 minutes of this episode.

"The Oasis," then, has a split personality. The first part is to be admired, enjoyed and – always a plus in moving pictures – even felt. The second part is something to merely be enjoyed … provided one doesn't think too hard about how much better this episode (and the series) could have been if Irwin Allen, Tony Wilson, and CBS had believed in the dramatic potential of the show and the characters as much as the kids watching at home did.

Script:

Story Assignment 8455 (Production #8509)
Peter Packer's treatment, and 1st and 2nd draft teleplays: Early to late September, 1965.
Reformatted Mimeo Department Shooting Final teleplay: September 29, 1965.
Tony Wilson's script polish (blue insert pages): October 1.
Additional page revisions by Wilson (pink insert pages): October 6.

The story assignment for "The Oasis" was given out during producer Buck Houghton's tenure at *Lost in Space*, perhaps explaining why the first two-thirds of the story deals with Man against Nature. The gimmick of turning Dr. Smith and Debbie into giants didn't kick in until late in the story. Regardless, he was still in his office through the first week of October, as the final draft of the script was being written. Whether he liked the idea of Smith – clothes and all – growing, or not, is unknown. Whether he could have done anything about it is also unknown. Houghton left behind very few memos to indicate his thinking, or influence. However, the rapid changes the series experienced after Houghton's exit, including the degradation of the Dr. Smith character, indicate that he did indeed have influence … even if it was waning.

Jonathan Harris had great fun with this role, perhaps more so than writers Packer and Wilson had intended. One example of how Harris enlarged his role – even before becoming a giant – can be found in Scene 50, when Smith first learns that he may have eaten poisonous fruit. Harris played it with an over-the-top reaction and, at the end of the scene, ran off in hysteria, very much the caricature of a coward in distress. The script, however, presented the scene in this way:

ROBINSON
(staring – then angrily to Smith)
Don't you ever pay attention to rules?

SMITH
(in terror now)
It – it was lying right there on the table. I was thirsty – and hungry. How was I to know –
(he stares at Robinson – a wild suspicion growing in his mind)
You left it there deliberately, didn't you? You <u>wanted</u> me to eat it!

ROBINSON
Don't be ridiculous, Smith. We did no such thing. We've only just found that fruit. If you'd stayed with us you'd have known that!

Smith backs away, a little like a man recoiling from his murderers.

SMITH
You took advantage of the way I felt to plant them there. You <u>knew</u> they'd be the first thing I'd see.

MAUREEN
Dr. Smith – that's not true!

SMITH
This is your revenge on me – because I used your drinking water to take a shower.

DON
That's crazy, Smith!

SMITH
Is it? I know how you all feel about me – another mouth to feed – another thirst to quench. Let's get rid of him – this is our chance. That's the way your evil minds worked, isn't it?
(suddenly he groans – clutches his stomach)
It's begun! I can feel it –
(groans again)
It's churning in my blood!

ROBINSON
(moving up)
Let's get you inside –

SMITH
Stay away from me!
(gasping for breath)
Leave me alone.

He retreats backward – staggering in toward the ship.

Note that there is no screaming; no running; not even an exclamation point after his last line, "Leave me alone." No hysterics whatsoever; merely understandable fear, along with the feelings of being both loathed and betrayed, as a personality of this type would likely experience.

Later in the story, as presented in Packer's script, much less was made of the sneezing fits. In fact, Smith only sneezed once during the scene when Maureen goes out to speak to him, and that was at the very end. There was no gush of wind knocking Maureen down, and the sneeze, both for this scene and the one to follow when it is established that Debbie is also sneezing, was merely there to reinforce the idea that the pituitary gland was affected by the consumption of the fruit. It was Jonathan Harris, with the approval of Tony Wilson, who turned the sneezing sequences toward camp.

It was also Wilson who changed the shower scene in the Teaser from Smith singing by himself to one where he and the Robot sing together.

However, Wilson's changes were not all detrimental. It was he who added in the poignant scenes when the Robinsons lament over how they have treated Smith, including Judy's guilt over things she said earlier, and Maureen's observations that Smith is a frightened and lonely man.

Although there is no record of CBS expressing concern over the pure fantasy in the last third of the story, the network did raise concerns over other aspects.

On October 4, 1965, Sam Taylor, Jr. of CBS Program Practices wrote:

> Scene 1-6: Please exercise care in filming the scene of Don being struck by the boulder and his eventual release, so that his agony is not too graphically portrayed.
>
> Scene 9 – 12: Please do not allow identification of the game which would include the commercial mention of "Monopoly."

Despite the network's concerns, Mark Goddard played the agony for all it was worth. However, the name of the game *was* modified – to "Inter Stellar Monopoly," with a change to both the board and the playing pieces so not to infringe on anyone's copyright.

Pre-Production:

Sutton Roley was 43 when he began directing for *Lost in Space*. He got his start as a television director working for Ziv Productions, with its low-budget half-hour shows such as *Highway Patrol* and *Harbor Command*. In 1959 he graduated to the Desilu-made half-hour western, *U.S. Marshal*, then stepped up to the hour-long western format, with *Wagon Train* and *Rawhide*. He directed World War II drama with *Twelve O'Clock High* and, with fifteen episodes, *Combat!* An invitation from Irwin Allen came next, leading Roley to direct four episodes of *Lost in Space* and three for *Voyage to the Bottom of the Sea*.

Hired to play the supersized Debbie, as well as creating the ape suit, was Janos Prohaska. He made a career out of designing ape and monster suits, and then wearing those suits in various TV series. He was Darwin the Monkey in "The Sixth Finger" episode of *The Outer Limits*; a big white ape in the "Fatal Cargo" episode of *Voyage to the Bottom of the Sea*; Bobo the Gorilla in an episode of *Land of the Giants*, as well as a second unnamed gorilla in another episode from the series; and he was Olga the Dancing Bear in an episode of *The Munsters*. For *Gilligan's Island* he appeared as an ape three times, once abducting 'Lovey' Howell and another time lobbing grenades in the castaways' direction. He played a bear and a gorilla and a Dodo Bird in various episodes of *Bewitched*. Prohaska was also one of the resident monster-makers/players on *Star Trek*, the man behind (and inside) the Horta in "The Devil in the Dark," the Mugato in "A Private Little War," and Yarnek, the super-hot, clawed, rock-based monster in "The Savage Curtain." His most steady work was on *The Andy Williams Show*, where he was a regular, playing Cookie Bear. Prohaska would return to *Space* to play the Giant Bird Monster, alongside guest star Wally Cox, in Season Two's "The Forbidden World."

Production Dairy:

Filmed October 8 – 18, 1965 (6 and ¾ days)

Filming the Teaser on Day 1. Don, suffering, with his foot caught under a rock, resulted in some curious letters from viewers. One is discussed in this chapter's "From the Mailbag" section.

Day 1: Friday, October 8. Work took place on Stage 11, with camera rolling at 8 a.m. The sets used on this stage during this first day, as well as on Day 4, included the upper deck of the Jupiter, and the exterior campsite. Also filmed: the Teaser, when the falling boulder pins down Don West.

Later in the day, the company moved to Stage 6. This was not one of the exclusively assigned stages for the series, but used in this episode to enlarge the areas of the landscape that would be covered while Smith evaded the Robinsons, and they conducted their search for him. Sutton Roley rolled camera until 6:25 p.m. He finished on schedule.

Day 2: Monday, October 11. Beginning on Stage 6, then moving to Stage 5, as the Robinson party continued to search for Smith, the camera rolled between 8 a.m. and 6:40 p.m.

Worked into the production schedule were allowances for Billy Mumy's and Angela Cartwright's school time. Mumy recalled, "School at the studio was great when Angela and I weren't filming. There was a permanent school room on the lot, and Frances Klampt was the Fox studio teacher. She'd been there since Shirley Temple first started making films. Frances was a sweet, warm, good-natured human and a very qualified teacher who encouraged our creativity instead of force-feeding us the curriculums our public schools were using. But when we were filming, Ange and I had to

Above: Sutton Roley used many camera tricks to create the illusion of a giant interacting with the normal size (yet seemingly tiny) people. Beside split-screen effects, Roley utilized "forced perspective," such as in the above shot in which he placed Harris (or more likely a double) on a camera crane, and then lifted him and camera high above the others actors. The camera would shoot over the "giants" shoulder, who was in extreme foreground, looking down at the other cast members, perhaps twenty feet away. Below: Guy Williams at the "Moat" location on the fourth day of production.

get our school requirements done in increments, with a different teacher, in a small trailer outside the sound stages." (BM-FM15)

When the camera stopped rolling at 6:40 p.m., Sutton Roley was one-quarter of a day behind.

Day 3: Tuesday, October 12. Work resumed on Stage 6, covering more territory on the sand-duned terrain, as well as the camera tie-down shots that enabled the split screen effect that placed a little Will opposite a giant Smith, and a big Smith talking with much smaller Maureen.

Jonathan Harris was getting creative with many of his scenes – not through rewrite but through liberal interpretation.

Sutton Roley said, "Jonathan Harris was wonderful. He would do anything you asked. You just had to restrain him a little. If you let Jonathan go, he would go absolutely ape. It's better to have an actor like that rather than one you have to keep pumping all the time."

As for the other cast members, Roley said, "Angela Cartwright was a lovely girl and a very good actress. Bill Mumy was a terrific, exceptionally talented kid. Mark Goddard and Marta Kristen were okay…. I found Guy Williams and June Lockhart very pretentious. They were always holding hands and playing it lovey-dovey. It got to be throw-up time. Whenever the kids were in peril, Guy and June raced for each other first. I would say, 'Forget that! Let's be concerned with the kids for a moment.'" (SR-SL95)

The company filmed from 8 a.m. to 6:16 p.m. Roley held at one-quarter of a day behind.

Day 4: Wednesday, October 13. The company was on the move, beginning on Stage 6, finishing up the scenes from the previous day, then on to Stage 5 for pickup shots to be added to the footage from Day 1. Finally it was time for new business: outdoors at the Moat location, as the Robinsons, with West and Debbie, came across the small pond with potentially life-saving fruit. They filmed from 8 a.m. to 6:10 p.m., but lost time as they covered ground and ended up one-half of a day behind.

"The Hungry Sea," the fifth broadcast episode of *Lost in Space*, had its only CBS airing on this night.

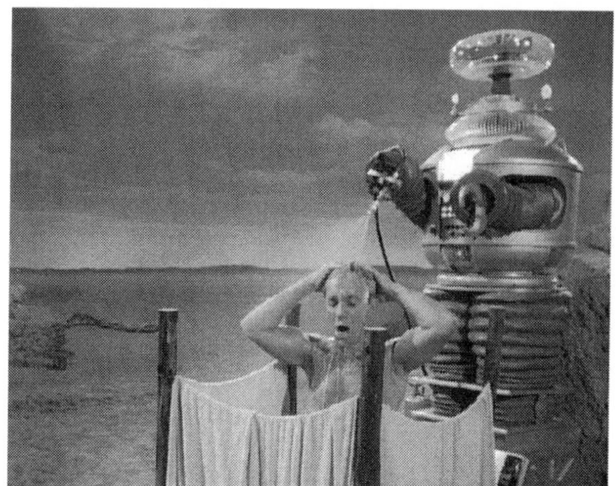

Day 5: Jonathan Harris gets to cool off under the hot lights with a shower.

Day 5: Thursday, October 14. A return to Stage 6 for more pickup shots, then on to Stage 11 where the company would remain until the end of the production filming in and around the Jupiter 2. Also filmed, Smith hitting the shower. They worked from 8 a.m. to 6:48 p.m., and held at one-half of a day behind.

Day 6: Friday, October 15. It was supposed to be the last day of production, but everyone knew better. The next planned episode, "The Sky Is Falling," was pushed back. Sutton Roley held at one-half of a day behind.

Promotional pictures taken on Day 6: The plot for "The Oasis" presented a challenge for the series' set photographer – how to stage a picture that CBS could use to promote the episode in newspapers and TV magazines. The split-screen shots of giant Smith and the comparatively tiny Robinsons wouldn't be processed in time for advance promotion. So, a "Beauty and the Beast" approach was used with Janos Prohaska, as giant Debbie, posing with pretty Marta Kristen.

Day 7: Monday, October 18. A final day on Stage 11. It would be a wet one, as the rain poured down from a sprinkler system mounted above the set. With the indoor downpour, this was a particularly traumatic day for Debbie the chimpanzee.

This caused concerns for Jonathan Harris. He admitted to interviewer William E. Anchors, Jr., "Debbie, the monkey, she terrified me. She terrified me and she loved me. *That* was a serious problem, I have to tell you…. You know a chimp is a very dangerous animal…. You know that scene where Debbie is playing in the sand with a pail and shovel? Louie [Schumacher] would put her there and say, 'Don't move or I'll kill you.' No sooner would Louie turn his back and she would scamper off. He'd yell, 'Get down here!'" (JH-IASB2)

Billy Mumy disputed Harris's assessment of Debbie, countering, "She was a great little professional animal… I've worked with so many animals in my career, seals and raccoons and bears and dogs, and Debbie was great. And that was her real name! That's the only reason she was named Debbie in the show. And there was only one of her -- it wasn't like, 'Well, Debbie's tired; get the other one.' It was just her."

Mumy did, however, confirm that Debbie wasn't always treated with kid gloves. He related sadly, "I never saw Lou Schumacher beat Debbie, but I will say that in that era of television and film – the late '50s and the '60s, which I worked prolifically in – they typically did not treat the animals with as much respect and gentle hand as they should. Today they wouldn't be allowed to treat them that way. Lou was okay, but he could have had a gentler hand. It's a weird thing to train an animal to be on camera, and to do things over and over again. I don't know; it's weird." (BM-AI15)

The day of the interior rain storm was especially difficult for Debbie.

Harris recalled, "We had one scene where there was a violent storm; a rainstorm. And I had to hug Debbie, and I thought, 'She'll kill me; she hates it, all that rain.' She'll get so nervous.' So I went to the director and said, 'Do you have to do this scene?' And he said, 'Are you serious? Go talk to Irwin. Of course we do. It's all Mr. Allen cares about – the flood, the earthquake, and the rainstorm.' I said, 'Doesn't he care about *me*?' Director said, 'No!'" (JH-IASB2)

Director Roley admitted, "Irwin Allen had a very cut-and-dried approach. He had his artists storyboard every shot beforehand. He wanted to know exactly how the show was going to look, because he hated surprises. If something caught him off-guard, he was quite a shouter…. What I didn't like was how Irwin treated his actors like buffoons." (SR-SL95)

Harris continued, "I practiced the shot, without Debbie, and then I thought, 'I'd better go play with her, to prepare her.' And she was very sweet for me, I have to tell you. So, I went, and Louie was there – her trainer – saying [to Debbie], 'Talk to Jonathan or I'll kill you!' He told me that he had to do that or she'd have never done one single thing right. He had to scare her into a fit. Chimps are like that, by the way…. Then we had to get ready to do the thing…. I have to tell you how stupid I was. I picked her up and I said, 'Debbie, this is a scene with a lot of water in it. You won't be mean to Uncle Jonathan? You're not going to hurt me or beat me, are you?' The cameraman was aghast. He said, 'Are you kidding?' I said, 'No.' We did the scene and she was so frightened that she clung on to me. I was her great protector. And I couldn't get rid of her and we did it in one take, which was wonderful." (JH-IASB2)

Roley directed from 8 a.m. to 4:10 p.m., at which time the company was handed off to Sobey Martin to begin "The Sky Is Falling." Roley had finished three-quarters of a day behind schedule, not entirely bad for the series at this time. Considering the trick shots, tying the camera down, the trick-perspective angles required, and the rain, Roley actually did remarkably well. His hard work would be rewarded with future assignments for Allen.

William Self wanted this one filmed for $141,610. The final cost came to $156,815. It could easily have been worse.

Release / Reaction:

(Only CBS broadcast: Wednesday, November 10, 1965)

The week "The Oasis" aired on CBS, the soap *Days of Our Lives* premiered on TV; the Rolling Stones had the top song on America's popular music radio stations, with "Get Off of My Cloud"; the Beatles still had the top-selling album, with *Help!*; the film making the most money in the movie houses was the WWII drama, *King Rat*, starring George Segal; and June Lockhart and Guy Williams appeared happily lost in space on the cover of *TV Guide*, in silver lamé spacesuits, and suspended by invisible wires.

The week "The Oasis" first aired, Guy Williams and June Lockhart had the cover of TV Guide - as photographed by the great Gene Trindl. Above and to the right: behind-the-scenes pictures from that photo session. Below: The end result.

Lockhart told *Starlog*'s Steve Swires, "When Guy and I posed for the *TV Guide* cover, we were swinging together, and then his wire *broke*.... But he was also very athletic, so he rolled with it and landed on his shoulder. After that accident, we didn't use the flying suits anymore." (JL-ST83)

"TV Scout," syndicated across America and in the November 10, 1965 edition of Illinois' *The Decatur Daily Review*, said of tonight's episode:

The family desperately looks for water and finds some strange gourd-like fruits with moisture inside. Smith gluts himself on them before they're tested and grows until he's almost as big as his ego – 18 feet tall, clothes and all. Now, that's not playing the game!

The picture above was the one many newspapers across America selected to use to represent the episode.

According to an A.C. Nielsen 30-City Ratings survey for November 10, 1965, *Lost in Space*, with "The Oasis," was the most-watched TV show across America during its time period.

Network / Program:	Rating	Audience Share:
7:30 – 8 p.m.:		
ABC: *Ozzie and Harriet*	13.1	22.2%
CBS: *Lost in Space*	**20.2**	**34.2%**
NBC: *The Virginian*	18.6	31.5%
8 – 8:30 p.m.:		
ABC: *The Patty Duke Show*	18.5	22.0%
CBS: *Lost in Space*	**21.6**	**35.2%**
NBC: *The Virginian*	19.0	30.9%

From the Mailbag:

From the November 27 issue of *TV Guide*:

> Thanks for the article on lovely June Lockhart ["Now She's the Fur-Bearing Animal," Nov. 6]. I've always hoped she would burst from the security bonds of *Lassie*. Why did she have to get *Lost in Space*? – William Glass, Jr., Salem, Oregon.

> Re: the *Lost in Space* episode last week, I can understand how the pituitary gland could cause "Dr. Smith" to grow larger than normal size, but tell me – which gland caused his clothes to grow with him? – (Name withheld), Milford, Ohio.

Regarding the mail, Jonathan Harris said, "We did a segment once where a great boulder came crashing down off a hill and landed on Mark's foot. A fake boulder, of course, and Mark acted up a storm. 'Oh, the pain! The pain!' About two weeks after that was on the air, Mark got a letter, which he quickly brought to my dressing room. He said, 'Read this.' So I did. It was from a gentleman who said, 'I just watched the segment where a terrible boulder came crashing down on your foot. The way you acted the pain was just wonderful. It was magnificent. I felt it. It was so real. If you would send me a picture of your foot, I would so much appreciate it.' I said, 'Oh?!' Mark said, 'Read on.' 'If you cannot send me a picture of your foot, could you possibly have a plaster cast made of your foot? I will pay the postage and I will pay for the plaster cast. And if you feel you cannot send a plaster cast, could you send me the measurements of your foot?' Well, we know all about that, don't we? I said to Mark, 'This is totally crazy; throw it away. Just forget it.' He said, 'No, I'm going to answer it.' I said, 'You're not!' He said, 'Yes, I am. I am going to send him the picture of a foot.' And he did. It was terrible; a wicked boy. I loved it.... I loved Mark. He had a wonderful, droll sense of humor. Very dry. And I like that a lot." (JH-IASB2)

20

Episode 10: "The Sky Is Falling"

Teleplay by Barney Slater and Herman Groves; story by Herman Groves

(Script polishing by Anthony Wilson)

Directed by Sobey Martin

Produced by Irwin Allen; with Jerry Briskin

From *Lost in Space* show files (Irwin Allen Papers Collection):

> Smith encounters a mysterious metallic object crawling along. It is evidently constructed for collecting data and soil samples. Everyone is interested as it must obviously have been sent by some "intelligent" form of life. The next day, Will comes across a humanoid boy, the same age as himself. They rapidly make friends and find they have much in common. The space boy and his parents are "Taurons" who are scouting out the planet to see if it is suitable for colonization. The second time Will sees the boy, he sneezes, and the Tauron, instantly contaminated by Will's Earth germs, falls seriously ill. Will helps him to a nearby cave and stays with him. Both families are highly concerned by the disappearance of their sons, and Smith, through his usual blunderings and deceit, sows seeds of doubt on both sides.

From the Script:

(Shooting Final teleplay, October 26, 1965 draft)

– *Smith (fearfully):* "Careful, Professor. It might suddenly attack." *Penny:* "It looks like a big bug…" *Smith:* "Don't be ridiculous, child – it's a monstrous, deadly creature capable of destroying us all."

– *Robinson:* "The central control unit is apparently activated by some kind of selective computer, giving it a form of free choice." *Don:* "That doesn't explain how it moved right through the hatch." *Robinson (shakes head):* "It must be some kind of matter transfer." *Will:* "Matter transfer?" *Robinson:* "It used to be a wild theory that somehow molecular structure could be broken up and re-assembled at another point." *Don (looks at object):* "Maybe it's not so wild anymore."

– *Smith:* "Who knows what terrible misfortune has befallen your young son. At this very moment he could be in the clutches of sinister beings, suffering indescribably torture." *Judy:* "Stop it!!"

– *Maureen:* "John, maybe you should go to the alien camp." *Robinson:* "I've been thinking of that too, honey. One moment I think, yes, and the next… no. If something like this had happened on Earth, I'd know exactly how to handle the situation. But here… in an alien world…. with alien people… and an alien morality, it's very easy to make mistakes. I just don't want to go jumping into anything we'll all be sorry for later."

Assessment:

"The Sky Is Falling" is not one of the more exciting episodes of *Lost in Space*, but it is somewhat profound and surprisingly adult for a series targeting youth, especially the under ten-year-old demographic. This may be this episode's most admirable aspect – that it presents a morality play much in the manner that *Star Trek* often did, to inspire and enlighten the young as well as the more mature viewers.

This story's theme promotes the possibility of trust and peace, even between strangers. This message was very relevant in 1965 when the Cold War between the United States and the Soviet Union was at a heightened level, the U.S. was escalating its involvement in Vietnam, and there was social unrest and racial strife in America. Smith makes the argument for the Hawks; John Robinson for the Doves. But John struggles with his beliefs and questions his lack of action, bringing forward the effective dramatic device of inner conflict.

Irwin Allen subscribed to the old Hollywood adage: "If you have a message, call Western Union." But "The Sky Is Falling" is clearly a message show. With this, we can get a sense of what *Lost in Space* may have been if producer Buck Houghton had stayed, for this story was first assigned during Houghton's tenure at *Space*. Smith's character is played straight, and the Robot is kept in the background, staying clear of comedy relief. The story's pace is deliberately slow, perhaps to emphasize its theme.

The production aspects are quite good throughout, with the possible exception of that crab-like environmental surveillance unit. Wardrobe and makeup for the Taurons, as well as set design for their very alien campsite, add greatly to the overall effect of the episode. The Taurons are indeed extremely alien in look and nature, and their silence is perhaps the most intimidating aspect about them, all the better to emphasize their difference from the voluble Smith and his intolerant attitudes.

Had there been more episodes like this, the ratings may have taken a dip, but as a change of pace, "The Sky Is Falling" is a nice addition to the series.

Script:

Story Assignment 8550 (Production #8510)
Story assigned to Herman Groves on June 24, 1965.
Groves' treatment and 1st draft teleplay: July - September 1965
Story cut-off of Groves' 1st Draft teleplay: September 28, 1965.
Barney Slater's rewrite (2nd Draft teleplay): Early October 1965.
Reformatted Mimeo Department Shooting Final teleplay: October 11, 1965.
Page revisions by Tony Wilson (blue insert pages): October 14.
Additional revisions by Wilson (blue insert pages): October 15.
Further revisions by Wilson (pink insert pages): October 19.
Further revisions by Wilson (pink insert pages): October 19.
Further revisions by Wilson (green insert pages): October 21.
Further revisions by Wilson (yellow insert pages): October 25.
Further revisions by Wilson (beige insert pages): October 26.

The script began with Herman Groves, who was 38 and in his fifth year as a TV writer, specializing in westerns (*The Restless Gun*, *The Gallant Men*, *Bonanza*), crime shows (*Surfside 6*, *The Untouchables*, and, featuring Mark Goddard, *The Detectives*), as well as far-fetched sitcoms (*Bewitched*).

"The Sky Is Falling" was actually Groves' second *Lost in Space* assignment. Prior to this, producer Buck Houghton assigned him Story #8546, "Refuge of the Damned." Groves wrote a treatment, followed by two drafts of a teleplay, before the script was put aside by Irwin Allen and left unproduced.

Following the unfilmed "Refuge of the Damned," Houghton gave Groves this second assignment. Two months later, on September 28, and after a treatment and a first draft teleplay had been written, Groves' assignment was cut-off by "mutual agreement." Houghton was preparing to exit the series and would be gone by the end of the first week of October. Meanwhile, Irwin Allen and Tony Wilson did not feel that Groves was connecting with the new direction they wished to take the series. Groves was given the option of doing a substantial rewrite or withdrawing from the assignment, with money already received but forfeiting half of the screen credit and the ensuing residuals paid for repeat airings. Groves chose to exit. The new writer would receive the $1,500 balance due for the script, for which he would rewrite Groves' first draft, addressing notes from Tony Wilson.

Writer Barney Slater was 42. He was highly respected as a screenwriter and someone Allen and Wilson felt fortunate to have. Slater began writing for the big screen, with medium budgeted films, such as the 1952 fantasy/comedy *It Grows on Trees*, starring Irene Dunn and Dean Jagger; the 1953 comedy *It Happens Every Thursday*, with Loretta Young and John Forsythe; the 1953 comedy *Mr. Scoutmaster*, starring Clifton

Webb; the 1954 film-noir mystery *Gorilla at Large,* starring Cameron Mitchell, Anne Bancroft, and a gorilla; and the 1956 western *Three Violent People*, starring Charlton Heston and Anne Baxter. He shared an Oscar nomination for co-authoring the story to 1957's *The Tin Star*, which starred Henry Fonda and Anthony Perkins, but Slater had already made the move into television, writing western scripts for *Zane Grey Theater*, *The Rifleman*, *Tombstone Territory*, *Bat Masterson*, and Mark Goddard's first series, *Johnny Ringo*. He also wrote juvenile tales for *Shirley Temple's Storybook*, including one called "The Return of Long John Silver." Irwin Allen and Tony Wilson figured that anyone who could write for kids, and had written dialogue for the character of Long John Silver, could also write for *Lost and Space* and Dr. Zachary Smith.

During his time with *Lost in Space*, Slater either wrote or co-wrote twenty-two episodes, making him the second most prolific writer on the series, next to Peter Packer (who wrote twenty-five), and Tony Wilson, who came up with story springboards and then handled all the script rewriting. Allen also tapped Slater to write one episode of *The Time Tunnel*.

As for Herman Groves, he moved on to take multiple assignments for *Hawaii Five-O* (with five scripts), *Harry O* (five scripts), *Vega$* (eight scripts), *Walt Disney's Wonderful World of Color* (eighteen scripts), and *Fantasy Island* (eighteen scripts).

Concerning Slater's second draft, delivered in October 1965, Irwin Allen wrote to Tony Wilson:

> P 40 – Sc 156: I am confused by the lack of interest on the part of Robinson and Don as to the presence of the aliens. Don seems to know the aliens came in "Capsules" and where and when they landed. This would have been the first place they would have looked for Will but they chose instead to comb the territory. Neither Robinson or Don have as yet seen the aliens. The ending of Act II and III are not very exciting.

Allen never would get more excitement added into the script; it wasn't that kind of story. However, there was a good bit of handwringing and debate among the characters, and lamenting, before a brief exchange of laser gun fire. This episode was not high on Allen's list of those to be repeated on CBS.

Pre-Production:

Director Sobey Martin returned to the series after impressing everyone with his work on "The Hungry Sea." More so, he had gained favor with Irwin Allen and 20th Century-Fox for being the first director to finish on schedule. This was his second of fourteen *Lost in Space* episodes.

Don Matheson was 36. He had served in the military during the Korean War, for which he was decorated with a Bronze Star and a Purple Heart. Matheson also served as a policeman in Detroit. Now he was an actor, having had small roles on *The Alfred Hitchcock Hour*, *McHale's Navy* and *The Gallant Men*. Irwin Allen and casting director Joe D'Agosta would bring Matheson back for a second *Lost in Space* (as IDAK Alpha 12 in the second season episode "Revolt of the Androids"), along with one guest spot on

Voyage to the Bottom of the Sea (the 1967 episode "The Deadly Amphibians"), before being cast as a regular in *Land of the Giants*. Matheson was paid $750 for his silent performance as Rethso.

Regarding getting the role, and the ordeal that followed, Matheson said, "It was the leading character and I was very pleased, until I got to the make-up department. There they applied a dead white make-up to my face and arms, sprayed my hair white, and I came out looking like a cross between a dead Inca Indian and an Apache." (DM-IPT68)

Françoise Ruggieri was born in Paris, France, but didn't have to worry about concealing her French accent when she played the mute alien wife and mother, Moela. She was 27, and had just completed her first of two episodes of *Voyage to the Bottom of the Sea* ("… And Five of Us Are Left," to be followed later in the year by "The Machines Strike Back"). Also from 1965: an episode of *The Wild, Wild West*, and playing a French Taxi Driver in the Jerry Lewis/Tony Curtis comedy *Boeing, Boeing*. Ruggieri was paid $350 to act without speaking.

Eddie Rosson played their son, Lunon. He was ten and worked in TV and films as a child actor from 1961 to 1968. He worked more days than Ruggieri, and was paid a bit more too – $400.

Production Diary:

Filmed: October 19 – 26, 1965

(6 ¼ days)

Work had finished on "The Oasis" three-quarters of a day late, at 4:10 in the afternoon. At that point, outgoing director Sutton Roley handed the production crew over to incoming director Sobey Martin, who had been patiently waiting through the day.

Day 1: Monday, October 18. Martin remained on the same set that Roley had been using on Stage 11, and ran the camera for a little more than two-and-a-half hours, from 4:10 to 6:59 p.m., filming the Teaser, with Judy's playful interaction with Dr. Smith, and then Smith being confronted by the crab-like mechanical creature.

Marta Kristen, "I had loved science fiction. I'd read, of course, Ray Bradbury and Isaac Asimov. Those were my favorite writers. That was a different kind of science fiction than most. I don't want to say intellectual, but it was more about the human condition than the science. But that's what *Lost in Space* was, too – it was about the human condition. It sounds sort of odd to talk about it in such a serious vein, because it turned out to be a little bit silly, but I really did feel that it was about a family. It was about the consequences of a family being alone and how they could survive, and interweave their lives in a way that was ultimately supportive. They had to hold each other up because no one else could, because the contacts that we had outside the family were always threatening. And, whatever happened, at the end of each show, we always ended up being together, whether it was Bill who saved us, or Mark, or Guy, we conquered everything by staying together, and being together, and holding each other up." (MK-AI15)

The theme to this story especially supported Kristen's assessment, with two separate families sharing the same experience.

Meanwhile, Sobey Martin considered the few hours of work on this day a gift – giving him a head start, and not being counted by the front office as one of his six production days.

Day 2: Tuesday, October 19. Work continued on Stage 11, both this day and the next. First up, filming Smith hightailing it back to the Jupiter 2 with the crablike creature after him, plus other scenes outside the Jupiter 2 and around the hydroponic garden. The camera rolled between 8 a.m. and 6:22 p.m.

Day 3: Wednesday, October 20. Another evenly-paced day of production under the direction of Martin. The camera filmed on and off between 8 a.m. and 6:25 p.m. Martin covered the remaining scenes at the Jupiter 2 campsite, as well as sequences on the top level of the ship.

"Welcome Stranger," the sixth episode to air, had its only CBS broadcast on this night. And, according to A.C. Nielsen, *Lost in Space* had its largest audience.

Day 4: Thursday, October 21. The company spent the first of two days on Stage 6, and the "Ext. Rocky Area" set. Filmed: the scene in which Will dashes up to tell his father and Don about seeing the alien camp; the castaways coming and going from the alien encampment; and John picking up the sick alien boy, and carrying him home. Martin stayed on schedule, again filming from 8 a.m. to 6:25 p.m.

Day 5: Friday, October 22. For the second day on Stage 6, the company filmed the sequences taking place at the Tauron camp. It went as smoothly as the three previous days, with Martin filming from 8 a.m. to 6:20 p.m., avoiding "golden hour" overtime pay, which would have kicked in at 6:30.

Françoise Ruggieri and Don Matheson.

Day 6: Monday, October 25. The company finished filming the Stage 6 sequences at the Tauron camp,

Above: Williams, Matheson and Ruggieri in action publicity photo. Below: Billy Mumy and Eddie Rosson demonstrating the story's theme of friendship and trust.

then moved to Stage 5 for the scenes on the Jupiter 2's lower deck. Martin finished at 7 p.m., half an hour into overtime but otherwise still on schedule.

Day 7: Tuesday, October 26. Officially, this was only Martin's sixth day of production, following the bonus time given to him at the end of Sutton Roley's last day on Monday, October 18th. This time was spent outdoors, at the Moat location on the 20th Century-Fox backlot. The scenes filmed included the sequence where Will threw the boomerang-like ball, and the alien boy fell ill.

Sobey Martin held the record for requiring the least amount of camera hours to finish a First Season episode of *Lost in Space* – 51.8 for "The Hungry Sea." That episode included a great deal of stock footage harvested from the pilot, so did not give a true indication of how economic Martin could be. "The Sky is Falling" did not utilize stock footage, but Martin finished it in only 58.9 camera hours, during a season in which the average was 68.3. Only one director had done better – Nathan "Jerry" Juran with "Return from Outer Space" (still to come), which was filmed utilizing only 54.2 camera hours. There was a reason why Martin would work often on *Space*, and this was it. Sadly, what Irwin Allen did not keep was a graph showing which episodes were the best directed.

William Self had approved $136,557 for the production. This, of course, was an impossible cost limitation for a one-hour science fiction episode. The company did well by bringing it in for only $150,557.

Release / Reaction:

(Only CBS broadcast: Wednesday, November 17, 1965)

The Beatles and their album *Help!* were finally knocked from the No. 1 spot in the Billboard magazine chart, by – of all people – Angela Cartwright … with a little help from Julie Andrews, for the soundtrack album to *The Sound of Music*. The song getting the most airplay on Top 40 radio stations was not "Edelweiss" or "Do-Re-Mi," which included Cartwright as one of the singers, but "Get Off of My Cloud" by the Rolling Stones. *King Rat*, starring George Segal, was still the top-grossing film in the movie houses. And Joey Heatherton, billed as a "swinging girl" modeling "swinging fashions," had the cover of *TV Guide*.

Eddie Rosson and Billy Mumy in promotional picture sent out by CBS to newspapers and TV magazines.

The syndicated "TV Key" column, carried by newspapers across America, including the November 17, 1965 issue of Ohio's *The Lima News*, gave "The Sky Is Falling" a thumbs up:

> Good adventure show for the youngsters. It's all about the alien family, a trio of strange creatures who talk in a puzzling [silent] language and have an eerie look about them. Not only do the aliens overshadow the story dialogue problems, but they're also a puzzle as to whether they're friend or foe.

A.C. Nielsen, with its 30-City Ratings survey for November 17, 1965, also gave the episode a thumbs up. The results:

Network / Program:	Rating	Audience Share:
7:30 – 8 p.m.:		
ABC: *Ozzie and Harriet*	11.8	19.1%
CBS: *Lost in Space*	**21.3**	**34.5%**
NBC: *The Virginian*	17.9	29.0%
8 – 8:30 p.m.:		
ABC: *The Patty Duke Show*	14.9	23.3%
CBS: *Lost in Space*	**23.6**	**36.9%**
NBC: *The Virginian*	18.6	29.1%

21

Episode 11: "Wish Upon a Star"

Written by Barney Slater
(with script polishing by Anthony Wilson)
Directed by Sutton Roley
Produced by Irwin Allen; with Jerry Briskin

From the *Lost in Space* show files (Irwin Allen Papers Collection):

> Smith and Will discover a strange box which has the power to materialize any object the holder has in mind. Immediately there is great competition amongst the whole family for its services. But instead of being a blessing, it only makes the users progressively more greedy. Quarrels break out as to whose turn is next and even cheating is resorted to, while necessary chores are left undone waiting for the box to do them instead. Robinson, anxious at this change in his family, orders Smith to take the box back to where he found it. Smith is secretly determined to keep it but an Alien creature appears and silently demands what is evidently his property.

From the Script:

(Shooting Final teleplay, November 2, 1965 draft)

– *Don (calls after Smith):* "And handle it carefully! That fuel can explode on contact with air!" *Smith (not listening):* "Never fear, Smith is here."

– *Robinson:* "I'm waiting for an answer, son." *Will (reluctantly):* "Well, Don asked Dr. Smith to get a new fuel pack. I guess it developed a leak." *Don:* "Because he was careless." *Smith:* "It was an accident due to a malfunctioning mechanism." *Robinson (deceptively mild):* "I'm sure it was. I suggest we forget the incident." *Smith (with triumphant vindication):* "You're a most understanding man, Dr. Robinson." *Robinson:* "And now let's discuss the accident at the hydroponic garden." *Smith (startled):* "Garden!?" *Robinson:* "Wasn't that responsibility delegated to you this week?" *Smith (fidgets nervously):* "As a matter of fact, it was. But I've been so busy…" *Robinson (finishing the thought):* "… you haven't had the time to give the garden the attention it deserves." *Smith (knows he's in hot water):* "That's very true. I was just about to go over there when you arrived. If you'll excuse me…" *Robinson (his voice is hard):* "You can save yourself the trip, Dr. Smith. We don't have a garden anymore." *Will:* "What happened to it?" *Robinson (stone cold):* "It died of neglect."

– *Penny:* "It's like Aladdin's lamp. Only instead of rubbing it, you just think of what you want." *Will (in disgust):* "We're trying to find a scientific explanation and you're giving us fairy tales. It's a thought translator, that's what it is." *Penny (fighting back):* "The trouble with you, William Robinson, is you've got <u>no</u> <u>imagination</u>. I don't care what you say, it's still a wishing machine!" *Smith (no attempt to hide his boredom):* "Theories and conjecture – nonsense and jabberwocky. We have the gift horse, let us not examine its mouth too closely."

– *Robinson:* "Now, let's see – where should we start? *(pretends to think hard)* The Chariot should be as good a place as any. *(beat)* I suppose you've finished putting in the new repressor unit, Don?" *Judy (off Don's discomfort):* "It's my fault. I asked Don to take me for a walk." *Robinson:* "But you were supposed to be working in the hydroponic garden. *(off the dead silence)* And, Will, you were supposed to be helping, Don. Isn't that so, son? *(off the group's embarrassment)* Does anyone care to make a comment? *(again, silence)* Then I will, and it can be said in three words – the cerebral machine!"

– *Will:* "I don't understand, Dad. Why did the alien give us things and then decide to take them away?" *Robinson:* "Because Dr. Smith asked for too much, Will. He could have had just about anything he wanted, but like most people it wasn't enough for him. He had to have more. When he tried to create a servant, the alien realized this."

Assessment:

"Wish Upon a Star" has it all – Smith being evicted and having to survive creatures of the night; the discovery of a haunted relic of an alien spaceship; the wonderment of a wish machine; a monster whose featureless plasticized face, elongated dagger-sharp fingers, eerie mummy-walk, and mournful moan cause sufficient chills; and a moral. As with "The Sky Is Falling," this one actually has a theme.

"Wish Upon a Star" was a 1965 television equivalent to an Aesop's Fable. The big payoff is when Smith asks for the one thing he should not have wished for – a slave. There are many smaller messages woven throughout the hour. John, the king Solomon in this story, is a symbol of wisdom. He says he is a pragmatic man and does not believe that you can get something from nothing – or, at least, something of true and lasting value. His lecture to Penny about lying and cheating is effective, as is her reaction to disappointing her father and coming to terms with how low she had sunk in his eyes. Will grows up a bit in this episode – and is rewarded in the end with one last apple. Smith does not grow. He is just happy to have survived. "It didn't harm me!" he rejoices after returning the wish machine to the alien. In a future episode, Maureen will lament: "Poor Dr. Smith. He just doesn't understand what moral integrity is." And this is the moment in *Lost in Space* when Will, the lonely boy who has been in search of a friend, learns that he has someone who is the equivalent to a ten-year-old already in his company – Dr. Smith. The bonding between these two characters happens here.

As a counterpoint to all the positive themes, there is the shadowy, cinematic, black-and-white photography. The series may have never looked darker … and better.

When *Lost in Space* used its position as a primetime network TV series with roughly 20 million people tuning in each week, and bothered to make a statement, it was a true treasure.

Script:

Story Assignment 8458 (Production #8512)
Barney Slater's story treatment, plus 1st and 2nd draft teleplays: September/October 1965.
Reformatted Mimeo Department Shooting Final teleplay: October 22, 1965.
Page revisions by Tony Wilson (on blue paper): October26.
Additional page revisions by Wilson (on pink paper): October 27.
Further revisions by Wilson (on green paper): October 29.
Further revisions by Wilson (on yellow paper): November 2.

"Wish Upon a Star" was Barney Slater's first assignment for *Lost in Space*. Story development began while Buck Houghton was still producing. By the time Slater delivered his second and final draft of the script, Houghton was gone.

Tony Wilson and Irwin Allen were so pleased with Slater's work that they immediately asked him to take over the writing of "The Sky Is Falling," replacing Herman Groves. That episode was filmed and aired first, but it only came to fruition as a result of Slater's excellent work here.

On October 20, after reading Barney Slater's second draft teleplay, Irwin Allen wrote to Tony Wilson:

> Page 35: Robinson should not ask Will if he has any ideas about the machine. This makes Robinson and Don look stupid. Will can, however, volunteer his ideas.
>
> Page 35 thru Page 48, all of Act II, is mostly talk. It is good dialogue but could bog down unless the pace is kept up. Could some action or excitement be inserted?

Page 56: Everyone seems to take their first sight of the Rubberoid for granted. Shouldn't all present comment on this unusual creature's presence.

Page 61: Why not have Robinson, Don and Smith continue on to the site of the old space ship. Robinson and Don have never seen it and it would be logical for them to go there, led by the reluctant Smith, to return the box.

Page 62: The Fourth Act should end as soon as the Rubberoid receives the box from Smith and the electrical current crackles between the two antennae. Make it a nervous fourth act curtain!

All of these changes came about as a result of Allen's notes and Wilson's script polishing. Wilson's script was the first version sent to CBS.

On October 25, 1965, regarding the October 22nd Shooting Final teleplay, Sam Taylor, Jr. of CBS Program Practices, wrote:

Per our discussion with Mr. Wilson, we understand the closing portion of the TAG sequence (where it appears WILL might be run over by the Chariot) will not be used, and that new script pages covering the end of the TAG sequence will be submitted.

For the Teaser, which also set up and then resolved the cliffhanger from the previous episode, Will was removed from danger per the network's request, and the rolling Chariot was taken out and replaced with Don risking his life to toss away the leaking fuel pack.

Pre-Production:

"Wish Upon a Star" was assigned the production number 8512, yet it was shot before "The Raft," which carried the production number of 8511. "Wish Upon a Star" was merely ready to begin filming sooner, while "The Raft" was held up with rewrites and preproduction.

Director Sutton Roley returned for his second of four *Lost in Space* assignments, interspersed between three for *Voyage to the Bottom of the Sea*. Regarding "Wish Upon a Star," he said, "That was the best script I ever had for *Lost in Space*. It had some heart to it and had something to say about family values." (SR-SL95)

This was quite high praise coming from Roley since one of the other episodes he would direct was "The Anti-Matter Man," considered by many fans, as well as the cast members, as being the best episode of the third season.

Dawson Palmer played the "Rubberoid," which was how the script identified the monster. This was his second job with *Lost in Space*, but the first time he was able to stand up straight. His previous role on the series was playing the "Bubble Creature" seen in "The Derelict." That costume was a tight fit for Palmer, who was a former basketball player, and was 6 foot 7 and ¾ inches tall. You can see how tall the 29-year-old Palmer looked in "The Space Croppers," when he played a human-like creature named Keel. Before that, however, Palmer would wear more monster suits for *Lost in Space*, playing the Bush Creature in "The Raft" and the Bog Monster in "Ghost in Space."

Production Diary:

Filmed October 27 – November 4, 1965 (7 days).

Above: Utilized for this shot, one of the Jupiter 2 models used in the filming of photographic effects as the ship flies through space. Below: Sutton Roley had a knack for staying on schedule by posing cast members as he did in this shot, saving time by not requiring additional "coverage," such as close ups on each of the players.

Day 1: Wednesday, October 27. Stage 11 was the setting for the "Ext. Jupiter 2 campsite." The entire cast was assembled at 8 a.m., with camera rolling at 9 a.m. and the final shot taken at 6:40 p.m. It was here that Zachary Smith first said the now famous line, "Never fear, Smith is here."

Sutton Roley recalled, "Early on, I said to him, 'Say the line, "Have no fear, Smith is here!" From then on, he said it all the time." (SR-SL95)

The line was in the script. But that didn't mean Roley remembered wrong about suggesting Harris say it. By this point, Harris had the ear of Tony Wilson and was making suggestions of his own for changes in the scripts. The cast members would be given a copy of the Shooting Final teleplay days before filming started. Then, as the production progressed, additional sets of page revisions would come down to the stage from Tony Wilson's office. In the case of this script, there were page revisions on October 27 and 29, and November 2. Many of these were a result of ideas from Harris which Wilson, and Irwin Allen, approved and had inserted into the shooting script.

Something Roley can indisputably be given credit for, in collaboration with cinematographer Gene Polito, is the wonderful use of the camera. Roley and Polito reach a zenith in this episode with hand-held/wide angle camerawork and zooms. In particular, when Smith wishes

for a new Jupiter II, the camera angle makes it almost look as though a full-size ship appears in the foreground, until the point of view angle cranes up and we realize it's a small ship. This was the actual fifteen-inch special effects filming miniature.

Later on this night, at 7:30 p.m. (6:30 Central), the whimsical "My Friend, Mr. Nobody" – the seventh broadcast episode of *Lost in Space* – had its only CBS airing.

Above: Dawson Palmer as the "Rubberoid," so frightening to young viewers that CBS almost didn't repeat this episode, and only did so as the very last of the First Season reruns. Below: Will wishes up something hot to eat for Dr. Smith ... alien-style.

Day 2: Thursday, October 28. Again, the entire cast was present on set at 8 a.m. as they continued to work on Stage 11 at the campsite outside the Jupiter 2. After rehearsing, and adjusting the lamps, the camera began rolling at 9:25 a.m., with the final shot of the day taken at 7:10 p.m. The production was still on schedule.

Day 3: Friday, October 29. Dawson Palmer (in his Rubberoid costume) joined the regular cast on Stage 11 for the nighttime shots in and outside the Jupiter 2.

The last shot was completed at 6:30 p.m. Sutton Roley had fallen to one-quarter of a day behind schedule.

Day 4: Monday, November 1. Work resumed on Stage 11 for more of the sequences staged on the upper deck of the Jupiter 2. Following this, there was a company move to Stage 6 to film on the "Ext. Bushy Area" set, as well as "Ext. Rocky Area" and "Ext./Int. Ghost Spaceship." Dawson Palmer continued to perform with Williams, Goddard, Mumy, and Harris. Not needed this day: Lockhart, Kristen, May, and Cartwright, although the latter was on the lot attending school.

Day 5: Tuesday, November 2. The same players from the previous day worked in and about "Ext. Rocky Area" and "Ext. & Int. Ghost Ship."

The cast and all else involved in the making of *Lost in Space* received good news on the set. CBS had increased its episode order beyond sixteen, renewing the series for the balance of the 1965-66 TV season.

Day 6: Wednesday, November 3. Only Williams, Goddard, Mumy and Harris were required, as they continued to work on Stage 6, with "Ext. & Int. Ghost Ship" (both "clean" and with "cobwebs"), and then a company move to Stage 5 for sequences in the lower deck of the Jupiter 2. The last shot was completed at 6:30 p.m., but the crew was kept until 8:30, preparing the set for the next day's work.

June Lockhart visits with two special guests to the set – her daughters: Anne and June Elizabeth.

"Wish Upon a Star" was supposed to finish but was now a full day behind. The crew, working late, would miss *Lost in Space* this night, as "Invaders from the Fifth Dimension," the eighth episode to air on CBS, had its first broadcast. It was the only episode aired up to this point that would later be given a repeat telecast by the network.

Day 7: Thursday, November 4. Director Sobey Martin was scheduled to begin work on "The Raft," but told the night before that he was being pushed back a full day. Sutton Roley, meanwhile, went into a seventh day of filming with the sequences needed on Stage 6 and the "ghost ship," then returning to Stage 5 for pickup shots on the upper deck of the Jupiter 2. He worked until 7:30 p.m., when the episode was finally wrapped.

20th Century-Fox Head of Television William Self approved a budget of $130,980 for this episode. The final cost, however, climbed to $149,655.

Post-Production:

Jack Gleason and Edit Team 3 handled the cutting, following their work on "The Hungry Sea" and "Invaders from the Fifth Dimension."

The score was made up of tracked music, and again demonstrates the talent of supervising music editor Leonard A. Engel and music editor Joseph Rudy. Note how pieces of music from other episodes are perfectly matched with newer footage here. To name only three: John Williams' "floating music" from the sequences in "The Reluctant Stowaway" when the children and Dr. Smith experienced weightlessness, now used as Dr. Smith glides around the area where he plans to wish into existence a replica of the Jupiter 2; Herman Stein's cowboy brawl music, which accompanied the fight between Jimmy Hapgood and Don West in "Welcome Stranger," used here when Will and Penny wrestle for possession of the wish machine; and Stein's hauntingly lovely melody first heard in "There Were Giants in the Earth," was now utilized during the scenes when John has heart-to-heart talks with his family.

Release / Reaction:

(CBS premiere broadcast: Wednesday, November 24, 1965)
(Network repeat airing: Wednesday, September 7, 1966)

When "Wish Upon a Star" first aired on CBS, it was the night before Thanksgiving. Most Americans had the next day off. On the radio, the Supremes had the most popular song with "I Hear a Symphony." In the stores, the soundtrack album from *The Sound of Music*, with Angela Cartwright among those singing, was the best-selling LP in the nation. In the movie houses, *King Rat*, starring George Segal, was still top film. On the *New York Times* Best Sellers List, Ian Fleming's *The Man with the Golden Gun* was in the Top Ten. On the cover of *TV Guide*, Efrem Zimbalist, Jr. of *The F.B.I.* Inside was a two-page article on Marta Kristen entitled "Norwegian Cinderella." She was described as "a slim, wide-eyed, flaxen-haired girl who looks like a combination of Mia Farrow and Tuesday Weld." Kristen talked about how she had been born Birgit Annalisa Rusanen in Norway during the final days of World War II, the daughter of a German soldier whom she would never meet, then placed in a Norwegian orphanage before being adopted by a Detroit couple and brought to America at the age of four. She told how she was taught to speak English and then had "the good luck to be an adaptable extrovert." A career in show business followed with all roads leading to *Lost in Space*.

Dawson Palmer and Jonathan Harris pose for a promotional photo. However, CBS preferred to distribute the one at the top of the chapter; it contained no stone-faced monster.

"Wish Upon a Star" offered newspapers a picture that was too good to ignore – Dr. Smith wearing the wish machine – something that looked like a space age dunce cap. As a result, *Lost in Space* got free promotion in countless newspapers across the United States and Canada. The photo caption read: "WISHFUL THINKING – Wishes come true when Dr. Zachary Smith (Jonathan Harris) wears a thinking cap from a cerebral machine he finds in a ghost spaceship, on *Lost in Space* Wednesday…"

Also during the week, a syndicated article on Jonathan Harris called "Though Harris Is a Hit, He Admits He's TV Stage-Struck" made the rounds to newspapers, including the November 20 edition of *The Times Record*, in Troy, New York. Hollywood correspondent Harold Stern wrote:

> There's only one thing wrong with Jonathan Harris's performance as the evil Dr. Zachary Smith on the CBS-TV *Lost in Space* series. He's so charming, you refuse to accept him as a villain. In real life, he isn't even close to the wonderful characterization of Mr.

> Philips he contributed in the late, lamented *Bill Dana Show*. His energy and effectiveness are almost beyond belief. He is a quicksilver conversationalist and one just doesn't interrupt.
>
> "I'm stage struck," he said as we began to make out each other's faces in the stygian gloom enveloping the "festive" Hollywood tavern where we met. "I love the word 'actor.' I still get nervous. Isn't that wonderful? It's standing in the wings waiting to go on, opening night with a death wish and then going on and giving the best performance of your life. I still get that feeling, even in TV. And you go out and do it, and you feel it isn't right or it isn't working, you blow it deliberately and force them to shoot it over."
>
> "Being an unemployed actor is disaster! Going to work every day is kicks. You learn something vital from each show. That's kicks for an old dog like me. And you can watch other actors and learn things *not* to do."
>
> "I never had any formal training. I learned by watching.... I've done so many of the shows where you read the script and you say, 'Oh, they're kidding!' But, they're not. And if you do the show, you must do your best. And for all that money, come on, you know you'll do your usual first-class job. It's your responsibility to your audience and to those important to you. Always do your best. I learned that in the theater. It's a question of pride in what you do. If you don't have it, you can't act. Never apologize for what you do or for the script. Just do it."
>
> "On the set I'm referred to as 'Himself.' It really swings when I'm there. Our producer Irwin Allen is called 'The Emperor' – the great 'Emperor Irwin, the First.' His energy is frightening, all the more so now that he knows he has a huge hit because of me. He's so inspired, he gets 28 hours of work into every day."

"TV Key-notes," appearing in the *Galveston Daily News*, said:

> This fantasy series comes up with inventive gimmicks to whet the appetites of youngsters. In this one, there's a new creature called Rubberoid, and a magic machine that can grant wishes. The only time the machine creates trouble is when greedy, villainous Dr. Smith asks for too many wishes.

A.C. Nielsen's 30-City Ratings survey for November 24, 1965 awarded the time period victory to *Lost in Space*:

Network / Program:	Rating	Audience Share:
7:30 – 8 p.m.:		
ABC: *Ozzie and Harriet*	12.5	23.1%
CBS: *Lost in Space*	**21.0**	**38.7%**
NBC: *The Virginian*	14.3	26.4%

8 – 8:30 p.m.:

ABC: *The Patty Duke Show*	13.3	23.2%
CBS: *Lost in Space*	**21.8**	**38.0%**
NBC: *The Virginian*	16.1	28.0%

Nielsen's National Index for the week ending November 21, as presented in the December 7, 1965 issue of *Daily Variety*, ranked the Top 40 primetime programs (out of more than 80) as follows:

1.	*Bonanza*	NBC	35.6
2.	*Gomer Pyle, U.S.M.C.*	CBS	29.1
3.	*The Lucy Show*	CBS	27.4
4.	*Walt Disney's World of Color*	NBC	27.4
5.	*The Andy Griffith Show*	CBS	26.6
6.	*The Beverly Hillbillies*	CBS	25.9
7.	*Hogan's Heroes*	CBS	25.4
8.	*Get Smart*	NBC	25.2
9.	*Gilligan's Island*	CBS	24.9
10.	*My Three Sons*	CBS	24.8
11.	*Branded*	NBC	24.3
12.	*The Red Skelton Show*	CBS	24.3
13.	*Bewitched*	ABC	24.2
14.	*Daniel Boone*	NBC	24.1
15.	Ringling Brothers Circus	NBC	24.0
16.	*The Dick Van Dyke Show*	CBS	23.8
17.	*The Munsters*	CBS	23.7
18.	*The Virginian*	NBC	23.6
19.	*Green Acres*	CBS	23.6
20.	*Lassie*	CBS	23.5
21.	*The Lawrence Welk Show*	ABC	23.4
22.	*The Ed Sullivan Show*	CBS	23.4
23.	*Candid Camera*	CBS	23.0
24.	*I've Got a Secret*	CBS	23.0
25.	Saturday Night Movie	NBC	22.9
26.	***Lost in Space***	**CBS**	**22.7**
27.	*The Man from U.N.C.L.E.*	NBC	22.5
28.	*The Wild, Wild West*	CBS	22.4
29.	Danny Thomas special	NBC	22.4
30.	*Flipper*	NBC	22.3
31.	*The Jackie Gleason Show*	CBS	22.2
32.	*I Dream of Jeannie*	NBC	21.8
33.	Thursday Night Movie	CBS	21.7
34.	*To Tell the Truth*	CBS	21.1
35.	*Petticoat Junction*	CBS	21.0
36.	*What's My Line*	CBS	20.9
37.	*Shenandoah*	ABC	20.6
38.	*Laredo*	NBC	20.3
39.	*Bob Hope Chrysler Theatre*	NBC	20.3
40.	*Legend of Jesse James*	ABC	20.2

Sometimes wishes do come true. Among the top third of all prime time programs, *Lost in Space* was assured a mid-season pickup.

22

Episode 12: "The Raft"

Written by Peter Packer
(with script polishing by Anthony Wilson)
Directed by Sobey Martin
Produced by Irwin Allen; with Jerry Briskin

From *Lost in Space* show files (Irwin Allen Papers Collection):

> Will has come up with an idea for building a small, two-man spaceship by utilizing parts from the Jupiter 2. Everyone gets to work on the project and soon a small spaceship is constructed and Don is due to fly it the following morning. But that night Smith sneaks out, planning to abscond with it. He takes the Robot along to release the lines for him at the right moment, but before he can get away he is surprised in the cabin by Will. While he is trying to convince the boy that he is only there to check on the safety factors, the Robot releases the lines and off they both go together. Eventually, far out in space, they fall asleep. When they wake, they find themselves coming down on another planet. Smith is convinced they have homed-in to Earth, and he goes off to look for people.

From the Script:

(Revised Shooting Final teleplay, November 11, 1965 draft)

– *Don:* "Are you writing a book?" *Smith:* "I am." *Don:* "What about?" *Smith:* "The social psychology of galactic castaways." *Robinson:* "That sounds interesting. Is there any particular point of view that you've settled on?" *Smith:* "My own. Naturally." *Maureen:* "Isn't that a little narrow, Dr. Smith?" *Smith:* "Not at all. I happen to have the gift of seeing myself as others see me… and vice versa." *Will (mystified):* "That's very confusing – especially that vice versa. Is it the same as E.S.P.?" *Smith (pats Will benevolently on the head):* "It is knowing who are your friends – *(glares at Don)* – and who are your enemies." *Don (shaking his head):* "Remind me to buy that book. I might sue him!"

– *Robinson:* "One of these days soon we might just witness a perfect lift off – our own." *Maureen (smiling):* "I guess it won't do any harm to admit now that I've never really liked this place." *Penny:* "But I'll bet you we'll miss it when we go." *Maureen:* "It's a bet!" … *(looking up):* "The night sky's always beautiful no matter where you are." *Robinson:* "It's more beautiful if you've <u>chosen</u> where you are." *Maureen:* "Have you chosen?" *Robinson:* "If it works – if we could get the Jupiter 2 into space, there's one place I think we ought to try for… *(hesitates, then)* Alpha Centauri."

– *Smith (recording):* "… and strange though it may seem to the dweller on our bounteous and hospitable Earth, the galactic castaway is likely to be affected by a form of insanity which distorts his values and urges him to prefer the hostile and uncharted wastes of deep space to the comfort and security of Earth. In the case history of the family 'R,' for example, a family which it has been my lot to observe scientifically at first hand, who have the absurd and utterly illogical resolve to continue on a voyage into space which can only end in even worse disasters than they have already endured."

Assessment:

"The Raft" is merely an average episode from this period in the series history, but, considering what would become the norm in Season Two, it is well above average *Lost in Space*.

The writers were still trying to feature the entire cast at this point in the series. Since the latter half of the episode would primarily focus on Dr. Smith and Will, the first half leaned toward John and Don's efforts to find a way off the planet, with the other cast members all figuring into the situation at hand. The character that is kept in the background, as it had been for the previous two episodes, is the Robot.

Will and Smith formed a bond in "Wish Upon a Star," and they take it a giant step forward here. One scene in particular, which is both humorous and touching, has Will ask Smith if he can stand in as his father.

The exterior shots of the shipwrecked Jupiter 2, with the space raft to its side, and the balloon floating above the raft, were beautifully executed for this era and medium. Camera angles of this type, with the added element of a matte shot, added greatly to the scope of the production.

The Bush Monster is effective, as well. In fact, so much so that it was also featured in episodes of *Voyage to the Bottom of the Sea*.

Early episodes included many firsts for the series, and this one is no exception. This was the first time we saw Dr. Smith clutch Will to himself, using the boy as a shield, and letting out a scream that at the time would be called womanly. The character is not yet camp, but the effort to soften his edges was accelerating.

Script:

Story Assignment 8457 (Production #8511)
Peter Packer's treatment, plus 1st draft teleplay: Early October 1965.
Packer's 2nd draft teleplay: October 14, 1965.
Reformatted Mimeo Department Shooting Final teleplay: Late October 1965
Tony Wilson's script polish (Rev. Shooting Final teleplay): October 28.
Page revisions by Wilson (blue insert pages): October 29.
Additional page revisions by Wilson (blue page inserts): November 2.
Further revisions by Wilson (pink insert pages): November 3.
Further revisions by Wilson (gold insert pages): November 9.
Further revisions of Wilson (green insert pages): November 11.

"The Raft" was one of the first story assignments given out after Buck Houghton stepped down as producer. This was Peter Packer's fifth assignment for *Lost in Space*, following "The Derelict," "Welcome Stranger," "The Oasis," and "Sorry, Wrong Planet," the latter being abandoned.

The script is nicely balanced to spread story and dialogue around to all the regulars. Included are some good old-fashioned sentimental moments, and family values. In one scene, writers Packer and Wilson deliver those values with a twist. Will and Smith have landed on a planet that Smith thinks is Earth. The delightful scene reads:

WILL
Dr. Smith – I don't think we're on Earth at all.

SMITH
You're just a little nervous – a little space-sickness perhaps after our ride. I'll prescribe something for you when we get to a drugstore.

Will sinks to the ground … squats there unhappily.

WILL
It isn't space sickness, Dr. Smith.

SMITH
Then what is it?

WILL
Homesickness, I guess.

SMITH
But this is home!

WILL

Supposing it's just another unknown planet like the one my parents are on. That means that you and I are all alone here and will have to go on living here … maybe forever. I'd probably live a bit longer because I'm not as old as you are.

SMITH

(icily)

Bully for you.

WILL

But until then – well, you're the only person I can rely on.

(simply)

Do you mind?

SMITH

Do I mind what?

WILL

Well – taking care of me – just like you were my father … seeing that I don't get into trouble and making sure I don't forget to eat … or get lost or anything –

Smith stares at him bewilderedly. This is the first time he has been asked to feel an emotion of which he would usually be incapable. It flusters him.

SMITH

Do you mean you actually want me to – to look after you?

WILL

Well, I – I don't have anyone else, Dr. Smith…

(smiles)

I'm sure you'd be pretty good at it –

SMITH

(astonished)

Do you really think so? Of course I haven't had too much experience with – uh – children.

WILL

It usually comes naturally to a grownup when there's someone young around.

SMITH

(thinking about this)

I guess it does. I hadn't really thought about it.

… Smith smiles as tenderly as he can – stretches out his hands and helps Will to his feet.

SMITH

(smiles benevolently)

I understand.

(then)

If you're tired I can carry you piggyback.

On October 18th, notes from an October 15th "Method Meeting" regarding Peter Packer's second and final draft script shared Irwin Allen's thoughts with the various department heads.

> Scene 17: It was decided that Tony Wilson would give the "plasma" a more futuristic title -- such as super-plasma, hyper-plasma, etc.
>
> Scenes 49/50: Will's last speech – re: building a small spacecraft out of parts of the Jupiter. Now that we are using the diving bell [from *Voyage to the Bottom of the Sea* as the raft], why couldn't John say that they could re-design the "space chamber" they presumably brought with them. Then, in the montage, we wouldn't have to show them tearing their spaceship apart. And we wouldn't have to show the bell in progressive stages of construction – just the remodeling stages.
>
> Scene 51: Change "Sketch" to "schematic plan."
>
> Scene 62: Why was the Robot programmed by Robinson to cast off the raft? He would have done this himself. Wouldn't Smith have already re-charted the raft to go to Earth instead of Alpha Centauri? If so, in Scene 62 he can now be programming the Robot to cast him off. Take Robot out of Scene 81 or family would learn what happened from it.
>
> Scene 63: Judy comes into Don's cabin. He was supposed to be trying to sleep for "14" hours. Wouldn't he be undressed? Pajamas? Censors! Judy says, "... your light was on." You can't see a light from outside.
>
> Scenes 74, 108: Rewrite interior raft action to conform to diving bell. No walking around.
>
> Scene 111: Delete piggyback business: Jonathan Harris's bad back.

The piggyback ride was stricken, but the line of dialogue when Smith offers one to Will was retained. Wilson merely wrote a line for Will, declining the invitation, thusly sparing Harris's delicate back.

On October 31, Irwin Allen commented on Tony Wilson's Revised Shooting Final teleplay, writing:

> Page 9, Scene 22: John states that there's only one place we can head for with any hope of making it – Alpha Centauri. How is it then possible that the smaller space craft has been programmed to take Don back to Earth?
>
> Page 33, Scene 83: It would seem that this is the first night after taking off and it seems a little strange that Smith and Will would

> be fooled into thinking the planet they see could be Earth. Will should bring up this point and Smith could find some explanation to give him (Possibly the fact that they have no way of knowing how long they've been traveling or sleeping or how fast the ship is going).

Wilson addressed Allen's notes for his page revisions dated November 2nd. There would be one more set of revisions to come from Wilson's typewriter before the episode began filming, and two more during the production period, no doubt the result of Jonathan Harris's suggestions for changes in his dialogue. More than mere suggestions, he was actually writing changes into his script.

This was not something allowed on most network shows – a notable exception having been for Steve McQueen on *Wanted: Dead or Alive*. Current examples of this kind of input were James Arness on *Gunsmoke*, and Robert Culp and Bill Cosby on *I Spy*. In McQueen's case, the actor felt the writers and the producer were giving him too many lines. He preferred his character, bounty hunter Josh Randall, to be less conversational – a man of few words and swift action. So McQueen would cross dialogue out, turning a paragraph of verbose speech into a single taut line accompanied by one of those famous McQueen looks. No one was going to dare argue with the star. In fact, two years into the run of *Wanted*, McQueen had producer John Robinson replaced. As for James Arness, he was one of the producers on the long-running *Gunsmoke*, a position which allowed him a say over his character's lines. And then there was the case of Culp and Cosby. They were filming *I Spy* overseas and, in an age before fax machines or the internet, NBC had no choice but to reluctantly release its right to approve dialogue changes. The actors, who were the true architects of the hip Kelly Robinson/Alexander Scott banter, routinely rewrote the dialogue, to the chagrin of writer/producers Mort Fine and David Friedkin and executive producer Sheldon Leonard. The execs supposedly in charge of the show wouldn't learn of the changes until the film was sent back to the United States for processing and screening.

In the same way, Jonathan Harris was changing his dialogue and actions the day before certain scenes were scheduled to be shot – but without the benefit of an insulating ocean. He was also starting to change the dialogue of the other characters interacting with him.

Interviewed for *A & E Biography*'s "Jonathan Harris: Never Fear, Smith Is Here," Bill Mumy said, "[W]e'd start working on a scene together and he'd have a line, and in the script I'd have my reply. And he'd say, 'No, no, no, dear boy. No, no, no. Before you say that, the Robot will say this, and then I will say this, this, this, this, and this. And then you will deliver your line." (BM-A&EB02)

Harris would bring Mumy into his dressing room and work out his ideas, then handwrite the changes into his copy of the script and send it back to Tony Wilson's office. Wilson would look it over and in most cases authorize the changes, having the pages retyped, then sent to CBS for approval, then distributed to the set to be inserted in the scripts.

Sheila Mathews, Irwin Allen's girlfriend, who also assisted Allen at the studio (and would one day become Sheila Mathews Allen), said, "The spark that Jonathan brought to the show was immediate and noticeable. There was no hiding it." (SMA-A&EB02)

Mumy said of Harris, "He truly, truly single handedly created the character of Dr. Zachary Smith that we know – this man we loved to hate; a coward who would cower behind the little boy – 'Oh, the pain; save me, William!' That's all him." (BM-A&EB02)

Pre-Production:

Sobey Martin returned for his third directing assignment on the series, following "The Hungry Sea" and "The Sky Is Falling."

Dawson Palmer was hired to play the Bush Creature. We last saw him (or a costume being worn by him) in "Wish Upon a Star," as the "Rubberoid."

Production Diary:

November 8 – 15, 1965 (7 days).

As was now the norm, the makeup calls were 6:30 for the women and 7 a.m. for the men.

Day 1, Friday, November 5. The entire cast (including the Robot) worked on Stage 11 filming the Teaser (which was also the previous episode's cliffhanger). They used the upper deck of the Jupiter 2, as well as outside the ship in the campsite area where Will's mini-rocket was attached to a balloon, with the Robot standing by to cast off. The work, as described in the shooting schedule: "Robot doing countdown, releasing the balloon, with Will & Penny; father running in to protect kids, other cast members watching from ship and reacting. Balloon explodes; fireball."

The fireball sequence is still impressive today.

Irwin Allen was always sure to be on set for effects shot such as this. June Lockhart said of Allen, "I always found him to be most interesting. We were very conscious of his presence all the time. He oversaw all the details; he's very gifted at that type of work. I enjoy anybody who has the ability to organize so many people and keep things running." (LJ-ST83)

Another impressive aspect of the wide angle shot which features the Jupiter 2 and the space raft (*Voyage to the Bottom of the Sea* diving bell), as well as the giant balloon floating above the raft, is the complexity used in getting this footage. These are not miniatures. To the contrary, this was the full size exterior of the spaceship on Stage 11, with the surrounding campsite area, and the full size space raft. The cyclorama in the background did not rise high enough to complete this shot, so the balloon was a miniature which was likely shot against the same background and then added in via a matte shot during post production. Even so, a wide angle shot of this type required extra time for lighting the entire set, and then tying down the camera in order for a matte process to be utilized later.

Above: From Day 2 of the production, Billy Mumy and Jonathan Harris with Dawson Palmer, this time playing the two-headed "Bush Monster." Below: From Day 3, Guy Williams to the rescue.

Sobey Martin got an earlier start, calling "Akchun" in his distinctive German accent at 7:18 a.m. It was 6:20 p.m. when he called out "Cut!" for the final time on this day. He was on schedule.

Day 2, Monday, November 8. Only Billy Mumy, Jonathan Harris and Dawson Palmer (in the "Bush Creature" getup) were needed, as they filmed on Stage 6, with "Ext. Space Craft (The Raft)," its landing site and the terrain surrounding it.

Martin again got an early start, rolling camera from 7:18 a.m. to 6 p.m. He was still on schedule.

Day 3, Tuesday, November 9. Another full day on Stage 6, this time with the sets for "Ext. Rocky Corridor" and "Ext. Narrow Rock Corridor." Guy Williams and Mark Goddard joined Mumy, Harris and Palmer. Also filmed, Don at the "Ext. Point" set, trying to get a fix on Will. Martin rolled camera from 7:18 a.m. to 6:20 p.m., and again stayed on schedule.

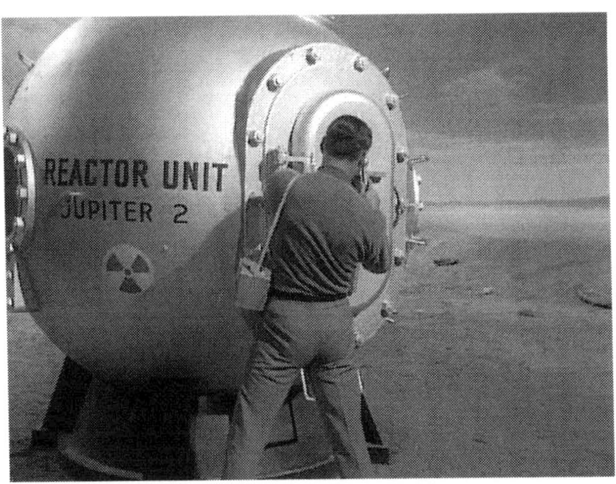

Above: Money was saved by using the diving bell from *Voyage to the Bottom of the Sea* as "the raft." Below: On the six day of production, Irwin Allen snuck in a little sexiness between Mark Goddard and Marta Kristen. As the publicity photo indicates, it was always Allen's intent to have plenty of romance between Don and Judy. However, after seeing the scene in which Judy visits Don in his cabin, CBS set forth a strict mandate: "No alluding to sex during the family hour."

Day 4, Wednesday, November 10. They worked on Stage 11, and the sets for "Ext. Jupiter 2 and Campsite" (including Don decontaminating the "raft"), "Int. Space Craft" with Will and Smith, and the Jupiter 2's upper deck. The entire cast were on hand. The camera began its roll at 8 a.m., with last shot completed at 6:10 p.m. Martin fell to one-quarter of a day behind.

"The Oasis," the ninth episode of *Lost in Space* to be filmed and aired, had its only CBS broadcast on this night.

Day 5, Thursday, November 11. Work began on Stage 11 and Jupiter 2's upper deck. Next, the company moved to Stage 5 for the ship's lower deck. Again, all eight recurring cast members were present as Martin rolled camera at 8 a.m. and completed his final shot at 7:25 p.m.. He was now a half a day behind.

Day 6, Friday, November 12. Work resumed on Stage 5, playing catch-up from the day before. All cast members were present except for Bob May. The sequences covered included those in Smith's and Don's cabin. In watching the scene between Don and Judy, it seemed a kiss was in order. But the mandate had come down from CBS: *Lost in Space* was to be a kiss-free series whenever Judy and Don were involved, or even married couple John and Maureen.

Marta Kristen lamented, "CBS really restricted us as to what we could do. Not only with what they felt would be too frightening for the kids watching, but Mark and I were never able to have our relationship develop. Irwin said, 'You and Mark will get married, and wonderful things will happen.' But it was CBS who said, 'No. No touching; no looking.' Even June and Guy couldn't." (MK-AI15)

June Lockhart sits in the driver's seat for a change. New footage was mixed in with stock shots from the pilot film, as well as from "Invaders from the Fifth Dimension" – another time we saw John and Maureen take the Chariot to search for Will.

It was an extremely long day, with the first camera shot taken at 7:18 a.m. and the last completed at 10:40 p.m., well into Golden Hour overtime pay. Martin was now a full day behind.

Day 7, Monday, November 15. They were still on Stage 5. Martin took some pickup shots on the Jupiter 2's lower deck, then moved across the stage to the process screen area for shots in the Chariot with Guy Williams and June Lockhart. If you thought all these shots were reused from "Invaders of the Fifth Dimension," think again. The ones of Don wearing the rocket belt, however, were.

It was another exceptionally long day, with Martin first saying "Akchun!" at 8:18 a.m., and, after a few naps in his director's chair, calling out "Cut!" for the last time at 8:04 p.m. He finished one day behind schedule, and had clocked up several hours of Golden Hour overtime pay for the crew.

The allocated First Season per-episode budget from 20th Century-Fox was $130,980. William Self agreed to a higher amount for this episode, set at $135,634. The final cost came to $161, 950, which was $23,220 over (equating to a $174,000 overage in 2015).

Some specific costs: Script: $1,500 for story, plus $6,280 for various drafts of the teleplay; Producer: $10,450 (including secretary); Director $3,000 (flat fee); Music: $2,500 (paid to the composers who had written the various sequences making up the "tracked" score); Sets: $8,912; Miniatures: $5,800 (including Will's small rocket and balloon, the space raft for its voyage through space, and the balloon which helped to launch it); Modification of diving bell: $1,302; Opticals: $1,630; Cast: $11,750.

Release / Reaction:

(Only CBS broadcast: Wednesday, December 1, 1965)

During the week that "The Raft" first aired, between 15,000 and 25,000 anti-war protesters marched on Washington D.C. Herb Alpert's Tijuana Brass had the top-selling album in the stores with *Whipped Cream & Other Delights*. Some said it was because of the peppy music; others bought it for the album cover. Dolores Erickson was the alluring model on the cover, apparently wearing nothing but whipped cream. In fact, she was wearing a straps-down bikini, and the white stuff was shaving cream. The Supremes' "I Hear a Symphony" was still the top song on the radio. *Harum Scarum*, starring Elvis Presley, was doing the best business in the movie houses. Bob Crane and Cynthia Lynn, of *Hogan's Heroes*, had the cover of *TV Guide*.

"TV Scout," syndicated to newspapers across America, including the December 1st edition of the Illinois *Edwardsville Intelligencer*, said:

> It looks for a moment that the Robinsons and Major West are finally going to get rid of the bad apple in their space trek. Old wily Dr. Smith (Jonathan Harris) steals the group's newly invented machine and whizzes off to what he thinks is Earth. But the planet he lands on seems mighty strange, especially to his young stowaway (Billy Mumy), who knows the difference between real life and Disneyland.

The A.C. Nielsen's 30-City Ratings survey for December 1, 1965 reported:

Network / Program:	Rating	Audience Share:
7:30 – 8 p.m.:		
ABC: *Ozzie and Harriet*	11.0	18.4%
CBS: *Lost in Space*	**21.5**	**36.0%**
NBC: *The Virginian*	20.4	34.2%
8 – 8:30 p.m.:		
ABC: *The Patty Duke Show*	12.7	19.6%
CBS: *Lost in Space*	**23.1**	**35.7%**
NBC: *The Virginian*	**23.1**	**35.7%**

Thinking ahead, from early November, the *Lost in Space* set photographer had Marta Kristen pose for some Christmas pictures while "The Raft" was filming.

23

Episode 13: "One of Our Dogs Is Missing"

Written by William Welch
(with script polishing by Anthony Wilson)
Directed by Sutton Roley
Produced by Irwin Allen; with Jerry Briskin

From the *Lost in Space* show files (Irwin Allen Papers Collection):

> While the men of the expedition, except Smith, are away, the women discover the wreckage of a space vehicle. On their return to the spaceship they find an intruder has looted their food supply. Later a small, friendly dog appears.... The dog is found to be the only occupant of the wrecked capsule; it had been sent up, frozen in suspended animation in an early space experiment, and became re-animated when the freezing tube broke on landing.... The mystery of the hidden intruder remains a frightening enigma. They do not know that it is a hideous mutant who has been secretly watching them.

From the Script:

(Revised Shooting Final teleplay, November 19, 1965 draft)

– *Maureen (into mike):* "John! Come in. Please… please… come in!" *Smith:* "It's no use, my dear. They can't hear you anymore." *Maureen:* "Now there's no sense borrowing trouble. Their radio probably went out during the storm. We'll make contact with them very soon." *Smith (steps forward to comfort her):* "'Storm,' madam?" *Maureen:* "A meteor storm. That's what it was, naturally." *Smith:* "Ridiculous! *(an expression of doom on his face)* If you want to spare the tender feelings of your little brood, go right ahead. I, at least, am willing to face the truth." *Judy (in annoyance):* "Suppose you tell us what the truth is, Dr. Smith." *Smith:* "Gladly. We have been through a barrage." *Judy:* "Barrage?" *Maureen:* "What's going on in that devious mind of yours, Dr. Smith?" *Smith:* "My dear madam, I could hardly expect you, as a non-military female, to comprehend, but it is painfully clear to me." *Judy:* "I'll tell you what's clear to me, Dr. Smith. You're a…" *Maureen (stops Judy with a gesture):* "Explain it to us then." *Smith:* "Very well. It is a universal military tactic to lay down a barrage before launching an invasion." *Judy (with scoffing amazement):* "Invasion! By whom?" *Smith:* "Ah, my girl, that is the terrifying question. Who knows what dreadful creatures inhabit the reaches of this galaxy. But I fear we are now about to find out."

Assessment:

Dependent on one's personal tastes, it could be argued that the decline of *Lost in Space* had begun. And we were only thirteen episodes in!

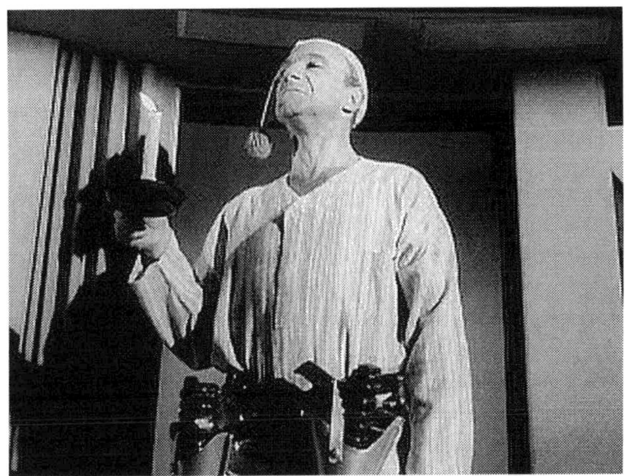

This episode was a giant step in changing the character of Dr. Smith. Jonathan Harris no longer had to sneak humor in; the writers were now fully on-board with the new direction, as this photo shows.

The writers, directors and Jonathan Harris had been playing Smith lighter in the last few installments – especially the last 15 minutes of "The Oasis" – but now, in many of this episode's scenes, he was portrayed as a buffoon. Of course, Smith had been becoming increasingly cowardly, beginning in 'The Raft," which included the first instance when he screamed and ducked to hide behind Will. Considering the frightening things he had recently experienced – the Bubble Creatures in "The Derelict"; those bodiless aliens from the fifth dimension; and a fruit that when consumed made him grow to three times his normal size – the poor man had every right to be close to a nervous breakdown. But the Smith we see here, who actually believes the little dog awkwardly holding a laser gun in its mouth is a true threat, and who, like an ostrich who buries its head in the sand, keeps running to his cabin to escape danger, is a great departure from the Smith seen in the first twelve episodes. Further, the imbecile who takes apart the ship's armament of weapons without a clue as to how to put them back together is not the trained Air Force Colonel with degrees in both science and medicine who had skillfully tampered with retro-rockets and later performed cyber-surgery on the Robot. When Smith appears in nightgown and cap, waving a brass candleholder, he looks like a refugee from *A Christmas Carol*, not a passenger in a space ship. The transformation of the suave, ruthless saboteur into a chattering nitwit was an effort to placate CBS. The pressure was on from the network after dark episodes such as "Invaders from the Fifth Dimension," in which Smith actually tricked Will into going with the frightening aliens in order to save his own skin. Sadly, the changes Allen was being asked to make in order to keep *Lost in Space*'s family hour time slot were making Smith a far less believable character, and eliminating the ability to use him as the catalyst for serious conflicts in the stories.

Further hurting this episode are the things that William Welch and Tony Wilson don't even try to explain. Was there a connection between the meteor shower and the arrival of the dog's space capsule? Did Maureen, Judy and Smith actually believe – if only for a while – that the little dog could have ripped apart those food tins? At the end of the episode, we see the Mutant crawl back into his sand pit, but couldn't someone in the party have at least suggested that the creature had learned a bitter lesson and would likely not return? Just because the Mutant has retreated does not mean it will not return. Another problem with the ending ... or the lack of an ending: The dog vanishes and is immediately forgotten about by all involved ... except the viewing audience. What happened to it?

Fortunately, this episode was an exception and not the rule at this stage of the series' development. There are many more serious episodes yet to come before the First Season would end.

Despite what doesn't work, there were several things to appreciate. The writers actually utilized the characters of Maureen and Judy; the night lighting and camerawork are beautiful, as always in these black-and-white episodes, to the credit of lighting director Clyde Taylor and cinematographer Gene Polito; the direction by Sutton Roley is fresh and inventive; art direction is also first-rate. Note in particular the smoldering meteorite pits and the sand-like material the Mutant is able to burrow in and out from.

"One of Our Dogs Is Missing" is missing much – including an ending – but it nonetheless entertains and is beautifully directed. Just don't expect it to make any sense.

Script:

Story Assignment 8452 (Production #8513)
William Welch's treatment, plus 1st and 2nd draft teleplays: October 1965.
Reformatted Mimeo Department Shooting Final teleplay: Early November 1965.
Tony Wilson's script polish (Revised Shooting Final teleplay): November 10, 1965.
Wilson's page revisions (purple page inserts): November 11.
Additional page revisions by Wilson (on yellow paper): November 15.
Further revisions by Wilson (blue paper): November 16.
Further revisions by Wilson (orange paper): November 19.

William Welch returned for his second *Lost in Space* script assignment. "One of Our Dogs Is Missing" was typical of many of the scripts from Welch, who wrote more episodes of *Voyage to the Bottom of the Sea* than any other writer. He was capable of good work, and did write many entertaining episodes for *Voyage*, but he was also prone to hurry through his script assignments. Allen kept Welch busy on *Voyage* (with a staggering thirty-four assignments), *The Time Tunnel* (with eight) and *Land of the Giants* (with ten). Welch would only write four scripts for *Lost in Space*, and the first of those – "The Hungry Sea" – was quite good. The next two – "The Lost Civilization" and "The Space Creature" – would not be as successful.

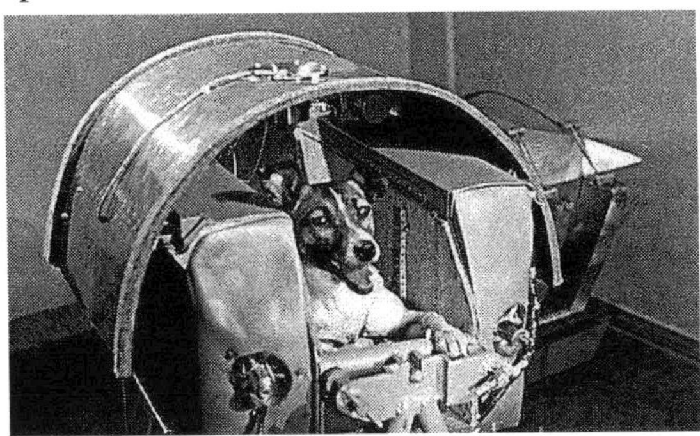

Strelka, along with travel companion Belka, were the first dogs to go into space, orbit the Earth, and return safely. Note the resemblance between Strelka and the dog in this episode of *Lost in Space*.

Welch's inspiration for the tale was the historical significance of several real-life dogs – Laika, the first sent into space and to orbit the Earth, by the Soviet Union on Sputnick 2 in 1957; and Belka and Strelka, who together in 1960 spent a day in space aboard Korabl-Sputnick 2 and orbited the Earth eighteen times before being returned home alive. The U.S.S.R. sent several other dogs into space throughout the early and mid-1960s.

On November 12, Sam Taylor, Jr., on behalf of CBS Broadcast Standards, sent in his notes. He wrote, in part:

> We noticed the revised script concluded Act II with the appearance of "the weird and frightening face of the MUTANT starring in at them." We would repeat our request that the appearance, actions, and sounds of the MUTANT be not so extreme as to unduly frighten the small children in your audience.

Taylor wrote again on November 18th, this time in response to Tony Wilson's rewrite. He said:

> As discussed with Mr. Wilson:
>
> In view of the fact that the MUTANT has been seen throughout a substantial portion of this episode, as he has been watching PENNY, and finally menacing JUDY and DON, we are concerned about his re-introduction and consequently the melee with JOHN and WILL (as described in Scenes A-154 – G-154).
>
> Earlier in the story, when MAUREEN reads JOHN's confidential files it is established that the MUTANT might try to "absorb" one of our space travelers.

> The struggle between JOHN and the MUTANT should not be too frightening; the MUTANT, which we understand will have fangs, should make no attempt to bite JOHN.
>
> We can merely repeat our earnest request made in previous reports that you avoid unduly frightening the small children in your audience.

Regardless, the Mutant was pretty frightening … to small children, anyway … and to CBS.

As it was becoming the norm, additional sets of page revisions were sent from Tony Wilson's office to the set after filming had begun on the episode, in this case on November 16th and 19th.

Pre-Production:

Sutton Roley returned for his third episode following "The Oasis" and the excellent "Wish Upon a Star."

Roley was one of the few *Lost in Space* directors to send script notes to Irwin Allen. In the "Method Meeting" as director and department heads discussed with Allen ways to realize the things called for in the script, Roley came prepared to make creative suggestions. Allen's response was for Roley to put his recommendations in a memo.

Regarding the November 11th draft, Roley wrote to Allen the following day:

> Here are my comments and suggestions for the Revised Shooting Final that you requested I put into writing:
>
> 1. Scene 40 – Suggest group starts back toward Jupiter at end of scene and CAMERA HOLDS on one of the meteor craters and we begin to HEAR some unseen creature (mutant) "moaning," deep inside the crater. Feel this will build needed suspense earlier in script.
>
> 2. Scene 42 – The conflict between Maureen and Penny [when they return to the Jupiter and find food missing] seems spurious and contrived to me. See no reason why Maureen should suspect Penny – makes for a rather trite situation. Suggest scene be written so Maureen and children immediately suspect someone or something has been in the Jupiter….
>
> 3. Scene 50 – During the dialogue in this scene, suggest cutting to a small rock above the people and having it begin to move. As the dialogue continues, the rock will move more and more until it topples, falling at their feet, revealing the dog that begins to "yelp" happily. Feel this will add counterpoint in scene and give the dog a more effective and exciting entrance….
>
> General comment – suggest it be clearly stated that the mutant came from under the ground and was freed when one of the

meteors opened the earth. Part of this could be covered nicely in Robinson's narration in Scene 65.

General comment – It seems incomprehensible that Maureen doesn't realize that the dog came from the space capsule when she first sees the capsule. The freezing unit is there inside the capsule for her to see the same as it is later when Robinson sees it.

For the most part, Roley's ideas were incorporated in the next draft of the script. Sadly, the last two notes, under "General Comment," were ignored.

Above: From this promotional picture, we clearly see that the Mutant was played by Charles Dierkop, and not Dawson Palmer, as many sources have indicated. Below: The pictures over the following pages demonstrate how the cast bonded with the little dog, who, at this point, was intended to remain with the series.

Many sources credit Dawson Palmer with playing the Mutant. This is incorrect. The production records say that actor Charles Dierkop was inside the monster suit and hidden behind all that makeup. Anyone familiar with Dierkop's appearance will easily recognize him.

Dierkop was 28. He'd just played the title character and assassin in "The Left-Handed Man," on *Voyage to the Bottom of the Sea*. Allen would bring him back for an episode of *Land of the Giants* and a 1971 pilot film/TV movie, *City Beneath the Sea*. In 1967, Dierkop played the jealous boyfriend of Victim #1 in *Star Trek*'s Jack-the-Ripper tale "Wolf in the Fold." One year later, he saddled up for *Butch Cassidy and the Sundance Kid*, as a character named Flat Nose Curry. Countless TV appearances followed, including 91 episodes of *Police Woman*, as Detective Pete Royster.

Production Diary:

November 16-24, 1965 (7 days).

Day 1, Tuesday, November 16. They began on Stage 5 for the scenes in the Chariot (filmed against the process screen). Sutton Roley took his first shot at 8 a.m. Present were Guy Williams, June Lockhart, Mark Goddard, Billy Mumy, and Bob May. Later, also on Stage 5, they filmed on the lower deck of the Jupiter 2, with Lockhart, Kristen, Cartwright and

Day 2: Filming on the lower deck set, and a series of scenes which redefined the character of Dr. Smith.

Harris. Roley completed his last shot at 6:43 p.m. He started strong, finishing this first day of production on schedule.

Roley said, "That was pure comic strip. Their adventures were pretty unbelievable. You had to treat it like *Macbeth*. You couldn't just say, 'This is garbage.' As a family show, it worked." (SR-SL95)

Day 2, Wednesday, November 17. Work resumed on Stage 5 and the lower deck of the Jupiter 2. Among the scenes filmed was the nonsensical one depicting Smith's disassembling the weapons. Charles Dierkop joined the cast for one of the sequences. It was a brief one – with the Mutant pulling open the crash shields on the lower deck's viewport and looking in. This was one of the scenes Sam Taylor at CBS had taken issue with. Nonetheless, as filmed, it might have generated a fair amount of fright … if it hadn't come at the end of the silly business involving Smith taking apart the weapons. Perhaps there was a method to the madness after all.

Regarding the makeup and costume, a different scene in the script described the Mutant this way:

> The earth behind some rocks begins to heave. Then a hairy hand emerges from the ground followed by the rest of the MUTANT. It crawls along the surface to the rocks, raises itself and looks beyond them to the group with cold, beady eyes. It is a monstrous-looking beast with a face resembling a gorilla's. On its sloping forehead are bony appendages like the horns of a goat. Its arms are long, hairy and dangling, its thick torso matted with coarse black hair, and its legs bent like the legs of a goat, ending in cloven hooves.

This was one reason why Irwin Allen liked to hire William Welch: Welch came up with good monsters.

Sutton Roley filmed between 8 a.m. and 6:30 p.m. He was still on schedule.

CBS aired "The Sky Is Falling," the eighth episode of *Lost in Space*, for the only time on this night.

Above and middle images: A big welcome to a new cast member. Far bottom: John Robinson to the rescue. Each laser beam used in the series cost $200 to animate.

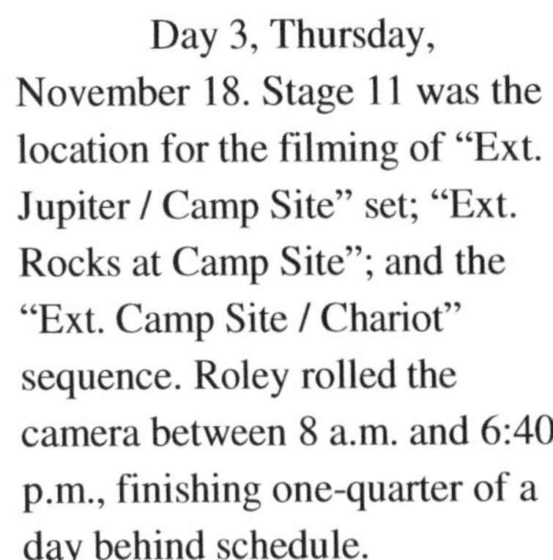

Day 3, Thursday, November 18. Stage 11 was the location for the filming of "Ext. Jupiter / Camp Site" set; "Ext. Rocks at Camp Site"; and the "Ext. Camp Site / Chariot" sequence. Roley rolled the camera between 8 a.m. and 6:40 p.m., finishing one-quarter of a day behind schedule.

Day 4, Friday, November 19. They continued to work on Stage 11, at the "Ext. Jupiter 2 and Camp Area" set; then onto the "Int. Jupiter 2 Upper Deck" set. Roley filmed between 8 a.m. to 8:10 p.m. He was into Golden Hours overtime when he called for a wrap, but otherwise held at one-quarter of a day behind schedule.

Day 5, Monday, November 22. They worked on Stage 6, at "Ext. Rugged Terrain & Craters" set. Next: the "Ext. Rock Terrain" set, with Kristen being pursued by the Mutant; followed by a scene featuring Williams and Goddard. Lastly, the "Ext. Desolate Area" set, requiring Williams, Goddard, Kristen and the Mutant. This was an extremely long and challenging day's work, with Roley filming from 8 a.m. to 11 p.m., deep into Golden Hours. It took all that time for him to hold at one-quarter of a day behind.

Day 6, Tuesday, November 23. Because of the late hour in which they had worked the night before, the camera didn't begin its roll until 9 a.m. They were back on Stage 6 for work on the "Ext. Rugged Terrain and Boulders" set with Lockhart, Kristen and the Mutant. Next: the "Ext. Rugged Grounds"; "Ext. Will's Trail"; and "Ext. Robinson's Trail." Present for the final sequence were Williams,

Goddard, Kristen, and Mumy. Roley filmed until 8:15 p.m., again into Golden Hours. When they called for a wrap, he had fallen to one-half of a day behind.

Day 7, Wednesday, November 24. The next episode to film, "Attack of the Monster Plants," was pushed back a day. Meanwhile, the company continued to work on Stage 6 with more action requiring the dog and the Mutant. Roley filmed from 8 a.m. to 11:28 p.m., deep into Golden Hours. He finished his episode a full day behind schedule, and had racked up over ten hours of overtime pay for the crew.

With the press of a finger, and the addition of the animated laser beam, another $200 would be spent. That equates to over $1,500 in 2016.

"Wish Upon a Star," the eleventh episode of *Lost in Space* (both in production and broadcast order) had its first of two CBS airings this night.

Post-Production:

The dog was planned to be a new member of the cast, and a "Tag" scene in the November 10th Shooting Final teleplay had Smith and the Robot watching as the entire family played with the dog near the Jupiter 2. The dog approached Smith to retrieve a toy that had been tossed by Will, then barked at Smith before running back to the others. The script read:

SMITH
What did he mean by *that*?

ROBOT
Meaning somewhat obscured.

SMITH
Well, it's altogether plain to me. This clever spy has wormed himself into their confidence now. No telling what foul deeds are hatching in that sinister brain. Mark my words, we haven't seen the last of this.
(darkly)
Not by any means.

HOLD ON Smith's dour expression as he looks with fear and distaste at the family group. FADE OUT.

This scene was removed from the episode. The dog had cost them time while filming, and, as Irwin Allen was fond of saying, "Time is money." Allen was known for tearing pages from a script to get a production back onto schedule. Removing a dog from the series was no worse … or so he thought.

Sutton Roley lamented, "You work a yard harder in TV, but by the time it's edited, your effort only shows an inch." (SR-SL95)

The mandated series budget for each episode set by 20th Century-Fox was $130,980. This episode was proposed to cost $135,817, which William Self approved. The final cost, however, climbed to $164,103.

Release / Reaction:

(CBS premiere air date: Wednesday, December 8, 1965)
(Network repeat broadcast: Wednesday, August 24, 1966)

The week "One of Our Dogs" first aired, Gemini 7 was launched by NASA; A *Charlie Brown Christmas* premiered on CBS; "Turn, Turn, Turn" by the Byrds was getting the most play on American Top 40 radio stations; *Whipped Cream & Other Delights* by Herb Alpert's Tijuana Brass remained the top-selling record album in the land; and the *Los Angeles Times* Sunday TV magazine (from December 5, 1965) featured an article on Jonathan Harris. Aleene MacMinn wrote:

The title character of this episode – that little dog – was hardly going to tease newspaper readers into watching tonight's episode, so CBS chose to distribute this picture instead. June Lockhart in danger! That might make for a good filler photo in TV listing sections of your local newspapers. And it did. The picture was widely circulated in print.

> Jonathan Harris claims he has the distinction of being the first spy in outer space. Not that he has sold out to some foreign power. Harris does his spying on *Lost in Space*, the adventure series which airs on CBS every Wednesday night. "I think this series presages things to come," commented Harris the other day. "I know that we're going to have spies in outer space. As for this series, I love being the villain or the heavy. And I think this particular villain comes out kind of funny. He's very hissable."
>
> *Lost in Space* is the third series for Harris and he says he's yet to play anything "really straight." "I never get the girl because I've always just killed her," he laughed. "It's fun being the character man, though, and when you're playing character parts, you don't have to worry about your looks. I don't have to fight the gray hair. In fact, I use a blue rinse to make it look grayer. I've been doing these roles for 20 years and finally I'm getting old enough to fit them."

Harris's hair had become noticeably grayer since we first saw him in "The Reluctant Stowaway." It was all part of the softening of the character of Dr. Smith. Gray-haired men seemed less threatening than dark-haired ones. Or so Harris believed.

When asked by MacMinn if he missed working on the stage, Harris answered, "It's good to face an audience *vis-à-vis*, because it's not scissors [cutting film], not a camera, it's you doing the work. But I refuse to team up with some of my confreres in knocking television. I love it. It pays lovely money and I don't feel I've sacrificed one thing. I'm doing the same thing I've always wanted to do – act – and I'm grateful that I've had three series. May it continue." (JH-LAT65)

"TV Key," a syndicated column carried in the December 8, 1966 issue of the Madison *Wisconsin State Journal*, among others newspapers, said:

> Meteor showers and new animals on the planet kindle interest for fans. One of the visitors is a dog, and the other a mutant, a real oddity to keep the kiddies properly puzzled. The plot isn't particularly suspenseful, but the new characters carry the show.

The A.C. Nielsen 30-City Ratings survey for December 8, 1965 reported that *Lost in Space* was still the show to beat during the family hour on Wednesday nights.

Network / Program:	Rating	Audience Share:
7:30 – 8 p.m.:		
ABC: *Ozzie and Harriet*	11.8	20.2%
CBS: *Lost in Space*	**21.5**	**36.9%**
NBC: *The Virginian*	17.7	30.4%
8 – 8:30 p.m.:		
ABC: *The Patty Duke Show*	12.9	21.5%
CBS: *Lost in Space*	**21.8**	**36.3%**
NBC: *The Virginian*	20.3	33.8%

Remarkably, this substandard episode was chosen for a network repeat airing, while the five-episode story arc that opened the series, as well as many other quality segments, such as "Welcome Stranger" and "My Friend, Mr. Nobody," were passed over. One reason those superior episodes did not repeat on CBS is that the characters of Smith and the Robot had been altered so greatly by the end of the season that televising the earlier segments might confuse newer audience members. It was one thing to gradually soften the Smith character and humanize the Robot over a period of six months, but to air an early episode in which Smith was his original sinister self – that might be too jarring to the audience. Besides, CBS preferred the lighter-toned episodes with the Smith-and-Robot comedy team.

24

Episode 14: "Attack of the Monster Plants"

Written by William Read Woodfield and Allan Balter
(with script polishing by Anthony Wilson)
Directed by Justus Addiss
Produced by Irwin Allen; with Jerry Briskin

From the *Lost in Space* show files (Irwin Allen Papers Collection):

> Dr. Robinson and Don have found a small vein of petroleum which they have mined for fuel to blast their spaceship off the planet. Unfortunately, a cyclamen-like plant, which has the power to ingest anything it finds and duplicate an image of it, swallows a can of deutronium hidden by Smith for use as a bargaining factor in case the Robinsons plan to leave him behind. The cyclamen, nourished by this element, starts growing rapidly. It lures Judy close enough to be ingested and turns out a duplicate image of her to steal the rest of the deutronium for its use. Now it grows so big that its tendrils completely envelop the spaceship.

From the Script:

(Revised Shooting Final teleplay, December 2, 1965 draft)

– *Will:* "Where did you get all these shaving kits? You only had one when you left the spaceship." *Smith:* "That's what I want to show you, young man. *(picks up shaving kit)* When I decided to set up my camp in this lovely, little garden, I started unpacking. I placed my shaving kit on this rock, thusly. *(places kit on rock)* I turned away to continue with my unpacking when I heard… *(we HEAR a soft, eerie SOUND)* … that. *(beat)* I turned… *(just as one of the Cyclamen plants sways and bends over the shaving kit)* … and saw the plant moving toward my shaving kit, just as it is now. Thinking the infernal thing was going to eat my shaving kit, I tried to grab it. *(he demonstrates, but the plant devours the kit)* For a moment, I was at a nonplus, torn between fear of the vegetaceous monster and the prospect of the loss of my shaving kit. Suddenly, I made a decision. I grabbed the thief… *(he does)* … forced it open… *(he does this)* … and plucked my shaving kit from its greedy mouth. *(removes the shaving kit)* I chanced to glance back inside the pod and … I saw that the plant had created an exact duplicate of my shaving kit. *(like a magician plucking a rabbit from a hat … he removes the other kit)* It was, my dear boy, a truly marvelous discovery. I spent all last night duplicating the luxuries and necessities of life. Look." *Will:* "Golly!"

– *Will:* "Too bad you couldn't find the deutronium, Dr. Smith. But you shouldn't have tried to trick me." *Smith:* "I didn't try – I succeeded. Let's not forget that." *Penny:* "Are you going to have to stay here, Dr. Smith?" *Smith (with great distaste):* "That question is still before the high tribunal." *Will (grins):* "That means Dad hasn't decided yet." *Penny:* "Well, I was wondering – if you <u>do</u> stay, would you tend my garden for me?" *Smith:* "Your garden will wither and die – that I can promise you."

Smith (swallows hard): "Good heavens! She's <u>one</u> <u>of</u> <u>them</u>!" *Judy (sees him; is undisturbed; smiles slightly; gestures to him):* "Come here." *Smith (terrified):* "No… no…" *Judy:* "Come here!" *Smith (inches forward; petrified):* "Well – isn't this a coincidence. You and I meeting out here like this?" *Judy:* "You followed me." *Smith (quickly):* "Nothing of the kind. No – I was just checking to make certain little Will hadn't left anything behind. Don't let me disturb you. I'll just toddle on back to the…" *Judy:* "Wait. *(off his weak smile; points to the plants)* You said I am one of them." *Smith:* "Well – I <u>did</u> see you go in there the other night – and they <u>are</u> duplicating plants. But – I'm probably wrong." *Judy:* "No." *Smith:* "Oh – right again am I? Well, good for me. *(he chuckles weakly)* They're certainly handsome plants. I'll say that."

Assessment:

"Attack of the Monster Plants" is a fan favorite, and for good reason. William Read Woodfield's and Allan Balter's script offers an intriguing science-fiction premise which glides along with briskly paced scenes, both rich with wonderment and conflict, and dialogue that is clever and memorable.

You may notice that this episode's concept – plants that can duplicate a person – is similar to the 1956 film *Invasion of the Body Snatchers*. As is appropriate for family

TV viewing, the idea is played more for comedy, as Smith makes duplicate shaving kits. But the undercurrent of uncertain identity is disturbing, even in this lighter treatment.

This episode stands apart from others in that it emphasizes the character of Judy, and in such a way as to offer Marta Kristen a chance to show her versatility as an actress – from sweet, caring Judy to the cold-hearted "Plant Judy," who distastefully views humans as creatures who are not only hard to fathom, but that kill and eat her fellow cyclamens. Kristen is excellent in delivering an appropriately unsettling performance.

Smith is utilized to perfection, and makes for a delightful catalyst that puts the story in motion, and Jonathan Harris's performance has been reined in by director Justus Addiss to avoid the campiness seen in "One of Our Dogs Is Missing." And his work here is on the level of that in the superb "Wish Upon a Star." Addis did more than maintain control over Harris. The performances are excellent throughout, indicative of a skilled director working with the performers rather than merely blocking their moves and photographing them.

The production values in this episode are also excellent and, considering the restrictions of 1965 TV, the drama is both intense and even somewhat risqué.

Sadly, the decision to cop out and not show the death of the Plant Judy marred this otherwise effective episode by leaving a giant hole in the story and denying the audience a proper resolution.

In the early drafts of the script, as John and Don froze the cyclamen, the duplicate Judy also withered and died. Imagine that, and you will have a complete story – one of *Lost in Space*'s very best.

Script:

Story Assignment 8548 (Production #8514)
William Read Woodfield's and Allan Balter's story assignment: June 9, 1965.
Woodfield's and Balter's treatment and 1st draft teleplay, "The Cyclamen": Date unknown.
Woodfield's and Balter's 2nd Draft teleplay: received November 16, 1965.
Reformatted Mimeo Department Shooting Final teleplay: Midday, November 16.
Woodfield's and Balter's additional material (Revised Shooting Final, 3rd Draft): also from November 16.
Page revisions by Tony Wilson (blue insert pages): November 22.
Additional page revisions by Wilson (green insert pages), now given the new title of "Attack of the Monster Plants": November 24.
Further revisions by Wilson (yellow insert pages): November 29.
Further revisions by Wilson (gold insert pages): November 30.
Further revisions by Wilson (green insert pages): December 2.

William Read Woodfield and Allan Balter had been writing for Irwin Allen's *Voyage to the Bottom of the Sea* – having provided scripts for more than a dozen episodes during that series' first and second seasons.

Woodfield was 37. Prior to writing for *Voyage*, he had been making a living as a photographer, and occasionally moonlighting as a TV writer. In the latter capacity, he sold two scripts to *Sea Hunt*, then two to *Everglades* (a short-lived syndicated series about a lawman patrolling the wilderness area in his airboat). He had also written *The*

Hypnotic Eye, a 1960 low-budget film concerning a serial killer. In 1964, Woodfield received a call from friend Allan Balter, who was the associate producer on *Voyage*.

Woodfield told interviewer Mark Phillips, "When Balter explained he was doing a TV series called *Voyage*, I asked him, 'How is it?' He said, 'Terrible. They've got no scripts. Why don't you write one?' He told me when it was on. I started to watch it and couldn't. I found it absolutely unwatchable. I thought it was a terrible show. I asked Balter, 'You'll pay me $3,500 to write one of *these*?,' and he said, 'Yeah. We need a script by next Monday.' I said, 'I'll give it to you in two days,' and I handed him 'Doomsday.'" (WRW-SL92)

"Doomsday" dealt with a "Dew Line" system warning of an impending attack, resulting in the U.S. activating its retaliatory nuclear missiles from bases all over the world, including Seaview. It was a false alarm, and quickly cancelled, but the system aboard Seaview shorts out and the missiles remain activated.

In his conversation with Phillips, Woodfield revealed, "I wanted to do *Dr. Strangelove*. Since Seaview was a nuclear submarine, I thought someone ought to show what Fail Safe was and the problem of turning the key. It made for an interesting episode, because showing people what they haven't seen is more interesting than showing what they have." (WRW-SL92)

In a different interview, Woodfield boasted, "'Doomsday' was a fine show. Richard Basehart and David Hedison both wanted to meet me after they read the script. They said, 'This is the best script we've ever had. Please stay and write more." (WRW-SL92)

Irwin Allen offered Woodfield a contract to be a staff writer on *Voyage*. Woodfield said of his new boss, "He was not a stupid man. He knew the difference between a good script and a bad script. If you had an argument of some substance to it, he found that better than whether there's a mountain ahead." (WRW-SL92)

Woodfield stayed clear of stories where the biggest threat was that the Seaview might slam into an underwater mountain. He preferred tales of moral dilemma and personal conflict. His next *Voyage* script, "Mutiny," was another of those – a powerful and adult drama in which Admiral Nelson, having suffered a trauma and being put on medication, begins behaving like a future-day Captain Bligh.

Richard Basehart and David Hedison enjoyed stories that challenged them as actors. Woodfield, however, didn't feel that writing for a series like *Voyage to the Bottom of the Sea* was serious work. He bemoaned, "I found it very lonely to sit there and write scripts for the first year. I knew Allan [Balter] wanted to write, so I said, 'Hey, why don't we write 'em together?' Allan said he would love to, and Irwin said, 'Over my dead body! Allan's an associate producer, Billy. You're a writer.' I said, 'We're gonna do 'em together or I walk and we'll write for someone else." (WRW-SL92)

This was a difficult ultimatum for Irwin Allen. *Voyage* director James Goldstone explained, "Allan Balter was really *the* producer as far as I was concerned. That is, he dealt with me because I wouldn't deal with Irwin..... I mainly dealt with Allan, and Billy Woodfield, who was a very good writer. We had as much fun as we could while trying to please this strange egomaniac in his lavish suite down the hall." (JG-SLP94)

Alan Balter was 40. Besides serving as associate producer on *Voyage to the Bottom of the Sea*, he had written two episodes of *The Outer Limits* – "The Hundred Days of the Dragon" and "The Mutant."

To avoid losing his best writer, Irwin Allen allowed Balter to leave his position as associate producer and become Woodfield's writing partner. One year later, as the team continued to crank out scripts for *Voyage*, Allen gave them an assignment on *Lost in Space*.

Woodfield and Balter pitched the idea for "The Cyclamen" in June 1965, while Buck Houghton was still the show-runner at *Lost in Space*. In fact, it was the first story bought after the initial five scripts that comprised the story arc that had the Jupiter 2 crash land on the alien planet. The serious handling of "The Cyclamen" story harkens back to episodes such as "Welcome Stranger," "My Friend, Mr. Nobody" and "Invaders from the Fifth Dimension," all developed during Houghton's tenure with the series. However, by the time the writers could free up enough time from *Voyage to the Bottom of the Sea* and deliver their script, Houghton was long gone.

After reading Woodfield's and Balter's 2nd draft teleplay, Irwin Allen wrote to Tony Wilson:

> Sc. 6: After it comes out that Smith never said anything about the peril Don and John were in, Don should get extremely angry and threaten bodily harm to Smith when he gets back. John should calm him down by saying he has a better way of teaching Smith a lesson he won't forget. Will asks what it is and John tells them that he intends to tell Smith that they can't trust him on the trip back to Earth so he'll have to stay behind. John makes it clear that he doesn't really mean this but only wants to put a good scare into Smith....
>
> It is unbelievable that the amount of fuel would be stated as the reason for not being able to take Smith back as it would be too easy for them to leave some of their unnecessary supplies like chairs and tables, etc., in order to lighten the load. This is why the fact that they can't trust him is a stronger excuse for leaving him. This problem comes up throughout the script....
>
> Sc. 86, P. 49: During this eating scene we should see that Smith is becoming suspicious of [Plant] Judy's true identity. This would tie in better with his stealthy departure from the ship later that night in Sc. 88, P. 50. His reason for going should be to check on the plants to see for sure if [the real] Judy really did manage to escape. It is unlikely that he would still have any of his belongings back at his campsite since he had Will working all that morning, putting his things back on the ship. It might lend some added excitement to the scene if Smith heard a sound just as he was about to leave the ship which forced him to hide behind a panel to avoid being seen. He would then witness Judy's departure and follow her.

Woodfield and Balter provided a third draft of their script, *gratis*, adding in the changes requested by Allen.

On November 16, also pertaining to Woodfield's and Balter's 2nd Draft teleplay, Sam Taylor, Jr., of CBS Practices and Standards, wrote:

> As discussed with Mr. Wilson:
>
> Page 20, Scene 23: In SMITH's line, please delete the mention of the Deity.
>
> Scenes 62-67: We assume the sequence wherein JUDY goes into the cyclamen pod will be handled in such a way that it will not be excessively frightening.
>
> Page 54, Scene 104: SMITH should not say "Good Lord!" Perhaps he could say, "Good heavens!"
>
> Page 62, Scene 119: Please do not allow the insert of the imprint of JOHN's fingers on the plant JUDY's arm to be unduly gruesome.
>
> Page 70, Scene 132: The death of the plant JUDY will not take place in the presence of WILL and PENNY. We would also strongly prefer that it be seen only in the distance.

Irwin Allen wanted more changes. He wrote to Wilson:

> Sc. 126, P. 67: Take out the death of the plant Judy as this would be too gruesome for the family to witness as well as the audience. Perhaps the men should take her with them or she should make good her escape so that we will not see her death.
>
> Sc. 132, P. 70: Death of the plant Judy is still bothersome. It would be better if she escaped somehow from the ship and disintegrated outside because of the cold. In this way only Maureen would be able to see her die and could keep Will and Penny from witnessing this.
>
> The problem of the two canisters which Smith has is still not resolved. Having them means that he would naturally think that the ship still could make it back to Earth. This point should be brought up in the tag and Smith would then be told that he was foolish to believe that the ship could work with only two canisters. The fact is they needed at least five for a lift off.

While the conversations would continue as to how to eliminate the "Plant Judy" without upsetting CBS, Tony Wilson ignored the latter note from Allen. With two series to oversee and a new pilot film for ABC (*The Time Tunnel*), Allen would often forget about the changes he had asked to see.

ABC executive Lew Hunter, the network liaison to *Voyage to the Bottom of the Sea*, *The Time Tunnel*, and *Land of the Giants*, was often a visitor to the Irwin Allen production offices. Regarding the working relationship between Allen and Wilson, an amused Hunter noted, "Irwin really admired Tony, and liked to have him around, because Tony gave him something that nobody else could give him, which was something called 'quality.' So he was very protective of Tony. And Tony was very acquiescent. He would say, 'Yeah, yeah, Irwin, that's great.' Then he would go ahead and do it his way. And Irwin wouldn't remember what he had asked for, and wouldn't know that he wasn't seeing what he had asked for. That was very much like Tony." (LH-AI15)

The following day, after reading Wilson's "Revised Shooting Final" draft, Allen wrote:

> Sc. 118, P. 61: Don says they don't have any more deutronium. When did they discover that their supply had been stolen? There should be a scene early in Act Four regarding this and the fact that now they can't leave the planet. It should also be remembered that Smith still has his two canisters. These could be done away with by having the plant Judy find them after she is told that Smith tried to trick her.

Wilson again ignored Allen. And Allen probably didn't have a clue.

Where in previous drafts, the "Plant Judy" had died on the Jupiter 2 in front of Maureen and the children, Tony Wilson followed his instructions and changed this, for the November 29 draft. The scene read:

> 132. INT. JUPITER 2 UPPER DECK – DAY
>
> MED. SHOT. Maureen, Will, Penny are grouped around the plant "Judy." She is panting for breath. Then, suddenly, she leaps to her feet and starts for the hatch. She dashes through it.
>
> A-132. ANGLE THROUGH HATCH
>
> "Judy" reaches the edge of the camp area then wavers for a moment, and sinks gently to the group and is still.
>
> B-132. BACK TO SHOT as Penny, Will and Maureen stare out the hatch. Penny runs to her mother's arms.
>
> MAUREEN
>
> I know, darling. I know. But it's going to be all right. I think this may mean Daddy's found our own Judy.

On November 29th, Sam Taylor, Jr. followed up with Wilson:

> Page 70, Scenes A-132 – B132: We had previously discussed with you our concern over the sequence where the plant JUDY dies in the presence of the children. You have assured us that scenes 122-124 when the plant JUDY reveals she is not the real JUDY, will take place in the presence of WILL and PENNY. If this is the case and the children knew that it is not their actual sister who is dying in front of their eyes, Scenes A-132 – B-132 will be acceptable.

They now had the blessing of CBS. So what went wrong? The answer: conflicting schedules. By including Billy Mumy and Angela Cartwright in the scene when Plant Judy is interrogated by John, Don and Maureen, would have necessitated taking Mumy and Cartwright out of the studio classroom for additional hours – and they were already needed for other scenes scheduled for that day. The easiest thing to do was just to drop the whole messy affair.

Plant Judy would have to shrivel up and die off camera. Or, at least, it would be up to the audience to make that assumption.

One more change, per Irwin Allen – the title had to go.

Lili Glinski Woodfield, Allen's secretary and later wife of William Read Woodfield, confessed, "Part of my job was to make up all of the names for *Lost in Space* episodes. The writers would always submit these stories, and Irwin liked the titles to have words in them like 'space,' 'monster,' 'creature,' etc. So, I would have to scan the script and see what the story was about and make up a list of five titles using Irwin's words and Irwin would choose the one he liked. It was funny, because the writers would see the new titles and they would come up to me and say, 'What the hell is this?' So, every week I had to go to the writer's office and make my apologies. The one that my husband Bill Woodfield wrote was called 'The Cyclamen,' and we ended up renaming it 'Attack of the Monster Plants.' I don't think he has really ever forgiven me for that one yet!" (LGW-LISF)

Pre-Production:

This was director Justus Addiss' first of two episodes for *Lost in Space*. During this same year, be began working for Allen's other series, *Voyage to the Bottom of the Sea*, where he would eventually direct sixteen episodes. Addiss was 49 and had worked as a dialogue coach on several movies in the 1950s before stepping up to directing for television anthology series such as *Schlitz Playhouse*, *Studio 57* and *Alfred Hitchcock Presents*. He worked frequently on westerns, including *The Restless Gun* and *Rawhide*, and directed three episodes of *The Twilight Zone*.

Ray Didsbury, who served as a lighting double on *Voyage to the Bottom of the Sea*, as well as playing one of crewmen, said, "One of my favorite directors was Justus Addiss. He was always prepared, and wasn't afraid to ask for help if he needed it. He was a sweet and sensitive person." (RD-FF01)

Guy Williams was scheduled to work five days; Lockhart, three, Goddard, six; Kristen, five; Mumy, five; Cartwright, three; Harris, six; May, three; and Debbie the Bloop, two.

Marta Kristen said, "I was happy to have a story. Finally, I got something to do. It reminded me of *Invasion of the Body Snatchers*, so I pretended I was part of that." (MK-SL88)

Production Diary:

Filmed November 26 – December 3, 1965 (6 days).

Work began on a Friday, following the Thursday Thanksgiving holiday.

Day 1: Friday, November 26, 1965. They filmed from 8 a.m. to 6:06 on Stage 6, for the Ext. Drill Site scenes, and ended the day on schedule.

Day 2: Monday, November 29. Still on Stage 6, filming the scenes on and around the Drill Site, which included the quicksand trap. Production went late, with filming not stopping until 8:14 p.m.

Day 3: Tuesday, November 30. They filmed on Stage 6, with Smith's temporary campsite, plus "Ext Rocks & Path," from 8 a.m. to 6:15 p.m., finishing on schedule.

Above: Mark Goddard and Guy Williams earning their salaries on the second day of production. Middle photo: Day 4, Smith reacts to seeing Judy interacting with the plants. Bottom: Billy Mumy gets into the act in this promotional photo featuring action not seen in the episode.

Day 4: Wednesday, December 1. The Unit was split into two on this day, with the Main Unit filming from 10 a.m. to 7:40 p.m. on Stage 11, for the Ext. Jupiter 2 campsite, while a Second Unit filmed from 8 a.m. to 6:40 p.m. on Stage 6, with Smith's campsite and the giant plants. The Main Unit worked with Guy Williams, June Lockhart, Mark Goddard, and Angela Cartwright. The other cast members – Marta Kristen, Jonathan Harris, Billy Mumy, and Bob May, worked with the Second Unit. This included the scenes in which Judy comes upon the giant plants in Smith's campsite for the first time, then returning later, as "Plant Judy."

Kristen said, "We were all good when we played bad. And I love when I just sort of sink into the flower. I look at it now and think, 'Oh, that's so graceful.' But it is sort of a ballet. And, because I was made up of vegetable matter, I love the moment when they ask me if I want salad." (MK-AI15)

Day 5: Thursday, December 2. Filming didn't begin until 8:45 a.m., and took

place on Stage 11 – Ext. Jupiter 2 Camp. It didn't stop until 7:25 p.m.

Day 6: Friday, December 3. Again, two units ran simultaneously -- a Main Unit from 8:45 – 6:50 p.m., filming on Stage 6, with the "Ext. Forest" and "Overgrown Terrain," while the Second Unit filmed on Stage 11 in the upper deck of the Jupiter 2. This lasted from 8 a.m. to 12:45 p.m.

Not a children's show this week, made evident by these dramatic images from "The Cyclamen," only later given the more kid-friendly title of "Attack of the Monster Planets."

Even though the production only spanned a six-day period, that didn't mean the episode was filmed in what equated to six days. Because a Second Unit was involved, it was considered a full seven days of filming, plus one and a half "Golden Hours" of double-time pay.

Billy Mumy said of director Justus Addiss, "I think we wore him out after seven days.... He never wanted to come back." (BM-LISBR-15)

Addiss may not have wanted to, but he did return – just once – to direct the Second Season episode "Curse of Cousin Smith."

William Self approved a budget of $136,272. The final cost was $170,264.

Marta Kristen felt the price was worth it. She said, "I thought "Attack of the Monster Plants" was good. And I so rarely had an opportunity to really do something that would be different from Judy. So, it was fun to be able to do that." (MK-AI15)

Post-Production:

Besides hacking off the ending of the episode during the writing phase, the story was hurt by some cuts made during editing. One such cut created confusion in the story as to why Judy is suddenly seen walking at night into the area where the giant duplicating plants are growing. The answer is in the original version of the shooting script.

In the completed episode, during the scene in which Dr. Smith is banished from the Jupiter 2 by Don, Judy says: "Don't you think you were too hard on him? I mean, I don't think he ever really means to harm anyone." Don replies: "Judy, you could find something decent in the worst human alive." What follows in the script:

JUDY
I'm going to find him and tell him Daddy won't leave without taking him.

DON
As far as I'm concerned he can just sweat it out.

JUDY
Well, I don't think it's right. I'm going to go tell him. He shouldn't have to go to sleep tonight believing he's going to be left behind.

DON
Then wait till tonight to tell him. At least let him sweat a little first.

Judy nods in agreement and the two move toward the Jupiter 2.

Now we know why Judy went to Smith's campsite after dark, where she encountered the giant plants for the first time. However, when the episode came in long, these lines were cut, along with several other trims.

In defense of film editor Jack Gleason and his team – who were on their fifth *Lost in Space* assignment, following "The Hungry Sea," "Invaders of the Fifth Dimension," Wish Upon a Star," and "The Raft" – the decision to make this cut came from higher up. Any cuts of this type had to be approved by the producer – meaning either Jerry Briskin or Irwin Allen. Briskin was not likely to stick his neck out. And that meant the buck stopped at Irwin Allen's desk.

Release / Reaction:

(CBS premiere broadcast: Wednesday, December 15, 1965)
(Network repeat air date: Wednesday, May 4, 1966)

During the week that "Attack of the Monster Plants" had its first of two CBS broadcasts, *Whipped Cream & Other Delights* by Herb Alpert's Tijuana Brass was still the top-selling record album in America. In second position: the soundtrack to *The Sound of Music*, featuring Angela Cartwright. "Turn, Turn, Turn" by the Byrds was in its second week as the song getting the most airplay on U.S. Top 40 radio stations. *A Patch of Blue*, starring Sidney Poitier, was the film doing the most business in movie houses. Judy Garland was the first performing artist to appear at the newly opened Astrodome in Houston, Texas. Her opening act was none other than the Supremes. The cheap seats only cost $1. Front and center was $7.50. Larry Storch, Forrest Tucker, Melody Patterson and Ken Berry of *F Troop* had the cover of *TV Guide*.

Above: "Attack of the Monster Plants" provided fans with a rare treat – an episode centered around Judy Robinson … and a first-rate performance from Marta Kristen. Her plant-Judy still creates chills.

Below: Promotional picture for the episode, circulated along with the one at the top of the chapter to newspapers for inclusion in their TV listing sections.

On the day "Attack" first aired, the manned spaceship Gemini 6A was launched by NASA, and would participate in the first manned rendezvous in space (with its sister ship Gemini 7). The following day, deep space probe Pioneer 6 was launched. It was last heard from in December 2000 (35 years after its launch), and is now considered to be "lost in space."

Days before "Attack of the Monster Plants" first aired on CBS, the *Los Angeles Times* devoted a full page to print three pictures under the heading, "They wish you a merry Christmas." Pictured giving Christmas Tidings were the casts from *Hazel*, *The John Forsythe Show* and *Lost in Space*. Curiously, two members of the *Space* cast were absent from the picture of the Robinsons and Major West (all in costume) gathered around a Christmas tree – Dr. Smith and the Robot. It was felt the warmth and sincerity of the holiday message would be dulled by the presence of a mechanical man and a villain.

The A.C. Nielsen 30-City Ratings survey for December 15, 1965 gave indication that most Americans were very much interested in the space program, both from NASA and from Irwin Allen. The survey said:

Network / Program:	Rating	Audience Share:
7:30 – 8 p.m.:		
ABC: *Ozzie and Harriet*	12.1	20.9%
CBS: *Lost in Space*	**22.6**	**39.0%**
NBC: *The Virginian*	18.0	31.0%
8 – 8:30 p.m.:		
ABC: *The Patty Duke Show*	13.6	23.0%
CBS: *Lost in Space*	**23.3**	**39.4%**
NBC: *The Virginian*	18.0	30.4%

From the Mailbag:

From the December 26, 1965 *TV WEEK* column, printed in the Pasadena *Independent Star News*, columnist Ernie Kreiling shared three letters reacting to his criticism of shows like *My Mother the Car* and *Lost in Space*:

> – In *TV WEEK* I saw two outrageous letters about *Lost in Space*. First of all, in Cover Closeup, when the parents called it "a frightening experience." That's the most ridiculous thing I've heard of. Second, a letter from Larry Baron. *Lost in Space* is no "advanced soap opera." It is an excellent show and my favorite program.... *My Mother the Car* is just unfunny comedy for two-year-olds. I'm eleven. John Mark.
>
> – I think that *Lost in Space* is fabulous because it is not scary and nobody ever gets killed except monsters. I especially like the way the scenery is set up because it looks so real. I do wish they would take off some of these programs like *The Edge of Night*, *As the World Turns*, and others based on the same thing. Frank Roberts.
>
> – Could it be that we grown-ups are being too critical of what is pleasing to the younger set? I've heard and read many comments on *My Mother the Car*. It seems only the kids are in favor of it. I have two boys, one 9 and one 16, and both enjoy it equally. *Lost in Space* is another favorite. I confess, I like it also. It really stimulates the imagination and each episode is full of adventure with the world of the unknown.... There's always a good moral. I'm afraid I fail to see anything frightening about it..... We adults have so many shows we can see. Let's let the kids have a few, even if we can't see much of them. One Family Mom.

Further Feedback:

While some 20 million of us loved *Lost in Space*, albeit a majority of those millions may have been only 10 years of age, some who were a bit older were struggling to understand the appeal. From the December 29 issue of *Variety* (as well as being reported in numerous other newspapers during this week):

> Prof. George Horsley Smith, chairman of the psychology department at Rutgers U. (New Jersey), has written an essay in praise of the sci-fi kidvider *Lost in Space* for CBS-TV. Previously, Smith authored a book commissioned by the Advertising Research Bureau titled *Motivation Research in Advertising and Marketing*. The prof's motivation for the *Space* piece, a CBS source reveals, was a fee in three figures. In what CBS calls the "latest attempt" at "some clinical observations on the reason for the rising popularity of the series," Smith declares, "In the CBS television series *Lost in Space* we see a classical fictional rehearsal for reality."
>
> Smith is from the if-you-can't-identify-forget-it school of literary pursuit. Says he, "Fiction has meaning only when it helps the reader – or viewer – to come to grips with something important in his own life: his wishes and fears, his sense of uncertainty, his impatience with the slowness of everyday happenings. Fiction often bodies forth the unconscious, rendering it more amenable to constructive speculation and action."
>
> "*Lost*," he says, "… catches up all the present uncertainties of the space age and 'jets' them ahead three decades, showing us how things are going to turn out, what the future will really be like." He thinks that many of the show's projections are plausible – a family space ship in the year 2,000, folks in a state of suspended animation via freezing, etc. He also thinks the Robinsons, the Space family, are "real" folk. He makes no mention of the show's heavy, Dr. Smith.

With all the talk from TV watchdogs about *Lost in Space* being too scary for its young audience, and CBS so bewildered by the success of the series that it would actually pay to have a professor of psychology prepare a report trying to explain it, we could expect more changes in the show. The series that followed *Lost in Space* on the network's Wednesday night schedule were *The Beverly Hillbillies* and *Green Acres*. Those programs CBS understood … without needed an explanation from a professor of psychology. Now, if only the network men could get *Lost in Space* to be more like those harmless sitcoms …

25

Episode 15: "Return from Outer Space"

Written by Peter Packer
(with script polishing by Anthony Wilson)
Directed by Nathan Juran
Produced by Irwin Allen; with Jerry Briskin

From the *Lost in Space* show files (Irwin Allen Papers Collection):

> Smith and Will find the matter-transfer unit that was used by the Taurons to travel from planet to planet via a maser beam. It is in bad disrepair but still seems to be working. Will, although forbidden by his father to tinker with it, cannot resist going back again later with the Robot whom he instructs to send him to Earth and recall him four hours later. The operation is successful. Will materializes in a little village in Vermont but he cannot get help for his family as he planned, because no one believes his story or will let him call Alpha Control.

Sound Bites:

– *Robinson:* "Extraterrestrials like the Taurons are way ahead of anything we know about the transfer of matter. Maybe they know how to break down their molecular structure and come and go as they please, but we don't. And until we do, let's forget it! It's too dangerous to fool around with!"

– *Smith (indicating machine):* "Your father was being too modest when he said that the Taurons are way ahead of us. If they can transfer themselves hither and yon, why can't we do the same? After all, who discovered that E equals MC squared – we or the Taurons?" *Will:* "I don't think we'd better monkey with it, Dr. Smith. We kind of promised." *Smith:* "Of course, we did! *(smiles at Robot)* But he didn't promise anything. *(to Robot)* Now then, my steely-eyed sorcerer, let's see you demonstrate your superiority over this container of molecular magic!"

– *Aunt Clara:* "Will dear, I know it's great fun being an astronaut and traveling through space and landing on strange planets…" *Davey (wincing):* "Aw Aunt Clara – do you have to?" *Aunt Clara:* "Be quiet, Davey. *(to Will)* I remember the Robinson family very well. They were the first family in space. I guess we all remember how exciting it was when they took off last year… but that seems like such a long time ago now. *(regretfully)* Things happen so fast in the world these days – and I'm afraid a lot of people have forgotten all about them. *(gently)* Maybe you ought to – well – just put them out of your mind for a spell and think about your own family. I'm sure they're wondering where you are. Why don't you call home now? Maybe they'll come and get you." *Will (passionately):* "The Robinsons are my own family! And they can't come and get me even if they knew where I was. The Jupiter 2 crashed into a hillside and that's where it is now!"

– *Lacy (grins):* "Sure would be funny if I put his story in the paper and it turned out to be true. *(a beat – then)* Guess I'd better call Alpha Control just to make sure it's not." *Aunt Clara:* "That's a good idea, Mr. Lacy." *Lacy (importantly):* "And I'm gonna do more than just write a weekend filler on it! I'm going to urge parents to watch out their children don't get too serious about all this science-fiction they read. It could have mighty serious consequences if a boy really believes he's from outer space!"

Assessment:

This episode struck a chord in the hearts of many of its young audience, whether they saw it on CBS four days after Christmas in 1965 or later in syndicated reruns. It's comfort food for the mind and soul, just as many holiday classics made during the 1940s and '50s were – featuring wonderful character actors with those great familiar faces from that bygone era, a Norman Rockwellesque wholesome town, photographed picture perfect in crisp black and white and bathed with the merriment of a sentimental musical score. Should some of the music in this episode remind you of the 1947 holiday chestnut *Miracle on 34th Street*, there is a reason – a portion of it was composed by Cyril Mockridge and lifted from that movie.

The striking visuals contrast beautifully between the scenes set on the Robinson's adopted home "Priplanus" and Hartfield Four Corners, Vermont. Viewed from a twenty-

Believe it or not, phone switchboards like the one in this episode were still active in rural America as late as 1998. As for this telephone Will is seen using – likely only by antique enthusiasts.

first century vantage point, it may seem improbable that a U.S. town in 1998 (the year after the Robinsons set off into space) would be this primitive, with some of the telephones dating back to the 1930s, and the type of phone company switchboard exchange that would seem more appropriate for a movie from the 1940s or '50s. But this *Lost in Space* was not that far off the mark. In our real world, the phone company servicing Bryant Pond, Maine kept a switchboard operator for hand-crank phones on the job until 1982, and manual central office switchboards continued in operation at some rural points, such as Kerman, California, until 1991. (As a ten-year old boy living on a dairy farm outside a small town in Oregon when "Return from Outer Space" first aired, this author experienced an antiquated culture first hand. Our nearest neighbor, a mile down the road, drove a 1920s Model T car. Another farmer, several miles away, drove a Model T truck from that same decade. The phone service – we all had Ma Bell then – provided our region with nothing more than a "party line." Sharing a telephone party line in the 1960s was similar to the sitcom stereotype of a household with one bathroom – if you wanted to use the facility, you had to wait until it was free. Although phone service reached many houses on a line, only one party could use the line at a time. At that time, in that place, long-distance calls were always placed through the operator (and these operators would sometimes listen into your conversations to hear all the gossip.)

Regardless, by keeping Hartfield Four Corners in the realm of that whimsical period of 1940s Americana, we were able to experience Will Robinson stepping into *It's a Wonderful Life*. And that was and still is priceless.

Script:

Story Assignment 8461 (Production #8515)
Story title: "Home Sweet Home."
Peter Packer's treatment and 1st Draft teleplay: November 1965.
Packer's 2nd Draft teleplay: November 24, 1965.
Reformatted Mimeo Department Shooting Final teleplay: Late November 1965.
Tony Wilson's script polish (Rev. Shooting Final teleplay): December 3.
Wilson's further polish (2nd Rev. Shooting Final): December 3.

This was Peter Packer's sixth *Lost in Space* script assignment, following "The Derelict," "Welcome Stranger," "The Oasis," "Sorry, Wrong Planet" (Story #8456, abandoned), and ""The Raft."

Packer, who was not a native of America, was fascinated by Americana. That passion comes across with this sentimental and nostalgic script. But not all that works here came from Packer's typewriter. Many good elements were added by Tony Wilson after Packer fulfilled his contract and moved on to his next *Lost in Space* assignment. And Irwin Allen contributed many of the ideas, as well.

On November 24, 1965, regarding Peter Packer's 2nd draft teleplay, Allen wrote to Wilson:

> After John finds Will's lunch box and becomes worried, Don should say something about getting rid of the MTU (which is why they came out there in the first place). Don should raise his gun and point it at the MTU [matter transfer unit] but John should stop him from firing at it at that time, as he is beginning to have an uneasy feeling about Will's disappearance. Even though he can't put it into words, he feels that in some way the MTU might be responsible. He wouldn't tell Don what he thinks but the audience should sense his fears. He tells Don they will take care of the MTU later but right now they'd better find Will. Don should sense John's uneasiness and decide not to put up any argument.
>
> P. 46, Sc. 51: Baxendale says Lacy is checking out Will's story but we only understand that he was going to print it in his paper, on P. 31, Sc, 27. Lacy should have said to himself that he better call Alpha Control as he might look awfully silly if someone thought he believed Will's story. Lacy's reason for even considering printing Will's story should be that he intends to do an article on the dangers involved in allowing children too much free time to spend on dreaming up fantasies which eventually they accept as reality, and the grief and worry which such children can cause their families. Otherwise Lacy seems like an idiot for paying any attention to Will and his problems.
>
> P. 63, Sc. 85: Considering the worry Will caused his family, John seems too lenient towards him once he is found safe and sound. The end of Act 4 should indicate that John intends to have more than a talk with him this time about his disobedience. Will would realize that not even his own family believes him.
>
> The Act 4 curtain is not very exciting. Perhaps it would be better if Will succeeded in bringing home the chemical and the Act ended on his producing the bottle as proof of his story. John would take the bottle from him in exasperation, as though he were going to toss it away, when his eye would catch sign of the printing on the bottle – "Bottled by Hatfield Hardware, Hatfield Corners, Vermont." Maureen and Smith would get a look at it and all three would stare at Will in astonishment as Smith would deliver his speech as written in Scene 86.

It is hard to imagine "Return from Outer Space" as being anywhere as successful without these additions to the script. Allen was very much on his game at this point in the series.

CBS Program Practices executive Sam Taylor Jr. wrote to Irwin Allen on December 3, 1965, saying:

> As discussed with Mr. Wilson:
>
> We are concerned with two portions of this episode. We do not feel that WILL should deliberately disobey his father a second time, as he apparently does beginning on Scene 16.
>
> WILL's attitude in obtaining the carbon-tetrachloride from the proprietor of the hardware store is one which might bring strong criticism from parental viewers. We would ask that the sequence be changed.
>
> When PENNY is entrapped with the laser beam and in the moments before she disappears, there should be no indication that she is terror-stricken or on a panic; both PENNY and WILL should be startled rather than fearful.

Surprisingly, the overworked Wilson didn't bother to make these changes to the script. He was already starting to not take the CBS censors as seriously. This was a mistake. One of the requests from the network that he ignored would come back to cause delays in getting the episode approved, thereby preventing it from airing before Christmas.

Pre-Production:

Nathan Juran was hired to direct. He was 54 and the makers of *Lost in Space* were happy to have him. Juran had directed classic sci-fi, with 1958's *Attack of the 50 Foot Woman*, and not-so-classic, but good fun, with 1957's *20 Million Miles to Earth* and *The Brain from Planet Arous*. Juran directed action/fantasy with 1958's *The 7th Voyage of Sinbad*, for which he received a Hugo Award nomination. On TV, he directed several episodes of a series that Irwin Allen may have enjoyed – 1959's *World of Giants*, which possibly planted a seed in Allen's mind for *Land of the Giants* – as well as episodes for another 1950s sci-fi that likely caught Allen's fancy, *Men into Space*. The parallels continued. One year before Allen made *Five Weeks in a Balloon*, Juran directed a film called *Flight of the Lost Balloon*. The next year he directed one called *Jack the Giant Killer*; two years after that, *First Men in the Moon*. Juran was also a writer, and had worked as an art director, winning an Oscar for 1941's *How Green Was My Valley*. Irwin Allen hired Juran to work not only for *Lost in Space* (with thirteen episodes) but for *Voyage to the Bottom of the Sea* (with three episodes), *The Time Tunnel* (with five), and *Land of the Giants* (also with five).

Juran told authors Joel Eisner and Barry Magen, "I much preferred directing television to feature films. TV is a shorter assignment. When you direct a film, you have one big problem to solve. With TV, you only have a little problem to solve.... You have to do ten pages a day to survive, [but] the TV actors are highly competent and know their stuff. They're playing the same character every day, so it's easy for them. You can get an awful lot done. It's not that tough, if you know what you're doing." (NJ-LISF)

Reta Shaw was 53 when hired to play Aunt Clara. She'd had a recurring role in 1958 on the *Ann Sothern Show* as Flora; then in 1960 on the *Tab Hunter Show* as Thelma; then in 1962 on *Oh, Those Bells* as Mrs. Stanfield. She excelled in roles as housekeepers, as in 1964's *Mary Poppins*, and, shortly after this *Lost in Space*, as Martha, for two seasons on *The Ghost and Mrs. Muir*. She would also pop up as Aunt Hagatha the witch in a couple of episodes of *Bewitched*. For "Return from Outer Space," she was paid $500 for two days' work.

Walter Sande played Sheriff Baxendale. He may look familiar – he had close to 300 TV and film roles between 1938 and 1972. Sande was perfect casting as the small-town sheriff, and did just that in episodes of *The Lone Ranger; The Texan; The Rebel; Wanted: Dead or Alive; Bronco; Maverick; Laramie; Bonanza;* and *A Man Called Shenandoah*. He played police detectives in fifteen episodes of *Dragnet*, and was Colonel Crockett, a regional boss of James West and Artemus Gordon, in several episodes of *The Wild, Wild West*. Irwin Allen and casting director Joe D'Agosta had Sande play an Admiral in an episode of *Voyage to the Bottom of the Sea*. Beyond all the guest spots, Sande was a series regular on 1957's *The Adventures of Tugboat Annie*, as a tugboat skipper, and he had a recurring role as Ingrid Stevens' father in a dozen episodes of the early 1960s series *The Farmer's Daughter*. He was 59 at this time when appearing in "Return from Outer Space," and was paid $400 for two days' work.

Donald Losby was fourteen when he played Davey Sims. Kurt Russell had originally been earmarked for this role, until it was decided to save him for "The Challenge." Losby had been performing in front of the camera since he was two, when he appeared in 1957's *Raintree County*. He played Prince Richard in 1962's *The Tower of London*, which starred Vincent Price, and he had just played the young Hank Williams in 1964's *Your Cheatin' Heart* (George Hamilton played the grownup Hank). Losby was also featured well in a 1968 film *How Sweet It Is!*, as the hippie son of James Garner and Debbie Reynolds. He worked for two days on "Return from Outer Space," and was paid $600.

Sheila Mathews was 36 when cast as Ruth Templeton. Allen had already cast her in *Five Weeks in a Balloon* and an episode of *Voyage to the Bottom of the Sea*. She was his girlfriend at this time, and in her immediate future there would be two more appearances on *Lost in Space* (as the singing Brynhilda in "The Space Vikings" and Aunt Gamma in "Princess of Space"), as well as two episodes of *Land of the Giants*. Also in Mathews' future, she and Allen would wed – in 1975.

Helen Kleeb was paid $200 for one day's work as the phone operator, Rachel. She had many little jobs like this, with 150 or so screen appearances. Maybe you'd remember her best from sixty-six episodes of *The Waltons*, as Mamie Baldwin.

Robert Easton was 35 when paid $150 for one day's work as the small town newspaper man, Lacy. Allen had hired him before to play "Sparks," the radioman in the feature film version of *Voyage to the Bottom of the Sea*. Baby boomers might remember him best as Lt. George Lee "Phones" Sheridan, in *Stingray*, a 1964-65

"Supermarionation" series by Gerry Anderson. Easton's likeness and distinctive voice were featured.

Harry Harvey, Sr. was 64 when he appeared as Grover, the hardware store proprietor. He was paid $200 for one day's work. Harvey had hundreds of these types of character roles in TV and films. Prior to this, he had played a sheriff in fifty-four episodes of *The Roy Rogers Show* and a town mayor in twenty-two episodes of *Man Without a Gun*. He was also a regular in the 1962-63 series *It's a Man's World*.

Keith Taylor was paid $200 for one day's work. He played Theodore, the bully kid. Taylor would return for another *Lost in Space*, as another rotten kid, in "The Promised Planet." You can also catch him as a rotten kid in "Miri," a 1966 episode of *Star Trek*. Taylor was featured as a friend of the Cleaver boys in several episodes of *Leave it to Beaver*. He played "Tubby" in a dozen episodes of a 1962-63 series called *McKeever & the Colonel*; "Chub" in an episode of *Mr. Ed*; and "Fat Boy" in an episode of *Here's Lucy*. Taylor, as you see, was typecast.

Ann Dore sat in as the "First Select-Person" at Will's hearing. She was paid $150 for her one day on set. It was a small role but worth mentioning because of some of her other appearances in TV and films. Dore had a walk-on as a car hop in 1952's *A Girl in Every Port*, one of Irwin Allen's first films (as an associate producer). She also had bit parts in Allen's *Dangerous Mission*, *The Big Circus* and *The Lost World*. Working for another famous moviemaker, she stood in for Anthony Perkins and played "Mother" for the shower sequence in *Psycho*. She was the one who stabbed Janet Leigh's character to death. Alfred Hitchcock put Dore in mother's getup at this early point in the film to prevent anyone in the audience from recognizing Perkins in drag. In TV, Allen cast Dore in five episodes of *The Time Tunnel*. He also cast her in the pilot for *Land of the Giants*, as "Giant Female."

Production Diary:

Filmed December 6 – 13, 1965 (6 days).

They would be cutting it close to get this one filmed and edited, with photographic and animated effects, and then delivered to CBS in time for a Christmas season broadcast. The race was on.

Day 1: Billy Mumy and Rita Shaw filming on one of the *Peyton Place* sets.

Day 1: Monday, December 6. Work began at 8 a.m. on Stage 9, where they filmed in the Farmhouse Living Room, Bedroom, and Hall to the bedroom. This soundstage was assigned to the TV series *Peyton Place*.

These were standing sets used in the series.

On the schedule, in the order they were filmed: "Will tries to call Alpha Control"; "Davey and Clara decide to see the Sheriff"; "Clara tries to comfort Will"; "Davey decides to help Will [and] they exit"; and "Davey enters to visit Will."

One of the difficulties in filming this episode was that it required Billy Mumy to be in most of the scenes – certainly most of those filmed on this day. In an article Mumy wrote for the March 2015 issue of *Famous Monsters*, he recalled, "Going to school when I was working at the time was the only thing I disliked. As Will Robinson, I carried a heavy amount of on-camera work, which I absolutely loved, but the child labor laws decreed that a minor has to get three hours of schooling in per day by four in the afternoon. It can be comprised of twenty-minute sessions. So we would block and rehearse a scene on the stage; then, when it was being lit, I would be rushed off the stage into the school trailer outside, and I'd have to switch my brain from thinking about my lines and the action on set and force myself to try and focus on Geography or Math or History, while the second assistant director would stand outside the trailer with a stopwatch. As soon as twenty minutes was up, he'd take me out of school and bring me back on set. That was always a drag, shifting gears in my brain so often." (BM-FM15)

Director Juran finished the last scene at to 5:40 p.m. Mumy had been overworked, but Juran was on schedule

Day 2: Tuesday, December 7. The company began working at 8 a.m. at the outdoor location on the backlot called "Stage Coach Street" for the scenes written for "Ext. Village Square" and the "Ext. Street with bus." This was Fox's western street and had been recently used in a remake of *Stagecoach*. This was where Bob May was talking with Red Buttons when he learned that Joe D'Agosta and Irwin Allen were looking to cast one last role for a new TV series called *Lost in Space* – that of the Robot.

Billy Mumy and Walter Sande on the Fox backlot (or what was left of it), in an area called "Stage Coach Street," which had been used in (and named after) the recent remake of *Stagecoach*.

Among the scenes filmed, as described in the shooting schedule: "Will appears on roof, meets Davey, climbs down tree"; "Davey helps Will to return to landing spot – Will vanishes [as] Sheriff, Lacy, Ruth and Clara come looking for [him]"; "Sheriff brings Will to school bus"; "Will gets quizzed by boys, fights Theodore – Ruth gets him off"; "Will runs to phone booth, has no dime, runs in – out of store – bumps into Sheriff."

Juran completed his last shot at 5:30 p.m.; still on schedule.

Day 3: Wednesday, December 8. Camera began rolling at 8 a.m. on the backlot location "Western Street," with the "Ext. Sloping Flaps of Cellar," "Int. Hardware Store,"

On Day 5 and 6: Filming at the "Ext. MTU Area" ["Matter Transmitter Unit"].

"Int. Sheriff's Office," followed by a company move to Stage 5 for "Int. Selectmen's Office."

Also filmed on Wednesday, two of the standing sets on Stage 5: Will's cabin on the Jupiter 2 and the lower deck of the ship, as well as a tiny new set – the "Rural Telephone Exchange."

The last shot was completed at 6:10 p.m., leaving the crew plenty of time to wrap the set and for the cast to have makeup removed and change into their own clothes, then make it home in time for the 7:30 p.m. start of Episode 13, "One of Our Dogs Is Missing."

Day 4: Thursday, December 9. Work began at 8 a.m. on Stage 11, for "Ext. Jupiter 2 Camp Area" and "Int. Jupiter 2 Upper Deck." Juran completed his last shot at 6 p.m. He was still on schedule.

Day 5: Friday, December 10. The set call was for 8 a.m. on Stage 6, for the "Ext. MTU Area." The last shot was in the can at 6:25 p.m. The company remained on schedule.

Day 6: Monday, December 13. Filming began at 8 a.m. on Stage 6, for the remaining "Ext. MTU Area" sequences, then on to film around "Ext. Barren Terrain," "Ext. Overgrown Terrain," "Ext. Rock Terrain," and "Ext. Rocky Concealment." Filming at these last two locations resulted in an impressive visual as Smith chased the Robot, which glided along on its tracks at a good clip while spinning its upper body and waving its arms. This was accomplished by having the Robot pulled by cables, and with the participation of a very dedicated Bob May.

The final shot was completed by 6:15 p.m. Nathan Juran had directed an excellent episode with no indication of being rushed. He finished on schedule.

Juran said: "I was always a company man and made it a point of pride to finish each TV episode within the allotted time schedule. This trait of a director is important and I was never at a loss for assignments." (NJ-LISF)

Filmed on Day 6, the Robot turns on Smith to help Will.

In fact, Juran required less "camera hours" to finish his first *Lost in Space* assignment than were required for any other First Season episode, except for one directed by Sobey Martin ("The Hungry Sea"). The average was 68.3 camera hours; Juran only took 54.2. He would be back.

William Self approved $137,198 for the production. Even with it finishing on schedule, the final cost was higher – reaching $149,120.

Billy Mumy thought it was money well spent, saying, "I love 'Return from Outer Space,' because Will truly DID get back and he DID get the carbon tetrachloride and without that, they would've died – that alone makes it a monumental story.... Of course, it's silly that it was so '40s or '50s-ish, when it was the 21st Century! But, it's still one of my favorite shows. It was great to shoot all over the 20th lot on that one, too. And I thought the guest cast was strong." (LISM.com)

Post-Production:

This episode was rushed through editing. A rough edit was delivered to CBS on December 17. On December 20, with the clock loudly ticking, Sam Taylor, Jr. wrote to the producers:

> As discussed with Mr. Wilson:
>
> In Scene 51 you have said that GROVER's line will be changed so that he will not say, "He stole it" (referring to WILL's acquisition of carbon tetrachloride).
>
> Upon editing of the film to accomplish the above mentioned deletion, the film will be approved for broadcast.

Tony Wilson had not satisfied the network's script notes asking that Will not be portrayed as a thief. Even though Wilson had the bottle of Carbon Tech retrieved by the shop owner, Will still had run from the store with it. There was no way to delete the scene without causing a gap in the episode, so the network was now wanting the words "He stole it" to be removed. Somehow this appeased CBS. (The scene was restored into the episode for the 2015 Blu-ray release.)

Release / Reaction:

(Only CBS air date: December 29, 1965)

CBS preempted *Lost in Space* on December 22, 1966 for a *National Geographic* special – probably because the series was falling behind in its deliveries to the network. The Christmas-themed "Return from Outer Space" didn't air until four days after Christmas. Even without a "special episode" right before the holiday, this picture appeared in many newspapers across America and in Canada – complete with an "alien" Christmas tree.

The week that "Return from Outer Space" had its only CBS broadcast, *A Patch of Blue*, starring Sidney Poitier, was tops in the movie houses; "Over and Over" by the Dave Clark Five was the song getting the most airplay on America's Top 40 radio stations; and *Whipped Cream & Other Delights* by Herb Alpert's Tijuana Brass was still No. 1 in stores. In Massachusetts, Mr. D's department stores (there were three) had it on sale for only $1.99. The album cover was worth at least that.

For anyone trying to decide what to watch on TV this Wednesday night in 1965, syndicated "TV Scout," carried in the December 29 issue of Wisconsin's Appleton *Post-Crescent*, among other newspapers, told them:

> *Lost in Space* gets around to celebrating the holidays with one of its more imaginative episodes. With the help of a "matter-transfer machine," little Will Robinson (Billy Mumy) is sent back to Earth. He arrives in snowy Vermont, whose citizens give a cold shoulder to his wild tales of outer space. To them, he's just like any boy who is lost.

Rival syndicated review column, "TV Key," in the December 29th edition of Pennsylvania's *Pittsburgh Post-Gazette*, also gave "Return from Outer Space" a thumbs-up:

> A surprise is in store for viewers as young Will Robinson gets back to Earth in time for Christmas. Will makes the trip by way of a strange machine, but has little success convincing people on Earth he's come from another planet. A good holiday episode the youngsters will enjoy.

A.C. Nielsen's 30-City Ratings survey for December 29, 1965 proclaimed *Space*'s Christmas season episode the winner by a wide margin:

Network / Program:	Rating	Audience Share:
7:30 – 8 p.m.:		
ABC: *Ozzie and Harriet*	8.4	16.1%
CBS: *Lost in Space*	**20.0**	**38.2%**
NBC: *The Virginian*	15.7	30.0%
8 – 8:30 p.m.:		
ABC: *The Patty Duke Show*	9.9	18.2%
CBS: *Lost in Space*	**21.0**	**38.7%**
NBC: *The Virginian*	16.6	30.6%

***

One day after "Return from Outer Space" aired on CBS, Hal Humphrey, entertainment critic for the *Los Angeles Times*, announced his choices for "Humphrey's Annual 10 Worst Awards" for 1965. The worst situation comedy, said "Hump," was *Camp Runamuck* on NBC, just barely nosing out *My Mother the Car*, the *Smothers Brothers* (sitcom, not the variety series to come later), *I Dream of Jeannie*, *Mr. Roberts*, and *O.K. Crackerby!* The worst adventure series, said Hump was *The F.B.I.* on ABC. Worst variety series host: Jimmy Dean on ABC. And the worst "single performance" during prime time award went to:

> Jonathan Harris, who portrays the villainous Smith on *Lost in Space* (CBS) with all the histrionics of the scenery-chewers from the old silent screen melodramas. Elmo Lincoln would have been ashamed of some of the faces Harris makes.

Two days after "Return from Outer Space" aired, the *El Paso Herald-Post* sampled quotes from an earlier syndicated article, saying:

> Just in case you are a *Lost in Space* fan and don't know why, here is the answer from Professor George Horsley Smith, chairman of the Department of Psychology at Rutgers University. In a five-page analysis of the CBS-TV series, the professor states "Fiction has a meaning only when it helps the reader – or viewer – come to grips with something important in his life.... In *Lost in Space*, we see a classic fictional rehearsal for reality. It catches up all the present uncertainties of the space age and "jets" them ahead three decades, showing us how things are going to turn out, what the future will really be like.... It provides us with useful information – or at least useful fantasy.

Speaking of useful fantasy, Billy Mumy remarked, "I like ["Return from Outer Space"] better because it was a concept that was only done by us once. Other things were repeated a lot." (BM-LISW)

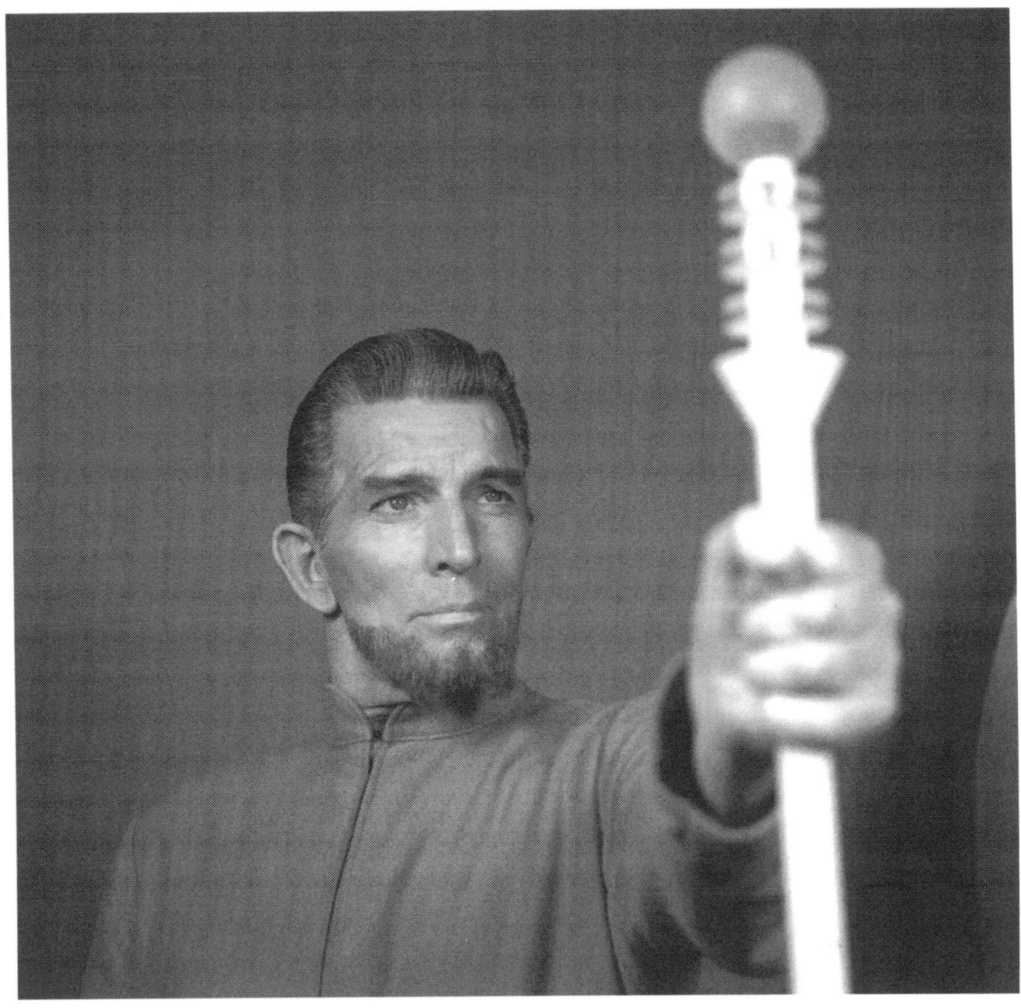

Episode 16: "The Keeper, Part 1"

Written by Barney Slater
(with script polishing by Anthony Wilson)
Directed by Sobey Martin
Produced by Irwin Allen; with Jerry Briskin

From *Lost in Space* show files (Irwin Allen Papers collection):

> An inter-galactic collector lands on the planet with a spaceship full of strange animals. He is looking for new specimens to add to his collection. Smith, with the Robot, tries to hi-jack his spaceship, planning to escape back to Earth on it. Fumbling with the controls, however, he inadvertently lets the animals out of their cages.

From the Script:

(Revised Shooting Final teleplay, December 16, 1965 draft)

– *Smith:* "You may now dig at a ninety-degree angle directly toward the hydroponic garden." *Robot:* "Instructions computed." *Will (with admiration):* "He sure works fast." *Smith:* "Another example of how man has freed himself from toil. We have harnessed the muscle of the machine thus giving ourselves more time for intellectual pursuits." *Will:* "Dad says we let machines do too much for us. He says it's good to get out and work." *Smith:* "Why work when it is so much easier to ride."

– *The Keeper:* "For a primitive people you have done well." *Smith (taking exception to the remark):* "My dear, sir, I resent the word 'primitive.' We are highly intelligent." *The Keeper (smiles, amused):* "I will not argue the point, Dr. Smith. Let us both be satisfied with our own opinions."

– *The Keeper:* "In my world, Will, the powers of nature are the servants of the people, not the masters. But we will speak of the miracles of science at another time. I have decided to make this a day of enjoyment for us. *(pleasantly, but watching the two children closely)* How would you like to come to my spaceship and see my collection of animals?" *Penny (exchanges a glance with Will):* "We'd love to, Mr. Keeper, but…" *The Keeper (breaking in):* "Hundreds and hundreds of animals, Penny. A butterfly that sings like a bird and a frog that laughs. There are creatures from every planet in the galaxy." *Will:* "Gee, I'd love to see 'em." *Penny (also intrigued):* "All right." *The Keeper (in triumph):* "Wonderful. Come, children, let us go."

Assessment:

"The Keeper, Part 1" would be a worthwhile *Lost in Space* episode even if Michael Rennie were not playing the title character. But Rennie's appearance here, partly because of his impeccable performance, partly because he had played Klaatu in *The Day the Earth Stood Still*, helps this episode score as one of the series' best. Beyond what Rennie brings to the party, the story certainly delivers the goods, as do the performances of many in the regular cast – all of whom are given their moments in the script. The score, some of it lifted from *The Day the Earth Stood Still*, adds to the overall effect, as does Gene Polito's excellent black-and-white photography.

The Twilight Zone had done a story about a human put on display in an alien zoo with the 1960 episode "People Are Alike All Over." The episode was based on Paul W. Fairman's "Brothers Beyond the Void," first published in the March 1952 issue of *Fantastic Adventures*. Another famous story featuring humans put into cages for the purpose of amusing their alien captors was 1964's "The Cage," the original pilot for *Star Trek*, although *Lost in Space* was not likely borrowing from that – "The Cage," reworked as the two-part "The Menagerie," wouldn't air until later in 1966. "The Keeper" was new enough territory on television in the first days of 1966, and certainly edgy with children being sought as the animals to be put on display.

Due to time and budget restraints, a miniature wasn't created. Instead, the artist's concept sketch was used when the Keeper's ship was supposed to appear.

Regardless, "The Keeper, Part 1" is flawed in several minor ways. The production seems a bit rushed in comparison to the episodes that preceded it – and for good reason: Director Sobey Martin, not the best of the series' directors, was under pressure to get back on schedule after falling behind. Note that there are very few "dirty singles" (over-the-shoulder shots). Sobey's work here is what people in the entertainment industry call "cookie-cutter direction," utilizing an establishing shot and then immediately going in for isolated "singles" and "two-shots," a means of speeding along the filming process as well as simplifying the editing. Missing are the effective but time-consuming crane and dolly (tracking) shots that we had seen in previous episodes under the guidance of other directors. Also indicative of a hurried production with an inattentive director are some of the performances, which appear rushed. This no doubt happened as a result of Martin telling cast members where to stand, when to speak, but giving them little if no guidance beyond that, and then trying to get everything in one take. Watch Angela Cartwright when Penny is under a trance, both on the Jupiter 2 and outdoors as she and Billy Mumy approach the Keeper's ship. Cartwright is clearly trying not to smile. Smirking like this is something a talented child actor such as Cartwright might do in a walk-through rehearsal, but certainly not for what would be deemed a useable take. Yet Martin did use this take. And then he moved on.

Beyond this, the establishing shot of the Keeper's immense space ark is immediately identifiable as an illustration over a location still photo.

These trifling flaws aside, "The Keeper, Part 1" will have you eager to see its conclusion. And isn't that the best compliment one can give?

Script:

Story Assignment 8459 (Production #8516)

Story title: "Twinkle, Twinkle Little Star."

Barney Slater's contract dated October 22, 1965.

Slater's treatment, and 1st and 2nd draft teleplays: November/December 1965

Reformatted Mimeo Department Shooting Final teleplay: Early December 1965.

Tony Wilson's script polish (Rev. Shooting Final; on pink paper): December 13, 1965.

Page revisions by Wilson (blue insert pages): December 13.

Additional revisions by Wilson (yellow insert pages): December 16.

This was writer Barry Slater's third *Lost in Space* assignment, following "Wish Upon a Star" and a rewrite of "The Sky Is Falling."

It was originally supposed to be a single episode, called "Twinkle, Twinkle Little Star." Irwin Allen and Tony Wilson were pleased by the script Slater turned in, so, when the series received its mid-season pickup from CBS, they asked him to extend the story into a second script, utilizing the same guest star, the same alien space ark, and most of the same monsters. Turning "Twinkle, Twinkle Little Star" into a two-parter would save the series money, which was vital at this stage of the First Season, since all of the fifteen episodes produced up to this time had exceeded their budgets. It also allowed the producers and their staffs to get the first episode of the CBS back-order of twelve into production quickly while more scripts were being prepared to fill out the rest of the season.

One admirable aspect of the episodes produced thus far was that *Lost in Space*'s creative staff were making efforts to explain something that even a more "realistic" science fiction like *Star Trek* would not – namely how aliens spoke English. The bubble creatures seen in "The Derelict" did not speak, nor did the giant in "There Were Giants in the Earth." Penny taught English to Mr. Nobody. The invaders from the fifth dimension explained how they had learned the language. The alien colonists in "The Sky Is Falling" were mute. The creature in "Wish Upon a Star" merely moaned a lot. And the creature in "One of Our Dogs Is Missing" just growled and howled. Now, with this script, the Keeper told us: "You would like to know how I learned to speak your language? Is that correct?... Your planet has been communicating to its astronauts for years. I simply recorded the speech patterns and broke the words down phonetically."

A little foreshadowing was also at play in this script offering explanation in advance as to why the Robinson party would be encountering many more aliens in the adventures to come. The Keeper told them: "You are not alone in space. All of the planets have eyes."

There were a couple of subtle themes woven into the story, one of which was pro-animal. After missing out when the Keeper first introduced himself to the others, Judy told Don: "I'm glad I wasn't there. I couldn't like anyone who locked up animals in cages."

The second theme harkens back to the old warning parents give their children about "Never talk to strangers." Watching how the Keeper tries to gain Will and Penny's trust, teasing them with stories of all the interesting animals they will meet back on his ship, and then offering to give Penny a miniature horse if she accompanies him there, certainly had to make an impression on many children watching … and many of their parents, too.

For the most part the script does not delineate the flamboyant Smith who is brought to life in the viewed version. In fact, examination of the shooting script gives evidence of the ways Jonathan Harris was taking liberty in altering his character. One example is in the Teaser. Harris hams it up when Smith is first cast under a spell. The December 16th final script described the action this way:

8. ANGLE SHOT – SMITH AND WILL

The boy thinks about this for a moment.

WILL

But you didn't tell him the Robot did all the work.

Smith puts a hand on Will's shoulder.

SMITH

Come, come, William. You're making a mountain out of...

Smith's voice trails off as suddenly there is a strong gust of wind.

9. MED. CLOSE SHOT – SMITH

He stiffens and his expression becomes dazed.

10. WIDER ANGLE TO INCLUDE WILL

as he stares bewildered at Smith's strange behavior.

WILL

Dr. Smith ... are you all right?

11. ANOTHER ANGLE

As in a trance, Smith begins to move stiffly away. Will moves over and tries to stop him.

WILL

Dr. Smith ... what's wrong?

Smith shoves the boy aside.

SMITH

(voice distant)

Out of the way. I am being summoned.

CAMERA PANNING, he moves out of the scene.

Jonathan Harris took liberties with the script, which did not describe his trance to this comedic degree. Director Sobey Martin, perhaps under a trance from Harris, went along with it.

Harris did more than stiffen and take on a dazed expression. The look on Smith's face is full-out comedy. Harris went beyond having his voice sound "distant" when he said, "Out of the way. I am being summoned," and then exited the scene. His line delivery leaned toward farce. And while the script merely said that Smith "moves out of scene," Harris decided to extend his arms straight out ahead of himself in a comedy take on a sleepwalker. Billy Mumy and Angela Cartwright did not do this when they were walking in a trance-like state. With these changes, a scene that was written with a tone leaning toward serious drama became one of silly comedy.

Moments later, Smith is in the cage and tormented by the "Animal-Monster." His arms are still stiffly extended out until he snaps out of the trance, and then, as he sees the monster, screams hysterically (his second time in the series, following the piercing scream in "The Raft," which was also not in the script). Again, here, the script gave no indication of comedy. It read:

> 22 MED. SHOT – THE ANIMAL-MONSTER
>
> It advances directly to the cage that houses Smith, and with a series of lunges begins to try and get in at him.
>
> 23. CLOSE SHOT – SMITH
>
> He has recovered from his trance-like state and is terrified.
>
> 24. WIDER ANGLE
>
> The animal-monster begins to batter at the cage door in an effort to get at Smith....
>
> 25. EXT. SMITH'S CAGE – DAY
>
> MED. CLOSE SHOT
>
> The animal-monster is growling savagely and trying to get at him.
>
> 26. CLOSE SHOT – SMITH
>
> He is cowering back in the cage in stark terror.
>
> 27. EXT. SMITH CAGE
>
> ANGLE SHOT – TOWARD NEARBY BUSHES
>
> A tall, bearded man materializes in front of the bushes. In his hand the KEEPER holds a long staff similar to the kind carried by shepherds. It is aglow with lights. Around the flowing robe which the Keeper wears is a wide belt which also is aglow with the lights. The wind whips the Keeper's robe.
>
> 28. MED. CLOSE SHOT – THE KEEPER
>
> He raises his staff in the direction of the animal-monster.
>
> 29. ANGLE SHOT
>
> The staff seems to affect the creature as it stops growling and moves toward the cage next to the one which houses Smith.

In television, actors rarely take liberties such as Harris's camping it up in this episode. At first, Harris didn't know if his arbitrary choices, toward which directors such as Sobey Martin turned a blind eye, would meet with the producers' approval. He said, "I did it hoping Irwin wouldn't notice, but he did notice! One day he came to my dressing room with that finger – which I always threatened to bite off – waving at me under my nose. He said, 'I know what you're doing.' I said, 'Yes.' He said, 'Do *more*,' and stormed out. And that was my *carte blanche*. Of course, Irwin had no loyalty to anything else but the ratings and the crazier I got, the higher the ratings went up. It worked. " (JH-SL98)

Allen said, "Smith was not originally created as a comedy character. He was just a villain, a constant threat in the first few episodes. Jonathan Harris was such a marvelous actor with great comedic overtones, he dictated what we should do with the character, and Dr. Smith became a villainous comic…. We loved it. We loved it right from the beginning. Smith eventually became the show's big draw." (IA-SL85)

Of course, a change in a series cannot be done without the approval of the network. CBS not only approved, but was encouraging the change. Allen later admitted, "I was always committed to CBS, from the very beginning." (IA-MC95)

What CBS wanted, CBS would get. But clearly Harris, Allen and Wilson weren't being forced by the network to shift *Lost in Space* from film noir action/adventure sci-fi toward fantasy/comedy. They embraced the change.

Pre-Production:

Michael Rennie as Klaatu, with Gort the robot, in the 1951 sci-fi classic *The Day the Earth Stood Still*.

Sobey Martin was hired to direct. William Read Woodfield, who was a staff writer for *Voyage to the Bottom of the Sea* (also writing for *Lost in Space*) and had an office next to Irwin Allen, told interviewer Mark Phillips, "Irwin either got very young directors, who were up-and-coming and good, or he got very old ones who shot *Voyage* [and *Space*] fast. Sobey Martin would line everybody up in a row of five and, when they had a speech, they would lean forward and Sobey would get the shot in one take." (WRW-SL92)

Marta Kristen said, "Sobey was a very good friend of Irwin's. Sobey would be sitting in his director's chair and he'd start falling asleep. He was not talented. Everybody else did their job, and did them well, and Sobey would just say, 'Okay, stand der, and der; okay, shoooot it.' He stayed on schedule. And he was under Irwin's thumb. And he just did what Irwin wanted him to do." (MK-AI15)

Michael Rennie was 56 when he played the Keeper. In the late 1950s and early '60s he starred as Harry Lime in the TV series *The Third Man*, which co-starred Jonathan Harris. The two became good friends. Besides *The Day the Earth Stood Still*, another top-billed role for Rennie was in an Irwin Allen film – 1960's *The Lost World*.

Wilbur Evans, the "Lighted Head" on the video screen in the Keeper's ship, was 60. This was a rare TV appearance for Evans, who had the male lead in the 1940 film *Her First Romance*, but primarily appeared on the stage as both an actor and a singer, often in Broadway plays and operas.

Stuntman Mike Donovan played the Animal-Monster that terrorized Dr. Smith in the episode's Teaser. He would return to play "Second Hairy Monster" in "All That Glitters" and "Hades Monster" in the Second Season episode, "A Visit to Hades."

Production Diary:
Filmed December 14 – 22, 1965 (7 days).

Day 1: Tuesday, December 14. The script was still being rewritten as the episode began filming. They assembled on Stage 6 for the first of three days and Sobey Martin "pulled trigger" at 8 a.m. with the scenes at the "Irrigation Project." This was for the Teaser, and featured Dr. Smith using the Robot to dig the irrigation ditch, then jumping in and doing a little digging himself in order to take credit for the work when John and Don arrive.

Look close at the back of Jonathan Harris's shirt when he is bending over with the shovel, then climbing out of the ditch with his back to camera. You can see the outline of his back brace (particularly on the Blu-ray release of this episode), with the top of the brace just above his shoulder blade and the

Day 1. Jonathan Harris remains dubious, although the irrigation trench has been dug for him! Smith's aversion to work was inspired by Harris's real-life, chronic back pain, which required a brace under his tunic. Note the stagehand in background – probably the actual ditch-digger. Bob May's legs are visible below the "Bermudas," as well as the electrical line into the Robot.

bottom of the brace causing a line on the seat of his pants. Dr. Smith wasn't the only one with a delicate back – Harris had one too. This was the primary reason it was written into the series that Smith had a weak back – or, at least, used back pain as a means of getting out of work.

Jonathan Harris was claustrophobic. The top of the acrylic cages were left open to alleviate his nervousness.

Next, onto the "Bushy Area" where Smith, in a trance, stepped into the cage, then was terrorized by the Animal-Monster. Sobey Martin did as expected, staying on schedule, as he covered seven and one-eighths pages from the script before stopping at 6:45 p.m.

Day 2: Wednesday, December 15. Six more pages of the script were filmed between 8 a.m. and 6:53 p.m. on Stage 6, including the scenes with the miniature horse, and the sequences outside the Keeper's spaceship. With the latter scenes, Harris and Rennie had their first opportunity to act opposite one another in several years.

Harris told interviewer William E. Anchors, Jr., "[W]hen I heard that we were going to do 'The Keeper,' I was quite ecstatic. [Michael Rennie and I] hadn't worked together since *The Third Man*. Well, it was quite a scene when he appeared, two grown

men hugging and kissing and screaming and howling. He was a marvelous, absolutely wonderful man." (JH-IASB2)

By the time they stopped, and perhaps because of all the kissing and hugging and screaming and howling, Sobey Martin had fallen to three-quarters of a day behind.

"Attack of the Monster Plants" premiered on CBS this night.

Above and to the right: From Day 4 of the production. Below (and top of following page): Day 5 was spent on the sets serving as the interior of the Keeper's space ship.

Day 3: Thursday, December 16. Filming continued on Stage 6 with the various scenes outside the Keeper's ship, and this brought Kristen's first opportunity to work with Rennie. She gushed, "I liked Michael Rennie a lot. He was a real nice person. He was erudite and I liked the way he carried himself, and flirted with me." (MK-LISF)

Rennie said, "I suppose women find me attractive because I am polite, charming, courteous – a gentleman. My romantic reputation is an exaggeration. The realities are a bit different." (MR-IMDB)

The company filmed from 8 a.m. to 7:05 p.m., during which time Martin, to the surprise of Irwin Allen, slipped to a full day behind schedule.

Day 4: Friday, December 17. They were still playing catch-up on Stage 6, with the scene in which the Keeper demonstrated the powers of his staff for Will and Penny, resulting in

thunder and wind. During the lunch break, the company moved to Stage 5 for the scenes on the lower deck of the Jupiter 2. Martin filmed until 6:50 p.m., and held at one day behind.

Day 5: Monday, December 20. A half-day on Stage 5, with new sets constructed for the interior of the Keeper's ship. At midday, the company moved to Stage 11 where the production would settle in until the episode was completed. First up, the Keeper outside the Jupiter 2, asking Don and Judy to go with him. They filmed until 7:02 p.m. Martin held at one day behind schedule.

Day 6: Tuesday, December 21. They filmed outside the Jupiter 2 on Stage 11. Among scenes covered was the one in which the Robot carries the cage containing the lizard back to the Jupiter 2. With this, Sobey Martin did as Jonathan Harris had, and took liberties with the action as described in the script.

Day 6 was spent on Stage 11 and the exterior Jupiter 2 campsite. This photo reveals the height of the cyclorama which surrounded the set.

As filmed, when the Robot releases the reptile, he passes his arm over the top of the cage, resulting in the transparent door in the front sliding opening and the lizard running off. The sensor device that would activate this door was in the front of the cage, not on the top, leaving one to wonder how the Robot did this trick. In the script it was no trick at all. The action began: "The Robot moves its arm toward the door of the cage." Then:

> 54. INSERT – ROBOT'S CLAW
>
> as it passes between the two lights on each side of the cage entrance.
>
> 55. WIDER ANGLE – FAVORING THE CAGE
>
> A moment and a small iguana makes its appearance. For a moment it stares outside, tongue flickering. Then it slides out of the cage and heads out of scene.

Director Martin, in a hurry to get the scene shot, didn't want to have to arrange for camera coverage of the Robot coming around to the front of the cage after setting it down, and then bending forward in order for its arm to be in position to pass in front of the sensor. Instead, Martin blocked and shot the action in a manner which violated continuity and even technical accuracy in respect to how the sensor on the cage worked.

Martin did it again later in the scene when the Keeper uses his staff to lure the lizard back into the cage. As filmed, the lizard just pops into the cage out of thin air, which is inconsistent with how we see the Keeper get all the other animals, as well as Will, Penny and Smith, to do as he wants. The script described the action this way:

> 77. CLOSE SHOT – THE KEEPER
>
> He slowly points the staff in the direction of the nearby bushes. A moment and the Keeper nods in satisfaction.
>
> 78. P.O.V. SHOT
>
> The iguanodon emerges from the bushes and, [with] CAMERA PANNING, comes toward the cage.
>
> 79. TWO SHOT – ROBINSON AND DON
>
> They stare fascinated at the approaching reptile.
>
> ROBINSON
> The staff emits a high frequency impulse.
>
> DON
> (nods)
> And the sonar receiver in the cage acts as a relay. Animals could be summoned from miles away.
>
> 80. CLOSE SHOT – THE IGUANODON
>
> As he crawls toward the cage.

81. CLOSE SHOT – THE KEEPER

He continues to hold the glowing staff up.

82. WIDER ANGLE

The iguanodon reaches the cage and enters. The door closes behind it. The Keeper lowers his staff and it becomes inactive.

A change this drastic, for which action was modified and dialogue cut, required approval from one of the producers – Jerry Briskin or Irwin Allen, more likely the latter. Time is money, as Allen so often would say, and getting a lizard to do the moves as described in the script was likely to eat up a great deal of production time. It was much easier, and cheaper, to tie down the camera and then pop the lizard into the cage. The result: more hocus pocus at the expense of story continuity.

Wrap time came at 6:45 p.m. Martin was still one day behind. The next episode to film, "The Keeper, Part II," assigned to director Harry Harris, was pushed back.

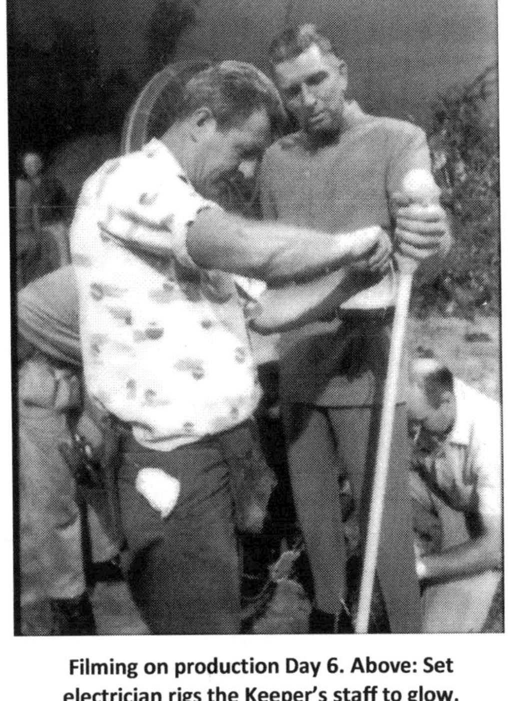

Filming on production Day 6. Above: Set electrician rigs the Keeper's staff to glow. Below: Dr. Smith is reluctant to place his hand into that of the Keeper's, and have his true character revealed.

Day 7: Wednesday, December 22. They filmed from 8 a.m. to 7:30 p.m., capturing on film the scenes on the upper deck of the Jupiter 2.

By the time the cast had changed into their own clothes and had their makeup removed, and the production crew had wrapped the set, it was close to 8 p.m. If *Lost in Space* had been on this night, cast and crew would have missed it. But CBS pre-empted the series for a National Geographic Special: "Miss Goodall and the Wild Chimpanzees." *Space* had been falling behind in its delivery of episodes to the network and producers Allen and Briskin could sigh a breath of relief that this pre-emption would buy them another week to make their next delivery.

To illustrate how bad the situation had become, "The Keeper, Part 1" finished filming on December 22. Each episode was allocated three weeks for post effects, editing, and audio work. But the CBS broadcast for this episode was scheduled for January 12, and only this late because the series had been pre-empted twice in the weeks prior (in late December and early January). CBS needed to screen the episode for its Broadcast Standards department, and the approved film – provided it *was* approved – would have to be delivered to the network several days prior to air time. This seemed impossible. The time between December 22 and January 12 was only twenty-one days. Everyone involved would have to work faster and put in extra hours in order to get this episode onto the air in time.

William Self had approved a budget of $137,858 for Part 1 of "The Keeper." With all the overtime pay kicking in as they rushed this one through the post-production process, the end cost climbed to $161,885.

One eleven-year-old boy felt the extra money was well spent. Billy Mumy said, "'The Keeper' and 'Return from Outer Space' are two of my very favorite *LIS* episodes of all time." (LISM.com)

Quality of product and popularity among the audience notwithstanding, something had to change soon regarding how long *Lost in Space* episodes were taking to film and post produce or the series would soon be missing air dates.

Michael Rennie had true star status in 1966, and this photo was issued by CBS to newspapers across America to promote "The Keeper, Part 1."

Release / Reaction:

(CBS premiere broadcast: January 12, 1966)

(Network repeat air date: May 18, 1966)

The week that "The Keeper, Part 1" was first televised on CBS, the Beatles had a lock on the top spot in the Billboard charts for their new album, *Rubber Soul*. No singles were issued from the album – something only the Beatles would dare do – but LP cuts immediately began getting airplay on radio stations, including "Norwegian Wood," "In My Life" and "Michelle." The new Beatles single, not found on the album, was a double-sided hit, with "We Can Work It Out" now the most played song on American Top 40 radio stations. The B-side, "Day Tripper," was not far behind. The sci-fi spy thriller *Agent for H.A.R.M.* was the film doing the best business in the nation's movie houses. H.A.R.M., by the way, was an acronym for

Human Aetiological Relations Machine. Eva Gabor and Eddie Albert of *Green Acres* had the cover of America's top-selling magazine – *TV Guide*.

Also during this week, *TV WEEK*, a television supplement carried by the Pasadena *Independent Star News* in California, printed the results of a TV poll. Editor Ernie Kreiling wrote:

> *I Spy*, *Get Smart*, and *Lost and Space* are very clearly your favorite new, regularly scheduled television programs. Almost 10,000 readers of *TV WEEK* participated in the "Be a TV Critic" poll which was published in mid-November. The ballots (rating just the NEW programs) were tabulated and analyzed by Audience Studios, Inc. of Hollywood and its IBM 440 computer.... The tabulation revealed that 61.38% of those who completed the *TV WEEK* ballot were women, 38.62% men. Three percent of *TV WEEK*'s critics were 9 or under; 36% were between 10 and 19 years of age; 45% between 20 and 49; and 16% over 50.

Of the 32 news primetime series that premiered in September 1966, the *TV WEEK* home critics ranked the Top 20 this way:

1. *I Spy*
2. *Get Smart*
3. ***Lost in Space***
4. *Hogan's Heroes*
5. *Run for Your Life*
6. *The Big Valley*
7. *The Smothers Brothers*
8. *Gidget*
9. *The FBI*
10. *The Dean Martin Show*
11. *I Dream of Jeannie*
12. *The Long, Hot Summer*
13. *Please Don't Eat the Daisies*
14. *My Mother the Car*
15. *The Wackiest Ship in the Army*
16. *F Troop*
17. *Honey West*
18. *The Wild, Wild West*
19. *Green Acres*
20. *Laredo*

It had been two weeks since the last episode of *Lost in Space* aired. CBS pre-empted the series on January 5 for a music special called "Young People's Concerts with Leonard Bernstein." Those kids – including the author – who tuned in to see their favorite sci-fi show instead caught 50 or so minutes of classical music. Actually, most of us changed the channel to *The Adventures of Ozzie & Harriet*, followed by *The Patty Duke Show*. In some homes, the parental units spoke up and the channel was turned instead to *The Virginian*.

One disappointed fan took pen in hand and wrote to the local newspaper. On January 24, the letter was published nationally in the "Ask TV Scout" column, carried by the *Abilene Reporter-News*, among other newspapers. The irritated young viewer complained:

> Why does the New York Philharmonic Young People's Concert sometimes preempt *Lost in Space*, my favorite show? Can't the concerts be on some other time? – Thomas Scott, Evansville, Indiana.

The "TV Scott" editor responded:

> They could be but it would only mean another series would have to be preempted. Only four concerts are presented this season.

Lost in Space would be preempted two more times in 1966 by the Young People's Concerts. CBS might have been trying to purge its lowbrow guilt for putting series like *Lost in Space*, *Gilligan's Island*, *The Wild, Wild West*, *Green Acres*, and *The Munsters* on the air that year, and for keeping shows like *My Favorite Martian* and *The Beverly Hillbillies* on the schedule. There was nothing like a classical music special during the "family hour" to atone for its corporate sins.

The two weeks did finally pass, and "TV Scout," also carried in the January 12, 1966 edition of *The Morning Herald*, from Hagerstown, Maryland, said:

> *Lost in Space* begins a two-parter which involves British actor Michael Rennie as a space traveler who pops into the Robinson colony with hopes of nabbing the family's two youngsters. At first, the lonesome clan welcomes him ("My gosh, it's good to see another human being again"), until they get wind of his mission: he collects creatures of the universe for a semi-scientific experiment [sic]. So, what else is new?

Rival "TV Key," syndicated to *The Bridgeport Post*, serving Bridgeport, Connecticut, among other newspapers, was more upbeat, with its assessment:

> Another new villain pops up in this two-parter to keep story interest alive. Michael Rennie plays the Keeper, an intelligent being who wants to capture the Robinson kids and use them as specimens. Rennie's performance as the wicked man is full of the kind of authority that will entrance the youngsters. Much as the character he played could entrance Will and Penny.

When *Lost in Space* returned after a two-week gap with "The Keeper, Part 1," it had a new fight on its hands. *Ozzie & Harriet* were out and a new series, *Batman*, had taken its place on ABC. "BAM! POW! ZWAP!" Worse for *Lost in Space*, it first episode was "Hey Diddle Diddle," featuring impressionist Frank Gorshin as the Riddler, and *TV Guide* gave it an attention-grabbing CLOSE-UP listing, on top of ABC's saturation promotional campaign – considered the most effective to be launched by a network up to this time. On NBC, Telly Savalas was one of the "Men with Guns" on *The Virginian*, something aimed at the mature crowd.

The A.C. Nielsen 30-City Ratings survey for January 12, 1966 gave *Lost in Space* the bad news … at least concerning the ratings for the first half-hour of its broadcast:

Network / Program:	Rating	Audience Share:
7:30 – 8 p.m.:		
ABC: *Batman*	**26.1**	**42.4%**
CBS: *Lost in Space*	14.3	23.3%
NBC: *The Virginian*	16.5	26.8%
8 – 8:30 p.m.:		
ABC: *The Patty Duke Show*	17.7	28.3%
CBS: *Lost in Space*	**19.8**	**31.6%**
NBC: *The Virginian*	18.7	29.9%

***Batman* delivered a sock in the kisser to *Lost in Space* in the ratings. But, the moment Batman cleared the air, Space rebounded as kids across America switched back to the Space Family Robinson (1966, 20th Century-Fox TV and ABC-TV).**

The Batman episode aired on this Wednesday night was the first of two parts, with the conclusion televised one day later. *The New York Times* summed up the ratings for the nights of January 12 and 13 with the headline: "Viewers Going Batty Over *Batman*."

Damaged worse than *Space* on Wednesday nights was *The Munsters* on Thursdays. It had always won its time slot, but now it dropped to third place. The *Times* reported:

> The highly publicized series based on Bob Kane's comic strip characters took over the network's 7:30 p.m. slot on Wednesdays and Thursdays last week and immediately jumped into an impressive lead over its network rivals. What is more, it ran up a higher rating on its second night than on its premiere. In a special 50-market Trendex survey, which assertedly covers about 70 percent of United States homes, *Batman* registered a 27.3 rating and had a 49.5 share of that viewing audience on Wednesday, but moved up to a 29.6 rating and 58.8 share of the audience on Thursday.

(To prevent confusion: The "special 50-market Trendex survey" was different than the "Nielsen 30-City Ratings survey," also presented here. Either way, America had a bad case of Batmania).

One day after "The Keeper, Part1" first aired, the *Los Angeles Times* ran the following blurb:

> Guy Williams is aboard Fox's *Lost in Space* but his biggest unhappiness with the show are its scripts. But producer Irwin Allen shrugs off such complaints and points to the high ratings."

From the Mailbag:

Form "Ask TV Scout," syndicated newspaper entertainment column, January 9, 1966, as carried in the *Waterloo Daily Courier*:

> Why don't Marta Kristen and Mark Goddard fall in love on *Lost in Space*? Also, do they date each other outside of the CBS series? – M.I.J., Norfolk, Vagina.

Answer:

> On the show the couple are too busy fighting villains to think of romance. And if they did, there is not a clergyman within several light years. Besides, the show is geared for youngsters who don't want their adventures messed up with love stories. Off the set, the two are married to other people.

27

The Inner Office and Inner Mind of Irwin Allen

By renewing *Lost in Space* for the balance of the First Season, the network demonstrated its approval for the new, less threatening Dr. Smith. Smith's new comedic role is seen in this network promotional photo. It's not hard to tell that Harris's image was added to an existing photo of the other cast members.

With the CBS backorder for thirteen more episodes of *Lost in Space*, Irwin Allen became something more than a television producer – he was now a TV mogul. *Voyage to the Bottom of the Sea*, now in its second year, had received its mid-season pickup as well, and ABC would soon place an initial order for sixteen episodes of a third series – *The Time Tunnel*.

While the fantasy worlds of Irwin Allen were certainly surreal, so were the inner processes of his office, reflecting the many splintered realms of his responsibilities and interests.

During the first season of *Voyage*, ABC had been doing what all three of the TV networks did back in that era – riding herd over all its series, and especially cracking the whip over the backs of the creator/producers who were new to the arena of television production. Irwin Allen, despite his early work in radio and TV, and his success as a film producer, was a freshman at producing a one-hour action-adventure. And there had never been anything quite like *Voyage*.

When the series first went into production, and before its hit status was known, Adrian Samish had been the primary liaison between Irwin Allen and the network. And Samish was a hands-on production manager. However, as the ratings reports came in, and *Voyage* was consistently winning its time slot and bringing in well above a 30% audience share, Allen started listening less to the requests of ABC and more to his own narrative instincts. At first, this change was not a dramatic one, with Samish attempting to keep a firm hand on both Allen and *Voyage*. However, by 1965, Samish had moved up at the network and Harve Bennett was in charge of overseeing the numerous details for many of ABC's series, including *Voyage*. Bennett soon learned that he wasn't going to make much headway in influencing the headstrong producer's decisions. He therefore took a step back and assigned one of his junior executives the headache of trying to pull the reins in on Irwin Allen. Handed this touchy job was Lew Hunter.

Allen admired Hunter. The two men had come from different parts of the United States but otherwise had much in common. Both were tireless workers. And both achieved what they had the hard way.

Hunter said, "Somehow, Irwin got hold of that information, and that gave him a little more respect for me. That energy that Irwin saw in me, from how I came out with no contacts and then worked my way up from the bottom, was something that he admired." (LW-AI15)

Like Hunter, Allen had been one of the few to conquer Hollywood without having had a leg up in the entertainment industry. Despite this, Allen harbored a fear that his position and success could suddenly slip away.

Vitina Marcus, Allen's close friend from this time, said, "Irwin told me he often had a dream that he was in a strange city without any money. There was no one he could go to; nowhere for him to turn. And no money to get him home. This was a recurring nightmare; he was always telling me about that dream. So this had been a big fear for him." (VM-AI15)

The fear drove Allen to push himself – and those who worked for him – relentlessly.

Even with his own work ethic of long days, Lew Hunter was in awe of the even longer days that Irwin Allen put in. He marveled, "Irwin worked eighteen hours a day. I can't imagine how he had time for anything else. I never got the impression that he had personal friends; only business friends. He wasn't married at that time, and he never did have children. His movies and television shows *were* his children. He was so consumed with what he did that it almost cut out everything else in his life. It was a seven-day-a-week gig. He just loved to work. And I did the same thing."

Despite feeling a kinship with Hunter, Allen wasn't about to put himself in another situation such as he'd had with Adrian Samish, in which a network man would have control over him – especially a network man who had far less experience in the business than he did. Hunter recalled, "I was going over the notes on this particular script with Irwin one day, and I said, 'We have to have this scene in the middle of the script moved toward the beginning of it, rather than so far back.' Irwin said, 'I'm not going to do it.' I said, 'Now, Irwin, you don't understand, I am the authority here; I am representing ABC, who funds your series.' 'No,' he says, 'I'm not going to do it.' He said, 'Let me tell you, Lew, I was dealing once with Columbia Pictures, and I was preparing a movie called *The Big Circus* [later to be released by Allied Artists], and I sat in a chair in [Columbia Head] Harry Cohn's office, and Cohn taught me a very important lesson.'

Harry Cohn, head of Columbia Pictures – loathed by many in Hollywood. Irwin Allen chose to imitate one Cohn practice: putting his desk on risers to intimidate others.

"Now, to Irwin's thinking, part of that lesson was how Cohn had set the stage for the meeting. He told me that Harry Cohn's desk was on a riser about a foot or a foot-and-a-half tall, so that people who sat in a chair across from the desk would be on the lower level. Not only on a lower level, but there was a spotlight aimed at their chair!

"So Irwin was sitting there, and Harry Cohn lifted up the script and said, 'Allen, this is a piece of shit!' He threw the script at Irwin, and then looked at him and said, 'You know how that asshole [character played by Gilbert Roland] walks across fucking Niagara Falls on a tightrope on Page 6?' And Irwin said, 'Yes, Mr. Cohn.' And Harry Cohn said, 'Put him on Page 45 and you got a deal.'

"Well, I broke out and laughed, because I knew exactly what he meant. Because, on Page 6, you don't give a shit if this character falls into Niagara Falls. You don't know this guy. But on Page 45, the audience is terrified, because they've invested themselves in the character. That was the kind of thinking that Irwin had. He was outrageous and wonderful."

What Allen *did* want to put on Page 6 was something that would grab his youthful audience. Hunter maintained, "Irwin did not want to do Hitchcock. He wanted to show the monster – 'Pow!' – right up front. Hitchcock liked to play with the audience, and then put the reveal of whoever it is that's the biggest threat as deep into the movie as possible. But Irwin wasn't that way. He was very frontal in his work. There was nothing subtle about him. He got a little calmed down with Stirling Silliphant, who wrote *The Poseidon Adventure* and *The Towering Inferno*, because Stirling had a good way of communicating and, basically, dealing with Irwin. So Irwin got a little subtler in both of those movies. But when it came to the TV shows, Irwin would say, 'I'm not serving caviar, I'm serving popcorn!' And it was hard to challenge that when you consider the content of *Voyage*. Or the other series he did. But especially *Voyage*. It was all action and stayed clear of philosophical statements. He'd say, 'You want to send a message, call Western Union. Now get out of the office.'" (LW-AI15)

When asked how the network felt about Allen, Hunter laughed, "We got a kick out of him! And I loved him because of his flamboyance. I think all the people around him were entertained by it. We of course would *never* give him that impression." (LW-AI15)

Regarding his visits to Irwin Allen's office, Bill Mumy said, "There was the physical impression that Irwin made on me when I was ten years old – that he was the first 'comb-over' that I'd ever experienced. I mean, physically speaking, I'd never seen anybody that presented himself like that. It was interesting, to say the least. He was a

Vintage *Lost in Space* merchandise: The Aurora model kit; Aladdin metal lunch box; Sawyer's View-Master 3-D; Remco motorized Robot and board game.

very, very colorful character. You know, Irwin always dressed in bright colors. In my mind, he was always wearing this bright yellow sweater. Or even a pinkish sweater. He liked big colors.

"I used to go into his office and he would have piles of merchandise, including *Lost in Space* merchandise. And he would always say, 'Billy, you can have *one*.' So I would get a box of cards, or a game board, or a model or something. But only one at a time, because I could only have *one*. So, I made it a point of going into his office as often as I could. And he would again say, 'Billy, you can have *one*.' And I'd take another!

"And Irwin liked power, because his desk was elevated. And so, everybody that came in to Irwin's office, had to kind of look up at him, because that's how it was physically placed." (BM-AI15)

For a ten-year-old boy on the small side of average, Allen appeared to be a giant of a man sitting at his desk on the risers. Or, perhaps, it would be more accurate to describe Allen as a giant child.

Mumy surmised, "I think Irwin was childlike in his own sense of what he liked, because if you look at the projects he made – dinosaur movies, circus movies, a television series going undersea, then one into space, then back in time – they were all the arenas that are so easy for a child to let his imagination run wild in. Those were the arenas he chose to play in. And I think he got a great pleasure out of those imaginative and boundary-less kind of canvases that he could paint." (BM-AI15)

T he

situation at ABC in respect to dealing with Irwin Allen and the boundary-less canvases he painted was not much different than that at CBS. The executives at ABC wanted more monsters on the canvas; Allen seemed to want that as well. At CBS, they wanted more comedy; Allen seemed fine with the request. Beyond that, and an occasional clash with the censors, Allen was left alone to make the series he wanted. The networks especially stayed clear of the class structure at Irwin Allen Productions. ABC and CBS felt it was none of their concern. Twentieth Century-Fox seemed happy to stay clear, as well.

Regarding Allen's staff, which he often moved from one series to another, Fox casting director Joe D'Agosta stated, "Everybody in his company – meaning his associate producers and his directors – were, in my observation, 'yes men.' You didn't have to salute when you entered Irwin's office, but yes, you basically *had to salute*. There was a certain protocol, because, after all, he *was* the emperor. I'd never met a man like him. I'd heard that expression about other people in this business – Louie B. Mayer, especially – but Irwin was the only emperor I had dealings with." (JDA-AI15)

Lew Hunter said, "There was definitely an imperial air about him. And every time he'd go someplace, he'd have about six people moving around the lot with him. He'd have Arthur Weiss, who was the story editor on one of his shows, and he had Jerry Briskin, who was one of his associate producers, and Frank La Tourette, who used to be at UCLA as one of the professors there. But they were all afraid of him. And they all knew exactly the breaking point with him, and they would back off the minute that was coming up. They all had love/hate for him. The love was the fact that they all knew that they were working for a very different sort of human being, and if they wanted to stick around, they *had* to love him.

"Before I came along, in his producing period, he probably fired a number of people in a flamboyant way, so they all knew the risk in displeasing him. The best way to put it is they were 'yes men.' But they did it in such a way that he respected them. He would say to me, 'Well, my associate producer here is one of the best men for the job.' He would praise them when he wanted to give them strength with the network. And they all wanted their jobs, so they did what he wanted." (LW-AI15)

D'Agosta added, "Everyone would shut up when he entered the room, or came onto the set. They were afraid he was going to criticize them. I mean, we're all very insecure, aren't we? 'Oh my God, he's going to see right through me.'" (JDA-AI15)

Hunter said, "He had a way of teasing people that was more of a threat than a tease. He would tease you in a negative way. 'You're out of the will.' And 'You just got yourself back in the will.' He wasn't profane, like some of those other guys, but he did intimidate people." (LW-AI15)

Allen had learned from one of the masters of intimidation. And as Harry Cohn did, Irwin Allen did. Hunter confirmed, "Irwin's desk was on a riser, too! I don't think it was as high up as Harry Cohn's desk, but it was enough so it certainly made him seem bigger. He was probably about five-foot-eight. And I was six-foot at the time. So he would find ways of rising above you." (LW-AI15)

Vitina Marcus said, "Irwin used to scare people. Everybody seemed to be frightened to talk to him, because he talked so fast and he went from one thought to another, like lightning speed. It's just that he thought really fast, and that's what happened – people were trying to keep up with him and it was a strain on them. And he went in to everybody's department. Nobody could escape him! He was in the makeup; the wardrobe; every department there was; he was in and out of them all. He didn't leave anyone alone!" (VM-AI15)

D'Agosta said, "I think he knew everybody's job. And he knew how to suck the last piece of energy out of you, and to get the best idea out of you. I think that was his talent, really. You knew Irwin Allen had a great mind. He was a determined, creative man. I might compare him to Orson Welles. He exuded that sense of command, and brilliance. You definitely got a sense of his creativity. And maybe he was always testing us as to what we would take and what we wouldn't take. The thing about men like that is they attract two kinds of people – strong people and weak people. The weak can be manipulated. And the strong people will make you look better. Anyone in between is just going to go away." (JDA-AI15)

It seemed everybody was tested to one extent or another. Lew Hunter recalled, "The only time I ever heard Irwin use profanity was during a screening. Clay Daniels, an editor friend of mine, and I were watching a rough cut with Irwin, and Irwin was screaming about the different things he thought were wrong. Clay was sitting there – just as an assistant editor; he didn't have anything to do with the cutting of this particular episode – but he saw how Irwin kept cursing at the screen. He did this as if he was yelling at whoever the editor was that made the cut. Finally, the lights came up, and the producer of the show – Jerry Briskin was his name – said, 'Hey, I want you to meet our new editorial assistant, Clay Daniels.' Irwin looked at Clay and said, 'Clay Daniels, huh? When are *you* going to fuck me?!'"

Jerry Briskin stayed silent. If anything, he, like the other associate producers on Irwin Allen's various series, stepped back an inch, shrinking in size, with a nonreactive expression frozen onto his face. Diplomatic silence was a survival trait among Allen's staff.

The contrast between this world and the one outside was immense. Beyond the studio walls: the Vietnam war; the chanting of draft protestors defying the system; the generation gap; the emerging drug culture; the riots on the Sunset Strip; racial unrest in Watts and countless other cities across the U.S.; the sudden roar of women's lib and its symbolic bra-burning; the shrieking of Beatlemania, and the toe-tapping too; pop art, political assassinations; advancements in science and the space race; and so much more. A country and a world were experiencing the turbulent change of the 1960s. However, within the inner sanctum of 20th Century-Fox, and deeper within, inside the twilight zone known as Irwin Allen Productions, there was only one force to contend with – writer, producer, director, creator, emperor Irwin Allen. He, along with Briskin, Tony Wilson and an emerging power named Jonathan Harris, were preparing to put the "Back Thirteen" of *Lost in Space*'s first season into production. As the nation and the world were changing, so was the series.

28

Episode 26: "The Keeper, Part II"

Written by Barney Slater
(with script polishing by Anthony Wilson)
Directed by Harry Harris
Produced by Irwin Allen; with Jerry Briskin

From the *Lost in Space* show files (Irwin Allen Papers Collection):

> The Keeper, furious at Smith's meddling, threatens to leave them all at the mercy of the dangerous, roaming animals unless they give him Will and Penny to add to his collection. They refuse, but in spite of all their precautions, he nearly succeeds in getting the children. Finally, impressed by the courage and love that the parents show for their children and their magnanimity towards him when he is in danger, he gives up his plan and, collecting his animals, departs, leaving them all once more safe and united.

From the Script:

(Shooting Final teleplay: December 13, 1965 draft)

– *Smith:* "Our unfortunate accident could prove beneficial." *Robot:* "I do not follow your reasoning." *Smith:* "Since all the Keeper's animals are released, he now has plenty of room for passengers. Perhaps he can be persuaded to take all of us back to Earth. After all, what else can he do?" *Robot:* "Destroy all of us for what you have done…" *Smith (reacts in alarm):* "What I have done? No, no, you must erase that from your memory banks. He must never know we were responsible." *Robot:* "Not we. You." *Smith:* "Don't quibble! Just erase everything that happened." *Robot (lights blink a moment, then):* "It is done. My memory banks have now eliminated all recorded events from 1710 hours to…" *Smith (reacts in terror to ROAR of an animal):* "Oh, shut up and come on!"

– *Robinson (to Keeper):* "I was hoping you would show up." *The Keeper:* "Were you?" *Robinson:* "If you hadn't come to see us, I was going to come to see you." *The Keeper:* "You are either a good liar, Professor Robinson, or you are innocent. I shall soon know which." *Don (temper begins to warm up):* "Now wait a minute!" *The Keeper:* "Silence! You try my patience! *(raises his staff)* I should destroy all of you now! Reduce you to pitiful grains of dust which the winds would blow away across the waste land of this planet!" *Smith (almost fawning):* "I'm sure the young man meant no harm. Let's try to keep our tempers and act like intelligent beings." *The Keeper (with a smile of contempt):* "You flatter yourself! Intelligent beings! You are less than the insect which I crush under my feet as I walk."

Assessment:

The theme is one of self-sacrifice. Don and Judy are ready to give up their freedom to spare Will and Penny from being imprisoned by the Keeper. So are John and Maureen. Meanwhile, Will and Penny go to the Keeper and give themselves up to spare the others from being preyed upon by the beasts that have escaped from the space ark. Also contributing to the theme is the one person who is *not* willing to make this sacrifice – Dr. Smith. We can learn by bad examples as well as good, especially when both are present in the same story.

Also present is the pro-animal, anti-captivity theme. More than this – a matter of how humans treat animals. The story also makes commentary on how humans treat one another. The Keeper has an intolerant air of superiority, yet he is every bit as susceptible to human frailties and outbursts of emotion as the Robinsons, Major West and Dr. Smith. The Keeper displays perhaps the greatest of all human faults – intolerance. He assumes that because of his presumed advanced refinement, he's more important than the humans. The payoff in this story is seeing the Keeper experience his character arc from stern intolerance to consideration and compassion.

While "The Keeper," Parts 1 and 2, make for an effective two-parter, and could easily combine together to form a decent late 1950s/early-1960s era sci-fi B-film, it contains one big but unintentional laugh – when the giant spider attacks the Chariot. That is one sorry-looking arachnid!

As bad as the monster is, the Fox effects men did a commendable job with the explosions as John tosses hand grenades at the beast.

Fulfillment of the CBS backorder of thirteen started off with a bang. "The Keeper, Part II," as well as its predecessor, is indeed a keeper.

Script:

Story Assignment 8463 (Production #8517)
Barney Slater's treatment, and 1st and 2nd draft teleplays: Early December 1965.
Reformatted Mimeo Department Shooting Final teleplay: December 13, 1965.
Tony Wilson's script polish, Revised Shooting Final (beige pages): December 20.
Page revisions by Wilson (pink insert pages): December 21.
Further revisions by Wilson (purple insert pages): December 21.
Further revisions by Wilson (blue insert pages): December 21.
Further revisions by Wilson (yellow insert pages): January 3, 1966.

Part 2 of "The Keeper" was assigned to Barney Slater after the script for Part 1 was being polished by Tony Wilson and the series received its pickup from CBS for additional episodes. Irwin Allen and Wilson felt the story was strong enough to be extended into a second segment. Doing so would help the company to glide along into the first episode of the backorder of thirteen. Most of the props had been designed already for Part 1, as well as special sets and wardrobe. Casting director Joe D'Agosta could shift his focus to *Voyage to the Bottom of the Sea* and other 20th Century-Fox TV series since Michael Rennie was already booked. Jerry Briskin would have to find a giant spider, but he didn't have to look far – *Voyage to the Bottom of the Sea* had one of those (for the episode "The Monster's Web"). All the producers needed was to get a script out of Slater fast.

Now that *Lost in Space* had its pickup for the remainder of the season, the mutation of the character of Dr. Smith was now in full swing. Jonathan Harris said, "I was very subtle. I snuck in all those goodies that you saw. The story editor … [Tony Wilson] … was a very, very brilliant, talented man. He saw the potential of what I was doing, and then had it written for me, because he saw the potential, and it worked." (JH-IASB2)

As discussed earlier (see "The Raft"), Harris was also handwriting suggested changes pertaining to his character into his copy of the script, then returning it to Tony Wilson for approval. Wilson would run the proposed changes by Irwin Allen and CBS, and then, with their blessing, send revised pages to the set to be inserted into all copies of the script.

Wilson was also encouraging Slater to alter the Robot's character, making it more human and comical. Slater, perhaps more than any other *Lost in Space* writer, would display a tendency to over-humanize the Robot. At first, while Irwin Allen was in favor of leaning the Smith character more toward comedy, he was resistant to changing the Robot.

On December 16, regarding Slater's second and final draft teleplay, Allen wrote to Wilson:

> P. 1, Teaser, Sc. 5 + 6: The Robot's lines are not written according to its usual characteristic fashion. They are too conversational; too human.
>
> P. 2, Sc. 6: Smith's last line should be more terrified and possibly funnier. Teaser should end on a shot of some terrifying monster about to attack Smith and the Robot….
>
> P. 22, Sc. 105: The Keeper says he can call all the animals back except for those which have been destroyed by the other animals. This statement is a direct contradiction of his speech in Scene 103. The Keeper should show his anger at what has happened [to his] wild animals. It is what such stupidity deserved. Or that it took him years to assemble his collection and will probably take as long this time.

Wilson made the changes, adding in the large flying creature at the end of the Teaser, prompting Smith to scream and dive for the ground, then having the Keeper become angered over the release of his animals. But some notes, such as Allen asking to keep the Robot more robot-like, were ignored. As it was happening with Dr. Smith and the Robot, Wilson was also going through a metamorphosis. He was testing the waters as to what he could get away with. In contrast, Allen was a reactive personality type. His reactions were sudden and often extreme, but, come a day or two later, whatever was so important to him earlier was no longer an issue. This gave Wilson great freedom in leaning the series in the direction he saw fit – and Wilson loved comedy.

In Barry Slater's final draft, the miniature horse seen in Part 1 made a return. The possibility of the horse remaining in the series as one of Penny's pets was established. But, after the trouble with the dog in "One of Our Dogs Is Missing" – delays in filming, as well as the cost of the animal and its handler – Irwin Allen nixed the idea and the scene was removed. Debbie the Bloop would remain Penny's sole pet and, in an effort to save time and money, even she would be seen less as the series progressed.

The assault on the Robinsons and Don and Smith wasn't only carried out by land animals, but also from the air. In one scene, while Maureen, Smith, Penny and the miniature horse are outside the Jupiter 2, "a huge, dark shadow is moving toward them." Smith's eyes widen. He points and exclaims, "Look!" The huge, dark shadow moves toward them. Everyone automatically looks upward. They see "a huge bird flying directly overhead." It emits a "high-pitched scream." The group immediately huddles together. Penny exclaims, "What a horrible-looking bird!" Maureen says, "It was big enough to carry off an adult." Smith speaks with urgency: "Ladies, let us go inside immediately." Maureen shivers, then says, "Perhaps we'd better. Strange, I suddenly feel frightened. Come on, Penny." Penny gives the small horse a final hug, and they head up the Jupiter 2 ramp.

Once Slater fulfilled his contract, Tony Wilson took over and did a fair amount of rewriting. As Slater left it, we never again see the Keeper after the end of Act III, when he is attacked by a "large tentacle creature" and slumps to the floor of his spaceship. The situation is never resolved. Also, Maureen doesn't go out looking for the children, but leaves that to John and Don. Therefore, there was no scene in which Maureen finds the Keeper on the floor of his ship, and, because of her compassionate treatment, he realizes that people from Earth are indeed an advanced and worthy race. With the Keeper out of the picture throughout the entire fourth act, as originally written left it, there was no scene where he uses his staff to drive "the giant tentacled creature" off after it attacks the Chariot and then turns on John. In Slater's final draft, John defeats the creature on his own, setting it on fire. At the end of Slater's script, we – as well as the Robinsons and Don – are left to assume that the Keeper recovered, called his animals back to the space ark, and then left the planet … while leaving behind a parting gift – Dr. Smith in a cage.

In Slater's defense, he had to write his treatment and the two drafts of the script in less than two weeks, as this story was rushed through the development stages.

Tony Wilson gave this story the proper resolution that it needed, as well as a pivotal scene for June Lockhart and a grand exit for Michael Rennie.

Production Diary:

Filmed December 23 – 31, 1965 (7 days).

Day 1: The Keeper learns a lesson in empathy from Maureen Robinson.

Day 1: Thursday, December 23, 1965. Filming began at 8 a.m. on Stage 5 for the Teaser, with the scenes inside the Keeper's ship as Smith and the Robot enter and Smith accidentally frees the creatures from their cages.

Jonathan Harris kept increasing the level of comedy. He admitted, "I began to do a little collusion with the story editor. Now it can be told. I said to the story editor, 'Now, why don't we do a little number? You know, we've got that crazy Robot. I'd like to play some games with that Robot. I would like to imagine him as a human being. I want to name him. I want to name him Claw-ed.' And somebody in the no humor department said, 'Claude?!' And that was the end of that. [But] then it became the show that you saw. Billy and Claw-ed and I, and that was the way that it worked and went. How did I pattern that part? It is a creation of mine of which I am inordinately proud, I have to tell you. I am very proud of that man. I dreamed up what you saw. I patterned him after every kid I've ever known. Quite seriously. You know what kids look like when they are upset. That's what I did. I wept, I cried, I lied, and I was the idol of every child in the world because I got away with it!... then I knew I had to use the robot for my ends. I dreamed up the alliterative, 'bald headed booby,' and 'Neanderthal ninny,' the 'parsimonious puppet.' That was one

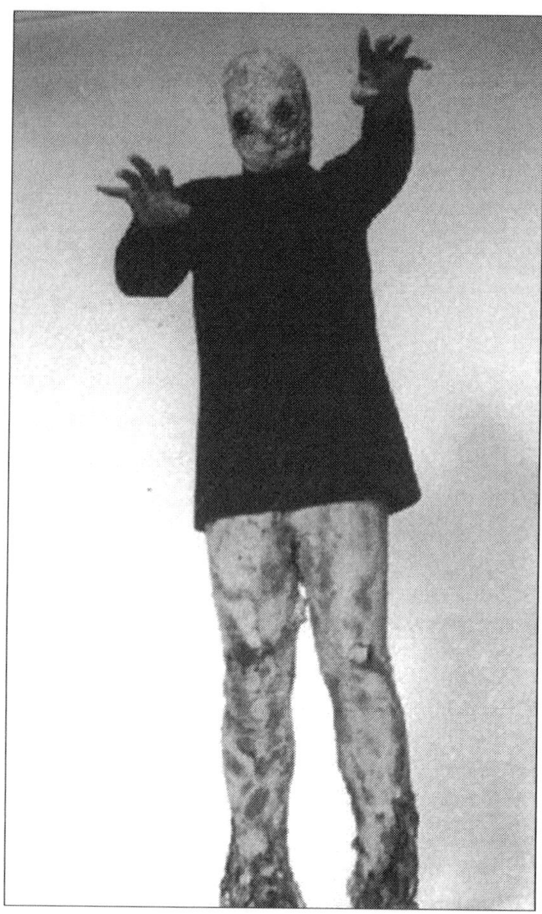

"The Keeper, Part 1" was originally planned as a standalone episode, the last for the initial CBS order of 16. For the first episode of the CBS backorder of 13, "The Keeper, Part II" saved money by utilizing sets from the first part of this now two-parter, as well as recycling monsters from past shows – all featured on the first day of production.

of my favorites. 'Pusillanimous pipsqueak' and things like that. And all that worked. It was craziness, you know. But within the framework of Dr. Smith, it all seemed to work. It all seemed to come together.... I knew that had tremendous potential and also it had never been done before. Quite seriously. So... it was a first and it worked. And Tony [Wilson] went right along with it because he knew it was good. If it had been bad, he never would have done it. Because Irwin would have breathed down his neck." (JH-IASB2)

Also filmed: the Keeper conferring with the Lighted Figure on the video screen; the Keeper ordering Smith to convince the Robinsons to give up the children; then, joined by John and Maureen, the Keeper refusing to accept the parents in exchange for the children. Last up for this location: the attack on the Keeper by the giant spider.

Moving to Stage 6, they filmed the remaining portion of the Teaser, as Smith and the Robot sneak onto the Keeper's ship, then, moments later, rush out, pursued by the "Two-Headed Bush," the "Cyclops," the "Rubberoid," and "Gillman's Bat." The names of the unsung, unthanked stuntmen inside these outfits are lost to history, a fact they might approve.

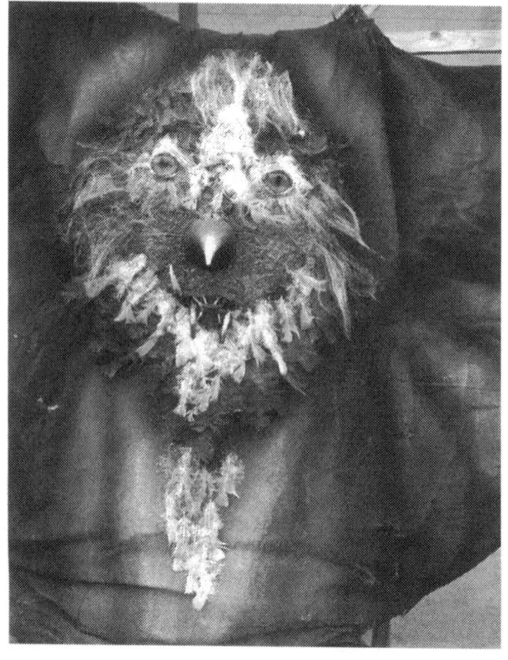

Work continued until 7:25 p.m.

Day 2: Friday, December 24. It was Christmas Eve. At 1 p.m., after finishing the scenes begun the day before on Stage 6, the cast and crew attended the company Christmas party on Stage 11, watched a blooper reel of outtakes from the episodes filmed thus far, which were projected on the large cyclorama surrounding the set, exchanged a few gifts, and then were dismissed for the holiday weekend.

Paul Zastupnevich wanted *Lost on Space* to be Christmas for everyone ... equally.

Paul Zastupnevich said of Irwin Allen, "With him, I always knew who was on top and who was on the bottom, because we had the 'A' list, the 'B' list, and the 'C' list, and I knew how to treat the certain people. Even at Christmastime, I would get very upset, because certain people would be dropped from the 'A' list to a 'C' list. They had irked him in some manner and so he would just drop them down a couple of pegs. Well, I would get the Christmas package ready, I would write all the Christmas cards for him, and I'd get the packages all wrapped. He'd come in and make an inspection. If I felt an individual was being slighted too much, then, while he was gone, I would take out some more cellophane, a few Christmas decorations, and gussy the basket back up to what the individual ordinarily would get. And it would always frustrate me because, no sooner than the Christmas package went out, at two o'clock or three o'clock, he expected his phone to ring with an acknowledgement from the individual that they had received the gift. So what I used to do was I would call the wives and I'd warn them. I'd say, 'The Christmas package is on its way; for God's sakes, please do me a favor and call him immediately, because you'll make your life miserable, and *mine*, if you don't acknowledge it.' He never knew. And that's how I kept him off of various people's backs." (PZ-KB95)

The Chariot is confronted by a giant spider, who would also make an appearance in *Voyage to the Bottom of the Sea* in a few weeks, for the Peter Packer scripted "The Monsters Web."

Day 3: Monday, December 27. It was a strange day of bouncing from one soundstage to another, with filming taking place on Stages 5, 6 and 11, between 8 a.m. and 7:06 p.m. The reason: They needed some pickup shots for Part 1 which was now being edited. After taking these, work continued on Part 2.

Day 4: Tuesday, December 28. From 8 a.m. to 6:33 p.m., they filmed on Stage 6.

NEA Hollywood correspondent Dick Kleiner visited the set with his children on this day. Later, for his syndicated "Show Beat" column, carried in the January 17, 1966 edition of North Carolina's *Gastonia Gazette*, Kleiner wrote:

A split-screen effect to make a lizard big enough to gobble up a couple humans worked well in T*he Lost World*, so Irwin Allen brought the trick back for "The Keeper, Part II."

> Mark Goddard raised his laser-beam ray gun and aimed at the giant lizard. Only there wasn't any lizard perched on the rock. Instead, was a man, stationed there so Goddard would have a target to aim at. "I'd better not really shoot this time," Goddard said. "Killing a giant lizard is one thing, but I don't want to kill any people." …
>
> Mark Goddard was playing a game for the benefit of my children. They went on the *Lost in Space* set to visit their favorite program and Goddard was making believe nicely. The children talked to him about the robot on the show and they said they knew there was really a man in the robot costume. (Daddy can be a terrible blabbermouth at times). "A man?" Goddard was aghast. "Nonsense. That's a real robot. Somebody's been putting out some bad stories. Come on, I'll show you there's no man in there." And they went over and saw the robot, and, as a matter of fact, there was no man in it – at that precise time. "See?" said Goddard. "I told you there was no man there."
>
> Then he had to go back into the scene, with Jonathan Harris and the *Lost in Space* kids, 13-year-old Angela Cartwright and 12-year-old Billy Mumy. They were supposed to be startled by the giant lizard (actually, they photographed a small lizard and they would blow it up and use a split screen).
>
> "How will we know when to look up there?" Jonathan Harris asked. "I'll make a noise," said director Harry Harris.
>
> It took them several retakes to get the scene right – a few times, they weren't sure of their lines, and then, when they did it perfectly, somebody opened a door to the stage and ruined the take.

A pair of outtakes from the production.

We all had lunch at the commissary with Angela and Billy and it was a wild scene. My three wanted to know how much allowance they got (Angela gets $1 a week when she isn't working and $5 when she is, and Billy is on $5 all the time); and what their middle names were (it's Angela Margaret Ann Cartwright and Charles William Mumy); and whether they went to school (they do, for three hours a day in a trailer on the set). Then they all got talking about the Beatles and we were a divided camp. Angela and my daughters think the four hairtops are "dreamy" and "the most" and talked about their collections of Beatles records and pictures and letters. Billy Mumy sneezed haughtily at this recitation. He saves up his allowance so he can buy Kingston Trio albums; he has 14 of them and he figures that's a fair assortment. He's a big folk song fancier and is learning the guitar himself.

Then we all went back to the set where the giant lizard was nowhere to be seen.

Day 5: Wednesday, December 29. A long day on Stage 6, filming to 7:28 p.m. By the time the set was wrapped, and the cast members had their makeup removed and they changed out of their costumes, then drove home, few were able to catch the only network airing of "Return from Outer Space." It would not play on television again until late 1968, in syndicated reruns.

Day 6: Thursday, December 30. It was to be the final day of production, but Harry Harris had fallen behind. Director Sobey Martin was asked to stand down and "The Sky Pirate" was pushed back to the following week.

Happy reunion for Jonathan Harris with Michael Rennie, who was among the favorite guest stars of the *Lost in Space* regular cast members.

Day 7: Friday, December 31. It took until 7:40 p.m., but Harry Harris finally finished filming "The Keeper, Part II." Most of the crew and cast members wouldn't leave the studio until past 8, and not arrive home until after 8:30 p.m. on New Year's Eve.

Recalling the experience of making "The Keeper":

Harry Harris said, "Jonathan was strictly professional. A *total* professional. He was also eccentric, and he set the ways of what he wanted to do. But he was terrific. And Billy Mumy knew everybody's lines, so you didn't have to worry about if they muffed a line – he'd just cue them. He knew the whole script before you shot it. They all were terrific – June and Guy, and Marta Kristen – they were all hardworking." (HH-KB95)

Billy Mumy said, "I liked working with Michael Rennie, because I thought he was a great actor, and he gave probably one of the best performances we had." (BM-LISW)

Jonathan Harris said, "Michael Rennie was a very lovely man … and a splendid actor … and we were devoted friends…. We used to see each other quite often over lunch where we would gossip a lot…. He was a devilishly wicked, intelligent and delightful man. When he appeared in *Lost in Space* it was the two happiest episodes in my life. It was as if we had never been apart despite [the] several years it had been since we worked on *The Third Man* series…. It was lovely to work with him again." (JH-LISF)

The second half of "The Keeper" was supposed to cost $139,655. The final toll was $177,507, which was $37,652 over.

Release / Reaction:

(CBS premiere broadcast: Wednesday, January 19, 1966)
(Network repeat airing: Wednesday, May 25, 1966)

The film doing the best business in movie houses across America was *Our Man Flint,* starring James Coburn. The Beatles still had a lock with the song getting the most airplay on American Top 40 radio stations, with "We Can Work It Out." The B-side "Day Tripper" held down the No. 6 spot. Even though neither song could be found on the group's new album, *Rubber Soul* was nonetheless the best-selling LP in the stores. The name "The Beatles" wasn't even on the cover, but the faces of John, Paul, George and Ringo were, and that was all it took in 1966 to sell a million dollars in record albums. The

"Hey, fellas, haven't I seen you two on the TV?"

faces of Robert Culp and Bill Cosby of *I Spy* had the cover of *TV Guide*. Their series was a hit, and *TV Guide* was out-selling *Life*, *Look*, *The Saturday Evening Post*, *Time*, *Newsweek*, and *Playboy*. Michael Rennie's face was very visible too, showing up in the TV section of newspapers around the country. The photo caption read: "Michael Rennie stars as the Keeper, a space traveler who collects creatures of the universe and visits the Robinson colony looking for a pair of human specimens on a two-part episode of *Lost in Space*."

Getting even more press than Rennie or *Lost in Space*, or, for that matter, on this week, even more than *Our Man Flint*, *I Spy* or the Beatles, was *Batman*. It seemed, after only four episodes having been aired (two per week for two weeks), that America was suffering an extreme case of *Batman* mania.

The syndicated entertainment column "TV Previews," carried in *The Daily Reporter*, serving Dover, Ohio, singled this episode of *Space* out as worth a look, saying:

> In this second of a 2-part story, the Keeper has enticed Will and Penny to his spaceship with his very odd assortment of animals from various planets – to which he wishes to add the children as fine specimens of Homo Sapiens. Wicked Dr. Zachary Smith (Jonathan Harris) lets the whole zoo go free, which so enrages the Keeper (Michael Rennie) that he threatens horrible revenge on Smith and the whole Robinson family as well. The best part of this episode is the really weird collection of animals.

.

Syndicated "TV Key," found in newspapers across America, including the Madison *Wisconsin State Journal*, said:

> Fascinating animals belonging to the villainous Keeper (Michael Rennie) walk off with the episode. Iguanas, lizards, and midget horses are just a few of the odd assortment of animals that break out of the Keeper's zoo and threaten the brave Robinson family. Clever special effects help, too.

The competition on ABC that night was "Fine Feathered Finks," introducing Burgess Meredith as the Penguin on *Batman. The Virginian* on NBC had guest star John Cassavetes.

George Laine, for his syndicated "Television View & Review" newspaper column, printed a letter sent to him by Irwin Allen. It read:

> George Laine, Wednesday night *Lost in Space* presents second part of "The Keeper," an hour dedicated to those who love way-out adventure. Last week, the Keeper, a strange alien who collects animal life throughout the far reaches of the galaxy, arrived on Robinsons' planet. He looms as most frightening threat yet to space family. When Keeper seeks to add Will and Penny to his animal collection, a surprise awaits our viewers. Guest star Michael Rennie joins Guy Williams, June Lockhart and Jonathan Harris Wednesday night. We hope you'll alert your readers to this episode, one of our best. Cordially, Irwin Allen, 20th Century-Fox-TV.

Laine knew it was a form letter with his name added at the top. His revenge was to print the reply: "Check, Irwin. I'll tune in the second half of it, right after *Batman*."

Laine wasn't alone in watching *Batman* at 7:30, then switching over to *Lost in Space* at 8 p.m. But some viewers – no doubt the ones without kids screaming for them to turn the channel knob to the local CBS station – stayed put in their seats and stuck with ABC.

A.C. Nielsen's 30-City Ratings survey for January 19, 1966, calculated the audience numbers this way:

Network / Program:	Rating	Share:
7:30 – 8 p.m.:		
ABC: *Batman*	**25.2**	**41.6%**
CBS: *Lost in Space*	13.3	21.9%
NBC: *The Virginian*	16.6	27.4%
8 – 8:30 p.m.:		
ABC: *The Patty Duke Show*	**19.1**	**30.9%**
CBS: *Lost in Space*	18.3	29.6%
NBC: *The Virginian*	17.9	29.0%

Irwin Allen's TV agent Herman Rush said, "Irwin respected Nielsen. You can be frustrated when you don't get a good rating, but you respect the fact that there is a reason for it. What is that reason; why? He would have brainstorming sessions with us on issues like that. I think every producer, every creator, worries when the numbers drop and there is competition that's eating into your audience. He wasn't any different." (HR-AI15)

The solution, thought Allen and CBS: Make *Lost in Space* more like *Batman*.

29

Episode 18: "The Sky Pirate"

Written by Carey Wilber
(with script polishing by Anthony Wilson)
Directed by Sobey Martin
Produced by Irwin Allen; with Jerry Briskin

From the *Lost in Space* show files (Irwin Allen Papers Collection):

> Tucker, a sky pirate, makes a forced landing on the planet as his spaceship is urgently in need of repairs. Holding Will as a hostage, he bargains with the Robinson to repair his ship in order to get the boy back. Will is fascinated by Tucker and his tales of pirate adventures in space. Tucker is being pursued by a "THING" from the Planet Cygnet 4, his last stopover. He doesn't know why. The "THING" tracks him down and, to escape it, Tucker and the family take refuge in the Jupiter 2. But when it looks as though they will all be destroyed, Tucker leaves the ship to save the others. In his headlong flight he drops a curious forecasting instrument he had picked up while on Cygnet 4.

From the Script:

(Shooting Final teleplay, January 6, 1966 draft)

– *Will:* "Why did you become a pirate?" *Tucker:* "What's wrong with bein' a pirate?" *Will:* "It's wrong, that's all." *Tucker:* "That depends on the kind of pirate." *Will:* "Is there more than one kind?" *Tucker:* "Why, sure there is. Why, there's land pirates an' stock market pirates an' railroad an' oil an' lumber pirates. An' when that kind gets tired of piratin' he sets up libraries an' foundations an' art galleries an' such an' then he's a philanthropist." *Will:* "What kind of pirate are you?" *Tucker:* "I'm an honest pirate."

– *Don:* "How long have you been in space, Captain Tucker?" *Tucker:* "Well now, let's see … what year is this, anyway?" *Smith:* "It is 1997." *Tucker:* "You don't say! More'n a hundred years…. Let's see … it was the year Custer got massacred by all them Injuns." *Don:* "You mean eighteen seventy-six?" *Tucker:* "Yup. Yup, that'd be about right. I was just crosin' the Buffalo Rochester an' Pittsburgh railroad tracks in Punxsutawney, PeeAye when…" *Smith:* "Captain Tucker, surely you are aware that no space ship left Earth until late in the 1950s." *Tucker:* "Callin' me a liar, Zach?" *Smith:* "Oh dear me, it's the farthest notion from my mind. I merely wanted to set forth the facts." *Tucker:* "Didn't say anything about leavin' Earth in an Earth ship, did I?" *Don:* "You mean you were picked up by aliens?" *Tucker:* "Yup. They was Tellurians. Nice folks when you got to know 'em." *Smith (hint of a sneer):* "I suppose they picked you up in a flying saucer, Captain?" *Tucker:* "That's right. That's what they did. Scooped me right up with a force ray. They cruised around for quite a spell pickin' up folks. They wanted 'em for study." *Robinson:* "According to that you're more than a hundred and forty years old." *Tucker:* "Born in eighteen fifty-eight, Perfessor." *Robinson:* "You're a very well preserved hundred and forty, Captain Tucker. May I congratulate you." *Tucker:* "No credit of mine, Perfessor. You see, them Tallurians kept us most of the time in a Time Freezer. Just hauled us out when they wanted to make a study."

Assessment:

Say what you will about "The Space Pirate" – that Albert Salmi's performance is way over the top (he's actually dong a parody of Robert Newton from *Treasure Island*); that his ship is too small on the outside to have the larger interior that we see; that Dr. Smith is out of character in the first half, fainting at the sight of a mere man, when he has already met things far more frightening; and that the alien blob is not one of the better monsters – but this one turns out to be a very enjoyable episode.

"The Sky Pirate" has many imaginative aspects, including the idea of humans being abducted by aliens, plucked off the Earth back in the 1800s; the talking mechanical parrot who can whip a gun out of an adversary's hand; and the alien forecasting machine that can project the thoughts one has about future actions.

Writer Carey Wilber even does a bit of forecasting toward *Star Trek*, still eight months away. John Robinson asks Tucker what happens when he hits a particular button on the control panel in his ship. Tucker answers: "Well, she starts a-shakin' an' a-quiverin' an' you start a-shakin' an' a-quiverin' – inside that is – like you been eatin' too many green apples or somethin' an' then all of a sudden she just goes zoop! An' the stars go out. They come back on when you reach where you're goin'." *Don:* "A star ship!" *Robinson:* "Hyper-space drive..." *Don:* "Faster than light..." *Robinson:* "Measure speed in parsecs.... Tucker, this ship could return us to Earth in a matter of seconds." *Tucker:* "It ain't big enough..." *Don:* "We could shuttle back and forth. The best brains on Earth could dismantle it and learn the secret of its drive. We could have star ships that would explore the farthest reaches of the galaxy..." *Robinson:* "The Universe! How about it, Tucker?"

The comedy in this episode also works, namely the aforementioned fainting spells by Smith. As silly as these scenes are – and while they do a bit of forecasting in their own way, giving us a preview of the Second Season – the running gag is nonetheless funny. The crowning moment: Tucker giving the fainted Smith a pitiful look and saying, "Tch-tch. Poor feller oughta do somethin' about his nerves."

What works best is that the story has heart. Will, the lonely boy who was longing for a playmate in many of the early episodes, trying to befriend the Robot, and then getting close to someone seemingly on his own juvenile level – Smith – has now found a friend in Tucker. The affection is returned. In the teleplay, it is stated this way: "Here is a man who has been playing on a child's credulity and interest for his own ends. Now his whole scheme has backfired on him and he doesn't know what to do. This kid really likes him and Tucker, for perhaps the first time in his life, likes somebody."

This brings forward the theme – a common one in television from this period, but always worth exploring – a lesson in self-sacrifice. Tucker is a ne'er-do-well, a man who was a drifter and thief, and who acquired no respect while on Earth. He clearly has not bettered himself since taking to space. But he becomes an unlikely hero when he risks his own life to protect the Earth people he has endangered, and save the boy who has touched his heart. In the final moments of the story, Tucker takes self-sacrifice one step further, as he, clearly a proud man, uses self-depreciation in order to lose Will's respect and thereby save the boy from feeling the full weight over losing a friend. In doing so, Tucker gives up the one thing he has never had, and clearly wanted, as indicated by his braggart ways – the respect and fondness of another. He does this because it is in the best interests of another.

Carey Wilber told an imaginative and touching story with "The Sky Pirate." It may have its detractors, and will likely not make many a fan's list of Top Ten favorite episodes, but it has something that overrides its faults – a good theme, and a warm heart.

Script:

Story # 8460 (Production #8518)

Carey Wilber's treatment and 1st draft script: November/December 1965

Wilber's 2nd Draft teleplay: December 19, 1965.

Reformatted Mimeo Department Shooting Final teleplay (pale green pages): Dec. 22, 1965.

Tony Wilson's page revisions (pink page inserts): December 31.

Additional revisions by Wilson (yellow page inserts): January 6, 1966.

This was Carey Wilber's third writing assignment for *Lost in Space*. His first was adapting Shimon Wincelberg's story for "There Were Giants in the Earth" into a teleplay, for which he wrote two drafts. Next, he was assigned Story #8454, "Curious Galactics," for which he wrote a treatment and three drafts of a teleplay before the story was abandoned. Wilber was then asked to write a story about a space pirate.

Wilber told interviewer James Van Hise, "That was about the time we started playing Dr. Smith as other than a straight villain and gave him the comedy bits. He became a funny character and he was the kind of guy who would say, 'Let you and he fight – I'll hold the coats.' I guess you could say that I was the first writer to play Smith that way in the script and Tony and Irwin both seemed to like it. I was kind of basing him on a character I used to do on the old *Captain Video* series, which I'd written for…. Tony Wilson was an absolutely wonderful guy, and, with Irwin Allen producing, he gave the writers so much leeway that it was really delightful to work on the show." (CW-LIS25)

Perhaps too much leeway. Fortunately, other than screaming when he first sees Tucker, and the fainting gag, Smith recovers his composure and during the last half of "The Space Pirate" is more like the Smith we knew from earlier episodes.

On December 19, 1965, concerning Wilber's 2nd Draft teleplay, Irwin Allen wrote to Tony Wilson:

> P. 2, Sc. 9: John's first speech: Change "Shut up, Smith" to something else, like "Be quiet" or "That's enough." …
>
> Penny and Judy are less than bit parts in this script….
>
> Shouldn't something be made of the [parrot] Nik? No one but Will ever remarks about it….
>
> Does Tucker have the Nik on his shoulder every time he is seen?

Allen would never get more of Penny and Judy in the script – a mere cameo from both Angela Cartwright and Marta Kristen at the conclusion of the episode is all we see. However, Wilson would make more of "the Nik." And the revised script clarified that the Nik would not always be on Tucker's shoulder – only when Tucker wished him to be.

The script timed out long and two scenes had to be cut. This is regretful, because one of these scenes would have helped explain why the idea of using Tucker's ship to shuttle the family back to Earth had been dropped, and even how Tucker came to land on this particular planet. It went like this:

> 158. INT. TUCKER'S SHIP – DAY
>
> Smith is standing at controls, studying them, making little tentative motions toward them. He turns as Tucker enters.
>
> TUCKER
> What're you doin' here, Zach?
>
> SMITH
> I've made up my mind to go with you.
>
> TUCKER
> Ye did?

(beat)

All right, make yerself to home.

SMITH

I knew you wouldn't mind. And when we reach Earth I shall make you a fortune. I promise you. You shall have everything your heart desires.

TUCKER

(preflighting controls)

Well, I'd settle right now fer a good navigation system.

SMITH

(alert)

Navigation system…? You mean your instruments are out of order?

TUCKER

What instruments? Never was any instruments in this runabout.

SMITH

There are navigation instruments in Jupiter 2. We could…

(breaks as Tucker shakes his head)

No…?

TUCKER

Earth-type instruments won't work with this drive. That's why I can't promise I'll send help from Earth – might not get there.

ANGLE ON TUCKER

as he starts activating things deliberately.

TUCKER

Oh, I just use the good Tucker system of navigation. You see, I kinda mentally imagine a map of Punxsutawney, PeeAye, laid over the sky. Now fer instance, to get us to Earth, I'll just head out North Findley Street past Buffalo, Rochester an' Pittsburg Railroad tracks an' turn left at the Fairgrounds. O'course, mebbe we won't make it to Earth, but we oughta come out some place, wouldn't ya think? Mebbe on Ganymede where them giant toads are. How's that sound, Zach?

There is silence. Tucker looks over with a grin to where Smith had been standing. Smith is gone.

The second deleted scene – the last in the script, excluding the cliffhanger – had offered the perfect ending for this boy-meets-pirate tale.

160. INT. JUPITER 2

All the family is inside looking at scanner except Will.

161. CLOSE ON SCANNER

As the o.s. SOUND of Tucker's ship taking off is HEARD and a blip slowly rises on scanner.

162. BACK TO FAMILY

watching scanner.

163. CLOSE SHOT – WILL

As he looks out window, his eyes following the departing ship. Then he waves just once and turns away.

FADE OUT.

On December 27th, and referring to the December 22nd "Shooting Final" teleplay, Sam Taylor, Jr. of CBS Program Practices wrote:

> As discussed with Mr. Wilson:
>
> Page 21, Scene 56: As WILL is hit by the light beam and frozen into motionless stasis, please do not show him in pain or terror stricken.
>
> Page 37, Scene 98: DON's line, "We could take this ship..." should not convey a malicious or unprincipled intention.

As for the cliffhanger, CBS took issue with it. The script described the action this way:

175. CLOSE – JOHN

Hammering the sign into place – unaware of the mist that is now all around him and beginning to creep up toward his head. Suddenly he begins to feel dizzy – he sways and staggers. He tries to shout – but his voice is choked in his throat. He turns to run – but falls to his knees – then falls prostrate trying to crawl out of the area as the poisonous mist envelops him, and we FREEZE FRAME.

On January 3, after receiving the Tag scene/cliffhanger, Sam Taylor, Jr. of CBS Program Practices wrote:

> Page 60, Scene 175: In order to avoid alarming younger members of your audience, we would request that JOHN's agonies, as he is enveloped by poisonous mist, not be too graphically portrayed.

Batman and Robin could "Pow," "Smash," "Bonk" and "Boff" all they wanted on ABC. But John Robinson couldn't even cough and fall down on CBS.

Pre-Production:

Sobey Martin was again in the director's chair, following his work on "The Hungry Sea," "The Sky Is Falling," "The Raft," and "The Keeper, Part 1."

NBC-TV promotional picture of Albert Salmi, sent to fans of *Daniel Boone* (NBC-TV, 1964).

Albert Salmi was 37 when he first played Alonzo P. Tucker. With close to 200 film and TV roles in a career that spanned the 1950s, '60s, '70s, and '80s, Salmi was usually cast as outdoorsmen, thugs and bandits. And pirates, too. Salmi received recognition in 1958 with a National Board of Review award as Best Supporting Actor for his work in two films from that year, *The Brothers Karamazov* and *The Bravados*. He stepped into *The Twilight Zone* three times, including twice in the lead, for "Execution," in which a scientist saves him from a hanging by bringing him forward in time, and, for "Of Late I Think of Cliffordville," as an aging tycoon who makes a deal with the devil to go back in time to visit his youth. When hired for *Lost in Space*, Salmi had just finished a year as a regular on *Daniel Boone*, playing Boone's companion Yadkin.

Production Diary:

Filmed January 4 – 12, 1966 (7 days).

Day 1: Tuesday, January 4. On Stage 11, the company filmed at the Ext. Jupiter 2 Camp, and, after a move to Stage 6, work continued with Ext. Tucker's Ship. Sobey Martin rolled camera from 8 a.m. to 6:44 p.m., covering seven and four-eighths pages.

The first day of production began with the discovery of Tucker's small ship.

Day 2: Wednesday, January 5. They were on Stage 6 from 8 a.m. to 7:05 p.m. Martin was a dynamo this day, covering eleven and three-eighths pages in 10.1 production hours, with the remaining scenes outside of Tucker's ship, plus the interior of his vessel. Also shot, the scene in which Will, Smith and the Robot first encountered the pirate and his mechanical parrot. The cast and crew may have been unhappy with the 7:05 p.m. wrap time (meaning they wouldn't be leaving the studio until around 7:30) if not for *Lost in Space* being preempted this night on CBS for a "Young People's Concert."

It was actually a blessing that *Lost in Space* had its second preemption of the season (in only three weeks). They didn't have a new episode ready, anyway.

Above: On Day 5. A crewmember readies Captain Tucker's future events forecaster.
Below: The object from the future that is causing all the drama. Its roar is worse than its bite.

Day 3: Thursday, January 6. Still on Stage 6, filming from 8 a.m. to 6:45 p.m. Martin covered eleven and three-eighths pages from the script, including the scenes in the cave with Will and Tucker. He finished on schedule.

Day 4: Friday, January 7. It was a long day on Stage 6 – into makeup at 6:30 a.m., filming from 8 a.m. to 7:53 p.m., then another 30 minutes needed to wrap the set and for the cast members to change and have makeup removed, then start the drive home. But Martin covered nine and six-eighths pages, including the balance of the scenes in the cave and the sequences outside the cave. He remained on schedule.

Day 5: Monday, January 10. They began work on Stage 11, where the company would remain for the remainder of the production. Martin shot from 8 a.m. to 7:10 p.m., with the night scenes on the upper deck of the Jupiter 2. Even though he covered eight pages from the script, it was only half the work planned for this ambitious day of production, and the company ended one-half day behind schedule.

Day 6: Tuesday, January 11. They began work on the daytime scenes on the Jupiter 2. The producers were expecting the impossible from Martin. It was a long script and, even though he covered ten and three-eighths pages, when the company stopped work at 7:05 p.m., they were a full day behind schedule.

Appropriately, the touching end to the story was filmed on the final day of production.

"Ghost in Space," the next episode planned for production, was pushed back a day.

Day 7: Wednesday, January 12. They filmed the balance of the daytime scenes on the Jupiter 2. It took a full day, rolling camera from 8 a.m. to 7:50 p.m.

"The Keeper, Part 1" had its first network airing on this night, starting in Los Angeles at 7:30 p.m. With the final shots of "Sky Pirate" not competed until 7:50 p.m., plus the additional time needed to wrap the set and, for the cast, change clothes and have makeup removed, few in the company were able to catch the broadcast. They would have to wait until the summer repeats.

Post-Production:

"The Space Pirate" had to be rushed through post-production. Even though the plan had always been to give each episode of *Lost in Space* three weeks for editing, audio work, and photo effects, this one would have to do it all in less than two weeks. When the last shot was taken at the end of the day on January 12, there were only fourteen days before the episode was scheduled to air on CBS. This did not mean they had fourteen days to do all the post work. CBS needed to screen the episode beforehand and have time for changes to be made should Broadcast Standards require them. And then the finalized episode needed to be at the network a few days before broadcast for insertion of commercials. At best, Fred Baratta and his editing team had a week and a half to do the cutting, while Don Hall added in all the sound effects and smoothed over the audio track, and Leonard Eagle put together a score made up of past music tracks plus additional library music owned by 20th Century-Fox. George E. Swink was the overworked post-production supervisor overseeing all aspects of this in half the normal allotted time.

William Self wanted "The Space Pirate" made for $133,856. By the time the film had been delivered to CBS, the cost had climbed to $150,916.

Release / Reaction:

(CBS premiere broadcast: Wednesday, January 26, 1966)
(Network repeat airdate: Wednesday, June 6, 1966)

The week "The Sky Pilot" first aired, "The Sounds of Silence" by Simon and Garfunkel was the most-played song on American Top 40 radio stations, displacing the

Tucker would be back in Season Two's "Treasure of the Lost Planet."

Beatles' "We Can Work it Out," which dropped to second position. However, the top-selling album honors still went to the Beatles, with *Rubber Soul*. In the movie houses, *The Ghost and Mr. Chicken*, starring Don Knotts, was doing the most business. A caricature of David Janssen of *The Fugitive* adorned the cover of *TV Guide*.

On January 23rd, three days before the airing of "The Sky Pilot," pretty Marta Kristen, in her silver fire retardant spacesuit, had the cover of Long Beach, California's *Independent Press-Telegram* Sunday "TeleVues" magazine. TV and Radio Editor Bert Resnik wrote:

> Marta Kristen doesn't remember too much about the orphanage. She knows she was there from the time she was two weeks old until she was adopted when she was 4 ½ years old. She knows her mother was Norwegian and her father a German soldier. She doesn't know their names. The name she was given was Birgit Annalisa Rusanen. Marta, now 20 and a gorgeous, blue-eyed blonde, currently has the role of Judy Robinson in CBS-TV's *Lost in Space* series. Her recollection of her orphanage years are mostly lost in 16 years of memory's space. But one memory is still strong. "The orphanage lacked the love of a real home," said Marta. "I think, perhaps, that's one reason why I'm an actress today. So many of us are insecure. We need attention of people. Somewhere along the line, we missed the feeling of real security and love."

Kristen told Resnik about being adopted by a Michigan couple, Professor and Mrs. Harold Soderquist, and her subsequent upbringing in the United States. She admitted that she often thought about her biological parents, saying, "I'm curious about them, but that's as far as it goes. I'm not planning on making any efforts to look them up. I think, if I did, it would hurt Mother (Mrs. Soderquist). I certainly wouldn't want to give her a feeling of insecurity." (MK-IPT66)

Kristen's Cinderella story was in full bloom. She added, "What's exciting for me is being recognized on the street. It's thrilling to me when someone says, 'Oh, I know you. You're the girl in *Lost in Space*." (MK-IPT66)

Also on Sunday, January 23rd, an interview with Mark Goddard was syndicated to newspapers, including Utah's *Ogden Standard-Examiner*. Goddard told interviewer Alice West, "Directing – that's the thing these days. I long for the time when I will have had enough experience as an actor to go into this field of show business. Acting comes first, of course, but many actors are going into producing and directing. Jackie Cooper directs now. I think a director who has had acting experience first, has a better opportunity because he knows what it's all about."

The mid-sixties had brought about an explosion of ideas and a change in attitudes that were influencing the various areas of pop culture. This included music, with the British invasion; films, with the popularity of the anti-hero; and now television, with series such as *Batman*; *The Man from U.N.C.L.E.; I Spy; Get Smart; The Wild, Wild West; Voyage to the Bottom of the Sea; The Addams Family; The Munsters; Bewitched; I Dream of Jeannie; Gilligan's Island; Hogan's Heroes;* and *Lost in Space*, all new in 1964, '65 and early '66. Many of the old Hollywood establishment were critical. Goddard wasn't. He said, "I don't know why there is so much 'kick' going on about the trend of show business. I think it's great. Everything is changing in these modern times – so why not TV and pictures. You've got to keep up with things – no matter what business you're in."

On the same day, the *Independent Star News*, serving Pasadena, California, printed Part 2 of its "Be a TV Critic" poll results. *Get Smart*, *Hogan's Heroes* and *I Spy* had been picked by the newspaper's readers as the best new series. The other series filling out the Top 10 favorites were *I Dream of Jeannie*; *The Smothers Brothers*; *The F.B.I.*; *Please Don't Eat the Daisies!*; *F Troop*; *The Dean Martin Show*; and *Lost in Space*. The newspaper reported:

> In last week's report showing the programs most frequently listed among the favorite new ones, *Lost in Space* ranked third. Measured by the Total Favorable votes this week, it dropped to 10th spot. Still more curious is the fact that it also ranks 3rd in Total <u>Un</u>favorable. We suspect this is accounted for by the fact that practically every young person listed it as a favorite, but that few adults did. Youngsters also probably marked it overwhelmingly Excellent or Very Good, but the adults almost unanimously considered it Poor or Fair, thereby running up its negative count (Adults accounted for over 60% of the ballots).

On January 22nd, in Maine's *Biddeford-Saco Journal*, a syndicated filler article began with the question:

> Who is the busiest guest star of the season? Your answer is wrong unless you said Jonathan Harris. Jonathan Harris is being billed as special guest star in every episode of *Lost in Space* – series of celestial cliff hangers.... Why is Jonathan Harris billed as a special guest star since he is as regular on the series as the others? The answer is that Harris is a unique passenger aboard the spaceship which the "space family Robinson" is using in its travels through the uncharted galaxies and of an unknown world. Harris plays a villainous stowaway who is a very special guest indeed. The casting of Harris as a permanent and uninvited guest aboard the spacecraft is a somewhat sardonic contrast to the role he played so merrily as the hotel manager on *The Bill Dana Show*. It may be

recalled that one of his principal jobs there was to make sure that there were no "stowaway" guests in the hotel.

On the day that "The Sky Pirate" first aired on CBS, Beulah Hill wrote in her "For the Homemaker" column for the January 26, 1966 edition of Ohio's *Wilmington News-Journal*:

> Our third grader is very space conscious lately so the TV show *Lost in Space* is one of his favorites. And I am watching too, each time it is on if I am home. You may wonder about my sudden interest – actually I began with a very negative attitude. But all at once I realized he was afraid to watch alone and felt much more secure if I was there. And I can say I really do like it now. No doubt we could talk about the pros and cons of this type show – but it seems to me it is making him more science-minded.

As for the episode itself, "TV Scout," carried by *The Edwardsville Intelligencer*, out of Edwardsville, Illinois, among other newspapers, picked it as a Wednesday night highlight, saying:

> Series is more spooky than usual with Albert Salmi hamming it up as the "terror of the space ways" – a pirate who crash-lands near the Robinsons. As terrifying as Captain Hook, he gives Will the pirates' oath and promises to take the lad on a voyage to a secret treasure.

The competition on ABC was *Batman*, with the introduction of the series' first guest villainess – Zelda the Great, a magician with glycerin tears and a bagful of tricks. Anne Baxter played the evil Zelda.

Did all the hype during the week about *Lost in Space* and its cast, as well as the good notice from "TV Scout," help? A.C. Nielsen had the answer with its 30-City Ratings survey for January 26, 1966:

Network / Program:	Rating	Share:
7:30 – 8 p.m.:		
ABC: *Batman*	**28.1**	**44.2%**
CBS: *Lost in Space*	13.5	21.2%
NBC: *The Virginian*	16.7	26.3%
8 – 8:30 p.m.:		
ABC: *The Patty Duke Show*	**21.0**	**30.9%**
CBS: *Lost in Space*	19.8	29.2%
NBC: *The Virginian*	20.8	30.6%

If a space pirate couldn't beat a bat man, what could? Perhaps a ghost in space. Irwin Allen would try that next.

End Note:

David Hedison and Albert Salmi on *Voyage to the Bottom of the Sea*.

Immediately following working on *Lost in Space*, Albert Salmi appeared in an episode of *Voyage to the Bottom of the Sea*, as a pirate again, in "Dead Men's Doubloons."

During the week that "The Space Pirate" first aired on CBS, the following filler piece turned up in numerous newspapers across America:

> No one can ever make the statement that producer Irwin Allen didn't make it easy for his guest stars.
>
> One of the briefest series switches in the annals of television acting assignments was made recently by former Broadway actor Albert Salmi. Producer Allen had cast him in the guest-starring stint in his exciting CBS-TV series, *Lost in Space* (seen each Wednesday at 7:30 p.m.) in the role of Captain Tucker, a space-age pirate. Salmi completed the assignment at 11:30 a.m. on a Thursday morning on Stage 11 at 20th Century-Fox studios. At 11:40 a.m., Salmi left the set, walked 50 feet to Stage 10 still in his pirate's costume and began fulfilling a guest-starring assignment in producer Allen's second series, *Voyage to the Bottom of the Sea*, with Richard Basehart and David Hedison (seen in color each Sunday at 7 p.m. over ABC-TV).
>
> Commented Salmi, "The only way Irwin Allen could have made it easier for me would have been to shoot the segments at my home."

And it was true! … except for a few details. The costume wasn't actually the same. And "The Space Pirate" finished filming on a Wednesday – January 12, 1966, at 8:50 p.m. – not on a Thursday, mid-morning. But it was on Stage 11. And it is true that "Dead Men's Doubloons" began filming the following morning – which was a Thursday, as reported (January 13, 1966). And it was indeed on Fox Stage 10.

30

Episode 19: "Ghost in Space"

Written by Peter Packer
(with script polishing by Anthony Wilson)
Directed by Don Richardson
Produced by Irwin Allen; with Jerry Briskin

From the *Lost in Space* show files (Irwin Allen Papers Collection):

> Smith gets rid of some blasting materials by throwing them into a nearby bog. The resulting explosion causes an angry, invisible presence to materialize from the marsh that night and make its way to the Jupiter 2 where it wreaks havoc until daylight. Smith, who has been trying to call up spirits with a Ouija board, thinks the manifestation is his dead Uncle Thaddeus. Believing that his uncle needs to be placated, he persuades Will to go to the marsh with him the following night to perform incantations. During the proceedings, Will drops the lantern and falls into the bog while looking for it. Although he clambers out again he has now become invisible. Smith discovers, to his terror, that the angry presence is not his uncle. As he is unable to see Will, he thinks that he has drowned.

From the Script:

(Revised Shooting Final teleplay, January 20, 1966 draft)

– *Smith:* "I must choose a medium from among you – a sensitive with the qualities of my Aunt Matilda. *(He looks at Penny; taking her hand)* Vital energy … great powers of concentration … a sympathetic heart. You'll do nicely, Penny – *(to Maureen)* With your permission, Mrs. Robinson." *Maureen (dubiously):* "Well – if it isn't going to frighten her." *Penny:* "Oh mother – I'm not a baby! *(to John)* It's really no different from a scientific experiment, Dad, is it?" *John:* "Science has been interested in psychical research for a long time, Penny … and there have been some phenomena which they haven't been able to explain. *(smiles)* All right, Smith – go to it!" *Smith (icily):* "You're too kind!"

– *Smith:* "Careful, boy! I almost fell into the bog!" *Will:* "You don't have to be so scared, Dr. Smith. It's not deep – just slimy." *Smith:* "That does not reassure me!"

– *Will:* "Do you recognize him?" *Smith (teeth chattering):* "Not exactly." *Will:* "You'd better start talking to him if you want him to let us by." *Smith (uneasily):* "He doesn't seem very friendly. He may be loaded with poltergeists." *Will:* "Are poltergeists dangerous?" *Smith:* "And unpredictable. You never know what they're going to do next. I'm afraid I'm going to have to exorcise them." *Will:* "But why would a ghost need exercise?" *Smith:* "No, my boy. Exorcise. It means to cast out evil. The evil demons."

Assessment:

"Ghost in Space" would have made an above average Second Season episode. As part of the First Season, and while entertaining and having plenty of spirit, it is below standard.

"Ghost" has many things going for it that were typical of the First Season – Gene Polito's excellent black-and-white photography (with the night scenes especially effective in this alleged ghost tale); a score that includes selected music tracks by Bernard Herrmann (taken from *The Day the Earth Stood Still*); and a script that, while favoring Smith and Will, nonetheless provides plenty of onscreen business for all the recurring characters.

One area where this episode gets off track is in story continuity. The invisible creature, when first "seen" near the bog, is identified by its thumping footsteps and the deep impressions of its three-toed feet appearing in the sand. Like a bull in a china shop, it kicks and throws objects out of its way – such as trees and that hand painted sign John made. Yet when the creature intrudes on the séance between Smith and Penny, there are no thumping feet or noticeable footprints in the soil. The tricks seen here seem more magical than the result of an invisible brute – including a shattering glass; a plant levitating, and then seeming to laugh before floating away; and a Ouija board that also levitates, with a sound suggesting ghostly playfulness instead of a monstrous assault. If this "thing" were standing right next to Penny and Smith – and had clearly tiptoed in – wouldn't they at least smell it? It's a bog monster! But it quietly enters and moves about instead of just crashing its way through the area as any good monster should.

Inquiring minds may also want to know how it got close enough to John and Don outside the Jupiter 2 to slug them around, again without them first hearing its approach?

Disjointed ideas such as these became common place in the Second Season when anything would go, and the first things that went was continuity, reason and logic.

The transformation of Smith and the Robot continue. Smith is now into the occult, and a believer in séances and communicating with the dead. Fair enough – a self-important individual such as Smith might believe in anything that would give him the comfort of thinking his life could go on beyond mortal years. And someone with his principles sure can't hope to make it to heaven.

But we do miss the Smith of episodes past – the more sensible and scientifically oriented Air Force Colonel and doctor.

The same could be said of the handling of the Robot in this episode. First, we see him playing guitar (as he had done in "Welcome Stranger," a result of Tony Wilson's script polish). The clawed hand of the Robot could not depress the strings on the instrument's neck in order to form chords. This is pure fantasy. And now Wilson had the Robot singing, too.

Along with a few too many "Warning! Warning!" alerts, as Dick Tufeld put a bit too much pitch in a voice that should have been less excitable, this wonderful creation that many kids watching believed could be real was now leaning toward something more suitable for the Saturday morning cartoons.

In a handful of previous episodes, the seeds had been sewed for a major shift in *Lost in Space*. Those seeds were now taking root and sprouting a beast of their own.

Script:

Story Assignment 8462 (Production #8519)
Peter Packer's treatment, and 1st and 2nd draft teleplays: December 1965.
Reformatted Mimeo Department Shooting Final teleplay: December 22, 1965.
Tony Wilson's script polish, Revised Shooting Final (green pages): January 7, 1966.
Page revisions by Wilson (blue inserts): January 11.
Additional page revisions by Wilson (pink inserts): January 12.
Further page revisions by Wilson (yellow inserts): January 13.
Further page revisions by Wilson (gold inserts): January 20.

Peter Packer was already on his fifth *Lost in Space* assignment. His association with the series began on a good note with "The Derelict," which Packer wrote in May and June of 1965. He continued strong with "Welcome Stranger," written from late June to mid July. For his third script, "The Oasis" (written in August and September), Packer had mixed results. The assignment he labored over in October, his script for "Sorry, Wrong Planet" was dead on delivery, and the assignment was cut off. Packer was back in good form during late October and the first half of November, writing the excellent "Return from Outer Space" script. In late November and early December, he wrote the atrocious "Monster's Web" episode of *Voyage to the Bottom of the Sea*. With this script, written during the last three weeks of December, Packer was again aiming low. But Irwin Allen and Tony Wilson loved it, and this episode served as a template for many scripts to follow during the second season.

The writing is not bad, *per se*. But the structure of the story is flawed and too many things are left unexplained.

With this story, there was a new ingredient in the caricature known as Dr. Zachary Smith – his belief in the occult. Also: a glimpse into the rotten fruit on his shaky family tree. In an amusing passage of dialogue, Smith tells the Robinsons and Major West: "I was afraid Uncle Thaddeus wouldn't like it here…. He was always a hot-tempered man in life. Always throwing things around when something didn't please him. Nice as pie on the surface, but very pugnacious underneath. Iron hand in a velvet glove. Tonight he was all iron hand."

Irwin Allen sent notes on Packer's second and final draft script to Wilson on December 28, 1965, saying:

> TEASER: P. 6, Sc. 24 thru P. 9, Sc. 30: A lot of this dialogue should be cut as it is too talky and makes the Teaser too long.
>
> Having Will serve coffee is unnecessary and Smith's attitude towards his task should be changed. Also, some of Don's sarcasm towards Smith should be cut as it is beginning to get boring and makes Don seem like a very petty person….
>
> Smith should resent this task from the beginning because he feels that they are wasting their time drilling in this area. This would help explain why he doesn't carry through with setting the charge in the proper place, and why he doesn't want Will with him. He should try to dissuade Will from accompanying him but when he can't, they should start out as they do but when Will suggests going by way of the bog, Smith should remind him of what happened to his father that morning. Will would then say he knows a safe way through it and this is what gives Smith the idea that this would be a good spot to dump the charge. Smith should find a stronger reason for sending Will back to the drill site then his concern for his health, which seems phony. He could send him back with a message of some sort for his father which would be logical and not arouse suspicion. This would cut down on some of the talkiness in Scene 30….
>
> P. 23, Sc 61: All should be dressed in night clothes, especially Smith, in his night shirt, which will add to the comedy effect when he is attacked by the ghost.

The ideas conveyed in these last two paragraphs were implemented in the next draft of the script. Allen's memo continued:

> Will there be wind accompanying the events with the ghost or not? There is a lot of dialogue referring to the high wind throughout the script….

> P. 48, Sc. 118: Smith should explain his strange [exorcism] get-up to Will so that the audience will understand why he is dressed this way.

On January 5, 1966, Sam Taylor, Jr., of CBS Program Practices in Hollywood, wrote:

> Page 17 & 18, Scenes 41-43: If the glass being used by SMITH is to rock and then shatter, we would wish it to be evident that the unseen PRESENCE has caused these movements. In other words, there should be no indication that the movements are caused by SMITH's use of the Ouija board.
>
> Page 37, Scene 77: As WILL and PENNY receive blows from the unseen PRESENCE, they should not appear to be seriously injured.
>
> Page 56, Scene 124: We would not wish the PRESENCE, now visible, to be excessively terrifying.
>
> Page 57: While this script does not indicate it, we would not wish WILL's disappearance into the bog to conclude an ACT.
>
> Page 61 & 62: As the visible PRESENCE menaces the now visible WILL, the boy's voice and the actions of the PRESENCE should not imply that he is being hurt.

On January 19, after receiving the pages for the cliffhanger that would end the episode and set up the story for "War of the Robots," Taylor wrote:

> Page 69, Scenes 165 thru 168: As WILL is alone and apparently being menaced by his own robot and another strange robot, we request special directorial care which will insure that the scenes not be so frightening as to seriously alarm younger members of your audience.

On January 24, Taylor added:

> As discussed with Mr. Wilson:
>
> Page 69, Scene 166: We would prefer the robot to say, 'Warning … alien presence …" rather than "danger." This may serve to soften the cliffhanger in which WILL is alone. We would hope that the episode would conclude with WILL being more surprised than fearful.

With CBS so determined that nothing frightening happen to the children in the series, and nothing happen to frighten the children watching at home, it had become even clearer that *Lost in Space* could not venture anywhere near true action/adventure life-and-death situations. Irwin Allen and Tony Wilson had good reason to believe that *Space* would have to be a show with intentionally non-horrific monsters and scenes that were played for laughs over thrills.

Seizing the opportunity, Jonathan Harris meddled further with the character. In the first minute of the episode, the tone was set as Harris overplayed the scene in which Smith tosses the blasting-pack into the bog. The idea that he would throw the pack, then turn to leave, then pause, then return to the edge of the bog to fling in the pin, is inane. But Harris thought it was funny, and so did first time *Lost in Space* director Don Richardson.

To appreciate how much Harris hammed it up, compare his behavior on the screen to the way the action was described in the script:

> 17. SMITH
>
> He looks around once more to make sure that Will is well on his way – then pulls the pin on the explosive and tosses it far out into the bog. He brushes his hands off with the satisfied smile of a job well done – then looks at his watch – and starts sauntering at a leisurely pace back to camp.

Regarding the continuing evolution of the character, Harris told interviewer Mike Clark, "I think he would be a bore. Comedic villainy is far more palatable than out-and-out villainy, which I don't think is interesting for more than 10 minutes. One could adore Dr. Smith while also screaming, 'I'm going to kill the S.O.B.!' And that's *exactly* what people did." (JH-SL85)

Pre-Production:

Director Don Richardson joins *Lost in Space* (third from left, with his arm around Jonathan Harris). Richardson would direct more episodes than anyone else, but it would be a love/hate relationship.

Don Richardson was 42 when first hired to direct for Irwin Allen. He was in his fifteenth year as a TV director, having began with sixteen episodes of *The Adventure of Ellery Queen* from 1950 through 1952. Other shows that employed him often included the sitcom *Margie* (sixteen episodes), the one-hour primetime hospital soap *The Doctors and the Nurses* (six episodes), and the courtroom drama *The Defenders* (six episodes). In 1964, with *The*

Virginian, Richardson directed his first western. Next, he moved into high concept and camp comedy with assignments on *Get Smart* and *The Munsters.* After directing a couple of episodes for the one-hour nighttime soap *The Long, Hot Summer* for 20th Century-Fox, he received an invitation to do an episode of *Voyage to the Bottom of the Sea.*

Richardson told authors Joel Eisner and Barry Magen, "I recall I was in a movie theater, and I used to, in those days, check with my agent once a day. I called in and he said that a man named Irwin Allen wanted me to do an episode of *Voyage to the Bottom of the Sea....* Then he said, 'There is one catch. He wants to meet you first.' I said, 'I don't meet anybody, because I don't appear on the screen. So there is no point in seeing what I look like. If he wants to see my work, he could watch the TV and it's there. Or he can call the networks and get an old show.' So my agent said to call him back in half an hour. I called back and he said, 'Mr. Allen said to go to hell.' So I said, 'It's mutual.'"

It was an introduction to Irwin Allen somewhat similar to that which Jonathan Harris had experienced. Allen had shown a similar dramatic reaction when Harris didn't immediately provide Allen with film of his acting when demanded. Beyond that, Harris behaved professionally and requested a meeting with Allen. Richardson did not. He was too busy going to a movie.

Allen had good reason in wanting to meet a director before hiring him, especially considering the unique aspects of *Voyage to the Bottom of the Sea* and *Lost in Space.* There rightfully would be much to discuss. But Richardson was already being difficult.

Richardson continued: "Two weeks later, I got called again. The agent said, 'Mr. Allen says would you do the show if he doesn't have to meet you?' I said, 'Sure. After I'm on salary I'll meet anybody, even the Devil himself.' So, I went to the studio on the appointed day and they put me in an office and gave me a script. About twenty minutes later, the associate producer came in. His name was Jerry Briskin, and he was a very nervous man; he would keep pulling at his collar all the time. He said, 'Mr. Allen says now that you are on salary are you willing to meet him?' So, I said, 'Sure,' and went with him to the stage where Irwin was directing the pilot to *The Time Tunnel.* There were hundreds of people running around on the Titanic in their underwear with water effects. I was led into a trailer on the stage where Irwin Allen was sitting. He was a tiny little man with about two feet of very Brillo-like hair on top of his head. He was wearing a puce shirt with a violet ribbon tied to a glass for looking through for color shots. He said, 'Sit down; sit down.' So I sat down and he briefed me on the cast. He told me this one is a lunatic and this one is an egomaniac and so on. Then he said, 'Good luck,' and I went back to my office. Then, after lunch, I came back and Briskin came in and said, 'Mr. Allen says now that you are on salary are you willing to meet him?' I said, 'We did that this morning.' He said, 'I told him, but he forgot.' So, we went back to the Titanic and the people in their underwear running around. This time Irwin had changed his shirt. He had on an orange shirt and a chartreuse ribbon tied to the seeing glass. He said, 'Sit down; sit down,' and, like nothing happened before, told me all about the *Voyage* cast. I looked at my notes and they all corresponded to what he told me before. And he said, 'Good luck.' And that's how I began working for Irwin." (DR-LISF)

This was not unlike the Irwin Allen that network executive Lew Hunter described, when explaining how Tony Wilson was able to get away with ignoring many of Allen's script notes. Wilson had learned that Allen simply wouldn't remember.

Richardson never did direct that episode of *Voyage to the Bottom of the Sea*. Allen pulled him off the job to do a *Lost in Space* instead. It would be Richardson's first of twenty-six episode for the series; making him *Lost in Space*'s most frequent director.

Dawson Palmer played the bog monster. Maybe you recognize him – he was the bubble creature in "The Derelict," the Rubberoid in "Wish Upon a Star" and "the Bush Creature" in "The Raft."

New wardrobe was introduced for the recurring cast members in this episode. In some scenes they wear them, in others they don't. Most liked their new duds. Up to this point, Smith had been costumed in more traditional bad-guy dark tones – black pants and a dark, burgundy sweater, which was set off by red piping and a light-blue turtleneck collar. It was designed to direct attention to Smith's villainous face. Now that was changed. Smith was given a beige/brown combination to wear.

Paul Zastupnevich said, "The cast got tired of wearing the same thing week after week, and the producers agreed to a change of colors. They said, 'Instead of having the villain in dark colors, let's do a reverse.'" (PZ-SL93)

Production Diary:

Filmed from January 13 – 21, 1966 (7 days).

Day 2 of the production – with Dawson Palmer as the "Ghost." The lines on the photo, creating a box around the bog monster, were drawn with a grease pencil. They indicated where to crop the picture for promotional purposes, as used at the beginning of this chapter. In the wider view, crew and lighting are visible.

Day 1: Thursday, January 13, 1966. They began filming at 8 a.m., as was the routine. Work took place on Stage 6. With the series behind in deliveries to CBS, first up was the sequence needed to be tagged onto "The Sky Pirate" as that episode's cliffhanger, which would air one week earlier. In the scene, John, Don, Will, and Smith are by the Chariot, then John heads toward the bog to plant a sign warning the others to stay clear. And then he gets gassed. Also filmed, Will and Smith crossing the bog with an explosive charge, and Smith ridding himself of that charge, then hurrying back to the Chariot. By 6:50 p.m. Richardson had covered only five and three-eighths pages from the script. He was one-quarter of a day behind. That meant that Allen came to the set to shout a bit and remind everyone that time was money.

Considering that no episode of *Lost in Space* had yet to be brought in on budget, Allen felt justified in doing a little shouting.

Day 2: Friday, January 14. It was another full day on Stage 6, with Will and Smith encountering the monster in the bog; and John and Don getting slapped silly by the invisible beast. Fortunately it didn't bite or claw. Or rip limbs out. It just hit.

Top and middle picture: Day 2, in the bog built onto Stage 6. Bottom picture: True chemistry ... even in the dressing room – and how many stars will do that?

The scenes with Smith and Will were intentionally played for laughs. The fight scene with John and Don was also laughable, but perhaps unintentionally so … at least by the actors. The man behind the camera felt differently about it.

Director Richardson said, "*Lost in Space* was always a space comedy adventure show. The story I was told by the story editor, Tony Wilson, who was a friend of mine from New York and was the one who got Irwin to hire me, was that when the pilot was made, Irwin, who had absolutely no sense of humor, thought he was making a very serious program. In the viewing room, the executives from the network who were watching the pilot were absolutely hysterical, laughing at this ridiculous thing. Irwin almost got furious and got up and wanted to stop the showing. Tony kicked him under the table and whispered, 'Never mind, they love it.' That's how it became a comedy and it stayed a comedy forever afterwards." (DR-LISF)

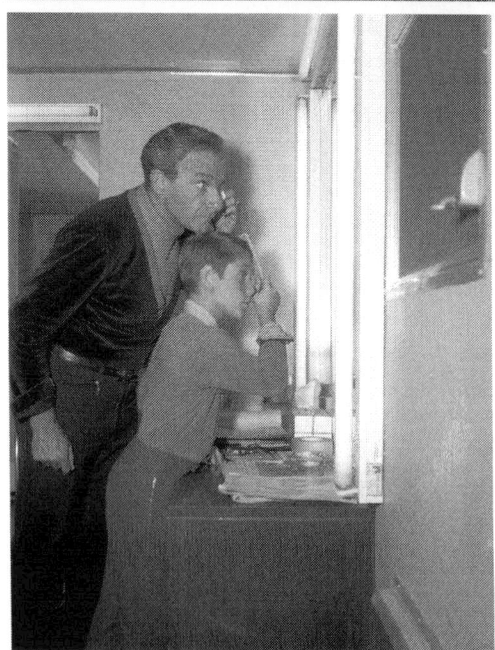

Concerning the comic chemistry between Smith and Will, Jonathan Harris told William Anchors, Jr., "We were very good friends, Billy and I, based on mutual

Now you see the new costume for Jonathan Harris ... now you don't. Harris hated his new yellow tunic and it would not last long.

need – *we needed each other*. I'm no fool, I needed that young boy. He was very, very important to me. He was also a wonderful actor, I thought.... You know, he had rules on how long he could act, and then he had to go to school. I used to go to the school, which was on the set. I would bribe [his female teacher] with a bottle of cologne and drag him off to my dressing room to work out the next scene. Oh, he was quick as could be. Of course, his dear mother was always hanging about until I barred her from the set. 'Out!' And out she went! She got in the way. I had no time for that nonsense. I really didn't. You know, it's a hard job. Really, it's very tough. Seven o'clock in the makeup chair, with your eyes totally closed. Toothpicks to hold them up, keep them open, so they could line your eyes; put mascara on. Then you come home at what – nine o'clock, nine-thirty, ten – just barely alive having survived the San Diego freeway, [then] to take a small glass of gin, a piece of steak, and you're dead; you're in bed. [Then] up again at 4:30, you see. So, you do what you have to. You need certain people to help you do what you're doing. So, you use each other. I don't know whether Billy felt that. He was very young. But I knew what I was doing. I was using him. For him and for me, it worked." (JH-IASB2)

From 8 a.m. to 6:50 p.m., Richardson covered nine and six-eighths pages from the script, and held at one-quarter of a day behind.

Day 3: Monday, January 17. The director seemed to have acquired his space legs. He filmed with the company on Stage 6 from 8 a.m. to 6:25 p.m., covering ten and one-eighths pages from the script, including the scenes at the Drill Site. Richardson continued to hold at one-quarter of a day behind.

Day 4: Tuesday, January 18. They worked on Stage 11, filming the séance scene and ensuing violence. Also filmed, many of the campsite scenes outside the Jupiter 2.

Between the hours of 8 a.m. and 7:05 p.m., Richardson was only able to film seven pages from the script. He fell to one-half of a day behind.

Day 5: Wednesday, January 19. Again on Stage 11, and the campsite outside the Jupiter 2, including the fight with the invisible monster. Richardson filmed from 8 a.m. to 6:27 p.m., covering nine pages from the script and holding at one-half of a day behind.

"The Keeper, Part II" aired on CBS this night from 7:30 to 8:30 p.m. With a 6:27 wrap time, most members of the cast and crew were able to make it home in time to see the entire episode. Billy Mumy was ecstatic. It was one of his favorites.

Day 6: Thursday, January 20. Again, they worked on Stage 11. This was meant to be the final day of production, but it was clear that goal would not be reached, so "War of the Robots" was delayed by one day. Don Richardson pushed the company to get ten and seven-eighths pages of script covered, finishing the Ext. Campsite scenes outside the Jupiter 2, and holding at one-half of a day behind. He completed his last shot at 7:15 p.m.

Day 7: Friday, January 21. They filmed on Stage 11, beginning at 8 a.m. with the upper deck of the Jupiter 2. Richardson covered eleven and one-eighths pages from the script, filming until 9:20 p.m.

William Self had approved $137,197 for the production. The final cost was $160,375.

Post-Production:

Some things are never made clear in this episode. Much of the confusion was the result of sound effects work during post production.

When Smith and Penny sit at the Ouija board, is it Uncle Thaddeus who causes the eerie-sounding wind, then the rustling of the bushes, then a bush to be levitated and seemingly laugh before flying off, then the glass to break, then the board was elevated and smashed against a rock? Or is it the creature from the bog? Or a combination of both? Sam Taylor of CBS had the same questions in one of his memos (printed earlier in the chapter), and asked that it be made clear to the viewing audience that it was the invisible bog creature creating the commotion and not a ghost or a demon. The network was okay with bog monsters during its family hour, but nothing to endorse the occult.

The decisions made during post-production didn't help the matter.

The sounds that accompanied the bog creature in a previous scene – the thumping of his heavy feet – are not present in this scene.

They are, however, present in the script. Peter Packer wrote:

9. THE TWO

As Smith looks at [Penny] hopefully.

SMITH
You are beginning to feel a presence.

PENNY
(shaking her head)
I just feel shivery.

SMITH

Good. That's how it begins.

CAMERA begins to creep in on the board and the glass. As it does so, we hear the remote approach of dragging, slithering footsteps, the labored respiration.

PENNY'S VOICE

Something's happening.

SMITH

What is it?

PENNY'S VOICE

It's moving, I think.

10. SMITH, PENNY

staring at the glass.

11. INSERT – THE GLASS

on the board. It is rocking a little – clattering faintly. The footsteps and the respiration are closer. The whine of the wind is louder.

42. SMITH, PENNY

staring at the rocking glass.

SMITH

(excited)

We are not alone. They are with us!

(sonorously)

Oh – eternal powers of the spirit world – grasp this humble artifact and materialize your presence so that we may recognize you.

43. INSERT – THE GLASS

rocking – clattering. Sounds of respiration and footsteps much closer. Suddenly – with a small explosive pop – the glass bursts into tinkling fragments!

44. SMITH, PENNY

staring, shocked at the fragments. And in that same instant there's an angry rumble of labored breathing – and the Ouija board is lifted from their legs. They jump to their feet and watch as the Ouija board floats away for a moment – then is suddenly dashed against a rock and splintered into pieces. The labored breathing is now fierce and very close – and the whine of the wind is terrifying. Smith – open-mouthed with fright – backs away from the shattered Ouija board – grabs Penny by the hand and both turn and run out of scene toward the camp area.

Release / Reaction:
(CBS premiere air date: February 2, 1966)
(Network repeat broadcast: June 8, 1966)

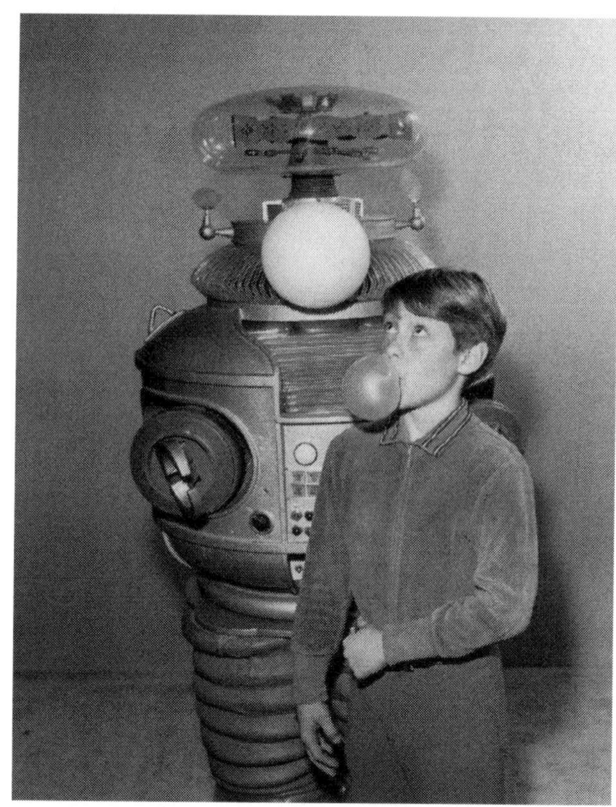

This was the week new publicity photos were released to newspapers by CBS and 20th Century-Fox. Instead of promoting an episode about a "Ghost in Space," the thinking was more directed to counter *Batman*'s silliness with some *Lost in Space* silliness – featuring the Robot.

The week that "Ghost in Space" had its initial broadcast, spacecraft Luna 9 was the first vessel made by man to make a soft landing on the moon. It was sent there by the Soviet Union. The Beatles still had the best-selling record album in department and record stores with *Rubber Soul*, keeping *Whipped Cream & Other Delights* by Herb Alpert's Tijuana Brass in second position. The Fab Four also had the song getting the most airplay on radio stations across the land, with "We Can Work It Out," having displaced Simon & Garfunkel's "Sounds of Silence" from the top spot, which in turn had displaced "We Can Work It Out" one week earlier. Meanwhile, *Dr. Zhivago* was doing the best business in the movie houses.

Also from this week – CBS began a new ploy to recapture the young viewers

who had abandoned the series for *Batman*. The subject of "Ghost in Space" was an indication of one technique used. The other was a picture of Billy Mumy and the Robot having a bubble-gum bubble-blowing contest, distributed to newspapers across the nation, and carried by many, including the *Arizona Republic*, in Phoenix, Arizona, with the caption: "'Anything you can do, I can do better,' Robot member of the CBS *Lost in Space* cast seems to be saying to Billy Mumy in a battle of bubble gum. The Robot has been adopted as mascot for the *Lost in Space* fan club at U.C.L.A. Westwood campus."

In another photo distributed to newspapers, and carried in Utah's *Ogden Standard-Examiner*, Jonathan Harris was shown playing chess with the Robot. The caption read: "PROGRAMMED FOR DEFEAT. Jonathan Harris (Col. Zachary Smith) is beside himself as his mechanical playmate, the robot, pulls a rare stratagem in a chess game. The only way Jonathan can get the better of his adversary is to program him to defeat with the robot mouthing the classic line, 'Will not compute.' The robot and the actor have roles in a CBS-TV series, *Lost in Space*."

Two days before the first broadcast of "Ghost in Space," a syndicated article by entertainment columnist Jay Fredericks, carried by the *Charleston Gazette Mail*, reported:

> The National Association for Better Radio and Television (NAFBRAT) has issued its 1966 edition of "Television for the Family," in which it rates programs as recommended or objectionable for teen and child viewing.

On the recommended list were *Bewitched*, which NAFBRAT found to be "beguiling, brightly written and produced," and *Bullwinkle*, which was deemed "satiric in a way easily understood by young viewers ... More organized and consistent than most series for children." Also given passing grades: *F Troop*, which was assessed as "pure hilarious farce ... well done and really funny," and *My Favorite Martian*, "done in good taste" and which "contrasts with most other 'space' programs because it generates a friendly curiosity rather than fear and hate toward the unknown elements and inhabitants of outer worlds."

The NAFBRAT report then turned to shows that were judged as "objectionable." For *Voyage to the Bottom of the Sea*, the NAFBRAT verdict said, "This series, strategically placed in the early evening to attract children, is far too tense and horror ridden for such an audience. The stories and situations are too ridiculous for anyone more mature." Of *The Wild, Wild West*," the prickly NAFBRAT people hissed, "[A]n outright horror show ... a disgrace to the Columbia Broadcasting System and a menace to American children." Even *Candid Camera* received criticism. NAFBRAT called it "tasteless ... [with] implications of invasion of privacy." Of *Gidget*, starring sweet young Sally Field, the not so sweet or young prudes from NAFBRAT said it was "a tiresome, pointless show in which the family is dominated unpleasantly by the youngsters." As for *Lost in Space*, the consumer watchdogs barked, "[C]liff hanger terror ... expensive production emphasizes the determination of the producer (and the network) to win a youthful audience, regardless of the consequences."

Come Wednesday night, and only a few clicks away on the channel dial: "The Joker Is Wild" on *Batman*, introducing Cesar Romero as the arch villain.

The A.C. Nielsen 30-City Ratings survey for February 2, 1966 awarded the win to the Joker, reporting:

Network / Program:	Rating	Share:
7:30 – 8 p.m.:		
ABC: *Batman*	**23.9**	**39.3%**
CBS: *Lost in Space*	16.0	26.3%
NBC: *The Virginian*	17.0	28.0%
8 – 8:30 p.m.:		
ABC: *The Patty Duke Show*	16.7	25.8%
CBS: *Lost in Space*	**22.3**	**34.4%**
NBC: *The Virginian*	20.8	32.1%

Compared to the previous few weeks, the numbers had improved for *Lost in Space* during its first half-hour, although the caped crusader and his boy wonder still dominated the time period. However, at 8 p.m., *Space* was now defying the rule of thumb concerning TV viewership from this era when most television sets did not come with remote controls. At the end of *Batman*, rather than enduring an episode of *The Patty Duke Show*, people were actually getting out of their chairs or off their couches to walk over to the TV set and switch the channel to a show that was already in progress.

More than likely, mom and dad stayed in their seats, and the small fry huddled on the floor a few feet in front of the television – the best place for kids ten and under to watch TV – looked back for permission, then spun that channel dial at record speed to CBS.

31

Episode 20: "War of the Robots"

Written by Barney Slater
(with script polishing by Anthony Wilson)
Directed by Sobey Martin
Produced by Irwin Allen; with Jerry Briskin

From the *Lost in Space* show files (Irwin Allen Papers Collection):

> Will discovers a rusty, abandoned alien Robot and insists on trying to put it together again in spite of warnings from our Robot that it is dangerous. He makes it work and everyone is delighted by its superior abilities. Our own Robot, now considered obsolete, is completely ignored and it finally wanders away. The alien Robot is secretly planning to get them all into its power and then turn them over to a "MONSTER" in outer space whom it serves. Will, who doesn't trust it, manages to get away when the alien Robot disarms the others and forces them into the spaceship.

From the Script:
(Shooting Final teleplay, February 1, 1966 draft)

– *Will:* "I'm going to get this Robot fixed and that's all there is to it!" *Robot:* "Correction: Not Robot … Robotoid." *Will (a bit irritated):* "Who cares what it's called. All I want to do is get it working." *Robot:* "A robot is a machine which performs as programmed. A robotoid is a machine which goes beyond programming. It has a free choice. *(singsong voice)* Good, bad – Wrong, right – Slow, fast – Hot, cold – loud…" *Will (breaking in):* "All right. Forget it." *Robot:* "Abandon this project." *Will:* "I know your problem. You're jealous. That's what's wrong – jealous!" *Robot:* "Jealousy – a human emotion. I am a machine." *Will (losing patience):* "Then what's the matter with you?" *Robot (voice low, barely audible):* "I do not know…. *(computers click and strange noises come from its inside)* … I am not jealous. It is a human emotion. I am not jealous. It is a human emotion."

– *Smith:* "You'll tell me what's been going on here or I'll take out your power-pak for a month! *(off Robot's silence)* All right. If that's what you want, that's exactly what you will get!" *Robinson:* "Take it easy, Dr. Smith. We can't find out anything if the Robot is deactivated." *Smith:* "Spare the punishment and spoil the robot. Is that what you want?" *Robinson:* "We're not dealing with a child but with a machine." *Will:* "The way he's been acting lately, Dad, I'm not so sure about that." *Robinson (with a disapproving look):* "I'm surprised at you, Will. We're talking about a piece of scientific equipment, not a flesh and blood creature."

– *Will (gets a thought):* "I've got it! I'll condition your memory bank. Now repeat after me – the Robotoid is a harmless machine. It offers no danger. *(off Robot's silence)* Well, go ahead." *Robot:* "I do not compute." *Will:* "You're just being stubborn, that's all." *Robot (mildly):* "As you suggested … an error in my programming." *Will (with hopeless gesture):* "I can't stand out here all night arguing with you. If you don't want to come with me, you don't have to." *Robot:* "You will go alone?" *Will:* "Sure." *Robot (as Will moves away):* "Stop, William Robinson … I will accompany you. *(walks toward Will)* You may need protection." *Will:* "I'm big enough to take care of myself." *Robot:* "True … but I am a little bigger."

– *Will:* "If we feed the Robotoid any more information, Dr. Smith, he's liable to explode." *Smith:* "Your fears are groundless, William. *(pats alien Robotoid affectionately)* The mental capabilities of this machine are unlimited. He's just devouring knowledge. *(looks toward the Robinson Robot with contempt)* Compared to that clumsy has-been over there, we have an absolute genius on our hands." *Will (looks concerned):* "You shouldn't talk that way in front of him, Dr. Smith. Even if he is a Robot he understands what we say and has a reaction." *Smith:* "Nonsense. The next thing you'll be telling me is he's thin-skinned."

Assessment:

It was a good idea to pit both of Robert Kinoshita's robot creations against one another. That in itself was the catalyst for story editor Tony Wilson and freelancer Barney Slater dreaming up this tale. With the menacing music from *The Day the Earth Stood Still* accompanying many of the shots of the Robotoid (aka Robbie the Robot from *Forbidden Planet*), the dark-colored, ominous looking mechanical man can still send a shiver up one's spine. In 1966, and especially for younger viewers, that shiver was electrifying.

In addition, since the creative staff – with both the blessing and much prodding from CBS – was determined to make the *Lost in Space* Robot more of a warm-hearted and comical character, this was as good a way to do it as any. We see the Robot acting more human than ever before, and even struggling to understand why he is behaving this way. He becomes fearful and hurt; lamenting like a mechanical Hamlet over his confused inner feelings and the weight he carries from believing he is no longer wanted. Self-conflict is always a plus in storytelling, and there is a hefty degree of it presented here. In fact, on February 9, 1966, when "War of the Robots" first aired, the self-tortured character of this tale came from a most unlikely recurring player.

An essential element in effective storytelling is to get the audience to feel empathy for the protagonist. And we do so for the Robot. As silly as this episode gets, it still brings forward a few "Aw, poor Robot" moments. It also presents an effective character arc, with the Robot learning and thereby changing through the course of the story. He experiences rejection, then indignation, then overcomes the anger and returns to risk destruction in order to protect the family he "loves."

Another plus is that we have the old Dr. Smith back. With the exception of a few brief moments, including the Tag scene when Smith is delegated the task of polishing the Robot's armor, his character is not played for laughs. He is nearly the cold-hearted Smith we saw in many of the first dozen episodes of the series. Consider the following passage of dialogue:

Robot: "Do you need any help, Dr. Smith?" *Smith:* "I can think of plenty of things which I would like done. Unfortunately, you are incapable of doing any of them." *Robot:* "No one requires my services anymore." *Smith:* "An astute observation. You've reached the end of the line. The joy ride is over. I had thought of redesigning you into a pleasure vehicle, but I'm sure you'd be substandard even as that."

These attributes noted, there are many unanswered questions. How does our Robot know the alien machine is a robotoid? Why is it that, in light of the behavior of our Robot, no one speculates that he too is a robotoid? How does the smokescreen emitted from the Robot's tracks (feet) prevent the Robotoid from using sensors to aim its weapons?

There are many artificial moments in this story about artificial intelligence as well. The Teaser, as with the conclusions of Acts I and III, each end with the same threat – the Robotoid firing its "neutron tube" at some object in order for the writers to convey danger and thereby create suspense. It's an unimaginative ploy.

Worse, Barney Slater's script is often shallow, as much of the dialogue leans towards one-dimensional characterizations with too many moments of dullness and clichés. In particular, many of the exchanges between the robots are downright trite.

Lost in Space never made a First Season episode that wasn't worth enjoying. That applies to this episode. But, despite all it has going for it, "War of the Robots" stumbles more than it sprints, much like another first season dog – "One of Our Dogs Is Missing." This is not *Space*'s First Season at its best.

Script:

Story assignment 8465 (Production #8521)

Barney Slater's treatment, and 1st and 2nd draft teleplays: December 1965/Early January 1966.

Reformatted Mimeo Department Shooting Final teleplay (light green pages): January 5, 1966.

Tony Wilson's page revisions (blue insert pages) January 17.

Additional page revisions by Wilson (pink insert pages) January 18.

Further page revisions by Wilson (dark green insert pages) January 19.
Further revisions by Wilson (yellow insert pages) January 20.
Further revisions by Wilson (gold insert pages) January 24.
Further revisions by Wilson (beige insert pages) January 27.
Further revisions by Wilson (blue insert pages) February 1.

A press release issued by the studio on October 4, 1965, announced:

> The public response to the robot in producer Irwin Allen's 20th Century-Fox Television series, *Lost in Space*, starring Guy Williams, June Lockhart, Jonathan Harris, Mark Goddard, Marta Kristen, Billy Mumy and Angela Cartwright, has become so great that Allen has instructed his team of writers to pen more scenes for the amusing "actor." Additionally, Allen will conduct a national contest later in the year to find a suitable name for his space "friend."

Irwin Allen and Tony Wilson didn't limit themselves to merely finding "more scenes for the amusing 'actor,'" they wanted a story built around the Robot as well.

Credit should be given to Allen, Slater, and Wilson: "War of the Robots" contains many story elements later found in the 2001 Kubrick-Spielberg film *AI: Artificial Intelligence*. On the other hand, a more cynical type might observe that this episode is a retelling of the Pinocchio story, or even the Greek myth of Pygmalion and Galatea. In all instances, an artificial construct yearns to attain human attributes. Shades of *Star Trek: The Next Generation's* Data!

Robot stories were nothing new by the time *Lost in Space* came along, but the concept of an artificial intelligence's ability to develop both human traits and affection toward its makers had perhaps never been explored to this degree. The Robot's personality development, as demonstrated here and in previous episodes, is certainly one brick in the edifice of fictional artificial intelligence.

The man inside the Robot, Bob May, put it this way: "Initially, our robot was just a General Utility Non-theorizing Environmental Control Robot, model B9, put aboard the Jupiter 2 with the responsibility of helping the Robinsons with their mission of colonizing and developing a new planet to alleviate Earth's overcrowding. Everything was fine until Dr. Smith reprogrammed the Robot to destroy the Jupiter 2.... Will, with his inquisitive mind, found out what Dr. Smith had done and proceeded to reprogram the Robot. But he changed something more than simple command sequences. From that moment on, the Robot started on his journey of self-awareness. The gradual change came from knowledge and positive data input from each member of the Robinson Family, Major West, and of course, Dr. Smith. [Acquired from] Maureen Robinson: Devotion to family; John Robinson: Responsibility and guardianship; Major Don West: Devotion to duty; Judy Robinson: Respect and kindness without reservation; Penny Robinson: Family loyalty and joy in diversity; Will Robinson: Love and friendship; Dr. Smith: Cheating, lying, buffoonery, complaining, excuses and cowardice. And, of course, encounters with aliens, friend and foe, contributed to his grasp of the fact that hopes and dreams are inherent in all creatures in the universe. All of this data enabled our Robot, in time, to develop feelings, attitudes, understanding and ambitions that no other robot or machine could ever have. The Robot is the protector of the family, and more importantly, he perceives this as his role in the family – it is not just simple programmed orders. Will and the Robot are like a boy and his dog." (LISM.COM01)

Two passages of dialogue in the script demonstrate the growing Will/Robot relationship. The first takes place after the Robot tells Will he wants to accompany him to see the Robotoid. Up until now, the Robot has always addressed Will by his full name – Will Robinson. Will tells the Robot: "I'm big enough to take care of myself." The Robot says: "True … but I am a little bigger." The scene continues:

> Will grins and looks at the Robot with affection.
>
> WILL
>
> Well, maybe a couple of inches or so. From now on, why don't you call me Will. We've known each other long enough to drop formalities.
>
> There is a brief silence and the Robot's computers click softly.
>
> ROBOT
>
> Will … Will. I shall call you Will.

The second passage occurs after the Robotoid has shown his true colors and taken the Robinsons prisoner. The dialogue reads:

Will: "You were right about the Robotoid. Repairing him was the worst thing I ever did." *Robot (half turns away from Will):* "You spoil our meeting with the discussion of this subject." *Will (moves around to face the Robot):* "But we've got to talk about him. You don't know what has happened." *Robot:* "It is not my concern. You forget that a Robot has no heart. I am only wires and cold metal parts." *Will:* "The Robotoid has everyone a prisoner in the Jupiter 2. And he's sending for some aliens to come and take them away. We need your help!" *Robot:* "It does not compute. I am sorry, but it does not compute." *Will (desperate):* "Yes, it does. You just don't want to listen." *Robot (computers click loudly)*: "The Robinsons are no longer my responsibility. They are no longer my family." *Will:* "What about Dr. Smith? I know you'll want to help him." *Robot:* "He has rejected me most of all. I will go now." *Will:* "No, wait! I'm your friend! You know that! Help them for me!" *Robot (hesitates as if thinking):* "You are my friend, Will. What do you wish done?"

The script has a split personality. While many scenes are effective, others are often pedestrian. Interwoven with the dialogue that works are complete passages that do not. Indicative of what doesn't work are the many scripted repartees between the robots, such as:

Robotoid: "You are obviously of very primitive design. From now on, I will serve the Robinsons. In all ways I am superior to you. Since there is no need for two of us, you will leave." *Robot:* "The Robinsons belong to me. I will not give up my family!" *Robotoid:* "The choice is not yours. Already you know what is happening. The Robinsons prefer me. In a short while I will be indispensable to them … while you will be relegated to the role of an inactive bystander." *Robot:* "You are mistaken. Your efforts will be resisted by me." *Robotoid:* "You are even more stupid than I first computed. My path is very clear, nothing can stop me." *Robot:* "I am very strong. I can stop you." *Robotoid:* "I am armed not only with superior mental powers but superior weapons as well." *Robot:* "You will be stopped." *Robotoid:* "I can destroy you easily."

Most Saturday morning cartoons are better-scripted than this. While we can easily imagine Slater and Tony Wilson chuckling over the idea of having the Robot make statement such as "I am very strong," from the perspective of a writer, dialogue this lacking in subtlety, this banal, is embarrassing by its lack of cleverness.

Wilson and Slater seemed to be kindred souls. In fact, Wilson liked Slater's script enough to feel it did not need a polish, therefore there was no "Revised Shooting Final" teleplay for this episode. This is one of a handful of episodes that went before the camera with the script still identified as a "Shooting Final" – so designated to identify it as the freelance writer's final draft after the pages were reformatted by the Mimeo Department. This draft would of course have selected page revisions by Wilson as he addressed the notes from CBS and Irwin Allen, and there were many of these – from January 17, 18, 19, 20, 24, 27 and February 1st – but Wilson never performed an overall script polish. Either Wilson was immensely impressed by Slater's writing, or he was merely too overworked to rework the script. Bet on the latter.

Pre-Production:

Robbie the Robot got around. Introduced in 1956 on *Forbidden Planet*, Robbie then popped up in other movies and TV shows, including with Rod Serling in *The Twilight Zone*, (above), with Ted Cassidy in *The Addams Family* (upper right), and even with Peter Falk in *Columbo* (right).

We first met Robbie the Robot in the classic 1956 MGM sci-fi film *Forbidden Planet*. The initial sketch design was from Arnold

Gillespie, then refined by production illustrator Mentor Huebner. It was *Lost in Space*'s own art designer Robert Kinoshita, and his team at the MGM prop department, that performed the actual building.

Eldon Hansen was the man inside the Robotoid for this episode. He would return to work inside the same robot housing for the Third Season episode "Condemned of Space."

Ollie O'Toole provided the voice of the Robotoid. Irwin Allen liked having the actors in the costumes provide the voices, but there was no way they were going to ask a professional voice actor to lug around a costume that weighed a few hundred pounds, and which also required technical skill to move all the working parts and flash the chest light to coincide with speaking.

Production Diary:

Filmed January 24 – 31, 1966 (6 days).

The situation regarding the late deliveries of new *Lost in Space* episodes to CBS was at a state of crisis. For this reason, it was decided that two episodes of the series would have to be filmed simultaneously. Production #8520, "The Magic Mirror," would be assigned to director Nathan Juran and guest director of photography Charles G. Clark. Production #8521, "War of the Robots," with director Sobey Martin and series regular cinematographer Gene Polito, would begin filming on the same day. For this reason, Angela Cartwright, featured prominently in "The Magic Mirror," does not appear in "War of the Robots." Accordingly, Billy Mumy and Bob May do not appear in 'The Magic Mirror." The remainder of the cast appeared in both episodes, although featured more prominently in "Robots."

It was an ambitious undertaking, with two corresponding production schedules intertwined. If either of the productions fell behind, both house of cards would collapse.

As for the production numbering, "The Magic Mirror" came first, as Production #8520, while "War of the Robots" was assigned the number 8521. However, "War of the Robots" finished filming one day earlier and entered into post-production first. It therefore aired first and is catalogued as *Lost in Space* Episode 26, with "The Magic Mirror" following as Episode 27.

Guy Williams was scheduled to work six days; Lockhart for four; Goddard for five; Kristen for four; Mumy for six; Harris for four; May for five; and Eldon Hansen, the man inside the Robotoid suit, for four. Hal John Norman, as the alien "monster" on the video screen, would only be needed for one day.

The new costumes for the recurring cast members, which were introduced and seen in approximately half of the previous episode, were now fully featured. Once Jonathan Harris saw the dailies and had a look at how he appeared in his new top, he was not pleased. Harris felt the lighter colored shirt made him look heavier around the middle. Also, in his opinion, it just wasn't an appropriate shade for a villain – even a funny villain. Most actors back in this day had little to no say regarding their wardrobe. But Harris was learning week by week that he could get away with things that other actors on other shows could not. The only question, then, was how long would the new attire stay?

Scenes filmed on Stage 11 during Day 1 of the production, by the *Lost in Space* production crew. The series had fallen behind on its deliveries to CBS, so "War of the Robots" and "Magic Mirror" had to be filmed simultaneously, splitting the cast between them, with the latter episode filmed by the *Voyage to the Bottom of the Sea* production team.

Day 1: Monday, January 24th. Sobey Martin had patiently waited an extra day to get started on his next *Lost in Space* assignment, as "Ghost in Space" had fallen behind schedule. Beginning at 8 a.m. on Stage 11, Martin and the production company worked on the "Ext. Jupiter 2" campsite set with Billy Mumy and Bob May. For part of the day, the cast was augmented with Guy Williams, June Lockhart, Mark Goddard, Marta Kristen, Jonathan Harris, and Eldon Hansen. The scenes filmed included Will running in and telling the family about the robot he had found; Will figuring how to fix the Robotoid and leaving with the Robot accompanying him for protection; the climactic fight between the two robots; and the Tag scene, with Dr. Smith polishing the Robot.

For the battle, a stuntman took Bob May's place inside the Robot. Jonathan Harris said, "Bobby was furious. He was on the sidelines during the fight, screaming, 'I look like a fake! Everybody will know I am a fake!'

"I used to throw him bodily out of my dressing room because he drove me mad. He was a most unfortunate young man, I have to tell you." (JH-IASB2)

Kevin Burns understood May's frustration. He said, "This was the first time the Robot had to be worn by a stuntman. Bobby was not a stuntman. So, for the first time on screen, Bobby wasn't in the suit. He was extremely upset that someone else was performing in the suit. So, he was standing there with the other cast watching the scene be shot, and he said, 'I'm a fake! I'm a fake! Everyone will know that I'm a fake!' And Jonathan was kind of like, '*I'm* a fake. Strange.' In other words, Bobby was so, by then, identifying with the character – he was so in love with this character; it gave him such a purpose, in terms of playing the Robot on *Lost in Space* – that he was upset that anyone else would be in the Robot. He was sure the people watching at home could discern that it wasn't him in that outfit. And that was his nature." (KB-AI16)

Sobey Martin filmed nine pages from the script, completing the last shot at 6:55 p.m. They were on schedule.

Meanwhile, Nathan Juran and the crew assigned to him for "The Magic Mirror" worked on Stage 6. They had Angela Cartwright for the entire day, and, off and on, Jonathan Harris, June Lockhart and Marta Kristen.

Above: From Day 2, not one of the better creatures on *Space*. Below: Filming on Stage 11 on Day 3.

Day 2: Tuesday, January 25th. A second day on Stage 11 for Martin and "War of the Robots," now on the "Int. Jupiter 2" upper deck set. Scheduled: The Robotoid talking to the alien on the video screen; the argument between the Robot and the Robotoid; Will catching the Robotoid with the ship's armament; the family discovering that the Robot is missing; and Maureen worried about the Robot, saying she was sorry they even found the Robotoid. Martin had Williams, Lockhart, Goddard, Kristen, Mumy and Hansen to direct, as he covered ten and sixth-eighths pages from the script, wrapping at 7 p.m. His unit was still on schedule.

Meanwhile, Nathan Juran was giving direction to Angela Cartwright, Jonathan Harris, and, for one scene, Guy Williams.

Day 3: Wednesday, January 26th. Martin again worked on Stage 11 at the Robinson's campsite outside the Jupiter 2. With his unit were Williams, Lockhart, Goddard, Kristen, Mumy, Harris, and Hansen. Among the scenes filmed was the sequence when Smith and Will feed information to the Robotoid; the discovery that numerous items were missing from the ship; then Will escaping. The timely although not terribly inventive director kept his unit filming from 8 a.m. to 6:55 p.m., finishing on schedule, with ten and one-eighth pages of the script covered. However, by the time the set was wrapped, and the cast members changed clothes and had makeup removed, then driven home, they would be missing the first part of "The Sky Pirate," having its CBS premiere on this night.

Meanwhile, on Stage 8, Nathan Juran continued filming "The Magic Mirror," with Angela Cartwright and Michael J. Pollard.

Day 4: Thursday, January 27th. This was the final day on Stage 11 for Sobey Martin and those assigned to his unit, including Williams, Lockhart, Goddard, Kristen, Mumy, Harris, May and Hansen. They filmed on the "Ext. Jupiter 2" campsite from 8 a.m. to 6:45 p.m. Martin covered all nine and five-eighths pages from the script that had been scheduled, including the scene when the Robot refuses to answer questions; the family feeling guilty over the Robot leaving; and the shots of the alien "Monster" for the "burn-in" sequences. Martin finished on schedule.

Meanwhile, on Stage 8, Nathan Juran worked with Cartwright and Pollard, and Jonathan Harris, who joined them in the afternoon.

Day 5 was planned for outdoor filming at the Fox "Moat" location, but rain forced this scene to be filmed on Stage 6 instead.

Day 5: Friday, January 28th. Martin and his unit were scheduled to work outdoors at the Moat location, but, due to rain, had to film on Stage 6 instead. The sequences planned for "Ext. Moat Area – Jungle Area (Day)," "Ext. Moat – Clearing (Day)," "Ext. Bushy Area – Another Section (Night") and "Ext. Moat Clearing (Night)" were now adapted for the soundstage, detracting from the production value of this episode. Martin had Williams, Goddard, Mumy, Harris, May and Hansen working with his unit. They covered nine and sixth-eighths pages, from 8 to 6:45 p.m. Scenes included Will finding the Robotoid in the Teaser; Will working on the Robotoid in the clearing; the search for the Robot; and the Robinson party stopping the Robot from destroying the Robotoid.

Jonathan Harris said, "The mobility of the Robot was difficult at best, because he was on wires controlled by the special effects off camera and there were certain things you couldn't do, because you had to pull him. And then you had to turn him around, because the track hadn't been laid for that yet. So we had to stop and re-set up, whatever.... Stuart Moody, who was special effects and a true genius – another crazy... wonderful man – dreamed up 'the bikini' – half the Robot. Bobby May wore the top half, [which was] very dreadful – it weighted about 80 pounds. They only shot to waist level, so you couldn't see that there was no bottom to the bikini. He would run around and climb up and down and do everything that we wanted him to do and it never cost a minute because Bobby did it. Eighty pounds! He loved it! I tell you, for the first month, I had such compassion for anyone who had to be in that thing, until I realized you couldn't get him out [of the suit or out of character]! You just couldn't get him out!" (JH-IASB2)

Bob May, carrying the top half of the Robot on his shoulders, fully operational, with his legs completely free, sans the "Bermuda shorts."

Wincing at some of the information conveyed by Harris, *Lost in Space* authority Mike Clark set the record straight: "The walking costume was known to cast and crew as "the Bermudas," named after shorts of the time. The upper costume in this process was borne by Bob May using a parachute-like harness and the whole thing weighed closer to 200 pounds due to the thickness of the fiberglass, batteries and accessories. And awarding Stu Moody the idea behind the Bermuda shorts seems off the mark to me. Stu did special effects and explosions, but I would think that Johnny Borgeze, Bill Myatt and Paul Skelton were more likely the inspiration for The Bermudas because they were directly involved with The Robot on a daily basis." (MC-AI15)

When they wrapped at 6:45 p.m., Martin was still on schedule.

Over on Stage 8, Nathan Juran continued working on the "Int. Magic Land" set with Cartwright and Pollard. Jonathan Harris divided his day between the two productions.

Day 6: Monday, January 31st. The location for this final day of production of "War of the Robots" was again supposed to be the outdoor Moat area, but, due to rain, was moved onto Stage 6. Martin worked with Williams, Mumy, May and Hansen for the scenes in which Will shows the Robotoid to his father and asks permission to try to repair it; Will activating the Robotoid; and the Robotoid uses the video screen to talk to the alien monster. Work began as usual at 8 a.m., but, according to production notes from the set, was delayed for 45 minutes "due to blinking light failure in Robot." Regardless, Martin resumed work and filmed until 7:40 at night, well into union overtime pay, but one of the few instances in the first season in which an episode wrapped within its allotted six-day production schedule.

William Self had approved $138,287 for "War of the Robots," which, despite finishing on schedule, ended up costing $148,303.

Release / Reaction:

(CBS premiere air date: Wednesday, February 9, 1966)
(Network repeat broadcast: Wednesday, June 15, 1966)

The week that "War of the Robots" had its first broadcast on CBS, Petula Clark's "My Love" was the song getting the most play on Top 40 radio stations. The Beatles still had the best-selling album in America, with *Rubber Soul.* A western called *The Rare Breed*, starring James Stewart, was doing the most business in movie houses. *The Source* by James Michener was No. 1 on the *New York Times* Best Seller List. The North Vietnamese captured a U.S. Green Beret camp at A Shau Valley, in South Vietnam. And Barbara Eden and Larry Hagman from *I Dream of Jeannie* had the cover of *TV Guide.* Inside the magazine, Cleveland Amory reviewed *Lost in Space.* He wrote, in part:

> Between the dark and the daylight, when night is beginning to lower, comes a pause in the adult viewing, which is known as the children's glower. And most shows designed primarily for children are not only written for them but also apparently – so it seems – by them. *Lost in Space*, at first brush, might appear to be no exception. For one thing, it was a science-fiction creation of Irwin Allen, whom you may forget – if not forgive – for having given us *Voyage to the Bottom of the Sea....* Don't let all this, however, keep you from this show. For the fact is Mr. Allen and his producer Buck (*Twilight Zone*) Houghton have going for them two basic ingredients which lift *Lost in Space* out of the ordinary into something remarkable.
>
> The first is our Emmy nomination for the best actor in any children's show this year – a robot. He knows his lines. He's appealing to both boys and girls, and he's even neat and well-mannered enough for the old folks to stand him. And when little Will is seized by an alien space craft and carried off to be a humanoid brain in *their* guidance-control system, who do the Robinsons turn to for their guidance? The robot, that's who. And when they ask him, "Which way did they go?" and he replies, "Insufficient data" – you somehow know that, when the chips are down, he'll do his duty, even if it means a hopeless charge against the alien space ship's "force field." Like the brave TV executives upstairs, his not to reason why, his but to program and die.
>
> Second only to the robot is a marvelous villain in this show in the person of Dr. Zachary Smith (Jonathan Harris). He is responsible almost every week for lousing up outer space with his innate rottenness, and you've

got to love him for it. Our favorite episode was the one in which Dr. Smith finds, on a nearby abandoned spaceship, a thought machine (it's like Aladdin's lamp, only instead of rubbing it you think what you want). At first everything is OK. Will thinks up apples, and apples come down; Mrs. Robinson thinks up something extra special for dinner, and it comes down; Judy thinks up a new dress, and it comes down; and Penny thinks up new tapes for her recorder, and they come down. But then greed takes over, and when greedy Dr. Smith thinks up a *servant* – well, there are some things these days, apparently, you can't even *think* up. Why then continue, week after week, to trust Dr. Smith beats us – and certainly Robinson and West don't. But you know women and children – always making decisions on insufficient data.

On the day "War of the Robots" first aired, Dave Kaufman wrote for his *Daily Variety* "On All Channels" column:

> Bill Dozier's *Batman* has created some ratings chaos, coming on in midseason with what CBS-TV program chief Mike Dann has admiringly commented "had the best campaign any TV show ever had." The ABC-TV cliffhanger has, at this stage of the game, dented CBS-TV's *Lost in Space*, which was sailing along with a healthy rating despite some scarcely flattering reviews when it opened last fall. In the latest national Nielsen, *Space*, which was a Top 20 with regularity, zoomed downwards to 52nd, direct result of the *Batman* [premiere]. Not hurt so much was the other competitor in the Wednesday night slot, *The Virginian*, on NBC-TV, but that figures, since it's not slanted for kiddies. That sudden hot competition doesn't disturb June Lockhart, one of the regulars in *Space*, who believes that "CBS is wise enough to want to protect its investment, and should *Batman* beat us in the long run, it will take steps to alleviate the situation – such as perhaps move us to a new time. At present, CBS doesn't regard it as a problem."

Kaufman noted that Lockhart's remarks were made before the latest Nielsens came out. She said of *Batman*, "We are on for the kids, and so are they. We expected to be hurt by *Batman* originally, and felt this would be reflected in the ratings. I don't know about the sustaining power of *Batman*. If I were that clairvoyant, I would be in another business." (JL-DV66)

A picture of Jonathan Harris and the villainous guest robot was circulated to newspapers, along with the caption: "AN ALIEN ROBOT focuses an eye on the villainous Dr. Zachary Smith (Jonathan Harris) as it plots warfare in the Robinson space colony on *Lost in Space* tonight…"

Syndicated "TV Scout," in the February 9, 1966 edition of Lumberton, North Carolina's *The Robesonian*, said:

> An episode about a rebuilt robot that outsmarts Dr. Smith's robot. Scenes between the competing mechanical wonders are fairly intriguing and outweigh all the by-play and dialogue given the human characters.

From "TV Key Previews," syndicated to newspapers across America, including the February 9th issue of Connecticut's *Bridgeport Telegram*, said:

> A hard choice for the kids – whether to watch *Batman* or this episode about a rebuilt robot that outsmarts Dr. Smith's robot. Scenes between the competing mechanical wonders are fairly intriguing, outweighing the dialogue and by-play of the humans in the cast.

A.C. Nielsen's 30-City Ratings survey for February 9, 1966, tallied the audience numbers this way:

Network / Program:	Rating	Share:
7:30 – 8 p.m.:		
ABC: *Batman*	**27.0**	**42.4%**
CBS: *Lost in Space*	17.8	27.9%
NBC: *The Virginian*	14.8	23.2%
8 – 8:30 p.m.:		
ABC: *The Patty Duke Show*	20.6	31.5%
CBS: *Lost in Space*	**23.7**	**36.2%**
NBC: *The Virginian*	16.4	25.0%

Quoted in the March 21, 1966 edition of Maryland's Annapolis *Capital*, Jonathan Harris said, "We will be around long after the *Batman* craze has worn off." (JH-AC66)

32

Episode 21: "The Magic Mirror"

Written by Jackson Gillis
(with script polishing by Anthony Wilson)
Directed by Nathan Juran
Produced by Irwin Allen; with Jerry Briskin

From the *Lost in Space* show files (Irwin Allen Papers Collection):

> Penny finds an ornate mirror abandoned in a remote area by some former space traveler. Smith also is interested in it because of the value of its solid platinum frame. During a storm the mirror is struck by a cosmic bolt and changes mysteriously. It has become the entrance to a world in another dimension. Falling through the mirror, Penny finds herself entrapped behind it and cannot get out. She meets a Peter Pan-like alien boy who tries to persuade her to stay there, where she will be free from adult authority and need never grow up. Then Smith turns up. He has also fallen in while tampering with the mirror's frame. Convinced that this is only a dream, Smith ignores the danger of a huge, hairy monster that is trying to get them. Penny is determined to get herself and Smith back safely into their own world.

From the Script:

(Revised Shooting Final teleplay, January 27, 1966 draft)

– *Judy:* "It's wonderful! A full-length mirror! Just what we need most! *(vainly primps at her hair)* Which reminds me, you promised you'd help me fix my hair." *Penny (loud groan):* "Oh, no, not <u>again</u>!" *Judy (glancing in mirror):* "I thought I'd try it a little higher on top this time, with maybe a softer roll." *Penny:* "Well, <u>I'm</u> going to cut my hair all <u>off</u>! Just like Will's!" *Judy:* "Go ahead – be ugly. Who cares? *(even before the flick of reaction in Penny's eyes; gives Penny a quick, apologetic hug)* Oh, I'm sorry, honey, but … *(glancing to mirror; starting to touch Penny's hair)* … if you'd just fix yourself up once in a while. It's just that I hate to ever see you – well, acting like a boy. You know what I mean." *Penny:* "What's wrong with boys?" *Judy (laughs):* "Nothing! But, honey, you could be so beautiful! You <u>are</u> so beautiful! It's time you started realizing it!" *Penny (beaks away):* "Why? Why's all that goop so important, anyway!" *Judy:* "Well, you are growing up, darling, and…" *Penny (lashing out stubbornly):* "So what? Why can't I be just the way I am? Maybe I like the way I am! Maybe I'll just stay this way forever!"

– *Penny:* "I just don't understand where all these things came from?" *Boy:* "They've always been here. Everything that gets lost or nobody wants any more ends up in here." *Penny:* "But how do they get into this world?" *Boy:* "It's not really a world. This is a dimension. That's better than a world. Anybody will tell you that…" *Penny (incredulously):* "<u>This</u> is where you live?"

– *Penny (stumbling over a pile, but politely):* "I thought you said you cleaned your house up a little." *Boy:* "I did! Oh, all except the dirt, and that doesn't hurt anybody." *Penny:* "No, of course not." *Boy:* "And you know what? Here you don't have to brush your teeth, you don't have to wash your face or pull up your socks – you don't have to do anything but have fun." *Penny (uncertainly):* "It – sounds wonderful!" *Boy (moves eagerly to her):* "Oh, it is! Penny, it's all anybody could want forever! You're going to love it!" *Penny:* "I – am?" *Boy (moving to 'flop' on his bed):* "Of course! With nothing to do except what you want and – *(embarrassedly)* – and none of that <u>goop</u> between people!" *Penny (also embarrassedly, but in quick agreement):* "Oh, yes, I hate goop! Like Judy and Don – well, I mean I just hate it, that's all!"

Assessment:

Alice through the Looking Glass meets *Peter Pan* meets "My Friend, Mr. Nobody." There is even a nod toward *The Wizard of Oz* as Maureen Robinson faces into the wind and wails "Penneee!" … just as Auntie Em had done when calling out to Dorothy. Then another, as Penny looks out from within the looking glass and calls to her mother and family, who cannot hear, as Dorothy had done to the image of her troubled aunt which then transformed into the Wicked Witch's leering face.

As with "Mr. Nobody," "The Magic Mirror" serves up a whimsical tale about a little girl awkwardly growing older, which in that more innocent time stirred something in the hearts of millions of *Lost in Space*'s young viewers … and perhaps a few adults, too.

The elements for success are all here. Writing, direction, acting, imaginative set design, artistic use of camera and lights, and an effectively multi-layered audio track combine together to create a never-never land that elevates TV to the best of all babysitters. It entertains its audience while sparking their imaginations and, as it happened with Penny, perhaps helping them to grow up … just a little. That's not bad for fifty minutes of TV from 1966!

Script:

Story Assignment 8464 (Production #8520)
Jackson Gillis's treatment, and 1st and 2nd draft teleplays: December 1965/January 1966.
Reformatted Mimeo Department Shooting Final teleplay: Mid-December 1965.
Tony Wilson's Revised Shooting Final teleplay (blue pages): January 17, 1966.
Additional page revisions by Wilson (pink insert pages): January 19.
Further revisions by Wilson (green insert pages): January 20.
Further revisions by Wilson (yellow insert pages): January 21.
Further revisions by Wilson (gold insert pages): January 21.
Further revisions by Wilson (yellow insert pages): January 25.
Further revisions by Wilson (pink insert pages): January 25.
Further revisions by Wilson (green insert pages): January 25.
Further revisions by Wilson (gold insert pages): January 26.
Further revisions by Wilson (pink insert pages): January 27.
Tag scene/cliffhanger from Barney Slater's script for "The Challenge" (pink insert pages): January 27.

This was Jackson Gillis's second *Lost in Space* assignment, following "My Friend, Mr. Nobody." With "Nobody," Jackson had written a charming tale that prominently featured Angela Cartwright. Gillis had been so successful with his first assignment that he was asked to write another story around the character of Penny.

Gillis's material succeeds in "Mr. Nobody," and here, because he was attentive in giving his stories a strong central theme. Penny is in no hurry to grow up – and why should she be? There are no boys to take an interest in her. Judy has Don, and Gillis implants subtle hints that suggest Penny is bothered over this – not that Penny desires Don, but she is clearly aware that there will be no Don in her adult love life. Therefore, the emotional display between Judy and Don, to Penny's thinking, is merely "goop." By the end of the story, after observing what happens to a boy who refuses to mature, and how meaningless and empty that sort of life would be, Penny experiences a character arc of her own. We first see this while she is still in "Mirror Land" with the "Boy." He begs her, "Stay here! Forever isn't such a long time. You'll like it and you'll never have to grow up." A nearly traumatized Penny responds: "But don't you see … I can't stay here. I don't want to be young forever!" The Boy is puzzled, and says, "But everybody does … I know, I listen to them through the mirrors…" Penny interrupts: "They just say that because they know they <u>have</u> to grow older!"

Later, after Penny is reunited with her family, she tells her mother: "How do you suppose my hair would look if I fixed it sort of soft up here and – shorter here, maybe?" A surprised Maureen asks, "What prompted that?" Penny answers: "I mean … well, you do have to grow up sometime, don't you?"

Also included in Gillis's script is a second look at the darkness inside Dr. Smith. In "My Friend, Mr. Nobody," Gillis showed Smith obsessively driven to accumulate material possessions. Here, Smith watches Penny and Judy as they prop up *his* platinum framed mirror. Gillis wrote a few jealous lines for Smith to utter to himself in a "murderously urgent whisper," hissing, "Get away from that mirror! It's *my* mirror! *My* platinum! Go play somewhere else, you nasty little girls." Harris delivered these lines beautifully. The look on his face is most certainly threatening – just as he had played the part Gillis wrote for him in "My Friend, Mr. Nobody" when diamond-fever strikes.

With his first two scripts for *Lost in Space*, Gillis proved that he understood Smith perhaps better than any other *Lost in Space* writer. He knew that the character could feel fondness for the Robinson children but, when under the spell of his craving for riches, he'd lose all reason and became potentially dangerous. If other writers, including Tony Wilson, had approached Smith in this manner, the character could have easily glided between serious-villain and comedic-villain without any loss of believability or continuity.

One delightful scene gives clear indication that Dr. Smith is on the verge of losing his marbles. After he falls through the mirror into Mirror Land, he encounters Penny as she is fleeing the "Hairy Monster." The scene continues:

Smith (has caught hold of her): "Now, now, my dear, I'm not angry anymore." *Penny:* "It's coming! It's coming!" *Smith (oblivious to her words):* "You see, I understand all this, now." *Penny (struggling, trying to push him):* "What are you talking about? Let go of me! Run!" *Smith (proudly stands fast):* "No! I will not run from my own nightmares!" *Penny (flabbergasted):* "What?" *Boy (disgusted yell):* "Hey, where'd he come from? *(upset and angry at the sight of Smith)* Did you let him in here?" *Penny:* "No!" *Smith:* "Of course not, my boy! I'm the one who let you in, don't you understand?" *Boy (seizing Penny's hand):* "He's goofy! Come on, he'll spoil everything!" *Penny (breaking loose):* "No, wait! Dr. Smith, there's an awful hairy beast running around…" *Smith (interrupting happily):* "A beast! Oh, yes, of course, of course, I would think of something like that, wouldn't I!" *Penny (worriedly):* "Do you feel all right, Dr. Smith?" *Smith:* "Yes, I do, surprisingly enough! *(moves to proudly inspect spaces around him)* And what a fascinating place I've created here for you! It's all a new dimension, isn't it? Behind all the mirrors in the universe, there's a new dimension which we've entered – oh, how clever of me!" *Penny (pointing to the boy; frightened wail):* "But he says we can't ever get out! We're trapped in the mirrors forever!" *Smith:* "Now, now, there's nothing for you to be frightened of, my dear. You're not really here – *(pointing to Boy)* – Neither is he!" *Boy (trying to grab Penny):* "And he's in loony-land! Come on, Penny!" *Smith (gives the Boy a distasteful glance):* "Though I must say I did a rather sloppy job in creating you, young man!" *Penny:* "Creating him! Oh, Dr. Smith, what's wrong with you!" *Smith:* "I'm dreaming, don't you see? All of it!"

Gillis was one of the few writers to give a possible explanation as to the change in Smith. The Boy tells us: "He's goofy…. And he's in loony-land."

Irwin Allen read the 2nd Draft script from Jackson Gillis, then sent his notes to Tony Wilson on January 17, 1966, saying:

> P. 8, Sc. 23-24: Note on previous week's Teaser ending: Teaser ending should be more frightening. We should see some visual effects of a monster seemingly reaching out of the mirror in anger as though to catch the lightning. The claws of the hairy monster [that] we see later in the script might be used here. Perhaps it could actually catch the lightning and draw it into the mirror. This accompanied with the screams of Penny from behind the mirror would be suitably frightening….

Bringing this idea to the screen would not only be frighteningly expensive, it would also likely scare the wits out of CBS's censors. Wilson felt it would be exciting and scary enough to have lightning strike the mirror and cause the demonic-looking face on the frame to snort smoke and have its eyes light up.

Allen's notes continued:

> Sc. 53 should start with a shot of Smith on his stomach peering down on the girls and then we should see the Bloop crawl up on his back and start jumping up and down. Smith would then push him off and start throwing pebbles at the Bloop as he says his 1st speech Sc. 53, and the Bloop, in trying to avoid being hit by the pebbles would cause the cluster of rocks which gets the attention of the girls.

Jonathan Harris was not going to tolerate Debbie the Chimp giving him a back-walking massage treatment. Wilson knew this and ignored the note.

Allen continued:

> Sc. 55: Penny – 1st speech should read: "Who cares! I'm not afraid of funny noises and I don't go around dreaming how pretty I am all the time."
>
> P. 19, Sc. 56: Penny – 2nd speech should read: "Why? What's so important about being beautiful, anyway?" …
>
> P. 20, Sc. 58: At the end of Smith's speech we should see him going to the back of the mirror with the rock he has found to start hammering on it. He should be seen hammering or we won't know what the noise is as described in Sc. 62.
>
> Sc. 63: Smith should come from behind the mirror and trip over the Bloop rather than bump him [sic] with his foot. He should not under any circumstances kick the Bloop. He can frighten him away just as easily with his loud voice and waving arms.
>
> P. 28, Sc. 93 & Sc. 94: Smith should <u>not</u> stick out his tongue. He can, instead, pull down the lower lid of his eyes and feel his brow.
>
> P. 34, Sc. 106: Don – 1st speech should be clearer. It has been quite a while since their last scene, so any reference to "a minute ago" SHOULD BE LEFT OUT. It should read: "Hey, did I say

> something wrong, or…" and Judy's answer should be: "Of course not, silly. It's what you didn't say, that's all."

Wilson addressed many of these notes in his numerous page revisions.

Another interesting note regarding the interplay between Don and Judy showed that Allen was not opposed to showing a little sexual tension on *Lost in Space*. He wrote:

> It would help give the proper feeling to this scene if Don had tried to take her hand or put his arm around her waist and Judy quickly evaded him by asking her mother if she wanted some help.

Of course, CBS would have none of it. No touching – especially male arms around female waists – was allowed. Previous expressions of affection, even between the Robinson parents, had been frowned upon by the network.

Allen's memo continued:

> P. 47, Sc. 138: Smith's speech is confusing because it was not made clear enough earlier on P. 26, Sc. 85 that Smith actually saw Penny disappear into the mirror.
>
> Shouldn't Act 4 open on a shot of Smith landing in a heap as the roar from the beast is heard off stage. At first he would be frightened and then he would talk to himself, telling himself that he must be dreaming. Since Act 3 closes on him and his predicament it seems strange to go to Penny and the boy immediately in Act 4.
>
> P. 53, Sc. 151: Smith – 2nd speech – add "…I want to see this wonderful creature of my imagination!"
>
> Every time Penny calls the boy "Boy," it seems reminiscent of the Tarzan pictures. If he has no name, why can't Penny give him one. Maybe "Charles" or something shorter.
>
> Throughout Penny's scenes with the boy, she uses the word "please" very often. It begins to get tiresome and should be deleted wherever possible.

Two days later, on January 19th, Sam Taylor, Jr., from CBS Program Practices, Hollywood, wrote:

> We are gravely concerned about this episode for one basic reason: as the script is written, PENNY would appear to be, periodically, in a state of terror for more than one-half of the program. Her terror is caused by the realization that she may be trapped forever in the mirror-world and by the menace of the loathsome HAIRY BEAST.
>
> There is slight indication toward the end of the script that the BEAST might be, after all, friendly. We would ask that you

explore the possibility of establishing the amiable part of his disposition much earlier in the script.

We would earnestly request that, throughout the episode, PENNY be more amazed than frightened by the strange surroundings and events....

Page 26, Scene 82: The huge staring eye should not be too gruesome.

Page 27, Scenes 86 & 87: PENNY should be amazed, possibly apprehensive, but not in great "terror."

Page 28, Scene 92: PENNY should not be in "Wild Panic." We would prefer that she not say, "Save me!" Perhaps she can say, "I'm in here!"

Page 29, Scene 95 & 96: We would not wish PENNY to be "frantic." The growl (of the BEAST) should here and in the future not be overly frightening.

Page 35, Scenes 110 through 113: The Boy has implied that he has been there forever and he tells PENNY that there isn't any way out. Perhaps these lines could be changed, because we would not want PENNY to be hysterical as she calls out to her mother. Please do <u>not</u> conclude the act with PENNY "collapsing in tears" or "sobbing hopelessly."

Instead of PENNY's lines "Let me out! Let me out!," perhaps she could say something of this nature: "Mother, I'm here! I'm all right but I'm trapped behind the mirrors." The girl's constant calls for help will only add to the alarm you may cause children in your audience.

Page 36, Scenes 114 and 116: PENNY should not be "sobbing broken heartedly." ...

Page 47, Scene 135: The claws of the HAIRY BEAST should not be excessively gruesome nor cause an "awful moment of horror" for the children.

Page 49, Scenes 142 thru 144: The mouth of the BEAST should not be excessively gruesome. We would insist that PENNY would show a certain amount of bravado and that she not merely "cower" and "whimper."

Page 53, Scene 152: PENNY should not "scream frantically."

Page 53, Scene 154: The BEAST's many clawed paw, approaching SMITH, should not be loathsome.

> Page 55, Scene 158: We do not wish PENNY to say "He'll eat him." Perhaps she could say, "He'll get him."
>
> Page 56, Scene 161: Please do not have the BEAST's huge tongue "munching" on SMITH's face.
>
> Page 57, Scene 163: Please do not let the audience believe the BEAST is about to eat SMITH.
>
> Scenes 168-173: This sequence in which various mirrors shatter and the BEAST keeps reappearing in different locations, could be very terrifying and we ask that you modify or change it.
>
> We understand the production exigencies which pertain to the shooting of this episode and thus we would request that any further script changes be cleared with this office as early as possible.

The "production exigencies" meant that the filming of "The Magic Mirror" would be advanced in the schedule to shoot simultaneously with "War of the Robots," and this meant less time to get changes cleared with the network.

More pages were rushed to CBS. On January 24th, Taylor wrote to Irwin Allen, Tony Wilson, and Boris Kaplan:

> As discussed with Mr. Wilson:
>
> Page 34, Scene 111: As the BOY has already told PENNY in Scene 100 that "there is no way out," we would prefer that he not reiterate the statement so close to the end of Act II.
>
> We would hope that PENNY's attitude at the end of Act II would be one of exasperation and frustration rather than one of hopelessness and abject resignation.

And now we know why it was that with each episode, *Lost in Space* shifted more from action/adventure sci-fi to kiddie comedy-fantasy. It's because the network's representatives demanded the change. After all, they were paying the bills.

Pre-Production:

Michael J. Pollard was cast as the Alien Boy. Pollard was 26, but playing much younger roles. His big break came in 1959 when Bob Denver, who played beatnik Maynard G. Krebs in TV's *The Many Loves of Dobie Gillis*, was drafted into the Army. Pollard was brought in to replace Denver as Maynard's weird cousin Jerome Krebs. It was a short stay – two 1959 episodes. Denver flunked out of the armed services as 4-F and returned to *Gillis*. Pollard's character was quickly written out, but the exposure helped catapult the oddball personality into other TV and film jobs. Later in 1966, Pollard played another teenager, this time in "Miri," an episode of *Star Trek*.

Casting director Joe D'Agosta said, "Michael was one of a kind. You either loved him or hated him, because he was so, for the lack of a better term, quirky. Odd. But interesting; unique. He brought that same performance to every job he did." (JDA-AI15)

Less than a year after getting "lost in space," Michael J. Pollard guest starred with Kim Darby in "Miri," a 1966 episode of *Star Trek*.

Director Vincent McEveety, who worked with Pollard in *Star Trek*'s "Miri," said, "Pollard is a very quirky fellow. But, after a while, you don't care how quirky actors are as long as they hit their mark and remember their lines. In his case, he could play it any way he chose because that was the character that they [the writer/producers] envisioned. They wanted that quirkiness and that nuttiness. So it was a very strange take on the character, but by an actor who was absolutely professional." (VM-AI13)

Next for Pollard came an uncredited scene-stealing performance in Carl Reiner's big screen 1966 comedy *The Russians Are Coming, the Russians Are Coming*. And he was already being considered by Warren Beatty for a prominent role in 1967's *Bonnie & Clyde*, for which he would receive a Golden Globe nomination and an Oscar nod, both in the category of Best Supporting Actor. (He was in good company; Gene Hackman was also nominated for Best Supporting Actor in that film.)

Mike Donovan was cast to be the man inside the hairy monster suit. He also played critters in "The Keeper, Part 1," "A Visit to Hades" and "All That Glitters."

Charles G. Clarke was brought in to serve as cinematographer on this episode so that it could be shot simultaneously with "War of the Robots," photographed by the series' regular director of photography, Gene Polito. Clarke had an impressive resume. His first film as D.P. had been *Son of Tarzan* in 1920. He shot another Tarzan film, 1934's *Tarzan and His Mate*, starring Johnny Weissmuller and Maureen O'Sullivan. He was also the director of photography on classic films such as 1937's *The Good Earth* and 1947's *Miracle on 34th Street*. Clarke was nominated for an Academy Award as Best Cinematographer on four occasions: 1943's *Moontide*; 1944's *Hello Frisco, Hello*; 1949's *Green Grass of Wyoming*; and 1950's *Sand*.

Clarke would be called back into service for *Lost in Space* to film "The Lost Civilization" later in the season. Irwin Allen would also tap him on three occasions for episodes of *Land of the Giants*.

Production Diary:

Filmed January 24 through February 1, 1966 (6 ¼ days).

The camera would roll on "The Magic Mirror" at the same time as another camera rolled on "War of the Robots" in order to catch up on productions and ensure to make deliveries to CBS on time. June Lockhart told interviewer Tom Weaver, "Sometimes we would finish on Monday and it would be on the air in Canada the following Saturday night. And if the show wasn't ready, 20th Century-Fox or CBS would have been fined $50,000. But we made it every time, because Irwin kept everybody there working 24 hours a day, practically – the post-production and everything." (JL-SL94)

Shooting two episodes at once was made possible since the Robot was not needed for this episode, while being a principal player in the other, and Angela Cartwright was excused from "War of the Robots" in order to be the primary focus in "The Magic Mirror." Billy Mumy, who was busy working on "War of the Robots," does not appear in "Magic Mirror" until the cliffhanger.

While "War of the Robots" filmed on Stage 11 (for four consecutive days), "The Magic Mirror" was shot on Stages 6 and 8. Then, during the latter days of the productions, the two units traded off, with director Sobey Martin and his team taking over Stages 8 and 6 for "War of the Robots," while director Nathan Juran, with cinematographer Charles Clarke and their unit, moved on to Stage 11 to film sequences involving the rest of the regular cast members for "The Magic Mirror." It was a shell game with one unit trying to stay out of the way of the other, and share cast members, as well as makeup service, set decorators, production manager, line producer, and lighting crew.

Shot simultaneously with "War of the Robots," cast members scrambled between two sound stages to allow *Lost in Space* to catch up on its episode deliveries to CBS. On the first day of production, Marta Kristen worked with Angela Cartwright on Stage 6.

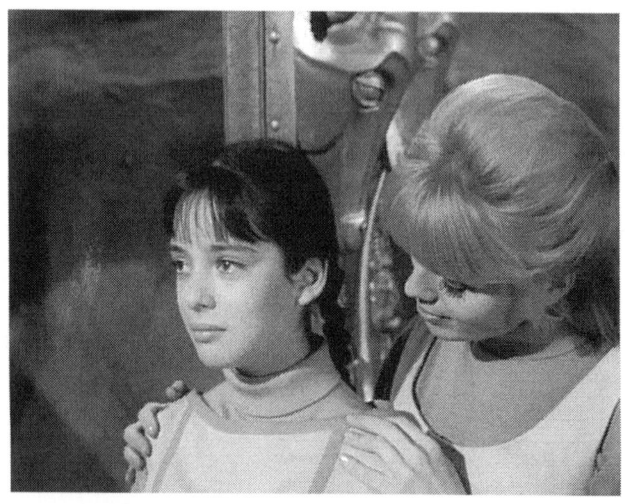

Day 1: Monday, January 24, 1966. Nathan Juran embarked on "The Magic Mirror" on Stage 6, with the "Rocky Area" where the alien mirror is discovered by Penny and Smith. Marta Kristen and Debbie the Bloop also

worked with Juran's unit. They filmed from 9:07 a.m. to 6:30 p.m., covering seven and six-eighths pages from the script.

Day 2: Tuesday, January 25. A second day on Stage 6 and the "Rocky Area" with the mirror. Cartwright was joined by Jonathan Harris and Guy Williams.

Day 2 of the production. Jonathan Harris, hiding under the mirror, hated the giant fans (Ritters) kicking up all the sand.

Nathan Juran told authors Joel Eisner and Barry Magen, "There was a scene in 'The Magic Mirror' in which Angela Cartwright fell through an alien mirror. There was a big commotion about how we could make the shot of her going through the looking glass. They were originally going to spend a lot of money in the lab, doing it with rotoscoping, but I felt that was unnecessary. I had an idea of how to do it, but I wanted to think about it some more. I said, 'Don't worry about it. We'll get it done one way or another.' And I got it done, in a unique way. I did it with the camera. It turned out great. [And] it was a good little episode." (NJ-LISF)

The trick with the camera was a split-screen effect that would not require post-production work in the lab. Jerry Finnerman, the talented cinematographer at *Star Trek*, used the same effect later in the year, and revealed, "You take the camera and you get a soft matte line in the middle of the scene [dividing the set], where the actor can't go over that line or he'll be in the [opposite] shot.... And you have to block the camera off with a solid [black opal]... so one side of the screen is black; you can't see anything.... Then you had to send the film to the camera department and they had to notch it.... Then we got the film back – notched... We put it in the camera, and we shot the scene, and Bill [Shatner] played to the mirror off stage.... 'Cut!... Okay, do the other side.'... Now, they have to rewind that film to where the notch is. Meantime, the camera's all tied off – locked off and braced – and we have to take the black opal and bring it over on the other side of the lens so that what was black is now clear and the side that was clear is now black.... And Bill played to the mirror off screen, and he was good.... I was beside myself, because I figured it wouldn't work.... And I went home and I thought about it all night. I really did.... And we ran it the next day. Oh, I was so proud. I mean, I was really proud. That stuff just came out perfect. I have to thank Lynn Dunn [of Film Effects of Hollywood] for that; for telling me how to do it, or I would have been in bad shape." (JF-AOT-02)

Juran and his share of the *Lost in Space* company filmed from 8 a.m. to 7:18 p.m. The director was under pressure to catch up or else the two co-existing production units might fall helplessly out of synch. He did, covering eleven and one-eighth pages from the script, as well as tying down the camera for a split-screen effect.

Day 3: Wednesday, January 26. Juran and his company moved to Stage 8 for the first of three days on the "Int. Mirror Land" set. Cartwright worked with Michael Pollard. Also present was Mike Donovan as the monster.

Above: Michael J. Pollard on the third day of filming in the "Int. Mirror Land." Below: On Day 4, Harris goes through the looking glass, and gets a hug by Mike Donovan ("Hairy Monster").

Angela Cartwright said, "I thought the concept of this show was terrific and I really enjoyed shooting this episode. Michael J. Pollard was a really low-key kind of guy and I remember I had a ton of lines to learn.

"There was one shot I remember shooting like it was yesterday. It was the shot over my shoulder at my Mom (June) and Judy (Marta) doing the laundry and I was banging on the glass yelling at them that I was right there. I remember thinking how frustrating that would be. To be so close and yet so far away, and the people on the other side of the glass not being able to hear you." (AC-LISM.com)

They filmed from 8 a.m. to 6 p.m., crossing off ten and three-eighths pages from the script and remaining on schedule. Those who worked on this crew, plus cast members, were able to get home in time for "The Sky Pirate." The same could not be said for those working Sobey Martin's side of the street on "War of the Robots."

Day 4: Thursday, January 27. A second day on Stage 8. Jonathan Harris did many of his scenes in the "Int. Mirror Land" dimension, working with Cartwright and Pollard … and the "Hairy Monster." They needed to shoot eight pages from the script to stay on schedule. And they did, finishing at 6:18 p.m.

Day 5: Friday, January 28. A third day on Stage 8, with Cartwright, Pollard, Harris and Donavan. They filmed from 8 a.m. to 7 p.m. It took an hour of overtime with the camera crew, but Juran stayed on schedule.

Day 6: Monday, January 31. It was a race to see who could finish their episode first. Sobey Martin won, wrapping "War of the Robots" on Stage 8 at 7:40 p.m. Nathan Juran shot with his unit on Stage 11, with Guy Williams, June Lockhart, Mark Goddard, Marta Kristen, Angela Cartwright and Jonathan Harris. They worked until 7 p.m. It was clear he was not going to finish, with a quarter-day's work left, so the company called it quits after one hour of "Golden Time."

Day 7: Tuesday, February 1. Juran finished "The Magic Mirror" on Stage 11, with all the cast members present other than Billy Mumy and Bob May, who sat this episode out.

This was the last time Jonathan Harris was seen in the yellow top he'd been wearing for the last three episodes. He said, "I had certain views about what I wanted to wear. I don't have the best figure in the world, God knows, and I knew I wanted it dark." (JH-IASB2)

Reverting back to dark colors for Smith wasn't only Harris's decision, at least according to Paul Zastupnevich. The wardrobe man later said that he, too, felt the lighter colors in his costume diffused Smith's character. He stressed, "Oh, I'm a real believer in color and how it affects your emotions. The experiment with Smith didn't work, so we went back to the dark shades." (PZ-SL93)

Harris disputed Zastupnevich's claim, and scoffed, "I had to fight the costume man, who wanted it light. So you have to stomp your foot, if necessary; stomp your foot and say, 'No, no, no, I want it dark!' And he said, 'Light makes you thinner.' And he complained, 'You're ruining my whole scheme.' 'Well, stick your scheme! I want it dark.' And so, it came to pass. It's as simple as that. You know, you have to think of things, not to be mean or rotten, but good things to help you or to help the show. I thought, quite honestly, that what helped *me* helped the show." (JH-IASB2)

Filming "War of the Robots" on another stage at the same time as "Magic Mirror," Jonathan Harris wears a look that can only represent his feelings about his new yellow tunic ... soon to go.

Now for the real reason:

Kevin Burns revealed, "I have no doubt that Paul Z. wanted to try something with giving Jonathan a lighter top. But I have no doubt that Jonathan hated it from Day 1. Originally, it was like a dark top and lighter pants, then they went to dark pants because Jonathan had a big behind, so he didn't like the way he looked in pants. The darker ones helped conceal this from the camera. But, as for the light top, the truth of it is that Jonathan didn't only wear a back brace, he wore shoulder pads, because he was very sloped shouldered, and Jonathan was very self-conscious about his frame. So, he always had shoulder pads put into his outfit, like George Reeves did. They weren't that noticeable, but they were there. Now, the problem was that the lighter tunic betrayed that he had shoulder pads. The dark color hid it. And that's why he preferred the darker top. It wasn't so much this notion that the villain has to wear black. Jonathan preferred wearing black, period." (KB-AI16)

Nathan Juran took his last shot at 10:30 a.m., and then made way for director Don Richardson, beginning his second *Lost in Space* episode, "The Challenge."

William Self had okayed a budget of $133,359 for "The Magic Mirror." The end toll came to $145,591.

Release / Reaction:

(CBS premiere broadcast: Wednesday, February 16, 1966)
(Network repeat airdate: Wednesday, June 22, 1966)

Dr. Zhivago moved back up to reclaim the top spot in the movie houses. *Rubber Soul* was still the top-selling album in America. It had been that way for six weeks. "My Love" by Petula Clark had another week at the top of Billboard magazine's Hot Singles chart. Despite Pet Clark's pop hit, the mood in Los Angeles wasn't all about love – race riots broke out in the Watts district of Los Angeles during this week. Also, a U.S. sub located a missing H-bomb in the Mediterranean Ocean, and Gemini 8 was launched with astronauts Neil Armstrong and David Scott, but then the mission was aborted after six and a half orbits of the Earth. America's top-selling magazine was *TV Guide*, and Ryan O'Neal and Barbara Parkins of *Peyton Place* had the cover. The series was filmed on the Fox lot near the *Lost in Space* stages.

Syndicated "TV Key Preview," in the February 16, 1966 edition of Connecticut's *The Bridgeport Post*, said of "The Magic Mirror":

> Youngsters will be interested in young Penny's problems in mirrorland – a dark, peculiar place containing another strange villain, the Alien Boy. Some of the moments are fairly spooky, thanks to good special effects and the unusual story idea.

The week "The Magic Mirror" had its premiere broadcast, a publicity picture of Angela Cartwright looking into a mirror and seeing Michael J. Pollard looking out received wide exposure in newspapers across America. The photo caption read: "SURPRISE REFLECTION – Angela Cartwright finds a boy (Michael J. Pollard) staring back at her when she looks into a magic mirror in tonight's episode of *Lost in Space*."

Did the striking visuals help the ratings? A.C. Nielsen felt it had the answer, with its 30-City Ratings survey for February 16, 1966. The results:

Network / Program:	Rating	Share:
7:30 – 8 p.m.:		
ABC: *Batman*	**26.4**	**41.1%**
CBS: *Lost in Space*	16.6	25.9%
NBC: *The Virginian*	15.9	24.8%
8 – 8:30 p.m.:		
ABC: *The Patty Duke Show*	18.1	27.8%
CBS: *Lost in Space*	**22.0**	**33.8%**
NBC: *The Virginian*	17.1	26.3%

Lost in Space was second during the first half of its time slot, and then claimed the lead spot over the rival networks during its final half-hour.

From the Mailbag:

The week after "The Magic Mirror" first aired, "You Said It," a letters column in the Pasadena *Independent Star-News*, printed the following:

> I am a boy of 11 years of age. There is a thing I can't understand – why *Lost in Space* came in third on your TV Critic Poll. I think *Lost in Space* is horrible! The acting is lousy. Same with the producing and directing. I'd rather watch *Batman* any day. – Stanley Brown, Pasadena, California.

The editor, who apparently hadn't looked at the latest Nielsen report, replied:

> *Lost in Space* is getting lost in the ratings since *Batman*, having dropped from the Top Twenty to 52nd spot. It ran high in *TV WEEK*'s reader poll because of the disproportionate number of young people who participated. But now, thousands are deserting it for *Batman*. One irony is that *Batman* is produced by 20th Century-Fox and is causing the most ratings damage to *Daniel Boone* [on Thursday nights] and *Lost in Space* [on Wednesdays] both produced by the same studio.

During the same week, for "Squawk Box," a readers' letters column syndicated to numerous newspapers, including the *Waterloo Daily Courier*, in Waterloo, Iowa, and the *San Antonio Express and News*, in Texas, the following appeared:

> *Lost in Space* is dull with the Robinsons stuck on that junky planet. Why can't they move? Why can't there be more romance? Why can't they meet some down-to-earth people. – Disgusted Viewer, Uvalde, Texas.

Reply from the editor:

> If the CBS-TV series adopted your suggestions it would be another type of show. It was designed for young people interested in far-out people involved in far-out adventure.

Angela Cartwright understood the appeal. She said, "Our show was set in the imaginary world of a child – a world that didn't say, 'No, you can't do that.' It said, 'If you can dream it, you can build it." (AC-TVG97)

33

Episode 22: "The Challenge"

Written by Barney Slater
(with script polishing by Anthony Wilson)
Directed by Don Richardson
Produced by Irwin Allen; with Jerry Briskin

From the *Lost in Space* show files (Irwin Allen Papers Collection):

> A mysterious thief who has been pilfering from the camp is finally caught by Smith. He is a defiant alien boy who proves to be thoroughly intractable and impossible to handle. Then the boy's father, a ruler from a distant planet, arrives and reveals that he has put his son there as a test to see how well he can fend for himself and thus prove if the boy is fit to succeed him. One test is to kill a giant monster. He insists that, to complete the tests, his son should challenge Will in a series of contests. Will, seeing himself as representing the planet Earth, is equally anxious to win. The boys tie in a number of events in spite of Smith's secret attempts to influence events in favor of the alien boy, hoping thus to win the father's approbation, but the final events confounds all Smith's secret schemes.

From the Script:

(Shooting Final teleplay, February 8, 1966 draft)

– *Don (re: Quano):* "I wonder what he's doing here?" *Smith:* "From his attitude, he's definitely not up to any good. I suggest we make sure the spaceship is well secured before we retire for the night." *Maureen:* "Surely you're not worried about an eleven-year-old boy, Dr. Smith." *Smith:* "My dear Mrs. Robinson. When you're dealing with a dangerous creature, age is of no consequence. A one-year-old viper is as dangerous as a ten-year-old one."

– *Maureen:* "What do you mean, 'challenge'?" *The Ruler (holds up a placating hand):* "This does not concern you, Mrs. Robinson. It is a matter for men to decide." *Maureen:* "I don't know about your world, Mr. Ruler, but in ours, women are treated as the equal of men." *The Ruler (laughs loudly):* "What a foolish arrangement." *Maureen (angry):* "I fail to see anything amusing." *The Ruler (still laughing):* "Women the equal of men – in what way? Are they stronger; more intelligent; do they make laws; fight wars? This will be an excellent story to tell when I return home." *Robinson (drily):* "I can hear the boys at the Club laughing now."

– *Smith:* "All right, turn on your long-range audio-detector. I want to hear what they are saying." *Robot:* "Such procedure is unethical. Their conversation may be highly personal." *Smith (with irritation):* "Never mind your misguided moral principles. All is fair in love and war." *Robot (puzzled):* "Love? That does not compute." *Smith:* "It never does."

– *Smith (as if to himself):* "The first time I set eyes on that boy I knew he was a savage." *Robot:* "Statement: If my programming is correct, he is much to be admired. He has principles." *Smith (coldly):* "And I haven't! Is that what you are implying?" *Robot:* "Do you insist on an answer?" *Smith:* "At once!" *Robot:* "And you will not remove my power pak if I speak the truth?" *Smith (glares at Robot):* "Just answer the question! *(There is a rapid whirring of the Robot's computers and a soft explosion from inside the mechanical man. Smoke escapes from its body and it becomes deactivated. Smith is furious.)* You evasive coward! You deliberately blew out your voltage regulators!"

Assessment:

"The Challenge" is quality *Lost in Space* in all regards. Here, we are given two impressive guest stars (Michael Ansara, having starred in two TV series by this time, and Kurt Russell, who was also the lead in a series, with motion picture stardom in his future); a compelling story by Barney Slater; competent direction by Don Richardson; and a script which blends drama and comedy, all the while sharing the action and dialogue evenly between very nearly all the recurring cast members (only Marta Kristen gets short-changed).

Of particular interest is the saber duel between Guy Williams and Michael Ansara. Back in 1966, it was a thrill to see the actor famous for playing Zorro engaging in electronically enhanced swordplay. That in itself, along with the high marquee value of the recurring cast and two guest stars, made "The Challenge" a highly promotable episode for the series. And one can't help but see the electric saber fight as a possible inspiration for *Star Wars* light-sabers a decade later.

Behind this inspired gimmick, there is a strong central theme present in the story, having to do with father/son relationships. One boy is desperate to gain approval, and under great pressure to live up to his father's expectations. After Quano's encounter with the monster in the cave, the Ruler asks with concern, "Are you all right? You were not injured in any way?" Quano answered, "No, father." The Ruler, speaking in anger, says, "Then I am free to say how much of a fool you are. What possessed you to confront such a formidable beast armed only with a wooden spear?" Quano avoids his father's stare, saying, "I wished to prove my courage to the Earth boy." His father scolds, "And instead, you displayed your stupidity!" Quano lowers his head and looks at the ground in shame, then says, "I am exceedingly sorry, Father. I only did so because I remembered that you killed such a beast when you were my age…" The script then describes how "the stern features of the Ruler soften and he places a gentle hand on the shoulder of the son." He merely says, "You are forgiven."

Later, Quano pleads with his father to remain in the competition. But his father has lost faith in the boy, fearing that he will lose and thereby suffer from wounded pride. He therefore removes Quano from the competition.

Robinson knows better. When learning that Will might have to compete against an older, stronger boy, he tells his wife, "I want him to meet the alien boy. I don't care if he loses or wins but he's got to have the opportunity." A surprised Maureen says, "I think you're almost glad Will is going to meet Quano!" Robinson responds: "Look at it this way, Maureen. No matter how civilized or primitive a man is, he welcomes a challenge. It's part of his nature to test his intelligence, and skills and strength. And without those things, we'd probably still be living in caves and cooking out of stone pots."

The Ruler comes to the same realization concerning his son, but too late. He admits, "In my desire to protect him, I made a mistake. I should have let him continue."

When the Ruler learns that Quano has returned to the cave to face the monster alone, he says, "Quano would not be so foolish after I warned him." Robinson says, "Can you think of a better way for a boy whose pride is hurt to prove himself to his father?"

Any story with a point is a story worth telling. "The Challenge" made for a worthwhile hour of television watching for young boys … and girls … and their parents, too.

Script:

Story assignment 8466 (Production #8522)

Barney Slater's treatment, and 1st and 2nd draft teleplays: January 1966.

Mimeo Department reformatted Shooting Final (white papers): January 28, 1966.

Page revisions by Tony Wilson (pink page inserts): February 1.

Additional page revisions by Wilson (blue page inserts): February 1.

Further page revisions by Wilson (yellow page inserts): February 2.

Further page revisions by Wilson (green page inserts): February 2.

Further page revisions by Wilson (beige page inserts): February 3.

Further page revisions by Wilson (blue page inserts): February 4.

Further page revisions by Wilson (pink page inserts): February 8.

In comparing Barney Slater, the second most prolific *Lost in Space* writer, to Peter Packer, who was the champ in respect to output, director Don Richardson said, "Barney Slater was an entirely opposite guy to Peter Packer. Barney was a very enthusiastic, very extroverted fellow who could drive you right up the wall, if you spent some time with him, because he would constantly tell you part of his next writing job. He would grab you, and whether you were having lunch with him or during the middle of rehearsal, you were stuck because he would tell you for two hours the entire plot of the movie he was writing." (DR-LISF)

"The Challenge" was Slater's sixth script for the series, following "Wish Upon a Star," "The Sky Is Falling," "The Keeper," Parts 1 and 2, and "War of the Robots."

On January 31, 1966, after reading Slater's final handling of the script, reformatted by the Mimeo Department and designated as the January 28, 1966 "Shooting Final," Sam Taylor, Jr., of CBS Program Practices, wrote:

> As discussed with Mr. Wilson:
>
> We do not wish the Act [I] to end as indicated on Page 18 with the two young boys menaced by the monster. You may wish to re-write the pertinent portion of the script so as to conclude the act in some new fashion. Barring this, however, the following are our suggestions based on the script now submitted:
>
> The Act could conclude at the end of Scene 39 on Page 17. So as to add suspense we would not object to growling sounds from the monster at this point. However, the monster should not appear on the screen....
>
> Page 18, Scene 47: Please do not allow this scene, where the monster receives the spear in his side and then tears it out, to be excessively gruesome.

The wording in the script caused the CBS censors great concern, and rightfully so. It read:

> 42. ANOTHER ANGLE – WILL AND QUANO
>
> The two boys begin to slowly back toward the cave exit. Without warning, the cave is filled with the fierce roar of a MONSTER. Will and Quano stop in fear and look in the direction of the sound.
>
> 43. REVERSE ANGLE
>
> A fantastic-looking Monster stands atop a rock. As we watch, it leaps to the ground with a growl.
>
> 44. MED. SHOT – WILL AND QUANO
>
> as they stare at the Monster. They are both backing away.

QUANO
(voice quaking)
Run! I will keep the creature at bay.

FAVORING THE MONSTER

Growling fiercely, it moves toward Will and Quano.

QUANO
Only one of us can make it! Go!

Will doesn't answer but raises the hunting knife to defend himself. The monster continues to advance and then suddenly, with a blood curdling growl, charges the two boys.

46. MED. CLOSE SHOT – WILL AND QUANO

as they brace themselves for the attack. Quano advances a couple of paces and hurls his spear.

47. CLOSE SHOT – THE MONSTER

The spear lodges in the fleshy part of the monster's side and, with a SCREAM of pain and fury, it tears the spear out, hurls it aside and continues toward Will and Quano.

48. INTERCUT THE ACTION

With a backward sweep of its hand, the monster sends Quano tumbling to the ground where he rolls against a rock and lies stunned. Then the monster directs its attention toward Will. Will, knife ready, retreats before the advance of the monster until his back is against the wall of the cave.

This presentation is dramatic and potentially frightening. CBS would have none of it. What we ended up getting was a roaring monster which stayed in the background, with Quano advancing on it, before tripping and hitting his head on a rock.

In fact, the peril toward the boys was so drastically curtailed that, in watching the scene, it is easy for many in the audience to actually empathize more for the beast than for the boys. After all, they are the aggressors, not it. It doesn't even come after them – it is merely trapped and treated as prey. Poor monster!

In Wilson's script polishing, the comedic impact of the Robot was increased, and this episode brought about the first instance of the Robot laughing at Smith. The scene plays it this way:

SMITH
What other work do I have on my schedule today?

The Robot turns toward Smith.

ROBOT
Correction: In reference to work, you should have referred to me instead of yourself.

SMITH
(drily)
If you have a complaint to make, try a different department.

ROBOT
It does not compute.

Smith gets to his feet.

SMITH
Never mind. What else do <u>we</u> have to do?

ROBOT
We?

There is a very rapid bubbling sound from the Robot's computers. (Similar to the laughter sound in "THE MAN IN THE WHITE SUIT".)

62. CLOSE SHOT – SMITH

He glares at the Robot.

SMITH
You ridiculous machine. Are you laughing at me?

63. WIDER ANGLE – THE ROBOT

ROBOT
You heard only my computers being cleared. I do not laugh.

SMITH
That's what you say. Now get on with our work.

ROBOT
Yes, <u>our</u> work.

Once again there is that rapid bubbling of the Robot's computers and it moves out of the scene. Smith stares after it.

SMITH
One of these days that over-sized sardine can will go too far.

Harris often took credit for not only the changes to his character, but the change pertaining to the interaction between Smith and the Robot. It is likely that much of the verbal sparring between the two in this episode came from suggestions made by Harris. As filming progressed, he continued to doctor the script and send handwritten changes to Tony Wilson. In respect to the shooting script for "War of the Robots," Wilson submitted page revisions to CBS while the episode filmed on February 1, 2, 3, 4, and 8. Once he had approval from the network, the revised pages were sent to the stage to be inserted into the numerous copies of the script. The other cast members were well aware by this point that many of the script changes were being prompted by Harris.

Elsewhere in the script, Wilson and his writers were still taking care to explain how the aliens who visited the planet spoke English. Robinson asks Quano: "How did you learn to speak our language?" Quano answers: "From my father. He knows many languages."

The aliens have also clearly been keeping an eye on Earth. Quano refers to how the Earth is ruled by kings, dictators and presidents, as opposed to his own world, and its single ruler-system.

On February 4, 1966, after reading Tony Wilson's page revisions dated February 2nd, Sam Taylor wrote:

> Page 58, Scene 148 thru 151: As you have substituted a duel, with electric swords, to replace the wrestling match between JOHN and THE RULER, we would request your usual directorial care so that the fight will not appear excessively violent or dangerous.

It was Wilson's idea to write a fencing match for Guy Williams, and then to take it one step further and turn the foils into electronic sabers for a sci-fi flavored clash of electricity.

Pre-Production:

Michael Ansara starred as Cochise in the 1950s TV series *Broken Arrow* (20th Century-Fox Television / ABC-TV, 1956).

Don Richardson returned for his second directing assignment on *Lost in Space*, following the so-so "Ghost in Space" (good direction, but inconsistent script). "The Challenge" was actually supposed to be directed by Tom Gries, with Richardson directing an episode of *Voyage to the Bottom of the Sea*, but Irwin Allen decided to swap the assignments and put Gries on *Voyage* instead. Now Richardson took his place alongside Sobey Martin, Nathan Juran, Ezra Stone, Harry Harris, and Sutton Roley as the series' most utilized directors. In time, Richardson would direct more episodes than anyone else (twenty-six, compared to fourteen for Martin, thirteen for Juran, eight for Stone, five for Harris, and four for Roley).

Both guest stars in this episode were indeed "stars" on television at this time.

Michael Ansara was 43 when cast to play the alien ruler. He had starred in two series of his own, as Cochise in the western *Broken Arrow* (1956-58), and Deputy Marshal Sam Buckhart in *Law of the Plainsman* (1959-60). He had played Judas in the 1953 film *The Robe* and was prominently featured in Irwin Allen's 1961 big-screen version of *Voyage to the Bottom of the Sea*. Allen also cast Ansara in two episodes of the TV version of *Voyage* and two for *The Time Tunnel*. Ansara later appeared in one episode of *Land of the Giants*.

One year before "The Challenge," Kurt Russell interacted with a different group of castaways, playing a jungle boy living on *Gilligan's Island*.

Ansara said, "I had worked for Irwin many times. He had a stock company and liked to use the same people over and over again.... I never had to audition for Irwin, he would just call on me and I would come on down." (MA-LISF)

In 1964, Ansara had the lead in "Soldier," a Harlan Ellison-scripted episode of *The Outer Limits*. His costume in "The Challenge" is reminiscent of the one he wore in "Soldier." Ansara also appeared as the Blue Djinn, opposite real-life wife Barbara Eden on her series *I Dream of Jeannie*. Three years after appearing on *Lost in Space,* Ansara played Klingon Commander Kang in the 1968 *Star Trek* episode "Day of the Dove."

Kurt Russell was cast as Quano. The script had Quano tell Will that he was eleven years old, the same age as Billy Mumy/Will Robinson at this point. However, once Russell was cast, it was felt that he could not pass for being so young, and it was decided to have Quano give his age as twelve. Russell was actually fourteen, and in his third year of television and film acting, having played the title character on a 1963-64 TV western series, *The Travels of Jaimie McPheeters*, as well as appearing in 1964 and '65 episodes of *The Man from U.N.C.L.E.*, *The Virginian* and *Gilligan's Island*, among other series.

Production Diary:

Filmed February 1 – 10, 1966 (7 days spanning 8).

Day 1: Tuesday, February 1st. On Stage 11, director Nathan Juran needed the first two-and-a-half hours of the morning to finish "Magic Mirror," at which point he turned the camera crew and cast over to Don Richardson. The company continued filming, from 10:30 a.m. to 6:44 p.m., covering five and three-eighths pages from the script. First up, the Teaser for "The Challenge" (which was also the Tag scene/cliffhanger for "Magic Mirror"). Filming of the Teaser first had become a must in scheduling the productions, since *Lost in Space* was so far behind in its

deliveries to CBS. A delay of mere days in finishing the editing of an episode could result in its not making the delivery deadline for air check and broadcast. The Tag scene for "The Magic Mirror" (but actually from the script and production for "The Challenge") involved Smith and Will sleeping outdoors, and setting a trap for the food thief, then their first encounter with the armed Quano.

Beyond making suggestions for script changes to Tony Wilson, Harris was modifying the behavior of his character even more while filming, turning dramatic scenes into comical ones. The first instance happened on this day, as they filmed the Teaser. The script said:

EXT. ROBINSON CAMP SITE – NIGHT

MED. SHOT

WILL and SMITH continue to watch the approach of QUANO. Suddenly the boy hurls the spear which he carries. Will jumps quickly to the side at the same time yelling to Smith.

WILL

Dr. Smith – look out!

Smith throws himself flat to the ground and the spear sails over his head.

Harris wasn't about to throw himself to the ground. And director Richardson didn't want to have to engage the services of a stuntman for the scene, which would require careful camera angles to conceal the switch of actor for stunt double. So Richardson and Harris decided to have Smith clutch Will and use the boy as a shield, and then scream.

February 1, 1966 was Billy Mumy's twelfth birthday. At the end of this first day, cake was served.

Day 2: Wednesday, February 2nd. Richardson filmed on Stage 11 from 8 a.m. to 6:50 p.m., shooting another nine pages from the script and more of the scenes taking place at the campsite outside the Jupiter 2.

From this day, there came another instance of Harris embellishing his role. It happened during the breakfast scene in which Quano reveals that his father is the ruler of their planet. The script underplayed Smith's reaction, as follows:

DON
What do you mean, "he is the ruler"?

QUANO
In your world there are presidents, kings, dictators. In mine there is only one – the ruler.

SMITH
(dubious)
Are you telling us your father is the head of your planet?

QUANO
(proudly)
And one day, I will take his place. My command will be law.

Don emits a low whistle.

DON
Well, what do you know. We're entertaining royalty.

Smith is stunned at the revelation. He gets quickly to his feet and gestures to his chair.

SMITH
My dear boy – why didn't you tell us who you were? Please, sit down. Can I get you anything?

QUANO
At the moment I am in need of nothing.

SMITH
(genially)
Well, if you do, just ask me for it.

DON
(with irony)
Quano has just added another abject subject to his kingdom.

The lines remained the same, but as played by Harris, Smith's reaction is over-the-top, as he bows and scrapes and even drapes a napkin over his arm as a waiter might.

Once filming stopped at 6:50 p.m., it would be a hard race for the crew to wrap the set, and for the cast to dress down and have makeup stripped off, then drive home in time for the 7:30 p.m. start time of the first CBS airing of "Ghost in Space."

Day 3: Thursday, February 3rd. A third day on Stage 11, filming from 8 a.m. to 6:35 p.m. Eight and one-eighths pages were filmed, with more of the scenes in and around the campsite outside the Jupiter 2. Richardson remained on schedule.

Day 4: Friday, February 4th. They started on Stage 11 at 8 a.m., with the balance of the Jupiter 2 campsite scenes, and ended on Stage 6 for the "Ext. Rocky Area" that was used for the training ground where Smith pushed Will to exhaustion, then Don intervened, sending Will to rest and reprimanding Smith.

All photos this page: Production Days 4 and 5.

Michael Ansara joined the cast this day. He later revealed, "Irwin Allen was a great one for shaving heads and things like that. I had a shaved head for the play *The King and I*, which Irvin had seen. When he cast me, he said, 'I want you to shave your head.' I said, 'No, I'm not going to shave my head unless you put me in a whole series.' So they put a rubber cap on my head, but you could see the wrinkles in it." (MS-LISF)

They finished at 6:40 p.m. Eleven and two-eighths pages from the script were put to film. Richardson was still on schedule.

Day 5: Monday, February 7. Another day split between two stages, with filming taking place on both Stage 6 ("Ext. Rocky Area," where Smith meets the Ruler, to the "Ext. Challenge Grounds," for the competition between Will and Quano), and then a company move to Stage 11 for pickup shots.

For the scene in which Smith first meets the Ruler, Harris made another enhancement to the script with approval from the front office, leaning his character even more toward comedy. It was the comical hand shake between Smith and the Ruler, sending Smith to his knees. The script described the action

this way:

65. GROUP SHOT – SMITH, THE RULER, AND QUANO

The Ruler shakes Smith's hand.

THE RULER
For a man, your grip is weak. You should exercise.

The Ruler pokes a finger into Smith's middle.

THE RULER
And there is fat around your middle.

SMITH
(lamely)
I'm a bit out of condition. But I haven't been well lately.

THE RULER
Exercise is a good cure for many ills.

SMITH
(as if to himself)
Not for me it isn't. The truth is, Mr. Ruler, it's this planet. I can't seem to acclimate myself. Now if I could get back to my own world…

THE RULER
(breaks in)
Another time, Dr. Smith. I want to speak to the father of the boy they call Will.

After reading Wilson's February 8th script polish, which included the above material, Harris went to work, coming up with ways to alter his role. It was at this point that the handshake became a comedy bit.

Nine and seven-eighths pages were filmed, but Richardson was one-quarter day behind when the order was given to wrap the set.

Day 6: Tuesday, February 8th. It was supposed to be the final day of production, but Richardson fell to one-half day behind after filming from 8 a.m. to 6:55 p.m. They worked on Stage 6 and the "Ext. Challenge Grounds" set, this time with the electronic sword fight between John and the Ruler. An arc welder was needed on set for the special effects-driven fight scene.

Michael Ansara said, "I recall I had a sword fight with Guy Williams, but I had done that sort of thing long before *Lost in Space*. I had trained in sword play when I went to the Pasadena Playhouse, where they trained us one hour a day." (MA-LISF)

Ansara held his own against the man who had played Zorro.

Shortly after this, June Lockhart was interviewed by Tom McIntrye, an editor for *The Gastonia Gazette*. For the newspaper's April 3, 1966 issue. McIntyre wrote:

> [Lockhart] said there is a show coming up soon on the air which she personally enjoyed watching being filmed. "Michael Ansara is

our guest star," she said. "He is a ruler from another planet. Guy Williams and he pair off for a duel to the death with electronic foils. Each time the foils touch, large electrical charges are given off. During the course of the battle they explode trees and rocks. It looked good while they were doing it and if the cutters do a good job it should look great on the air."

With the electrical component, however, the duel took extra time to film and "The Space Trader," planned to begin production the next morning, was pushed back.

Day 6: Guy Williams and Michael Ansara, both skilled swordsmen, were doing most of their own stunts. And these weren't just sabers, but electrified ones. The two actors were truly sticking their necks out. Note June Lockhart (right of truck) watching from the sidelines.

Day 7: Wednesday, February 9th. They remained on Stage 6 and filmed from 8 a.m. to 6:55 p.m., finishing the sword fight sequence, then moving to the "Ext. Rocky Area, Cave Opening" set. Richardson fell further behind and "The Space Trader" was again pushed back. By filming until 6:55 p.m. (with another half-hour needed to wrap the set and for cast members to dress down and have their makeup removed), many didn't leave the studio until close to 7:30 p.m., meaning they were not able to make it home in time for the start of "War of the Robots," aired this night on CBS.

Day 8: Thursday, February 10th. It took two-and-a-half hours to film the four remaining pages from the script, with the "Int. Cave" set built onto Stage 6. Richardson was a full day behind when he wrapped his second assignment and handed

Day 7: Filming inside the cave on Stage 6. The "bug creature" wears a recycled fly mask from 20th Century-Fox's *Return of the Fly*.

the production crew off to director Nathan Juran, allowing him to begin filming "The Space Trader."

This wouldn't sit well with Irwin Allen. It was Richardson's friend Tony Wilson who had brought him onto *Lost in Space*, and no doubt protected his job during his first few assignments.

Marta Kristen recalled, "Tony Wilson and Don Richardson got along well. And Don was into the three martini lunches, as was Tony. And they would laugh. And Tony would laugh all during lunch at the script he was working on. He admired and respected Irwin, but he was very smart, and Irwin respected that. And he knew how to survive with Irwin. I don't think Tony was under anyone's thumb. He had power and he knew how to work it." (MK-AI15)

Jonathan Harris told interviewer Ian Spelling, "On a series, after a while, we all get pretty much set in what we're doing. It was the director's job, for the most part, to be a good manager on *Lost in Space*. You see, Irwin was a very tough taskmaster. We had six-day shoots, period. Not six-and-a-half days. He was very adamant about that. So, our directors had to bring the show in on schedule. If you watch the shows, they amounted to scenes with a master shot, and over-the-shoulder shot, a two-shot and a close-up. Irwin very much liked to feature the scenery. At the drop of a hat, he would use the master and cut in to close-ups. The directors managed as best they could, and some were better than others at doing that. Still, they were all at the mercy of Irwin, who was a tough cookie. We did have some very good directors, though. I recall Harry Harris, Jerry [Nathan] Juran, and a slew of others. We had Don Richardson, who really understood the craziness and the joy of what we were all working [at], and he played to that." (JH-SL98)

Michael Ansara said, "I enjoyed working with Jonathan. He was just wonderful. I enjoyed everyone on that show. They were all very nice and, as I recall, they were also a very easy group to work with. The director, the producer and the production people were all wonderful." (MA-LISF)

Billy Mumy said, "I liked working with Kurt Russell because he and I worked together on Disney films when I was a kid. It was nice to work with him." (BM-LISW)

William Self targeted this episode for a $137,190 budget. It finished having cost $150,635.

Release / Reaction:

(CBS premiere broadcast: Wednesday, March 2, 1966)

(Network repeat air date: Wednesday, June 29, 1966)

Guy Williams – the man who played Zorro – back in action, in a futuristic saber fight! It was a press agent's dream come true, and it didn't take much work from CBS or 20th Century-Fox to get newspapers across America and Canada to run this promotional picture in their TV listings section.

The amount of U.S. soldiers deployed to South Vietnam climbed to 215,000 during the week when "The Challenge" first aired. Nancy Sinatra's "These Boots Are Made for Walkin'" was top song on the radio. Whipped Cream & Other Delights by Herb Alpert's Tijuana Brass reclaimed the top spot in the record album charts, dethroning the Beatles' Rubber Soul. Paul Newman had the top-grossing movie in America with a detective tale, Harper.

The day that "The Challenge" first aired, and despite the threat of *Batman* and a downturn in the ratings, the first round of network schedules for the fall TV season were released to the press. *Lost in Space* was penciled in for continuing on Wednesday nights opposite *Batman*. CBS was betting that *Batman* would overstay its welcome, and that *Lost in Space* would have longer legs.

During this week, and perfectly timed with the airing of "The Challenge," United Press International syndicated an article to newspapers across America focusing on Guy Williams. Included in the February 27, 1966 editions of Kannapolis's *The Daily Independent*, UPA Hollywood Correspondent Vernon Scott wrote:

> Guy Williams spent two years in a cape and mask as Zorro and now finds himself encased in a space suit for *Lost in Space*. Between the two he managed to star in a few European movies (*Captain Sindbad* and *Damon and Pythias*), still romping around in hokey costumes. It's no wonder then that Williams enjoys lounging around home in slacks, sports shirts and sweaters. Home is a Mediterranean mansion in the Hollywood hills. It's a solid 30-year-old stucco with 14 rooms and six baths. He and his wife Jan have decorated the place in period furniture picked up in Italy and France during their motion picture junkets aboard.... Married 15 years, the Williams have a son, Steve, 12, and a daughter, Toni, 6, who joined their parents in Europe. At home Guy escapes the normal family uproar in a combination study-library equipped with tape machines. It is off limits for all but the family feline, an animal of dubious antecedents who goes by the name of "Cat." There is also a swimming pool which serves as Williams' main source of exercise and relaxation. "I used to own a sailboat," he says, "but I've been working so hard and traveling so much that I

> sold it. [And] because horseback riding and fencing are so much a part of my business I wouldn't think of doing either one for recreation." Williams is up by 6 a.m. weekdays in time to arrive at 20th Century-Fox by 7 for the CBS-TV series which co-stars June Lockhart. He's rarely home before 7 o'clock in the evening, and sometimes as late as 11 p.m.

Jonathan Harris was given equal time with a filler piece of his own, carried in newspapers such as the *Abilene Reporter-News*, the *El Paso Herald-Post*, both out of Texas, and the *North Adams Transcript*, serving North Adams, Massachusetts. Erskine Johnson wrote:

> A funny thing happened to Jonathan Harris while he was *Lost in Space* on television. A Los Angeles TV critic voted him the "worst" actor of the year. On the same day, another newspaper critic of equal stature acclaimed Harris "the most delightful and best tongue-in-cheek villain on television." The clash of views, we are happy to report, was no traumatic experience for Harris, the New York pharmacist who became an actor with a multitude of characterizations. "Let's face it," he laughed between scenes for the far-out CBS-TV series in which he plays the evil Col. Zachary Smith, "I'm playing this role with my tongue so far in my cheek it hurts to talk. It's all spoof. I just can't understand a critic trying to take the part seriously. I'm having a ball playing Smith; he's such a nut. And I'm not really overplaying him, he's just over extended. He's such a pompous ass, but he's really a simple soul who is a dreadful coward. The combination, I think, would work out very well because the show is part reality and part fantasy."

Harris told Johnson, "I've never been one of those artsy-craftsy actors and this role I love because I'm an actor performing in my craft every day. As an actor I guess I'm limited, I can play heavies and I can be funny. In this role I combine both."

Also during the week, *TV Guide*'s letter column included:

> You are missing a good bet. Thought sure you'd have a profile on Dr. Smith of *Lost in Space*. My family agrees he is the funniest arch villain on TV. – Lee Biggs, Reno, Nevada.

The Editor that *TV GUIDE* had an article on Jonathan Harris coming up soon.

On March 2, 1966, Betty Marsh, for her "Looking at TV" column in the *Medina County Gazette*, serving Medina, Ohio, commented on the latest *Lost in Space* episode:

> A fighting 11-year-old boy gives the Robinson family a run for their money on *Lost in Space* at 7:30 on channel 8. Seems the lad feels that this group of space travelers are inferior people. (I'm with him!). Stars June Lockhart, Guy Williams and Kurt Russell.

For his television column in Ohio's *The Akron Beacon Journal*, TV-Radio-Film critic Dick Shippy wrote:

Lost in Space: Let's hear no more about the loneliness of space. The Robinsons' supposedly deserted planet continues to swarm with strangers. This time, it's the ruler of another planet out to prove his superiority over Earth people.

The A.C. Nielsen's 30-City Ratings survey for March 2, 1966 reported:

Network / Program:	Rating	Share:
7:30 – 8 p.m.:		
ABC: *Batman*	**25.0**	**40.1%**
CBS: *Lost in Space*	16.1	25.8%
NBC: *The Virginian*	15.9	25.5%
8 – 8:30 p.m.:		
ABC: *The Patty Duke Show*	18.6	29.9%
CBS: *Lost in Space*	**21.4**	**34.3%**
NBC: *The Virginian*	16.6	26.2%

Nielsen also conducted a national survey for the two-week period ending March 6, 1966 (as presented in March 22, 1966 issue of *Daily Variety*). *Lost in Space* aired only once during the two weeks. A special presentation of "Cinderella" was televised over CBS on Wednesday during Week 1, and was the second most-watched primetime program during the two-week period. *Lost in Space*, with "The Challenge," aired the following Wednesday night, ranked at No. 40. According to Nielsen, the Top 40 programs for the two-week period stacked up this way:

1. *Bonanza*	NBC	31.5
2. *Cinderella* (special)	CBS	30.9
3. *The Lucy Show*	CBS	29.7
4. *The Beverly Hillbillies*	CBS	29.2
5. *Green Acres*	CBS	28.2
6. *The Andy Griffith Show*	CBS	28.5
7. *Batman* (Thursday)	ABC	28.4
8. *Gomer Pyle, U.S.M.C.*	CBS	27.8
9. *Bewitched*	ABC	27.6
10. *The Ed Sullivan Show*	CBS	27.0
11. *Hogan's Heroes*	CBS	27.0
12. *The Dick Van Dyke Show*	CBS	26.6
13. *Get Smart*	NBC	26.2
14. *The Red Skelton Show*	CBS	26.2
15. *The Man from U.N.C.L.E.*	NBC	26.0
16. *My Three Sons*	CBS	24.4
17. *The Jackie Gleason Show*	CBS	24.3
18. *Batman* (Wednesday)	ABC	24.1
19. *I Dream of Jeannie*	NBC	23.9
20. *The Wild, Wild West*	CBS	23.6
21. *I've Got a Secret*	CBS	23.6
22. *The Lawrence Welk Show*	ABC	23.4
23. *Combat!*	ABC	23.1

24. *Daktari*	CBS	23.0
25. *Flipper*	NBC	22.4
26. Tuesday Night Movie	NBC	22.3
27. *Petticoat Junction*	CBS	22.3
28. *My Favorite Martian*	CBS	22.1
29. *The Dean Martin Show*	CBS	22.1
30. *Lassie*	NBC	22.1
31. *Peyton Place* (Thursday)	ABC	22.0
32. Thursday Night Movie	CBS	21.9
33. *Hollywood Palace*	ABC	21.9
34. *Gilligan's Island*	CBS	21.8
35. *Gunsmoke*	CBS	21.7
36. *Peyton Place* (Monday)	ABC	21.3
37. Saturday Night Movie	NBC	21.2
38. *The Big Valley*	ABC	21.1
39. *Candid Camera*	CBS	20.9
40. *Lost in Space*	**CBS**	**20.9**

Making the Top 40 (out of more than 80 primetime programs) qualified a series as a hit show. In fact, some shows considered hits didn't even make the Top 40. These series, which would continue for at least one additional TV season, but ranked under *Lost in Space*, included, *Voyage to the Bottom of the Sea*, *The F.B.I.*, ABC Sunday Night Movie, *Walt Disney's Wonderful World of Color*, *Twelve O'Clock High*, *Run for Your Life*, *F Troop*, *The Fugitive*, *I Spy*, *The Virginian*, *Laredo*, *Daniel Boone*, and *Please Don't Eat the Daisies!*

34

Episode 23: "The Space Trader"

Written by Barney Slater
(co-written with Anthony Wilson, uncredited)
Directed by Nathan Juran
Produced by Irwin Allen; with Jerry Briskin

From the *Lost in Space* show files (Irwin Allen Papers Collection):

> A violent, cosmic storm devastates the family's hydroponic garden, leaving them woefully short of food. This has been done deliberately by a sinister Space Trader who now sets up a store full of exotic merchandise. The Robinsons do not trust him and will not deal with him, but Smith secretly swaps the Robot for a private supply of food. When the family discovers this, none of them will speak to him. To get the Robot back, Smith, who has nothing else to offer, carelessly agrees to the Trader's suggestion that he trade in himself. He does not think he will ever have to honor the bargain but the contract, a card with an electronic imprint of his hand on it, gives the Trader power over him. When the Trader announces that he is leaving and taking Smith with him, the doctor is unable to refuse to go.

From the Script:

(Shooting Final teleplay, February 2, 1966 draft)

– *The Trader:* "Humanoids! A man and a boy! How absolutely delightful! I'm overjoyed! I'm ecstatic! *(with a flourishing bow)* The Trader … at your service, sirs." *Smith:* "I'm Dr. Zachary Smith from the planet Earth. And this young man is William Robinson." *The Trader (impressed):* "From the planet Earth. My, you are a long way from home, aren't you." *Will:* "Where do you come from, sir?" *The Trader:* "Me? From everywhere. A citizen of the whole galaxy is what I am. *(with a big smile)* I was beginning to think I was all alone here. There are two things the Trader loves most – good company and good business." *Will:* "What is your business, Mr. Trader?" *The Trader:* "Come into my store, young man, and I'll show you."

– *Will:* "What does this do, Mr. Trader?" *The Trader:* "Controls the weather. Makes the climate cool in the summer; warm in the winter." *Smith:* "Too bad we didn't have this earlier today. We could have diverted the storm." *The Trader (looks sympathetic):* "How unfortunate. Perhaps you would like to trade me something for it?" *Will:* "We don't need it now. The damage is done." *The Trader (as if to himself):* "Yes, so it is."

Assessment:

"The Space Trader" is a familiar type, the rambling merchant who supplies frontiers people with staples or exotic items. Such rovers, from the tinkers and Gypsies of Western Europe to the stereotypical traveling salesman, are an easy way to introduce a mischievous idea or an intriguing device into a group of established characters. *Star Trek* would feature several, including Cyrano Jones and Harry Mudd.

This story contains an assortment of plot devices and gimmicks which mar many an episode of *Lost in Space* – some found here for the first time in the series, others already familiar filler items.

Smith acts the complete moron more than once – first in the Teaser, as he risks his safety by chasing after his "masterpiece," then by planning his life only days at a time (he trades the Robot for a mere ten days' worth of food).

The dumbing down of the Robot continues. He is now a rather crass art critic. Despite his lack of tact while critiquing Dr. Smith's attempt at painting, the Robot has also become so hyper sensitive that his feelings are hurt merely because Smith insults him back … as if an insult from Smith hasn't happened before.

Even though the Trader boasts how valuable and formidable his dogs are, they fall for the old "distract-the-dogs-by-throwing-a-stick" routine. It makes for rather dull stuff.

Speaking of dull, Smith runs for twenty seconds, or is it only ten, before plopping himself down on a rock, exhausted and ready to give up. We've seen this before and will see it again … often.

The episode brings forward more recycling – this time with the language translator device, last seen as the wish machine in "Which Upon a Star," and the Trader's ship, last seen as Tucker the Pirate's ship.

Speaking of the ship: How in the world – or galaxy – did the Trader fit all his wares into that itsy-bitsy craft? Perhaps he uses relativistic physics to make it larger inside than out – like Dr. Who's TARDIS.

All in all, "The Space Trader" makes for a mediocre episode. Yet it received a network repeat airing while more intriguing episodes, such as "Welcome Stranger" and "My Friend, Mr. Nobody," were passed over. Worse, this episode, perhaps more so than any other produced up until this time, would serve as a template for many Second Season stories – and many of those would be among the worst in the series.

"The Space Pirate" does redeem itself on occasion. The alien language – both spoken and written on the electronic sign posts – is a nice addition, as is a machine that can alter the weather, and another that can instantly teach one a new language. Another plus is the contract solemnized by one's handprint, which can glow and summon the signer even against his or her or its will. Interwoven among the less inspired moments is the delightful interaction between Torin Thatcher, as the Trader, and Jonathan Harris. Beyond this, the overall cast is well utilized. And you'll likely need to interrupt the viewing of this episode to raid the refrigerator. Watching Smith crave food can have a contagious effect on the more impressionable in the audience, this author included.

The simple directions for enjoying this episode: Don't think, or question, or scoff; just watch, enjoy, and, when it's over, *bon appétit*.

Script:

Story assignment 8467 (Production #8523)
Barney Slater's story treatment, plus 1st and 2nd draft teleplays: January 1966.
Mimeo Department's reformatted Shooting Final teleplay: February 2, 1966.
Tony Wilson's rewrite, Revised Shooting Final teleplay (on blue paper): Date unknown.
Page revisions by Wilson (inserts, on green paper): February 8, 1966.
Wilson's rewrite, 2nd Rev. Shooting Final (all new printing on pink paper): February 10.
Additional page revisions by Wilson (inserts, on blue paper): February 11.

Barney Slater was already on his seventh *Lost in Space* writing assignment.

As soon as the mid-season pickup from CBS came in December 1965, Slater was put on assignment to write "The Space Trader." His two-page springboard from the early days of January 1966 read:

> A howling storm sweeps down on the Jupiter 2 and, when it departs, the hydroponic garden has been destroyed, and the water supply polluted. Realizing the desperate straits of his party, John Robinson puts everyone on short rations. Smith, a voice of doom, says that it was only a matter of time until the planet got them all and now it has.
>
> It is later that day that Smith and Will encounter The Trader. The alien (perhaps Michael Dunn), good-humored individual, has landed his spaceship and set it up as a trading post not far from the

Jupiter 2. Will and Smith gaze in awe and wonder at the wonderful things which The Trader has to sell. Not only is there food and water, but fabulous contrivances from all over the galaxy. Two huge chained, dog-like monsters guard the store.

Smith is delighted. They are saved. But The Trader, despite his good nature, is a man of business. He will give them nothing without trade in return. Smith is willing to give up anything for the luxuries of food that he is accustomed to. He is willing to barter the Chariot, weapons, even the spaceship to get food and some of the wonderful inventions which The Trader has. But Robinson pulls back – no one will starve, with rationing. They have enough to get by. Smith refuses to believe him. Secretly, Smith trades the Robot to The Trader for a huge eight-course dinner.

The family is horrified, but Smith shrugs off their disapproval. Not only does he have food, but other alien luxuries. The Robot, however, refuses to stay with The Trader. He comes back to the Robinsons. The Trader is not far behind. If he cannot keep the Robot, then Smith must give him something else. When Smith can think of nothing, The Trader suggests that Smith offer himself. At first, Smith is frightened at that prospect. But, as usual, he thinks he has a way out … he just won't pay off. The Trader makes Smith put his hand print in a glowing tablet to seal the bargain. The Robinsons are suspicious of a plump, happy Smith, but he assures them that he got all of his supplies by shrewd bargaining.

When the time comes for The Trader to leave and Smith to pay off, Smith flees to the Robinsons for help – they can't let the alien take him away.

Holding the two dog-like monsters on a chain, The Trader shows up at the spaceship. The alien holds up the glowing tablet which has Smith's hand print on it. This is the contract; Smith belongs to him. A bargain has been made and it must be kept. If the Robinsons do not turn Smith over, then he will destroy them all. As the family deliberates their problem, the Robot solves the dilemma by picking up the kicking, screaming Smith and carrying him out to The Trader.

As the family watches horrified, the Robot proceeds to renegotiate the deal, convincing The Trader that Smith is the worst of possible bargains.

This was an easy one for the CBS censors to say "yes" too. There were no horrifying monsters coming toward camera, and the Robinson children, although hungry, were not otherwise threatened.

However, there was one little thing that turned up in Slater's script that the network watchdogs took issue over. During the Teaser, as Smith paints his "masterpiece," the Robot says, "I would like to express an opinion." Smith replies, "You have my permission." Slater then wrote: "From inside the Robot there is a SOUND which resembles someone regurgitating. Smith fails to get its meaning." He says, "If you have a comment to make – make it!" The Robot says, "I already have."

Sam Taylor, Jr., of CBS Program Practices, wrote:

> If the Robot were to make a sound "which resembles someone regurgitating," we feel this would be in poor taste and request a change in the business.

The sound was changed to something less vulgar.

Tony Wilson earned his pay as story editor with all the rewriting he did for this episode. With his Revised Shooting Final teleplay, then a 2nd Revised Shooting Final teleplay, followed by a series of page revisions, Wilson wrote close to half of the dialogue heard in the episode, as well as substantially restructuring the last half of the story.

During the first half, it was Wilson who wrote the scene in which the Robinsons, West and Smith sit around the dining table and are given protein pills to eat. He also added the business with the electric sign posts leading to the Trader's store, and the idea of having the Trader speak in an alien tongue when we first meet him, then using the translator "thinking cap" unit and, presto, acquiring the English language.

The second half of the script constituted very nearly a complete rewrite from Wilson. As Slater left it, the Robot was only in the possession of the Trader for a short while before running away and returning to the Jupiter 2 camp. In Slater's version, the Robinsons and West discover that Smith has acquired food from the Trader, but believe his story about trading labor for the food. At no time does Smith tell them that he traded the Robot, nor does the Robot reveal this to the Robinsons or West after returning. In fact, Slater wrote scenes in which Smith shared his food with the others. After a feast, Don says, "I ate too much. Much as I hate to admit it, for once I was wrong about Smith." Robinson asks, "Think we should apologize?" Don replies, "In my contented condition, I am at peace with the universe … Smith included."

There are no scenes in Slater's final handling of the script in which the family stops talking to Smith, thereby prompting him to feel ostracized and attempt to retrieve the Robot. In Slater's script, Smith does return to see the Trader, but only to tell him that the Robot will not return and there is nothing that he can do about it. The Trader then decides that he will take an Earthling in exchange for the Robot and has Smith place his hand on the contract. Smith is pressured into doing so. Unlike in Wilson's rewrite and the filmed episode, the Trader does not con Smith into doing this, and there is no discussion of the Trader waiting 200 years before collecting on the contract; nor does he use the contract to cast a spell over Smith and force him to return.

As Slater left it, the Robot does not save the day, but, instead, John and Don out-con the Trader. Robinson says, "You just traded a lot of good food for a completely useless object, that's all. Just ask yourself one question – why would anyone want Dr. Smith? He won't work, he's too lazy. He's always getting in trouble. And he'll eat you right out of business." The Trader says, "I hadn't thought of that." Robinson adds, "Even if you do succeed in selling Smith off to someone, it won't be good for you. The buyer will find out you cheated him and demand a refund." Don injects, "If you've got a good business reputation, Smith will ruin it."

Robinson ends up giving the Trader a solar heating unit in exchange for Smith, and the Trader contently leaves. It was all quite anticlimactic.

Wilson's rewrites, as documented in the *Lost in Space* show files, provide for much of what works in the latter half of "The Space Trader."

Pre-Production:

Torin Thatcher was sixty-one when cast as the Trader. Born and raised in England, where he began his career on the stage in London, Thatcher excelled at playing villains. One such role was as Sokurah the Magician in 1958's *The 7th Voyage of Sinbad*, in which he shrank female lead Kathryn Grant to the size of a Barbie doll.

Thatcher was a favorite of director Nathan Juran, and it was Juran's idea to bring Thatcher to *Lost in Space*. The director said, "Irwin thought Torin Thatcher must have been my brother-in-law, because I asked for him so often." (NJ-LISF)

Thatcher appeared in two other Irwin Allen productions – in one episode each for *Voyage to the Bottom of the Sea* and *Land of the Giants*. One year after *Space*, Thatcher appeared in the 1967 *Star Trek* episode "The Return of the Archons."

Production Diary:

Filmed February 10 – 18, 1966 (6 ½ days).

Production began on Thursday, February 10, 1966, on Stage 11, for the "Ext. Jupiter 2" set, with the fall of the water tower. Don Richardson needed approximately three hours in the morning to finish "The Challenge," therefore Nathan Juran wasn't able to begin filming "The Space Trader" until 11:45 a.m.

As it was now customary, the Teaser was filmed first, allowing the previous episode to have its cliffhanger added, and be shipped off to the network, barely arriving in time for broadcast. This was an especially difficult day's work, with wind machines blowing brush and leaves and sand, then the water tower collapse and the rolling of the hollowed drum. Stunt men were needed, as well as extra stand-ins for the wind sequences.

Watch closely as the Robot moves up the ramp leading into the Jupiter 2. Pulled by cables, it begins to tilt backward, then starts to fall, just as the scene is cut.

Bob May said, "There was one time that [Nathan Juran] wanted me to go up the ramp into the Jupiter 2 along with some other people.... I did not want to do it in the full outfit with the cable; I wanted to do it in the Bermudas. I could see it was a dangerous thing. Juran wouldn't change this camera angle, and insisted I do it his way. That's when I flipped up in the air and went completely 360 – and I was *out*. I was knocked out, and the Robot was busted up a little bit. But it could have been disastrous. If I didn't duck down, and if I didn't pull my arms in, I would have busted both my arms and my neck." (BM-SL94)

Kevin Burns said, "It fell over hard. Not 360 degrees, as Bobby has said, but he was on a ramp, so it probably would be, not 45 degrees, but maybe a 50 degree angle. But it was scary. You know, he was knocked out. And they did take the suit off him, and he was a little woozy, and June was there, asking, 'Are you okay?'" (KB-AI16)

Journalist Mike Clark interviewed numerous witnesses to the accident, and revealed, "I was told by more than one cast member that June Lockhart cradled the unconscious Bob May after the prop guys pulled the top of the costume off him. When Bob awoke, he surveyed the damage and said 'Is the Robot alright?!'" (MC-AI15)

Above: The series struggles to stay on budget by recycling (the "wishing cap" from "Wish Upon a Star" and Captain Tucker's spaceship, from "The Sky Pirate"). Below: A *Lost in Space* first – Dr. Smith trades the Robot for food.

May concluded, "I was all right. And the crew guys fixed the Robot up again, and soon we were back working." (BM-SL94)

With the late start, and the mishap concerning the Robot, Juran didn't complete his final shot until 7:14 p.m.

For the second and third day, and part of the fourth, the company was on Stage 6 with the "Ext. Trader Store."

Nathan Juran said, "The little bitty ship Torin travelled around in was sort of ridiculous. But, on the other hand, what the hell. It's just imagination, isn't it?" (NJ-LISF)

Regarding the chemistry between Harris and Thatcher, Juran said, "I thought Torin fit very well into 'Space Trader.' His scenes with Jonathan Harris were great fun. They were like two old hams chewing up the scenery together." (NJ-LISF)

Days 5 and 6 were spent back on Stage 11 for more shooting outside the Jupiter 2 camp, plus the hydroponic garden.

On that fifth day, Wednesday, February 16th, "The Magic Mirror" aired on CBS. Few got home in time to see it, since Juran didn't complete his last shot until 7:14 p.m.

"The Space Trader" was filled with many clever touches. Above: Smith is bound by a futuristic contract. Below: The future of advertising.

By Day 6, Nathan Juran had fallen half a day behind and was unable to put the episode to bed.

Jonathan Harris said, "I liked Nathan Juran very much, but he was a very hysterical man. He was a very talented director and he did excellent work. I don't know whether Irwin made him hysterical, but it is entirely possible because Irwin was a director killer. Irwin's spies would call him up and say the director was falling behind schedule. Irwin would come down and walk over to Juran, or whoever, and look at his watch and then at the director, meaning, 'Time is money,' which would make Juran hysterical. He was a brilliant director who put together a wonder show." (JH-LISF)

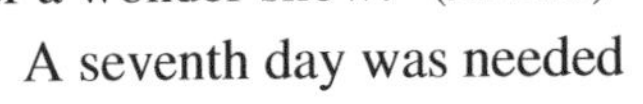

A seventh day was needed to finish, filming on Stage 6 for "Ext. Bushy Area," then back to Stage 11 for additional sequences and pickup shots at the Jupiter 2, both inside and out. Juran completed his final shot at 6:34 p.m.

While filming "The Space Trader," June Lockhart was interviewed by Tom McIntyre, the "Weekender Editor" for *The Gastonia Gazette.* For an article in that newspapers April 3, 1966 issue, McIntyre wrote:

> Viewing television night after night, week after week, can become the most maddening, frustrating thing anyone ever suffered. Do you ever get the feeling you'd like to see some of the actors appearing regularly in series just step out of character and blow the roof off the house?... June Lockhart is one on my list. Miss Lockhart, who portrays Maureen Robinson on *Lost in Space*, seen locally on WBTV Wednesdays at 7:30, has so much more depth than she is allowed to display as the faithful wife of space explorer John Robinson. That is what is so frustrating. Week after week she has to play her role in subdued tones. Never raising her voice in anger, never displaying deep emotion…. This apparently doesn't bother Miss Lockhart. "I must prefer a series than now and then guest shots on other series," she said. "I adapt well to a series and

> we have a great company working on our show.... You might as well forget trying to satisfy your acting ego with any television part," she added, "because all shows are designed for one thing. Sell the 'soap.' So if you're going to appear on television, a series of your own is the best way."

After six seasons on *Lassie*, and now half a season for *Lost and Space*, and counting, Lockhart knew what she spoke of. It was a little before eight in the morning as McIntyre interviewed her, and she told him, "The technicians are lining up the lights on our standings. They'll call us any minute now to begin. I've been up since five. It's a daily ritual. Get up, feed the cats, and drive to the studio for makeup, and on the set ready to work by eight."

Asked to compare her new job to the one on *Lassie*, Lockhart said, "*Lost in Space* is much more demanding. I have to suffer through sand and wind storms on our little planet and help fight off all sorts of monsters and space creatures."

Perhaps the worst ordeal was premature aging. Lockhart said, "As far as me having a daughter as old as the one on the show, well, people have more or less accepted it. Does seem strange though since I am supposed to have gone through college and became a biochemist and still had time to raise a large family. Maybe I was a youngster when I went to the altar."

McIntyre wrote:

> If you watch the show you might get the impression on occasion even the actors don't believe what's happening. Before the season began it was given to believe *Lost in Space* would be a straight drama, but more and more the approach appears to be tongue-in-cheek.

Lockhart responded, "That may be because of the character of Dr. Smith. In the first episode he was a karate chopping villain who stowed away on our ship to sabotage the mission. Since then he has evolved into a comic character. I don't think it was intentional, but sometimes in television things just work out for the better that way."

Interviewed by Dave Kaufman for a February 9, 1966 *Daily Variety* article, Lockhart described the plot of "Space Trader" as a Faust yarn, saying, "We run out of food and water. Things look very bleak. An itinerant peddler lands on the planet. His space ship is full of food and all the things we need. The only way we can get it is by selling our souls to him." (JL-DV66)

Lockhart's description of the plot sounded better. CBS, however, would never have approved it.

What was approved, by William Self, was a budget of $135,456 (above the studio per-episode wish budget of $130,980). By the time all was said, and shot, and done, the costs climbed to $145,020.

Release / Reaction:

(CBS premiere broadcast: Wednesday, March 9, 1966)
(Network repeat airdate: Wednesday, July 7, 1966)

During the week in which "The Space Trader" had its first broadcast on CBS, *Whipped Cream & Other Delights* by Herb Alpert's Tijuana Brass finally was knocked from the top spot in record album sales charts. The new top-seller was *Going Places* ... by, you guessed it, Herb Alpert's Tijuana Brass. *Whipped Cream & Other Delights* moved down to second place. The TJ Brass also had two other albums in the Top 20 of Billboard's album chart – *South of the Border* and *The Lonely Bull.* At this particular moment of the 1960s in the U.S., TJ Brass-mania was outselling Beatlemania. The song getting the most attention on the radio was "The Ballad of the Green Berets" by Staff Sgt. Barry Sadler, a former Green Beret himself. Top film in the movie houses: *The Group*, a social satire about a group of female college students, including Candice Bergen and Joan Hackett. On the cover of *TV Guide*: Barbara Feldon of *Get Smart.*

The A.C. Nielsen 30-City Ratings survey for March 9, 1966 reported:

Network / Program:	Rating	Share:
7:30 – 8 p.m.:		
ABC: *Batman*	**25.0**	**38.6%**
CBS: *Lost in Space*	17.5	27.0%
NBC: *The Virginian*	16.1	24.8%
8 – 8:30 p.m.:		
ABC: *The Patty Duke Show*	17.5	27.3%
CBS: *Lost in Space*	**22.4**	**34.9%**
NBC: *The Virginian*	17.3	27.0%

35

Episode 24: "His Majesty Smith"

Written by Carey Wilber
(with script polishing by Anthony Wilson)
Directed by Harry Harris
Produced by Irwin Allen; with Jerry Briskin

From the *Lost in Space* show files (Irwin Allen Papers Collection):

> Smith and Will are approached by some handsome aliens whose leader, Nexus, says they have come from the planet Andronica looking for a king. When Smith hears that their world is filled with every imaginable luxury, he arranges to get himself chosen for this role. Attended by Andronicans in regal style, Smith is preparing to leave for his new kingdom when an ugly, hairy creature appears and tells him that these handsome people are not the inhabitants of Andrinica but human-like robots made in order to deceive him into becoming their king. When he arrives he is to be sacrificed to ensure prosperity for his subjects. The Robinsons are uneasy about Smith's future and have prevented the androids from contacting their spaceship. To allay their suspicions the ugly Andronican creates an exact robot replica of Smith which he sends to the Robinsons.

From the Script:

(Shooting Final, February 24, 1966 draft)

– *John:* "Something tells me Smith has gotten himself into deep trouble." *Don:* "Let him stay there." *John:* "Whether we like him or not, Smith is a human being and a member of this expedition. He's entitled to our help."

– *Smith:* "Then I really am king?" *Alien:* "Oh yes. You are king for festival of sacrifice." *Smith:* "Festival? Sacrifice?" *Alien:* "Big festival. Everybody come. Drink glooog. Make sleemoth." *Smith:* "Drink glooog ... make sleemoth..." *Alien:* "Very happy." *Smith:* "Very happy..." *Alien:* "Then make sacrifice." *Smith:* "One of your quaint religious rites, no doubt. Purely symbolic in nature?" *Alien:* "No. Sacrifice king so everybody be happy, well, prosperous in year to come." *Smith:* "Sacrifice the king?" *Alien:* "Skin him. Stuff him. Very good stuffing. Last many years. Ten thousand years from now, you look same. Stand in hall of immortal kings. Very great honor."

Assessment:

As with "The Space Trader," this is an episode which would serve as a template for many to come, especially during the second season – Smith bribed or conned by aliens with promises of riches and power ... or, in the case of "Trader," merely some food, all of which of course leads to Smith getting himself into deep trouble. "His Majesty Smith" was also the first of several instances in the series in which Smith would be replicated. However, unlike "Trader," and a handful of other episodes that were later made that featured a similar theme, this one sparkles with fresh ideas; a strong central theme; many surprises; and some truly humorous moments – as opposed to ones which merely attempt to be funny.

"Daddy Zach," Smith's clone, is a delight, as are the reactions from the Robinsons, Major West and the Robot to this changed Smith, who is selfless and hardworking, and which, as the Robot says, "Does not compute." Jonathan Harris shines in this episode, playing two very different Smiths. Guest player Kevin Hagen also turns in an original take on the old monstrous alien role. Credit must also go to writers Carey Wilber and Tony Wilson – the quirkiness of the characterizations is well in place on the written page.

The dual themes in this story have to do with identifying the positive virtues in humankind, and the heroic trait of self-sacrifice.

Script:

Story Assignment 8470 (Production #8524)

Carey Wilber's treatment, and 1st and 2nd draft teleplays: January and early February 1966.

Mimeo Department reformatted Shooting Final teleplay: February 14, 1966.

Page revisions by Tony Wilson (blue insert pages): February 15.

Additional page revisions by Tony Wilson (pink insert pages): February 15.

Further revisions by Tony Wilson (yellow insert pages): February 16.

Further revisions by Tony Wilson (green insert pages): February 16.

Further revisions by Tony Wilson (gold insert pages): February 17.

Further revisions by Tony Wilson (beige insert pages): February 22.
Further revisions by Tony Wilson (pink insert pages): February 23.
Further revisions by Tony Wilson (dark green insert pages): February 24.

Carey Wilber returned for his fourth *Lost in Space* assignment (third to be produced, with one abandoned). By this time, Wilber had written "Space Seed," his one and only script for *Star Trek*, which *Trek* producers Gene Roddenberry and Gene L. Coon rewrote. The rewrite was substantial enough for both producers to request screen credit from the Writers Guild of America Arbitration Board. After reading all drafts of the script, Roddenberry's name was omitted and the screen credit read: "Teleplay by Gene L. Coon and Carey Wilber. Story by Carey Wilber." Wilber was more fortunate with his scripts for *Lost in Space*. In fact, even though Tony Wilson contributed eight different sets of page revisions between February 15th and 24th, there was never a complete rewrite, therefore it was primarily Wilber's version of the script which went before the camera.

Wilber does well at defining Smith, and explaining how the Robinsons can have affection for him despite his many faults. In one scene, Will, baffled by the behavior of "Daddy Zach," asks, "Do you suppose there's something wrong?" Don answers: "With Smith? If there is I hope it's lasting. You know, I could actually almost like the guy." Will says, "I don't know. The way he was before… Oh, I know he was lazy and greedy and an awful liar, but there was just something so darn human about him."

In another scene, John tells the "Second Smith," aka "Daddy Zach," "I don't think there's room in this group for two Smiths." The Second Smith says, "I couldn't agree more. You'll have to get rid of him." When John reacts in concern, the Second Smith adds, "Well, you certainly don't want him around, do you?" John explains: "He was here first. He's our friend." The Second Smith says: "Makes no difference, John. None at all. I was created from the essence of the original Smith … with a few of his worse characteristics omitted. But I am just as much Zachary Smith as he is. Just as human. Just as real. Now which one are you going to keep?" John answers: "Zach, with all his faults, Dr. Zachary Smith is our friend. We don't want to lose him."

One of the two themes in the story – the value of the individual, whether or not that person is likable – has the real Smith ask the Alien, "Why take a rascal when there are such noble minds as Professor Robinson, or physical courage like Major West, or incipient genius like little Will available?" The Alien answers: "They are useful creatures. You are useless creature. It is wasteful to sacrifice useful creatures as king." A shocked Smith asks, "You mean, you select your kings because they are useless?" The Alien replies: "Yes. They will not be missed."

Regarding the second theme, self-sacrifice, Smith (the real one, posing as the imposter) tells Will: "Dear little nipper! My mind is made up. I shall give myself to save those whom I have grown to love. 'But whether on the scaffold high, or in the battle's van, the fittest place a man can die … is where he dies for man.' Oh, the beauty of it!"

The poem "The Place Where Man Should Die" was written by Michael Joseph Barry and published in 1844.

On February 13, 1966, after reading Carey Wilber's 2nd draft teleplay, Irwin Allen wrote to Tony Wilson:

P. 26, Sc. 52: Smith's last speech seems to be a complete switch from earlier in the scene in which he had decided to pass judgment on the Robinsons and take Will with him – now he accepts the fact that they are not going with him. This change in plans should be clarified.

John said he was going to keep the appointment because he felt Smith didn't know what trouble he was getting into – yet John says nothing of his fears to Smith and nothing seems to have been accomplished in this scene. John should at least request to speak with Smith alone and Smith could refuse him an audience.

P. 51 & 52, Sc. 120 & 121 & 122: John's attitude should be changed. He should be obviously joking when he acts bemused by the problem of which Smith [real or double] to keep. Otherwise he'll sound stupid. We should know that he will obviously keep the real Dr. Smith.

This was the first episode in the series to have aliens speaking English without explaining how this was possible. However, to the credit of writers Carey Wilber and Tony Wilson, the alien does speak a type of Pidgin English, making it clear that this is not their native language. As for his android replicas, it would stand to reason that they would be programmed to speak English since they and the alien admit Smith had been under observation.

In the end of the story, the Second Smith (Daddy Zach) sacrifices himself for the real Smith and the Robinson party. CBS wasn't about to allow the story to end on such a somber note, with the audience believing that Daddy Zach would likely be killed, and then skinned and stuffed. A line of dialogue was added to the script to eliminate this concern. Smith tells the others: "If it's any comfort to you, both I and my alter ego are quite certain nothing horrible will happen to him. You see, the Andronicans have a horror of waste and when they discover he is really a useful sort they will alter their plans and release him."

Liam Sullivan in the 1968 *Star Trek* episode "Plato's Stepchildren."

Pre-Production:

Harry Harris returned to the series for his second directing assignment, following "The Keeper, Part II."

Liam Sullivan was forty-two when he played Nexus. His career spanned nearly 150 TV and film appearances. Sullivan took two trips into *The Twilight Zone*, including "The Silence," in which his talkative character accepts a bet that he can go a year without speaking; to ensure winning the bet, he has his vocal chords removed. Jonathan Harris played a part in that episode. Irwin Allen had previously cast Sullivan in an episode of *Voyage to the Bottom of the Sea*, "Leviathan." Sullivan's appearance there is noteworthy, among other reasons, because he played a giant in fright makeup and was placed into the Green Tank to wrestle with the Seaview miniature. Paul Zastupnevich revealed to interviewer Mike Clark that Sullivan performed the underwater stunt without a double. In order to do so, the crew had to weigh down his clothes so he wouldn't float upwards. They lowered the level of the tank water to just a few inches above Sullivan's head in case anything went wrong. How they got him air is unknown. Clark commented, "I've never heard of a more difficult guest role." (MC-AI15)

Above: Actor Kevin Hagen as he appeared at this time without all the makeup.
Below: Hagen on *Lost in Space*.

Two other memorable pop-culture TV appearances in Sullivan's immediate future: playing a Timothy Leary-type guru and LSD advocate in a 1968 episode of *Dragnet*, and portraying the leader of a band of sadistic Plato-worshipping aliens in "Plato's Stepchildren," a 1968 episode of *Star Trek*.

Kevin Hagen was thirty-six when he played the alien "Master." Prior to this, he had played John Coltor in thirty-one episodes of the 1958-59 western series *Yancy Derringer*. He took two journeys into *The Twilight Zone*, including "Elegy," in which he was one of three astronauts who land on an Earth-like planet where they find a town of people who appear to be frozen in time. Irwin Allen liked Hagen and cast him in four episodes of *The Time Tunnel*, two for *Voyage to the Bottom of the Sea*, and nine for *Land of the Giants*, where he played the recurring role of Inspector Dobbs Kobick.

An effort was made to obtain permission to use the song "Heigh-Ho" from Walt Disney Productions' 1937 animated film *Snow White and the Seven Dwarfs*, so that Daddy Zach could sing it whenever marching off to work. To save money, however, Irwin Allen settled for a public-domain folk song from an unknown writer dating back to the nineteenth century – "I've Been Working on the Railroad."

Above, On Day 1, filming the Teaser on Stage 6. Middle image: From Production Day 3, split-screen effect of the real Dr. Smith and his double, Daddy Zach. Bottom image: Production Day 4, with the "Int. Alien Laboratory" set.

Production Diary:

Filmed February 18 through March 2, 1966 (8 days, spanning 9).

Production began on Friday, February 18, 1966. Harry Harris filmed from 8 a.m. to 12:15 p.m. on Stage 6, covering the three and three-eighths pages that made up the cliffhanger for "The Space Trader" and the Teaser for "His Majesty Smith." Once this scene was in the can, filming of "His Majesty Smith" was suspended so that the company could move to Stage 11 to get pickup shots for "The Space Trader." All the footage shot on this day was urgently needed so that "Trader" could be rushed through editing and delivered to CBS for broadcast.

Day 2: Monday, February 21st. Director Harris shot from 8 a.m. to 6:10 p.m., covering seven and six-eighths pages from the script on Stage 11. Among scenes shot at the Ext. Jupiter 2 campsite: Smith working and singing; the Second Smith and Will returning to the ship, singing; and Daddy Zach serving breakfast to the family.

Harry Harris, as with all the directors, was charged by the antics of Jonathan Harris, and the chemistry between him and Billy Mumy, and even between Smith and the Robot. He said, "Billy and the Robot and Jonathan were – let's face it – they were outstanding." (HH-A&EB02)

Day 3: Tuesday, February 22nd. A long day of production – 8 a.m. to 7:18 p.m. on Stage 11. Seven and one-eighths pages of the script were filmed. It was difficult

Above: Filming on the "Int. Alien Laboratory" set during Production Day 3. Below: Onto the "Int. Alien Spacecraft" set for Days 4 and 5.

material to cover, requiring the camera to be tied down numerous times for split-screen and optical effects shots. Included were scenes on the upper deck of the Jupiter 2 and the campsite outside the Jupiter 2, where John converses with both Smiths, and Smith pleads with his own double to save him. Also filmed this day: the aliens attacking and one of the two Smiths (guess who?) giving himself up to save the others.

Day 4: Wednesday, February 23rd. They filmed from 8 a.m. to 7:50 p.m. on Stage 11, including the "Int. Alien Laboratory" and "Int. Alien Spacecraft."

Kevin Hagen said, "I had this great big wig on for that episode and they accidentally set this thing on fire during the scene. We were doing this shot and the wig actually caught on fire." (KH-LISF)

Harry Harris finished one-half of a day behind schedule.

Day 5: Thursday, February 24th. Harris filmed from 8 a.m. to 7 p.m. on Stage 6, covering another seven pages from the script. He fell to a full day behind schedule while filming scenes in the alien spacecraft, as well as "Ext. Clearing" where Smith meets Nexus and gives a report, while Will watches from cover.

Liam Sullivan told interviewer Flint Mitchell, "Everybody else knew who they were as characters, and had been playing the parts long enough. I mean, you didn't have to tell Jonathan Harris how to do anything… All Harry really had to do was tell them where to stand and when to come in. With us [guest players], he had a chance to spend more time to help us with mannerisms, with things that these bizarre people [would do] to give them some kind of thrust. And he was very good at that, and he was very helpful at that. He had a sense of style, and he had a sense of knowing what was too much and what was not enough. He would give us a chance to try something, and if it worked, he'd use it, and if it wasn't, he'd say, 'Can we heighten that a little, or square that off a little,' something like that…. I'd never played the role of a non-human before. Nexus was an android; a sort of manufactured person. I was intrigued with a way to play a character that seemed to be human enough that he fooled Dr. Smith and the other people on the show, but that it came out later that he was an android and he was a made-up kind of character. [The challenge was] to find ways either vocally or in physical movements to indicate that he was not quite a mechanical man, but the audience would not be taken aback to discover later on that he was not a real, living human being. Harry Harris and I tried several things with the voice to try to give it a sort of a flat tone. Nexus' reactions were never normal highs and lows and surprise or anger, or whatever. Everything was pretty much flattened out as though he was computing what to do next, and so on. And the arm movements were kind of mechanical…. and that turned out to be fun to do. But it was a whole new set of circumstances in acting, mannerisms and things that I hadn't had a chance to try before." (LS-LISF8)

By the time the set was wrapped and the cast had changed out of their wardrobe and had their makeup removed, it was well past 8 p.m. on Wednesday. No one minded too badly – *Lost in Space* was preempted on this night by a TV musical version of "Cinderella." One reason for all the preemptions: *Lost in Space* was late in its episode deliveries.

Day 6: Friday, February 25th. Pickup shots were needed on Stage 11, then back to Stage 6 where the company would remain through the end of the production. Covered on this day: the scene where Nexus offers the crown to Will, and he refuses. Director Harris covered only six pages, with the lost time involved in the move from one stage to another. He finished one-and-a-quarter days behind. "The Space Croppers" was supposed to start production on Monday. Director Sobey Martin was told to stand down until Tuesday morning.

Harry Harris said, "They didn't build too many new sets, but they had the space ship and all that other stuff and, the sets were big and it took a long time to light them. Irwin would take up the whole stage with all this stuff. And you'd get up on cranes and he'd get up on cranes – those big titan cranes – and shoot the whole thing. This is what he wanted – he wanted big, big, big scope. And it takes a long time to light. And some of the cameramen he had were very slow. And then he had to find guys that could light it up a lot faster, because some guys took forever, and you'd sit there. Then he'd come down. You know, they'd say, 'Eight pages a day keeps Irwin away.' But, you couldn't get eight pages a day because it took too long to light and you couldn't say, 'Hey, this guy's killing me.' Well, what can I tell you? But he always came to the director and beat the hell out of him. He didn't want to hear about actor problems, or anything else. It was always the director. And he always came down with an entourage. He had about six guys with him, and he would pin you in the corner and say, 'Do you know what time it is? Do you know how many pages you've got?'"

Harris added, "But the studio was pressuring him, because his shows cost a lot of money. He had a lot of production going; he was keeping that whole studio going over there, and if it wasn't for him, that place would have closed down at one time. But his things cost money." (HH-KB95)

Day 7: Monday, February 28th. Harry Harris was being pushed to finish. He worked late in hopes of doing so, filming from 8 a.m. to 8:25 p.m. Add to that an hour of makeup in the morning, and another 30 minutes at the end of the day for dressing down

Scenes filmed on Production Days 7 and 8.

of cast and wrapping of the set, and this was more than a fourteen-hour day for most in the company. Despite this, Harris fell further behind, now by one-and-a-half days. Sobey Martin was told his start date was being pushed back again, now likely to be Wednesday.

Day 8: Tuesday, March 1st. It was another long day, with filming lasting from 8 a.m. to 7:10 p.m. Harris was one-and-three-quarters days behind at wrap time. Sobey Martin and his guest cast would be standing by patiently in the wings in the morning, waiting for Harris to finish.

Day 9: Wednesday, March 2. A final day on Stage 6. Harris filmed from 8 to 11 a.m. with scenes on the Jupiter 2's lower deck. Martin took over after that and finally broke ground on "The Space Croppers."

When it finally ended, Liam Sullivan said, "[M]y recollection was that it was a very warm and tight family of actors on that show. They all seemed to get along well, they liked each other, June Lockhart and Guy Williams and so on. It was a joy to do, because Jonathan was funny and we knew each other [from *The Twilight Zone* episode, "The Silence"], and the whole thing was a very pleasant memory for me. And I had worked for Irwin Allen before … on *Voyage to the Bottom of the Sea*." (LS-LISF8)

Jonathan Harris said, "Another one of my favorites was probably 'His Majesty Smith.' It was great fun. I did have *carte blanche* to sort of play games and I always did things within the framework of what was good for the show. And was it good for the show? Yes, it was." (JH-IASB2)

William Self had approved $144,952 for the production. The final cost came to $172,787.

Release / Reaction:

(CBS premiere broadcast: Wednesday, March 23, 1966).
(Network repeat airing: Wednesday, July 13, 1966).

"His Majesty Smith" was supposed to air on March 16, but was preempted by a news special. Only hours into its flight orbiting the Earth, Gemini 8 had lost 30% of its fuel reserve and had to make an emergency re-entry into the Earth's atmosphere. At this point, it went into an uncontrolled and violent spin, reaching one revolution per second. Aboard the space capsule were astronauts Neil Armstrong and David R. Scott. The crisis would later be called "The Vomit-Inducing Gemini 8 Mission." Armstrong and Scott made it back to Earth and splashed down in the ocean very near to their designated landing spot. And TV covered it to the best of its ability in 1966.

Two days later, the Madison *Wisconsin State Journal* ran the headline "*Lost in Space* Tops Reality for Some." The article said:

> Channel 3 reported numerous calls of complaint Wednesday night because *Lost in Space* had been preempted by a telecast of the Gemini 8 space flight. "But this is the real thing!" one distraught father protested in answer to the loud wails of protest from his young. However, reality was a pale substitute for their favorite program. "Why can't they just run the real thing in little writing along the bottom?" the astute 10-year-old demanded. "*Lost in Space* is a lot more interesting."

The complaints weren't only coming from Madison, Wisconsin. *TV Guide*, for its March 26th issue, reported:

> When Gemini 8 ran into trouble, the men in charge of the networks were faced with a dilemma. The first word on the spaceship's problems came just a few minutes before the normal Wednesday schedule of entertainment programs was to begin. Should they go with their regular (and revenue-producing) shows or the space story? CBS decided first. At 7:22 (ET) Walter Cronkite broke into the evening-news program with a report on Gemini's woes, and CBS stayed with its space coverage all the way through to the small hours of the morning. NBC and ABC started their 7:30 programs, as usual, but NBC cut away from *The Virginian* at 7:41 and spent the next six hours covering Gemini 8. ABC tried dauntlessly to get all the way through *Batman* before tuning in permanently on the real world at 8, but it did interrupt *Batman* and the Catwoman often enough with news bulletins to keep viewers up-to-date – and make a hash of the plot. CBS reported that its stations had received hundreds of calls from viewers complaining that they had preempted *Lost in Space*, of all things.

As for the news coverage, a handful of letters in the April 2nd issue of *TV Guide* summed up what the network news divisions were capable of in 1965.

> Congratulations to all associated with TV coverage of the Gemini VIII recovery on March 16. The mass of drivel, repetitive information, verbal fumbling, and the efforts of news commentators to sound as though they possessed the highest degree of scientific technical knowledge was wonderful to behold. – Thomas E. Booth, Lawton, Oklahoma.

> … It seems the powers that be could have kept the people informed and still had the regular programs by running the tape across the bottom of the screen, or waiting until they had definite information. – Thomas Raphael, Saint Joseph, Montana.

> Concerning Gulf's not showing commercials during NBC's nighttime coverage of the Gemini splashdown, this was one of the few times that I would gladly have welcomed a commercial just to relieve the boredom. – Ronald Stinnett, Knoxville, Tennessee.

Taking the counterpoint, and clearly in the minority, one letter said:

> I was shocked, and I mean really shocked, to learn that people were more interested in *Batman* and other programs than they were in the fate of these brave men who are serving their country. – Ubaldo T. Dominguez, Niagara Falls, New York.

The CBS and 20th Century-Fox PR people were building the Robot up as a new top TV star.

"His Majesty Smith" was pushed back one week and aired on the night that *TV Guide* and many other television directories said "The Space Croppers" would be broadcast. David McCallum and Robert Vaughn of *The Man from U.N.C.L.E.* had the cover of *TV Guide*.

On the morning that "His Majesty Smith" did make it onto the air, the CBS promotion team was working feverishly to win more audience members back from *Batman*. The *Los Angeles Times* ran a picture article showing the *Lost in Space* Robot being made up for his close-up. Other photos depicted Billy Mumy playing guitar while Marta Kristen and the Robot danced; and the Robot playing tick-tac-toe with Angela Cartwright.

The PR men told us:

> The younger generation – below teens – can have Lassie and Flipper. The other kids – the college set – have a new hero. It's the robot on CBS' *Lost in Space*. Psychologists might analyze this as the trend toward progressive thinking, or the herd complex with futuristic leanings. Whatever the reasoning, this 7-foot bucket of bolts has become the campus idol. At UCLA's Westwood campus there's a fan club with an enrollment of 4,500 students. The robot is not only their official mascot, but it is also their cheerleader, credited with helping the Bruins win the Rose Bowl game. Ah, this misguided generation. The one they really should be cheering for is the prop man inside working the crazy robot.

The A.C. Nielsen 30-City Ratings survey for March 23, 1966 reported:

Network / Program:	Rating	Share:
7:30 – 8 p.m.:		
ABC: *Batman*	**26.9**	**42.6%**
CBS: *Lost in Space*	15.3	24.2%
NBC: *The Virginian*	16.2	25.6%
8 – 8:30 p.m.:		
ABC: *The Patty Duke Show*	17.5	27.3%
CBS: *Lost in Space*	**22.4**	**35.0%**
NBC: *The Virginian*	16.6	25.9%

From the Mailbag:

From the week following the first broadcast of "His Majesty Smith," received by "TV Answer Man," a syndicated letters column carried by, among other newspapers, the *Dover Daily Reporter*, from Dover, Ohio:

> Will *Lost in Space* be back again next year? I understand it took a ratings beating from *Batman* and won't be back. – D.S., Tacoma, Washington.

The Answer Man said:

> The *Lost in Space* show is penciled in for the same time and day next season.

36

Episode 25: "The Space Croppers"

Written by Peter Packer
(with script polishing by Anthony Wilson)
Directed by Sobey Martin
Produced by Irwin Allen; with Jerry Briskin

From the *Lost in Space* show files (Irwin Allen Papers Collection):

> Smith and the children, trying to track down a werewolf, find a strange family consisting of a mother and son and daughter, all dressed in rags with a dilapidated spaceship resembling a hillbilly shack. They are planting crops and as soon as their harvest is in, they say they will be moving to another planet. Smith, who sees a chance to get back to Earth with them, begins courting the mother. Meanwhile, the plants, nurtured by strange rites and incantations, grow rapidly, and produce exotic fruits and shining silks. On Smith's next visit he finds the family all elegantly dressed and ready to depart. All set and ready to leave with them, Smith refuses to listen to Will who has discovered that the son is the werewolf they saw and that the plants, after producing all that the alien family needs, will be left to take over and devour everything that remains alive on the planet.

From the Script:

(Revised Shooting Final. March 9, 1966 draft)

– *Smith (beaming):* "What strength of purpose you have, Madam! There's nothing I admire more in a woman than rugged individualism and determination!" *Sybilla (eyeing him up and down):* "I can't return the compliment – if that's what it's supposed to be. I can't see one thing about you worth admiring." *Smith:* "Ah – Madam – if you knew me better…" *Sybilla:* "I'd rather not."

– *Smith:* "It's you who are in my heart, Sybilla. The other night when I first set eyes on you, I said to myself – there's a woman for a man to cherish and be proud of. A woman alone – close to the soil – providing for her loved ones by the labor of her own dear hands – happy, uncomplaining, radiant with the joy of watching little green things grow." *Sybilla (chuckling):* "I like that – watching little green things grow." *Smith:* "Yes – I've thought about you a lot, Sybilla – of the burden of responsibility which you carry alone." *Sybilla:* "I'm not complaining." *Smith:* "But what an added joy it would be if you had companionship – someone to stand beside you as you traveled Earthward … *(hastily)* … or anywhere else in the galaxy – someone to share your labor in the fields – be a father to your children … *(as he says this, Sybilla yawns loudly)* … Perhaps I spoke too soon." *Sybilla (yawning again):* "Not too soon, Zachary – too long!"

– *Effra (re: makeup):* "What you foolin' with that stuff for, Maw? You purty enough the way you are." *Sybilla:* "There's always a little room for improvement. *(smiles)* He said I looked radiant with the joy of watching little green things grow." *Effra (giggling):* "You gonna tell him the truth about them little green things if he comes again?" *Sybilla:* "What he doesn't know won't hurt him." *Effra:* "That sweet-talk of his'n been doing things to you, Maw." *Sybilla:* "Rubbish! *(softening)* Although I must say – it's been too long since I've been flattered so much. If our little green growing things would settle for six delicacies instead of seven, I might take him along. A woman needs a little sweet-talk once in a while."

– *Smith:* "Did your parents tell you that Sybilla and I are betrothed?" *Will (unhappily):* "I can see that for myself. But I still don't think much of it." *Sybilla:* "No one's asking for your opinion – sonny. *(he stares at her)* Don't you know it's rude to stare?" *Will:* "I'm just trying to figure out what you want with <u>him</u>." *Sybilla:* "You're very precocious for an Earthling child. I can dispose of you very quickly, you know. *(to Smith)* You're the master of this house now, Zachary. Send the child packing!" *Smith:* "Yes, Will – be a good little boy and go back home." *Will:* "Gosh, Dr. Smith – I don't think you realize what you're doing!" *Smith (angrily):* "I'm afraid I can't discuss that with a child." *Will:* "But you don't belong with her – or with <u>them</u>. You belong with us! You don't know what terrible things might happen to you if you go with her … and you'll be too far away for us to help you!" *Sybilla:* "I could swat him very easily from here – squash him flat."

Assessment:

"The Space Croppers" is an atypical episode of *Lost in Space*, particularly for the First Season. This one is almost all comedy and aimed more toward the mature audience members instead of the core audience of small fry. For an adult, there is much to appreciate, including a delightfully sardonic performance from Mercedes McCambridge; the sparkling chemistry between her and Jonathan Harris; the light-hearted sexual tension between Sherry Jackson and Mark Goddard; and a fairly good job at making those "little green things" actually come to life (after a test run with the same type of effect in "Welcome Stranger" and "Attack of the Monster Plants").

Regardless, this episode was certainly a strange concoction which attempted to serve up something for everybody, even if the various elements mixed as well as oil and water.

- Two of CBS's biggest hits, which directly followed *Lost in Space* on Wednesday night, were *The Beverly Hillbillies* and *Green Acres*. So, "The Space Croppers" gave us hillbilly space travelers.
- Werewolf movies had always been popular, so we got that, too. And two full moons!
- *Bewitched* was ABC's top show, so we got witches.
- "Attack of the Monster Plants" had been one of *Lost in Space*'s highest-rated episodes, so we had a return of killer plants.
- Sherry Jackson was sure to please the males in the audience who were over the age of eleven, so they were given a generous dose of her.
- Dr. Smith was catching on, so this story leaned heavy on Jonathan Harris – although, as with most First Season entries, it still utilized the entire recurring cast.
- And Mercedes McCambridge was a heralded star of film and stage whom the adult viewers might appreciate, so she was added to give the show a little class amidst the madness.

It was a strange witch's brew, but was off-kilter enough, witty enough, charming enough, and even sexy enough to actually work. After all, who couldn't love an episode in which Mercedes McCambridge (later the voice of the demon in *The Exorcist*) tells her werewolf son (who has returned home from a night of howling at the moons and who knows what else), "And don't forget to brush your teeth!"

Script:

Story Assignment 8474 (Production #8525)

Peter Packer's treatment, and 1st and 2nd draft teleplays: Late January through late February 1966.

Mimeo Department reformatted Shooting Final teleplay: Late February 1966.

Tony Wilson's script polish, Revised Shooting Final (blue pages): February 28, 1966.

Page revisions by Wilson (pink page inserts): March 1.

Additional page revisions by Wilson (green page inserts): March 2.

Further revisions by Wilson (yellow page inserts): March 3.

Further revisions by Wilson (gold page inserts): March 4.
Further revisions by Wilson (beige page inserts): March 7.
Further revisions by Wilson (pink page inserts): March 8.
Further revisions by Wilson (green page inserts): March 9.

"The Space Croppers" was Peter Packer's ninth *Lost in Space* writing assignment, following a script he had just completed – "Blast Off into Space" – which would be held until the Second Season as the kickoff (or blastoff) episode, when the Jupiter 2 finally lifts off from the planet where it had been wrecked for a year.

Peter Packer's original story for "The Space Croppers" was very different than the final product. From February 1966, Packer wrote:

> As the Robinsons soon learn, to their dismay, the space folk who arrive in a rattle-trap vehicle which barely manages to touch down without falling apart, are a shaggy, shiftless, backwoods lot from way down south in the galaxy, who'd rather loaf than labor. Yet all four of them – LOD, the father; EFFIE, the ma; KEEL, the son; and LUTI, the young daughter, are as likable and friendly as could be.
>
> They are share-croppers, nesters who've been everywhere. They plant a planet, harvest a crop, then wander on, always looking for a nice piece of land that allows for a little less work. And this planet looks like it might be it. For Lod, it's got everything he desires – God's little acre, the rich lode of Tobacco Road, the climate and the quiet – although being an alien these are hardly the phrases he uses to describe this land. As for the Robinsons, they're right nice neighbors to have – like having calabash and kissing cousins in his own back yard!
>
> Yet, as the days go by, and Lod and his brood continue to accept the hospitality of the Robinsons, including borrowing figurative cups of sugar and flour as well as small pieces of equipment (ostensibly for repairs, but really for Lod to make himself a jug or two of space brew), this endearing alien family does absolutely nothing in the way of cultivating anything but Maureen's pantry and some useful gadgetry on the control deck of the Jupiter. They even "borrow" the Robot, but can do nothing with him since he doesn't seem to dig their philosophy of life.
>
> Keel, the son, a tall, handsome if grimy hunk of a man in his early twenties, spends most of his time making music on an odd-looking guitar, while his mangy hound whines an accompaniment and Keel himself sings in a lyrical and poetic way of wanderin' and searchin' amid the stars. His music fascinates Judy, who pays him much more attention than Don cares for – and this leads to a couple of heated arguments and almost to a fight, except that Keel don't cotton to fighting – it's too tiring. He backs off rather than fight …

Miracle though it is to the Robinsons that this alien family's vehicle ever got anywhere, to Smith it is an opportunity to depart … if only he can instill some discipline into these drifters in return for a mortgage on their rickety spaceship. Smith provides them with some seeds he found that the Robot guaranteed as quick-growing although potentially dangerous. Smith's discipline program starts the shiftless family off with early rising… followed by plowing and planting … but somehow Lod and his family manage to see to it that Smith does most of the hard work – including the planting. Smith also encourages them to do as much "borrowing" as they can from the Jupiter – of spare parts which will give their craft enough git-up-and-go to get him to Earth. But without him knowing it, the spare parts go into making toys for Luti, who has been making [away] with Penny's and Will's toys, and wrecking them when she got bored.

For a few brief hours, when things begin to sprout from the seeds which Smith has planted, Lod becomes an enthusiastic dirt-farmer – hoeing and weeding and watering. And to Smith's disgust, he says he never wants to leave. Smith tries to poison and kill the new crop but to no apparent effect. Lod is determined to stay for good with the growing crops that will keep his family fed and himself contented.

Smith can do nothing to persuade him otherwise, but Keel, who has developed a real thing for Judy, asks Smith to act as Cupid, in return for which he'll fix up his pa's spaceship good enough for Smith to take off. Determinedly, Smith sets out on his match-making activities, and Keel does what he can to fix up the ship when he isn't busy romancing Judy.

But Lod's energy and enthusiasm don't last very long and much as he sings the praises of growing things, it is Luti, helped by Will and Penny, who goes to work cultivating the crop.

The children work with a will, especially Will who likes the idea of being calabash cousin to Luti … unaware of the fact that very soon, the seeds which Smith has sown and then tried to poison will mutate into a crop of huge, plant monsters.

After reading Packer's story, an underwhelmed Tony Wilson wrote to Irwin Allen:

Irwin: Take the men with Will and the Robot out – leaving Smith and the woman – then make the share-croppers all male with one son for Penny and one for Judy and the father for Maureen and you might have half a twist.

Numerous story conferences between Allen, Wilson and Packer brought forth the story that was eventually filmed. Wilson instructed Packer to drop Lod, the father; drop the idea of Judy being smitten with Keel; have Luti smitten with Don instead … except

Luti would be older than Packer had originally indicated, and her name would become Effra. Meanwhile, the mother would get a name change to Sybilla – and a romance between her and Smith would bloom … along with all those people-eating plants. The idea of Smith doing any work was dropped, and Keel was no longer depicted as lazy, but a hardworking plow-boy … and werewolf.

At least the title remained unchanged … and Packer – the Englander with a fascination for American western and backwoods culture – got to write a story about hillbillies in space.

Packer had fun describing the hillbilly aliens. Regarding Keel, Packer wrote: "By Earth standards he's probably in his early twenties – and his blank, impassive features are about as animated as a cold potato."

Effra was described as seeming "to be about seventeen, clad in space rags, but *very attractive ones*, and her eyes as sharp and glittering as onyx buttons which look as though they could cast a spell with a single, flashing glance."

Packer described Sybilla as "a dynamic, handsome woman of about forty – dressed in tattered-but-regal robes – an overpowering and commanding presence as she moves up to them and cocks her gun."

As for the spaceship, Packer wrote: "On a bare patch of land sits an alien spaceship like no spaceship they ever saw. It looks more like a space version of a hillbilly shack – complete with what could be a chimney (if we didn't know it was the exhaust stack for its drive unit). Out front there's a kind of porch – unpainted – dilapidated – scarred with the markings of a thousand flights through meteor dust and space debris."

Upon first seeing the strange craft, Will exclaims, "Golly! What is it?" Effra answers, "It's a spaceship. Don't you know nothin'?" A bewildered Will observes, ""But it's all open." Effra explains, "We got ways of closing it up. We just like to keep it sociable."

All but one of the scripts written up to this point included an explanation as to how the aliens spoke English. This one does, too. Smith scolds, "My dear young lady, I don't know where you've come from or what you're doing here, or how you happen to speak our language – but…" Effra cuts in, "Speak all kinds of language, we do. Got to, when you're on the go as much as we are." Effra tells Smith she and her family had visited Earth once, then adds, "Didn't like it, though – too many people like you – too many laws – too much fightin' and feudin'."

Tony Wilson probably had a ball reworking Packer's script.

Appreciative of Wilson's surreal take on life, Marta Kristen fondly recalled, "I had lunch with Tony at least a couple times a week. And it would become a three martini lunch. Honestly. Not for me, because I didn't drink, but Tony did. And he would smoke these little black cigars. And he was just so funny, and so smart, and he had this attitude where he would joke about things, but not care, really. Life was something that he would view with a great sense of humor. And he was very cynical in some ways. And he, of course, was responsible for all the writing, and he knew that making the show lighter would work. Remember, we had *Batman* opposite us, and so that changed the nature of a lot of television. It became, "Wham" and "Pow," comic-book style. Every show took on that look. So Tony, I think, really enjoyed making this really crazy, silly show, as far out as he could possibly make it. He was just having the time of his life. And, frankly, it was easier for him to do it that way. It wasn't as much work for him to write about things that weren't overly serious, and to let Jonathan take the lead and write his own material. And, after the three martini lunches, logic would just go out the window." (MK-AI15)

Amongst all the silliness, there are some nice moments of series continuity. Items added into the time capsule by Penny, Will and Smith include the "portable thruster – employed in rocket belt flight by Dr. John Robinson, circa 1997," Maureen Robinson's "space gauntlets," which Penny tells us were worn when the Jupiter 2 left Earth; and a manuscript for a book which Dr. Smith dictated onto a spool of recording tape, called "Meditations of a Galactic Castaway: An Account of the Courage, Fortitude and Personal Sacrifice of Dr. Zachary Smith" – no doubt a continuation of the book he was recording in "The Oasis."

On March 2, 1966, regarding Tony Wilson's script polish of Packer's teleplay, Sam Taylor, Jr. of CBS wrote:

> Page 5: In this sequence WILL, DR. SMITH and the ROBOT are menaced by the wolf, please exercise your customary care so younger members of your audience will not be terrified.
>
> Pages 52 & 53: Please do not show WILL as terror-stricken as he is enveloped by the plants and menaced by the wolf.

Billy Mumy did his best to not act too "terror-stricken" while being menaced and cornered by a werewolf, and then tumbling into a people-eating plant.

Pre-Production:

Sobey Martin returned for his seventh directing assignment on *Lost in Space*.

Broderick Crawford and Mercedes McCambridge with director Robert Rossen, all Oscar winners for 1949's *All the King's Men*.

Mercedes McCambridge (Sybilla) had taken over the lead in the Broadway production of *Who's Afraid of Virginia Woolf!* in 1964, which won her rave notices. Before that, McCambridge gained the respect of film critics and an Academy Award in 1950 as Best Supporting Actress, for *All the King's Men*. In the same category, she was nominated for a second Oscar in 1957, for *Giant*. McCambridge was 49 at the time of her trip into *Space*.

Interviewed just prior to her beginning work on "The Space Croppers," McCambridge admitted to *Los Angeles Times* entertainment correspondent Hal Humphrey that *Lost in Space* was not likely to add anything of merit to her professional resume. For a short article with the heading of "Mercedes Lost a Little in Space," Humphrey wrote:

> After winning an Oscar in movies and critical praise on Broadway, what does an actress do on the day her agent calls to say he can get her a one-shot guest role on CBS-TV's *Lost in Space* as a hillbilly? "Well," says actress Mercedes McCambridge, "first I cry a little bit. Then I begin thinking what I can do with the $2,500 – doctor bills, clothes and so on – but by the time the money gets to me it will be only 60% of $2,500. So now the ham in me takes over, and I say to myself, 'By golly, this will be the damnedest hillbilly anybody's ever seen on TV or anywhere else,' and I tell my agent to go ahead."

Six months after filming "The Space Croppers," Sherry Jackson, as an android, would have a fling with Captain Kirk in the 1966 *Star Trek* episode "What Are Little Girls Made Of?"

Sherry Jackson had just turned twenty-four when she played the flirtatious Effra, and proved just how good a girl could look in rags. Jackson began working in front of the camera at age six. By the time she hit the ripe old age of seven, she had a recurring role as little Suzie Kettle in the popular *Ma and Pa Kettle* film series. Three years later, at age ten, Jackson began a half-decade stint on *The Danny Thomas Show* as daughter Terry. Angela Cartwright appeared with Jackson in the series.

Guest spots on TV shows followed, such as *77 Sunset Strip* and *The Twilight Zone*, and Jackson played a sexy android in the 1966 *Star Trek* episode "What Are Little Girls Made Of?" By the mid-1960s, she had blossomed and steamier roles were coming her way.

Casting Director Joe D'Agosta was the one who recommended Jackson for both her *Lost in Space* and *Star Trek* episodes. He had met her while casting an episode of producer Gene Roddenberry's first series, *The Lieutenant*. With Jackson's memorable 36-22-35 measurements, D'Agosta felt Jackson was perfect for the sexy females described in both the *Lost in Space* and *Star Trek* scripts. Others still thought of her as Danny Thomas's TV daughter, but not D'Agosta. He confessed, "I was madly in love with her. I never saw a figure like that in my life. And such a sweet face." (43-4)

Sherry Jackson said, "I was very shy and never picked up the signals. I just couldn't believe that there were so many people that had crushes on me that I didn't even know about. I didn't know anything about Joe D'Agosta having a crush on me. I never even picked up a cue. I just figured he was a happy man." (90-1)

Dawson Palmer played Keel, the son by day, werewolf by night. He was twenty-nine, and a former basketball player. A syndicated article on *Lost in Space* made the rounds in newspapers across America in May and June 1966, with the title "Dawson Palmer: Now You See Him, Now You Don't." Hollywood entertainment correspondent Erskine Johnson wrote:

> At 25 [sic] and with a Hollywood heritage (his grandmother was a movie executive and his father was C.B. DeMille's personal film projectionist), Dawson Palmer has been *Lost in Space* in more ways than one. You have been seeing young Dawson without seeing him on *Lost in Space* all this TV season. He's the man behind the horror masks on the show, now a 40-foot, one-eyed monster, now a two-headed bushman, now a frightening rubberoid creature. Dawson's height, 6 feet 7 ¾ inches, won him his first monster role on the show and eventually led him to a straight role in one episode as a dim-witted, hillbilly son of Mercedes McCambridge. The show, he admits, has done a great deal for his morale.
>
> "Everyone told me I was too tall to be an actor and I had a terrible complex about it," he explains. "I'm really not much taller than Jim Arness and Clint Walker, but until *Lost in Space* no one would hire me. It got to the point where I was bending over to appear shorter and pleading for a chance. But all the time I went on studying acting to be prepared when the break came.... I no longer have this complex; I'm not convinced now that my height is against me. I feel now that there are all kinds of roles I can play, on *Gunsmoke*, on *Gomer Pyle*, and on a lot of other shows. I'm even up for a continuing role in a new series. I've never stopped studying acting and when the big break comes I'll be ready."

As for the down side to playing all those monsters, Dawson said that there was only one: "They cover your face with so much makeup you can't see where you're going. It's like flying blind without instruments."

Dawson played at least sixteen roles (nearly always uncredited) on *Lost in Space*, one on *Voyage to the Bottom of the Sea* (as a monster) and *Land of the Giants* (as a scientist). Of his *LiS* roles, Dawson was able to show his face two more times, in "The Lost Civilization," as one of the soldiers, and in "Revolt of the Androids," as IDAK Omega 17, albeit covered in silver makeup. Also in the future, but again hidden under a monster suit or wearing heavy makeup that rendered him nearly unrecognizable, Dawson appeared in Season Two's "The Dream Monster" (as the android Raddion); "The Treasure of the Lost Planet" (as alien pirate Izralim); and "The Astral Traveler" (as Angus, the loch monster).

Production Diary:

Filmed March 2 – 11, 1966 (7 days, spanning 8).

Above: On Day 1 of the production, Dawson Palmer (both in and out of a monster suit for this episode) played a space werewolf. Below: Things heat up between Mark Goddard and Sherry Jackson during the third day of filming.

Day 1: Wednesday, March 2, 1966. Director Sobey Martin waited patiently as the production for "The Space Croppers" was delayed one day at a time, times three, while "His Majesty Smith" fell further and further behind. On the third day, Martin was finally able to begin at 11 a.m. on Stage 6, where the previous episode had finished filming. The Tag scene for "His Majesty Smith" (and Teaser for "The Space Croppers") was up first. For this scene, Smith, Will, Penny, and the Robot bury a time capsule. And then they see a werewolf. Next, Smith and Will go on safari, and follow the paw prints of a giant wolf, and then meet Keel.

Martin's production schedule had been modified to take into account a shortened first day of filming. When he finished at 6:45 p.m., having covered six pages from the script, the production was on schedule. Most members of the cast and crew were able to make it home in time for the start of "The Challenge" on CBS, airing at 7:30 p.m. in Los Angeles on KNXT-2.

Day 2: Thursday, March 3rd. Filming took place on Stage 11, lasting from 8 a.m. to 7 p.m., filming at the Ext. Jupiter 2 campsite, then on the upper deck of the ship. This included the scene where the men gas the rapidly growing plants. Martin remained on schedule.

Day 3: Friday, March 4th. They began on Stage 11 at 8 a.m., with more shooting around the Jupiter 2 campsite, including Effra and Keel's visit. Next, a move to Stage 6, for action on the trail through the boulder-strewn area that leads to the Space Croppers' ship, and then the ship itself, with "Smith speaking love to Sybilla," as the shooting schedule described it.

Jonathan Harris was stretching the character of Dr. Smith more with each new episode. Harris said, "He was an interesting man, Dr. Smith. He had all these facets to his nature, carefully thought up. These things are not random. You have to work. And I did. I worked very, very hard finding new things for him to do. Always within the framework of what he was. That, you must not violate. He would always have to be what he was. But he had other things that could be introduced. So I did that. And it was very, very satisfying to me." (JH-IASB2)

It was especially satisfying for Harris to see changes he requested for the script implemented by Tony Wilson. As "The Space Croppers" filmed, Wilson sent revised pages to CBS on March 2, 3, 4, 7, 8, and 9. Many of these were a result of suggestions made by Harris for both dialogue and action in scenes featuring Dr. Smith.

The camera stopped rolling at 6:50 p.m. on Stage 6. Martin covered ten and two-eighths pages, despite the company move. Even so, this was less than had been scheduled and he finished one-quarter of a day behind.

Day 4: Monday, March 7. Martin filmed on Stage 6 from 8 a.m., including the "Ext. Plowed Field" scene in which Will has to choose between facing carnivorous plants or a werewolf. They filmed until 6:55 p.m. Martin only managed to cover eight and five-eighths pages from the script, thereby finishing three-quarters of a day behind schedule.

Day 5: Tuesday, March 8. Another long day on Stage 6, filming from 8 in the morning

until 7 in the evening. Shooting out of sequence, the scenes covered on this day included Will and Smith first encountering the Space Croppers' ship and meeting Effra and Sybilla, then John, Don, and Smith entering the area where Effra and Sybilla are chanting. Martin held at three-quarters of a day behind.

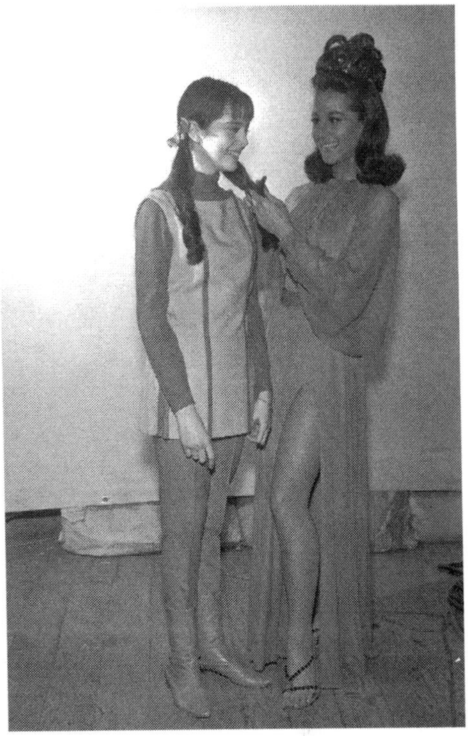

Day 6: The company filmed from 8 a.m. to 6:50 p.m. on Stage 6. More scenes at the "Ext. Plowing Field" (John, Don and Will spraying the plants), as well as "Ext. Open Trench" (Robot working in the trench) were filmed. Martin managed to shoot ten pages from the script.

Day 7: It was a final day on Stage 6, filming from 8 a.m. to 5:15 p.m., on the lower deck of the Jupiter 2, as well as in Smith's cabin.

Day 8: They began early in hopes of not delaying the next episode too much. The "Tag" scene for "The Space Croppers" was filmed on Stage 11, on the "Ext. Campsite" set, from 7:18 a.m. to 11:15 p.m., at which point Sobey Martin turned over the company to director Harry Harris so that he could begin filming "All That Glitters."

"The Space Croppers" was the last episode to be photographed by Director of Photography Gene Polito, who had served as camera operator on the pilot film, and cinematographer on twenty-four of the first twenty-five episodes. The series had fallen behind, resulting in the one episode Polito did not film ("Magic Mirror") having to be shot by a Second Unit crew while Polito filmed "War of the Robots." Then the series fell further behind, risking missing network airdates and then incurring large penalties from CBS. Polito missed the next episode due to illness, and then found himself permanently replaced (see Pre-Production of "All That Glitters").

Marta Kristen said, "Gene Polito was good. He did really good work. But I think he took too long. Irwin never should have let Gene go. Gene was an artist. He was just wonderful. And when you're that creative, it's not just that you're a creative person, but you're creative all down the line. You recognize that each person has a place. And it's a team." (MK-AI15)

"The Space Croppers" had been budgeted by William Self at $136,543. The final cost was $148,456.

Post-Production:

Sam Taylor, Jr., of CBS Program Practices, viewed the rough edit of the episode on March 14, 1966 with Tony Wilson and film editor Roland Gross. The following day he wrote Irwin Allen:

As discussed with Mr. Wilson & Mr. Gross:

> We feel the conclusion of Act III, which depicts WILL falling into the carnivorous plants with the Wolfman apparently going into the plants after him, would prove unnecessarily alarming for younger members of your audience.
>
> We understand you will edit the film in such a manner as to conclude the Act immediately after the closeup of WILL which shows him looking back at the Wolfman. Thus, we will not see WILL fall back into the plants nor will we see any further movements by the Wolfman until after the commercial break.

The network, always loyal to their sponsors, did not want to risk having any young viewers run from the room *before* the commercial.

Release / Reaction:

(CBS premiere broadcast: Wednesday, March 30, 1966).
(Network repeat airdate: Wednesday, July 20, 1966).

"TV Scout," syndicated to numerous U.S. newspapers, including the *Southwest Times*, in Pulaski, Virginia, said:

> *Lost in Space* has one of its better episodes, featuring Mercedes McCambridge, as a "space cropper" – a frontier-type squatter who doesn't fancy the invasion of outsiders like the Robinsons. Only youngsters will take her rebuttals seriously, but adults may get a chuckle or two out of the Oscar winning actress' far-out role.

It was going to be extra difficult on this night. Adam West of *Batman* was giving the cover of *TV Guide* a "POW." And most everyone's favorite guest villain, the Riddler (played by Frank Gorshin), was going to go head-to-head with *Lost in Space*.

A.C. Nielsen 30-City Ratings survey for March 30, 1966, ranked the shows as follows:

Network / Program:	Rating	Share:
7:30 – 8 p.m.:		
ABC: *Batman*	**28.8**	**49.1%**
CBS: *Lost in Space*	12.6	21.5%
NBC: *The Virginian*	14.6	24.9%
8 – 8:30 p.m.:		
ABC: *The Patty Duke Show*	**31.7**	**45.2%**
CBS: *Lost in Space*	15.7	22.8%
NBC: *The Virginian*	17.9	26.0%

During the week following the airing of "The Space Croppers," "TV Key" syndicated an article to newspapers across America. Entertainment columnist Charles Witbeck wrote:

> While TV's winter wonder, *Batman*, clobbered its opposition – *Lost in Space*, *The Munsters*, *The Virginian*, and *Daniel Boone* – small whimpers from the wounded are heard in the enemy camp. Herman Munster sounds like a bleating sheep. Only *Lost in Space* people appear to have any confidence in outlasting the Cowled Crusader and Boy Wonder, for their spies optimistically report kiddies under 12 prefer the weird monsters and the Robinson family in outer space to the far-out absurdities on the comic book series.
>
> "We have no doubt about *Lost in Space* surviving against *Batman*," bravely asserts assistant producer Paul Zastupnevich, the man who designs and constructs the marvelous mutant monsters, plants and machines on the Wednesday night space show. Perhaps Paul is the pigeon, but somebody has to stand up and fight back, even if the rebuttal has a hollow sound.
>
> Taking a poll on the kids in his block, Paul says *Lost in Space* is regaining its hold on youngsters after *Batman*'s opening bombardment. The novelty is wearing off after the first two weeks. Perhaps this is wishful thinking. But Paul believes he has reason on his side.
>
> "Strange as it may seem, our space villains are quite realistic compared to these comic book characters," he explained. "We may be far-out, but we do relate to current space ideas."
>
> The Robot is a good example of fans' fascination with the series, Paul believes. "Children love that robot," he says. UCLA college students have gone so far as to adopt the metal marvel, and the show term, "does not compute," apparently is a favorite with high school and college students. While nobody is fascinated by the weekly wooden dialogue, it is an accepted basic ingredient.

In the April 3, 1966 "You Said It" letters column of the syndicate "TV Scout" newspaper supplement, the subject of *Lost in Space* versus *Batman* was debated.

> I am a boy of 10 years old. I think you should keep *Lost in Space* on because I like the show and lots of other people do too. Another thing, too: There are different programs on instead of *Lost in Space* to stay on, and give the boot to *Batman*. – Dirk Zimmerman, Altadena, California.

And:

> *Batman* is horrible! *Lost in Space* is the best program I have ever seen.... I am fighting for my rights. Really, I want *Lost in Space* to stay on for years to come. I think anybody that likes that rubbish [on *Batman*] is nuts in the head. They need a psychiatrist. Will *Lost in Space* stay on and *Batman* go off? – Dennis Maldonado, Whittier, California.

The editor responded:

> TV WEEK apparently caused near-panic among the youngsters a few weeks ago. We wrote that *Batman* was giving *Lost in Space* ratings troubles, but we didn't mean to suggest *Lost in Space* was going off. It isn't. *Lost in Space* will be back on CBS next season as far as anyone knows now. So relax, kids.

When CBS repeated "The Space Croppers" on July 20, 1966, A.C. Nielsen reported that it received a 33.2% audience share, making it the third highest rated episode during the summer repeat months (following "The Lost Civilization," with 34.4%, and "Follow the Leader," with 33.5%).

37

Episode 26: "All That Glitters"

Written by Barney Slater
(with script polishing by Anthony Wilson, uncredited)
Directed by Harry Harris
Produced by Irwin Allen; with Jerry Briskin

From the *Lost in Space* show files (Irwin Allen Papers Collection):

> Ohan, a galactic burglar, arrives, closely pursued by Officer Bolix of the Galaxy Law Enforcement Agency. Afraid of being caught with his loot, Ohan leaves a mysterious stolen object with Penny. Smith discovers its secret. It leads him to a hidden ring, just large enough to fit around his neck, which has the property of turning anything he touches into platinum. Smith betrays Ohan to Bolix in order to keep the ring. At first, he is enthralled by it, but when his food turns to metal before he can eat it and he finds he cannot take the ring off, he is terrified. Too dangerous to the family to be allowed to stay with them, he wanders into the forest to die. Penny, finding Smith in the forest, forgets the danger of coming too close and is also turned into platinum.

From the Script:

(Revised Shooting Final teleplay, March 15, 1966 draft)

– *Judy:* "What happened to the alien?" *Penny:* "Oh, I brought him back to the spaceship with me. *(off their stunned silence)* He's below deck … asleep in Dr. Smith's quarters. *(with compassion)* He just fell into the bed. The poor man was at the end of his strength." *Smith (sputtering):* "You … you placed him in my quarters … my bed?" *Penny:* "I couldn't very well let him go to sleep on the floor." *Smith (quite upset):* "Penny, how could you! He was absolutely filthy!" *Penny:* "Not any more he isn't. He took a shower. And I gave him some of your clothes. I hope you don't mind." *Smith (makes a hopeless gesture):* "Why not! Share my meager possessions with every hobo that wanders by. What do I care?! I have plenty of everything." *Penny:* "Ohan isn't a hobo. He's a fugitive from justice." *Smith (in disbelief):* "I must be hearing things. This can't be true. A criminal is sleeping in my bed … wearing my clothes!"

– *Smith (brokenly):* "Oh, Penny … forgive me for what I have done … forgive me. *(eyes brimming with tears, Smith kisses Penny tenderly on the cheek. … turns away … sinks to his knees)* Death … where are you!" *Voice:* "Foolish, foolish man. You had everything necessary for happiness. And you gave it all up for what – a cold, unfeeling metal?" *Smith (looking upward):* "I know … I deserve to be punished! *(raises his arms, pleading)* But Penny … the child is innocent … she shouldn't suffer because of my folly." *Voice:* "You should have thought of that earlier." *Smith:* "Yes … yes … and now it's too late. What a miserable wretch I am." *Voice:* "Perhaps you have learned a lesson, Dr. Smith." *Smith:* "Oh, I have … I have." *Voice:* "Then for once I will make an exception. I will spare you." *Smith:* "I don't care about myself. It's only Penny I want saved. *(there is no answer)* Where are you? Don't leave! You've got to make Penny normal again!"

Assessment:

"All That Glitters" stumbles, right out of the gate. An alien on the run – who looks, talks and behaves like a twentieth-century American – seeks asylum in the Jupiter 2 … just for the night, you see, until he's rested and then can retrieve the treasure he stashed away somewhere. Then we meet the law – in fact, an officer of the Galaxy Law Enforcement Agency, no less. He of course speaks English, too. And he's played by the actor who was also playing Colonel Klink on *Hogan's Heroes* at this time, who was brilliant there but sadly miscast here. This Enforcer use a couple of monsters as hired muscle – played by the hapless Dawson Palmer and Mike Donovan, in hairy "creature" costumes. They growl a lot. Meanwhile, Smith has picked up the scent of a hidden treasure.

So far, this sounds like a typically not-so-good episode from Season Two. It continues to underwhelm for the first half hour. Then things improve. For the last half, Barney Slater and Tony Wilson serve up a retelling of the old story about King Midas. As you may recall, Midas turned everything he touched to gold, including his daughter. Similarly, Dr. Smith turns everything he touches into platinum, including Penny.

The script for "All That Glitters" was unashamed thievery. But, in this case, the thievery ranks as inspired. The set decoration with platinum trees and bushes and rocks is a wonder to behold. And platinum Angela Cartwright certainly would have won the "Best Child Performer Standing Still Without Blinking" award, if there were such a thing. There should have been, for few could go that long without blinking. The best is saved for last – the final moments of this episode are remarkably touching. After Smith accidentally transforms Penny into platinum, he seems to experience true sorrow and regret. For once, a Smith scene is not played for laughs. He says that he wants to die, and we believe him. Jonathan Harris delivers a heartfelt performance. Smith begs for death to deliver its "sting" (a line Harris contributed). He cannot bear another moment of life. Then Penny's hand reaches out from off camera and touches his shoulder. You are completely justified in finding your emotions cresting … and perhaps letting a bit of moisture collect in your eyes. This may be Jonathan Harris's best moment on film. It is arguably Dr. Smith's.

Script:

Story Assignment 8468 (Production #8526)
Barney Slater's treatment, and 1st and 2nd draft teleplays: February 1966.
Mimeo Department reformatted Shooting Final teleplay: Late February 1966.
Tony Wilson's script polish, Revised Shooting Final (blue pages): March 2, 1966.
Page revisions by Wilson (pink insert pages): March 9.
Additional page revisions by Wilson (gold insert pages): March 10.
Further revisions by Wilson (green insert pages): March 10.
Further revisions by Wilson (yellow insert pages): March 15.

This was Barney Slater's eighth *Lost in Space* script assignment. He had spun an effectively magical allegory with his first – "Wish Upon a Star" – and does so again here during the second half of this story.

One thing that Irwin Allen did not care for was the original name of the fugitive from the law – "Wohan."

On March 1, 1966, Allen wrote to Tony Wilson:

> The name "Wohan" is not good – change it – sounds too much like "woman." …

Wilson wrote onto the first page of his final script polish: "NOTE: THE CHARACTER NAME WOHAN HAS BEEN CHANGED TO OHAN THROUGHOUT THE SCRIPT IN BUSINESS AND DIALOGUE. THIS IS IMPORTANT!"

Allen's notes to Wilson continued:

> P. 13, Sc. 25: Penny mentions the "Galaxy Law Enforcement Agency" – we have never heard of this before and it seems strange that no one shows any curiosity or surprise that such an organization exists (or is it supposed to be well known by space travelers from Earth?).

P. 16, Sc. 28: Smith's second speech -- he should continue the speech with "and consider that rather unusual occupation of this 'Wohan' fellow, I think it would be a good idea to check our possessions. We may have been robbed!" -- (This will eliminate the unfeminine attitude which Maureen's speech has when she questions him as to where he's going.) …

P. 27, Sc. 41: Maureen says it's good to know there is someone they can call on in case of trouble – yet she never asks Bolix anything about his organization:

a) Where is he from?
b) How does he know so much about Earth?
c) If he can help them get back to Earth or Alpha Centauri?
d) Where they really are, etc.

P. 36, Sc. 54: Smith's attitude toward Wohan staying around the Jupiter 2 has undergone a drastic change since P. 13, Sc. 25. He now suggests that Wohan be careful or he will be apprehended. Why is Smith now so concerned about Wohan's safety?

It is never established how Ohan talks like the American actor that Larry Ward was. However, per Irwin Allen, lip-service was given as to just how Galaxy Law Enforcement Officer Bolix speaks English. He explains: "I've had special training. We've been expecting travelers from Earth for a long time. But never mind that."

In nearly all the episodes to come, Tony Wilson would never mind about it, too, and just let the alien visitors speak colloquial Yankee English without question or explanation.

Warner Klemperer was in his first season of playing Colonel Klink on *Hogan's Heroes*, also for CBS-TV.

Pre-Production:

Harry Harris returned to direct his second of five episodes for *Lost in Space*. He said, "Irwin loved fantasy. He loved to frighten people with monsters and throw hooks into people for suspense. His thing was, in a way, science fiction. But, really, it was [science fiction] and it *wasn't*. It was fantasy." (HH-KB95)

Werner Klemperer was forty-five when he signed on for a trip into fantasy as Intergalactic Enforcer Bolix. Irwin Allen was fond of Klemperer, having hired him to stand in for Theodore Marcuse as Dr. Gamma in the *Voyage to the Bottom of the Sea* pilot film, then featuring him prominently as another villain in the series' first season, the

1964 episode "The Blizzard Makers." Klemperer often played bad guys. He had the look for it, and was cast as a Nazi on trial for war crimes in the 1961 film *Judgment at Nuremberg*. Then he broke out of the typecasting in the fall of 1965 on CBS, as bumbling Colonel Wilhelm Klink, commandant of German prisoner-of-war camp Stalag 13. CBS liked the idea of Klemperer guest-starring on another of its series, even if the role didn't seem an ideal match for him. As Colonel Klink, Klemperer would win two Emmy awards, plus three additional nominations. As Bolix, well, Klemperer took home a $2,500 paycheck.

Above: the cast of ABC-TV's *The Dakotas*: (L-R) Michael "Whisky" Greene, Jack Elam, Larry Ward, Chad Everett (Warner Bros., 1962). Below: tonight's monster.

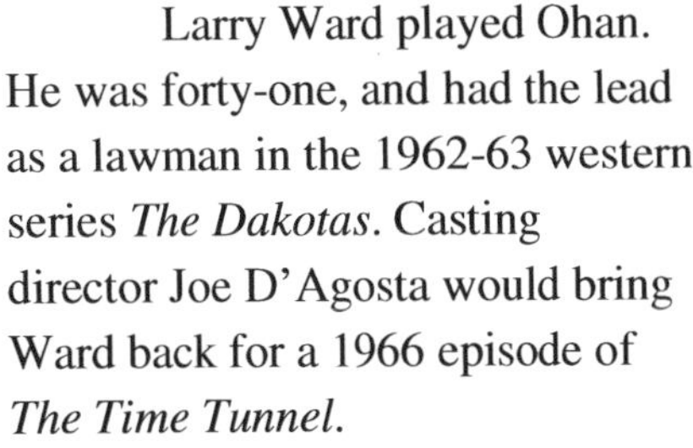

Larry Ward played Ohan. He was forty-one, and had the lead as a lawman in the 1962-63 western series *The Dakotas*. Casting director Joe D'Agosta would bring Ward back for a 1966 episode of *The Time Tunnel*.

Theodore Lehmann provided the voice of the glowing object that Smith uses to find the treasure. Lehmann had appeared on *Lost in Space* once before, as one of the aliens from "Invaders from the Fifth Dimension."

Lost in Space's resident director of photography, Gene Polito, missed out on all the fun. He said, "I had gotten very sick. I think I came down with the flu or something. So, while I was sick, they brought in another cameraman." (GP-LISF5)

The replacement was Winton Hoch, the director of photography on *Voyage to the Bottom of the Sea,* which had finished filming its second season. Hoch had also been the cinematographer on the *Lost in Space* pilot film, "No Place to Hide," for which Polito had served as camera operator.

Polito told writer Flint Mitchell, "I had lit this big set a certain way with arc lights – that was how I got my single source shadows all the time. And the other fellow [Hoch] elected to do it a different way, by not using those kinds of lamps, which in turn required a couple less electricians." (GP-LISF5)

It also saved time.

Polito continued, "So… I was without a

job because this other guy had proved to them that he could shoot it cheaper somehow; I don't know. But that's par for the course. So, I went on to do something else." (GP-LISF5)

The "something else" was a feature film western, called *Ride to Hangman's Tree*, starring Jack Lord. Immediately following that assignment, Polito served as director of photography on eight episodes of a new CBS series, *Mannix*. He then moved over to *It Takes a Thief*. More films followed, including the 1970 TV movie *My Sweet Charlie* – for which he was nominated for an Emmy award. Also for 1970, the sci-fi movie *Colossus: The Forbin Project*. After serving as director of photography on *The Bold Ones*, followed by *Alias Smith and Jones,* Polito left television for several years to film numerous hit movies, including the 1973 sci-fi classic *Westworld*, and its 1976 sequel, *Futureworld*.

Winton Hoch stayed on to finish *Lost in Space*'s First Season.

Production Dairy:

Filmed March 11 – 18, 1966 (6 days).

As with "War of the Robots" and "The Magic Mirror," which were shot simultaneously by two different crews, *Lost in Space* would again have to build a two-episode house of cards production schedule in order to catch up on its deliveries to CBS. "All That Glitters" would begin filming on the same day as the next episode on the production roster – "The Lost Civilization."

Irwin Allen and his staff had learned from the previous experience of filming "Robots" along with "Mirror" to be a bit less ambitious. First, there would be very little sharing of sets between the two productions. One unit would stay on *Lost in Space*'s home turf – Stages 6 and 11. This would be the crew normally assigned to the series. The other company, filming "The Lost Civilization," would be comprised of the production crew from *Voyage to the Bottom of the Sea*. They would have limited time on Stages 6 and 11 (only a partial day on each), with most of their production filmed on Stage 10 and Stage B (both usually assigned to *Voyage*), and Fox Stage 19. Second, there would be no sharing of cast members – other than for the cliffhanger for "The Space Croppers" (filmed as part of the Teaser for "All That Glitters"). The women, with Smith, would be featured in "All That Glitters," while the men (including the Robot) would carry "The Lost Civilization."

As stated earlier, a change took place on the production crew – cinematographer Gene Polito fell ill and had to be replaced with Winton Hoch, the director of photography for *Voyage to the Bottom of the Sea*. Hoch was intended to be in charge of his regular camera crew on "The Lost Civilization," but made the move since the *Lost in Space* producers felt "All That Glitters" was the better of the two episodes being filmed and warranted the cinematographer that Irwin Allen knew best and therefore trusted the most.

As a result, Charles Clarke, a D.P. from outside of the company, was hired on short notice to film "The Lost Civilization."

Day 1: Friday, March 11, 1966. Work began on "All That Glitters" on Stage 11. The company filmed the Ext. Jupiter 2 campsite, with the men leaving in the Chariot, thereby "leaving Smith in charge"; Penny bringing Ohan to meet the family; and Smith trying on the ring. Harry Harris filmed from 8 a.m. to 7:25 p.m., over an hour into union overtime pay, but otherwise on schedule.

Above: Production began on Stage 11, Friday, March 11, 1966.
Below: Cross-promotion – CBS 1966 style.

Day 2: Monday, March 14th. A second day on Stage 11, at the Hydroponic Garden, where Smith gets the disk to glow, hears a voice, and, after Penny joins him, searches for hidden treasure; as well as the first breakfast scene, when Bolix appears with his monsters, introducing himself, then searches the ship.

Interviewed for a syndicated newspaper article from April 1966, Werner Klemperer said he was delighted with the role of a galaxy enforcement officer. He told the reporter, "I'm appearing on *Lost in Space* for several reasons. It's a fairly straight part, and I needed a change of pace after a season of comedy. It's also a reunion with some old friends -- June Lockhart, Guy Williams, Jonathan Harris, and director Harry Harris. June was one of my victims when I played one of the heaviest of heavies on a *Studio One*. Guy and I share a strong interest in classical music, and I've known Jonathan for a long time. Harry Harris and I are in a director's study group together. And, frankly, the salary will help finance my trip to Europe in a few weeks. I'm going to visit my family in Zurich and see my father [orchestra conductor Otto Klemperer] conduct in Munich." (WK-BC66)

Director Harris filmed from 8 in the morning until 6:50 in the evening. He managed to cover twelve and two-eighths pages from the script. Again, he transgressed into "golden hour" pay, but stayed on schedule.

Day 3: Tuesday, March 15th. The company filmed from 8 a.m. to 6:58 p.m., still on Stage 11 and the upper deck of the Jupiter 2, as well as the campsite area. This work included the second breakfast scene, battle stations (turning on the force field and taking refuge in the ship), and the scene during which Bolix and his monsters capture Ohan.

Above: Jonathan Harris's discarded yellow tunic and lighter pants just fit Larry Ward. And Harris was right about that top – it didn't look good on Ward either. Below: the Midas touch.

Tony Wilson sent revised script pages to the stage on this day, some of which were no doubt prompted by suggestions from Jonathan Harris, designed to enlarge Harris's role and amplify the comedy elements. Director Harry Harris said of Jonathan Harris, "If he had played that straight, he would have had nothing. But he had the eyebrow go up, and they let him emote, and it worked." (HH-A&EB02)

Harry Harris covered eleven and seven-eighths pages. Again, he dipped into union overtime, but he otherwise stayed on schedule.

Day 4: Wednesday, March 16th. "His Majesty Smith" aired this night on CBS. The race was on to get everyone home in time to be able to see how their efforts had come together. Harry Harris filmed on Stages 6 and 11, from 8 a.m. to 6:30 p.m., covering eleven and four-eighths pages from the script. The scenes included those at the Ext. Campsite for the scene when Bolix arrests the women, then a despondent Smith returns and threatens to turn Bolix into platinum.

Day 5: Thursday, March 17th. It was a long day – filming from 8 a.m. to 7:10 p.m., on Stage 6, for the "Ext. Bushy Area" where Maureen pleads with Bolix; Ohan grabs Penny by the wrists; Penny searches for Smith, sees the platinum bushes and rocks; then back to Stage 11 for pickup shots. The director again covered eleven and four-eighths pages from the script. The production remained on schedule.

Day 6: Friday, March 18th. The longest day yet – filming on Stage 6 from 8 a.m. to 8:07 p.m., with the scenes in which Penny is turned to platinum.

Angela Cartwright said, "The part that sticks out in my mind on this episode was the silver makeup I had to wear [which photographed as "gold" in black and white]. It took hours for them to put it on, and it's lucky I didn't have an allergic reaction to the silver paint. It's not like makeup is nowadays – this makeup was horrible, thick and heavy. Thank goodness I only had to wear it one day." (LISM.com)

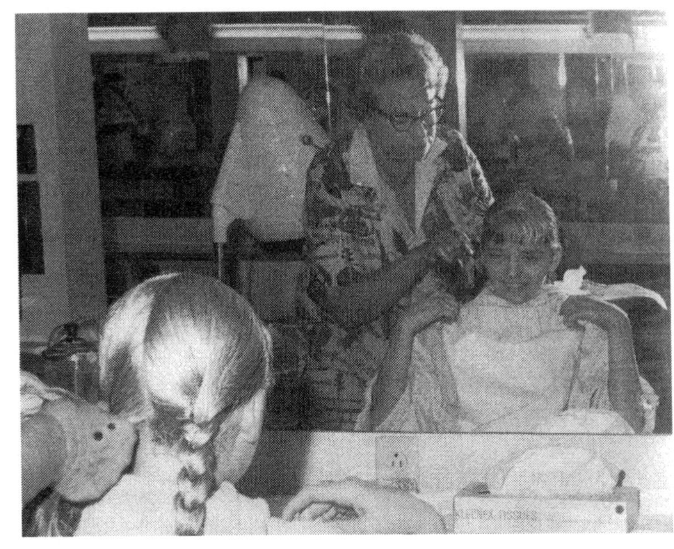

How to turn a thirteen-year-old girl platinum (above and left-hand photo by John V. Cartwright)

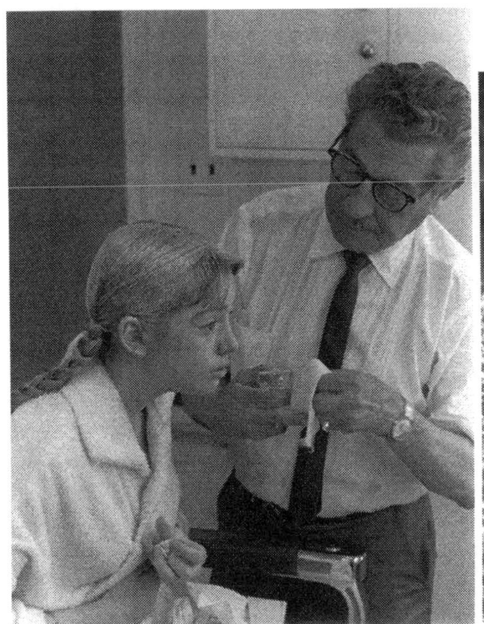

After makeup was removed, and the stage wrapped, it had been a fourteen-hour work day, but Harry Harris finished within the mandated six-day production schedule, albeit with a fair amount of "golden hour" pay going to the crew.

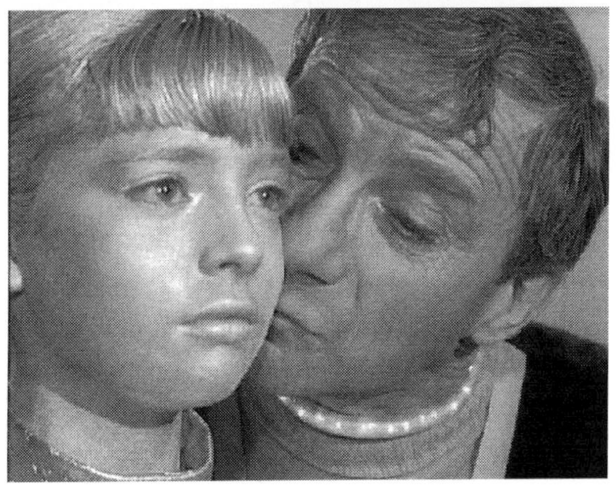

Above two images: Final day of production, with great patience from Angela Cartwright, and an Emmy-worthy performance from Jonathan Harris.

Release / Reaction:

(CBS premiere broadcast: Wednesday, April 6, 1966)

(Network repeat air date: Wednesday, July 27, 1966)

During the week that "All That Glitters" had its initial network broadcast, the Soviet Union's Luna 10 became the first spacecraft to orbit the moon. The top-grossing movie in America was *Frankie and Johnny*, starring Elvis Presley and leading lady Donna Douglas (Elly May from *The Beverly Hillbillies*). "The Ballad of the Green Berets" by Staff Sergeant Barry Sadler was still the song getting the most air play on Top 40 radio stations – now in its fifth week at the top. For over a month, the former Green Beret took turns keeping the Rolling Stones' "19th Nervous Breakdown," Herman's Hermits "Listen People," and the Beatles' "Nowhere Man" from reaching the summit. Sadler also had the top-selling record album in America for five weeks. The albums taking turns sitting underneath it were all former Number Ones – *Whipped Cream & Other Delights* and *Going Places*, both by Herb Alpert's Tijuana Brass; the soundtrack to *The Sound of Music*, which included the singing of Angela Cartwright; and Cartwright's favorite band at this time – the Beatles, with *Rubber Soul*. Dean Martin didn't have an album in the top of the music charts, but he did have a hit TV show, and the cover of *TV Guide*.

Promotional picture to capitalize on the pairing of two CBS stars.

On the day "All That Glitters" first aired, the editor of the *Daily Review*, in Hayward, California, wrote:

> This science fiction series has sent chills up and down the spines of millions of children. It is well produced, is played by an accomplished cast, and contains the only honest-to-goodness scenery-chewing villain left in television. Jonathan Harris, who portrays the villainous Dr. Zachary Smith, is cowardly, completely selfish, and doesn't hesitate to leave a couple of kids to strange fates every few episodes. Tonight, Werner Klemperer, on leave as the funny Nazi prison camp officer of *Hogan's Heroes*, portrays a Galaxy Enforcement Officer who pursues an interplanetary crook to the Robinson camp, where the crook's booty gets Dr. Smith into trouble, as usual.

That same day, entertainment correspondent Bob Hull wrote in his "TV Talk" column, featured in the *Los Angeles Herald-Examiner*:

> Werner Klemperer and Jonathan Harris have played some of the nastiest characters on stage and screen, yet today they're famous as a pair of TV villains idolized by the youngsters. Harris is the wicked Dr. Smith of the *Lost in Space* series, a pseudo-comedy of

> a science-fiction nature in which all manner of weird creatures wander around as background to his hateful efforts to thwart a modern Swiss Family Robinson trying to get back to Earth. Klemperer, son of the famed symphony conductor, currently draws the hisses and boos of the audience watching the *Hogan's Heroes* comedy series. He plays the monocle-sporting Col. Klink, commander of the prisoner of war camp in Nazi Germany. For some reason, and despite his diabolical looks, Werner has become one of the hit personalities of the year as far as the school kids are concerned. Tonight, the pair of veteran monsters get together for their first reunion since some of the post-war Nazi films, this time on the *Lost in Space* episode beaming at 7:30 on Channel 2.
>
> In real life, Klemperer and Harris are as scary as a couple of puppy dogs. Both dote on long-hair music; each is a gourmet in his own way; and either is happy to tell what a delight it is to receive the recognition of successful TV series actors.
>
> "I was happy to come out of retirement to do *Lost in Space*," Harris remarked stentorianly at a luncheon with Klemperer and this writer. "And I'm glad to see that you have come out of obscurity, too, old boy," he added, pointing to Werner.
>
> "We're both slightly manic at times," Werner apologized. "Actually, they should never let both of us on the sound stage at the same time. We do cut up a bit."
>
> In the show tonight, the "cut-up" bits are for insiders who know the pair. For instance, it was Harris who insisted that Klemperer's character in the teleplay, that of an intergalactic space patrolman, be called Officer Bolix, which is another way to spell a word meaning "fouled up."
>
> "Ah," said Harris, "it is a pleasure to finally find our niche as comedy heavies. Villains don't usually get the chance to be *heroes*."
>
> "Thanks for the mention of the last half of the name of our show," Werner chimed in. "I always mention the first part of yours when I talk about you."
>
> If the show is half as good as their friendly repartee off the set, it should be worth forgoing *Batman* to see. And, truth to tell, if they didn't have their own series, they'd be playing comedy heavies [on *Batman*]. But they sort of started the trend.

Klemperer actually *would* appear on *Batman*, in December 1966 … as Colonel Klink. The cameo occurred while Batman and Robin were climbing the side of a building. A window opened and Colonel Klink popped his head out and talked to the Dynamic Duo. It was a surreal moment, having the heroes talk to a character from a different time period … and a rival network.

As for "All That Glitters" and its *Hogan's Heroes* connection, stunt casting to help cross-promote two CBS shows seemed a good idea. Unfortunately, the role of Bolix did not utilize either Klemperer's villainous looks or comedic talents. It was a rather characterless role.

Syndicated "TV Scout," included in the *Edwardsville Intelligencer*, from Edwardsville, Illinois, also took notice of "All That Glitters," saying:

> Series borrows Werner Klemperer, the pompous Kommandant Klink from *Hogan's Heroes*, for a slightly amusing spoof on *The Fugitive*. Klemperer plays a glazy law-enforcement officer hunting the skies for Larry Ward, a thief with a key to some wild treasures.

The big question: Would all the hype make a difference in the ratings? A.C. Nielsen's 30-City Ratings survey for April 6, 1966 provided the answer to that question.

Network / Program:	Rating	Share:
7:30 – 8 p.m.:		
ABC: *Batman*	**24.2**	**41.2%**
CBS: *Lost in Space*	15.2	25.9%
NBC: *The Virginian*	14.3	24.3%
8 – 8:30 p.m.:		
ABC: *The Patty Duke Show*	18.5	31.3%
CBS: *Lost in Space*	**20.1**	**34.0%**
NBC: *The Virginian*	15.1	25.5%

Batman was still the winner from 7:30 to 8 p.m. But, come eight o'clock, perhaps a million people switched channels from ABC to CBS to catch the last half of *Lost in Space*. The person credited the most by the producers and the network for helping this this happen was Dr. Zachary Smith.

A few days after "All That Glitters" first aired, TV correspondent Allen Rich, writing for the *Pasadena Independent Star-News*, said:

> One suspects that *Lost in Space* would have become just that were it not for that delightful villain Dr. Smith, portrayed by Jonathan Harris. Harris' interpretation – ham or tongue-in-cheek – and I prefer the latter designation, has given viewers a rooting interest in the series. You know, a hiss-the-villain sort of thing.

With all the praise Harris was receiving from the press, CBS and Irwin Allen were sure of one thing – Dr. Smith should feature strongly in every single episode of Season Two.

38

Episode 27: "The Lost Civilization"

Written by William Welch
(with script polishing by Anthony Wilson)
Directed by Don Richardson
Produced by Irwin Allen; with Jerry Briskin

From the *Lost in Space* show files (Irwin Allen Papers Collection):

> John, Don, Will and the Robot are out searching for a fresh water supply. While Don and John are repairing the Chariot in a cave, Will and the Robot explore. They fall down a crevice and find a vast inland sea and jungle. There, in a clearing, is a young girl of Will's age, fast asleep. The Robot directs Will to wake her with a kiss, which he does. She tells them she is a princess, and takes them to her kingdom. On arriving, they find John and Don who, while searching for them have been taken prisoners. The Major Domo of the kingdom reveals that a vast army has been put into a state of suspended animation for generation after generation, waiting for the day when a traveler from another planet should arrive. He is to marry the princess. Then, the warriors will be awakened and will conquer the whole universe, starting with the planet from which the traveler came. Will tells the Princess that he doesn't want to get married and, with her connivance, and the help of a planet quake, they all make their escape and the Princess goes back to sleep again.

From the Script:

(Revised Shooting Final, March 18, 1966 draft)

– *Robot:* "Kiss her." *Will (horrified by the suggestion):* "Kiss her?" *Robot:* "It is the only way to wake her up." *Will:* "Then let her sleep." *Robot:* "It is necessary to kiss the girl." *Will:* "All right then, you do it." *Robot:* "It is necessary that you do it." *Will (in stubborn defiance):* "How do you know what is necessary for me to do?" *Robot:* "Dr. Smith has programmed into my sensors the plots of every story in literature. This is one of them." *Will (suspiciously):* "Which one?" *Robot:* "Sleeping Beauty." *Will (casts a quick glance at the girl):* "She doesn't look like any 'Beauty' to me."\

– *Girl:* "Where do you come from, Will?" *Will:* "Well … originally I came from a place called Earth." *Girl (her expression clouds faintly):* "Earth? Oh … that's too bad." *Will (surprised):* "You mean you know about Earth?" *Girl:* "I have been taught about it." *Will:* "And why did you say it's too bad?" *Girl:* "Well, I suppose it's all right as long as you come from there … and you aren't going back."

– *Will (to Robot):* "You made me kiss that girl. A fine mess you made of everything. All on account of that story. What happened anyway after he kissed that girl?" *Robot:* "They were married and lived happily ever after." *Will (incredulous):* "Married … and lived happily ever after?" *Robot (clicks and whirs for a moment):* "You are correct. It does not compute."

Assessment:

Reading the synopsis for this episode from the *Lost in Space* show files signals the trouble ahead. From that ill-conceived foundation, the domino effect from sci-fi adventure series to juvenile fantasy had begun. Misstep No. 1: Hiring William Welch to write the script.

Welch, as demonstrated by his work on the various Irwin Allen television series, was in danger of becoming a true TV hack. By this point in his career, Welch's work rarely had heart … or logic … or even common sense. His dialogue almost always rang wooden, spoken without conviction by characters lacking depth while engaged in artificial conflicts. The villains in Welch's stories were often one-dimensional megalomaniacal clichés, usually not even clever enough to provide any real threat to the series' heroes. Generally, Welch's stories lacked theme, therefore they made for pointless (and often mindless) entertainment. Finally, many of his stories didn't even offer a proper resolve.

The dominos continued to tumble.

The direction by Don Richardson was substandard; the performance by guest villain Royal Dano was stiff as a board; the role of the sleeping beauty princess was poorly cast (little Kym Karath was a bit too young and missing a few too many front teeth to pull it off); the stock footage of the volcano and flowing lava was both crudely filmed and completely incompatible with the new shots of the *Lost in Space* cast members in the Chariot; and the Seaview sets from *Voyage to the Bottom of the Sea* were not sufficiently disguised.

One can only wonder how an imaginative and well executed series like *Lost in Space* could deteriorate so badly in a single season.

Some of the answers:

- CBS seemed to be doing everything possible to dumb the show down, resulted in less compelling drama, and little purpose. Perhaps what the network really wanted was *Gilligan's Island* in outer space.
- Irwin Allen, despite being a brilliant creator/producer, had spread himself thin with too many TV projects.
- Tony Wilson, overworked and understandably burned out by the season's end, had stopped taking the series seriously. By this point, he was not even trying to have the stories and characters make sense.

You may now wish to skip watching "The Lost Civilization" and go directly to the next episode.

Script:

Story Assignment 8478 (Production #8527)

William Welch's treatment, and 1st and 2nd draft teleplays: February 1966.

Mimeo Department reformatted Shooting Final teleplay: Early March 1966.

Tony Wilson's script polish, Revised Shooting Final (blue pages): March 8, 1966.

Page revisions by Wilson (pink insert pages): March 8.

Additional page revisions by Wilson (green insert pages): March 9.

Further revisions by Wilson (pink insert pages): March 16.

Further revisions by Wilson (green insert pages): March 18.

This was William Welch's third of four script assignments for *Lost in Space*. That was three too many. Only the first ("The Hungry Sea") had merit.

Ignoring all that went wrong with the actual production, and focusing merely on what does not work in the script:

Doesn't it seem odd that Don, John and Will constantly belittle the Robot in this story? It seemed out-of-character to Irwin Allen too, as you'll soon read.

Next, the Robot locates water in the underground world, saves Will from a trap, is right about a kiss being the thing to wake a sleeping beauty, and is also proven right about there being "alien" humans in the area. Yet Will continually challenges the Robot concerning this information, even suggesting that his circuits must be damaged. Now Will is the one who behaves foolishly.

It all becomes rather tiresome.

Note how the erupting volcano and flowing lava, have nothing to do with the story about to be told, and are therefore an artificial jeopardy which comes and goes, and is forgotten, in a matter of minutes.

Note how the Princess wakes up and immediately talks in English, without a question from Will as to how she knows the language and would speak it even before hearing what language he speaks! Major Domo seems to have been raised and educated in the United States, too.

Note that the portion of the story involving the Princess has no proper resolution, nor does the subplot concerning the vast army. Does this "planet-quake" kill them? All we know is that the Princess intends to go back to sleep and wait to be kissed again, and that the army will stay dormant in their freezing tubes until another adventurer and princess-kisser happens along. In the end, John merely states that he hopes that the Princess won't be awakened any time soon, and that the army won't be sent out to attack Earth in his lifetime. Let Earth be invaded on someone else's watch, he implies.

Beyond all of this, we are given the cliché of aliens set on invading the Earth and conquering the universe. Why? They never really say. It's just what alien armies do. Right?

More banality:

Why does the Princess sleep? Why does a kiss wake her up? Perhaps she read *Sleeping Beauty*, too.

Lastly, the whole point to this story – that of searching for drinking water – is dropped and forgotten by the end. The underground world and sea is sealed off, so John drives the Chariot back to the Jupiter 2 and Will and Don tell everyone about the princess and the army, then Don chews out Dr. Smith for tampering with the Chariot's air conditioning unit. Apparently, they really didn't need any water after all.

On March 3, 1966, after reading Welch's second draft (reformatted as the Shooting Final teleplay), Irwin Allen wrote to Tony Wilson:

> P. 7, Sc. 18: John's line seems silly coming from John who should be well aware of the possibilities of underground water in desert terrain.
>
> P. 13, Sc. 29: John's second speech seems strange since he really means they can't continue looking for water even in the Chariot without the air conditioner. Why doesn't John suggest opening the windows so that they at least get a breeze, even if a hot one.
>
> P. 14, Sc. 29: Don's second speech – It's inconsistent to doubt the Robot now because of the water episode since the Robot was correct about the water where he said it would be. The fact that it was not drinkable was not his fault….
>
> P. 18, Sc. 39: Cut Will's last speech. He is usually the champion of the Robot, not his detractor.
>
> P. 20, Sc. 45: Shouldn't Will call up to the Robot or at least yell for help? Then, not receiving an answer, Will should proceed to investigate the tunnel.
>
> P. 35, Sc. 88: The Robot's overhaul remarks are beginning to get tiresome.

Tony Wilson made changes to the script on March 8th and 9th, and after the episode had started filming, on March 16th and 20th. But he failed to address many of Allen's concerns about the story and the foolish behavior of the characters. Wilson was more attentive to changes CBS wanted to see made. Concerning these, note how Don's injured foot is a false jeopardy. Immediately following the accident, it is determined by John and Don that the foot is not broken. Why tell us this? Why have it be merely a sprain, which is far less problematic and, therefore, less dramatic? The answer – a broken foot might upset the audience. Better let it be a sprain.

In the script, Major Domo heals Don's foot with the touch of his hand. But this act hinted toward divine intervention, or the occult. CBS wanted this changed, so Domo uses a machine to fix the foot. As a result, this action is rendered as inconsequential to the story as nearly everything else in the script.

One thing that the two writers cannot be blamed for is how in the world a planet-quake can shake up Will and the Robot so badly but not even be felt by John and Don back at the Chariot. The script had a brief scene in which John and Don do feel a quake, although a minor one. John says, "That's the second small quake. I don't want to stay in here any longer than we have to." Don, working hard under the Chariot, says, "You and me both!"

Will and the Robot couldn't have wandered far from where John and Don are working on the Chariot. Why wouldn't the effects of the quake have been as strong in both places? And John would certainly have immediately wanted to know if Will was all right, rather than continuing to watch Don work.

Maybe the writers should be blamed after all.

Pre-Production:

Kym Karath had appeared as one of the von Trapp children in 1965's *The Sound of Music*. She is second from right in front row, next to Angela Cartwright.

Don Richardson returned for his third directing assignment, following "Ghost in Space" and "The Challenge."

Winton Hoch, the director of photography for *Voyage to the Bottom of the Sea*, was intended to film this one, leading the production unit from *Voyage* on the same days that Gene Poltio and the *Lost in Space* unit filmed "All That Glitters." When Polito fell ill with the flu, Hoch was moved over to the "All That Glitters" production, which Irwin Allen, Jerry Briskin and Tony Wilson felt was the better of the two episodes. A cinematographer from outside Allen's circle was hired to take over the filming of "The Lost Civilization."

Charles G. Clarke, who had served as cinematographer on *Lost in Space*'s "The Magic Mirror" only two months previously, was once again brought back to help the company catch up.

Kym Karath was seven when she played the sleeping-beauty princess. She had been acting in films since age three, when she appeared in 1963's *Spencer's Mountain* as one of the daughters to stars Henry Fonda and Maureen O'Hara. Also from 1963 was *The Thrill of it All*, starring James Garner, and, one year later, *Good Neighbor Sam*, starring Jack Lemmon. Later in 1964, Karath was cast as Gretl, the youngest von Trapp daughter in *The Sound of Music*, which also featured Angela Cartwright in the cast. Karath had also appeared in an episode of *Lassie* during June Lockhart's tenure with the series.

Royal Dano in the 1956 Alfred Hitchcock film, *The Trouble with Harry* (Paramount Pictures, 1955).

Character actor Royal Dano played Major Domo. He was forty-three and appeared in approximately 200 movies and TV shows between 1949 and 1993. For Major Domo, Dano was made-up to stir memories of Charles B. Middleton's performance as Ming the Merciless in the *Flash Gordon* serial from the 1930s.

Dawson Palmer appeared as one of the soldiers.

Production Diary:

Filmed March 11 – 21, 1966, with pickup shots taken on March 22 & 23 (7 days, plus 2 partial days for pickup shots).

Stock footage filmed for the pilot, of the Chariot driving at night, helped to keep costs down on "The Lost Civilization."

Lost in Space again had to shoot two episodes simultaneously in an effort to catch up on production and make its delivery dates to CBS. This had been done once before, with the overlapping production schedules for "War of the Robots" and "The Magic Mirror." This time, greater care was taken to allow the two film units to stay out of each other's way. There was less sharing of sound stages and regular cast members. While June Lockhart, Marta Kristen, Angela Cartwright, and Jonathan Harris worked in "All That Glitters," Guy Williams, Mark Goddard, Billy Mumy, and Bob May appeared in "The Lost Civilization."

Another case of two episodes being shot simultaneously in order to help *Lost in Space* make its network deliveries. The female cast members, and Dr. Smith, carried the story for ""All that Glitters," while the men were away. And here the men are – male Robot included – for "The Lost Civilization," filmed by the *Voyage to the Bottom of the Sea* company. Above: The interior Chariot scenes were filmed on Day 1. Below: On Day 2, they took the Chariot into cavernous Stage 19.

Day 1: Friday, March 11th. A full day was spent on Stage 6, filming from 8 a.m. to 5:48 p.m., with the scenes of the Chariot being subjected to a meteor storm … or was it raining chunks of volcanic ash? We had seen it before, in the Teaser of "One of Our Dogs is Missing" The new footage was limited to the actors' reaction shots from within the Chariot. But Don Richardson did get one striking shot, from inside the Chariot as a fireball comes toward the vehicle and John and Don quickly turn away from it and toward camera. Otherwise, the scenes with Williams, Goddard, Mumy, and May are plagued by the stilted dialogue.

Mark Goddard told interviewer Tom Weaver, "Doing a show like that is very difficult. I used to always put myself down. I would say, 'Gee, I'm not very good; this is tough to do.' Then one day, years later, I was on the set of *The Towering Inferno* [1974] and I stood there and watched Irwin directing Paul Newman and Steve McQueen in an office scene. Paul Newman is one of my favorite actors and one of the best actors who has ever been around, and one of the great thing that you have to do as an actor is to be relaxed. That's very important. I was watching that scene being done, and I watched the tension in Paul Newman grow. I couldn't believe that *he* -- even *he* -- was having a hard time with this kind of dialogue, with this kind of directing, and what was happening. Of course, he was doing it because he was getting a million dollars – he did it for the money; he wasn't doing it because he wanted to work with Irwin Allen. But I saw that tension and I said, 'Boy, even with Paul Newman. Words that don't work are even hard for him. I guess I'm not doin' such a bad job after all!' That puts things in perspective." (MG-SL93)

Richardson stayed on schedule.

Day 2: Monday, March 14th. The company was supposed to spend only a half-day on Stage 19, filming the Chariot being driven into a

Top and middle photos: On Day 3, filming on Stage 6 in the deeper caverns. Bottom photo: Day 4 was spent on *Voyage to the Bottom of the Sea*'s Stage B for jungle sets as well as a beach … and a sleeping beauty.

cavern, then the group exiting the vehicle, and Don, with John watching, making the repairs. Also to be covered: the action in which Will and the Robot wander off, and then John and Don exit in search for the others. It ended up taking the entire day, setting the production one-half of a day behind.

The company soldiered on with the substandard material, filming from 8 a.m. to 6:15 p.m., covering seven-point-six pages from the script from "The Lost Civilization," plus a couple of pickup shots for "All That Glitters."

Day 3, Tuesday, March 15th. Stage 6 was the location. Richardson again had to pause from making "The Lost Civilization" to get additional footage for the Tag scene to "All That Glitters." For his own episode, he covered thirteen and five-eighths pages, including scenes in the "Int. Cavern" and "Int. Tunnel Cave" sets. Richardson improved his standing to one-quarter of a day behind schedule.

Day 4: Wednesday, March 16th. Work began on Stage 6 for more scenes in the "Int. Tunnel Cave" set, then the company moved to Stage "B" for "Ext. Beach." Richardson covered thirteen and six-eighths pages from the script, putting the production back on schedule. Filming stopped at 5:10 p.m., allowing plenty of time to wrap the familiar *Voyage to the Bottom of the Sea* set and get everyone home in time for the network premiere of "His Majesty Smith" … except it never took

place. Gemini 8 was in trouble and *Lost in Space* was pre-empted for the real space drama.

Day 5: Thursday, March 17th. Richardson filmed from 8 a.m. to 6:50 p.m., beginning on Stage B, for the "Ext. Jungle" and "Ext. Jungle Clearing," then moving to Stage 10 for "Int. Detention Area" – a redress of the Missile Room from *Voyage*. The company covered eight and five-eighths pages of the script, falling behind again by one-quarter of a day.

Day 6: Friday, March 18th. It was supposed to be the final day of filming on Stage 10, for more scenes on the "Int. Detention Area" set, but Richardson fell further behind. Come 5:55 p.m., when they wrapped, a half-day's work had to be carried over to the new week, pushing back the start of the next episode – "A Change of Space."

Above: Kym Karath gets a lift to the set on the shoulders of Guy Williams. What little girl wouldn't love that?! Middle image: with studio teacher Francess Klampt. Bottom photo: the things they made poor Billy Mumy do in the name of publicity.

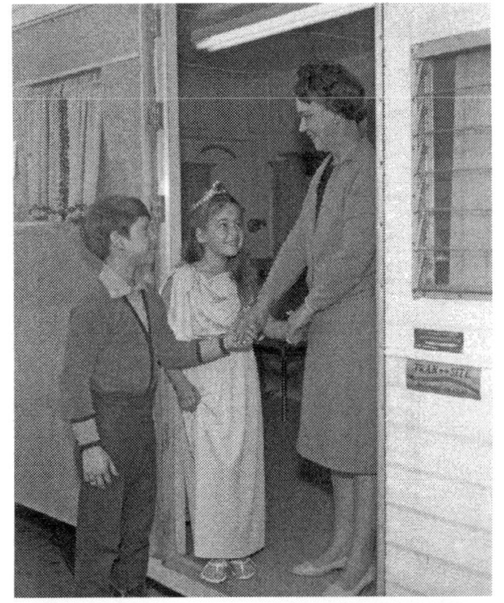

Day 7: Monday, March 21st. What was planned to take a half-day's work ended up requiring an entire day, and an hour's overtime pay, with filming going from 8 a.m. to 7:04 p.m. on Stage 10, for the "Int. Control Center." Anyone who ever saw *Voyage to the Bottom of the Sea* will recognize this set immediately – it was the Control Room from the submarine Seaview.

Major Domo had his death scene on this day. Royal Dano told authors Joel Eisner and Barry Magen, "I know that we used a lot of fireworks during the electrocution scene, and they had a lot of problems setting that up, because at the first rehearsal when he threw me, I was going back into the control panel where I could have gotten tangled up in the explosives. As it turned out, I hit the panel slightly off mark, but I caught myself and moved into position, where I was electrocuted. It was all a matter of timing, to being in the correct spot

Day 6 and 7 were spent filming the "Int. Detention Area" and "Int. Control Room." Royal Dano had to take care not to get a *real* shock out of the below scene.

when the explosives went off and not get hurt in the process." (RD-LISF)

Don Richardson was sent into post-production to try to help film editor Fred Baratta cut the mess together. Meanwhile, the regular *Lost in Space* production crew, with D.P. Winton Hoch, having finished filming "All That Glitters" and standing by to begin "A Change of Space," took over filming the rest of "The Lost Civilization" under the direction of Sobey Martin.

Day 8: Tuesday, March 22nd. The episode's Tag scene was shot.

Day 9: Wednesday, March 23rd. Pickup shots were taken on Stage 11 for the "Ext. Campsite" set, again utilizing the director and crew from "A Change of Space."

William Self wanted this one made for $130,980. With all the stock footage used, and borrowing sets from *Voyage*, they came close. Final cost was $133,851.

Release / Reaction:

(CBS premiere broadcast: Wednesday, April 13, 1966)
(Network repeat airing: Wednesday, August 3, 1966)

The week that "The Lost Civilization" had its first of two CBS broadcasts, another bomb was dropped. In fact, many bombs, as the U.S. launched the first B-52 bombing missions over North Vietnam. "The Ballad of the Green Berets" by Staff Sergeant Barry Sadler was *still* the top-selling album in America. At least we had a new top song on the radio – "(You're My) Soul and Inspiration" by the Righteous Brothers. The top-grossing film in the movie houses was *The Singing Nun*, starring Debbie Reynolds. (And you thought this episode of *Lost in Space* was bad!)

None of the syndicated newspaper television review columns bothered with this episode.

The A.C. Nielsen 30-City Ratings survey for April 13, 1966 reported the audience estimates as follows:

Network / Program:	Rating	Share:
7:30 – 8 p.m.:		
ABC: *Batman*	**25.6**	**42.3%**
CBS: *Lost in Space*	16.1	26.6%
NBC: *The Virginian*	15.8	26.1%
8 – 8:30 p.m.:		
ABC: *The Patty Duke Show*	17.0	27.4%
CBS: *Lost in Space*	**22.1**	**35.6%**
NBC: *The Virginian*	18.7	30.1%

"The Lost Civilization," arguably the single worst episode from *Lost in Space*'s First Season, was given a network repeat airing, while fan favorites such as "Welcome Stranger" and "My Friend, Mr. Nobody" were not. The rerun schedule was decided by Irwin Allen and CBS, but all indications are the network did not want to repeat the earlier episodes which depicted Smith and his henchman, the Robot, as being a direct threat to the children in the series.

With an audience share of 34.4, "The Lost Civilization" received the highest Nielsen rating of all the summer repeats.

39

Episode 28: "A Change of Space"

Written by Peter Packer
(with script polishing by Anthony Wilson)
Directed by Sobey Martin
Produced by Irwin Allen; with Jerry Briskin

From the *Lost in Space* show files (Irwin Allen Papers Collection):

> Smith and Will discover an ultra-sophisticated spaceship which the Robot reports is capable of circumnavigating the universe at the velocity of light squared, but warns that there could be great hazards in such a flight. Will gets in, and inadvertently sets it in flight. He returns shortly with his intellect tremendously stimulated. Smith, wanting the same advantages, also takes a flight but he returns just a doddering old man. Will thinks that another trip, with the ship's guidance system in reverse, might return Smith to the way he was. Smith says he is too old and frail to take the risk so Will agrees to try it first. The alien owner of the spaceship appears, angrily demands the return of his ship and seizes Smith as a hostage.

From the Script:

– *Maureen (off Will staring coolly, almost arrogantly)* "Will – what is it? Are you all right?" *John (quietly):* "Your mother asked you a question, Will." *Will (smiles coolly):* "Not really, Dad. She was just expressing her momentary emotional anxiety in rhetorical terms. Certainly the state of my physical well-being should be apparent to all." *Maureen (bewildered):* "Will – I don't understand. Why are you speaking that way?" *Will:* "What way, Mother?" *Maureen:* "Well – it just isn't like you to answer my questions with an analysis of my feelings." *Will:* "I'm sorry if the operation of my mind doesn't please you. But it happens to be the way I am." *Smith (smiles):* "The boy is showing a remarkably independent spirit. Rather like mine." *John:* "Shut up, Smith. *(to Will)* Did you go up in that ship, Will?" *Will (casually):* "As a matter of fact, I did. *(then)* Incidentally, you've been conditioned to accept the velocity of light as a limiting factor in space travel. My flight disproved that theory." *John:* "Yes – I'm beginning to see that. *(cautiously)* I – uh – I'd like to talk to you about it – and about your experience." *Will:* "Certainly, Dad. *(frowns)* It might be a little hard for you to understand. *(smiles)* But I'll try and simplify it for you." *John (drily):* "Thanks."

– *Maureen:* "What happened in here? Will was almost in tears." *John:* "At least he hasn't forgotten that primitive emotion. He's still a boy." *Maureen (quietly):* "Has he given you reason to doubt it?" *John:* "Not to doubt it – Maureen, but to recognize that there's been a tremendous acceleration in his intellectual maturity because of that flight he took. He's way ahead of <u>us</u> in many respects." *Don:* "Yeah – I might have to bone up a little on multi-dimensional flight phenomena before he'll talk to <u>me</u> again." *Maureen (to John):* "It can't be harmful to him – can it?" *John:* "Only in relationship to us."

– *Old Smith:* "I'm in the last stage of the seven stages of man…" *Will (the brisk scientist):* "Tomorrow, I'll conduct a few tests on molecular reversibility … but I doubt whether they will be successful." *Old Smith:* "That's not very hopeful, is it?" *Will:* "Hope is an opiate for the lazy and the uninformed." *Old Smith (shaking his head – a lament):* "Where is the Will I used to know? Where has he gone – that sympathetic, optimistic little chap who admired me so – drank wisdom from my utterances – played and laughed with me – brought joy to my heart – not the chilling predictions of his icy intellect? Where is that blithe young spirit?" *Will (momentarily uncertain of himself):* "Gosh – I guess I was like that once."

Assessment:

Lost in Space seemed to be back on track with this episode, after the misfire called "The Lost Civilization." The story is imaginative and well structured. There is even a character arc for Will, as he realizes that he may have lost as much as he gained in becoming a sudden genius. And he is willing to risk losing his newfound enhanced intellect, by making another test flight in the alien ship – and all in order to perhaps save the life of another. Will is very much the hero in this episode in that he is willing to sacrifice himself for someone else.

In addition to what works on a story level, the dialogue is sharp, and that means the characters come off as smart – something they most certainly did not in William Welch's script for "The Lost Civilization."

Writer Peter Packer utilized the cast members well, and even brought back the sense of family – Judy recording her audio diary; Maureen and Penny bonding as Mother/Daughter; Will and Penny playing chess; Don and Penny trying to find a little alone time for romance. Moments such as these had been missing from several of the recent episodes.

The alien ships (even though clearly a modified versions of the Seaview's diving bell from *Voyage to the Bottom of the Sea*) are inspired in design and execution. The space travelling creature himself (again, modified from one seen on *Voyage*) is also effectively alien … and frightening. And it speaks in a foreign tongue! Bravo to Peter Packer.

The wart on the skin of this episode is that Jonathan Harris plays his old-man-Smith way over the top. It's silly and hammy to the point of annoyance. Fortunately, the Old Smith doesn't make his entrance in the story until the curtain of the Second Act.

"A Change of Space" is a change in the right direction after "The Lost Civilization."

Script:

Story Assignment 9543 (Production #8528)
Peter Packer's treatment, and 1st and 2nd draft teleplays: February/March 1966.
Mimeo Department reformatted Shooting Final teleplay: March 14, 1966.
Page revisions by Tony Wilson (light green insert pages): March 14.
Additional page revisions by Wilson (blue insert pages): March 15.
Further revisions by Wilson (pink insert pages): March 16.
Further revisions by Wilson (beige insert pages): March 18.
Further revisions by Wilson (blue insert pages): March 21.
Further revisions by Wilson (purple insert pages): March 22.
Further revisions by Wilson (dark green insert pages): March 25.

This was already Peter Packer's tenth *Lost in Space* script. All had been produced except for "Sorry, Wrong Planet," which had been abandoned, and "Blast Off into Space," which was being held to launch the Second Season.

Tony Wilson felt Packer had done well – to the extent Wilson did not put the script through a rewrite, opting instead for a series of page revisions as notes came in from Irwin Allen, CBS and Jonathan Harris.

On March 17, 1966, Sam Taylor, Jr. of CBS Program Practices to Irwin Allen:

> As discussed with Mr. Wilson:
>
> When WILL visits the alien spaceship (scene 39) for the second time, he is acting imprudently; however, when he again goes to the ship (after scene 83) he seems to be committing a deliberate act of disobedience. We would ask that you alter the situation by deleting the last sentence ("but Dad won't allow it") in WILL's speech, Page 45, Scene 83.

The following day, Taylor added:

> As discussed with Mr. Wilson:
>
> Page 14, Scene 28: Will's speech indicates that he realizes he is being disobedient. We would request it be changed so as to indicate apprehension. Perhaps he could say, "I shouldn't get too close, but …"

Pre-Production:

Sobey Martin returned to direct. This was already his eighth episode of *Lost in Space,* with another six to go. At this time, he was well along the way in directing fourteen episodes of *Voyage to the Bottom of the Sea*, with fourteen episodes still ahead for *The Time Tunnel*, and then twenty-one for *Land of the Giants*.

Paul Zastupnevich said of Irwin Allen, "He didn't like to make changes. Once he found someone that adapted to his way of thinking, and did things the way he wanted them to, he kept them. But if you did something that irked him, he dumped you." (PZ-KB95)

Frank Graham was the man in the alien monster suit. He was an actor and a stuntman who often appeared as a cowboy or horse soldier in movies starring John Wayne, whom Graham stunted for.

The monster costume, resembling a fish-man covered with loosely attached scales, was reminiscent of one of the low-budget imitators of *The Creature from the Black Lagoon*'s gillman. Regarding the frantic pace needed in turning out monster suits for both *Voyage to the Bottom of the Sea* and *Lost in Space*, and the necessity to often use the same costume in both series, Paul Zastupnevich told interviewer Mike Clark, "What can you do when you have a segment that's shooting in three or four days, and you get the actor the day before he's to step in front of the camera? The only basic thing we did was use a diver's wetsuit as a basis for the monster costumes. The suits have a certain amount of 'give' to them, which makes it easier to adjust. You can zip it up and overlap a piece, and if you have to let it out, you can cut a seam up the back. I would coordinate with the makeup and special FX department on the monster costumes, and between the three of us, we would reach an understanding as to who did what." (PZ-SL93)

Zastupnevich would sketch out his ideas, then turn the sketches over to John Chambers and Dan Striepeke to create the mask or face parts. Then one of the three would busy himself by applying gills or scales, or other features, made from rubber or plastic, to the basic wetsuit.

This particular monster, with only minor adjustments, had already appeared in *Voyage to the Bottom of the Sea*, as the "fish-man." Zastupnevich said, "What are you going to do? There was no time or money. I figured a fish-man was a fish-man whether on land or sea. If I could cut a dollar off somewhere, I would do it. Generally, we were given about $250 to work up a costume. I defy you to try and do that today. You can't even buy a cashmere sweater for that price."

The bottom line was an ongoing directive from Irwin Allen's office to shave costs. In twenty-first-century terms, "reduce, reuse, recycle." So Allen's office was where the fish-man and many other creatures would be taken for approval. Zastupnevich said, "You would see me leading an actor wearing a fish-man costume over to Irwin's office. He would approve it, and I would lead the fish-man back to wardrobe. It became a running gag to see who I would be dragging through the Fox lot next." (PZ-SL93)

Production Diary:

Filmed from March 22 to March 30 (7 days).

The chemistry on the screen – as a tight-knit family – was just as present away from the set.

Day 1: Tuesday, March 22nd. Sobey Martin filmed from 8 a.m. to 5:35 p.m. on Stage 6, covering eight pages and staying on schedule. Covered on this day, the scene that would end the previous episode, "The Lost Civilization," and open "A Change of Space": On a "Rocky Plateau," while looking for treasure, Smith falls into a pit; Will helps him out; then they leave to investigate an alien space ship. Also: "Ext. Trail Approaching Promontory" for the various comings to and goings from the alien ship throughout the episode.

While filming this episode, *TV Guide* writer Dwight Whitney visited the set to do a feature article. The topic was not Guy Williams, the star, or June Lockhart, the other star, but Jonathan Harris … the "special guest star." In the article (included in the magazine's June 18th issue), Whitney wrote that Harris had stolen the show. After asking Guy Williams what he thought of Harris's sudden rise in status, Whitney wrote:

> "It isn't so much that he *steals* the show," said Williams wistfully one day last spring. "It's that they [the producers] give it to him. But we're working on that now." He furrows his brow. "We have to – uh, open up the material. Next week's show ["Follow the Leader"] is better. I have something to *do*."

Playing an aged version of the already prissy Smith, Harris took the character into the comic book world that would be embellished even further in the coming Second Season. Harris told Dwight Whitney, "Irwin wasn't always that sure what was going on. He used to come to the set on a day when I was playing Shakespeare. I could do anything I wanted with Dr. Smith, I really could, because it all worked, you see, because I invented this crazy man, and Irwin would gape and say to the director, 'What is he doing?' And the director would say, 'Don't talk to him or he will stop doing it.' And he [Allen] would go." (JH-IASB2)

Above: Day 2 of the production, both inside and outside the Jupiter 2, was spent filming most of the scenes in which Will is a genius. Below: *Lost and Space* and *Batman* may have been in a fight for ratings, but the cast members were friendly neighbors. Burt Ward poses with Billy Mumy and Angela Cartwright. Bottom right: A clever redesign of the diving bell from *Voyage to the Bottom of the Sea* helped to save money.

Day 2: Wednesday, March 23rd. Work commenced on Stage 11, filming from 8 a.m. to 5:45 p.m., for the "Ext. Hydroponic Garden," where Will bores Judy with his intellectual prowess; and "Another Part of Camp Area," where Will irritates Penny with super-knowledge of chess; and "Ext. Jupiter 2 Campsite," where Will confesses that Smith may have taken off in the alien craft. Also filmed, the scenes on the upper deck of the Jupiter 2. Ten and a quarter pages were covered and the production remained on schedule.

"His Majesty Smith" aired on this night at 7:30 p.m. in Los Angeles.

Day 3: Thursday, March 24th. The company was back on Stage 6, where they would remain for the rest of the production. Sobey Martin filmed from 8 a.m. to 6:55 p.m., covering ten and four-eighths pages. He was on schedule.

Day 4: Friday, March 25th. Work continued on Stage 6, filming from 8 in the morning to 6:55 in the evening, covering seven and three-eighths pages, and falling behind by one-quarter of a day. Covered: the "Int. Promontory & Alien Spaceship," as Smith and Will discover the spacecraft; the family join Will and Smith at the craft and John decides they should not tamper with it; Smith attempts to diagnose the ship with the reluctant help of the Robot, who is then kayoed out by an alien power beam; Will repairs the Robot; Will flies the ship; and the family meets Will as he exits the ship and demonstrates his new intellectual prowess to them.

The diving bell wasn't the only thing borrowed from *Voyage to the Bottom of the Sea*. This monster came from there, too.

Day 5: Monday, March 28th. Director Martin filmed from 8 in the morning until 6:40 p.m., covering nine and two-eighths pages, and falling behind by one-half of a day. The scenes shot included Smith flying in the ship, then returning as an old man.

Day 6: Tuesday, March 29th. The company filmed from 8 a.m. to 6:55 p.m. Scenes shot included encountering the agitated alien. When they stopped filming, Martin was a full day behind.

The start of production for "Follow the Leader" was pushed back a day, now set to begin on Thursday.

Day 7: Wednesday, March 30th. A final day on Stage 6, shooting eleven and one-eighths pages from the script, and finishing the episode at 6:15 p.m. At 7:30 p.m., CBS aired "The Space Croppers."

Post-Production:

On April 5, 1966, after viewing the rough cut of the episode, Sam Taylor, Jr. wrote:

> As discussed with Mr. Wilson:
>
> The film shown to this editor contained the incorrect footage from Scene 80. You have said that the correct footage will be inserted into the film as per Page 41 (revised 3/25/66). In other words, JOHN's line, "No, Will – no more flights" will be deleted; MAUREEN's line will be changed to, "I don't want to hear anymore talk about test flights," and WILL's line will be changed to, "But, Mom…"
>
> As you know, the purpose of this request is to eliminate what would later appear to be a deliberate act of disobedience by WILL.

The budget 20th Century-Fox allocated was $130,980. The end result was $134,196.

Release / Reaction:

(CBS premiere broadcast: Wednesday, April 20, 1966)

(Network repeat airing: Wednesday, August 19, 1966)

Promotional picture circulated to newspapers by CBS and 20th Century-Fox.

"(You're My) Soul and Inspiration" by the Righteous Brothers had another week as the most-played song on the radio across America. But the "brothers" didn't have the top LP. That honor went to Herb Alpert's Tijuana Brass, back on the top again with *Going Places*. The top-grossing film in the movie houses was *Doctor Zhivago*. Those incredible girls from *Petticoat Junction* – Lori Saunders, Linda Kaye, and Gunilla Hutton (the reason teenage boys watched the show) – had the cover of *TV Guide*. Where was Meredith MacRae, you may ask. She was still a season away, when she would replace Hutton.

The TV editor for the Monessen, Pennsylvania *Valley Independent* picked this episode as a highlight for the evening, saying:

> Little Billy Mumy, playing with an alien space ship on the Space Family Robinson's planet, rockets into space and returns a blooming genius. So greedy Dr. Smith, avid for additional knowledge, takes a ride in the ship and returns an old man. Jonathan Harris is very funny, hamming it up like a far-out King Lear.

Syndicated "TV Scout," carried in Illinois in the April 20th edition of *The Edwardsville Intelligencer*, said:

> Little Billy Mumy, playing with an alien space ship on the Space Family Robinson's planet, rockets into space and returns a blooming genius. So greedy Dr. Smith, avid for additional knowledge, takes a ride in the ship and returns an old man. Jonathan Harris is very funny, hamming it up like a far-out King Lear.

Now you know why Harris was allowed to push his campy performance to the limit … and beyond. At this point in the series, the critics, as well as the viewing audience – at least those who kept Nielsen ratings logs or wrote letters to the network – seemed to be eating it up.

A.C. Nielsen 30-City Ratings survey for April 20, 1966 counted the audience members' noses as follows:

Network / Program:	Rating	Share:
7:30 – 8 p.m.:		
ABC: *Batman*	**24.1**	**42.3%**
CBS: *Lost in Space*	15.0	25.8%
NBC: *The Virginian*	12.9	22.6%
8 – 8:30 p.m.:		
ABC: *The Patty Duke Show*	15.9	26.2%
CBS: *Lost in Space*	**22.0**	**36.3%**
NBC: *The Virginian*	15.5	25.6%

40

Episode 29: "Follow the Leader"

Written by Barney Slater
(with script polishing by Anthony Wilson)
Directed by Don Richardson
Produced by Irwin Allen; with Jerry Briskin

From the *Lost in Space* show files (Irwin Allen Papers Collection):

> John, caught in a cave by a rock fall, hears a voice coming from an old sarcophagus. It is the spirit of Canto, a former warrior from the planet Quasti, who wants to take over John's body and thus live again. The voice tells him that it will gain possession of his mind bit by bit, until John will be completely under his control. Back with the family, John bewilders them by acting like a ruthless dictator. With Canto using John's voice, the family are forced to work night and day repairing the spaceship as he plans to return to Quasti in it. When the ship is ready, John, under Canto's control, imprisons Maureen, Judy and Don in the cave, then, wearing a helmet and mask, tricks Smith and Penny into believing he is an alien who will take them to find their father. Only Will isn't deceived, so Canto makes John take the boy to a steep precipice, planning to hurl him over.

From the Script:

(Revised Shooting final teleplay, April 1, 1966 draft)

– *Smith:* "Before we go any further, Professor Robinson, I wish to state that I did everything in my power to help you yesterday." *Robinson (mildly):* "Of course you did, Dr. Smith." *Smith (surprised):* "Then you aren't angry at me?" *Robinson (smiles deceptively, gestures to nearby vacant chair):* "Not in the least. Sit down, have some breakfast." *Smith (greatly relieved):* "Why thank you, Professor Robinson. I am a little hungry this morning. *(reaches for a platter of food)* I'll just have a little of this…" *Robinson (brings a clenched fist down on the table; he has suddenly become savagely angry):* "Don't touch that food!!" *Smith (freezes in mid-action):* "But you just said…" *Robinson (in fury):* "You're not going to have anything to eat at this table today. And if you fail to join us on time for breakfast tomorrow, you won't get anything to eat for another twenty-four hours. Do you understand me, Dr. Smith!!" *Maureen:* "John, aren't you being unreasonable? I'm sure Dr. Smith…" *Robinson (interrupting):* "This doesn't concern you, Maureen." *Don (voice placating):* "Take it easy, John. Are you sure you're feeling all right?" *Robinson (snapping at him):* "I'm perfectly fine. Just because I expect a little discipline and routine from that man is no reason to think I'm sick."

– *Will:* "How do you feel, sir?" *Robinson (voice a little drowsy):* "Like a prize idiot. I made a fool of myself, didn't I?" *Will:* "No, you didn't, sir. Everyone understands." *Robinson:* "You're a good boy, Will. Sometimes I feel you're a better son than I am a father." *Will (sheepishly):* "I think it's the other way around." *Robinson:* "Instead of being lost out here in space, you should be living the life of a normal boy. Playing with youngsters your own age, going to ball games ... doing all the things a boy needs to do before growing up." *Will:* "I like what I'm doing better." *Robinson (sighs):* "You're saying that, Will, because you don't know what you've missed. *(lies back; closes his eyes)* It's my fault. I should have insisted you stay on Earth … the girls too. It's not fair … there's so much they haven't experienced … so much."

– *Will:* "It's all right now, Dad. He's gone forever." *Robinson:* "Yes, Will … he's gone." *Will:* "What do you think chased him off, sir?" *Robinson:* "Love, Will. In all the worlds and galaxies of the universe, there's nothing stronger."

Assessment:

Jon Abbott, in *Irwin Allen Television Productions 1964-1970: A Critical History*, referred to "Follow the Leader" as "A dry run for the third season's 'Anti-Matter Man,' and a rather good one."

This was an especially frightening episode for children watching the loving and devoted father change before their eyes and even take young Will to the edge of a cliff where he orders the boy to jump … and it is clear that he is willing to push Will if need be. Love is the weapon that defeats the intruder possessing John Robinson's body. Although a few cynical audience members might call this a trite resolution, it's still a satisfying one for those of us who more familiar with the power of affection.

Another effective and startling scene comes when John invites Smith to join the family for breakfast. All seems forgiven, until John slams his fist on the table and sends a chill down the not-so-good doctor's spine.

Also dramatic: The family working relentlessly through the night to dig the rubble from the mouth of the cave; the worry conveyed for their lost one; and standout moments for both the character of John Robinson and Guy Williams, allowed to portray something other than the constant hero and proper father. Williams was very much in his element when playing against the heroic type.

While time has corroded some of the elements in this episode, "Follow the Leader" nonetheless remains among the series' best and, as the last produced and aired for the First Season, a sad reminder of things past and what could and should have been in the future.

Script:

Story Assignment 8477 (Production #8529)
Barney Slater's treatment, and 1st and 2nd draft teleplays: February/March 1966.
Mimeo Department reformatted Shooting Final teleplay: Mid-March 1966.
Tony Wilson's script polish, Revised Shooting Final (blue pages): March 24, 1966.
Page revisions by Wilson (green insert pages): March 31.
Additional page revisions by Wilson (green insert pages): April 1.

This was Barney Slater's ninth *Lost in Space* writing assignment, which included standout episodes such as "Wish Upon a Star" and the two-parter "The Keeper."

On March 31st, during the episode's first day of filming, Sam Taylor, Jr. of CBS Program Practices, Hollywood, wrote:

> As discussed with Mr. Wilson:
>
> Throughout the episode we would not wish JOHN, possessed by an alien spirit, to evidence extreme ferocity or malice toward his family and friends. With such attitude displayed, the effect on younger members of the audience might be a disturbing one. Specifically we would ask for directorial care in the following sequences: Scene 51, when JOHN threatens to destroy SMITH; Scene 69, when JOHN discovers WILL has been following him; Scene 77-81, when JOHN threatens MAUREEN, JUDY and DON, and then fights with DON; and, finally, in scene 96, 98, when JOHN takes WILL to the edge of the cliff. You have told us that during this latter sequence the ALIEN's voice will emanate from JOHN [rather than JOHN speaking].

Taylor wrote again on April 4th, saying:

> Pages 61, 61A & 62: As you have changed the point at which you will conclude ACT IV, we will reiterate our request in connection with the voices and actions in the final sequence of the Act and the sequence which follows. As ROBINSON, wearing the mask, takes WILL to the edge of the abyss, the voice of the ALIEN will be

emanating from him. The Act should not be concluded with any movement by ROBINSON through Page 61-A and that ROBINSON's own voice will not be heard until the mask has been removed and he speaks at the top of Page 62.

Pre-Production:

Don Richardson returned for his fourth assignment on *Lost in Space*, making amends for his directing-by-the-numbers effort during "The Lost Civilization." He was, of course, benefited by a good script and first-rate performances from all the cast members.

Gregory Morton provided the voice of Canto of Quasti. He was an actor with nearly 100 known screen credits in films and television from the early 1950s through the mid-1970s. He would also provide the voice of Judge Iko of the tribunal space court in the second season entry, "The Prisoners of Space." Irwin Allen would cast Morton in "End of the World," an episode of *The Time Tunnel*, where he is seen as an astronomer.

Production Diary:

Filmed from March 31 through April 8, 1966 (7 days).

Day 1: Thursday, March 31st. The company filmed on Stage 11 from 8 a.m. to 6:20 p.m., covering ten and seven-eighths pages from the script, exclusive to scenes at the Jupiter 2 campsite, including John's outburst during the family's breakfast.

Day 2: Friday, April 1st. The Tag scene from "A Change of Space" had to be filmed in order for that episode to be hurried through post-production and delivered to the network. The "Ext. Cave," as John and Smith enter, and then the "Int. Cave" as John ties a line to a rock and has Smith lower him into the pit, were filmed. Following this, the company made a move to Stage 11 for scenes staged on the "Ext. Jupiter & Camp" set, including the group looking worried as the Robot tells them that John is possessed by an alien spirit, then the scene from Act IV when Robinson, wearing the mask and dressed as the alien warrior, arrives to tell Will, Penny, Smith and the Robot that he is a friend and they will all leave together in the Jupiter 2. More scenes were planned, but, after filming the cliffhanger for "A Change of Space," Don Richardson was only able to cover four and four-eighths pages from the "Follow the Leader" script. They worked from 8 a.m. to 6:30 p.m., finishing one-quarter of a day behind schedule.

Day 3: Monday, April 4th. The company shot on Stage 11 from 8 a.m. to 6:50 p.m., covering eleven and one-eighth pages from the script and holding at one-quarter of a day behind schedule. Sequences filmed included those at the Garden outside the Jupiter 2, as well as John showing the others his plans for a machine that could refine fuel; and the masked John inviting Will to follow him to some unknown destination in order to see proof that he speaks the truth.

Day 4: Tuesday, April 5th. The company filmed from 8 a.m. to 6:48 p.m. at Stage 11 on the upper deck of the Jupiter 2. Richardson covered nine and two-eighths pages, but fell to a half-day behind schedule.

Day 5: Wednesday, April 6th. Work started on Stage 11, finishing up the scenes needed on the upper deck of the Jupiter 2, followed by a company move to Stage 6 where they would remain for the next two days. Among sets utilized and scenes filmed: "Ext. Bushy Area" as John takes Will to the Promontory, and then at the "Ext. Promontory & Rocky Area," when Will's love allows John to overthrow the intruder's influence. Canto wants to throw Will into the pit, but John reasserts control just in time – after the Act Break, of course. They filmed from 8 a.m. to 6:45 p.m., with Richardson covering nine and two-eighths pages from the script, and holding at one-half of a day behind schedule.

Work on Production Day 4 included the dramatic scenes on the "promontory" where Canto of Quasti plans to send Will to his death. It was one of the most moving scenes in the series between Guy Williams and Billy Mumy.

"All That Glitters" aired on CBS this night.

Day 6: Thursday, April 7th. A great deal of dirty work was covered on the "Ext. Cave" set, as the family tried to dig their way into the cave. The outdoor Moat location would have been an ideal setting for this scene … except that the action was written for night … and there was a great deal of dialogue to be recorded – too much to successfully achieve at this outdoor location after dark.

This was supposed to be the final day of production on "Follow the Leader" … and for the season. However, Don Richardson was three-quarters of a day behind when he finished. The cast and crew had to be held over for a seventh day of filming.

Middle photo: The final scene of the production – and the season – gave us another heartfelt moment between Williams and Mumy.

Day 7: Friday, April 8th. Richardson filmed another ten pages from the script between 8 a.m. and 7:34 p.m. The "Int. Cave" – the tomb of Canto – were covered, as well as sequences on the lower deck of the Jupiter 2. For the scene when John is in the cabin alone and conversing with the alien, it was Richardson's idea to get a shot of the chair to give a sense of where the voice was emitting from. It was not written that way in the script – the voice was all around John. Would this particular alien – a proud warrior -- sit in a chair to have his chat with John? Richardson felt so.

The filming for the First Season was finally over – for the production crew, anyway. Post-production work would continue for another three weeks.

Post-Production:

The episode ran long and there were a few significant cuts of dialogue made during the editing phase.

Act One of the episode opens with Will replacing the Robot's power-pak, and telling him, "This is the second time this week I've recharged your power-pak. You're sure using up a lot of energy." The Robot says: "It is Dr. Smith's fault. He is constantly talking to me." Judy, having heard this while exiting the Jupiter 2 with Don, tells the Robot: "Well, you don't have to reply." Don says, "Judy's right. All you have to do is tune him out by shutting off your audio unit."

The lines that were to follow, and were filmed but left out of the episode, continued with the Robot saying, "I did. Dr. Smith discovered my deception." Judy asked, "What did he do?" The Robot answered, "He made me open my audio unit. I had to listen to him for a full day." Don quipped, "I can think of no greater torture." The Robot bemoaned, "A very trying experience. My computers are still all shook up."

Another cut removed a portion of the scene in which John returns to the Jupiter 2 after being sealed in the cave. As aired, no one in the family, nor Don, wonder how John could have gotten out of the cave when several feet of rock and dirt still blocked the entrance. All we saw was Maureen rush to her husband, embrace him, then ask, "John, are you all right?" The dialogue that followed, but was cut from the episode, went like this:

Robinson (attempting at lightness): "Remind me to get trapped in a cave more often. The homecoming is well worth the trouble." *Judy:* "Are you sure you're all right?" *Robinson:* "Fine. Except for a slight headache." *Don:* "You had us pretty worried there. How did you ever get out?" *Robinson:* "Walked. The entrance was open." *Don (puzzled):* "But it was blocked with ten feet of rock." *Robinson (shrugs):* "The last thing I remember was the cave-in and then falling. A stone must have struck me in the head." *Don:* "That would account for the headache, but not the escape." *Maureen:* "Who cares how he got out. He's back, and that's all I care about." *Don (nods):* "Sure. I was just curious, that's all." *Maureen:* "Well, you can puzzle it out tomorrow. Right now, my husband needs some rest." *Robinson (ruefully):* "I am a little beat. *(rubs back of his head)* I really must have taken a crack on the head. And I had the strangest nightmare while I was unconscious." *Don:* "You'll feel fine in the morning." *Robinson:* "Sure I will. Good night, Don." *Don:* "Sleep well."

WARNING! Do not try this at home! If you take "a crack on the head" by a stone, and feel "beat" after being unconscious, do not sleep. Go to a doctor!

Another scene left on the cutting room floor had Maureen exit John's cabin. Will greets her, asking, "Mom, how is he?" Maureen says, "I gave him a sedative. Your father will be fine. He just needs rest." Will asks, "Do you think it would be all right if I kept him company for awhile?" Maureen hesitates, but, seeing the expectancy in Will's face, relents. This leads to the scene in which Will enters John's cabin, then sits with his father while he falls to sleep.

CBS was happy to see the scene – and the reference to Maureen giving John a sedative – remain on the editing room floor.

The biggest cut was an entire scene in Tag. After John embraced Will while standing on the precipice, the story was intended to continue with the following scene:

101. EXT. ROBINSON CAMP SITE – DAY

MED. SHOT
Robinson and Don stand at table, studying plans that Robinson drew up. Maureen enters with a tray of coffee mugs. The men each take one, go back to studying plans.

ROBINSON
(tossing them down resignedly)
It's no use. All these plans that I drew up when I was under Canto's control make no sense at all to me now.

DON
Too bad. Somewhere in there is the secret that could get us off this planet.

PAN with Maureen as she crosses to where Dr. Smith can be seen by the gardens. The Robot is stretched out on a tilted platform. There is a pillow under his head. Smith sits in a nearby chair, a pad and pencil in his hands. Will and Judy watch.

MAUREEN

(surprised)

Dr. Smith, is there something wrong with the Robot?

SMITH

I don't know yet, Mrs. Robinson. But he has been acting very strangely.

JUDY

He seemed perfectly all right this morning.

SMITH

(with foreboding)

Your father seemed perfectly normal too, young lady. And then...

(snaps his finger)

Off the deep end he went.

WILL

Dr. Smith doesn't believe the alien sprit is gone. He thinks it left Dad and took possession of one of us.

SMITH

And well it may have, William. At this very moment, that monster may be waiting in someone's brain, ready to take over.

WILL

(strongly)

He's not in my brain, Dr. Smith. I'm clean.

Smith studied the boy thoughtfully.

SMITH

We will know the answer to that after you have undergone psycho-analysis, William.

(looks at Robot)

And now if you will excuse me, I must get back to my work.

102. ANOTHER ANGLE – FAVORING SMITH

He takes up the pad, poises his pencil. The others stand watching.

SMITH

Now tell me the first thing you can remember.

ROBOT

It was a warm, spring day. My mother was pushing me down the street in a baby carriage...

The Robot starts that gurgling laughter.

SMITH

Stop laughing, you mechanical manic depressive. This is important! What was the first thing you recall?

ROBOT

The day they installed my memory banks. I remember it well. The mechanic's name was Alfred and he … No, Alfred was the second day. He installed my linear computers.

SMITH

Yes, yes, go on! Concentrate – this could be very important.

Maureen, Judy and Will burst into laughter and we DISSOLVE TO:

CLIFFHANGER SCENE LEADING INTO "ATTACK OF THE MONSTER PLANTS."

That was how the First Season was supposed to end.

With the cuts made, work began on the soundtrack, adding sound effects and music. It was decided that this moody episode was a good fit for the foreboding score from *The Day the Earth Stood Still*, which was heavily sampled here.

The "wish budget" from 20th Century-Fox was $130, 980. The final cost was $135,189.

Release / Reaction:

(CBS premiere broadcast: Wednesday, April 27, 1966)

(Network repeat broadcast: Wednesday, August 17, 1966)

The week the final First Season episode of *Lost in Space* first aired on CBS, Herb Alpert's Tijuana Brass remained the rage in the stores, with *Going Places* topping the Billboard album sales chart. "(You're My) Soul and Inspiration" by the Righteous Brothers was still the song receiving the most airplay on Top 40 radio stations. The next two ranking songs on the charts were "Daydream" by the Lovin' Spoonful and "Bang Bang" by Cher. Where was Sonny? He wrote and produced. *Dr. Zhivago* was still champ in the movie houses. Andy Williams had the cover of *TV Guide*.

The A.C. Nielsen's 30-City Ratings survey for April 27, 1966 estimated the audience percentages this way:

Network / Program:	Rating	Share:
7:30 – 8 p.m.:		
ABC: *Batman*	**24.0**	**41.9%**
CBS: *Lost in Space*	14.4	25.1%
NBC: *The Virginian*	13.6	23.7%
8 – 8:30 p.m.:		

ABC: *The Patty Duke Show*	18.6	31.7%
CBS: *Lost in Space*	**20.2**	**34.4%**
NBC: *The Virginian*	12.0	20.4%

***

This was the last black-and-white episode. The original cliffhanger shown by CBS was the setup for "Attack of the Monster Plants," the first *Lost in Space* episode to be repeated by the network.

When "Follow the Leader" aired again over CBS on August 17, 1966, it had an audience share of 33.5, giving it the second highest Nielsen rating of all the summer repeats (just below the rerun of "The Lost Civilization").

The last black-and-white episode to repeat on CBS was "Wish Upon a Star," on Wednesday, September 7, 1966. The cliffhanger inserted at the end of that episode was for the Second Season kick-off, "Blast Off Into Space." And this cliffhanger was in color!

One reason for the success of *Lost in Space* was a strong sense of family – which existed both in front of and behind the camera. This was evident from Day 1. Pictured: Guy and Janice Williams, with children Steven and Toni (holding hands with Debbie).

41

That's a Wrap!

Irwin Allen invites Billy Mumy to help him cut the first piece from a cake celebrating the sell of *The Time Tunnel* to ABC-TV. Staring in the fall of 1966, Allen would have three hour-long series on the air. No other producer in TV was as busy.

As early as the final days of January, 1966, while "War of the Robots" and "The Magic Mirror" were interwoven into the desperation tactic of a parallel shooting schedule, Irwin Allen's TV agent was putting pressure on CBS to make a decision about renewing *Lost in Space* for a second season. It was clear to all involved that a demanding series of this type needed an earlier pickup from the network than more conventional shows. To avoid a repeat of having to film two episodes simultaneously, Herman Rush believed that *Lost in Space* should get writers working on scripts well in advance of the other shows on the network, and have episodes into production at the earliest possible date.

On January 27, Rush wrote to Allen:

> I have requested immediate pickup from CBS on *Lost in Space* for 1967. They have replied that it will take well into the middle – end of Feb., 1966. I have also requested [money for] ten scripts immediately. [They] promise fast answer.

At this time, *Batman* had only been on the air for four weeks. CBS had yet to determine whether *Lost in Space* was performing well enough against the much-hyped new series to warrant a second season on the network. Within weeks of Herman Rush's letter, however, the renewal had come.

In its February 23, 1966 issue, *Variety* announced that *Lost in Space* would return to CBS in the fall. A week later, on March 2, the trade magazine printed the "first round" draft of all three networks' schedules for the new season. *Lost in Space* would remain in the 7:30 to 8:30 p.m. time slot, against NBC's *The Virginian* and ABC's *Batman* (with a new western series, *The Monroes*, following on ABC at 8 p.m.). The initial order was for sixteen episodes, with CBS reserving the right to order as many as sixteen more. Even with the damage *Batman* had inflicted on *Lost in Space*'s ratings, CBS was not about to ditch a series that lured viewers by the millions back to the network at 8 p.m., as soon as the Caped Crusader cleared the airwaves. From that point on, *Space* won its time slot and delivered a sizable audience to the CBS series which followed – *The Beverly Hillbillies*, *Green Acres* and *The Dick Van Dyke Show*, allowing the Columbia Broadcasting System to claim Most-Watched Network honors for a two-hour block of the Wednesday primetime period. Come 10 p.m. Eastern and Pacific Time, when *The Danny Kaye Show* aired, the mass audience abandoned CBS for the super-hip and much talked about *I Spy*, with its landmark interracial pairing of Robert Culp and Bill Cosby, and location production from around the world. But that was Danny Kaye's problem. He wouldn't have to worry about it for much longer, having been given his pink slip from the network at roughly the same time that *Lost in Space* received its renewal.

On the day the cast and crew of *Lost in Space* finished filming "Follow the Leader," they knew they would be back.

Many would see one another again on May 22 at the Emmy Awards ceremony. With *Voyage to the Bottom of the Sea* and *Lost in Space*, Irwin Allen's technicians and craftsmen garnered seven Emmy nominations. Only one, however, was for *Lost in Space*. L.B. Abbott and Howard Lydecker received a nomination for their photographic effects. They didn't win for *Space* because they were also nominated in the same category for *Voyage* – for which they indeep took home the Emmy.

Between Allen's two series, *Voyage to the Bottom of the Sea* proved the clear favorite at the Emmys. Besides the award won by Abbott and Lydecker, Winton Hoch won an Emmy for Individual Achievement in Cinematography. Others from *Voyage* were nominated: William J. Creber for art direction; Norman Rocket for set decoration; James Baiotto, Robert Belcher and Dick Wornell for film editing; and Don Hall, Don Higgins, Elwell Jackson, and Bob Cornett for sound editing.

During the summer repeat months, the editor of the 'You Said It' letters column in the TV WEEK newspaper supplement printed the following letters:

> I am a girl fourteen years old, and I absolutely love *Lost in Space*. It's the greatest program that ever came out. And your TV WEEK is really something. I used to live in Kansas, where they don't have anything like it out there. I also like it out here better. Now back to *Lost in Space*. Could you please tell me where or help me with this problem: Do you know if "they" have anything out "of" *Lost in Space*? Such as pictures, autographed or something out of them? … Oh, yes, here's a poem of *Lost in Space*:
>
> In space they roam,
> Far, far from home.
> On a planet they stay
> With Dr. Smith in their way.
> They hope they will leave
> For where they have started.
> If they will get enough petroleum to go,
> So they and the planet will be departed.
>
> Gail Mitchell, Pomona.

And, from the producer of a yet-to-be-seen television sci-fi series, telling TV WEEK editor Ernie Kreiling:

> First, I want to thank you very much for running a two-part column on *Star Trek.* We do indeed appreciate the space. However, may I take friendly issue with your preface ... in which you say, "...*Star Trek* strikes TV WEEK as a *Lost in Space* for adults ... " Of all things *Star Trek* is, it is not in any way a *Lost in Space*. I am certain you did not mean this comment to be caustic. However, we are naturally anxious that it not be thought we are a copy of any show. *Star Trek,* in fact, was conceived long before *Lost in Space* and was in script form a year earlier than that show. We do not criticize that series. It does what it sets out to do, but *Star Trek* is as different from *Lost in Space* as *Gunsmoke* is from *Lassie*... Gene Roddenberry, Producer, *Star Trek.*

Kreiling responded:

> Roddenberry's new series, *Star Trek,* premieres on NBC in September. Having seen the pilot film, we are still inclined to think that the audience will make somewhat the same comparisons we did.

A few weeks after "Follow the Leader" first aired on CBS, a syndicated newspaper filler article was picked up by the Pasadena, California *Independent Star-News*, reading, in part:

> Jonathan Harris, admitting to a healthy streak of ham, loves applause as well as any actor. But this season, as television's original special resident villain, he has found something he likes better.... His special appeal was dramatized the other day when Harris dined at a Hollywood restaurant, which happens to be an "in" place for the younger set. A table of teen-agers kept staring, and Harris stared back as only he can. Finally he decided to ignore them. That did it. They began hissing, first almost inaudibly, then building to a crescendo of hisses. Harris rose from his table, faced his audience and hissed back. "They loved it, and so did I," he said, never once questioning that his hissers were ardent fans. Harris knows, as does every villain worth a sneer, that a hiss can be more flattering than the most thunderous applause.

Days later, Harris was profiled in a UPI syndicated article. Clearly enjoying the perks of his newfound status as a network TV series "lead," Harris rejoiced, "I live in Encino on a hilltop overlooking the world.... This is the first time I've ever lived in a house. And I've gone mad about working in the soil. I was born in New York and lived my life in apartments. I hope I never have to move back to New York. And I'll never live in an apartment again."

Harris loved his new kitchen as well. He said, "I adore cooking French and Italian dishes. But I'm also famous for my baked steaks."

His home in Encino was a half-hour drive from the 20th Century-Fox studio in Westwood. Harris added, "I don't get home much before 7:40 in the evening. It just gives me enough time for a couple of glasses of booze, a steak and bed." (JHRDN66)

With the series now on summer hiatus, Harris would have a few months off, with time to garden, cook, enjoy his home, and not have to hurry to bed. A few months would be long enough for Harris's liking. Come June 21, he would be back on the 20th Century-Fox lot doing the thing that he had grown to love most – playing Dr. Smith on *Lost in Space*. And for this new season, the colorful character would be seen in all his glory.

Stay tuned.

And that's a wrap! See you all next season!

Appendix

Season One Episodes

1	1-01	8501	09/15/65	The Reluctant Stowaway
2	1-02	8502	09/22/65	The Derelict
3	1-03	8503	09/29/65	Island in the Sky
4	1-04	8504	10/06/65	There Were Giants in the Earth
5	1-05	8505	10/13/65	The Hungry Sea
6	1-06	8506	10/20/65	Welcome Stranger
7	1-07	8507	10/27/65	My Friend, Mr. Nobody
8	1-08	8508	11/03/65	Invaders from the Fifth Dimension
9	1-09	8509	11/10/65	The Oasis
10	1-10	8510	11/17/65	The Sky is Falling
11	1-11	8512	11/24/65	Wish Upon a Star
12	1-12	8511	12/01/65	The Raft
13	1-13	8513	12/08/65	One of Our Dogs Is Missing
14	1-14	8514	12/15/65	Attack of the Monster Plants
Pre-emption		-	12/22/65	*"National Geographic Special: Miss Goodall and the Wild Chimpanzees"*
15	1-15	8515	12/29/65	Return from Outer Space
Pre-emption		-	01/05/66	*"Young People's Concerts"*
16	1-16	8516	01/12/66	The Keeper (Part 1)
17	1-17	8517	01/19/66	The Keeper (Part 2)
18	1-18	8518	01/26/66	The Sky Pirate
19	1-19	8519	02/02/66	Ghost in Space
20	1-20	8521	02/09/66	War of the Robots
21	1-21	8520	02/16/66	The Magic Mirror
Pre-emption		-	02/23/66	*Entertainment special: "Cinderella"*
22	1-22	8522	03/02/66	The Challenge
23	1-23	8523	03/09/66	The Space Trader
Pre-emption		-	03/23/66	*Pre-empted by Gemini 8 splashdown*
24	1-24	8524	03/16/66	His Majesty Smith
25	1-25	8525	03/30/66	The Space Croppers
26	1-26	8526	04/06/66	All That Glitters
27	1-27	8527	04/13/66	The Lost Civilization
28	1-28	8528	04/20/66	A Change of Space
29	1-29	8529	04/27/66	Follow the Leader
(repeat)	-	-	05/04/66	Attack of the Monster Plants
(repeat)	-	-	05/11/66	Return from Outer Space
(repeat)	-	-	05/18/66	The Keeper, Part 1
(repeat)	-	-	05/25/66	The Keeper, Part 2
(repeat)	-	-	06/06/66	The Sky Pirate
(repeat)	-	-	06/08/66	Ghost in Space
(repeat)	-	-	06/15/66	War of the Robots
(repeat)	-	-	06/22/66	The Magic Mirror
(repeat)	-	-	06/29/66	The Challenge

(repeat)	-	-	07/06/66	The Space Trader
(repeat)	-	-	07/13/66	His Majesty Smith
(repeat)	-	-	07/20/66	The Space Croppers
(repeat)	-	-	07/27/66	All That Glitters
(repeat)	-	-	08/03/66	The Lost Civilization
(repeat)	-	-	08/10/66	A Change of Space
(repeat)	-	-	08/17/66	Follow the Leader
(repeat)	-	-	08/24/66	One of Our Dogs is Missing
(repeat)	-	-	08/31/66	Invaders from the Fifth Dimension
(repeat)	-	-	09/07/66	Wish Upon a Star

Season Two Episodes

30	2-01	9501	09/14/66	Blast Off Into Space
31	2-02	9502	09/21/66	Wild Adventure
32	2-03	9503	09/28/66	The Ghost Planet
33	2-04	9504	10/05/66	Forbidden World
34	2-05	9505	10/12/66	Space Circus
35	2-06	9506	10/19/66	The Prisoners of Space
36	2-07	9507	10/26/66	The Android Machine
37	2-08	9508	11/02/66	The Deadly Games of Gamma 6
38	2-09	9509	11/09/66	The Thief of Outer Space
39	2-10	9510	11/16/66	Curse of Cousin Smith
Pre-emption		-	11/23/66	*"Young People's Concert"*
40	2-11	9512	11/30/66	West of Mars
41	2-12	9513	12/07/66	A Visit to Hades
42	2-13	9514	12/14/66	Wreck of the Robot
43	2-14	9511	12/21/66	The Dream Monster
44	2-15	9515	12/28/66	The Golden Man
44	2-16	9516	01/04/67	The Girl from the Green Dimension
46	2-17	9517	01/11/67	The Questing Beast
Pre-emption		-	01/18/67	*"Cinderella" repeat*
47	2-18	9518	01/25/67	The Toymaker
48	2-19	9519	02/01/67	Mutiny in Space
49	2-20	9520	02/08/67	The Space Vikings
50	2-21	9522	02/15/67	Rocket to Earth
51	2-22	9525	02/22/67	The Cave of the Wizards
52	2-23	9521	03/01/67	Treasure of the Lost Planet
53	2-24	9524	03/08/67	Revolt of the Androids
54	2-25	9526	03/15/67	The Colonists
55	2-26	9527	03/22/67	Trip Through the Robot
56	2-27	9528	03/29/67	The Phantom Family
57	2-28	9523	04/05/67	The Mechanical Men
58	2-29	9529	04/12/67	The Astral Traveler
Pre-emption		-	04/19/67	*"Young People's Concert."*
59	2-30	9530	04/26/67	The Galaxy Gift
(repeat)	-	-	05-03-67	Blast Off Into Space
(repeat)	-	-	05-10-67	Wild Adventure
(repeat)	-	-	05-17-67	The Ghost Planet
(repeat)	-	-	05-24-67	Forbidden World
(repeat)	-	-	05-31-67	Thief of Outer Space
(repeat)	-	-	06-07-67	A Visit to Hades
(repeat)	-	-	06-14-67	Wreck of the Robot
(repeat)	-	-	06-21-67	The Golden Man
(repeat)	-	-	06-28-67	The Girl from the Green Dimension
(repeat)	-	-	07-05-67	West of Mars

(repeat)	-	-	07-12-67	The Space Vikings
(repeat)	-	-	07-19-67	Revolt of the Androids
(repeat)	-	-	07-26-67	Mutiny in Space
(repeat)	-	-	08-02-67	The Cave of the Wizards
(repeat)	-	-	08-09-67	Rocket to Earth
(repeat)	-	-	08-16-67	Trip Through the Robot
(repeat)	-	-	08-23-67	The Phantom Family
(repeat)	-	-	08-30-67	The Mechanical Men

Season Three Episodes

60	3-01	1501	09/06/67	Condemned of Space
61	3-02	1505	09/13/67	Visit to a Hostile Planet
62	3-03	1506	09/20/67	Kidnapped in Space
63	3-04	1502	09/27/67	Hunter's Moon
64	3-05	1503	10/04/67	The Space Primevals
65	3-06	1508	10/11/67	Space Destructors
66	3-07	1509	10/18/67	The Haunted Lighthouse
67	3-08	1507	10/25/67	Flight into the Future
Pre-emption		-	11/01/67	*National Geographic: "Grizzley!"*
68	3-09	1510	11/08/67	Collision of Planets
69	3-10	1511	11/15/67	Space Creature
70	3-11	1504	11/22/67	Deadliest of the Species
71	3-12	1514	11/29/67	A Day at the Zoo
Pre-emption		-	12/06/67	*Entertainment special: "Aladdin"*
72	3-13	1515	12/13/67	Two Weeks in Space
73	3-14	1513	12/20/67	Castles in Space
74	3-15	1512	12/27/67	The Anti-Matter Man
75	3-16	1516	01/03/68	Target Earth
76	3-17	1519	01/10/68	Princess of Space
77	3-18	1518	01/17/68	The Time Merchant
78	3-19	1520	01/24/68	The Promised Planet
79	3-20	1522	01/31/68	Fugitives in Space
Pre-emption		-	02/07/68	*News special: "Destination North Pole"*
80	3-21	1523	02/14/68	Space Beauty
81	3-22	1517	02/21/68	The Flaming Planet
82	3-23	1521	02/28/68	The Great Vegetable Rebellion
83	3-24	1524	03/06/68	Junkyard in Space
(repeat)	-	-	03/13/68	Visit to a Hostile Planet
(repeat)	-	-	03/20/68	Condemned of Space
(repeat)	-	-	03/27/68	Kidnapped in Space
(repeat)	-	-	04/03/68	Hunter's Moon
(repeat)	-	-	04/10/68	The Space Primevals
(repeat)	-	-	04/17/68	Space Destructors
(repeat)	-	-	04/24/68	The Haunted Lighthouse
(repeat)	-	-	05/01/68	Flight into the Future
(repeat)	-	-	05/08/68	Collision of Planets
(repeat)	-	-	05/15/68	Space Creature
(repeat)	-	-	05/22/68	Deadliest of the Species
(repeat)	-	-	05/29/68	A Day at the Zoo
(repeat)	-	-	06/05/68	Two Weeks in Space
(repeat)	-	-	06/12/68	Castles in the Sky
(repeat)	-	-	06/19/68	The Anti-Matter Man
(repeat)	-	-	06/26/68	Target: Earth

(repeat) -	-	07/03/68	Princess of Space
(repeat) -	-	07/10/68	The Flaming Planet
(repeat) -	-	07/17/68	The Great Vegetable Rebellion
(repeat) -	-	07/24/68	The Time Merchant
(repeat) -	-	07/31/68	The Fugitives in Space
Pre-emption	-	08/07/68	*Republican Presidential Convention*
(repeat) -	-	08/14/68	Space Beauty
(repeat) -	-	08/21/68	Junkyard in Space
(repeat) -	-	09/04/68	The Promised Planet
(repeat) -	-	09/11/68	A Visit to Hades (second repeat)

Bibliography

Books:

Billboard Hot 100 Charts, edited by Joel Whitburn (Record Research, Inc., 1990)
Billboard Pop Album Charts, edited by Joel Whitburn (Record Research, Inc., 1993)
Complete Directory to Prime Time Network TV Shows, by Tim Brooks and Earle Marsh (Ballantine Books, May 1979)
Hitchcock's Partner in Suspense: The Life of Screenwriter Charles Bennett, by Charles Bennett (University Press of Kentucky, 2014)
Irwin Allen Scrapbook, Volume Two, Edited by William E. Anchors, Jr. (1992, Alpha Control Press)
Irwin Allen Television Productions, 1964-1970: A Critical History, by Jon Abbott (2006, McFarland & Company, Inc.)
LISFAN ONE, edited by Flint Mitchell (Summer 1981)
LISFAN3, edited by Flint Mitchell (1984)
LISFAN4, edited by Flint Mitchell (1986)
LISFAN5, edited by Flint Mitchell (1988)
LISFAN6, edited by Flint Mitchell (1990)
LISFAN8, edited by Flint Mitchell (1994)
Lost in Space Design: "No Place to Hide," by Robert Rowe (2011, ARA Press)
Lost in Space Encyclopedia II, Edited by Flint Mitchell and William E. Anchors, Jr. (2012, LISFN Press and Alpha Control Press)
Lost in Space Forever, by Joel Eisner and Barry Magen (1992, Windsong Publishing, Inc.)
Lost in Space: The True Story, by Ed Shifres (1996, Windsor House Publishing)
Lost in Space 25th Anniversary Tribute Book, by James Van Hise (1990, Pioneer Books, Inc.)
Rachel Carson: Witness for Nature, by Linda Lear (Mariner Books, 2009)
Science Fiction Television Series, Volume 1, by Mark Phillips and Frank Garcia (1994, McFarland & Co.)
Science Fiction Television Series, Volume 2, by Mark Phillips and Frank Garcia (1996, McFarland & Co.)
Seaview: A 50th Anniversary Tribute to Voyage to the Bottom of the Sea, by William E. Anchors and Frederick Barr (2012, Alpha Control Press)
Special Effects: Wire, Tape and Rubber Band Style, by L.B. Abbott (ASC Press, 1984)
Talks with the Dead, by William Welch (Pinnacle Books, 1975)

Websites:

CinemaRetor.com
Classicfilmtvcafe.com
ChrisPappas.com
Cultbox.co.uk
Diaboliquemagazine.com
Iann.net (IrwinAllen.com)
Latimes.com
Mike'svoyagetothebottomofthesea.zone at vttbolts.com
popcultureaddict.com
sci-fi-online.com
thunderchild.com

Newspaper & Magazine Articles:

Hollywood Feature Syndicates, 1943, "On the Set," with Irwin Allen.

Daily Variety, November 10, 1943, Irwin Allen's radio work discussed in "First Lit Up Preem Since Jap Attack Set for Diary."

Daily Variety, February 2, 1944, "New contracts," Irwin Allen's KMTR radio gossip show renewed for fifth year.

Daily Variety, August 9, 1945, ad for new radio series, *Story of a Star*, with Irwin Allen, on KECA.

Daily Variety, February 8, 1946, blurb concerning Irwin Allen initiating his association with the Orsatti literary agency.

Daily Variety, April 5, 1946, *She-Wolf of London* film review.

Brooklyn Daily Eagle, June 2, 1947, "Richard Basehart, Hedgerow Actor, Now on the First Rung of Film Stardom," by Herbert Cohn.

Daily Variety, July 21, 1947, "Orsatti Agency to NY, London," identifying Allen's title as head of radio department and story editor.

Joplin Globe, November 19, 1947, "Jimmie Fidler in Hollywood."

The Brooklyn Daily Eagle, November 20, 1947, "Being the Rage of Broadway Leaves No Time to Buy Lipstick," by Shiela McKeon.

Syracuse Herald Journal, November 23, 1947, "New Broadway Star," by Jean Meegan.

Los Angeles Times, December 14, 1947, "June Lockhart Considers West Coast Stock, Films," by E.J. Strong.

Charleston Gazette, January 4, 1948, "Critic Applauds Stage Poise of Youthful June Lockhart," by Louella O. Parsons.

Daily Variety, May 3, 1948, "Allen Quits Orsatti for His Own Agency."

The Evening News, May 18. 1948, "Studio Recalls June Lockhart."

Daily Variety, September 13, 1948, "Hollywood Inside," reporting Allen's KLAC *Hollywood Merry-G-Round* radio program going national.

Daily Variety, September 24, 1948, "Television Reviews: *Hollywood Merry-G-Round*."

Variety, September 28, 1948, TV review of *Hollywood Merry-Go-Round*, by "Frce."

Daily Variety, October 15, 1948, "RKO Deal Brewing with Cummings."

Daily Variety, November 22, 1948, "'Only Money' Getting Gun at RKO Today."

TELE-Views magazine, November 26, 1948. "Stars Are Coming Your Way!", by Albert H. Grogan.

Daily Variety, December 17, 1948, "Cummings' Canning 'Money' Under Sked."

Evening Journal. January 4, 1949, "Film Stars Coming Your Way in Effort to Boost Pictures," by Bob Thomas.

Variety, January 26, 1949, "Inside Stuff – Pictures," "It's Only Money" wrapping three days early.

Daily Variety, April 25, 1949, ad for the *Irwin Allen Show* on KLAC-TV.

Daily Variety, May 6, 1949, "RKO Releasing 'Julie'."

Denton Record Chronicle, May 20, 1949, announcement that June Lockhart hasn't worked in a year.

Daily Variety, August 19, 1949, "On the Air Waves," Charles Bennett as guest on *Irwin Allen Show*.

Daily Variety, September 6, 1949, "Short Shorts," Charles Bennett status, "White Rose for Julie."

Daily Variety, October 13, 1949, "E-L Lops Lockhart; Has Only 3 Players."

The Billboard, December 10, 1949, "Irwin Allen's *H'wood Party*" TV review.

Daily Variety, December 21, 1949, "Mitchum, Domergue for 'White Rose'."

Daily Variety, December 27, 1949, "RKO Launching Steady Prod'n Program for the New Year," announcing "A White Rose for Julie," with Cummings, Jr. and Allen to produce.
Daily Variety, January 9, 1950, "'Rose for Julie' Rolling Today at RKO."
Daily Variety, January 26, 1950, "Hollywood Inside," reporting film crew for "White Rose for Julie" appearing on new KLAC-TV program, *Irwin Allen's House Party.*
Daily Variety, March 15, 1950, "Hollywood Inside," regarding efficiency of production on "A White Rose for Julie" (AKA *Where Danger Lives*).
Daily Variety, May 19, 1950, announcement of Allen resuming his TV talk show.
Independent Film Journal, June 1, 1950, *Where Danger Lives* film review.
Daily Variety, June 16, 1950, "TRADE SHOW: *Where Danger Lives*" film review.
Variety, June 21, 1950, TRADE SHOW: *Where Danger Lives* film review, by "Brog."
Variety, November 15, 1950, *Where Danger Lives* full-page ad.
Daily Variety, November 15, 1950, "Just for Variety" by Mike Connolly.
Los Angeles Times, November 17, 1950, *Where Danger Lives* film review, by Philip K. Scheurer.
Los Angeles Daily News, November 17, 1950, *Where Danger Lives* film review, by Darr Smith.
Hollywood Citizen-News, November 17, 1950, *Where Danger Lives* film review, by Lowell F. Redelings.
Los Angeles Examiner, November 17, 1950, *Where Danger Lives* film review, by Louella O. Parsons.
Variety, November 29, 1950, "Picture Grosses" for *Where Danger Lives.*
TIME, December 18, 1950, *Where Danger Lives* film review.
Cue magazine, January 6, 1951, *Where Danger Lives* film review, by Jessie Zunser.
The Terre Haute Tribune, May 20, 1951, RKO press release for *Where Danger Lives.*
Variety, May 23, 1951, "House of Seven Gables" TV review.
Los Angeles Daily News, June 23, 1951, Darr Smith column covering filming of *A Girl in Every Port.*
Variety, November 7, 1951, *Double Dynamite* film review, by "Brog."
Daily Variety, November 7, 1951, *Double Dynamite* film review.
Boxoffice, November 17, 1951, *Double Dynamite* film review.
TIME, November 26, 1951, *Double Dynamite* film review.
The Salt Lake Tribune, December 19, 1951, RKO promotional piece for *Double Dynamite.*
Daily Variety, December 20, 1951, TRADE SHOW: *A Girl in Every Port* film review.
Hollywood Reporter, December 20, 1951, *A Girl in Every Port* film review.
The New York Times, December 26, 1951, *Double Dynamite* film review, by "H.H.T."
Variety, December 26, 1951, *A Girl in Every Port* film review, by "Brog."
Daily Variety, December 27, 1951, "RKO Fuses *Dynamite* with 85G Ad Budget."
Boxoffice, January 5, 1952, TRADE SCREENING: *A Girl in Every Port* film review.
The Salt Lake Tribune, February 1, 1952, RKO press release for *A Girl in Every Port.*
Los Angeles Times, February 4, 1952, *Double Dynamite* review, by Philip K. Scheuer.
Los Angeles Daily News, February 4, 1952, *Double Dynamite* film review, by Howard McClay.
Los Angeles Mirror, February 4, 1952, *Double Dynamite* film review, by Fred W. Fox.
Variety, February 6, 1952, "Jan. Golden Dozen," with *Double Dynamite* at No. 5, and "National Boxoffice Survey" with movie at No. 6.
Cue magazine, February 16, 1952, *A Girl in Every Port* film review.
Beatrice Daily Sun, February 24, 1952, RKO press info for *Double Dynamite.*
Los Angeles Examiner, March 22, 1952, *A Girl in Every Port* review, by Kay Proctor.
Los Angeles Times, March 22, 1952, *A Girl in Every Port* film review, by John L. Scott.
TIME, February 25, 1952, *A Girl in Every Port* film review.
Variety, March 5, 1952, "National Boxoffice Survey," including *A Girl in Every Port.*
Joplin Globe, April 4, 1952, "Jimmie Fidler in Hollywood."

The Holland Evening Sentinel, June 27, 1952, book review of *The Sea Around Us* by Arnold Mulder.
The Edwardsville Intelligencer, October 29, 1952, "*Dear Ruth* at Empress Features June Lockhart."
Daily Variety, October 30, 1952, "*Sea* to Flow in Dec."
Daily Variety, December 17, 1952, "Manpower Problem Besets RKO Board in Revving Prod'n."
Variety, December 31, 1952, "20 for RKO in '53, Tevlin Announces."
Daily Variety, January 14, 1953, *The Sea Around Us* film review, by "Brog."
Boxoffice magazine, January 17, 1953, *The Sea Around Us* film review.
Daily Variety, January 19, 1953, two full-page ads with review blurbs for *The Sea Around Us.*
Daily Variety, January 28, 1953, "Chatter."
Daily Variety, January 29, 1953, "Chatter."
Lubbock Avalanche-Journal, February 15, 1953, UP wire story: "Scientists in 14 Countries Took Pictures for Hollywood Film, *The Sea Around Us*."
United Press syndicated article, April 1953, "Award-Winning Film *Sea* Cost RKO Studio $200,000."
Los Angeles Times, July 3, 1953, *The Sea Around Us* film review.
Variety, July 15, 1953, "National Boxoffice Survey," including *The Sea Around Us.*
Daily Variety, July 20, 1953, "Vincent Price Legit for 'Rangers'."
The Mason City Globe-Gazette, December 22, 1953, RKO press release for *The Sea Around Us.*
Daily Variety, January 13, 1954, "Allen, Wiesenthal Quit RKO."
Variety, February 24, 1954, *Dangerous Mission* film review.
Hollywood Reporter, February 24, 1954, *Dangerous Mission* film review by "M.L."
Boxoffice, February 27, 1954, *Dangerous Mission* film review.
Variety, March 3, 1954, "Irwin Allen's Own Co."
Daily Variety, March 9, 1954, "Indie Haven."
New Yorker, March 13, 1954, *Dangerous Mission* film review, by John McCarten.
Los Angeles Times, March 17, 1954, *Dangerous Mission* review, by Edwin Schallert.
TIME, March 22, 1954, *Dangerous Mission* film review.
Variety, March 31, 1954, "National Boxoffice Survey," including *Dangerous Mission.*
Shamokin News-Dispatch, April 22, 1954, RKO press release for *Dangerous Mission.*
Filmindia, May 1954, *Dangerous Mission* film review.
Daily Variety, September 2, 1954, "Irwin Allen Grooming *Animal* for WB Release."
Variety, December 6, 1954, "Great Talent Makes Great Pictures!"
The New York Times, February 13, 1955, "From Primordial Ooze to Primates," by Oscar Godbout.
Daily Independent Journal, February 19, 1955, "June Lockhart Joins *Who Said That* Panel."
Logansport Pharos-Tribune, April 27, 1955, UP wire story: "Hollywood's Newest Stars Made Entirely of Rubber."
Daily Variety, July 29, 1955, "Can *Animal World* After 18 Mos. In Prod'n."
Los Angeles Times, January 18, 1956, "*Animal World* Producer Faces Big Human Issues."
Variety, March 16, 1956, "Nature Widens '7 Basic Plots'," by Fred Hift.
Los Angeles Times, March 21, 1956, "*Story of Mankind* Put on Full-Scale Footing," by Edwin Schallert.
Daily Variety, April 18, 1956, *The Animal World* film review, by "Whit."
The Hollywood Reporter, April 18, 1956, *The Animal World* review, by James Powers.
Daily Independent Journal, May 18, 1956, United Press wire story: "Science Goes to Hollywood."
Daily Variety, May 29, 1956, "Chatter," reporting Allen's 28-day cross-country tour for *Animal World.*

Cue magazine, June 2, 1956, *The Animal World* film review, by Jesse Zunser.
Los Angeles Times, June 21, 1956, *The Animal World* film review, by Edwin Schallert.
Los Angeles Mirror, June 21, 1956, *The Animal World.*
The Paris News, June 24, 1956, Warner Bros. press release for *The Animal Planet.*
Variety, June 27, 1956, "National Boxoffice Survey," including *The Animal World.*
Films in Review, June/July 1956, *The Animal World* film review.
Variety, July 4, 1956, "National Boxoffice Survey," including *The Animal World.*
The Index-Journal, August 15, 1956, "June Lockhart Shows Hollywood She Is 'The Type,'" by Gene Handsaker.
Los Angeles Times, November 9, 1956, "Groucho, Cesar Romero Aid Story of Mankind," by Philip K. Scheuer.
Los Angeles Times, November 18, 1956, "*Mankind* to Tour History of Humans in Three Hours," by Philip K. Scheuer.
Moberly Monitor-Index, November 26, 1956, "Film Maker Maps Entire Story of Man," by Bob Thomas.
Kalamazoo, Mich. Gazette, December 9, 1956, "Stars in Sky Talk and *The Story of Mankind* Becomes Star-Studded Movie."
The Billboard, February 16, 1957, "*Zorro* to Try Out Cliff-Hanger Idea."
Daily Variety, March 4, 1957, "Just for Variety," by Army Archerd, reporting that Allen owns 25% of *The Story of Mankind.* And unlikely to renew Warners' pact.
New York Herald Tribune, March 10, 1957, "*Story of Mankind* Filmed as a Trial," by Thomas Wood.
Los Angeles Times, March 19, 1957, "Hedda Hopper: "June Lockhart's TV Role Wins Her Film."
Newsweek, May 6, 1957, "Movies: Everything, Then Some."
The Courier News, May 20, 1957, "Woman TV Commentators? Why Not, Says June Lockhart," by Charles Mercer.
Daily Variety, May 22, 1957, "Just for Variety," by Army Archerd on preview of *The Story of Mankind.*
Variety, July 3, 1957, "Irwin Allen Doing a Todd with 62 Speaking Stars for *The Big Circus.*"
Daily Variety, October 8, 1957, "WB *Story* Wins A-Bomb Pix Race, Declares Allen."
Variety, October 9, 1957, "Irwin Allen's Slants on Stars and Trademark Value with Age."
Daily Variety, October 9, 1957, *The Danny Thomas Show* review, by "Daku."
Los Angeles Times, October 10, 1957, "*Zorro* Will Take Viewers Back to Pueblo La Reina," by Walter Ames.
Daily Variety, October 14, 1957, *Zorro* TV review, by "Daku."
Daily Variety, October 14, 1957, "Light and Airy," by Jack Hellamn; *Zorro* ratings.
The Billboard, October 14, 1957, *Zorro* TV review, and "ABC Makes Gains 8-9 on Thursdays."
Daily Variety, October 21, 1957, "Light and Airy," by Jack Hellamn; *Zorro* TV ratings.
Daily Variety, October 23, 1957, "Top 20 New shows Based on Trendix Ratings for Oct. 4-10."
Variety, October 23, 1957, "Getcha Latest Trendix Figures," with *Zorro* TV ratings.
Daily Variety, October 23, 1957, *The Story of Mankind* film review.
The Hollywood Reporter, October 23, 1957, *The Story of Mankind* film review, by James Powers.
The Independent Film Journal, October 26, 1957, *The Story of Mankind* film review.
Daily Variety, October 28, 1957, "Light and Airy," by Jack Hellamn; *Zorro* TV ratings.
Variety, November 6, 1957, "National Boxoffice Survey," with *The Story of Man.*
Cue magazine, November 9, 1957, *The Story of Mankind* film review, by Jesse Zunser.
Los Angeles Times, November 10, 1957, "June Lockhart Moves Ahead," by Edwin Schallert.
Daily Variety, November 11, 1957, "Light and Airy," by Jack Hellamn; *Zorro* ratings.
Variety, November 13, 1957, "National Boxoffice Survey," with *The Story of Man.*

Los Angeles Mirror-News, November 14, 1957, *The Story of Man* film review, by Dick Williams.
Los Angeles Times, November 14, 1957, *The Story of Mankind* film review, by Philip K. Scheuer.
Los Angeles Examiner, November 14, 1957, *The Story of Mankind* film review, by S.A. Desick.
The Wisconsin Jewish Chronicle, November 15, 1957, review of *The Story of Mankind*, by Hubert C. Luft.
New Yorker, November 16, 1957, *The Story of Man* film review.
The Bridgeport Post, November 17, 1957, Warner Bros. press release for *The Story of Mankind.*
Newsweek, November 18, 1957, *The Story of Man* film review.
Daily Variety, December 4, 1957, "Thomas Tops Monday's Trendex."
Broadcasting, December 16, 1957, *Zorro* TV review.
The Amarillo Globe-Times, December 18, 1957, review of *The Story of Mankind* by Bill McReynolds.
Variety, February 19, 1958, *Brothers Karamazov* film review, by "Pow."
Variety, March 5, 1958, "CITY-BY-CITY PROGRAM CHART," with *Zorro* TV rating.
Daily Variety, May 6, 1958, "Leachman No 2nd Fiddle to Canine, Boy; Quits *Lassie.*
Los Angeles Times, May 18, 1958, "WHHHTT, WHHHTT, WHHHTT! Williams Making Mark (Z) as Zorro," by Boots Lebaron.
Daily Variety, June 3, 1958, "On All Channels," by Dave Kaufman.
Daily Variety, September 9, 1958, *Lassie* TV review, by "Chan."
Daily Variety, October 13, 1958, "Light and Airy," by Jack Hellamn; *Zorro* TV ratings.
Variety, October 15, 1958, *Zorro* TV review, by "Les."
Daily Variety, November 3, 1958, "Light and Airy," by Jack Hellamn; *Zorro* TV ratings.
Variety, November 19, 1958, "CITY-BY-CITY PROGRAM CHART," with *Zorro* rating.
Daily Variety, November 25, 1958, "Light and Airy," by Jack Hellamn, regarding Guy Williams' merchandising deal with Disney.
Variety, December 17, 1958, "CITY-BY-CITY PROGRAM CHART," with *Zorro* TV rating.
Daily Variety, December 1, 1958, "Light and Airy," by Jack Hellamn, about Williams appearance at Disneyland.
Variety, December 10, 1958, "Allen's *Circus* Becomes Allied Artists Partnership."
Corsicana Daily Sun, December 30, 1958, "June Lockhart Without Fears of Being typed," by Charles Mercer.
Daily Variety, January 2, 1959, "Light and Airy," by Jack Hellamn; Williams' fan mail.
New York Times, January 11, 1959, "*Big Circus* Troupe Works to Equal Bit Top's Authenticity and Color," by Thomas M. Pryor.
Daily Variety, January 12, 1959, "Light and Airy," by Jack Hellamn; *Zorro* TV ratings.
Variety, January 28, 1959, "CITY-BY-CITY PROGRAM CHART," with *Zorro* TV rating.
Variety, February 18, 1959, "CITY-BY-CITY PROGRAM CHART," with *Zorro* TV rating.
Los Angeles Times, February 27, 1959, "*The Big Circus* Set Magnificent," by Hedda Hopper.
Monroe Evening Times, March 14, 1959, "June Lockhart Keeps Tradition," by Hal Boyle.
Variety, April 15, 1959, "Best Foods May Get ABC Bounce."
Daily Variety, April 20, 1959, "Light and Airy," by Jack Hellamn; *Zorro* TV ratings.
Anderson Daily Bulletin, April 20, 1959, Louella O. Parson's column, regarding David Nelson in *The Big Circus.*
Daily Variety, April 24, 1959, "Sponsors Balk Over *Zorro*' Price Hike."
Variety, May 6, 1959, "CITY-BY-CITY PROGRAM CHART," with *Zorro* and *Lassie* TV rating.
Los Angeles Times, May 10, 1959, "Romping Young Publicists Beat the Drums for Zorro," by Carl Swenson.
Daily Variety, May 20, 1959, "ABC Says Tag Too High So Disney Kills *Zorro.*"

Hollywood Reporter, May 26, 1959, "Irwin Allen Will Remake A. Conan Doyle's *Lost World* on $3 Million Budget in Todd-AO."

The Billboard, June 8, 1959, "Ft. Smith Rodeo, Zorro Top Record."

Daily Variety, June 26, 1959, "Sound and Pictures," by Bob Chandler.

Rocky Mountain News, June 30, 1959, "Producer 'Careful Shopper.'"

Denver Post, July 1, 1959, "Producer Allen Beats Drum for His Circus Extravaganza," by Larry Tajiri.

Daily Variety, July 2, 1959, Disney Antitrust Suit Vs. ABC," reporting battle over *Zorro*.

Broadcasting. July 6, 1959, "ABC-TV, Disney Go to Court."

Variety, July 8, 1959, *The Big Circus* film review.

The New York Times, July 18, 1959, *The Big Circus* film review, by Bosley Crowther.

The Paris News, July 19, 1959, press release for *The Big Circus*.

Variety, July 22, 1959, "National Boxoffice Survey," including *The Big Circus*.

Variety, July 22, 1959, "National Boxoffice Survey," including *The Big Circus*.

Variety, July 29, 1959, "TELEPOSE CITY-BY-CITY PROGRAM CHART," with *Zorro* rating.

TIME, August 3, 1959, *The Big Circus* film review.

The Corpus Christi Caller-Times, August 4, 1959, with syndicated *Chicago Daily News* story, "Advice to Would-Be Actresses: 'Stay Home,'" by Pat Dalton.

Daily Variety, August 5, 1959, "20th Mulls Buy Up of *Zorro* Williams Pact from Disney."

Los Angeles Times, August 6, 1959, *The Big Circus* film review, by Philip K. Scheuer.

Daily Variety, August 14, 1959, "Record Teleseries Productions Here Will Top 100 Next Week," by Larry Tubelle.

Daily Variety, October 1, 1959, "Irwin Allen Set to Film Lost World for 20th Release."

Daily Variety, October 6, 1959, *Five Fingers* TV review, by "Tube."

Variety, October 7, 1959, *Five Fingers* TV review, by "Trau."

Daily Variety, October 19, 1959, "Light and Airy," by Jack Hellman," ratings for *Johnny Ringo*.

Daily Variety, October 26, 1959, "Light and Airy," by Jack Hellman," ratings for *Johnny Ringo*.

Daily Variety, October 27, 1959, "The Weekend Arbitrex."

Daily Variety, October 28, 1959, "*Zorro* Feature In Offing As 3 Segs Spliced Together."

Daily Variety, November 6, 1959, "Kiddin' Kids Takes More Coin These Days, Sez Irwin Allen," by Ron Silverman.

Daily Variety, November 9, 1959, "TV Ratings" for *Johnny Ringo*.

Daily Variety, January 5, 1960, "*Ringo* Best, Sez *Fast Draw* Survey."

Daily Variety, February 3, 1960, "Out of the Tube," by Larry Tubelle, on Guy Williams.

Daily Variety, February 8, 1960, "Untouchables Is Just That In Rates," ratings for *Johnny Ringo*.

Los Angeles Times, May 11, 1960, "Disney Will Expand *Zorro*," by Philip K. Scheuer.

TV Month, June 1960, article concerning David and Ricky Nelson's flying trapeze act, inspired by *The Big Circus*.

El Paso Herald Post, June 11, 1960, "Zorro Appears Here in World Premier Movie," by Barbara Causey.

Austin Summer Texan, June 14, 1960, Zorro to Appear in Austin."

San Antonio Light, June 14, 1960, "Star Will Appear on Stage."

Variety, June 22, 1960, "Picture Grosses," tracking *The Sign of Zorro*.

Daily Variety, June 28, 1960, "In L.A. Film B.O. Upbeat," with *The Sign of Zorro*grosses.

Variety, June 29, 1960, "Picture Grosses," tracking *The Sign of Zorro*.

The Hollywood Reporter, July 1, 1960, *The Lost World* film review, by James Powers.

The Film Daily, July 1, 1960, *The Lost World* film review, by Mandel Herbstman.

Variety, July 6, 1960, "Better if Producer Directs, Too – Allen,' regarding *The Lost Wolds*, and film review of *The Lost World*, by "Tube."

Motion Picture Herald, July 9, 1960, *The Lost World* film review.
Los Angeles Times, July 14, 1960, "*Lost World* Notable for Special Effects," by John L. Scott.
Hollywood Citizen News, July 14, 1960, *The Lost World* review, by Lowell E. Redelings.
Los Angeles Mirror News, July 14, 1960, *The Lost World* review, by Margaret Harford.
Los Angeles Examiner, July 14, 1960, *The Lost World* film review, by Ruth Waterbury.
The New York Times, July 14, 1960, *The Lost World* film review, by A.H. Weiler.
Cue magazine, July 16, 1960, *The Lost World* film review.
TIME, July 18, 1960, *The Lost World* film review.
Variety, August 3, 1960, "National Boxoffice Survey, including *The Lost World.*
Arlington Heights Herald, August 4, 1960, review of *The Lost World* by Jim Phillips.
Variety, August 10, 1960, "National Boxoffice Survey, including *The Lost World.*
Variety, August 17, 1960, "National Boxoffice Survey, including *The Lost World.*
The Anniston Star, August 28, 1960, 20th Century-Fox press release for *The Lost World.*
Daily Variety, September 19, 1960, "Telepix Reviews," for *The Detectives*, by "Helm."
Variety, September 21, 1960, review of *The Detective*, by "Art."
Shamokian News-Dispatch, September 22, 1960, "June Lockhart, Star of *Lassie*, Leads Double Life," by Vernon Scott.
Variety, September 28, 1960, "Picture Grosses," tracking *The Sign of Zorro.*
Hollywood Reporter, October 5, 1960, "Irwin Allen Aims for Program of Features and TV at 20th."
Variety, October 5, 1960, *Adventures in Paradise* TV review, by "Bill."
Daily Variety, October 11, 1960, "Dinah Shore and Jackie Gleason Shows Tie," with ratings for *The Detectives.*
Variety, October 12, 1960, "Irwin Allen in $9-Mil Program."
Lubbock Avalanche-Journal, November 1, 1960, Louella O. Parsons announced *Voyage to the Bottom of the Sea* as Allen's next movie for Fox.
The Daily Herald, December 12, 1960, preview of "The Mormon" on *Zane Grey Theatre.*
Variety, November 9, 1960, "Picture Grosses," tracking *The Sign of Zorro.*
Daily Variety, November 20, 1960, "Ax Threatens More Than Half 90 TV Shows," with ratings for *The Detectives.*
Daily Variety, December 30, 1960, *How to Make a Man* stage review, by "Tew."
Tucson Daily Citizen, February 11, 1961, "He Came and Conquered," by Micheline Keating.
The Daily Herald, April 3, 1961, Outlaws' episode "Outrage at Pawnee Bend" TV preview.
Daily Variety, April 10, 1961, "Reach *Bottom*; 20th Spends 860G on Special Effects."
Press Telegram, June 2, 1961, "Found: A Modest Actor! Goddard – Still Learning," by Terry Vernon.
Boxoffice, June 5, 1961, "Exhibitors to Meet Allen Promoting His *Voyage*."
Variety, June 7, 1961, "Irwin Allen's Road: Embassy vs. 20th."
The Evening Bulletin, June 13, 1961, "Director Must Rise Early for Today's Movies," by Rex Polier.
The Boston Globe, June 14, 1961, "Producer's Nightmare Science-Fiction Epic," by Kevin Kelly.
Quincy Patriot Ledger, June 15, 1961, "*Bottom of Sea* Science Thriller, by Mabelle Fullerton.
Los Angeles Times, June 18, 1961, *Voyage to the Bottom of the Sea* review, by Philip K. Scheuer.
The Charlotte News, June 21, 1961, "Pressure's On in Hollywood," by Brooks Yarborough.
Chicago's American, June 21, 1961, "Irwin Allen Wooing Girl Movie Patrons," by Ann Masters.
Variety, June 21, 1961, "Allen's Round Fugures; $250,000 for TV Plugs of 20th's *Bottom Sea*."
Christian Science Monitor, June 1961, "Technicolor Visions Mean Business to Irwin Allen," by Nora E. Taylor.

The Hollywood Reporter, June 23, 1961, *Voyage to the Bottom to the Sea* film review, by James Powers.
Motion Picture Herald, June 24, 1961, *Voyage to the Bottom of the Sea* film review.
Boxoffice magazine, June 26, 1961, *Voyage to the Bottom of the Sea* film review.
Los Angeles Mirror, July 27, 1961, *Voyage to the Bottom of the Sea* review, by Dick Williams.
Los Angeles Times, June 28, 1961, "Irwin Allen Signs Multiple Film Deal."
Los Angeles Times, July 28, 1961, *Voyage to the Bottom of the Sea* film review, by John L. Scott.
Variety, June 28, 1961, *Voyage to the Bottom of the Sea* film review, by "Tube."
Motion Picture Limelight, June 29, 1961, *Voyage to the Bottom of the Sea* film review, by Jack Moffitt.
The Hollywood Diary, July 1, 1961, *Voyage to the Bottom of the Sea* film review, by Jonah M. Ruddy.
Variety, July 19, 1961, "National Boxoffice Survey," *Voyage to the Bottom of the Sea.*
The New York Times, July 20, 1961, *Voyage to the Bottom of the Sea* film review, by Howard Thompson.
TIME, July 21, 1961, *Voyage to the Bottom of the Sea* film review.
Variety, July 26, 1961, "National Boxoffice Survey," *Voyage to the Bottom of the Sea.*
Hollywood Citizen-News, July 27, 1961, *Voyage to the Bottom of the Sea* film review, by Lowell E. Redeling.
The Galveston Daily News, July 30, 1961, 20th Century-Fox press release for *Voyage to the Bottom of the Sea* feature film.
Variety, August 2, 1961, "National Boxoffice Survey," *Voyage to the Bottom of the Sea.*
Boxoffice, August 6, 1962, *Two Weeks in a Balloon* film review.
The Plain Speaker, August 4, 1961, "Hollywood Today!" by Erskine Johnson.
Variety, August 9, 1961, "National Boxoffice Survey," *Voyage to the Bottom of the Sea.*
Daily Variety, August 11, 1961, "*Bottom* Hits Top B.O."
Variety, August 16, 1961, *Marines, Let's Go* film review.
Variety, August 16, 1961, "National Boxoffice Survey," *Voyage to the Bottom of the Sea.*
Variety, August 23, 1961, "National Boxoffice Survey," *Voyage to the Bottom of the Sea.*
Daily Variety, September 12, 1961, *Lassie* TV review, by "Helm."
Variety, October 4, 1961, "Television Reviews," including *Robert Taylor's The Detectives.*
Daily Variety, November 22, 1961, TV ratings for *Robert Taylor's Detectives.*
The Times Recorder, November 26, 1961, "There's Only One Lassie But He Has Three Aides."
Sunday Gazette-Mail, December 3, 1961, "June Lockhart Happy in Secondary Role."
Long Beach Independent Press Telegram, March 11, 1962, "Ex-Zorro TV Duels Again," by Rob Thomas.
Los Angeles Times, March 20, 1962, "June Lockhart Finds *Lassie* a Belssing," by Hedda Hopper.
Daily Variety, March 22, 1962, "Bricken Talks Deal 'On Bitter' Fruit, Filming with 20th," mentioning *White Crocus* novel by Peter Packer.
Los Angeles Times, April 24, 1962, *Five Weeks in a Balloon* film review, by Margaret Harford.
Variety, May 2, 1962, "Status of the Telefilm Majors."
Daily Variety, May 2, 1962, *Lad: A Dog* film review, by "Tube."
Los Angeles Times, June 29, 1962, *Captain Sinbad* film review.
Daily Variety, July 24, 1962, "Allen's *Balloon* Campaign Follows *Voyage* Pattern.
The Hollywood Reporter, August 13, 1962, *Five Weeks in a Balloon* film review.
The Film Daily, August 14, 1962, *Five Weeks in a Balloon* film review.
Variety, August 15, 1962, *Five Weeks in a Balloon* film review, by "Tube."
Variety, August 15, 1962, "National Boxoffice Survey," with *Five Weeks in a Balloon.*

Cue, August 18, 1962, *Five Weeks in a Balloon* film review.
Variety, August 22, 1962, "National Boxoffice Survey," with *Five Weeks in a Balloon.*
Los Angeles Herald-Examiner, August 23, 1962, *Five Weeks in a Balloon* film review, by Harrison Carroll.
Hollywood Citizen-News, August 23, 1962, *Five Weeks in a Balloon* review, by Hazel Flynn.
Variety, August 29, 1962, "National Boxoffice Survey," with *Five Weeks in a Balloon.*
TIME, August 31, 1962, *Five Weeks in a Balloon* film review.
Variety, September 5, 1962, "National Boxoffice Survey," with *Five Weeks in a Balloon.*
Daily Variety, September 10, 1962, *Damon and Pythias* film review, by "Pit."
The Daily Herald [Provo, Utah], September 23, 1962, 20th Century-Fox press release for *Five Weeks in a Balloon.*
Cedar Rapids Gazette, September 23, 1962, "Marta Kristen: Disney's Newest Discovery," by Lloyd Shearer.
Boxoffice magazine, "October 15, 1962, "*Five Weeks in a Balloon* Wins Sept. Blue Ribbon Award," by Velma West Sykes.
Big Springs Daily Herald, October 28, 1962, *Damon and Pythias* press release.
Variety, April 17, 1963, "Foreign Television Reviews," with review of *The Third Man*, by "Otta."
Daily Variety, May 22, 1963" *Savage Sam* film review, by "Tube."
Los Angeles Times, July 4, 1963, "Newcomer Sacrifices for Her Art."
Los Angeles Times, July 13, 1963, "Marta Kristen's Life Like a movie," by Art Seidenbaum.
Variety, August 21, 1963, "Irwin Allen, 20th in *Voyage* Series."
Daily Variety, September 23, 1963, "Just for Variety," by Army Archerd; Walter Pigeon in TV *Voyage.*
Daily Variety, September 25, 1963, "Maggie Brown" TV pilot review, by "Tube."
Variety, September 25, 1963, *The Bill Dana Show* TV review, by "Herm."
The Gettysburg Times, September 28, 1963, "Busy Sunday" for Jonathan Harris.
Daily Variety, October 1, 1963, *Lassie* TV review, by "Helm."
Variety, October 2, 1963, TV ratings for *Lassie* and *The Bill Dana Show.*
Variety, October 9, 1963, TV ratings for *Lassie* and *The Bill Dana Show.*
Great Bend Daily Tribune, October 20, 1963, *Captain Sinbad* press release.
Daily Variety, October 30, 1964, "*Voyage* Starts Nov. 18."
Daily Variety, November 11, 1963, "20th-TV Rolling 3 Pilots This Month."
Broadcasting, November 18, 1963, "20th Century-Fox Starts Work on Pilots."
Los Angeles Times, November 23, 1963, "Four Feet in the Morning" review, by Cecil Smith.
Daily Variety, November 26, 1963, "Four Feet in the Morning" TV review by "Tube."
Daily Variety, December 20, 1963, "5 Nations South of Border to Co-op with Lubin in Biopicturing Bolivar," mentioning Peter Packer novel *Love Thieves.*
The Manhattan Mercury, January 10, 1964, "Critics Examine Programs," with *Bill Dana Show* TV review.
Variety, April 15, 1964, "No Tint for 20th's *Bottom of the Sea.*"
Provo Daily Herald, April 20, 1964, preview for "The Senior Prom" episode of *Mr. Novak.*
Daily Variety, May 5, 1964, "On All Channels: Irwin Allen 20-Year TVet," by Dave Kaufman.
Los Angeles Times, May 24, 1964, "June Fleas *Lassie* Show," by Aleene MacMinn.
Sunday Gazette-Mail, May 24, 1964, "June Lockhart Seeks Sexy Role," by Charles Wilbeck.
Bristol Daily-Courier, May 30, 1964, "Actor Bets Future on New Series."
Lebanon Daily News, June 6, 1964, "Freckled American Boy, 10, Plays Love Scene with Bardot," by Vernon Scott.
Los Angeles Times, June 28, 1964, "Fox Suddenly Jumps into the Series Picture," by Cecil Smith.
Abilene Reporter News, July 7, 1964, "Submarine Rates as Scene-Stealer," by Erskine Johnson.

Daily Variety, July 9, 1964, "Light and Airy," by Jack Hellman, on Allen and *Voyage*.
The Indiana Gazette, August 14, 1964, AP article on filming the *Voyage* miniatures, by Cynthia Lowry.
Daily Variety, August 14, 1964, "Buck Houghton Joins 20th-TV."
Los Angeles Times, August 23, 1964, "June Sitting Pretty On TV Panel Shows," by Hal Humphrey.
Valley Morning Star, August 27, 1964, "In Hollywood," syndicated column by Hedda Hopper.
Biddeford-Saco Journal, September 12, 1964, ABC press release for *Voyage* premiere episode "Eleven Days to Zero."
Tucson Daily Citizen, September 14, 1964, "TV Key" preview of "Eleven Days to Zero."
Lima News, September 14, 1964, "TV Scout" review of "Eleven Days to Zero."
Warren Times Mirror, September 15, 1964, review of "Eleven Days to Zero" by Cynthia Lowry.
The San Mateo Times, September 15, 1964, "TV Screening," by Bob Foster.
Variety, September 16, 1964, *Voyage to the Bottom of the Sea* TV review, by "Pit."
Daily Variety, September 16, 1964, *Voyage to the Bottom of the Sea* TV review, by "Daku."
Petersburg Progress Index, September 17, 1964, "*Voyage* Actors Upstaged by Sub."
Long Beach Press Telegram, September 21, 1964, "Tele-Vues" review of "Eleven Days to Zero," by Terry Vernon.
Lake Charles American-Press, September 21, 1964, "TV Key" preview of *Voyage* episode "City Beneath the Sea."
San Antonio Express, September 21, 1964, "TV Scout" review of "City Beneath the Sea."
Monessen Valley Independent, September 28, 1964, "TV Scout" review of *Voyage* episode "The Fear-Makers."
The Daily Reporter, September 28, 1964, "TV Key" preview of "The Fear-Makers."
Cullman Times, October 4, 1964, "TV Tonight" preview of *Voyage*'s "The Mist of Silence."
Tucson Daily Citizen, October 5, 1964, "TV Key Preview" review of *Voyage* episode "The Mist of Silence."
Broadcasting, October 12, 1964, TV ratings with *Voyage* at No. 16.
Doylestown Intelligence, October 12, 1964, "TV Key Preview" review of "The Price of Doom."
Daily Variety, October 15, 1964, "Just for Variety," by Army Archerd; Goddard wants out of *Many Happy Returns*.
The Times Record, October 17, 1964, "$1,000,000 Set Enjoyed in *Voyage*."
Cullman Times, October 18, 1964, *Voyage* episode "The Sky is Falling" preview, by Bill Shelton.
Tucson Daily Citizen, October 19, 1964, "TV Key Preview" review of "The Sky is Falling."
Monessen Valley Independent, October 19, 1964, "TV Scout" review of "The Sky is Falling."
Beckley Post-Herald and *The Raleigh Register*, October 24, 1964, review of *Voyage* episode "Turn Back the Clock."
Waterloo Daily Courier, October 25, 1964, "TV Keynotes: High Adventure Series," by Charles Witbeck.
Monessen Valley Independent, October 26, 1964, "TV Key Previews" review of "Turn Back the Clock."
The Daily Reporter, October 26, 1964, "TV Previews" review of "Turn Back the Clock."
Variety, October 28, 1964, "Nielsen Top 50" ratings, with *Many Happy Returns* and *Voyage to the Bottom of the Sea*.
The Kansas City Times, November 7, 1964, "Letters" section, concerning *Voyage* episode "Turn Back the Clock" using sequences from *The Lost World*.
Daily Variety, November 11, 1964, announcement that *Voyage* is picked up for full season.
Biddeford Journal, November 14, 1964, "Jonathan Harris is Correct Manager."
TV Guide, November 14, 1964, Letters" about *Voyage* taking footage from *The Lost World*.

Greenville Delta Democrat, November 15, 1965, UPI story: "TV Ratings Executioners."
Daily Variety, November 17, 1964, "Just for Variety," by Army Archerd; Goddard released from *Many Happy Returns*.
The North Adams Transcript, November 19, 1964, Erkine Johnson column, with a letter concerning *Voyage*'s "Turn Back the Clock" recycling from *The Lost World*.
Variety, November 25, 1964, "20th's 5 New Shows Rack Up O'seas Sales" and "New Nielsen: Top 20."
Variety, December 9, 1964, "*Lost in Space* as CBS-TV Entry."
TV Guide, December 12, 1964, "Letters" section, "*Outer Limits* Out" and "Weekly Panic."
Winona Daily News, December 20, 1964, "TV Key" Mailbag.
Broadcasting, December 28, 1964, "Entertainment: Goal and Glory of William Self."
Daily Variety, December 30, 1964, "Angela Cartwright into *Space* at 20th."
Portsmouth Times, January 4, 1964, "*Bonanza* Tops List of TV's '10 Worst,' by Hal Humphrey.
Daily Variety, January 4, 1965, "Five Latch *Lost* Roles."
The Bridgeport Post, January 7, 1965, "TV Key Mailbag."
The Fresno Bee / The Republican, January 10, 1965, "*Voyage* Series is British Hit."
Idaho State Journal, January 12, 1965, AP story, "Monday Night TV Watchers Face Decision," by Cynthia Lowry.
Tucson Daily Citizen, January 18, 1965, "TV Key" review of *Voyage* episode "Doomsday."
The News-Palladium, January 19, 1965, "Hollywood Today!," by Dick Kleiner.
Bakersfield Californian, January 23, 1965, "Atom Sub Leads Fan Mail Race."
TV Guide, January 30, 1965, "Down to the Sea in a Hollywood Moat."
Monessen Valley Independent, February 1, 1965, "TV Key Preview" review of *Voyage* episode "The Indestructible Man."
Redlands Daily Facts, February 1, 1965, "Show Beat," by Dick Kleiner.
Variety, February 10, 1965, "1965-66 Networks' Checkerboard (First Draft)," and "*Variety*-ARB Syndication Chart."
Variety, February 24, 1965, "1965-66 Networks' Checkerboard (Semi-Finals)."
Daily Variety, February 24, 1965, "Nets Neck 'n' Neck in Tightest Nielsen Competish Ever."
Daily Variety, March 4, 1965, "*Lost in Space* Refound by CBS."
The Fresno Bee/The Republican, March 7, 1965, "*Voyage* Series Goes Over Big On Japan TV."
Variety, March 10, 1965, "It's Paley & Schneider & Dann: Troika Revamps CBS' Fall Sked."
Long Beach Press Telegram, March 29, 1965, "Tele-Vues," by Terry Vernon.
Variety, March 31, 1965, "1965-66 Networks' Checkerboard."
Abilene Reporter-News, April 8, 1965, "Ask TV Scout" letters column about *Outer Limits* cancelled, and *Voyage* being only sci-fi non network TV, but pilots having been filmed for *Lost in Space* and *Star Trek*.
Daily Variety, April 7, 1965, "Houghton on *Space*."
The Bridgeport Post, April 7, 1965, "TV Key Mailbag."
Variety, April 7, 1965, *Beach Blanket Bingo* film review by "Dale."
Los Angeles Times, April 9, 1965, *Beach Blanket Bingo* film review, by Margaret Harford.
TV Guide, May 1, 1965, *Voyage* series review by Cleveland Amory.
Daily Variety, May 4, 1965, "Wilson *Lost* Story Ed."
Variety, May 13, 1964, "*Variety*-ARB Syndicated Chart."
Daily Variety, June 1, 1965, "On All Channels: Allen's 1997 *Space* Shot 1st Primetime Cliffhanger," by Dave Kaufman.
Daily Variety, June 3, 1965, "Just for Variety," by Army Archerd, reporting *Lost in Space* "space-walk."
Daily Variety, June 15, 1965, "Set 6 *Space* Scribes."

TV Guide, June 19, 1965, "Well, Of Course, It Isn't Exactly Hamlet...," by Marian Dern.
Daily Variety, June 23, 1965, Irwin Allen casting Long John Silver villain role.
Daily Variety, July 7, 1965, "Harris into *Space*."
Daily Variety, July 16, 1965, "Cartwright into *Space*."
New Castle News, July 22, 1965, UPI story, "June Will Tackle New Role on TV," by Vernon Scott.
Variety, July 29, 1965, "The Season's Nielsen Wrap-up."
New York Daily News, August 3, 1965, "CBS Cliff-Hanger Solves World Population Crises," by Kay Gardella.
Bristol Daily Courier, August 7, 1965, "*Lost in Space*: Fun and Fantasy," by Don Royal.
North Adams Transcript, August 21, 1965, "Wonderful Swimmer."
Courier Times, August 21, 1965, syndicated story: "New Show 'Wired' to Space Age," by Erskine Johnson.
Las Vegas Review Journal, cover of *The Nevadan TV Week*, August 29, 1965, showing Cyclops creature attacking chariot.
Variety, September 1, 1965, "TV's Daytime Rises & Shines," by Bill Greeley) with price tags of four most expensive pilot films in TV history).
Galveston Daily News, September 3, 1965, "Guy Williams in *Space* for New Series on TV."
Syracuse Herald-American, September 5, 1965, "Cliffhangers Are in Vogue on Television This Season," by Joan E. Vadeboncoeur.
Huntington Daily News, September 10, 1965, "Notes for Watching Television" regarding Debbie the Chimpanzee.
TV Guide, September 11, 1965, *Lost in Space* series description.
Emporia Gazette, September 15, 1965, "A Season of Duds," by Richard K. Doan.
Kokomo Morning Times, September 15, 1965, *Lost in Space* series preview.
Syracuse Herald Journal, September 15, 1965, "A Cliff-Hanger: *Lost in Space*."
Middletown Times Herald Recorder, September 15, 1965, "Suspended Animation."
Big Springs Daily Herald, September 15, 1965, CBS "HEY, look us over!" ad.
Lima News, September 15, 1965, "TV Key" preview of "The Reluctant Stowaway."
Morgantown Post, September 16, 1965, *New York Times* syndicated review of preem Episode, by Jack Gould.
Chicago Tribune, September 16, 1965, *LIS* review by Clay Gowran.
New York Telegram, September 16, 1965, *Lost in Space* review, by Al Salerno.
Fort Worth Star-Telegram, September 16, 1966, review of *Lost in Space*, by Jerry Coffey.
Daily Variety, September 17, 1965, *Lost in Space* preem review, by "Daku," and "CBS-TV Wins Both Heats of Wednesday Ratings Race."
Hollywood Reporter, September 17, 1965, *Lost in Space* review by Frank Barron.
Appleton Post Crescent, September 17, 1965, *Lost in Space* series review (screening of first three episodes), by "Jingo."
Galveston Daily News, September 18, 1965, *Lost in Space* review by A.C. Becker, Jr.
Biddeford Journal, September 18, 1965, "Television Notes and Anecdotes," about Guy Williams choosing chess moves for Robot.
Citizen-News, September 20, 1965, *Lost in Space* review by Allen Rich.
Broadcasting, September 20, 1965, "Early Ratings Give CBS Edge" and "Sample Reviews."
Daily Variety, September 21, 1965, Trendix and Arbitron ratings reports for September 19, and review of *Voyage* episode "Jona and the Whale," by "Daku.".
The Edwardsville Intelligencer, September 21, 1965, "TV Scout Reports," review of "The Derelict."

Variety, September 22, 1965, *Lost in Space* preem review, by "Horo" and "National Boxoffice Survey."
Oakland Tribune, September 23, 1965, "Bob McKenzie … On Television," with review of *Lost in Space.*
The Bershire Eagle, September 23, 1965, *Lost in Space* review, by Milton R. Bass.
The News, September 23, 1965, *Lost in Space* review, by Ernie Kreiling.
Lowell Sun, September 23, 1965, "Nominees for Quick Cancellation," by William E. Sarmento.
Daily Variety, September 24, 1965, "*Dick Van Dyke* Wins Both Wednesday Ratings Races."
Charleston Gazette Mail, September 26, 1965, *Lost in Space* series review, by Jay Fredericks.
The Lincoln Sunday Journal and Star, September 26, 1965, series review by Ginny Fisher.
Broadcasting, September 27, 1965, "NBC Gets Nielsen Nod in 30-Market Average."
Eureka Humboldt Standard, September 27, 1965, "Actors Timetable Off," by Dick Kleiner.
Steubenville Herald Star, September 29, 1965, *L.A. Times*' "Who's *Lost in Space*?" by Hal Humphrey.
Appleton Post Crescent, September 29, 1965, "TV Scout" preview of "Island in the Sky."
Galveston Daily News, September 29, 1965, "TV Keynotes" preview of "Island in the Sky."
Bristol Daily Courier, September 30, 1965, "*I Spy* Delightful Action Adventure and Humor," by Rick du Brow.
Los Angeles Times Sunday TV magazine, October 3, 1965, "Marta: A Space Saver," by Hal Humphrey.
Broadcasting, October 4, 1965, "Arbitron Places Two Networks in Tie."
Syracuse Herald Journal, October 6, 1965, "TV Tonight" preview of "There Were Giants in the Earth."
Galveston Daily News, October 6, 1965, "TV Keynotes" preview of "There Were Giants in the Earth."
Dover Daily Reporter, October 6, 1965, "TV Previews" review of "There Were Giants in the Earth."
Variety, October 13, 1965, "National Boxoffice Survey."
Syracuse Herald Journal, October 13, 1965, "TV Tonight" preview of "The Hungry Sea."
Galveston Daily News, October 13, 1965, "TV Key-notes" preview of "The Hungry Sea."
Broadcasting, October 17, 1965, "The Nielsen nighttime List."
Star News, October 18, 1965, "TV Viewers Favor New CBS Shows," by Jack Boyle.
The Daily Herald, October 18, 1965, CBS press release for "Welcome Stranger."
The Ottawa Journal, October 18, 1965, Photo and caption for "Welcome Stranger."
Daily Variety, "On All Channels," by Dave Kaufman, announcing *Time Tunnel* pilot.
Abilene Reporter News, October 20, 1965, "TV Scout" preview of "Welcome Stranger."
Variety, October 27, 1965, "The Hungry Sea" episode review, by "Horo."
Abilene Reporter News, October 27, 1965, "TV Scout" preview of "My Friend Mr. Nobody."
Galveston Daily News, October 27, 1965, "TV Key-notes" preview of "My Friend, Mr. Nobody."
New York Journal American TV Magazine, October 31, 1965, "*Lost in Space* Proud of its Scenic Tricks," by Frank Judge.
Broadcasting, October 31, 1965, "NBC Leads Second Nielsen."
Daily Variety, November 1, 1965, "NBC Leads Latest 30-Mkt. Nielsen."
Variety, November 2, 1966, announcing *Lost in Space* renewal for balance of season.
San Antonio Light, November 3, 1965, "TV Key" preview of "Invaders from the 5th Dimension."
The Daily Mail (from Hagerstown, Maryland), November 3, 1965, "TV Scout" review of "Invaders from the 5th Dimension."
Scottsdale Daily Progress, November 3, 1965, "Wednesday Highlights" preview of "Invaders from the 5th Dimension."

TV Guide, November 6, 1965, "Now She's the Fur-Bearing Animal," by Melvin Durslag.

Syracuse Post Standard, November 7, 1965, "Sexy Feet?"

Broadcasting, November 8, 1965, "CBS-TV Makes 13 of Arbitron Top 20."

Daily Variety, November 9, 1965, "Only 8 New Shows in Latest, Crucial National Nielsen."

The Decatur Daily Review, November 10, 1965, "TV Scout" review of "The Oasis."

Lima News, November 17, 1965, "TV Key" preview of "The Sky is Falling."

TV Guide, November 20, 1965, "Norwegian Cinderella."

The Times Record, November 20, 1965, "Thought Harris Is a Hit, He Admits He's TV Stage-Struck," by Harold Stern.

The Edwardsville Intelligencer, November 11, 1965, "TV Scout" preview of "The Raft."

Los Angeles Times, December 5, 1965, "Playing Spy in Space," by Aleene MacMinn.

Daily Variety, December 7, 1965, Nielsen report.

Madison Wisconsin State Journal, December 8, 1966, "TV Key" preview of "One of Our Dogs is Missing."

Joplin News Herald, December 20, 1965, Associated Press syndicated article, "Television Show Proves Exciting," by Cynthia Lowry.

Independent Star News, TV WEEK, December 26, 1965, "You Said It" letters column.

Variety. December 29. 1965, "*Lost* in the Horsley Platitudes."

Appleton Post Crescent, December 29, 1965, "TV Scout" preview of "Return from Outer Space.

Pittsburgh Post-Gazette, December 29, 1965, "TV Key Previews," review of "Return from Outer Space."

Los Angeles Times, December 30, 1965, "'65 Worst awards Cup Runneth Over," by Hal Humphrey.

El Paso Herald Post, January 1, 1966, "Things to Know About People in the Show."

Hutchinson News, January 1, 1966, "Wish Upon a Star" press photo caption, and "Drydocked Sailor."

Waterloo Daily Courier, January 9, 1966, "Ask TV Scout."

The Morning Herald, January 12, 1966, "TV Scout" preview of "The Keeper, Part 1."

The Bridgeport Post, January 12, 1966, "TV Key" preview of "The Keeper, Part 1."

Los Angeles Times, January 13, 1966, blurb about Guy Williams being unhappy with the scripts.

Gastonia Gazette, January 17, 1966, "Show Beat: *Lost in Space* is Good Fun," by Dick Kleiner.

Independent Star News, TV WEEK, January 18, 1966, TV WEEK's "Be a TV Critic" poll results.

Biddeford Journal, January 22, 1966, "Jonathan Harris is Busiest Guest Star."

Ogden Standard Examiner, January 23, 1966, "Behind the Scenes," by Alice Pardoe West.

Independent Press Telegram, January 23, 1966, "Tele Vues" cover story on Marta Kristen, by Bert Resnik.

Pasadena Independent Star News, January 23, 1966, "Part II – TV Week's 'Be a TV Critic' Poll Results."

Oxnard Press Courier, January 23, 1966, "Viewers Going Batty Over Batman Series (*New York Times* syndicated story).

San Antonio Express and News, January 23, 1966, "Why Some Fans Get Lost in Television Shows."

Abilene Reporter News, January 24, 1966, "Ask TV Scout" letters column.

Wilmington News-Journal, January 26, 1966, "For the Homemaker" by Beulah Hill.

Ogden Standard Examiner, January 27, 1966, "Programmed for Defeat" photo caption, Jonathan Harris playing chess with the Robot.

Arizona Republic, January 30, 1966, photo of Billy Mumy and Robot in bubble-gum blowing contest.

Charleston Gazette Mail, January 30, 1966, "TV Group Rates Kiddie Programs." By Jay Fredericks.
Waterloo Daily Courier, January 30, 1966, NEA syndicated article, "Cliff-Hanger in Space," by Don Royal.
Broadcasting, January 31, 1966, "*Batman* Adds Muscle to ABC-TV Ratings."
Daily Variety, January 31, 1966, "Just for Variety," by Army Archerd.
TV Guide, February 5, 1966, "REVIEW by Cleveland Amory: *Lost in Space*."
Arizona Republic, February 6, 1966, TV Time Service syndicated article: "New Game: Psychoanalyzing Viewers of Various shows," by Mimi Mead.
Daily Variety, February 9, 1966, "On All Channels," by Dave Kaufman.
Sandusky Register, February 9, 1966, "War of the Robots" press photo and caption.
Bridgeport Telegram, February 9, 1966, "TV Key" preview of "War of the Robots."
North Carolina's *The Robesonian*, February 9, 1966, "TV Key" review, "War of the Robots."
Joplin Globe, February 13, 1966, "Guy Williams Prefers Space for Emoting."
The Bridgeport Post, February 16, 1966, "TV Key Previews," review, "The Magic Mirror."
North Adams Transcript, February 19, 1966, "Jonathan Harris, Good-Bad Actor *Lost in Space*," by Erskine Johnson.
San Antonio Express and News, February 20, 1966, "Squawk Box" letters column.
Variety, February 23, 1966, "New Season at First Blush," announcing *Lost in Space* renewal.
TV Guide, February 26, 1966, "Letters."
Kannapolis Daily Independent, February 27, 1966, "Guy Williams from Cape and Mask to Space Suit," UPI syndicated article by Vernon Scott.
Pasadena Independent Star-New, February 27, 1966, "TV Week" "You Said It" letters column.
Variety, March 2, 1966, "Next Season's 3 Net Schedule – First Round."
Medina County-Gazette, March 2, 1966, "Looking at TV" preview of "The Challenge."
Madison Wisconsin State Journal, March 18, 1966, "*Lost in Space* Tops Reality for some."
Los Angeles Times, March 20, 1966, "Everybody Loves a Robot" picture article.
Annapolis Capitol, March 21, 1966, "Show Beat," by dick Kleiner.
Los Angeles Times, March 21, 1966, "Mercedes: Lost a *Little in Space*," by Hal Humphrey.
Daily Variety, March 22, 1966, "CBS-TV Solidifies Nielsen Lead in Latest Survey."
Dover Daily Reporter, March 23, 1966, "TV Answer Man," letter about *Lost in Space* renewal.
TV Guide, March 26, 1966, "For the Record," about preemption due to Gemini 8 crises.
Morning Herald, March 30, 1966, "TV Scout" preview for "The Space Croppers."
Variety, March 30, 1966, Network schedules for fall 1966; "Irwin Allen Firms 3 Shows with 20th; Budget at $12-Mil."
The Galveston News, April 2, 1966, "Weird Monsters Give Batman Fits in Battle for TV Ratings," by Charles Witbeck.
The Gastonia Gazette, April 3, 1966, "*Lost in Space* -- And Enjoying Every Thrilling Minute of It," by Tom McIntyre.
Daily Review, April 3, 1966, TV WEEK "You Said It" letters column.
Los Angeles Herald-Examiner, April 6, 1966, "TV Talk" with Bob Hull, for *LiS* episode "All That Glitters."
Bakersfield Californian, April 9, 1966, "*Heroes*' Star Plans Travel."
The Winona Daily News, April 10, 1966, "Monsters Figure in Ratings Battle," by Charles Witbeck.
Pasadena Independent Star-News, April 10, 1966, "TV Week," by Allen Rich.
Monessen Valley Independent, April 20, 1966, preview, "A Change in Space."
The Edwardsville Intelligencer, April 20, 1966, "TV Scout" review of "A Change in Space."
Richardson Daily News, April 28, 1966, "*Lost in Space* Doctor Finds Kitchen."

Anderson Daily Bulletin (Indiana), May 14, 1966, "Exciting Adventure of Two Scientists in *Time Tunnel*."
Pasadena Independent Star-News, TV WEEK, May 15, 1966, "You Said It."
Pasadena Independent Star-News, May 22, 1966, "Jonathan Harris: Hisses Sweeter Than Wine."
Broadcasting, May 23, 1966, two-page ad for *Time Tunnel.*
Madison Wisconsin State Journal, May 25, 1966, "TV Key" preview of "The Keeper, Part 2."
The Daily Reporter, May 25, 1966, "TV Preview" review of "The Keeper, Part 2."
The Edwardsville Intelligencer, June 1, 1966, "TV Scout" preview of "The Space Pirate."
North Adams Transcript, June 4, 1966, "Dawson Palmer, You See Him, Now You Don't," by Erskine Johnson.
TV Guide, June 18, 1966, "One Case Where Evil Triumphs," by Dwight Whitney.
Manfield News Journal, June 22, 1966, "Magic Mirror" photo caption.
Daily Variety, June 29, 1966, "Meriwether Time'd."
Daily Variety, July 1, 1966, "33 Scribes at work on 3 20th-Fox Vidpix Series."
Variety, July 6, 1966, "CBS in Comic Strip Stakes Via Development Deal for 'The Spirit.'"
The Indianapolis Star, July 9, 1966, "Irwin Allen's *Time Tunnel* Set Has Never Never Land Talking," by Julia Inman.
Colorado Springs Gazette-Telegraph, July ,9, 1966, "Science Fiction Thriller Stars James Darren."
The Daily Review, July 17, 1966, TV WEEK, "You Said It" letters column.
Daily Review, July 24, 1966, preview of "All That Glitters."
Edwardsville Intelligencer, July 27, 1966, "TV Scout" preview of "All That Glitters."
Biddeford-Saco-Journal, July 29, 1966, CBS press release for "Blast Off into Space."
San Antonio Express and News, July 31, 1966, "Teen TV Actress Has Novel Dating Problem."
The Daily Herald (Provo, Utah), August 7, 1966, "Dirty Work Afoot for J. Darren."
TV Guide, August 27, 1966, "Letters."
The Indiana Gazette, September 1, 1966, Associated Press wire article: "TV Producer Typecast," by Cynthia Lowry.
The Tennessean, September 4, 1966, "*Time Tunnel* Offers Infinity of Entertainment," by Irwin Allen.
Variety, September 7, 1966, "Clearance Follies of '66-'67," by Murray Horowitz.
Galveston Daily News, September 7, 1966, "TV-Key-notes" preview of "Wish Upon a Star."
The Edwardsville Intelligencer (Illinois), September 8, 1966, "TV Scout" review of *Time Tunnel* premiere episode.
Hutchinson News, September 10, 1966, "Fading Freckles."
Hammond Times, September 11, 1966, "Animal Actors No Different."
The Victoria [Texas] Advocate, September 11, 1966, "Show Beat," by Dick Kleiner.
Galveston Daily News, September 11, 1966, "TV Key-notes," preview of "Blast Off Into Space."
The Post-Crescent (Appleton, Wisconsin), September 12, 1966, review of *Time Tunnel*, by "Jingo."
Variety, September 14, 1966, "The Overnight Scores," with Trendex and Arbitron ratings for *Time Tunnel*; and review of *The Time Tunnel*, by "Mor."
Hagerstown Daily Mail, September 14, 1966, "TV Scout" preview of "Blast Off into Space."
Daily Variety, September 16, 1966, "NBC continues to Pace Primetime Wed. Ratings Race"; "Blast Off into Space" episode review, by "Beig."
The Pittsburgh Press, September 16, 1966, "TV Scout" review of *Time Tunnel* "One Way to the Moon" episode, by Joan Crosby.
Courier-Post (Camden, New Jersey), September 17, 1966, "*Time* Will Tell," by Beth Gillin.

The Edwardsville Intelligencer, September 21, 1966, "TV Scout Reports," with preview of "Wild Adventure."

The Edwardsville Intelligencer, September 23, 1966, "TV Key" preview of Time Tunnel's "End of the World."

TV Guide, September 24, 1966, "When Guy Hisses the Villain – HE MEANS IT," by Michael Fessier, Jr.

Pulaski Southwest Times, September 25, 1966, "Show Boat," by Dick Kleiner.

Waterloo Daily Courier, September 25, 1966, "No Scene-Stealing on *Lost in Space*."

Detroit Free Press, September 25, 1966, "A Celebrity in Detroit: Marta Kristen," by Ellen Goodman.

Broadcasting, September 26, 1966, ratings for *Voyage*, *Lost in Space*, and *Time Tunnel.*

Daily Variety, September 26, 1966, "Light and Airy," by Jack Hellman, *Time Tunnel* ratings.

Salt Lake Tribune, September 28, 1966, "Blastoff Making Williams Happy."

Variety, September 28, 1966, "Wild Adventure" episode review, by "Syd."

Fremont, California's *The Argus*, September 28, 1966, "Mr. Peepers in Space" article.

Daily Variety, September 29, 1966, Irwin Allen's "The Spirit" and "Journey to the Center of the Earth" TV projects.

Laurel Leader Call, September 30, 1966, AP syndicated review: "Bob Hope Jokes Weak," by Cynthia Lowry.

Pittsburgh Post-Crescent, September 30, 1966, "TV Key" preview of *Time Tunnel*'s "The Day the Sky Fell In."

Independent Star-News (Pasadena, California), October 2, 1966, "Will *Time Tunnel* Stand the Test of Time?," by Marian Dern.

The Courier-Journal (Louisville, Kentucky), October 3, 1966, "*Time Tunnel* Seems to Be Top Notch Show," by Bill Ladd.

Broadcasting, October 3, 1966, Trendex TV ratings.

Bridgeport Telegram. October 5, 1966, "TV Key" preview of *LiS* "The Forbidden World."

Galveston Daily News, October 7, 1966, "TV Key" preview of *Time Tunnel*'s "The Last Patrol."

Detroit Free Press, October 9, 1966, "This Chimp's No Chump" feature on Debbie the Bloop.

Variety, October 12, 1966, "TV's New Top 40"; "Eight New Shows in TvQ's Top 20; Teens Favor 16.

Pennsylvania's *The News-Herald*, October 12, 1966, "TV Scout" review, "Space Circus."

The Edwardsville Intelligencer, October 14, 1966, "TV Scout" preview of *Time Tunnel*'s "Crack of Doom."

Broadcasting, October 17, 1966, "The Ratings: A Photo Finish."

The Edwardsville Intelligencer, October 19. 1966, "TV Scout" review of "Prisoners of Space."

The Bridgeport Telegram, October 19, 1966, "TV Key Preview" review of "Prisoners of Space."

Daily Variety, October 21, 1966, "ABC-TV Axes *Shane* and *Hawk*, Whets Blade for More Programs."

The Edwardsville Intelligencer, October 21, 1966, "TV Scout" preview of *Time Tunnel*'s "Revenge of the Gods."

Beckley Post-Herald / The Raleigh Register, October 22, 1966, "Creator of Time Tunnel Probes Space for Ideas."

The Ogden Standard-Examiner (Utah), October 23, 1966, "Imagination Helps *Time Tunnel* Tick," by Don Royal.

San Antonio Express and News, October 23, 1966, "Unhappy Star."

Daily Variety, October 24, 1966, "ABC-TV Orders 9 More *Tunnel* Segs."

Daily Variety, October 25, 1966, "Nielsen's Year of the Rat."

Appleton Post Crescent, October 26, 1966, "TV Scout" preview of "The Android Machine."

The Kokomo Tribune, October 26, 1966, "TV Key" review of "The Android Machine."

The Decatur Herald (Illinois), October 28, 1966, "TV Key" preview of *Time Tunnel*'s "Massacre."

The Pittsburgh Press, October 28, 1966, "TV Scout" preview of *Time Tunnel*'s "Massacre."

Daily Review, October 30, 1966, TV WEEK, "You Said It" letters column.

Ogden Standard Examiner, October 30, 1966, "Acting Breeds Complexity, Star Asserts."

Broadcasting, October 31, 1966, "NBC Leads Second Nielsen."

Rebesonian, November 2, 1966, "Deadly Games of Gamma 6" preview.

Nashua Telegraph, November 2, 1966, "TV Highlights" review of "Deadly Games of Gamma 6."

The Decatur Herald, November 3, 1966, filler piece, Mark Klemperer prefers *Time Tunnel* over *Hogan's Heroes.*

Pasadena Independent Star-News, November 6, 1966, "Jonathan Harris: He Likes Being Despicable."

Dover Daily Reporter, November 8, 1966, "Answer Man" letters column.

The Post-Crescent (Appleton, Wisconsin), November 11, 1966, "TV Scout" preview of *Time Tunnel*'s "Devil's Island."

Albuquerque Journal, November 11, 1966, "TV Key" preview of *Time Tunnel*'s "Devil's Island."

The Pittsburgh Press, November 14, 1966, "TV Scout preview of *Time Tunnel*'s "Reign of Terror."

The Courier-Journal (Louisville, Kentucky), November 15, 1966, *Time Tunnel* review by Bill Ladd.

Daily Variety, November 16, 1966, "On All Channels" by Dave Kaufman, interview with William Self.

The San Antonio Light, November 16, 1966, "TV Key" preview of "Curse of Cousin Smith."

Arizona Republic, November 20, 1966, AP News syndicated story, "Jonathan Harris to Play 4 Roles" and "Poor Robot, He Needs Tear Ducts," by Richard K. Shull.

Abilene Reporter News, November 21, 1966, "Ask TV Scout" letters column.

Daily Variety, November 22, 1966, "New Shows Continue to Descend Nielsen Ladder."

The Coe Cosmos, November 25, 1966, *Time Tunnel* review by Ed Gorman.

TV Guide, November 26, 1966, "What Are a Few Galaxies Among Friends?," by Isaac Asimov.

Galveston Daily Review, November 27, 1966, "TV Week: You Are the Critic" letters column.

TV Guide, November 27, 1966, "Letters."

The Salt Lake Tribune, November 27, 1966, "*Time Tunnel* Costumes Are Tough."

Abilene Reporter News, November 27, 1966, "Harris Playing Quartet of roles in Space Western."

Louisville, Kentucky's *The Courier-Journal*, November 27, 1966, Bill Ladd's "Critic's Choice" ` review of "West of Mars."

Arizona Republic, November 27, 1966, "*Time Tunnel* from the Epics," by Charles Whitbeck.

Mansfield, Ohio's *News Journal*, November 30, 1966, Photo caption for "West of Mars."

Lima News, November 30, 1966, "TV Key" preview of "West of Mars."

The News-Herald, December 2, 1966, "TV Scout" preview of *Time Tunnel*'s "The Death Trap."

Nashua Telegraph, December 2, 1966, "TV Key" preview of *Time Tunnel*'s "The Death Trap."

The Ogden Standard-Examiner, December 4, 1966, Steven H. Scheuer's "TV Mailbag"

The Corpus Christi Caller-Times, "December 4, 1966, "School Drop-ups."

Bridgeport Post, December 9, 1966, "TV Key Mailbag."

Pittsburgh Post-Gazette, December 9, 1966, "TV Key" preview of *Time Tunnel*'s "The Alamo."

Advocate, December 11, 1966, "Sunday's Mailbag."

Syracuse Herald Journal, December 11, 1966, "Mohr's 'Heavy'."

The Edwardsville Intelligencer, December 14, 1966, "3-Part *Batman* Stories Slated," by Dick Kleiner.

News Journal, December 14, 1966, preview of "Wreck of the Robot."
Tucson Daily Reporter, December 14, "Santa Has Your Letters Kids, So You Can Relax."
Elwood, Indiana's *The Call-Leader*, December 14, 1966, "Letters to Santa."
The Edwardsville Intelligencer (Illinois), December 14, 1966, "3-Part Batman Stories Slated," by Dick Kleiner.
The Daily Mail (Hagerstown, Maryland), December 16, 1966, "TV Key" preview of *Time Tunnel*'s "The Night of the Long Knives."
Mattoon, Illinois *Journal Gazette*, December 17, 1966, "Santa Letters."
Pasadena Independent Star-News, December 18, 1966, "TV Week," by Allen Rich.
The Cincinnati Enquirer, December 18, 1966, ad for Mattell *Lost in Space* Roto Gun.
The Corpus Christi Caller-Times, December 18, 1966, "Soprano Plays 'Space Viking.'"
Abilene Reporter News, December 21, 1966, "TV Scout" preview of "The Dream Monster."
Mansfield, Ohio's *News-Journal*, December 21, 1966, "TV Key" review, "The Dream Monster."
Delaware County Daily Times, December 21, 1966, "Letters to Santa."
Mattoon, Illinois *Journal Gazette*, December 21, 1966, "Santa Letters."
Statesville Recorder & Landmark, December 21, 1966, "Dear Santa, Christmas Eve Is Just Three Day Away, So Hurry And Read Those Letters."
Albuquerque Journal, December 23, 1966, "TV Key" preview of *Time Tunnel*'s "Invasion."
Abilene Reporter-News, December 23, 1966, "TV Scout" preview of "Invasion."
Daily Review, December 25, 1966, "You Said It" letters column.
Independent Star-News (Pasadena, California), December 25, 1966, *Time Tunnel* review by Mike Sollenberger.
The Indianapolis Star, December 30, 1966, "TV Key" preview of *Time Tunnel*'s "The Revenge of Robin Hood."
Long Beach Independent, January 3, 1967, "Tele-Vues," by Terry Vernon.
Pittsburgh Post-Gazette, January 4, 1967, "TV Key Previews" review of "The Girl from the Green Dimension."
The News-Herald (Franklin, Pennsylvania), January 6, 1967, "TV Scout" preview of *Time Tunnel*'s "Kill Two By Two."
Independent Star-News, January 8, 1967, "Hippity Hop, From Catfood [sic] to Lily Pad" article on Ron Gans guest player in "The Golden Man."
Long Beach *Independent Press-Telegram*, January 8, 1967, "Pan and Fan" letters column.
The Indianapolis Star , January 8, 1967, "Ex-Henry Aldrich Has Fun Directing."
Variety, January 11, 1967, "ABC-TV May Flit *Hornet* in Spring; Mulls 3rd Season."
Madison Wisconsin State Journal, January 11, 1967, "TV Key" preview of "The Questing Beast."
The Independent Star, January 22, 1967, "Albert Salmi Sports Curls As Buccaneer."
The San Bernardino County Sun, January 23, 1967, "Just Who Are Shows Trying to Reach?" by Vernon Scott.
Broadcasting, January 23, 1967, "Second Season Loses to Movies," ratings report.
Kokomo Tribune, January 25, 1967, "TV Scout" preview of *LiS* episode "The Toymaker."
Beckley Post-Herald, January 25, 1967, preview of "The Toy Maker."
Hagerstown *The Daily Mail*, Wednesday 25, 1967, "TV Key" review, "The Toymaker.
The Akron Beacon Journal, January 25, 1967, "Radio-TV Mailbag," by Dick Shippy, with "Dear Fat Head" letter about *Lost in Space*.
The Daily Reporter (Dover, Ohio), January 27, 1967, "TV Key" preview of *Time Tunnel*'s "The Walls of Jericho."
Democrat and Chronicle, January 29, 1967 "More Honest Than Batman," by John Heisner.
Los Angeles Times, February 1, 1967, "New Strategy in the War of Ratings," by Hal Humphrey.
The Bridgeport Post, February 1, 1967, Steven H. Scheuer's "TV Key Mailbag."

Pasadena Independent, February 1, 1967, "Jack Bradford Notes from Hollywood."
Medina County Gazette (Ohio), February 1, 1967, "Need Information? Ask a Child," by Barbara Buda.
The Decatur Daily Review (Illinois), February 3, 1967, "TV Key" preview of *Time Tunnel*'s "Idol of Death."
Pulaski Southwest Times, February 8, 1967, "TV Scout" preview of "Mutiny in Space" and "Series Indicate Silver Surplus," by Dick Kleiner, with photo and caption.
Variety, February 8, 1967, "TV Webs Sight $1."
Pittsburgh Post-Gazette, February 8, 1967, "TV Key Previews" review of "Mutiny in Space."
The Daily Mail (Hagerstown, Maryland), February 10, 1967, "TV Key" preview of *Time Tunnel*'s "Billy the Kid."
Los Angeles Herald Examiner, February 11, 1967, "Letters to the Editor" concerning *LIS*.
The Sandusky Register, February 14, 1967, photo and caption for "Rocket to Earth."
Medina County Gazette, February 15, 1967, "Looking At TV" preview of "Rocket to Earth."
Madison Wisconsin State Journal, February 15, 1967, "TV Key" preview of "Rocket to Earth."
The Indianapolis Star, February 17, 1967, "TV Key" preview of *Time Tunnel*'s "Pirates of Deadman's Island."
Medina County Gazette, February 22, 1967, "Looking At TV" by Barbara Budu, review of "Cave of the Wizards."
Pittsburgh Post-Gazette, February 22, 1967, "TV Key Previews," review, "Cave of the Wizards."
The Daily Reporter (Dover, Ohio), February 24m 1967, "TV Key" preview of *Time Tunnel*'s "Chase Through Time."
The News Journal, February 24, 1967, "TV Scout" preview of *Time Tunnel*'s "Chase Through Time."
Detroit Free Press, February 26, 1967, "It's All in the Family for June Lockhart."
The Edwardsville Intelligencer, February 28, 1967 and March 1, 1967, "TV Scout" review of "Treasure of the Lost Planet."
The Bridgeport Telegram, March 1, 1967, "TV Key Previews" review, "Treasure of the Lost Planet."
Medina County Gazette, March 1, 1967, "Looking At TV" by Barbara Budu, review of "Treasure of the Lost Planet."
The News-Herald, March 3, 1967, "TV Scout" preview of *Time Tunnel*'s "The Death Merchant."
The Sandusky Reporter, March 3, 1967, "Billy Mumy: Juvenile Idol."
Los Angeles Times, March 5, 1967, "He's An Earthbound Spaceman," by Aleene MacMinn.
Variety, March 8, 1967, "TV Nets 1967-68 Season Blueprint."
The Morning Herald, March 8, 1967, "TV Scout" review of "Revolt of the Androids."
The Bridgeport Telegram, March 8, 1967, "TV Key Previews" review, "Revolt of the Androids."
The Decatur Daily Review, March 10, 1967, "TV Key" preview of *Time Tunnel*'s Attack of the Barbarians."
The Cincinnati Enquirer, March 10, 1967, review of sci-fi series by Martin Hogan, Jr.
Anaheim, California Bulletin, March 11, 1967, promotional story for "The Astral Traveler."
The Corpus Christi Caller-Times, March 12, 1967, photo and picture caption for "The Colonists."
Daily Variety, March 14, 1967, "On All Channels," by Dave Kaufman, about *Time Tunnel* and *Lost in Space* being scheduled opposite one another.
Madison Capitol Times, March 15, 1967, "TV Scout" preview of "The Colonists."
Pittsburgh Post-Gazette, March 15, 1967, "TV Key Previews" review of "The Colonists."
Nashua Telegraph, March 18, 1967, "Inter-Galactic Mailings from *Lost in Space*."
The Sunday Herald (Provo, Utah), "March 19, 1967, "Inter-Galactic Mail from *Lost in Space*."

The Indianapolis Star, March 19, 1967, cover of *TV Week* supplement featuring Guy Williams and June Lockhart.

Las Cruces Sun-News, March 19, 1967, AP wire story, "Matt Dillon to Be Back at New Stand," by Cynthia Lowry, mentioning ratings and renewal for *Lost in Space.*

Abilene Reporter-News, March 21, 1967, "TV Scout" preview of "Thief from Outer Space."

Pulaski Southwest Times, March 22, 1967, "TV Scout" preview of "Trip Through the Robot."

Pittsburgh Post-Gazette, March 22, 1967, "TV Key Previews" review, "Trip Through the Robot."

Variety, March 22, 1967, "ABC-TV Going Dark…" and cancelling *Time Tunnel.*

Alton Evening Telegraph (Illinois), March 24, 1966, *Time Tunnel* to be replaced by *Custer.*

The Morning Herald, March 24, 1967, "TV Scout" preview of *Time Tunnel*'s "The Kidnappers."

Variety, March 29, 1967, "TV Nets 1967-68 – At NAB Time."

The News-Herald (Franklin, Pennsylvania), March 29, 1967, "TV Scout" review, "The Phantom Family."

The Bridgeport Telegram, March 29, 1967, "TV Key Previews" review, "The Phantom Family."

Toledo Blade, April 3, 1967, listing for *The Red Skelton Show* with LIS comedy skit, featuring June Lockhart and the Robot.

The Edwardsville Intelligencer, April 7, 1967, "TV Scout" preview of *Time Tunnel*'s "Town of Terror."

Pasadena Independent, April 24, 1967, "The Galaxy Gift" promo photo and caption.

San Antonio Express and News, April 29, 1967, review of "The Galaxy Gift."

Daily Variety, May 10, 1967, "20th to animate Verne *Journey* for ABC-TV."

Daily Herald, May 15, 1967, blurb about Vincent Price imitating Dr. Smith on *The Red Skelton Show.*

Madison Capitol Times, May 17, 1967, "TV Scout" preview of "The Ghost Planet."

Advocate, May 21, 1967, "Show Beat" piece on June Lockhart and *LiS* format change.

Hamilton Daily News Journal, May 23, 1967, "Dr. Smith Helping English Teachers."

Daily Variety, May 24, 1967, "*Center of Earth* Vidpix Alter Cartooney Method."

Abilene Reporter-News, May 24, 1967, "Forbidden World" preview.

Hutchinson News, May 28, 1967, "Forbidden World" promotional pix and caption.

Ogden Standard Examiner, May 28, 1967, "He's Popular in Bangkok, But at Home?"

Port Arthur News, May 28, 1967, "*Lost in Space* Cast on Vacation."

Madison Capitol Times, May 31, 1967, "TV Scout" preview of "The Thief of Outer Space."

Madison Capitol Times, June 7, 1967, "TV Scout" preview of "A Visit to Hades."

The Anderson Herald, June 17, 1967, promo photo and caption for *LiS*'s "The Golden Man."

Abilene Reporter-News, June 21, 1967, "TV Scout preview of "The Golden Man."

Arizona Republic, June 21, 1967, listing for "The Golden Man."

The Daily Reporter, June 26, 1967, "TV Closeup," by Marilyn Beck.

Morning Herald, June 28, 1967, "

Wisconsin State Journal, July 1, 1967, "*Lost in Space* Robot a Real Show Biz Buff," by Vernon Scott.

Arizona Republic, July 2, 1967, "He Likes Series Role," by Harvey Pack.

Pulaski Southwest Times, July 5, 1967, "TV Scout" preview of *LiS* episode "West of Mars."

Deseret News (Utah), July 6, 1967, Howard Pearson column with *LiS* item.

The Indianapolis Star, July 9, 1967, "Dr. Smith Takes Viewing Over Singing."

The Edwardsville Intelligencer, July 12, 1967, "TV Scout" preview of *LiS* "Mutiny in Space."

Albuquerque Tribune, July 19, 1967, "TV Scout" preview of "Revolt of the Androids."

Edwardsville Intelligencer, August 1, 1967, "TV Scout" preview of "The Cave of the Wizards."

Deseret News (Utah), August 1, 1967, Howard Pearson column with *LiS* item.

Daily Kennebec Journal, August 9, 1967, "TV Scout" preview of *LiS* episode "Rocket to Earth."

Independent Press-Telegram, August 13, 1967, "Evil Triumphant -- Jonathan Harris: Deliciously Wicked."
Salt Lake Tribune, August 28, 1967, "Why Not Lose the' Quack in Space?" by Harold Schindler.
Madison Capitol Times, August 30, 1967, "TV Scout" preview of "The Mechanical Men."
Wisconsin State Journal, September 3, 1967, "TV KEY Mailbag."
North Adams Transcript, September 7, 1967, "TV Scout" preview of "Condemned of Space."
Variety, September 13, 1967, *LIS* episode "Condemned of Space" episode review by "Frie."
The Indianapolis Star, September 24, 1967, "*Time Tunnel* Revival Planned by Allen," by Harvey Pack.
Edwardsville Intelligencer, September 27, 1967, "TV Scout" preview of *LiS* "Hunter's Moon."
San Antonio Express, October 4, 1967, "TV Scout" preview of *LIS* "The Space Primevils."
Wisconsin State Journal, October 11, 1967, "TV Key" preview of "The Space Destructors."
Kenosha News, October 11, 1967, "TV Scout" preview of "The Space Destructors."
Broadcasting, October 17, 1966, Nielsen ratings.
San Antonio Express and News, October 17, 1967, "Authenticity Strong Point of TV Show."
Variety, October 25, 1967, "Nat'l Nielsen Boxscore."
Los Angeles Times, November 12, 1967, "Love and Hisses for the Villain," by Walt Dutton.
Madison Capitol Times, December 13, 1967, "TV Scout" review of "Two Weeks in Space."
Daily Variety, December 14, 1967, "Tenn. Ernie Wins Nielsen's Latest Nat'l; *Family* 2nd."
The Daily Mail, December 20, 1967, "TV Scout" review of "Castles in Space."
Morning Herald, December 27, 1967, "TV Scout" review of "The Anti-Matter Man."
Variety, December 27, 1967, "Silverbach Eyes 20th-TV corp. O'seas; Sees Changing Global Mkt.," by Dave Jampel.
North Adams Transcript, January 10, 1968, "TV Scout," preview of "Princess in Space."
Variety, January 17, 1968, "*Thief* and *Avengers* Off to Good Start as ABC Jan. Replacements."
Pulaski Southwest Times, January 17, 1968, "TV Scout" preview of "The Time Merchant."
Madison Capitol Times, January 24, 1968, "TV Scout" preview of "The Promised Land."
Variety, January 31, 1968, "TV's Un-Roaring 20s (rating shares)."
Madison Capitol Times, January 31, 1968, "TV Scout" preview of "Fugitives in Space."
Appleton Post Crescent, February 14, 1968, "TV Scout" preview of "Space Beauty."
Daily Variety, February 20, 1968, "CBS-TV Axes 4, Buys 6 New Fall Shows."
Syracuse Herald Journal, February 21, 1968, "TV Scout" preview of "The Flaming Planet."
Syracuse Herald Journal, February 28, 1968, "TV Scout" preview of "The Great Vegetable Rebellion."
News Journal, February 28, 1968, preview of "The Great Vegetable Rebellion."
Daily Variety, February 28, 1968, Mark Goddard on cancellation of *Lost in Space*.
TV Guide, March 2, 1968, "The Doan Report," with word of *Voyage* being cancelled.
The Akron Beacon-Journal, March 6, 1968, Dick Shippy's Letter's Column, about *Lost in Space*.
Variety, March 13, 1968, "Night of Specs Puts ABC on Top in N.Y. Overnights."
Ogden Standard-Examiner, March 17, 1968, "TV Key Mail Bag," by Steven H. Scheuer.
TV Guide, March 30, 1968, "Letters" column.
Broadcasting, April 1, 1968, "National Ratings."
Democrat and Chronicle (Rochester, New York), April 7, 1968, TV letters column, re: cancellation of *Lost in Space*.
Auburn Citizen Advertiser, April 10, 1968, "TV Key" preview of *LiS* "The Space Primevils."
The Ogden Standard-Examiner (Utah), April 14, 1968, "Ask Them Yourself" letters column, with June Lockhart regarding beauty pageants.
Madison Capitol News, May 15, 1968, "TV Scout" preview of *LiS* "Space Creature."
Abilene Reporter News, May 22, 1968, "TV Scout" preview of *LiS* "Deadliest of the Species."

The Ogden Standard-Examiner (Utah), May 27, 1968, AP syndicated column: "Some Series About to Fade From View," by Cynthia Lowry.

Madison Capitol Times, May 29, 1968, "TV Scout" preview of *LiS* "A Day at the Zoo."

Democrat and Chronicle (Rochester, New York), June 2, 1968, TV letters column with *Lost in Space* mail.

Madison Capitol Times, June 26, 1968, "TV Scout" preview of *LiS* "Target: Earth."

Madison Capitol Times, July 3, 1968, "TV Scout" second review of *LiS* "Princess of Space."

The Daily Reporter (Dover, Ohio), July 5, 1968, "TV Answer Man," letter about *Lost in Space*.

News-Journal, July 6, 1968, "TV Key Mail Bag."

Akron Evening Telegram (Illinois), July 6, 1968, "Top View Voters Favor Dropping *Lost in Space*," by Clarke Williamson.

Seattle Post-Intelligencer Viewer Mail, August 1968, letter about *LiS* cancellation.

The Cincinnati Enquirer, September 3, 1968, "The Long and Short of It" by Martin Hogan Jr., interview with Irwin Allen.

Waterloo Daily Courier, August 16, 1968, "Ask TV Scout" letters column, regarding cancellation.

Madison Capitol Times, August 21, 1968, "TV Scout" preview of "Junkyard in Space."

Dallas Morning News, August 21, 1968, "Now It's Giants," by Bevo Baker.

St. Louis Post-Dispatch, August 23, 1968, "Television's Master of the Hokus Pokus," on Irwin Allen.

Madison Capitol Times, September 11, 1968, "TV Scout" preview of "A Visit to Hades."

Nashua Telegraph (New Hampshire), September 20, 1968, Associated Press syndicated article, "*Petticoat Junction* to Star June Lockhart as Doctor," by Bob Thomas.

The Raleigh Register (Beckley, West Virginia), September 24, 1968, "Hollywood" by Vernon Scott, with interview of Irwin Allen regarding *Land of the Giants*.

The Akron Beacon Journal, October 6, 1968, "New Lady in Town," by Bob Thomas.

The Cumberland News (Maryland), October 26, 1968, "Old Home Week for Jon Harris."

Pittsburgh Post-Gazette, November 4, 1968, from the syndicated "TV Key Mail" column on cancellation of *Lost in Space*.

The Times Record (Troy, New York), November 9, 1968, "Lost in Space" reference in synopsis for *Star Trek*'s "The Tholian Web" episode.

The Indianapolis Star, November 10, 1968, "Wholesome June Lockhart New Additions to *Petticoat Junction*," by Charles Witbeck.

Detroit Free Press, November 10, 1968, "The Starlet Who Isn't Too Inhibited," by George Christian, interviewing Edy Williams about appearance on *LiS*'s "Two Weeks in Space."

The Daily Herald (Provo, Utah), November 11, 1968, CBS press release: "June Lockhart New Doctor on *Petticoat* Tale."

The Campus Christi Caller-Times, November 16, 1968, "TV Scout," by Joan Crosby.

Independent Press-Telegram (Long Beach, California), November 17, 1968, Don Matheson interview.

Beckley Post-Herald, November 18, 1968, "*Petticoat Junction Adds* Doctor (June Lockhart)," by Hal Humphrey.

The Raleigh Register (West Virginia), September 24, 1968, Vernon Scott interview with Irwin Allen.

The Ottawa Journal, November 26, 1968, "June 'Lost' and Found," by Sandy Gardiner.

The North Adams Transcript, November 30, 1968, article on Jonathan Harris by uncredited writer/interviewer.

The Tennessean, January 18, 1969, "TV Scout" synopsis of *My Three Sons* episode with Angela Cartwright.

The Corpus Christi Caller-Texas, January 21, 1969, "TV Scout" review of *Lancer*, with guest star Jonathan Harris.

The Daily Mail (Hagerstown, Maryland), January 23, 1969, Associated Press syndicated story: "Astronauts Lost in Space Provided New Movie Theme," by Bob Thomas.

Hartford News, April 2, 1969, "Producer Irwin Allen Follows in Footsteps of Jules Verne," by Allen M. Widem.

Variety, June 11, 1969, film review of *Rascal* (starring Billy Mumy), by "Tone."

The Courier-Journal (Louisville, Kentucky), film review of *Rascal* by William Mootz.

The Racine Journal-Times Sunday Bulletin (Wisconsin), August 10, 1969, regarding Jonathan Harris in *Damn Cardinals*, and touring NASA in Houston, Texas.

Los Angeles Times, August 14, 1969, Charles Chaplin film review of *Rascal*, starring Billy Mumy.

Eugene Register Guard, August 17, 1969, Leonard Stone comment about appearing on *LiS*.

Simpson's Leader-Times (Kittanning, Pennsylvania), November 22, 1969, "June Lockhart, Mike Douglas Thanksgiving Parade Hosts."

The Troy Record (New York), December 27, 1969, NEA syndicated newspaper filler piece: "Fans Confused About Actors," concerning Jonathan Harris and Ray Walston.

Florence Morning News, January 10, 1970, "Jonathan Harris Finds Chair Waiting on Space Show Set."

The Odessa American, January 11, 1970, "TV Scout" preview for *Land of the Giants* episode with guest star Jonathan Harris.

St. Louis Post-Dispatch, January 28, 1970, review of *Visit to a Small Planet*, starring Jonathan Harris.

The News-Herald (Franklin, Pennsylvania), review of *Get Smart*, featuring guest star Jonathan Harris.

The Daily Reporter (Dover, Ohio), April 14, 1970, UPI article, "June Lockhart is 'Free' Again, by Vernon Scott.

The Anniston Star (Alabama), May 28, 1970, NEW syndicated article: "June Lockhart Jr. Follows Acting Mom," by Stan Maays.

Variety, September 17, 1969, review of *Make Room for Granddaddy*, by "Swis."

Daily Variety, September 30, 1970, review of *Make Room for Granddaddy*, by "Mor."

The Kansas City Times, March 5, 1971, "No Star Illusions for Youthful Actress," by Joyce Wagner.

St. Louis Post-Dispatch, May 16, 1971, "No Make-believe Off-stage," by Margaret McManus.

Progress Bulletin (Pomona, California), May 17, 1971, "Not All Hollywood Gals Empty Shells."

The Indianapolis Star, May 23, 1971, "June Lockhart Wants To Shed Lingering Lassie's Mother Image," by Harvey Pack.

Variety, July 14, 1971, film review: *Bless the Beast and Children* (with Bill Mumy), by "Hawk."

The Daily Chronicle (De Kalb, Illinois), October 23, 1971, review of *Affairs of State*, starring June Lockhart.

Arizona Daily Sun, October 29, 1971, film review: *Bless the Beasts and Children.*

Detroit Free Press, November 10, 1971, film review of *Bless the Beasts and Children* (co-starring Bill Mumy), by John Weisman.

Detroit Free Press, November 10, 1971, film review of *Bless the Beasts and Children*, by Hiley H. Ward.

The Corpus Christi Caller-Times (Texas), November 17, 1971, film review: *Bless the Beasts and Children*, by Roger Greenspun.

Democrat and chronicle (Rochester, N.Y.), November 18, 1971, film review: *Bless the Beasts and Children*, by Bernard Drew.

The Akron Beacon Journal (Ohio), November 27, 1971, film review: *Bless the Beasts and Children*, by Dick Shippy.

The Cincinnati Enquirer (Ohio), November 27, 1971, film review: *Bless the Beasts and Children*, by Paul Kreft.

Prospector (El Paso, Texas), December 2, 1971, film review: *Bless the Beasts and Children*, by Robert Dahl.

The Cumberland News (Maryland), December 11, 1971, "Daddy Dan's Little Angela Big Girl Now."

Echoes-Sentinel (Warren Township, New Jersey), February 3, 1972, "Meadowbrook Comedy Stars June Lockhart & Daughter," by Allen Crossett.

The Daily Herald (Provo, Utah), March 27, 1972, "June Lockhart Keeps Busy in Acting Jobs," by Alice Pardue West.

Traverse City Record-Eagle, June 20, 1972, "Lockhart Show Biz Lineage Dates to Last Century," by Vernon Scott.

The Roselle Register (Illinois), July 21, 1972, listing for "Honeymoon Sweet," co-starring June Lockhart.

Los Angeles Times, October 17, 1972, "Getting Back in Shape," by Lydia Lane, interviewing Marta Kristen.

The Times Recorder (Troy, New York), February 23, 1973, review of *Sanford and Son* with guest star Jonathan Harris.

Detroit Free Press, June 10, 1973, print ad for *Terminal Island*, co-starring Marta Kristen.

Daily Variety, September 10, 1973, review of animated *Lost in Space*, by "Tone."

Variety, October 3, 1972, film review by "Besa" for *Once*, co-starring Marta Kristen.

The Lowell Sun (Massachusetts), January 2, 1973, "TV Scout" preview of *Sunshine* (with Bill Mumy).

Fredericksburg Standard (Texas), October 31, 1973, "*Sunshine* – A True Love Story."

The Journal News (White Plains, New York), November 4, 1973, "Letting a Little *Sunshine* In," by Charles Witbeck (TV Movie featuring Bill Mumy).

The Charleston Daily Mail, November 9, 1973, "*Sunshine* Unusual Love Story, review by Bill Garrett.

The Cincinnati Enquirer, December 1, 1973, "Monday's Role [in *I Never Said Goodbye*] Reminds June of Past," by Steve Hoffman.

Los Angeles Times, December 26, 1973, review, *Once*, by Charles Chaplin, co-starring Marta Kristen.

Daily Variety, January 8, 1974, *The Death Squad* (with Mark Goddard) review by "Tone."

Los Angeles Times, August 30, 1974, "Hot New Series That Never Was," by Cecil Smith (on *Sunshine*, with Bill Mumy).

Boxoffice, September 2, 1974, film review: *Terminal Island*, co-starring Marta Kristen.

Piano Daily Star-Courier (Texas), September 22, 1974, review of *My Daughter's Rated X*, starring Jonathan Harris.

Variety, December 18, 1974, film review: *Once*, co-starring Marta Kristen, by "Robe."

The Gallup Independent (New Mexico), March 6, 1975, "Odds against NBC's *Sunshine*."

Variety, March 17, 1975, review of TV series *Sunshine* (with Bill Mumy), by "Bill."

The Palm Beach Post (Florida), March 19, 1975, review of *Irene*, co-starring Jonathan Harris.

The Indianapolis Star, March 28, 1975, review of *Sunshine* series, by Julia Inman.

News-Journal (Mansfield, Ohio), April 30, 1975, "*Sunshine* Gets Fine Reviews, 'Pink Slip,'" by Charles Witbeck.

St. Louis Post-Dispatch, June 26, 1975, "Hair's Cut Short But Not Career," by Judy J. Newmark.

The Pantagraph (Bloomington, Illinois), March 11, 1976, UPI filler piece on Jonathan Harris.

The Daily Reporter (Dover, Ohio), January 28, 1977, "TV Fans' Mailbag," with letter concerning Jonathan Harris being absent from TV.

The Daily Herald (Provo, Utah), August 8, 1977, CBS press release announcing *Space Academy*, starring Jonathan Harris.

Daily Variety, September 1, 1977, "Just for Variety," by Army Archerd, saying *The Act*, with Mark Goddard undergoing changes in San Francisco, headed for L.A., plus review.

Variety, November 2, 1977, review of *The Act* (with Mark Goddard) by "Hobe."

The Oil City Derrick (Pennsylvania), December 6, 1977, article on *Sunshine Christmas* TV movie (with Bill Mumy).

Los Angeles Times, December 9, 1977, "Make Room for Angela," by Teri Lobree Ritzer.

The Independent Star (Indianapolis, Indiana), December 12, 1977, review of *Sunshine Christmas.*

Los Angeles Times, December 12, 1977, review of *Sunshine Christmas* by Cecil Smith.

Starlog, April 1979, "*Lost in Space* Lives," by Ted Michael Hruschak & Richard Meyers.

The Journal News (White Plains, New York), May 25, 1979, review of *Beyond the Poseidon Adventure*, by Bernard Drew.

Variety, May 30, 1979, review of *Beyond the Poseidon Adventure*, by "Poll."

Boxoffice, June 4, 1979, film review for *Beyond the Poseidon Adventure.*

The Independent Film Journal, July 1, 1979, film review for *Beyond the Poseidon Adventure*, by E.P.

Screen International, August 11, 1979, review of *Beyond the Poseidon Adventure.*

Detroit Free Press, August 12, 1979, review of *Beyond the Poseidon Adventure*, by Jack Mathews.

Los Angeles Times, August 17, 1979, film review for *Beyond the Poseidon Adventure*, by Kevin Thomas.

The Sydney Morning Herald (Australia), October 14, 1979, review of *Beyond the Poseidon Adventure.*

Variety, December 19, 1979, review of *Roller Boogie* (with Mark Goddard), by "Cart."

Variety, June 30, 1980, *Battle Beyond the Stars* film review by "Sege."

Arizona Republic. September 10, 1980, *Battle Beyond the Stars* review by Michael Maza.

The Pittsburgh Press, September 26, 1980, review of *Battle Beyond the Stars* by Ed Blank.

LISFAN ONE, 1981, "An Interview with Jonathan Harris," by Jeff Blair, foreword by Flint Mitchell.

Variety, July 14, 1982, "Mark Goddard Joined the Cast of NBC-TV's *The Doctors.*"

The Morning News (Wilmington, Delaware), April 6, 1983, review of *Zorro and Son*, by Bill Hayden.

Variety, April 13, 1983, Nielsen ratings for *Zorro and Son*, reported by Bob Knight, plus review of series by "Bok."

Broadcasting, May 16, 1983, TV ratings for *Zorro and Son.*

Broadcasting, June 13, 1983, TV ratings for *Zorro and Son.*

Starlog, July 1983, "June Lockhart, America's Favorite Mother," by Steve Swires."

Daily Variety, September 12, 1983, review of *Strange Invaders* (with June Lockhart) by "Loyn."

LISFAN3, 1984, "A Discussion with June Lockhart, by Ken Holland and Flint Mitchell.

Daily Variety, July 5, 1984, stage review of *The Love Suicide at Schofield Barracks*, co-starring Marta Kristen.

Variety, November 14, 1984, film review by "Lor" of *Gemini Affair – A Diary*, starring Marta Kristen.

Daily Variety, November 28, 1984, review of *Never Say Die*, by "Edwa."

The Salina Journal (Kansas), January 1985, announcing June Lockhart as a regular on *General Hospital*.

Starlog, July 1985, "Jonathan Harris: He's Dr. Smith -- Still *Lost in Space*," by Mike Clark; "Interview: L.B. Abbott," by Jeff Blair.

Starlog, November 1985, "Irwin Allen Remembers *Lost in Space*," by Mike Clark.

LISFAN4, 1986, "A Conversation with Marta Kristen," by Barry Magen; "Warning! Warning! – An Interview with Dick Tufeld," by Barry Magen.

Starlog, October 1988, "Marta Kristen: 'Viking Princess' of the 'All-American Space Family Robinson,'" by Mike Clark.

LISFAN5, 1988, "Interview with Marcel Hillaire," by Flint Mitchell; "Interview: Ezra Stone," by Flint Mitchell; "Interview with Gene Polito," by Flint Mitchell.

Starlog, April 1990, "The Cat with Nine Lives," by Kyle Counts.

The Akron Beacon Journal. September 6, 1990, "*Lost in Space* popular in revival," by Juan Carlos Coto.

Starlog, October 1990, "They Wrote Land of the Giants," by Mark Phillips, and "Misplaced Among the Stars," by Mike Clark.

LISFAN6, 1990, "Interview: Simon Wincelberg," by Flint Mitchell; "Interview: Robert Drasnin," by Flint Mitchell; "Interview: Gerald Fried," by Flint Mitchell; "Interview: Paul Zastupnevich," by Flint Mitchell.

Starlog, February 1991, "Will Power," by Kyle Counts.

Starlog, July 1991, "Bill Mumy," by Bill Cotter & Mike Clark.

Starlog, September 1991, "A Brief History of *Time Tunnel*, by Mark Phillips.

Starlog, March 1992, "The Master of Disaster," by Mike Clark.

Starlog, June 1992, "Captain of Television," by Pat Jankiewicz; "Time Traveler," by Kyle Counts.

Starlog, July 1992, "A Time to Remember," by Kyle Counts.

Starlog, August 1992, "Giant Jellyfish & Time-Lost Dinosaurs," by Mark Phillips.

Starlog, September 1992, "Giant Jellyfish & Time-Lost Dinosaurs, Part 2," by Mark Phillips.

Starlog, October 1992, "Giant Jellyfish & Time-Lost Dinosaurs, Part 3," by Mark Phillips.

Starlog, February 1993, "Designing Man," by Mike Clark.

Starlog, May 1993, "Space Duty," by Tom Weaver.

Starlog, August 1993, "The Oldest Working Screenwriter Explains It All," by Tom Weaver.

Starlog, January 1994, "Outrageous Original," article on June Lockhart, by Tom Weaver.

LISFAN8, 1994, "Interview: Liam Sullivan," by Flint Mitchell; "Interview: Malachi Throne," by Flint Mitchell; "Interview: John Abbott," by Flint Mitchell; "Interview: Jack Turley," by Flint Mitchell.

Starlog, April 1994, "The Man in the Bubble-Headed Mask," by Tom Weaver.

Starlog Platinum, 1994, "Voyages Long Past," by Mark Phillips.

The Indianapolis Star, February 18, 1996, "Mumy Keeps Kid Stardom in Perspective," by Steve Hall.

Daily Variety, August 23, 1996, "Hopkins Nabs *Space* Helm for New Line, by Dan Cox.

Daily Variety, January 22, 1997, "Oldman May Get *Lost* at NL," by Dan Cox.

Daily Variety, February 19, 1997, "New Line Find Russo for *Lost*," by John Dempsey.

Daily Variety, March 12, 1997, "Fill-In LeBlanc Spells Flanery in *Space*," by Dan Cox.

Asbury Park Press, May 25, 1997, "Why Harris Nixed *Lost in Space* Film," by Mark Voger.

TV Guide, October 11, 1997, "Space Odyssey," by Michael Logan.

The Akron Beacon Journal, October 15, 1997, "Laughs in Space," by Mark Dawidziak."

Pittsburgh Post-Gazette, October 15, 1997, "Lost in Space Finds its Way Back to TV," by Sharon Eberman.

Daily Variety, November 18, 1997, "DISH" by Michael Fleming.
Starlog, March 1998, "Dr. Smith, I Presume," by Ian Spelling.
Los Angeles Times, April 3, 1998, review of *Lost in Space* movie by Kenneth Turan.
Arizona Republic, April 3, 1998, "Allure of Cheesy Robot Hasn't Mellowed With Age," by Don Renfore, and film review for *Lost in Space* movie, by Bob Fernster.
Variety, April 13, 1998, Box office returns for *Lost in Space* film, knocking *Titanic* out of top Spot, reported by Leonard Klady.
The News Journal (Wilmington, Delaware), April 3, 1998, review of *Lost in Space* movie by Marshall Fine.
Chicago Tribune, April 3, 1998, review of *Lost in Space* movie, by Roger Ebert.
Variety, April 6, 1998, *Lost in Space* movie review, by Dennis Harvey.
Pittsburg Post-Gazette, April 7, 1998, "*Lost in Space* Actor Turned Down a Role in Movie Remake."
Screen International, April 10, 1998, film review of *Lost in Space* movie.
The Pantagraph (Bloomington, Illinois), April 10, 1998, film review of *Lost in Space*, by Dan craft.
Boxoffice, May 1, 1998, *Lost in Space* film review, by Wade Major.
Film Journal International, May 1, 1998, *Lost in Space* film review, by R.G.
Asbury Park Press (New Jersey), January 3, 1999, SECTION X syndicated story: "TV Wife Gathered Real and 'Reel' Families," by Mark Voger.
Daily Variety, January 5, 1999, "New Line Rushes to B.O. Riches," with final tally on *LiS* movie.
Variety, January 11, 1999, with list of the Top 250 domestic box office grosser of 1998, including *Lost in Space* at No. 26.
TV Collector magazine, February 1999, "Do You Remember…" by Mark Phillips.
TV Zone, February 1999, "Fantasy Flashback: 'My Friend, Mr. Nobody," by Jon Abbott."
Asbury Park Press, April 7, 2000, "Page X: Danger, Will Robinson," by Mark Voger.
Film Fax, 2001, "Charting a *Voyage to the Bottom of the Sea*!, by Mark Phillips.
Daily Variety, January 8, 2002, "Peacock Back to the Future," by Josef Adalian.
Daily Variety, March 5, 2002, "Fox TV Rewinds Allen's Sci-Fi Hits," by Josef Adalian.
Asbury Park Press, November 10, 2002, "Colleagues Recall TV's Dr. Smith," by Mark Voger.
Ashbury Park Press (New Jersey), December 27, 2002, Mark Voger last interview with Jonathon Harris.
Starlog Yearbook, February 2003, "Man Down Under," by Mark Phillips.
Daily Variety, September 24, 2003, "*Lost* is Found Again," by Josef Adalian.
Daily Variety, October 9, 2003, "WB Wins *Space* Race," by Josef Adalian.
Starlog, January 2007, "Rendezvous with Yesterday," by Tom Weaver; "Cast a Giant shadow," by Mark Phillips.
Famous Monsters, March/April 2015, "Black Hole Son," by Bill Mumy, and "*Lost in Space* Odyssey" by Kevin Burns.

Quote Index:

Abbott, John	JA-LISF. *Lost in Space Forever*, by Joel Eisner and/or Barry Magen (1992, Windsong Publishing, Inc.)
Abbott, John	JA-LISF8. *LISFAN8*, 1994, "Interview: John Abbott," by Flint Mitchell.
Abbott, L.B.	LBA-SE84. *Special Effects: Wire, Tape and Rubber Band Style*, by L.B. Abbott (ASC Press, 1984)
Abbott, L.B.	LBA-SL85. *Starlog*, July 1985, "Jonathan Harris: He's Dr. Smith – Still *Lost in Space*," by Mike Clark; "Interview: L.B. Abbott," by Jeff Blair.
Abbott, L.B.	LBA-LISF. *Lost in Space Forever*, by Joel Eisner and/or Barry Magen (1992, Windsong Publishing, Inc.)
Adams, Stanley	SA-LISF. *Lost in Space Forever*, by Joel Eisner and/or Barry Magen (1992, Windsong Publishing, Inc.)
Allen, Irwin	IA-TV48. *TELE-Views* magazine, November 26, 1948. "Stars Are Coming Your Way!", by Albert H. Grogan.
Allen, Irwin	IA-UP3. United Press wire story: "Scientists in 14 Countries Took Pictures for Hollywood Film, *The Sea Around Us*", in *The Lubbock Avalanche-Journal*, February 15, 1953.
Allen, Irwin	IA-UP53-2. United Press syndicated article, April 1953, "Award-Winning Film Sea Cost RKO Studio $200,000."
Allen, Irwin	IA-LPT55. United Press wire story: "Hollywood's Newest Stars Made Entirely of Rubber," *The Logansport Pharos-Tribune*, April 27, 1955.
Allen, Irwin	IA-UP56. United Press wire story: "Science Goes to Hollywood," from *Daily Independent Journal*, May 18, 1956.
Allen, Irwin	IA-KG56. *Kalamazoo, Mich. Gazette*, December 9, 1956, "Stars in Sky Talk and *The Story of Mankind* Becomes Star-Studded Movie."
Allen, Irwin	IA-NW57. *Newsweek*, May 6, 1957, "Movies: Everything, Then Some."
Allen, Irwin	IA-NWT59. *New York Times*, January 11, 1959, "*Big Circus* Troupe Works to Equal Bit Top's Authenticity and Color," by Thomas M. Pryor.
Allen, Irwin	IA-ADB59. *Anderson Daily Bulletin*, April 20, 1959, Louella O. Parson's column, regarding David Nelson in *The Big Circus*.
Allen, Irwin	IA-RMN59. *Rocky Mountain News*, June 30, 1959, "Producer 'Careful Shopper.'"
Allen, Irwin	IA-DP59. *Denver Post*, July 1, 1959, "Producer Allen Beats Drum for His Circus Extravaganza," by Larry Tajiri.
Allen, Irwin	IA-CDN59. Chicago Daily News syndicated story in *The Corpus Christi Caller-Times*, August 4, 1959, "Advice to Would-Be Actresses: 'Stay Home,'" by Pat Dalton.
Allen, Irwin	IA-EB61. *The Evening Bulletin*, June 13, 1961, "Director Must Rise Early for Today's Movies," by Rex Polier.
Allen, Irwin	IA-BG61. *The Boston Globe*, June 14, 1961, "Producer's Nightmare Science-Fiction Epic," by Kevin Kelly.

Allen, Irwin — IA-QPL61. *Quincy Patriot Ledger*, June 15, 1961, "*Bottom of Sea* Science Thriller, by Mabelle Fullerton.

Allen, Irwin — IA-CN61. *The Charlotte News*, June 21, 1961, "Pressure's On in Hollywood," by Brooks Yarborough.

Allen, Irwin — IA-CA61. *Chicago's American*, June 21, 1961, "Irwin Allen Wooing Girl Movie Patrons," by Ann Masters.

Allen, Irwin — IA-AJC61. *Atlantic Journal-Constitution*, June 1961, "Producer Irwin Allen" His Movies Are Potboilers, But He's Honest About Them," by Betty Carrollton.

Allen, Irwin — IA-CSM. *Christian Science Monitor*, June 1961, "Technicolor Visions Mean Business to Irwin Allen," by Nora E. Taylor.

Allen, Irwin — IA-EH62. Syndicated newspaper article by Elinor Hughes, 1962.

Allen, Irwin — IA-IAPC62. Irwin Allen Papers Collection belonging to Kevin Burns, 1962 file for *Five Weeks in a Balloon* -- newspaper clippings.

Allen, Irwin — IA-DV64. *Daily Variety*, May 5, 1964, "On All Channels: Irwin Allen 20-Year TVet," by Dave Kaufman.

Allen, Irwin — IA-TR64. *The Times Record*, October 17, 1964, "$1,000,000 Set Enjoyed in *Voyage*."

Allen, Irwin — IA-WDC64. *Waterloo Daily Courier*, October 25, 1964, "TV Keynotes: High Adventure Series," by Charles Witbeck.

Allen, Irwin — IA-DV65. *Daily Variety*, June 1, 1965, "On All Channels: Allen's 1997 *Space* Shot 1st Primetime Cliffhanger," by Dave Kaufman.

Allen, Irwin — IA-NYJM65. *New York Journal American* TV Magazine, October 31, 1965, "*Lost in Space* Proud of its Scenic Tricks," by Frank Judge.

Allen, Irwin — IA-TVG65. *TV Guide*, June 19, 1965, "Well, Of Course, It Isn't Exactly Hamlet…," by Marian Dern.

Allen, Irwin — IA-KG67. *Kingston Gleaner*, January 22, 1967, "Monsters, Adventure on JBC-TV."

Allen, Irwin — IA-IS67. *The Indianapolis Star*, September 24, 1967, "*Time Tunnel* Revival Planned by Allen," by Harvey Pack.

Allen, Irwin — IA-DMN68. *Dallas Morning News*, August 21, 1968, "Now It's Giants," by Bevo Baker.

Allen, Irwin — IA-RR68. *The Raleigh Register* (West Virginia), September 24, 1968, Vernon Scott interview with Irwin Allen.

Allen, Irwin — IA-HT69. *Hartford News*, April 2, 1969, "Producer Irwin Allen Follows in Footsteps of Jules Verne," by Allen M. Widem.

Allen, Irwin — IA-LISF1. *LISFAN ONE*, 1981, "An Interview with Jonathan Harris," by Jeff Blair; foreword by Flint Mithell.

Allen, Irwin — IA-SL85. *Starlog*, November 1985, "Irwin Allen Remembers *Lost in Space*," interviewed by Mike Clark.

Allen, Irwin — IA-SL92. *Starlog*, March 1992, "The Master of Disaster," by Mike Clark.

Allen, Irwin — IA-MC95. Twentieth Anniversary Interview with Irwin Allen, conducted by Mike Clark, 1995 (*Lost in Space* Blu-ray box set special feature, 2015).

Allen, Irwin — IA-TC09. Thunderchild.com, July 2009, "Underwater Adventures with the Crew of the Seaview," by Linda A. Delaney.

Allan, Michael — **MA-AI15. Author interview, 2015.**

Ansara, Michael	MS-LISF. *Lost in Space Forever*, by Joel Eisner and/or Barry Magen (1992, Windsong Publishing, Inc.)
Apstein, Theodore	TA-SL91. *Starlog*, September 1991, "A Brief History of *Time Tunnel*, by Mark Phillips.
Aubrey, Jim	JA-LAT86. *Los Angeles Times*; "Aubrey: A Lion in Winter," by Paul Rosenfield, April 27, 1986.
Basehart, Richard	RB-HT-60. *The [Hammond] Times*, March 22, 1960, "TV Keynotes: Richard Basehart is a Jet-Age Actor," by Harvey Pack.
Basehart, Richard	RB-ARN64. *Abilene Reporter News*, July 7, 1964, "Submarine Rates as Scene-Stealer," by Erskine Johnson.
Basehart, Richard	RB-LAT66. *Los Angeles Times*, January 23, 1966, "Basehart Changes Mind About TV," by Hedda Hopper.
Beck, Vincent	VB-LISF. *Lost in Space Forever*, by Joel Eisner and/or Barry Magen (1992, Windsong Publishing, Inc.)
Bennett, Charles	CB-SL92. *Starlog*, August 1992, "Giant Jellyfish & Time-Lost Dinosaurs," by Mark Phillips.
Bennett, Charles	CB-SL92. *Starlog*, October 1992, "Giant Jellyfish & Time-Lost Dinosaurs, Part 3," by Mark Phillips.
Bennett, Charles	CB-SL93. *Starlog*, August 1993, "The Oldest Working Screenwriter Explains It All," by Tom Weaver.
Bennett, Charles	CB-LISTTS96. *Lost in Space: The True Story*, by Ed Shifres (1996, Windsor House Publishing)
Bennett, Charles	CB-HPIS14. *Hitchcock's Partner in Suspense: The Life of Screenwriter Charles Bennett*, by Charles Bennett (University Press of Kentucky, 2014)
Bloom, Harold Jack	HJB-SL91. *Starlog*, September 1991, "A Brief History of *Time Tunnel*, by Mark Phillips.
Bloomfield, Robert	RB-SL92. *Starlog*, October 1992, "Giant Jellyfish & Time-Lost Dinosaurs, Part 3," by Mark Phillips.
Burns, Kevin	KB-DA02. *Daily Variety*, March 5, 2002, "Fox TV Rewinds Allen's Sci-Fi Hits," by Josef Adalian.
Burns. Kevin	KB-DA03. *Daily Variety*, September 24, 2003, "*Lost* is Found Again," by Josef Adalian.
Burns, Kevin	KB-FM15. *Famous Monsters*, March/April 2015, "*Lost in Space* Odyssey" by Kevin Burns.
Burns, Kevin	**KB-AI16. Author interview, 2016.**
Carmel, Roger C.	**RCC-AI. Author interview, 1982.**
Carradine, John	JC-IS67. *Indianapolis Star*, March 26, 1967.

Cartwright, Angela	AC-SAE66. *San Antonio Express and News*, July 31, 1966, "Teen TV Actress Has Novel Dating Problem."
Cartwright, Angela	AC-KCT71. *The Kansas City Times*, March 5, 1971, "No Star Illusions for Youthful Actress," by Joyce Wagner.
Cartwright, Angela	AC-CN71. *The Cumberland News* (Maryland), December 11, 1971, "Daddy Dan's Little Angela Big Girl Now."
Cartwright, Angela	AC-SLDP75. *St. Louis Post-Dispatch*, June 26, 1975, "Hair's Cut Short But Not Career," by Judy J. Newmark
Cartwright, Angela	AC-SL79. *Starlog*, April 1979, "*Lost in Space* Lives," by Ted Michael Hruschak & Richard Meyers.
Cartwright, Angela	AC-LISF. *Lost in Space Forever*, by Joel Eisner and/or Barry Magen (1992, Windsong Publishing, Inc.)
Cartwright, Angela	AC-TVG97. *TV Guide*, October 11, 1997, "Space Odyssey," by Michael Logan.
Cartwright, Angela	AC-LISM. LostInSpaceMemories.com.
Cartwright, Angela	AC-EPT13. *El Paso Times*, "Angela Cartwright Looks Back on *Sound of Music*," by Doug Pullen, August 7, 2013.
Cartwright, Angela	AC-CAFE13. Café.com, "Angela Cartwright Talks with Café about Danny Thomas, *Lost in Space*, *The Sound of Music*, and Her Artwork," May 15, 2013.
Cartwright, Angela	AC-SFO14. Sci-fi-online.com, interview from April 6, 2014.
Cartwright, Angela	AC-WB15. Angela-Cartwight.com website, updated 2015.
Cartwright, Angela	AC-AF15. Angelfire.com, "Interview(s) with Angela Cartwright (Brigitta)," updated 2015.
Cartwright, Angela	AC-LISBR15. *Lost in Space* Blu-ray box set, special features commentary, 2015.
Cassidy, Ted	TC-LISF. *Lost in Space Forever*, by Joel Eisner and/or Barry Magen (1992, Windsong Publishing, Inc.)
Catalano. Terri	TC-LISBR15. Bonus feature interview, *Lost in Space* Blu-ray box set, 2015.
Chambers, John	JC-LISF. *Lost in Space Forever*, by Joel Eisner and/or Barry Magen (1992, Windsong Publishing, Inc.)
Clark, Mike	**MC-AI15. Author interview.**
Colbert, Robert	RC-AR66. *Arizona Republic*, November 27, 1966, "*Time Tunnel* from the Epics," by Charles Witbeck.
Colbert, Robert	RC-SL92. *Starlog*, June 1992, "Time Traveler," by Kyle Counts.
Colbert, Robert	RC-SL07. *Starlog*, January 2007, "Rendezvous with Yesterday," by Tom Weaver.
Comi, Paul	**PC-AI13. Author interview.**

Connell, Dell	DC-LISTTS. *Lost in Space: The True Story*, by Ed Shifres (1996, Windsor House Publishing)
Conrad, Michael	MC-LISF. *Lost in Space Forever*, by Joel Eisner and/or Barry Magen (1992, Windsong Publishing, Inc.)
Coon, Gene	GC-TMOST68. Interviewed by Stephen Whitfield for *The Making of Star Trek* (Ballantine Books, 1968)
Crawford, John	JC-SL96. *Starlog*, February 1996, "Merchant of Menace," interviewed by Joel Eisner.
D-Agosta, Joe	**JDA-AI15. Author interview, 2015.**
Dano, Royal	RD-LISF. *Lost in Space Forever*, by Joel Eisner and/or Barry Magen (1992, Windsong Publishing, Inc.)
Darren, James	JD-CP66. *Courier-Post* (Camden, New Jersey), September 17, 1966, "*Time* Will Tell," by Beth Gillin.
Darren, James	JD-SL92. *Starlog*, July 1992, "A Time to Remember," by Kyle Counts.
De Luca, Michael	MDL-DV96. *Daily Variety*, August 23, 1996, "Hopkins Nabs *Space* Helm for New Line, by Dan Cox.
Disney, Roy	RD-DV59. *Daily Variety*, July 2, 1959, Disney Antitrust Suit Vs. ABC," reporting battle over *Zorro*.
Douglas, Robert	RD-SL95. *Starlog*, November 1995, "Space Families Found, Part Two," interviewed by Mark Phillips.
Drasnin, Robert	RD-LISF6. *LISFAN6*, 1990, "Interview: Robert Drasnin," by Flint Mitchell.
Duncan, Bob	BD-SL90. *Starlog*, October 1990, "They Wrote Land of the Giants," interviewed by Mark Phillips.
Duncan, Bob	BD-SL91. *Starlog*, October 1991, "Time & *Time Tunnel* Again," interviewed by Mark Phillips.
Duncan, Bob	BD-SL95. *Starlog*, October 1995, "Space Family Lost, Part One," interviewed by Mark Phillips.
Eden, Barbara	**BE-AI15. Author interview, 2015.**
Ellerbe, Harry	HE-LAT47. *Los Angeles Times*, December 14, 1947, "June Lockhart Considers West Coast Stock, Films," by E.J. Strong.
Ellison, Harlan	**HE-AI13. Author's interview.**
Feld, Frtiz	FF-LISF. *Lost in Space Forever*, by Joel Eisner and/or Barry Magen (1992, Windsong Publishing, Inc.)

Finnerman, Gerald	JF-AOT-02. Interviewed for Archive of Television, October 8, 2002.
Fried, Gerald	GF-LISF6. *LISFAN6*, 1990, "Interview: Gerald Fried," by Flint Mitchell.
Gail, Al	AG-SL92. *Starlog*, March 1992, "The Master of Disaster," by Mike Clark.
Gail, Al.	AG-SL92. *Starlog*, October 1992, "Giant Jellyfish & Time-Lost Dinosaurs, Part 3," by Mark Phillips.
Gail, Al	**AG-KB95. Interview by Kevin Burns, 1995.**
Gaspin, Jeff	JG-DV02. *Daily Variety*, January 8, 2002, "Peacock Back to the Future," by Josef Adalian.
Giler, Berne	BG-TVG66. *TV Guide*, September 24, 1966, "When Guy Hisses the Villain, he Means It," by Michael Fessier, Jr.
Goddard, Mark	MG-TDC61. *Tucson Daily Citizen*, February 11, 1961, "He Came and Conquered," by Micheline Keating.
Goddard, Mark	MG-PT61. *Press Telegram*, June 2, 1961, "Found: A Modest Actor! Goddard – Still Learning," by Terry Vernon.
Goddard, Mark	MG-OSE66. *Ogden Standard Examiner*, January 23, 1966, "Behind the Scenes," by Alice Pardoe West.
Goddard, Mark	MG-TVG66. *TV Guide*, September 24, 1966, "When Guy Hisses the Villain -- HE MEANS IT," by Michael Fessier, Jr.
Goddard, Mark	MG-DV68. *Daily Variety*, February 28, 1968, Mark Goddard on cancellation of *Lost in Space*.
Goddard, Mark	MG-LISF. *Lost in Space Forever*, by Joel Eisner and/or Barry Magen (1992, Windsong Publishing, Inc.)
Goddard, Mark	MG-SL93. *Starlog*, May 1993, "Space Duty," by Tom Weaver.
Goddard, Mark	MG-TVG97. *TV Guide*, October 11, 1997, "Space Odyssey," by Michael Logan.
Goddard, Mark	MG-LISM. LostinSpaceMemories.com.
Goddard, Mark	MG-TSAB08. To Space and Back: A Memoir by Mark Goddard (2008, iUniverse).
Goddard, Mark	MG-LISBR15. *Lost in Space* Blu-ray box set, special features commentary, 2015.
Grant. David	DG-DV02. *Daily Variety*, March 5, 2002, "Fox TV Rewinds Allen's Sci-Fi Hits," by Josef Adalian.
Hagen. Kevin	KH-LISF. *Lost in Space Forever*, by Joel Eisner and/or Barry Magen (1992, Windsong Publishing, Inc.)
Hagen, Kevin	KH-SL07. *Starlog*, January 2007, "Cast a Giant shadow," by Mark Phillips.
Hamner, Robert	RH-SL92. *Starlog*, August 1992, "Giant Jellyfish & Time-Lost Dinosaurs, Part 2," by Mark Phillips.

Hamner, Robert RH-SL92. *Starlog*, October 1992, "Giant Jellyfish & Time-Lost Dinosaurs, Part 3," by Mark Phillips.

Hamner, Robert RH-SL95. *Starlog*, November, 1995, "Space Families Found, Part Two," interviewed by Mark Phillips.

Hamner, Robert RH-LISF. *Lost in Space Forever*, by Joel Eisner and/or Barry Magen (1992, Windsong Publishing, Inc.)

Hamner, Robert RH-VTTBOTS. Mike'svoyagetothebottomofthesea.zone at vttbolts.com, interviewed by Mark Phillips.

Harris, Harry HH-KB95. Interviewed by Kevin Burns, 1995.

Harris, Harry HH-A&EB02. *A & E Biography*: "Jonathan Harris: Never Fear, Smith Is Here," 2002.

Harris, Jonathan JH-LAT65. *Los Angeles Times*, December 5, 1965, "Playing Spy in Space," by Aleene MacMinn.

Harris, Jonathan JH-AC66. *Annapolis Capitol*, March 21, 1966, Harris quite on *Batman*.

Harris, Jonathan JH-WDC66. *Waterloo Daily Courier*, September 25, 1966, "No Scene-Stealing on *Lost in Space*."

Harris, Jonathan JH-RDN66. *Richardson Daily News*, April 28. 1966, "*Lost in Space* Doctor Finds Kitchen."

Harris, Jonathan JH-IS67. *The Indianapolis Star*, July 9, 1967.

Harris, Jonathan JH-NAT68. *The North Adams Transcript*, November 30, 1968, article on Jonathan Harris by uncredited writer/interviewer.

Harris, Jonathan JH-LISF. *Lost in Space Forever*, by Joel Eisner and/or Barry Magen (1992, Windsong Publishing, Inc.)

Harris, Jonathan JH-IASB2. *The Irwin Allen Scrapbook, Volume Two: Lost in Space*, Edited by William E. Anchors, Jr.

Harris, Jonathan JH-SL85. *Starlog*, July 1985, "Jonathan Harris: He's Dr. Smith – - Still *Lost in Space*," by Mike Clark.

Harris, Jonathan JH-MMM88. Interviewed for *Mancow's Morning Madness*, 1988.

Harris, Jonathan JH-ABJ90. *The Akron Beacon Journal*. September 6, 1990, "*Lost in Space* popular in revival," by Juan Carlos Coto.

Harris, Jonathan JH-APP97. *Asbury Park Press*, May 25, 1997, "Why Harris Nixed *Lost in Space* Film," by Mark Voger.

Harris, Jonathan JH-TVG97. *TV Guide*, October 11, 1997, "Space Odyssey," by Michael Logan.

Harris, Jonathan JH-ABJ97. *The Akron Beacon Journal*, October 15, 1997, "Laughs in Space," by Mark Dawidziak."

Harris, Jonathan JH-SL98. *Starlog*, March 1998, "Dr. Smith, I Presume," by Ian Spelling.

Harris, Jonathan JH-PPG98. *Pittsburg Post-Gazette*, April 7, 1998, "*Lost in Space* Actor Turned Down a Role in Movie Remake."

Harris, Jonathan JH-A&EB02. *A&E Biography*: "Jonathan Harris: Never Fear, Smith Is Here," 2002.

Harris, Jonathan JH-APP02. *Ashbury Park Press* (New Jersey), December 27, 2002, Mark Voger last interview with Jonathon Harris.

Harris, Jonathan JH-LISM. BM-LISM. LostInSpaceMemoreis.com.

Hartford, Dee	DH-LISF. *Lost in Space Forever*, by Joel Eisner and/or Barry Magen (1992, Windsong Publishing, Inc.)
Hedison, David	DH-SL86. *Starlog*, July 1986, "David Hedison: Submarine Hero," by Mike Clark.
Hedison, David	DH-TCF07. Twentieth Century Fox bts material, 2007 DVD set.
Hedison, David	DH-LAT11. From latimes.com, July, 2011, 'David Hedison Looks Back On Periscope," by Susan King.
Hedison, David	DH-CB12. Cultbox.co.uk, "David Hedison, James Bond, *Voyage to the Bottom of the Sea*, by William Martin.
Hedeson, David	DH-DM13. Diaboliquemagazine.com, 2013, interviewed by Harvey Chartrand.
Herbert, F. Hugh	FHH-LAT47. *Los Angeles Times*, December 14, 1947, "June Lockhart Considers West Coast Stock, Films," by E.J. Strong.
Hewitt, Alan	AH-LISF. *Lost in Space Forever*, by Joel Eisner and/or Barry Magen (1992, Windsong Publishing, Inc.)
Hillaire, Marcel	MH-LISF5. *LISFAN5*, 1988, "Interview with Marcel Hillaire," by Flint Mitchell.
Hillaire, Marcel	MH-LISF. *Lost in Space Forever*, by Joel Eisner and/or Barry Magen (1992, Windsong Publishing, Inc.)
Hiller, Arthur	AH-A&EB02. *A & E Biography*: "Jonathan Harris: Never Fear, Smith Is Here," 2002.
Hunter, Lew	**LH-AI15. Author interview, 2015.**
Jashni, Jon	JJ-DV02. *Daily Variety*, March 5, 2002, "Fox TV Rewinds Allen's Sci-Fi Hits," by Josef Adalian.
Juran, Nathan	NJ-LISF. *Lost in Space Forever*, by Joel Eisner and/or Barry Magen (1992, Windsong Publishing, Inc.)
Katz, Oscar	OK-STC94. *Star Trek Creator*, by David Alexander (Penguin Books, 1994)
Keelin, Mike	MK-LISF. *Lost in Space Forever*, by Joel Eisner and/or Barry Magen (1992, Windsong Publishing, Inc.)
Kinoshita, Bob	BK-ICONS-08. Interviewed by icons in 2008 for b9rbs.com.
Klemperer, Werner	WK-BC66. *Bakersfield Californian*, April 9, 1966, "*Heroes*' Star Plans Travel."
Kranzler, Bryna	**BK-AI16. Author interview, January 2016.**

Kristen, Marta	MK-CRG62. *Cedar Rapids Gazette*, September 23, 1962, "Marta Kristen: Disney's Newest Discovery," by Lloyd Shearer.
Kristen, Marta	MK-LAT65. *Los Angeles Times* Sunday TV magazine, October 3, 1965, "Marta: A Space Saver," by Hal Humphrey.
Kristen, Marta	MK-TVG65. *TV Guide*, November 20, 1965, "Norwegian Cinderella."
Kristen, Marta	MK-IPT66. *Independent Press Telegram*, January 23, 1966, "Tele Vues" cover story on Marta Kristen, by Bert Resnik.
Kristen, Marta	MK-LG68. Leo Guild syndicated column, "A Look at TV" -- "Lost in Space Takes Walk After 3 Years."
Kristen, Marta	MK-LAT72. *Los Angeles Times*, October 17, 1972, "Getting Back in Shape," by Lydia Lane, interviewing Marta Kristen.
Kristen, Marta	MK-LISF4. *LISFAN4*, 1986, "A conversation with Marta Kristen," by Barry Magen.
Kristen, Marta	MK-SL88. *Starlog*, October 1988, "Marta Kristen: 'Viking Princess' of the 'All-American Space Family Robinson,'" by Mike Clark.
Kristen, Marta	MK-LISF. *Lost in Space Forever*, by Joel Eisner and/or Barry Magen (1992, Windsong Publishing, Inc.)
Kristen, Marta	MK-TVG97. *TV Guide*, October 11, 1997, "Space Odyssey," by Michael Logan.
Kristen, Marta	MK-APP02. *Asbury Park Press*, November 10, 2002, "Colleagues Recall TV's Dr. Smith," by Mark Voger.
Kristen, Marta	MK-LISM. LostInSpaceMemoreis.com.
Kristen, Marta	**MK-AI15. Author interview, 2015.**
Kristen, Marta	MK-LISBR15. *Lost in Space* Blu-ray box set, special features commentary, 2015.
Leader, Tony	TL-LISF. *Lost in Space Forever*, by Joel Eisner and/or Barry Magen (1992, Windsong Publishing, Inc.)
Lehmann, Theodore	TL-LISF. *Lost in Space Forever*, by Joel Eisner and/or Barry Magen (1992, Windsong Publishing, Inc.)
Levin, Jordan	JL-DV03. *Daily Variety*, October 9, 2003, "WB Wins *Space* Race," by Josef Adalian.
Lewis, Al	AL-MMM88. Interviewed for *Mancow's Morning Madness*, 1988.
Lewis, Al	AL-LISF. *Lost in Space Forever*, by Joel Eisner and/or Barry Magen (1992, Windsong Publishing, Inc.)
Lockhart, Gene	GL-SHJ47. JL-SHJ47. *Syracuse Herald Journal*, November 23, 1947, "New Broadway Star," by Jean Meegan.
Lockhart, Gene	GL-LOP48. Louella O. Parsons' column, *Charleston Gazette*, January 4, 1948, "Critic Applauds Stage Poise of Youthful June Lockhart."
Lockhart, June	JL-BDE47. *The Brooklyn Daily Eagle*, November 20, 1947, "Being the Rage of Broadway Leaves No Time to Buy Lipstick," by Shiela McKeon.

Lockhart, June	JL-SHJ47. *Syracuse Herald Journal*, November 23, 1947, "New Broadway Star," by Jean Meegan.
Lockhart, June	JL-LAT47. *Los Angeles Times*, December 14, 1947, "June Lockhart Considers West Coast Stock, Films," by E.J. Strong.
Lockhart, June	JL-LOP48. Louella O. Parsons' column, *Charleston Gazette*, January 4, 1948, "Critic Applauds Stage Poise of Youthful June Lockhart."
Lockhart, June	JL-LAT57. *Los Angeles Times*, November 10, 1957, "June Lockhart Moves Ahead," by Edwin Schallert.
Lockhart, June	JL-DV58. *Daily Variety*, June 3, 1958, "On All Channels," by Dave Kaufman.
Lockhart, June	JL-CDS58. *Corsicana Daily Sun*, December 30, 1958, "June Lockhart Without Fears of Being typed," by Charles Mercer.
Lockhart, June	JL-MET59. *Monroe Evening Times*, March 14, 1959, "June Lockhart Keeps Tradition," by Hal Boyle.
Lockhart, June	JL-SNB60. *Shamokian News-Dispatch*, September 22, 1960, "June Lockhart, Star of *Lassie*, Leads Double Life," by Vernon Scott.
Lockhart, June	JL-TR61. *The Times Recorder*, November 26, 1961, "There's Only One Lassie But He Has Three Aides."
Lockhart, June	JL-SGM61. *Sunday Gazette-Mail*, December 3, 1961, "June Lockhart Happy in Secondary Role."
Lockhart, June	JL-LAT62. *Los Angeles Times*, March 20, 1962, "June Lockhart Finds *Lassie* a Belssing," by Hedda Hopper.
Lockhart, June	JL-LAT64. *Los Angeles Times*, May 24, 1964, "June Fleas *Lassie* Show," by Aleene MacMinn.
Lockhart, June	JL-SGM64. *Sunday Gazette-Mail*, May 24, 1964, "June Lockhart Seeks Sexy Role," by Charles Wilbeck.
Lockhart, June	JL-LAT64a. *Los Angeles Times*, August 23, 1964, "June Sitting Pretty On TV Panel Shows," by Hal Humphrey.
Lockhart, June	JL-NCN65. *New Castle News*, UPI story, "June Will Tackle New Role on TV," by Vernon Scott, July 22, 1965.
Lockhart, June	JL-DV66. *Daily Variety*, February 9, 1966, "On All Channels," by Dave Kaufman.
Lockhart, June	JL-TA67. *The Advocate*, May 21, 1967, "Show Beat."
Lockhart, June	JL-OSE68. *The Ogden Standard-Examiner* (Utah), April 14, 1968, "Ask Them Yourself" letters column, with June Lockhart regarding beauty pageants.
Lockhart, June	JL-ABJ68. *The Akron Beacon Journal*, October 6, 1968, "New Lady in Town," by Bob Thomas.
Lockhart, June	JL-BPH68. *Beckley Post-Herald*, November 18, 1968, "*Petticoat Junction Adds* Doctor (June Lockhart)," by Hal Humphrey.
Lockhart, June	JL-OJ68. *The Ottawa Journal*, November 26, 1968, "June 'Lost' and Found," by Sandy Gardiner.
Lockhart, June	JL-SLPD71. *St. Louis Post-Dispatch*, May 16, 1971, "No Make-believe Off-stage," by Margaret McManus.
Lockhart, June	JL-PB71. *Progress Bulletin* (Pomona, California), May 17, 1971, "Not All Hollywood Gals Empty Shells."
Lockhart, June	JL-CE73. *The Cincinnati Enquirer*, December 1, 1973, "Monday's Role Reminds June of Past," by Steve Hoffman.

Lockhart, June	JL-SL83. *Starlog*, July 1983, "June Lockhart, America's Favorite Mother," interviewed by Steve Swires.
Lockhart, June	JL-LISF3. *LISFAN3*, 1984, "A Discussion with June Lockhart, by Ken Holland and Flint Mitchell.
Lockhart, June	JL-LISF. *Lost in Space Forever*, by Joel Eisner and/or Barry Magen (1992, Windsong Publishing, Inc.)
Lockhart, June	JL-SL94. *Starlog*, January 1994, "Outrageous Original," by Tom Weaver.
Lockhart, June	JL-TVG97. *TV Guide*, October 11, 1997, "Space Odyssey," by Michael Logan.
Lockhart, June	JL-APP99. *Ashbury Park Press* (New Jersey), January 3, 1999, SECTION X syndicated story: "TV Wife Gathered Real and 'Reel' Families," by Mark Voger.
Lockhart, June	JL-APP02. *Asbury Park Press*, November 10, 2002, "Colleagues Recall TV's Dr. Smith," by Mark Voger.
Lockhart, June	JL-LISM. LostInSpaceMemoreis.com.
Lockhart, June	JL-PCA. Popcultureaddict.com.
Lockhart, June	JL-YT. June Lockhart interview on YouTube.
Luna, BarBara	**BL-AI15. Author interview, 2015.**
Lupiz, Fernando	FL-GW:MBTM05. Interview from *Guy Williams: The Man Behind the Mask*, by Antoinette Girgenti Lane (BearManor Media, 2005)
Maffei, Robert	RM-LISF. *Lost in Space Forever*, by Joel Eisner and/or Barry Magen (1992, Windsong Publishing, Inc.)
Mandelick, Gilbert	GM-LISF. *Lost in Space Forever*, by Joel Eisner and/or Barry Magen (1992, Windsong Publishing, Inc.)
Marlo, Steve	**SM-AI15. Author interview, 2015.**
Matheson, Don	DM-IPT. *Independent Press-Telegram* (Long Beach, California), November 17, 1968, Don Matheson interview.
Mathews, Sheila	SM-CCCT66. *The Corpus Christi Caller–Times*, December 18, 1966.
Mathews-Allen, Sheila	**SMA-KB95. Interviewed by Kevin Burns, 1995.**
Mathews-Allen, Sheila	SMA-DV02. *Daily Variety*, March 5, 2002, "Fox TV Rewinds Allen's Sci-Fi Hits," by Josef Adalian.
May, Bob	BM-LISF. *Lost in Space Forever*, by Joel Eisner and/or Barry Magen (1992, Windsong Publishing, Inc.)
May, Bob	BM-SL94. *Starlog*, April 1994, "The Man in the Bubble-Headed Mask," by Tom Weaver.
May, Bob	**BM-KB95. Interviewed by Kevin Burns, 1995.**
May, Bob	BM-LISM01. LostInSpaceMemoreis.com, message from Bob May, July 24, 2001.
May, Bob	BM-APP02. *Asbury Park Press*, November 10, 2002, "Colleagues Recall TV's Dr. Smith," by Mark Voger.

McEveety, Vincent	**VM-AI13. Author interview, 2013.**
McClory, Sean	SM-LISF. *Lost in Space Forever*, by Joel Eisner and/or Barry Magen (1992, Windsong Publishing, Inc.)
Melchior, Ib J.	IJM-LISTTS96. Interviewed by Scott Halper on TV program *Around the Mind Bend*, as printed in *Lost in Space: The True Story*, by Ed Shifres (1996, Windsor House Publishing).
Meriwether, Lee	LM-SL90. *Starlog*, April 1990, "The Cat with Nine Lives," by Kyle Counts.
Meriwether, Lee	**LM-AI15. Author interview, 2015.**
Mintz, Robert	RM-VTTBOTS. Mike'svoyagetothebottomofthesea.zone at vttbolts.com, interviewed by Mark Phillips.
Mohr, Gerald	GM-SHJ66. *Syracuse Herald Journal*, December 11, 1966, "Mohr's 'Heavy'."
Monty, Harry	HM-LISF. *Lost in Space Forever*, by Joel Eisner and/or Barry Magen (1992, Windsong Publishing, Inc.)
Mumy, Bill	BM-UPI64. *Lebanon Daily News*, June 6, 1964, UPI syndicated story: "Freckled American Boy, 10, Plays Love Scene with Bardot," by Vernon Scott.
Mumy, Bill	BM-HH64. *Valley Morning Star*, August 27, 1964, "In Hollywood" syndicated column, by Hedda Hopper.
Mumy, Bill	BM-SL81. *Starlog*, July 1981, "Bill Mumy," by Bill Cotter & Mike Clark.
Mumy, Bill	BM-LISBM#13. Interviewed by Robert Coyle for Lost in Space B-monthly, #13, 1980s.
Mumy, Bill	BM-SL91. *Starlog*, February 1991, "Will Power," by Kyle Counts.
Mumy, Bill	BM-LISF. *Lost in Space Forever*, by Joel Eisner and/or Barry Magen (1992, Windsong Publishing, Inc.)
Mumy, Bill	BM-IS96. *The Indianapolis Star*, February 18, 1996, "Mumy Keeps Kid Stardom in Perspective," by Steve Hall.
Mumy, Bill	BM-TVG97. *TV Guide*, October 11, 1997, "Space Odyssey," by Michael Logan.
Mumy, Bill	**BM-KB95. Interviewed by Kevin Burns, 1995.**
Mumy, Bill	BM-APP00. *Ashbury Park Press*, April 7, 2000, "Page X: Danger, Will Robinson," by Mark Voger.
Mumy, Bill	BM-APP02. *Asbury Park Press*, November 10, 2002, "Colleagues Recall TV's Dr. Smith," by Mark Voger.
Mumy, Bill	BM-FM15. *Famous Monsters*, March 2015, "Black Hole Son," by Bill Mumy.
Mumy, Bill	BM-LISM. LostInSpaceMemoreis.com.
Mumy, Bill	BM-LISW. *Lost in Space* Wikipedia, including interview conducted by Robert Coyle, Jeff Blair, and David Krinksy.

Mumy, Bill	**BM-AI15. Author interview, 2015.**
Mumy, Bill	BM-FM15. *Famous Monsters*, March/April 2015, "Black Hole Son," by Bill Mumy.
Mumy, Bill	BM-LISBR15. *Lost in Space* Blu-ray box set, special features commentary, 2015.
Newman, Gary	GN-DA02. *Daily Variety*, March 5, 2002, "Fox TV Rewinds Allen's Sci-Fi Hits," by Josef Adalian.
Newman, Gary	GN-DV03. *Daily Variety*, October 9, 2003, "WB Wins *Space* Race," by Josef Adalian.
Ormond, John	JO-GW:MBTM05. Interview from *Guy Williams: The Man Behind the Mask*, by Antoinette Girgenti Lane (BearManor Media, 2005)
Penn, Leo	LP-SL92. *Starlog*, June 1992, "Captain of Television," by Pat Jankiewicz.
Petrie, Doug	DP-DV03. *Daily Variety*, October 9, 2003, "WB Wins *Space* Race," by Josef Adalian.
Polito, Gene	GP-LISF5. *LISFAN5*, 1988, "Interview with Gene Polito," by Flint Mitchell.
Rennie, Michael	MR-imdb. Quote posted on Internet Movie Data Base.
Richardson, Don	DR-LISF. *Lost in Space Forever*, by Joel Eisner and/or Barry Magen (1992, Windsong Publishing, Inc.)
Robbie, Seymour	SR-SL95. *Starlog*, "Space Families Found, Part Two," interviewed by Mark Phillips.
Robotham, George	GR-SFTS2. *Science Fiction Television Series*, Volume 2, by Mark Phillips and Frank Garcia (1996, McFarland & Co.)
Robotham, George	GR-TVC99. *The TV Collector* magazine, February 1999, "Do You Remember…" by Mark Phillips.
Roddenberry, Gene	GR-MOST68. *The Making of Star Trek*, by Stephen E. Whitfield (Ballantine Books, 1968)
Roley, Sutton	SR-SL95. *Starlog*, November, 1995, "Space Families Found, Part Two," interviewed by Mark Phillips.
Roley, Sutton	SM-SFTS2. *Science Fiction Television Series*, Volume 2, by Mark Phillips and Frank Garcia (1996, McFarland & Co.)
Rush, Herman	**HR-AI15. Author interview, 2015.**
Salmi, Albert	AS-IS67. *Indianapolis Star*, January 22, 1967.

Saperstein, Richard	RS-DV96. *Daily Variety*, August 23, 1996, "Hopkins Nabs *Space* Helm for New Line, by Dan Cox.
Self, William	WS-LAT64. *Los Angeles Times*, June 28, 1964, "Fox Suddenly Jumps into the Series Picture," by Cecil Smith.
Self, William	WS-B64. *Broadcasting*, December 28, 1964, "Entertainment: Goal and Glory of William Self."
Self, William	WS-DV66. *Daily Variety*, November 16, 1966, "On All Channels" by Dave Kaufman, interview with William Self.
Silver, Steve	SS-GY:TMBTM05. Steve Silver interview in *Guy Williams: The Man Behind the Mask*, by Antoinette Girgenti Lane (2005, BearManor Media)
Slade, Mark	MS-SFTS2. *Science Fiction Television Series*, Volume 2, by Mark Phillips and Frank Garcia (1996, McFarland & Co.)
Slade, Mark	MS-TVC99. *The TV Collector* magazine, February 1999, "Do You Remember…" by Mark Phillips.
Slade, Mark	MS-VTTBOTS. Mark Phillips' interview posted at Mike'svoyagetothebottomofthesea.zone at vttbolts.com.
Stadd, Leonard	LS-SL91. *Starlog*, September 1991, "A Brief History of *Time Tunnel*, by Mark Phillips.
Stewart, Larry	LS-LISF. *Lost in Space Forever*, by Joel Eisner and/or Barry Magen (1992, Windsong Publishing, Inc.)
Stewart, Larry	LS-SFTS2. *Science Fiction Television Series*, Volume 2, by Mark Phillips and Frank Garcia (1996, McFarland & Co.)
Stewart, Margaret	MS-SL95. *Starlog*, October 1995, "Space Family Lost, Part One," interviewed by Mark Phillips.
Stone, Ezra	ES-IS67. *The Indianapolis Star*, January 8, 1967.
Stone, Ezra	ES-LISF5. *LISFAN5*, 1988, "Interview: Ezra Stone," by Flint Mitchell.
Stone, Ezra	ES-SL95. *Starlog*, "Space Families Found, Part Two," interviewed by Mark Phillips.
Stone, Leonard	LS-LISF. *Lost in Space Forever*, by Joel Eisner and/or Barry Magen (1992, Windsong Publishing, Inc.)
Sullivan, Liam	LS-LISF. *Lost in Space Forever*, by Joel Eisner and/or Barry Magen (1992, Windsong Publishing, Inc.)
Sullivan, Liam	LS-LISF8. *LISFAN8*, 1994, "Interview: Liam Sullivan," by Flint Mitchell.
Sullivan, Liam	LS-SFTS2. *Science Fiction Television Series*, Volume 2, by Mark Phillips and Frank Garcia (1996, McFarland & Co.)
Swink, George	GS-LISF. *Lost in Space Forever*, by Joel Eisner and/or Barry Magen (1992, Windsong Publishing, Inc.)

Throne, Malachi	**MT-AI. Author's interview, 2011.**
Throne, Malachi	MT-SL93. *Starlog*, May 1993, "Throne of Villainy," interviewed by Joel Eisner.
Throne, Malachi	*LISFAN8*, 1994, "Interview: Malachi Throne," by Flint Mitchell.
Tigerman, Gary	GT-LISF. *Lost in Space Forever*, by Joel Eisner and/or Barry Magen (1992, Windsong Publishing, Inc.)
Tufeld, Dick	DT-LISF4. . *LISFAN4*, 1986, "Warning! Warning!' – An Interview with Dick Tufeld," by Barry Magen.
Tufeld, Dick	DT-LISF. *Lost in Space Forever*, by Joel Eisner and/or Barry Magen (1992, Windsong Publishing, Inc.)
Turley, Jack	JT-SL90. *Starlog*, October 1990, "They Wrote for Giants," interviewed by Mark Phillips.
Turley, Jack	JT-LISF8. *LISFAN8*, 1994, "Interview: Jack Turley," by Flint Mitchell.
Vennari, Rith	RV-A&EB02. *A & E Biography*: "Jonathan Harris: Never Fear, Smith Is Here," 2002.
Wagner, Lou	LW-LISF. *Lost in Space Forever*, by Joel Eisner and/or Barry Magen (1992, Windsong Publishing, Inc.)
Welch, William	WW-TWTD75. *Talks with the Dead*, by William Welch (Pinnacle Books, 1975)
Wickerman, Sven	SW-VTTBOTS. Mike'svoyagetothebottomofthesea.zone at vttbolts.com, interviewed by Mark Phillips.
Wilbur, Carey	CW-LIS25. *Lost in Space 25th Anniversary Tribute Book*, by James Van Hise (1990, Pioneer Books)
Williams, Edy	EW-DFP68. *Detroit Free Press*, November 10, 1968, "The Starlet Who Isn't Too Inhibited," by George Christian, interviewing Edy Williams about appearance on *LiS*'s "Two Weeks in Space."
Williams, Guy	GW-LAT58. *Los Angeles Times*, May 18, 1958, "WHHHTT, WHHHTT, WHHHTT! Williams Making Mark (Z) as Zorro," by Boots Lebaron.
Williams, Guy	GW-LAT59. *Los Angeles Times*, May 10, 1959, "Romping Young Publicists Beat the Drums for Zorro," by Carl Swenson.
Williams, Guy	GW-DV58. *Daily Variety*, November 25, 1958, "Light and Airy," by Jack Hellamn.
Williams, Guy	GW-IPT62. Long Beach *Independent Press Telegram*, March 11, 1962, "Ex-Zorro TV Duels Again," by Rob Thomas.
Williams, Guy	GW-NP65. *The News-Palladium*, January 19, 1965, "Hollywood Today!," by Dick Kleiner.

Williams, Guy	GW-SHA65. *Syracuse Herald-American*, September 5, 1965, "Cliffhangers Are in Vogue on Television This Season," by Joan E. Vadeboncoeur.
Williams, Guy	GW-TVG66. *TV Guide*, September 24, 1966, "When Guy Hisses the Villain -- HE MEANS IT," by Michael Fessier, Jr.
Williams, Guy	GW-LAT67. *Los Angeles Times*, March 5, 1967, "He's An Earthbound Spaceman," by Aleene MacMinn.
Williams, Guy	GW-TVG78. Interviewed for Argentina's *TV Guia*, March 1978, as translated for *Guy Williams: The Man Behind the Mask* (BearManor Media, 2005)
Williams, Guy	GW-TVG78. Interviewed for Argentina's *Daily Popular*, May 11, 1978, as translated for *Guy Williams: The Man Behind the Mask* (BearManor Media, 2005)
Williams, Guy	GW-SL87. *Starlog*, January 1987, "Guy Williams: Relaxed, Retired & *Lost in Space,"* by Mike Clark.
Williams, Jr., Guy	GWJ-GW:MBTM05. Interview from *Guy Williams: The Man Behind the Mask*, by Antoinette Girgenti Lane (BearManor Media, 2005)
Williams, Jr., Guy	**GWJ-AI15. Author interview, 2015.**
Williams, Jr., Guy	GWJ-LISBY15. Bonus feature interview, *Lost in Space* Blu-ray box set, 2015.
Williams, Janice	JW-GW:MBTM05. Interview from *Guy Williams: The Man Behind the Mask*, by Antoinette Girgenti Lane (BearManor Media, 2005)
Wincelberg, Shimon	SW-LISF. *Lost in Space Forever*, by Joel Eisner and/or Barry Magen (1992, Windsong Publishing, Inc.)
Wincelberg, Shimon	SW-SL85. *Starlog*, November 1985, "Irwin Allen Remembers *Lost in Space*," interviewed by Mike Clark.
Wincelberg, Shimon	SW-SL90. *Starlog*, October 1990, "Misplaced Among the Stars," interviewed by Mike Clark.
Wincelberg, Shimon	SW-LISF6. *LISFAN6*, 1990, "Interview: Simon Wincelberg," by Flint Mitchell.
Wincelberg, Shimon	SW-SL91. *Starlog*, September 1991, "A Brief History of *Time Tunnel*, by Mark Phillips.
Wincelberg, Shimon	SW-SL95. *Starlog*, November, 1995, "Space Families Found, Part Two," interviewed by Mark Phillips.
Wincelberg, Shimon	**SW-KB95. Interviewed by Kevin Burns, 1995.**
Woodfield, Lili Glinski	LGW-LISF. *Lost in Space Forever*, by Joel Eisner and/or Barry Magen (1992, Windsong Publishing, Inc.)
Woodfield, William Read	WRW-SL92. *Starlog*, August 1992, "Giant Jellyfish & Time-Lost Dinosaurs," by Mark Phillips.
Woodfield, William Read	WRW-SL92-2. *Starlog*, August 1992, "Giant Jellyfish & Time-Lost Dinosaurs, Part 2," by Mark Phillips.
Woodfiled, Willima Read	WRW-SFTS2. *Science Fiction Television Series*, Volume 2, by Mark Phillips and Frank Garcia (1996, McFarland & Co.)

Woodfield, William Read	WRW-LISF. *Lost in Space Forever*, by Joel Eisner and/or Barry Magen (1992, Windsong Publishing, Inc.)
York, Francine	**FY-AI. Author's interview, February 2015.**
Zastupnevich, Paul	PZ-WDN66. *The Winona Daily News*, April 10, 1966, "Monsters Figure in Ratings Battle," by Charles Witbeck.
Zastupnevich, Paul	PZ-SLT66. *The Salt Lake Tribune*, November 27, 1966, "*Time Tunnel* Costumes Are Tough."
Zastupnevich, Paul	PZ-LISF6. *LISFAN6*, 1990, "Interview: Paul Zastupnevich," by Flint Mitchell.
Zastupnevich, Paul	PZ-LISF92. *Lost in Space Forever*, by Joel Eisner and/or Barry Magen (1992, Windsong Publishing, Inc.)
Zastupnevich, Paul	PZ-SL93. *Starlog*, February 1993, "Designing Man," by Mike Clark.
Zastupnevich, Paul	**PZ-KB95. Interviewed by Kevin Burns, 1995.**
Zastupnevich, Paul	PZ-S50. *Seaview: A 50th Anniversary Tribute to Voyage to the Bottom of the Sea*, by William E. Anchors and Frederick Barr (2012, Alpha Control Press).

Printed by Amazon Italia Logistica S.r.l.
Torrazza Piemonte (TO), Italy